Anti-Personnel Mines under Humanitarian Law

A View from the Vanishing Point

Anti-Personnel Mines under Humanitarian Law

A View from the Vanishing Point

Stuart Maslen

Intersentia – Transnational Publishers
Antwerp – Oxford – New York

Distribution for the UK:
Hart Publishing
Salter's Boat Yard
Folly Bridge
Abingdon Road
Oxford OX1 4LB
UK
Tel: + 44 1865 24 55 33
Fax: + 44 1865 79 48 82

Distribution for North America:
Transnational Publishers
410 Saw Mill River Road
Ardsley
New York 10502-2615
USA
Tel: + 1 914 693 5100
Fax: + 1 914 693 4430

Distribution for Switzerland and Germany:
Schulthess Verlag
Zwingliplatz 2
CH-8022 Zürich
Switzerland
Tel: + 41 1 251 93 36
Fax: + 41 1 261 63 94

Distribution for other countries:
Intersentia Publishers
Churchilllaan 108
2900 Schoten
Belgium
Tel: + 32 3 680 15 50
Fax: + 32 3 658 71 21

Anti-Personnel Mines under Humanitarian Law
A View from the Vanishing Point
Stuart Maslen

ISBN 1-57105-244-5
ISBN 90-5095-189-9
D/2001/7849/30
NUGI 698

TABLE OF CONTENTS

List of Abbreviations xi

Introduction 1
0.1. The Development and Use of Anti-Personnel Mines 3
0.2. The Development of International Humanitarian Law Applicable to Weapons 12
0.3. The Development of International Humanitarian Law Applicable to Anti-Personnel Mines 14
0.3.1. The Role of the International Committee of the Red Cross 14
0.3.2. The Role of the International Campaign to Ban Landmines 16
0.4. Statistics and the Development of International Humanitarian Law Governing Anti-Personnel Mines 19

Chapter 1
Anti-Personnel Mines on the Battlefield under the 1980 Convention on Certain Conventional Weapons 25
1.1. The Historical Background to the Convention 25
1.2. The Negotiation of the 1980 Convention on Certain Conventional Weapons 29
1.3. The Structure of the Convention 30
1.4. The Scope and Applicability of the Convention 31
1.5. The Implementation of the Convention 33
1.6. The Adoption and Entry Into Force of the Convention 34
1.7. Protocol II on Mines, Booby-Traps and Other Devices 35
1.7.1. The Historical Background to Protocol II 35
1.7.2. The Provisions of Protocol II 38
A. Key Definitions 38
(i) Mine 38
(ii) Remotely-Delivered Mines 39
(iii) Booby-Traps 40
(iv) Military Objective 40
B. Prohibitions and Restrictions on the Use of Mines 41
(i) General Prohibitions and Restrictions 41
(ii) Recording of Mines and Mine Clearance 43
C. The Implementation of the Protocol 45
D. Entry into Force of the Protocol 46
1.8. The First Review Conference of the Convention on Certain Conventional Weapons 46
1.8.1. The Provisions of Amended Protocol II 52
A. The Scope of Amended Protocol II 52
(i) The Application to Internal Armed Conflicts 52
(ii) Application to Peacetime 54
B. Key Definitions 55
(i) Mine and Remotely-Delivered Mine 55

(ii) Anti-Personnel Mine 56
(iii) Anti-Handling Device 57
C. General Prohibitions 58
(i) Mines causing 'Superfluous Injury or Unnecessary Suffering' 58
(ii) Mines Designed to be Detonated by Mine Detectors 58
(iii) 'Long-Lived' Anti-Handling Devices on Self-Deactivating Mines 59
(iv) The Indiscriminate Use of Anti-Personnel Mines 60
D. The Prohibition of Certain Anti-Personnel Mines 60
(i) 'Undetectable' Anti-Personnel Mines 60
(ii) 'Long-Lived' Remotely-Delivered Anti-Personnel Mines 63
E. Restrictions on the Use of Other Anti-Personnel Mines 64
(i) Manually-Emplaced 'Long-Lived' Anti-Personnel Mines 64
(ii) Remotely-Delivered Anti-Vehicle Mines 65
F. Prohibitions and Restrictions on the Transfer of Anti-Personnel Mines 66
G. The Recording and Removal of Landmines 69
H. The Implementation of Amended Protocol II 70
(i) The Annual Conferences of States Parties 72
1.9. The Second Review Conference of the Convention on Certain Conventional Weapons 73
1.10. Concluding Remarks 74

Chapter 2
Anti-Personnel Mines on the Battlefield under the Convention on the Prohibition of Anti-Personnel Mines 77
2.1. Introduction 77
2.2. The Negotiation of the Convention on the Prohibition of Anti-Personnel Mines 79
2.3. Discussions in the UN Conference on Disarmament 88
2.4. The Content of the Convention on the Prohibition of Anti-Personnel Mines 93
2.4.1. Scope and Application 93
2.4.2. Key Definitions 96
A. 'Anti-Personnel Mine' and 'Anti-Handling Device' 96
B. Anti-Vehicle Mines 98
C. Anti-Vehicle Mines Equipped with Anti-Handling Devices .. 99
D. Claymore Mines 103
E. Other Weapons 104
F. Summary 105
2.4.3. Prohibitions 106
A. Prohibition on the Use of Anti-Personnel Mines 106
B. The Prohibition on the Production of Anti-Personnel Mines 111
C. The Prohibition on the Transfer of Anti-Personnel Mines .. 111
D. The Prohibition on the Stockpiling of Anti-Personnel Mines 113

E. Prohibition on Assisting, Encouraging or Inducing Others to Violate the Convention 115
2.4.4. Implementation of the Convention 119
A. The Destruction of Stockpiles 119
B. Mine Clearance 125
C. International Co-operation and Assistance 128
D. National Legislation 131
2.4.5. Adoption and Entry into force 137
A. Signature 137
B. Entry Into Force 138
C. Ratification by Signatories 140
D. Non-signatories 141
(i) Africa 141
(ii) The Americas 143
(iii) Asia 146
(iv) Europe 154
E. Reservations 158
F. Provisional Application 160
G. Withdrawal 160
H. Amendments 161
I. Review Conference of States Parties 161
2.4.6. Promoting Compliance 162
A. Transparency measures 162
B. The Compliance Mechanism 163
C. Annual Meetings of States Parties 165
D. Landmine Monitor 168
2.5. Conclusion 169
2.5.1. Does the Convention Effectively Prohibit the Use of Anti-Personnel Mines? 169
A. The Reach of the Convention 169
B. The Implementation of the Convention 172
2.5.2. The Implications for International Humanitarian Law of the Ottawa Process 175

Chapter 3
Anti-Personnel Mines on the Battlefield under Customary International Humanitarian Law 179
3.1. Introduction 179
3.1.1. Basic Rules Governing the Use of Weapons on the Battlefield 183
3.1.2. Criteria to Assess the Legality of the Use of Anti-Personnel Mines 186
3.2. Anti-Personnel Mines and the Principle of Distinction 187
3.2.1. The Principle of Distinction and Conventional Weapons 187
3.2.2. Application of the Principle to Anti-Personnel Mines 190
3.2.3. Conclusion 193
3.3. Anti-Personnel Mines and the Principle of Proportionality 194
3.3.1. Introduction 194

3.2.2. The Humanitarian Impact of Anti-Personnel Mines 198
A. The Impact on the Individual 198
B. The Socio-Economic Impact of Anti-Personnel Mines 199
C. The Impact on the Environment 200
3.3.3. The Military Utility of Anti-Personnel Mines 202
A. Alternatives to Anti-Personnel Mines 206
3.3.4. Conclusion 208
3.4. Anti-Personnel Mines and 'Superfluous Injury or Unnecessary Suffering' 210
3.4.1. Introduction 210
3.4.2. Criteria for the Assessment of 'Superfluous Injury or Unnecessary Suffering' 214
3.4.3. Weapons Causing Superfluous Injury or Unnecessary Suffering 217
A. Exploding Bullets 217
B. Expanding Bullets 218
C. Chemical and Bacteriological Warfare 220
D. Non-Detectable Fragments 221
E. Blinding Laser Weapons 221
3.4.4. The Application of the Principle to Anti-Personnel Mines 222
3.4.5. Conclusion 223
3.5. Environmental Protection 224
3.5.1. 1977 Additional Protocol I 225
3.5.2. Applicability to Internal Armed Conflict 228
3.5.3. Conclusion 229
3.6. The Laws of Humanity and the Dictates of the Public Conscience 229
3.6.1. The Martens Clause 229
3.6.2. Applicability to Internal Armed Conflicts 231
3.6.3. Conclusion 232
3.7. The Convention on the Prohibition of Anti-Personnel Mines ... 232
3.8. The ICRC Customary Law Study 235

4. **Concluding Remarks** 239
4.1. The Development and Use of Anti-Personnel Mines 239
4.2. The Legality of Anti-Personnel Mines on the Battlefield Under International Humanitarian Law 240
4.2.1. Customary International Humanitarian Law 240
4.2.2. Conventional International Humanitarian Law 241
4.3. The Implications for International Humanitarian Law of the Ottawa Process 243

5. **Bibliography** 245
5.1. Publications 245
5.2. Articles, Monographs, Reports, and Statements 248
5.3. United Nations Documents, Resolutions and Judicial Decisions 261

5.4. Press Articles and Releases ... 262
5.5. E-mail correspondence and Websites ... 267

6. Appendices ... 269
6.1. Declaration Renouncing the Use, in Time of War, of Certain Explosive Projectiles ... 269
6.2. Project of an International Declaration Concerning the Laws and Customs of War ... 270
6.3. Convention (II) with Respect to the Laws and Customs of War on Land and its Annex: Regulations Concerning the Laws and Customs of War on Land ... 271
6.3.1. Annex to the Convention Regulations Respecting the Laws and Customs of War on Land ... 272
6.4. Declaration (IV, 3) Concerning Expanding Bullets ... 273
6.5. Convention (IV) Respecting the Laws and Customs of War on Land and its Annex: Regulations Concerning the Laws and Customs of War on Land ... 274
6.5.1. Annex to the Convention Regulations Respecting the Laws and Customs of War on Land ... 274
6.6. Convention (VIII) Relative to the Laying of Automatic Submarine Contact Mines ... 275
6.7. Convention Relative to the Treatment of Prisoners of War ... 278
6.8. Convention (III) Relative to the Treatment of Prisoners of War . 278
6.9. Draft Rules for the Limitation of the Dangers Incurred by the Civilian Population in Time of War ... 279
6.10. 'Human Rights in Armed Conflicts' Resolution XXIII Adopted by the International Conference on Human Rights ... 280
6.11. Respect for Human Rights in Armed Conflicts Resolution 2444 (XXIII) of the United Nations General Assembly ... 282
6.12. Resolutions of the Diplomatic Conference of Geneva of 1974-1977 ... 283
6.13. Resolution on Small-Calibre Weapon Systems ... 285
6.14. Convention on Prohibitions or Restrictions on the Use of Certain Conventional Weapons which may be Deemed to be Excessively Injurious or to have Indiscriminate Effects ... 286
6.14.1. Protocol on Non-Detectable Fragments (Protocol I) ... 290
6.14.2. Protocol on Prohibitions or Restrictions on the Use of Mines, Booby-Traps and Other Devices (Protocol II) ... 290
A. Technical Annex to the Protocol on Prohibitions or Restrictions on the Use of Mines, Booby-Traps and Other Devices (Protocol II) ... 293
(i) Guidelines on recording ... 293
6.14.3. Protocol on Prohibitions or Restrictions on the Use of Incendiary Weapons (Protocol III) ... 294
6.14.4. Protocol on Blinding Laser Weapons (Protocol IV) ... 295

6.14.5. Protocol on Prohibitions or Restrictions on the Use of Mines, Booby-Traps and Other Devices as amended on 3 May 1996 (Protocol II to the 1980 Convention as amended on 3 May 1996) 295
6.14.6. Technical Annex 304
6.15. Convention on the Prohibition of the Use, Stockpiling, Production and Transfer of Anti-Personnel Mines and on their Destruction 306
6.16. UN General Assembly Resolution 52/38A 316
6.17. UN General Assembly Resolution 53/77N 318
6.18. Meeting of the States Parties to the Convention on the Prohibition of Anti-Personnel Mines 320
6.18.1. Part I Organization and work of the first meeting 320
6.18.2. Part II Maputo Declaration 324

7. **Acknowledgements** 327

LIST OF ABBREVIATIONS

AFP	Agence France Presse
AP	Associated Press
APM	Anti-personnel mine
ATM	Anti-tank mine
AVM	Anti-vehicle mine
CCW	Convention on Certain Conventional Weapons
CD	United Nations Conference on Disarmament
DMZ	Demilitarised Zone
ECOMOG	ECOWAS Ceasefire Monitoring Group
ECOWAS	Economic Community of West African States
EOD	Explosive ordnance disposal
EU	European Union
FRY	Federal Republic of Yugoslavia
HI	Handicap International
HRW	Human Rights Watch
ICBL	International Campaign to Ban Landmines
ICJ	International Court of Justice
ICRC	International Committee of the Red Cross
IED	Improvised explosive device
IMSMA	Information Management System for Mine Action
IRIN	Integrated Regional Information Network (UN)
KLA	Kosovo Liberation Army
LSN	Landmine Survivors Network
MAC	Mine Action Centre
MAG	Mines Advisory Group
MI	Medico International
NATO	North Atlantic Treaty Organization
NGO	Non-governmental organisation
NSA	Non-State actor
OCHA	Organisation for the Coordination of Humanitarian Affairs (UN)
OSCE	Organization for Security and Cooperation in Europe
PHR	Physicians for Human Rights
POW	Prisoner of war
RAF	Royal Air Force (UK)
ROK	Republic of Korea
SAC	Survey Action Center
SCE	Standing Committee of Experts
UK	United Kingdom of Great Britain and Northern Ireland
UN	United Nations
UNDP	United Nations Development Programme
UNGA	United Nations General Assembly
UNICEF	United Nations Children's Fund
UNMAS	United Nations Mine Action Service
UNOPS	United Nations Office for Project Services

US	United States of America
UXO	Unexploded ordnance
VVAF	Vietnam Veterans of America Foundation

INTRODUCTION

The late Sir Hersch Lauterpacht once famously declared that 'if international law is, in some ways, the vanishing point of law, the law of war[1] is, perhaps even more conspicuously, at the vanishing point of international law.'[2] Taking this claim a stage further, it has been asserted that 'the law on the battlefield would be at the vanishing point of the law of war.'[3] With this healthy scepticism at the forefront of our minds, here opens consideration of the legality of the use of anti-personnel mines on the battlefield under prevailing international humanitarian law.

In 1997, the international community witnessed the adoption and signature of a new international legal instrument, the Convention on the Prohibition of the Use, Stockpiling, Production and Transfer of Anti-Personnel Mines and on their Destruction.[4] As its name indicates, the Convention prohibited not only the use

---

1 A number of military lawyers still tend to prefer the term law (or laws) or war to international humanitarian law when referring to the body of international law that governs the lawful conduct of warfare (*jus in bello*). According to Professor Christopher Greenwood: 'International humanitarian law includes most of what used to be known as the laws of war, although strictly speaking some parts of those laws, such as the law of neutrality, are not included since their primary purpose is not humanitarian.' Greenwood, C., "Historical Development and Legal Basis", in Fleck, D. (ed.), *The Handbook of Humanitarian Law in Armed Conflicts*, Oxford University Press, US, 1995, p. 9; Condorelli, L., "Le droit international humanitaire, ou de l'exploration par la Cour d'une *terra* à peu près *incognita* pour elle", in Boisson de Chazournes, L. *et al.* (eds.), *International Law, the International Court of Justice and Nuclear Weapons*, Cambridge University Press, Cambridge, 1999, p. 231. See also Roberts, A. and Guelff, R. (eds.), *Documents on the Laws of War*, 2nd edn., Clarendon Press, Oxford, UK, 1989, pp. 1-2. (Hereinafter, this work, in its second edition, will be referred to as *Documents on the Laws of War*.)

According to the International Committee of the Red Cross: 'International Humanitarian Law (IHL), or the Law of War as [it] is known in the armed forces, is a set of rules established by treaties or custom, which are specifically intended to solve humanitarian issues directly arising from international or non-international armed conflicts. They limit, for humanitarian reasons, the right of the parties to a conflict to choose the methods and means of warfare and they protect persons and property which are, or may be affected by conflict. IHL is composed of the Geneva Conventions and their Additional Protocols of 1977, which aim to safeguard military personnel who are placed "hors de combat" and persons not taking part in hostilities, and the Law of the Hague, which determines the rights and duties of belligerents in the conduct of operations and limits the choice of methods of warfare.' See for instance *ICRC Newsletter*, ICRC Sri Lanka, No. 2, December 1997, p. 2, <http://www.icrc.org>.

2 Lauterpacht, H., "The Problem of the Revision of the Law of War", *British Yearbook of International Law*, Vol. 29, 1952, p. 382.

3 Rogers, A.P.V., *Law on the Battlefield*, Manchester University Press, Manchester, 1996, p. 3. Commander Bill Fenrick makes a similar claim, declaring that the vanishing point of the law of war is most likely to be found in the body of law regulating combat operations, 'because it is at that point that law most clearly confronts force.' Fenrick, Lt.-Col. W.J., "New Developments in the Law Concerning the Use of Conventional Weapons in Armed Conflict", *Canadian Yearbook of International Law*, Vol. 19, No. 19, 1981, p. 229.

4 Hereinafter, for reasons of brevity, the Convention is generally referred to as the *Convention on the Prohibition of Anti-Personnel Mines*. This designation has no legal status.

of anti-personnel mines[5] but also their production, stockpiling and transfer (as well as their development, acquisition and retention, whether direct or indirect).[6] This achievement represented the culmination of energetic campaigns over several years by hundreds of non-governmental organisations (NGOs) belonging to the International Campaign to Ban Landmines (ICBL), the International Committee of the Red Cross (ICRC), and the United Nations (UN).

But with States currently outside the legal purview of the Convention representing more than one-half of the world's population and allegedly holding more than 200 million anti-personnel mines in stockpiles,[7] and with anti-personnel mines continuing to be laid in a number of conflicts around the world,[8] we are entitled to ask how far the 'vanishing point' of the law of war has effectively put an end to the threat of anti-personnel landmines, variously termed a scourge,[9] a plague,[10] a deadly legacy,[11] or, in terms of the human cost, a worldwide epidemic.[12]

This work, then, has as its aims to consider the current legality of the use of anti-personnel mines on the battlefield under customary and conventional humanitarian law, as well as the prospects for the law being respected in practice – both by governmental and non-governmental armed forces and groups. It further seeks to consider the development of the law regulating anti-personnel mines within the wider context of the future development of international humanitarian law itself. It is intended that the information contained herein be accurate as of end March 2001, unless otherwise stated.

---

5 As will be seen *infra*, international humanitarian law has traditionally concentrated on the use of a given weapon; other issues, such as production, stockpiling and transfer have generally fallen within the ambit of arms control and disarmament fora.

6 Article 1(1)(a) and (b), *Convention on the Prohibition of Anti-Personnel Mines*.

7 See for instance Landmine Monitor, "New study reveals 250 million stockpiled landmines in 104 countries, 19 million destroyed to date", *Press release*, Geneva, 15 December 1999.

8 Between May 1999 and August 2000, for example, the International Campaign to Ban Landmines (ICBL) reported, *inter alia*, extensive use of anti-personnel mines in the conflicts in Chechnya and Kosovo, continued use by treaty signatory Angola, likely use by treaty signatories Burundi and Sudan, and alleged use by Ethiopia and Rwanda, both signatories, and by Uganda and Zimbabwe, both States Parties. See ICBL, *Landmine Monitor Report 2000, Toward a Mine-Free World*, Human Rights Watch, Washington DC, August 2000, pp. 1-2, 4-6, 158. (Hereinafter, this report will be referred to as *Landmine Monitor Report 2000*.) For the most comprehensive overview of the reported use of anti-personnel mines in 1998 – March 1999, see ICBL, *Landmine Monitor Report 1999, Toward a Mine-Free World*, Human Rights Watch, Washington, April 1999. (Hereinafter, this report will be referred to as *Landmine Monitor Report 1999*.)

9 See for instance UNICEF, *Anti-Personnel Mines, A Scourge on Children*, UNICEF New York, 1994.

10 See for instance ICRC, *A Silent Menace: Landmines in Bosnia and Herzegovina*, ICRC, Geneva, March 1998.

11 See for instance Human Rights Watch and Physicians for Human Rights, *Landmines, A Deadly Legacy*, New York, October 1993. Hereinafter, this work will be referred to as *A Deadly Legacy*.

12 See for instance ICRC, *The worldwide epidemic of landmine injuries: The ICRC's health oriented approach*, ICRC, Geneva, 1995.

0.1. The Development and Use of Anti-Personnel Mines

Landmines[13] may be 'concisely defined as mass-produced, victim-operated, explosive traps.'[14] This definition 'excludes booby-traps by virtue of the term "mass-produced", although in reality the difference between landmines and booby-traps can be academic.'[15] Likewise, the distinction between anti-personnel[16] and anti-tank or anti-vehicle mines,[17] improvised explosive devices[18] and even certain sub-munitions, can be, and is, fiercely debated.[19] The simplest blast anti-personnel mine comprises four elements: a case, a fuze, a detonator, and an explosive filling.[20]

The precise origin of the anti-personnel mine is a moot point. To date, the most authoritative work on the subject, Mike Croll's *The History of Landmines*, published in 1998, claims that modern landmines 'trace their lineage from non-explosive predecessors such as the spikes and stakes that were employed by ancient armies.'[21] Croll asserts that the term 'mine' is derived from the Latin *mina* – meaning a vein of ore[22] – and 'was originally applied to the excavation of minerals from the earth. The technique and the term were borrowed by military engineers who dug mines during sieges and packed them with explosives to cause the collapse of fortifications (...) the expression was close enough

---

13 The term *landmine* is often used interchangeably with anti-personnel mine, most notably by the ICBL. *Stricto sensu*, of course, a landmine includes anti-tank/anti-vehicle mines, which are not the primary subject of this work, as well as anti-personnel mines. Hereinafter, where the word landmine is used, other than in the context of the ICBL, it refers to all landmines, not merely anti-personnel mines.

14 Croll, M., *The History of Landmines*, Leo Cooper, UK, 1998, p. ix. Hereinafter, this work is referred to as *The History of Landmines*.

15 *Ibid.* See *infra* Chapter 2 for a further discussion of this issue.

16 The term *personnel* originates in the early nineteenth century, coming from French, and means people engaged in an organised undertaking (such as military service), being distinguished from the *matériel* used in the undertaking. See for instance *The New Oxford Dictionary of English*, Clarendon Press, Oxford, UK, 1998, p. 1386.

17 The definition of an anti-personnel mine, and the legal distinction between anti-personnel and anti-vehicle mines, are discussed in both Chapter 1 and Chapter 2 *infra*, as seemingly different definitions of what constitutes an anti-personnel mine are contained in two existing international legal instruments. There are no legal definitions of what constitutes an anti-vehicle or an anti-tank mine, though a simple working definition could be 'a landmine other than an anti-personnel mine'. Increasingly, anti-vehicle mine is used rather than anti-tank mine; the term is employed in both major international legal instruments governing landmines.

18 Similarly, the issue of improvised explosive devices (IEDs) is discussed in both Chapter 1 and Chapter 2 *infra*. At least one commentator seemingly regards IEDs as being synonymous with booby-traps. Wyatt, Maj. (ret.) J.D.R., "Land mine warfare, recent lessons and future trends", *International Defense Review*, Vol. 22, No. 1, 1989, p. 1499.

19 See for instance McGrath, R., "Definitions and Anti-Handling Devices", *Discussion Paper*, Mines Advisory Group, Cockermouth, UK, August 1997.

20 Cornish, P., *Anti-Personnel Mines, Controlling the Plague of 'Butterflies'*, Royal Institute for International Affairs, London, 1994, p. 11. Cornish records that: 'The explosive filling may have three elements, a primary charge or detonator; a secondary or booster charge, and a main charge. Various types of explosive are used, such as RDX, TNT, trotyl, trialene and tetryl.' *Ibid.*

21 *The History of Landmines*, p. ix; see also pp. 1-8.

22 According to the New Oxford Dictionary of English, however, the word mine is from Old French *mine* and perhaps of Celtic origin. *New Oxford Dictionary of English*, *op. cit.*, pp. 1176-7.

to apply to the process of burying victim activated explosive charges and from around 1880 onwards the word landmine gained common usage.'[23]

The 'so-called "mine" was a common feature of medieval siege warfare. (...) The besieger removed as much earth as he could carry away from beneath some exposed corner of the fortifications, and shored up the hole with beams. He then filled the space between the beams with straw and brushwood, and set fire to it. When the supports were consumed, the wall crumbled downwards into the hole, and a breach was produced. (...) Over time, gunpowder and explosives took the place of fire, but the essentially medieval technique was retained, and was used as recently as the First World War.'[24]

In April 2001, it was reported that archaeologists in northern China's Inner Mongolia Autonomous Region had discovered more than 20 ancient "landmines" dating back over 600 years to the early Ming Dynasty.[25] But the earliest known description of a pressure-operated landmine seemingly comes from a book by a German military historian entitled *The Perfect German Soldier*, published in 1726.[26] The author, Freiherr von Flemming, talks of the use of a *fladdermine* (literally, a flying mine), which consisted of a ceramic container with glass and metal fragments embedded in the clay containing 2lb of gunpowder, buried at a shallow depth in the glacis[27] of a fortress and activated by someone stepping on it or touching a low-strung wire.[28]

It was not until the American Civil War, however, that widespread use occurred on the battlefield of what may justly be termed anti-personnel mines.[29] Badly outnumbered in their struggle with the Unionists, Confederate troops needed to reinforce their defences to delay and imperil the Union forces; anti-personnel mines also permitted a withdrawal without sacrificing precious manpower in rearguard actions. 'Thus the demand for landmines coincided with a period in which technology was sufficiently advanced to fulfil it.'[30]

---

23 See *The History of Landmines*, p. ix; see also pp. 8-9.

24 Cornish, P., *Anti-Personnel Mines, Controlling the Plague of 'Butterflies'*, *op. cit.*, p. 18, citing Oman, C., *The Art of War in the Middle Ages, Volume One: 378-1278AD*, Greenhill, London, 1991, p. 133.

25 "600-Year-Old Mines Unearthed in Inner Mongolia", *Xinhua Press Agency*, Hohhot, Mongolia, 11 April 2001.

26 *The History of Landmines*, p. 10.

27 A glacis is a sloping bank around a fort that exposes attackers to the defenders' missiles. See for instance *New Oxford Dictionary of English*, *op. cit.*, p. 777.

28 See Kreuzfeld, U., in Dupuy, T.N. (ed.), *The International Military and Defence Encyclopaedia*, Vol. 4, Brassey's, London, 1993, pp. 1757-8, cited by *The History of Landmines*, p. 15.

29 *The History of Landmines*, p. 15. Thus, as Croll points out, the oft-made claim that anti-personnel mines were first laid to protect anti-tank mines in the First World War, is clearly incorrect. *Ibid.*, p. 31. See for instance *A Deadly Legacy*, pp. 16-17.

30 *The History of Landmines*, p. 15.

The invention of these 'infernal machines'[31] is usually attributed to Brigadier-General Gabriel Rains of the Confederate Army.[32] In the spring of 1862, when commanding a garrison of 2,500 men at Yorktown, Rains ordered his troops to prepare artillery shells so that they could be exploded by pulling trip-wires or by being stepped on.[33] The first casualties of these early anti-personnel mines were reported on 4 May 1862; even some of the Confederate troops deemed the devices 'barbaric'[34] and Rains' commanding officer forbade their further use, declaring them neither a 'proper nor effective method of war'.[35] Yet, despite concerns on both sides, use of the weapons continued and in 1864 at Fort McAllister, near Savannah, mines killed 12 men and wounded 80 others during the Union assault.[36] It was following this battle that the commander of the Union Army, General William T. Sherman uttered his now famous dictum that the use of mines 'was not war, but murder'.[37]

Croll claims that not more than 20,000 mines were used during the entire war and that they probably inflicted only a few hundred casualties in all, but he notes that the figures 'conceal the importance of the lessons they demonstrated: the delays they imposed, the caution they induced and the acceptance of an extremely distasteful manner of killing one's enemies[.] (...) It would be another 76 years before they were again used by an American soldier.'[38] But in a salutary indication of the problems that would subsequently be confronted as a result of the use of anti-personnel mines on the battlefield, he notes that in 1960 five landmines with Rains' fuzes were recovered in Alabama. Nearly 100 years after they were laid, the powder was 'still quite dangerous'.[39]

Largely as a result of the static trench warfare in which the machine gun ruled supreme, anti-personnel mines were not extensively deployed on the battlefield in Europe during the First World War.[40] Apparently, tripwire-

---

31 The Unionist General who captured Yorktown, George B. McClellan, is alleged to have written to his wife that mine warfare 'is the most murderous and barbarous thing I ever heard of.' Perry, M.F., *Infernal Machines. The Story of Confederate Submarine and Mine Warfare*, Louisiana State University Press, Baton Rouge, US, 1985, p. 22.

32 Rains would subsequently lose the forefinger and thumb of his right hand while experimenting with a fuze designed to 'explode from the slightest pressure.' *The History of Landmines*, p. 17.

33 *Ibid.*, p. 16.

34 'Said one [Confederate] infantryman while being led though the minefield at Yorktown: "This is barbarism."' Minnich, "Incidents of the Peninsular Campaign", *Confederate Veteran*, 1922, p. 53, cited by Perry, M.F., *Infernal Machines*, *op. cit.*, p. 25.

35 Indeed, Croll reports that the debate reached the Southern Secretary of War who vindicated Rains by declaring that landmines could be used along roads to delay pursuit, in front of defences to repel attack, and in rivers and harbours to attack warships. *The History of Landmines*, p. 16.

36 *Ibid.*, p. 18.

37 *Ibid.*, although Sherman later records his belief that the use of mines (called torpedoes) was justifiable in war in advance of an enemy. See *infra* Chapter 1, p. 36, footnote 275.

38 *The History of Landmines*, p. 20.

39 Perry, M.F., *Infernal Machines*, *op. cit.*, p. 206, cited by *ibid.*, p. 20.

40 *The History of Landmines*, p. 25. It is alleged that landmines were used more extensively in German East and South-West Africa both as defensive barriers and as a way of closing roads. *Ibid.*, p. 27. These included so-called 'pipe' mines, which were the first designed specifically to wound rather than to kill. *Ibid.*, pp. 27-8.

activated mines were laced within wire entanglements early in the war but they were often as dangerous to the side that laid them as to the enemy and they were quickly phased out.[41] However, anti-personnel mines and booby-traps were laid in abandoned positions in anticipation of an enemy advance.[42] These weapons were adapted from artillery shells, with specially-designed fuzes screwed into the bottom of the shell.[43]

In the Second World War, however, landmines, both anti-personnel and anti-tank, were used on a huge scale.[44] According to the US Defense Intelligence Agency, more than 300 million anti-tank mines were used during the war, including 220 million by the Soviet Union.[45] Landmines were integral to the famous battles at El Alamein[46] and Kursk,[47] among others. It is claimed that one

---

41 School of Military Engineering (SME), *The Work of the Royal Engineers in the European War 1914-19*, SME, Chatham, UK, 1924, p. 257, cited by *ibid.*, p. 26.

42 *The History of Landmines*, p. 26; see also pp. 27-28.

43 *Ibid.*, p. 26. Under Article 8 of the Armistice Agreement of 11 November 1918 the Germans were required to hand over plans showing where mines had been laid. *Ibid.*, p. 27.

44 According to Croll, by the end of the war, the Germans had manufactured 16 different types of anti-tank mine, 10 different types of anti-personnel mine, and used many different types of improvised devices and captured mines. *The History of Landmines, op. cit.*, p. 37; see also pp. 38-52. This included the development and incorporation of the anti-handling device, and the first use of an aerially-delivered scatterable anti-personnel mine. *Ibid.*, pp. 39, 46-7. Towards the end of the war, the Germans experimented with magnetic-influence, vibration-sensitive, radio-controlled and frequency-induction fuzes. *Ibid.*, p. 48.
Croll, however, notes that while many advances in mine warfare were the result of German innovation, it was in fact the British who first started laying mines *en masse* during the Second World War, with around 350,000 mines laid on the south and east coast of England in around 2,000 individual fields. Pakenham-Walsh, Maj.-Gen. R.P., *The History of the Corps of Royal Engineers*, Vol. X, Institute of Royal Engineers, Chatham, 1986, p. 288, cited by *The History of Landmines*, p. 54.

45 US Defense Intelligence Agency and US Army Foreign Science and Technology Center, *Landmine Warfare – Trends and Projections*, December 1992, DST-1160S-019-92, p. 2-1, cited in *A Deadly Legacy*, p. 16. Given the discussion of statistics *infra*, the accuracy of these estimates remains unclear. In this regard, Croll cites Soviet sources which reported a figure of 67 million Soviet-laid mines. Zatylkin, B.V., *The Occupation of Sapper*, Dosaaf SSR, Moscow, 1978, p. 23, cited in *The History of Landmines, op. cit.*, p. 37.

46 See *The History of Landmines*, pp. 61-63; *Landmine Monitor Report 1999*, p. 880. Though, interestingly, Field Marshal Montgomery, the commander of the allied forces in North Africa, barely mentions landmines in his work on the history of warfare. He does, though, point out that 'minefields were laid in the desert very much as they were in the sea.' See Field-Marshal Viscount Montgomery of Alamein, *The History of Warfare*, The World Publishing Company, Cleveland, 1968, p. 512.
For details of the use of mines in North Africa see for instance Ceva, L., "The Influence of Mines and Minefields in the North African Campaign of 1940-1943", Paper presented to the Symposium on Material Remnants of the Second World War on Libyan Soil, Geneva, 28 April to 1 May 1981; Vines, A., "The Crisis of Anti-Personnel Mines", in Lawson, R.J. *et al.*, (eds.), *To Walk Without Fear, The Global Movement to Ban Landmines*, Oxford University Press, Toronto, 1998, p. 119. (Hereinafter, this work will be referred to as *To Walk Without Fear*.)
Following the difficulties encountered in clearing mines left over from the battles in North Africa, a British report entitled "Engineer Lessons from the North African Campaign" recommended the design of a new form of mine capable of 'self-destroying after a certain period to avoid the need for lifting'. *Ibid.*, p. 65.

47 *The History of Landmines*, p. 66. See also Healy, M., *Kursk 1943, The Tide Turns in the East*, Osprey Military, pp. 31, 33, 36, 38, 41, 57, 64, 69.

German anti-personnel mine, the *Schrapnellmine 35* or S mine as it was later called, 'was probably the most feared device encountered by Allied troops' in the Second World War.[48]

In late 1943, when given the task of preparing defences against the expected Allied invasion of France, Field-Marshal Rommel gave the following instructions to his chief engineer officer General Wilhelm Weise:

> *'Our only possible chance will be at the beaches – that's where the enemy is always weakest. I want anti-personnel mines, anti-tank mines, anti-paratroop mines. I want mines to sink ships and mines to sink landing craft. I want some minefields designed so that our infantry can cross them, but no enemy tanks. I want mines that detonate when a wire is tripped; mines that explode when a wire is cut; mines that can be remotely controlled and mines that blow up when a beam of light is interrupted.'*[49]

Following the end of the Second World War, demobilised soldiers introduced the term 'minefield' into everyday parlance, meaning a situation beset with problems.[50] And more than 50 years later, many countries are still clearing anti-personnel mines (and, of course, other unexploded ordnance) left on the former battlefields.[51] These include Albania (which is also clearing anti-tank mines from the First World War),[52] Belarus,[53] Belgium,[54] Denmark,[55] France,[56] Moldova,[57] Niger,[58] the Russian Federation,[59] the Solomon Islands,[60] and Ukraine.[61] On the other hand, it was reported that within two years of the cessation of hostilities, by using mostly prisoner of war (POW) labour, some 90 million landmines had been cleared.[62]

---

48 Sloan, Lt.-Col. C.E.E., *Mine Warfare on Land*, Brassey's, London, 1986, p. 36, cited in *The History of Landmines*, p. 42.

49 See Ambrose, S.E., *D-Day June 6, 1944: The Climactic Battle of World War II*, Simon & Schuster, New York, 1994, p. 588, cited in *The History of Landmines*, p. 74.

50 *The History of Landmines*, p. 53.

51 On this issue see for instance Norwegian People's Aid, "Humanitarian Mine Action", Landmine Monitor Fact Sheet prepared for the Meeting of the Standing Committee of Experts on Mine Clearance, Geneva, 13-15 September 1999. In early October 2000, it was reported that German chemical weapons sunk by the Allies in the Baltic after the Second World War are beginning to disintegrate, releasing deadly poisons into one of the world's most heavily fished seas. See Chazan, G., "Dumped World War II Shells", *Daily Telegraph*, 8 October 2000.

52 *Landmine Monitor Report 1999*, p. 701.

53 *Ibid.*, p. 773.

54 *Ibid.*, p. 547.

55 *Ibid.*, p. 584.

56 Webster, D., "One Leg, One Life at a Time", *New York Times Magazine*, 23 January 1994, pp. 26-33.

57 *Landmine Monitor Report 1999*, p. 745.

58 These mines are apparently among those laid in Libya near the frontier with Niger, but which have moved over the border due to the slow movement of sand dunes over the decades. *Ibid.*, p. 74.

59 *Ibid.*, p. 811.

60 *Ibid.*, p. 374.

61 *Ibid.*, p. 579. Casualties continue to this day. See for instance "World War II mine explodes in Ukraine, killing three children", *AP*, Kiev, 8 August 1997.

62 *The History of Landmines*, p. 94. See also *infra* footnote 135; Chapter 1, p. 36, footnote 275.

Since 1945, the design of mines is said to have concentrated on five criteria: effectiveness, size, detectability, logistic effort, and speed of laying.[63] But bounding technological advance has also resulted in rapid obsolescence and by the 1990s more than 600 types of landmine had been produced.[64] Anti-Personnel mines were used widely in both the Korean and Vietnam Wars, for example, and both of these wars led to the specific development of new anti-personnel mines. In Korea, landmines accounted for just under 5 per cent of US troop casualties,[65] and many UN casualties resulted from UN-laid minefields that were unrecorded.[66] Uncleared mines remaining from the conflict still remain on Korean territory to this day.[67]

As a result of experiences during the Korean War, in particular following human-wave attacks against UN positions, the US developed the M18 Claymore directional fragmentation mine.[68] When detonated, either by trip-wire or by electric command wire, hundreds of steel ball bearings are hurled out in a 60-degree arc. The lethal radius is 50 metres.[69]

The Vietnam War saw the first widespread use of remotely-delivered or 'scatterable' mines by US forces[70] seeking to stop the flow of men and material from North to South Vietnam through Laos and Cambodia.[71] Aerially-delivered anti-personnel mines had a number of obvious advantages of their manually-emplaced counterparts: they could be deployed rapidly, required little logistic support, and could be laid deep within enemy-held territory, causing disruption in troops movements and supply lines, all with minimal risk to the air-crews.[72] But at the same time, they represented a substantial danger to advances by friendly forces.[73] Thus, without a self-destructing or self-neutralising mechanism and in the absence of straightforward and effective clearance techniques, remotely-delivered mines represented 'a modern version of the ancient, reviled practice of poisoning wells or ploughing salt into farmland.'[74]

Indeed, one of the reasons advanced for the US defeat in Vietnam is its inability to cope with the Vietcong's method of offensive mine warfare, which

---

63 *Ibid.*, p. 96.

64 *Ibid.* Anti-personnel mines are commonly divided into four categories: blast, fragmentation, bounding, and directional fragmentation, based on their primary method of causing injury.

65 But anti-tank mines resulted in 38 per cent of tank losses. *Ibid.*, p. 97.

66 Engineer Agency for Resource Inventories, *Landmine and Countermine Warfare, Korea, 1950-54*, Vol. 5, p. A3, cited in *ibid.*, p. 99. See also *Landmine Monitor Report 1999*, p. 477.

67 See for instance *Landmine Monitor Report 1999*, p. 478; *Landmine Monitor Report 2000*, p. 501.

68 *The History of Landmines*, p. 100. See also *A Deadly Legacy*, p. 20.

69 *Ibid.*

70 It is reported that between 1966 and 1968, the US Department of Defense procured more than 114 million anti-personnel mines for use in the Vietnam War. Cornish, P., *Anti-Personnel Mines, Controlling the Plague of 'Butterflies'*, *op. cit.*, p. 7.

71 See *A Deadly Legacy*, pp. 17-18; *The History of Landmines*, pp. 107-8. For details of the long-term impact on Vietnam of the use of anti-personnel mines see for instance Handicap International, *Landmines in Vietnam, The Coward's War*, Brussels, 1996.

72 *The History of Landmines*, pp. 107-8; *A Deadly Legacy*, p. 17.

73 *A Deadly Legacy*, p. 18.

74 *The History of Landmines*, p. 108.

at times paralysed US forces.[75] Thus, in 1965, 65-70 per cent of US Marine Corps casualties were caused by mines and booby-traps.[76] As Croll notes:

> *'As the Second World War saw the mixed minefield firmly embedded into the defensive doctrine of conventional armies, so the Vietnam War established the mine as a major offensive weapon of guerrilla forces. Technology and manpower could be countered by simplicity and stealth.'*[77]

During the 1970s Italian companies in particular developed and 'market[ed] aggressively state-of-the-art fuze mechanisms and modern plastics.'[78] One such anti-personnel mine was Misar's virtually undetectable SB33, 'which featured an anti-shock device that made it insensitive to explosive clearance. Optional extras included a choice of colour, a special paint that made it undetectable to infra-red equipment and an anti-handling device.'[79] Meanwhile, the US, based on its experiences in Vietnam, poured 'billions of dollars into corporate research and development laboratories' to develop mines that would self-destruct within a pre-set time (usually 4-48 hours).[80] It even developed landmines that served as chemical weapons, each mine containing a quantity of VX nerve gas.[81]

The Gulf War saw extensive use of anti-personnel mines by both Iraqi and Coalition armed forces.[82] Although initial estimates of seven million Iraqi-laid mines subsequently appeared to be an exaggeration,[83] the minefields confronting the Coalition were a matter of considerable concern. In fact they were breached relatively quickly, using a variety of existing and improvised clearance techniques.[84] For its part, the Coalition forces used aerially-delivered GATOR mine systems and the British deployed its JP233 runway-denial system on Iraqi airfields.[85] The true effectiveness of these scatterable mines, however, remains a matter of some dispute,[86] but certainly the much-vaunted self-destruct mecha-

75 *The History of Landmines*, pp. 102, 107. To make up for their lack of resources, the Vietcong frequently resorted to 'stealing' from minefields. As a result, it is estimated that 16 per cent of US mine casualties, and 50 per cent of total Australian casualties, were caused by US-manufactured mines. *Ibid.*, p. 104. See also *Landmine Monitor Report 1999*, p. 384.

76 US Defense Intelligence Agency and US Army Foreign Science and Technology Center, *Landmine Warfare – Trends and Projections, op. cit.*, p. 2-1, cited in *A Deadly Legacy*, p. 18.

77 *The History of Landmines*, p. 108.

78 *Ibid.*, p. 112.

79 *Ibid.*

80 *Landmine Monitor Report 1999*, pp. 322-3.

81 On 30 November 2000, the Department of Defense reported the successful destruction on Johnston Atoll in the Pacific of more than 13,000 landmines filled with VX gas. "Chemical Weapons Destruction Complete on Johnston Atoll", *Press release No. 715-00*, Office of the Assistant Secretary of Defense (Public Affairs), Washington DC, 30 November 2000.

82 *The History of Landmines*, pp. 118-23.

83 See for instance *Landmine Monitor Report 1999*, p. 15. See also *infra* Chapter 3, pp. 203-4.

84 *The History of Landmines*, p. 120.

85 *Ibid.*, p. 121.

86 See for instance Gard, R., "The Military Utility of Anti-Personnel Mines", in *To Walk Without Fear*, pp. 142-4.

nisms had a relatively high failure rate,[87] resulting, as in the Vietnam War, in danger to the advancing troops.[88]

Yet, while mine technology advanced rapidly, the typical use of landmines involved the manual emplacement of 'long-lived'[89] anti-personnel mines in internal armed conflicts by both government armed forces and armed opposition groups.[90] In Angola,[91] Cambodia,[92] Ethiopia, Mozambique,[93] Nicaragua,[94] Iraq,[95] Somalia,[96] Sudan and many other countries, mines were used to terrorise civilians and control their movements.[97] Proliferation was fuelled by low cost of anti-personnel mines, with average prices ranging from US$3-15.[98] And as the Soviet Union crumbled, bitter conflicts in the Caucasus and the former Yugoslavia,[99] which included some of the world's leading landmine producers, saw widespread use of anti-personnel mines. Half a century on from the appalling destruction inflicted by the Second World War, battlefields in Europe were once more littered with explosive remnants of war.

But the increasingly widespread use of anti-personnel mines was not limited to armed forces and armed groups. By the 1990s, civilians in many countries

---

87 Estimated to be at least 10 per cent. *The History of Landmines*, p. 121.

88 *Ibid.*, p. 143. According to a paper by two Pentagon officials, landmines caused 34 per cent of US casualties in Operation Desert Storm. A former US Assistant Secretary of Defense who served in the Gulf War, 'was also struck by the fact that US minefields were unmarked; that no minefield maps were available; that the US could not even provide a general area description of where the mines were supposed to have landed, let alone where they actually did.' *Landmine Monitor Report 1999*, p. 336.

89 That is, without any self-destruct or self-neutralisation mechanism incorporated. Such mines are sometimes referred to as 'dumb' or 'persistent' mines. A self-destruct mechanism is, as the name suggests, an automatically functioning device incorporated into the mine that causes it to explode after a pre-set period of time; self-neutralisation, on the other hand, uses a chemical process to render the mine inert.

90 For instance, the ICBL's Landmine Monitor Report for 2000 reports that 76 different types of anti-personnel mine from 22 countries have been deployed in Angola alone. *Landmine Monitor Report 2000*, p. 130.

91 See for instance Africa Watch, *Landmines in Angola*, New York, 1993; Human Rights Watch Arms Project, *Still Killing: Landmines in Southern Africa*, US, 1997.

92 See for instance Asia Watch and Physicians for Human Rights, *Land Mines in Cambodia, The Coward's War*, US, 1991, pp. 21-58; Davies, P., *The War of the Mines: Cambodia, Landmines and the Impoverishment of a Nation*, Pluto Press, Colorado, 1994.

93 See for instance Human Rights Watch, *Landmines in Mozambique*, New York, 1994; Human Rights Watch Arms Project, *Still Killing: Landmines in Southern Africa*, US, 1997.

94 Americas Watch, *Landmines in El Salvador and Nicaragua: The Civilian Victims*, Human Rights Watch, New York, December 1986.

95 See for instance Middle East Watch, *Hidden Death: Land Mines and Civilian Casualties in Iraqi Kurdistan*, New York, 1992.

96 See for instance African Rights and Mines Advisory Group, *Violent Deeds Live On – Landmines in Somalia and Somaliland*, London, 1993; Physicians for Human Rights, *Hidden Enemies: Land Mines in Northern Somalia*, Boston, November 1992.

97 *A Deadly Legacy*, *op. cit.*, p. 23; see also *Landmine Monitor Report 1999*, p. 447.

98 See for example DHA Factsheet on Manufacturing and Trade, New York, 1996; *Landmine Monitor Report 1999*, pp. 457, 458, 496. Hi-tech mines are, however, considerably more expensive.

99 See for instance *The Silent Menace – Landmines in Bosnia and Herzegovina*, ICRC/UNHCR, Geneva, 1997.

were laying mines for their own purposes.[100] In Cambodia, for instance, they have been used to protect homes and livestock, for fishing, even to settle local disputes.[101] In Colombia and the Casamance region of Senegal, anti-personnel mines are allegedly used to protect illegal drug plantations.[102] And in Georgia, landmines are reportedly used to uproot trees![103]

In Kosovo, which saw extensive minelaying by Yugoslav forces and Serb paramilitaries and, though to a lesser extent, by the Kosovo Liberation Army (KLA) in 1998 and 1999,[104] even children were schooled in the art of mine warfare, presumably in preparation for the expected ground assault by NATO forces. According to a British KFOR soldier who found instructional equipment intended for children in a school: 'They have the information here to learn over and above what a skilled Class 1 Royal Engineer with two years' experience would know, more on a par with an Explosive Ordnance Disposal specialist. (...) They have been in a state of war for ten years, and it is quite rational to assume that once they leave school they are going to defend their country.'[105] And even though the war between the Federal Republic of Yugoslavia and the North Atlantic Treaty Organization (NATO) was formally ended in June 1999, anti-vehicle and anti-personnel mines continued to be laid in the province in furtherance of ethnic strife.[106]

Based on an historical assessment of the use of all landmines (*i.e.*, not merely anti-personnel mines), Croll asserts that given the range of tactical situations, terrain and types of forces that used them, mines have undoubtedly been one of the most flexible weapon systems of the late 20th Century.[107] He claims that the 'intelligent' mine is 'perhaps the "perfect soldier": it does not sleep, require feeding or paying and is unable to feel pain.'[108] More controversially, he goes on to claim that the mine, 'the silent sentinel, may become the war hero of the 21st Century[.] (...) After 2,500 years the evolution of the victim-operated trap is not complete, the "infernal machine" is here to stay.'[109]

---

100 See also *Landmine Monitor Report 1999*, pp. 183, 698, 700.

101 See for instance Davies, P., "Mines and Unexploded Ordnance in Cambodia and Laos: Understanding the Costs", in Kumar, K. (ed.), *Rebuilding Societies After Civil War, Critical Roles for International Assistance*, Lynne Rienner, US, 1997, p. 243. See also *Landmine Monitor Report 1999*, pp. 389, 393.

102 *Landmine Monitor Report 1999*, p. 299; *Landmine Monitor Report 2000*, p. 98.

103 *Ibid.*, p. 794.

104 See for instance *Explosive Remnants of War, Cluster Bombs and Landmines in Kosovo*, ICRC, Geneva, August 2000, pp. 17-18; see also "Four deaths in blast show risk to refugees", *Irish Times*, 22 June 1999.

105 Farrell, S., "Serb pupils learnt tactics of terror", *Times*, 29 June 1999. See also "Youngsters given lessons in how to make landmines", *Scotsman*, 29 June 1999.

106 See for instance *Explosive Remnants of War: Cluster Bombs and Landmines in Kosovo*, ICRC, Geneva, August 2000.

107 *The History of Landmines*, p. 123.

108 *Ibid.*, p. 147.

109 *Ibid.*, pp. 147, 152.

0.2. The Development of International Humanitarian Law Applicable to Weapons[110]

As Professor Greenwood remarks: 'Throughout its history, the development of international humanitarian law has been influenced by religious concepts and philosophical ideas.[111] Customary rules of warfare are part of the very first rules of international law.'[112] In India, in the fourth century BC, for example, literature and laws contained provisions that forbade the use of certain means of combat, such as poisoned or burning arrows.[113] Likewise, the Greeks[114] and Romans customarily observed a prohibition against the use of poison or poisoned weapons.[115] In 1132, the Lateran Council declared that the crossbow and arbalest were 'unchristian' weapons,[116] though their use continued, seemingly unarrested by this sacred prohibition.

It was not until the latter half of the 19th Century that a written international agreement first prohibited a specific weapon or war. The *1868 St Petersburg Declaration Renouncing the Use, in Time of War, of Explosive Projectiles Under 400 Grammes Weight*[117] was negotiated by 16 States,[118] at an International Military Commission convened at the invitation of the Russian Tsar.[119] It prohibited the use of a newly-developed 'exploding' bullet designed to destroy ammunition wagons but which also exploded upon impact with a soft surface (such as, for instance, the human body).[120] But in the words of Professor Greenwood:

---

110 For a thoughtful introduction to this issue see for instance Oeter, S., "Methods and Means of Combat", in Fleck, D. (ed.), *The Handbook of Humanitarian Law in Armed Conflicts*, *op. cit.*, pp. 105-10; Greenwood, C., "Humanitarian Law and Laws of War", *Centennial of the First International Peace Conference, Preliminary Report*, June 1998. For a more general overview of the development of international humanitarian law, see for instance Münsch, F., "History of the Laws of War", *Encyclopaedia of Public International Law*, Vol. 4, North Holland, Amsterdam, pp. 326-9.

111 On this point see also Johnson, J.T., *Can Modern War Be Just?*, Yale University Press, New Haven and London, 1984, pp. 86-104. Johnson, at p. 89, cites the philosopher Locke's *Essay Concerning Civil Government*, wherein Locke strongly condemns means of war that have effects of war enduring after the war has end. Johnson gives the example of a scorched-earth policy, though the example of anti-personnel mines would also appear appropriate. See also Rogers, A.P.V., *Law on the Battlefield*, Manchester University Press, Manchester, 1996, p. 1.

112 Greenwood, C., "Historical Development and Legal Basis", *op. cit.*, p. 12.

113 *Ibid.*, p. 13; *Documents on the Laws of War*, p. 29.

114 'When Odysseus had gone to Ephyra to procure a deadly drug for smearing his arrows, Ilus refused to give it to him on the ground that the gods would not sanction such an act.' Phillipson, C., *International Law and Custom of Ancient Greece and Rome*, Macmillan & Co. Ltd., 1911, p. 209, cited by Robblee Jr., Capt. P.A., "The Legitimacy of Modern Conventional Weaponry", *The Military Law and Law of War Review*, Vol. XVI, No. 4, 1977, p. 403.

115 *Documents on the Laws of War*, p. 29.

116 *Ibid.* See also Greenwood, C., "Historical Development and Legal Basis", *op. cit.*, p. 15.

117 Hereinafter, this instrument will be referred to as the 1868 St Petersburg Declaration.

118 Austria-Hungary, Bavaria, Belgium, Denmark, France, Great Britain, Greece, Italy, Netherlands, Portugal, Prussia and the North German Confederation, Russia, Sweden and Norway, Switzerland, Turkey, and Wurtemberg. *Documents on the Laws of War*, p. 32.

119 *Ibid.*, p. 29; see also Greenwood, C., "Historical Development and Legal Basis", *op. cit.*, p. 19.

120 *Documents on the Laws of War*, p. 29.

> *'The importance of the 1868 Declaration lies not so much in the specific ban which it introduced as in its statement of the principles on which that ban was based. The Preamble to the Declaration reflects the theories developed by Rousseau nearly a century earlier and is the classic statement of the principle that it is prohibited to employ weapons or methods of warfare which are likely to cause unnecessary suffering. Humanitarian law accepts that one of the legitimate objects of warfare is to disable enemy combatants (and in many cases this necessarily involves killing) but it rejects the use of weapons which cause additional suffering for no military gain. That principle remains important today. It is one of the general principles of humanitarian law, by which the legality of all weapons and means of warfare fall to be measured. It also inspired a number of other international agreements banning specific weapons, such as poison gas and soft-headed or "dumdum" bullets.'*[121]

In 1899, at the First Hague Peace Conference,[122] two further international agreements sought to prohibit, with varying degrees of success, the 'use of projectiles the sole object of which is the diffusion of asphyxiating or deleterious gases',[123] and 'the use of bullets which expand or flatten easily in the human body, such as bullets with a hard envelope which does not entirely cover the core or is pierced with incisions.'[124] Indeed, it was the failure of the *1899 Hague Declaration Concerning Asphyxiating Gases* to stop the use of chemical warfare during the First World War[125] that resulted in the negotiation of the 1925 Geneva Protocol for the Prohibition of the Use in War of Asphyxiating, Poisonous or Other Gases, and of Bacteriological Methods of Warfare.[126]

Despite the horrific impact on civilians of weaponry used during the Second World War, efforts to prohibit specific weapons were stymied until the adoption, in 1980, of the *United Nations Convention on Prohibitions or Restrictions on the Use of Certain Conventional Weapons Which May be Deemed to be Excessively Injurious or to Have Indiscriminate Effects.*[127] Three protocols originally annexed to this Convention, respectively, prohibited the use of 'any weapon the primary effect of which is to injure by fragments which in the human body escape detection by X-rays';[128] restricted the use of mines, booby-traps and other

---

121 Greenwood, C., "Historical Development and Legal Basis", *op. cit.*, pp. 19-20, footnotes omitted.

122 See for instance *Documents on the Laws of War*, p. 35.

123 Hague Declaration (IV, 2) Concerning Asphyxiating Gases. See *Documents on the Laws of War*, pp. 35-7.

124 That is, the infamous 'dumdum' bullets. See *infra* Chapter 3, pp. 217-9. Hague Declaration (IV, 3) Concerning Expanding Bullets. *Documents on the Laws of War*, pp. 39-41.

125 It is alleged that chemical warfare in the First World War resulted in some 1.3 million casualties, including 100,000 fatalities. Krutzsch, W. and Trapp, R., *A Commentary on the Chemical Weapons Convention*, Martinus Nijhoff, Dordrecht, 1994, p. 1.

126 Hereinafter, this instrument is referred to as the 1925 Geneva Gas Protocol. See Krutzsch, W. and Trapp, R., *A Commentary on the Chemical Weapons Convention, op. cit.*, pp. 137-46.

127 This Convention, which is generally hereinafter referred to as the 1980 Convention on Certain Conventional Weapons or 1980 CCW,.is considered in detail in Chapter 1 *infra*.

128 Protocol I. *Documents on the Laws of War*, p. 479.

devices;[129] and restricted the use of incendiary weapons.[130] A Protocol IV outlawing the use of laser weapons specifically designed to blind was added in September 1995 at the First Review Conference of the Convention, and in May 1996, the same Conference adopted an amended Protocol II.[131]

The only other significant international humanitarian law agreement governing a specific weapon[132] is the *Convention on the Prohibition of the Use, Stockpiling, Production and Transfer of Anti-Personnel Mines and on Their Destruction.*[133] It is possible, however, that a number of additional Protocols will be adopted by the Second Review Conference of the 1980 Convention on Conventional Weapons, due to take place in Geneva in December 2001.[134]

0.3. The Development of International Humanitarian Law Applicable to Anti-Personnel Mines

Although the relevant instruments of international humanitarian law applicable to anti-personnel mines are discussed in detail in Chapters 1 and 2 *infra*, in understanding the development of the law during the 1990s, it is essential first to consider the respective roles of the ICRC and the ICBL. Both of these organisations have been hugely influential in the recent evolution of international humanitarian law governing the use of anti-personnel mines.

0.3.1. The Role of the International Committee of the Red Cross

The ICRC first raised concerns about landmines – anti-tank as well as anti-personnel – in 1955, following the use of POW labour for clearance during and following the Second World War.[135] But following unsuccessful attempts to include the regulation of specific conventional weapons in the 1977 Additional Protocols to the Geneva Conventions, the ICRC maintained a relatively low

---

129 Protocol II. See *ibid.*, pp. 479-84.

130 Protocol III. See *ibid.*, pp. 484-5.

131 See *infra* Chapter 1.

132 Of course, other instruments of international law are also applicable to the use of weapons. See for instance *Documents on the Laws of War*, pp. 17-18. Thus, for example, arms control and disarmament agreements prohibit the development, production and stockpiling of biological weapons (the Convention on the Prohibition of the Development, Production and Stockpiling of Bacteriological (Biological) Weapons and on their Destruction) and the production, and the development, production, stockpiling and use of chemical weapons (the Convention on the Prohibition of the Development, Production, Stockpiling and Use of Chemical Weapons and on their Destruction). See for instance Krutzsch, W. and Trapp, R., *A Commentary on the Chemical Weapons Convention, op. cit.*, pp. 1-5.

133 Hereinafter, this instrument is generally referred to as the Convention on the Prohibition of Anti-Personnel Mines.

134 See *infra* Chapter 2 and the Concluding Remarks. The ICRC, for instance, has proposed a new Protocol to regulate 'explosive remnants of war' (although it is unlikely that an agreement will be adopted in 2001), and the US has proposed increased regulation of remotely-delivered landmines, particularly anti-vehicle mines.

135 It had previously insisted that the compulsory use of prisoners of war for mine clearance be explicitly outlawed in the Third Geneva Convention of 1949, after the implicit prohibition in the corresponding 1929 Geneva Convention was not respected during and after the Second World War. See *infra* Chapter 1, p. 36, footnote 275.

profile as States negotiated and adopted under UN auspices the 1980 Convention on Certain Conventional Weapons (1980 CCW) including its annexed Protocol II which regulated the use of landmines, booby-traps and other devices.

As the 1980s wore on, and the number of casualties due to anti-personnel mines grew and grew, ICRC field surgeons, reportedly sick of amputating the limbs of young children and other civilians, asked the organisation's Geneva headquarters to promote the need for effective preventive action through a change in international law.[136] A number of carefully-planned meetings and seminars followed, beginning with the Montreux Symposium on Mines, held in 1993. Then in February 1994, as States were preparing to attend intergovernmental meetings of experts in Geneva to prepare the First Review Conference of the 1980 CCW, the then President of the ICRC, Cornelio Sommaruga, astonished many, including within the institution itself, when he declared that from a 'humanitarian point of view' a 'world-wide ban on anti-personnel mines is the only truly effective solution [to the landmine crisis].'[137]

In the autumn of 1995, as negotiations in Vienna at the first session of the CCW Review Conference staggered on inexorably towards deadlock,[138] the ICRC decided to launch, for the first time in its history, a public media campaign in favour of the total prohibition of anti-personnel mines, with the ultimate goal of stigmatising the weapon in order to make its use 'unconscionable'. With targeted regional seminars and workshops, some devoted to assessing the military utility of anti-personnel landmines, others looking at their humanitarian impact, the ICRC and certain national Red Cross societies contributed significantly to raising the consciousness of the world to the consequences of the widespread and indiscriminate use of the weapon.

The publication in 1996 of a study commissioned by the ICRC into the military effectiveness of anti-personnel mines in 26 armed conflicts beginning with the Second World War marked one of the turning points in the effort to stem the use and proliferation of landmines.[139] Its central conclusions were that: 'Although the military value of anti-tank mines is acknowledged, the value of [anti-personnel] mines is questionable. (...) The limited military utility of [anti-personnel] mines is far outweighed by the humanitarian consequences of their use in actual conflicts. On this basis their prohibition and elimination should be pursued as a matter of utmost urgency by governments and the entire international community.'[140] Largely as a result of the ICRC's work, ministries of defence were less able to continue to justify their retention of anti-personnel mines on the basis of an overriding, but unspecified, military utility.

---

136 See for instance the Foreword by Cornelio Sommaruga in Maresca, L. and Maslen, S. (eds.), *The Banning of Anti-Personnel Landmines, The Work of the International Committee of the Red Cross 1955-1999*, Cambridge University Press, Cambridge, UK, October 2000, p. xvii.

137 See *ibid.*, p. 264.

138 In fact, only one session of the Review Conference had originally been envisaged, but the failure to reach agreement led to two further sessions in 1996.

139 *Anti-Personnel Landmines: Friend or Foe, A Study of the Military Use and Effectiveness of Anti-Personnel Mines*, ICRC, Geneva, 1996.

140 See Maresca, L. and Maslen, S. (eds.), *The Banning of Anti-Personnel Landmines, op. cit.*, pp. 418-9.

Thereafter, from the launch of the 'Ottawa Process'[141] in October 1996 until the adoption of the Convention on the Prohibition of Anti-Personnel Mines in September 1997, the ICRC participated in meetings as an Expert Observer lending its unequalled knowledge of international humanitarian law to the movement to prohibit the weapon. In accordance with its role – 'to work for the faithful application of international humanitarian law applicable in armed conflicts'[142] –, the ICRC is currently engaged in promoting the ratification and implementation of both the 1980 Convention on Conventional Weapons and the Convention on the Prohibition of Anti-Personnel Mines. Notwithstanding the increasingly professional involvement in international humanitarian law[143] of non-governmental organisations (NGOs), such as Human Rights Watch, the ICRC will once again be called upon to play a pivotal role in promoting new international law in the Second Review Conference of the 1980 Convention on Conventional Weapons.

0.3.2. The Role of the International Campaign to Ban Landmines[144]

The ICBL was born out of the work of field- and human-rights-based NGOs that became increasingly concerned by the dramatic effects of anti-personnel mines on communities in conflict and post-conflict settings. The ICBL's own 'ban movement chronology'[145] records the first notable event in the putative campaign as the publication in September 1991 by Asia Watch of Human Rights Watch and Physicians for Human Rights (PHR) of *Land Mines in Cambodia, The Coward's War*, in which both organisations called for 'consideration of an unconditional ban on the manufacture, possession, transfer, sale and use of land mines and other devices that detonate on contact in all international and internal conflicts.'[146]

In November 1991, Vietnam Veterans of America Foundation (VVAF), Washington, and Medico International (MI), Frankfurt, agreed to launch jointly a campaign of advocacy to bring together NGOs in a co-ordinated effort to ban landmines. The following year, Handicap International (HI), Human Rights Watch (HRW), MI, Mines Advisory Group (MAG), PHR and VVAF all met in New York and agreed to co-ordinate campaigning efforts and to co-sponsor a

---

141 See for instance Lawson, R.J., "The Ottawa Process and the International Movement to Ban Anti-Personnel Mines", *To Walk Without Fear*, pp. 160-84.

142 See for instance the amended Statutes of the International Committee of the Red Cross, which came into force on 20 July 1998. "Statutes of the International Committee of the Red Cross", *International Review of the Red Cross*, No. 324, 1 September 1998, pp. 537-43.

143 See for instance Sandoz, Y., *The International Committee of the Red Cross as guardian of international humanitarian law*, ICRC, Geneva, March 1998.

144 Unless otherwise stated, this section is based on information contained in the ICBL's own 'Ban Movement Chronology'; see <http://www.icbl.org>.

145 See <http://www.icbl.org>.

146 Asia Watch and Physicians for Human Rights, *Land Mines in Cambodia, The Coward's War*, *op. cit.*, pp. 102-3.

first NGO Conference on Landmines in London in 1993.[147] The six NGOs issued a 'Joint Call to Ban Anti-Personnel Landmines', the founding document of the ICBL.[148] The 1993 conference brought together 50 representatives of 40 NGOs to strategise on building the campaign to ban landmines. HI, HRW, MI, MAG, PHR and VVAF were formally recognised as the Steering Committee of the ICBL and VVAF was named as its Co-ordinator.

The same year, following lobbying by HI,[149] the French Foreign Ministry sent a letter to the UN Secretary-General officially requesting a review conference of the 1980 CCW.[150] In the autumn of 1993, the 48th session of the UN General Assembly adopted a resolution formally calling for the review conference.[151] The same session also adopted a resolution calling for a moratorium on the export of anti-personnel mines.[152]

In 1994, the UN Secretary-General submitted his first report on mine clearance, noting that the 'best and most effective way' to solve the global landmine problem was a complete ban of all landmines.[153] Before the UN General Assembly that year, and following extensive pressure by the US Campaign to Ban Landmines and Patrick Leahy, the Democrat Senator of Vermont, US President Bill Clinton called for the first time for the 'eventual elimination' of landmines.

In 1995, Belgium became the first country to pass domestic legislation banning landmine use, production, procurement, sale and transfer, including components, parts and technology. But whereas a growing number of States were by then supporting a total prohibition of anti-personnel mines, the 1995 Review Conference of the 1980 CCW was unable to reach consensus. The decision was taken to suspend proceedings and to reconvene with two further sessions of the Conference in 1996.

In March 1996, prior to the adoption by consensus of amended Protocol II annexed to the 1980 CCW, VVAF sponsored two full-page advertisements in the *New York Times* calling on the US President to ban anti-personnel mines

---

147 See for instance Chabasse, P., "The French Campaign", *To Walk Without Fear*, p. 60. According to Chabasse, the idea for a NGO network came from Rae McGrath, the founder of Mines Advisory Group.

148 See for instance Williams, J. and Goose, S., "The International Campaign to Ban Landmines", *To Walk Without Fear*, p. 22; *Landmine Monitor Report 1999*, p. 928. The joint call was for:
An international ban on the use, production, stockpiling, and sale, transfer or export of anti-personnel mines;
The establishment of an international fund, administered by the United Nations, to promote and finance landmine awareness, clearance and eradication programmes worldwide; and
Countries responsible for the production and dissemination of anti-personnel mines to contribute to the international fund.
See for instance *A Deadly Legacy*, pp. 361-2.

149 According to one of HI's Co-Directors, Philippe Chabasse, the idea came from Senator Leahy who wrote to the organisation asking them to push the government to call for the Review Conference. Chabasse, P., "The French Campaign", *To Walk Without Fear*, p. 62.

150 In accordance with the procedure laid down in Article 8 of the Convention. See *infra* Chapter 1, p. 46-7.

151 UN General Assembly resolution 48/79, paras. 5-7. See *infra* Chapter 1, p. 47-8.

152 UN General Assembly resolution 48/75K of 16 December 1993.

153 *UN Doc. A/49/357* of 6 September 1994.

immediately. The second of these advertisements was an open letter to the President signed by retired General Norman Schwarzkopf and 14 other high-ranking officers.[154] The military case for anti-personnel mines was coming under ever-increasing scrutiny.

In 1997, media attention given to landmines increased exponentially following high-profile visits to Angola and Bosnia-Herzegovina by the late Princess of Wales.[155] Following the successful adoption of the Convention on the Prohibition of Anti-Personnel Mines, the Nobel Peace Prize was awarded jointly to the ICBL and its Co-ordinator, Jody Williams.[156] The same year, on 10 December, a few days after the signature by 123 States of the Convention, the ICBL and Ms Williams received the prize at the formal ceremony held in Oslo.[157]

In September 1998, following an energetic campaign in favour of ratification of the Convention on the Prohibition of Anti-Personnel Mines by both the ICBL and the ICRC, Burkina Faso became the 40th country to deposit its instrument of ratification with the UN Secretary-General thereby triggering the Convention's entry into force on 1 March 1999. This landmark event was celebrated by bell-ringing and campaign events in more than 30 countries; and by this time, the ICBL had grown into a coalition of more than 1,300 NGOs in more than 75 countries.[158]

The most significant event in ICBL's recent history has been the publication in April 1999 and August 2000 of *Landmine Monitor*, the ICBL's 'unprecedented initiative (...) to monitor implementation of and compliance with' the Convention. In this impressive research document, which is revised, updated and reissued annually,[159] the objectives of the ICBL are now stated to be:

- *An international ban on the use, production, stockpiling, and sale, transfer, or export of anti-personnel mines;*

[154] Though a number, including General Schwarzkopf, have since distanced themselves from the letter.

[155] Somewhat surprisingly, these events are absent from the ICBL's own chronology. Although the first visit to Angola in January 1997 was made at the invitation of the British Red Cross, the visit to Bosnia-Herzegovina in August 1997 was organised by the Landmines Survivors Network (LSN), a member of ICBL's steering committee.

[156] An article in the Seattle Post-Intelligencer by a member of the editorial board declared that 'it wasn't just the bunny-hugging peaceniks who backed Williams. A driving force in the movement was Bobby Muller, president of the Vietnam Veterans of America Foundation – himself rendered paraplegic in that war.' Shapley, T., "Clinton's cruel decision on land mines risks too many lives", *Seattle Post-Intelligencer*, 17 April 2000.

[157] In an article for the Canadian book, *To Walk Without Fear*, Williams and Steve Goose of Human Rights Watch claim that the Nobel Peace Prize convinced Japan to sign the treaty. See Williams, J. and Goose, S., "The International Campaign to Ban Landmines", in *To Walk Without Fear*, p. 46.

[158] ICBL, "Mine Ban Treaty Enters Into Force – ICBL Praises Progress, Condemns Users", *Press release*, Oslo, 1 March 1999. There are now said to be 1,400 member organisations in 90 countries. *Landmine Monitor Report 2000*, p. 981.

[159] Each annual report is published just prior to the Annual Meeting of States Parties of the Convention on the Prohibition of Anti-Personnel Mines.

- *The signing, ratification, implementation, and monitoring of the 1997 Mine Ban Treaty;*[160]
- *Increased resources for humanitarian demining and mine awareness programmes; and*
- *Increased resources for landmine victim rehabilitation and assistance.*

0.4. Statistics and the Development of International Humanitarian Law Governing Anti-Personnel Mines

Given the widespread use of figures in the campaigns to prohibit anti-personnel mines, it is appropriate, before concluding this introduction, to address briefly the accuracy of statistics. Figures relating to the estimated number of mines uncleared, the number of mines being emplaced, the number of mines stockpiled, and the number of mine victims annually worldwide, have all played a prominent role in both the ICBL and the ICRC campaigns and were widely reported in the media.[161] The issue has become increasingly embroiled in controversy, with particular concern being raised by former military figures[162] and a number of deminers, especially those linked with the UK-based mine clearance organisation, the Halo Trust.[163]

In 1993, the US Department of State conducted enquiries through its embassies and concluded in a report to Congress that there were between 65 and 110 million uncleared anti-personnel mines affecting 62 countries.[164] The second report, issued the following year, concluded that some 80-110 million anti-

160 The term favoured by ICBL for the *Convention on the Prohibition of the Use, Stockpiling, Production and Transfer of Anti-Personnel Mines and on Their Destruction.*

161 See for instance the preface in King, C. (ed.), *Jane's Mines and Mine Clearance 1997-1998*, Jane's, UK, 1998. Note also the caution about statistical accuracy already expressed in 1994. See Cornish, P., *Anti-Personnel Mines, Controlling the Plague of 'Butterflies'*, *op. cit.*, p. 5.

162 Lynch Jr., Maj.-Gen. J.D., "Landmines, Lies, And Other Phenomena", *Proceedings (US Naval Institute)*, May 1998, p. 44. Yet, the apparently strong case being made of deliberate, or at least reckless exaggeration of figures, was sometimes weakened by the proponents themselves engaging in a similar enterprise. Thus, for example, Lynch cites Frank Gaffney, the Director of the extreme right-wing think-tank, the Center for Security Policy, as justification for the claim that some US$30 million of US taxpayer's money was spent by the ICRC in its 'public relations' campaign supporting the landmine ban. Likewise, Mike Croll claimed incorrectly that the cost of the Oslo Diplomatic Conference was US$25 million and that none of the Can$100 million pledged by Canada for landmines was intended for clearance. Croll, M., "Wrong turning in a minefield: Diana was wrong", *The Independent*, 20 August 1998.

163 See for instance *The History of Landmines*, pp. 131-2. It appeared, though, that other deminers did not share the views of Halo Trust. Halle J. Hansen, Director of Norwegian People's Aid, the world's largest humanitarian mine clearance organisation, declared in an ICBL press release: 'We have always viewed demining and the ban as two essential, mutually reinforcing goals and activities. There is no question that a political ban – stopping new production, trade, stockpiling and use – is a pre-requisite to successful long-term global mine clearance. The attention to the issue generated by the ban movement has been nothing but beneficial to deminers. The number of organisations and individuals in our profession who think otherwise is very small.' ICBL, "Mine Ban Treaty Enters Into Force – ICBL Praises Progress, Condemns Users", *Press release*, Oslo, 1 March 1999.

164 United States Department of State, *Hidden Killers: the Global Problem with Uncleared Landmines, a Report on International Demining*, Washington DC, 1993.

personnel mines were littered across 64 countries.[165] These figures were adopted by the United Nations, and the ICBL and the ICRC decided to use generally a figure of 100 million landmines in their advocacy work.[166]

Although no one, even today, can give an accurate, verifiable figure for the number of uncleared anti-personnel mines worldwide,[167] it was apparent to many from the early days of the campaigns, that the figures were exaggerated.[168] They included, for instance, a reported 23 million mines in Egypt,[169] a figure possibly inflated by the authorities for political purposes,[170] and which also seemingly encompassed a very high percentage of other unexploded munitions.[171] Likewise, in Bosnia-Herzegovina, estimates went as high as six million mines,[172] but it is now reliably believed, based on recovered minefield maps, that somewhere around 750,000 anti-personnel mines remain to be cleared.[173] In Cambodia, where estimates are of 6 million mines, Halo Trust confidently asserts that there are no more than 300,000.[174] In Afghanistan, an initial estimate of 35 million mines was downgraded to 10 million,[175] after it was pointed out that this would have involved the Soviets laying some 10,000 mines per day, every day of its

---

165 United States Department of State, *Hidden Killers: the Global Landmine Crisis*, Washington DC, 1994, p. v. See also Williams, J., "Landmines and measures to eliminate them", *The International Review of the Red Cross*, No. 305, July-August 1995, p. 379.

166 Following public discussion of the figures, the ICBL talked of 'tens of millions' of mines and then of 'millions' of uncleared landmines in 'as many as' 70 countries. See Williams, J. and Goose, S., "The International Campaign to Ban Landmines", *To Walk Without Fear*, p. 21; International Campaign to Ban Landmines, campaign leaflet, Human Rights Watch, Washington, March 1999. The ICRC now refers to 'millions' of mines. See for instance <http://www.icrc.org>.

167 In terms of numbers – though these are not necessarily reflected in the impact on the civilian population –, the most affected countries are probably Afghanistan, Angola, Bosnia-Herzegovina, Cambodia, Chad, Egypt, Iran, Iraq, Libya, and the Republic of Korea.

168 See for instance Flynn, M., "Politisches Minenfeld", in *Der Überblick*, No. 2, 1999, pp. 86-9.

169 Germany is reported to believe that there are no more than 1.5 to 2 million landmines (*i.e.*, including anti-tank mines) uncleared from World War II in Egypt. There are, though, landmines also remaining from subsequent conflicts. See *Landmine Monitor Report 2000*, p. 922. It was previously reported that the US Central Intelligence Agency believed there were no more than one million landmines uncleared in Egypt. Windrem, R., "How bad is the problem?", *NBC News*, 17 September 1997. See also "Egypt to Ask WWII Rivals to Clear Landmines", *Xinhua*, Cairo, 20 October 1997; "Egypt's landmines are old and hard to locate in The Devil's Garden", *Arabic News*, 9 October 1997.

170 Egypt has repeatedly called for US$250 million from the UK and Germany to clear landmines left over from the Second World War. See *Landmine Monitor Report 2000*, p. 923; see also *Landmine Monitor Report 1999*, p. 15.

171 According to Landmine Monitor, Egypt includes all unexploded ordnance within these figures. *Landmine Monitor Report 2000*, p. 922.

172 See for instance Parliamentary Assembly of the Council of Europe, *Recommendation 1343 (1997) on anti-personnel landmines and their humanitarian implications*, adopted on 24 September 1997.

173 See *The Silent Menace op. cit.*, pp. 5, 15. In late 1999; it was reported, that 120,000 anti-personnel mines had been cleared since 1996. See for instance "Ridding the world of land mines", *Chicago Tribune*, 27 November 1999.

174 Alford, P., "Cambodia's landmine myths exploded", *Australian*, 3 June 2000, <http://www.news.com.au>.

175 See *The History of Landmines*, p. 131.

nine-year military involvement. Halo Trust asserts that there are fewer than one million anti-personnel mines on Afghan soil.[176]

Moreover, estimates of the numbers of mines being laid each year also varied widely. The UN claimed in 1994 that between two and five million landmines were being laid each year,[177] but that only 100,000 were being cleared. The former figure is no longer believed valid (if ever it were),[178] and it is now asserted that more mines are being cleared than laid[179] (although the statistical basis for this assertion is also noticeable by its absence).[180]

Certain mine clearers objected strongly to these over-estimates,[181] which they blamed for causing donors to shy away from adequately funding mine clearance,[182] and they variously criticised the ICBL, the ICRC and the UN for the situation. Thus, in early 2000, a study published on behalf of the Pro Victimis Foundation, a financial supporter of the Halo Trust, found that the UN estimate of how many mines were buried in the ground were 'overly inflated' and called upon the organisation either to revise and update its estimates or to drop the use of figures.[183] But little evidence was produced to justify their claims that donors were actually being deterred.[184] In fact, the excessively high costs of mine clearance as a result of bloated expatriate salaries and the problems of re-mining in certain countries such as Angola, may be more responsible for any diversion of funding away from mine clearance operations. There was also a suspicion that former soldiers, as Western deminers tend to be, were less than

176 See for instance Lynch Jr., Maj.-Gen. J.D., "Landmines, Lies, And Other Phenomena", *op. cit.*, citing Jefferson, P., "A Political Minefield", *The Wall Street Journal*, 15 October 1997. The Halo Trust was presumably the source for the Washington Post estimate of between 500,000-800,000 landmines (anti-vehicle as well as anti-personnel mines) used during the conflict. Since 1990, Halo Trust claims to have found and destroyed more than 22,000 landmines. See Constable, P., "Afghan minefields go to the dogs", *Washington Post*, 6 March 2000, p. A16.

177 See for instance "Assistance in Mine Clearance", Report of the Secretary-General, issued as *UN Doc. A/49/357* on 6 September 1994, p. 7.

178 Though, the Landmine Monitor still claimed in 2000 that millions of mines had been laid each year in the 1970s, 1980s and early 1990s. *Landmine Monitor Report 2000*, p. 5.

179 See for instance US Department of State, *Hidden Killers*, Washington DC, September 1998, p. v.

180 In the view of the author, even this assertion may be wrong, at least for 1999. In 1999, substantial numbers of anti-personnel mines were used in Angola, the Eritrea-Ethiopia conflict, the Federal Republic of Yugoslavia (Kosovo), the Russian Federation (Chechnya), and unknown numbers of mines were being used in the Democratic Republic of Congo, Sri Lanka, Uganda, among other countries.

181 See for instance "Landmine numbers 'hugely exaggerated'", *Sunday Telegraph*, 29 November 1998.

182 *The History of Landmines*, p. 131.

183 Bottagliero, I., *120 Million Landmines Deployed Worldwide: Fact or Fiction*, Fondation Pro Victimis Geneva, UK, 2000, pp. 79-80.

184 In fact, the opposite appears to be true, as funding for mine clearance appears (it is rather difficult to know for certain) to have risen dramatically over the past five years. The question of how effectively these additional resources have been targeted is, however, a different kettle of fish.

enthralled at the prospect of civilian, particularly NGO, intervention in military affairs.[185]

Furthermore, the organisations and agencies under attack appeared unrepentant. In 1999, the ICBL, for instance, pointed out, somewhat disingenuously: 'Nobody knows how many mines there are in the ground, and that number is not very relevant, despite the attention given to the issue. What is relevant is how many people are affected by the presence of mines, which are obstacles to post-conflict reconstruction and socio-economic development.'[186] A spokesman for MAG, the UK-based mine clearance organisation, said the UN figures 'might be inflated' but added that, 'this does not mean the problem is not a major one.'[187] A representative of the UN's Mine Action Service, the UN focal point for mine action, stated that 'All we can do is make intelligent guesses.'[188]

On the other hand, original ICBL estimates of 100 million anti-personnel mines in stockpiles have been revised sharply upwards to the current estimate of 250 million lying in the arsenals of 108 countries.[189] And in response to attacks on the use of estimates of mine numbers, the British Red Cross, stood its ground. A spokesman declared: 'Every 20 minutes someone somewhere is injured by a landmine. That's all that matters.'[190]

Yet, concern was even expressed at the accuracy of the estimated figures of landmine victims. In 1999, according to the Landmine Monitor: 'Just as with the number of landmines in the world, the number of landmines survivors remains difficult to definitively answer. Even more daunting is trying to get a complete picture of landmine casualties. Victim profiles vary from country to country – but what is consistent is that the vast majority of mine victims are civilians.'[191] Between March 1999 and May 2000, the Landmine Monitor believed that there were new landmine and UXO victims in 71 countries.[192] In 1999, the ICRC

185 According to Croll, for instance: 'Most of the bodies that work in the field are humanitarian groups, and are by nature pacifist and suspicious of the military. Most deminers are former soldiers like myself. It makes communication very difficult.' See Croll, M., "Wrong turning in a minefield: Diana was wrong", *Independent*, 20 August 1998.

186 *Landmine Monitor Report 1999*, pp. 13, 14, 15. For the ICBL's present position see for instance the Statement of Facts issued by the ICBL Mine Action Working Group in 1998.

187 Ngqiyaza, B., "Landmines: UN figures exaggerated, group says", *Johannesburg Business Day*, 4 May 2000.

188 See for instance "Landmine numbers 'hugely exaggerated'", *Sunday Telegraph*, 29 November 1998.

189 "New Study reveals 250 million stockpiled landmines in 105 countries, 17 million destroyed to date", *Landmine Monitor press release*, Geneva, 9 December 1999. See also *Landmine Monitor Report 1999, op. cit.*, p. 11; see also Vines, A., "The Crisis of Anti-Personnel Mines", *To Walk Without Fear*, in which Vines points out that only 'a very small number of States around the world, such as San Marino, Andorra, and Saint Lucia, appear never to have maintained [anti-personnel mine] stockpiles.'

190 See for instance "Landmine numbers 'hugely exaggerated'", *op. cit.*

191 *Landmine Monitor Report 1999*, p. 23. Even this last statement is open to question. During armed conflict, such figures as may be reliable suggest that combatants are often the more frequent victims. See for instance *The Silent Menace*, *op. cit.* See also *Landmine Monitor Report 1999*, pp. 95, 566.

192 *Landmine Monitor Report 2000*, p. 23.

produced nearly 9,000 prostheses for mine victims,[193] though according to LSN, there were some 300,000 living landmine victims globally.[194]

In 1994, the US State Department quoted a figure of 500 people killed or injured each week (*i.e.*, 24,000 each year),[195] a number supported by the ICRC.[196] The ICBL and the UN appeared to favour an estimate of 26,000 per year.[197] Initially at least, these figures did not seem excessive.[198] However, by 1998, numbers appeared to be falling.[199] In Cambodia, for instance, it was claimed that the number of mine victims annually had fallen from about 3,000 in 1996 to 1,012 in 1999.[200]

In 1997, at the *International Conference for a Global Ban on Anti-Personnel Landmines* held in Brussels, the ICRC announced that they had been compiling a registry of landmine incidents from 'credible sources' throughout the world. In 1996 alone, it recorded incidents in which 7,404 people had been killed or injured from landmine explosions. It noted that it was likely that the statistics record but a small fraction of the human cost, and suggested that 24,000 might actually be an under-estimate.[201] Based on available information, however,[202] the author estimates that around 12,000 individuals are being killed or injured each year by anti-personnel mines (*i.e.*, as opposed to anti-vehicle mines or unexploded ordnance).

193 *Ibid.*, p. 1057.

194 "Press Conference on Anti-Personnel Mine Convention", 1 March 2000. It is believed that this figure pertains only to 'direct' anti-personnel mine victims. See *Landmine Monitor Report* 2000, pp. 989-90, for the ICBL's expanded definition of who constitute mine victims.

195 United States Department of State, *Hidden Killers: the Global Landmine Crisis*, Washington DC, 1994, p. v.

196 See for instance ICRC website: <http://www.icrc.org>.

197 See for instance ICBL website: <http://www.icbl.org>.

198 In 1996, for instance, South Sudanese mine victims alone were reported to number 1,725. *Landmine Monitor Report 1999*, p. 159.

199 See for instance *Landmine Monitor Report 1999*, p. 24.

200 Though these figures, as in a number of cases, included all landmine and also UXO casualties. See *Landmine Monitor Report 2000*, p. 395. See also Alford, P., "Cambodia's landmine myths exploded", *Australian*, 3 June 2000, <http://www.news.com.au>; "Only 30 Years: Cambodia's Landmines", *Economist*, 7 November 1998.

201 Maresca, L. and Maslen, S. (eds.), *The Banning of Anti-Personnel Landmines*, *op. cit.*, pp. 543-4.

202 See *Landmine Monitor Report 2000*, pp. 23-6, for the best summary of available data.

CHAPTER 1
ANTI-PERSONNEL MINES ON THE BATTLEFIELD UNDER THE 1980 CONVENTION ON CERTAIN CONVENTIONAL WEAPONS[203]

1.1. THE HISTORICAL BACKGROUND TO THE CONVENTION[204]

The experiences of the Second World War, with its quantum leap in weapons technology, had graphically demonstrated the need for strengthened legal protection of the civilian population against modern warfare and its many excesses. In June 1955, the International Committee of the Red Cross (ICRC) issued its *Draft Rules for the Protection of the Civilian Population from the Dangers of Indiscriminate Warfare*,[205] elaborated following a meeting of experts held in Geneva the previous year.[206] With weapons of mass destruction and specific conventional weapons clearly in mind, the 1955 Draft Rules sought to prohibit weapons 'contrary to the laws of humanity', whose consequences were 'unpredictable and uncontrollable'.[207]

Of the draft rules, two provisions are particularly relevant to the use of landmines and could even be considered as a precursor to their future regulation under the 1980 Convention on Certain Conventional Weapons (CCW):

---

203 As noted above, the formal title is the *United Nations Convention on Prohibitions or Restrictions on the Use of Certain Conventional Weapons Which May be Deemed to be Excessively Injurious or to Have Indiscriminate Effects*. The simplified formulations, *Convention on Certain Conventional Weapons* or *CCW*, which have no formal legal status, are used in this work for the sake of brevity. For a discussion on the background to the adoption of the formal title see Roach, Capt. J.A., "Certain Conventional Weapons Convention: Arms Control or Humanitarian Law?", *Military Law Review*, Vol. 105, Summer 1984, pp. 16-17; Kalshoven, F., "The Conventional Weapons Convention: Underlying Legal Principles", *International Review of the Red Cross*, 1990, No. 279, p. 515.

204 For an interesting personal account of the background to the adoption of the 1980 Convention on Conventional Weapons (CCW) see Kalshoven, F., "Conventional Weaponry: The Law from St Petersburg to Lucerne and Beyond", in Meyer, M.A. (Ed.), *Armed Conflict and the New Law: Aspects of the 1977 Geneva Protocols and the 1981 Weapons Convention*, British Institute of International and Comparative Law, London, 1989, pp. 251-70. See also UN, "Summary of Negotiations Leading to the Conclusion of the Convention on Prohibitions or Restrictions on the Use of Certain Conventional Weapons Which May Be Deemed to Be Excessively Injurious or to Have Indiscriminate Effects and of Subsequent Developments Related to the Convention", *UN Doc. CCW/CONF.I/GE/5*, 6 May 1994 (hereinafter, UN, *Summary of Negotiations*).

205 Hereinafter, the *1955 Draft Rules*.

206 For further background on the elaboration of the *1955 Draft Rules* and its subsequent revision see *Draft Rules for the Limitation of the Dangers Incurred by the Civilian Population in Time of War*, 2nd edn., ICRC, Geneva, April 1958, pp. 21-6.

207 See Article 10, *1955 Draft Rules*. See also Roach, Capt. J.A., "Certain Conventional Weapons Convention", *op. cit.*, p. 7. Yves Sandoz, the ICRC's Director of International Law and Policy, stated that the Draft Rules were drawn up because it was felt that civilians were inadequately protected against the effects of hostilities by the Geneva Convention Relative to the Protection of Civilian Persons in Time of War of 12 August 1949 (hereinafter *1949 Geneva Convention IV*). Sandoz, Y., "Prohibitions or Restrictions on the Use of Certain Conventional Weapons", *International Review of the Red Cross*, January-February 1981, p. 4.

'The use of so-called delay-action projectiles is only authorized when their effects are limited to the objective itself.[208]
Weapons capable of causing serious damage shall, so far as possible, be equipped with a safety device which renders them harmless when they can no longer be directed with precision against a military objective. '[209]

In its commentary of these articles, the ICRC noted that 'since war is carried on everywhere, the use of the weapons prohibited by the laws of humanity is even more dangerous to the civilian population than to the combatants[.] (...) And civilians will often be completely without any material protection against such weapons.'[210]

Following comments, and not a little concern, from a number of national Red Cross and Red Crescent societies,[211] the ICRC revised the 1955 Draft Rules and transmitted them for consideration to the 19th International Conference of the Red Cross, held in New Delhi, in October-November 1957.[212] The Conference in turn formally requested the ICRC to submit to governments the revised Draft Rules, a record of the discussions on the issue at the Conference, and the text of proposals and amendments contributed by the national societies.[213] But governmental reaction to the proposals remained muted.[214] Certainly few were eager to consider the adoption of new international legislation based on the Draft Rules, and the question of regulation of weaponry fell into abeyance for a decade.

Renewed interest in adopting further international standards governing means of warfare followed the 1968 International Conference for Human Rights held in Tehran.[215] The Conference adopted a resolution calling upon the UN General Assembly to request the Secretary-General to study 'the need for additional humanitarian international conventions or for possible revision of existing Conventions to ensure the better protection of civilians, prisoners and combatants in all armed conflicts and the prohibition and limitation of the use of certain methods and means of warfare.'[216]

Following the resolution, the same year the UN General Assembly adopted Resolution 2444 (XXIII) entitled 'Respect for Human Rights in Armed Con-

---

208 Article 10(4). See *Draft Rules for the Limitation of the Dangers Incurred by the Civilian Population in Time of War*, 2nd edn., ICRC, Geneva, April 1958, p. 9.

209 Article 11. See *ibid.*, p. 10.

210 *Ibid.*, p. 76.

211 The often close relationship between a national society and its respective government means that the reaction of a national society to a certain proposal may also predict the government views on the subject matter.

212 The amended Draft Rules were renamed the *Draft Rules for the Limitation of the Dangers Incurred by the Civilian Population in Time of War.*

213 See ICRC, *Final Record concerning the Draft Rules for the Limitation of the Dangers Incurred by the Civilian Population in Time of War*, ICRC, Geneva, April 1958, p. 141.

214 Despite the Second World War, few governments were enthusiastic to accept the prohibition of weapons they regarded as militarily useful.

215 See for example Roach, Capt. J.A., "Certain Conventional Weapons Convention", *op. cit.*, p. 7. The UN convened the Conference to commemorate the International Year for Human Rights and the 20th anniversary of the Universal Declaration of Human Rights.

216 Operative Paragraph 1, Resolution XXIII, "Human rights in armed conflicts" of 12 May 1968 of the International Conference on Human Rights, Tehran, 22 April to 13 May 1968, *UN Doc. A/CONF.32/41*.

flicts'[217] calling upon the Secretary-General to prepare a study on this issue for its consideration. The study, which was submitted on 20 November 1969,[218] reviewed previous efforts to restrict the use of weapons and proposed that the legality of napalm be the subject of further detailed study.[219]

In parallel with the work of the UN, and following the 21st International Conference of the Red Cross held in Istanbul in 1969,[220] the ICRC had renewed its interest in the regulation of the use of weapons, as well as the broader development of international humanitarian law, and decided to convene a *Conference of Government Experts on the Reaffirmation and Development of International Humanitarian Law Applicable in Armed Conflicts.* In 1972, at the second session of the Conference, the experts of 19 governments proposed in writing that the ICRC should convene a separate meeting of experts specifically to discuss the regulation of conventional weapons under international humanitarian law. The following year, the ICRC convened two meetings (hereinafter *the 1973 ICRC Experts Meetings*), which included experts from 21 countries as well as a number of representatives of the UN and non-governmental organisations. The experts discussed general legal issues governing means of warfare, and the possible regulation of weapons of mass destruction, small-calibre projectiles, blast and fragmentation weapons, time-delay weapons, incendiary weapons and potential future weapons, particularly lasers.[221]

Subsequently, repeated attempts were made to prohibit or restrict the use of specific conventional weapons in the two 1977 Additional Protocols[222] although at least one observer felt that in designing the Protocols the ICRC 'seemed to have decided not to touch the law relating to different types of weapons.'[223] A number of governments were also markedly unenthusiastic about regulating

---

217 See Shaw, M., "The United Nations Convention on Prohibitions or Restrictions on the Use of Certain Conventional Weapons, 1981", *Review of International Studies*, Vol. 9, No. 2, 1983, p. 110; Roach, Capt. J.A., "Certain Conventional Weapons Convention", *op. cit.*, p. 7.

218 *UN Doc. A/8052.*

219 *UN Doc. A/8803.* See Roach, Capt. J.A., "Certain Conventional Weapons Convention", *op. cit.*, p. 7.

220 The ICRC submitted a report to the 21st International Conference concluding that 'belligerents should refrain from using weapons:
of a nature to cause unnecessary suffering;
which, on account of their imprecision or their effects, harmed civilian populations and combatants without distinction;
whose consequences escaped from the control of those employing them, in space or time.'
See ICRC, *Weapons that may Cause Unnecessary Suffering or have Indiscriminate Effects. Report on the work of Experts*, ICRC, Geneva, 1973, pp. 1-2 (hereinafter, *Weapons that may Cause Unnecessary Suffering*).

221 See generally *Weapons that may Cause Unnecessary Suffering.*

222 Protocol Additional to the Geneva Conventions of 12 August 1949, and Relating to the Protection of Victims of International Armed Conflicts (Protocol I) and Protocol Additional to the Geneva Conventions of 12 August 1949, and Relating to the Protection of Victims of Non-International Armed Conflicts (Protocol II). (These instruments are hereinafter referred to as 1977 Protocol I and 1977 Protocol II.) See Carnahan, Lt.-Col. B.M., "The Law of Land Mine Warfare: Protocol II to the United Nations Convention on Certain Conventional Weapons", *Military Law Review*, Vol. 105, Summer 1984, p. 75 *et seq.*

223 Draper, G.I.A.D., "The Emerging Law of Weapons Restraint", *Survival*, International Institute for Strategic Studies, January/February 1997, p. 10.

specific weapons in the Protocols. One view, particularly prevalent in Western countries, was that this was outside the scope of the Geneva Diplomatic Conference and should 'properly' be dealt with in a disarmament forum.[224]

Yet, at the 22nd International Conference of the Red Cross, held in Tehran in November 1973, agreement had apparently been reached that discussions on the international legal regulation of certain conventional weapons could continue without prejudicing the negotiation of the Additional Protocols.[225] Accordingly, the 22nd International Conference adopted a resolution by consensus urging the *Diplomatic Conference on the Reaffirmation and Development of International Humanitarian Law applicable in Armed Conflicts*, convened by the Swiss government, to consider, at its first session in early 1974, 'the question of the prohibition or restriction of the use of conventional weapons which may cause unnecessary suffering or have indiscriminate effects'. The resolution further invited the ICRC to convene, also in 1974, a conference of government experts 'to study in depth' the issue and to submit a report to the Diplomatic Conference.[226]

Thus, in 1974 the Diplomatic Conference established an *Ad Hoc Committee on Conventional Weapons* and the ICRC, for its part, agreed to convene a *Conference of Governmental Experts on the Use of Certain Conventional Weapons*. A first session of the Conference was held in Lucerne from 24 September to 18 October 1974[227] and a second session from 28 January to 26 February 1976 in Lugano.[228] Participants were asked to consider the possible specific legal regulation of a number of categories of weapons, including incendiary weapons, small calibre projectiles, blast and fragmentation weapons, and delayed action and treacherous weapons.

---

224 Roach, Capt. J.A., "Certain Conventional Weapons Convention", *op. cit.*, p. 9. But note his subsequent claim at p. 10 that the US also doubted whether the United Nations was the appropriate forum for work on specific conventional weapons. Roach further claims, somewhat unconvincingly in the view of the author, that the US did not wish to see the progress towards the adoption of the Protocols delayed by discussions on weapons. *Ibid.*, p. 9.

225 *Ibid.*, p. 12. According to Roach, who cites as authority the report of the US delegation to the subsequent experts conference in Lucerne, Switzerland: 'Doubts about the forum in which the work should be carried on were subordinated at that time.'

226 Resolution XIV, 22nd International Conference of the Red Cross. The United Nations General Assembly 'took note' of the decision of the International Conference of the Red Cross and invited the Diplomatic Conference 'to consider (...) the question of the use of napalm and other incendiary weapons, as well as other specific conventional weapons which may be deemed to cause unnecessary suffering or to have indiscriminate effects, and to seek agreement on rules prohibiting or restricting the use of such weapons.' *UN General Assembly Resolution 3076 (XXVIII) of 6 December 1973*, adopted by 103 votes to 0, with 18 abstentions, including France, the United Kingdom (UK), the US and the USSR. See also Roach, Capt. J.A., "Certain Conventional Weapons Convention", *op. cit.*, p. 12; De Mulinen, F., "A propos de la Conférence de Lucerne et Lugano sur l'emploi de certaines armes conventionelles", *Annales d'études internationales 1977, Droit humanitaire et protection de l'homme*, Vol. 8, p. 111 *et seq.*

227 Hereinafter, the 1974 Lucerne Weapons Conference. *Conference of Government Experts on the Use of Certain Conventional Weapons (Lucerne, 24.9 – 18.10.1974)*, Report, ICRC, Geneva, 1975 (hereinafter, *Report on the 1974 Lucerne Weapons Conference*).

228 Hereinafter, the 1976 Lugano Weapons Conference. *Conference of Government Experts on the Use of Certain Conventional Weapons (Lugano, 28.1 – 26.2.1976)*, Report, ICRC, Geneva, 1976 (hereinafter, *Report on the 1976 Lugano Weapons Conference*).

According to one participant, the most significant progress was achieved with respect to mines and booby-traps, and particular difficulties were encountered regarding the use of incendiary weapons.[229] At the 1976 Lugano Weapons Conference, the UK delegation, with support from the Dutch and French delegations, tabled a set of draft proposals for the regulation of mines and booby-traps, which would later form the basis for the Protocol on Prohibitions or Restrictions on the Use of Mines, Booby-Traps and Other Devices (Protocol II) annexed to the 1980 CCW.[230]

Following lengthy negotiations during the four sessions of the Diplomatic Conference in its *Ad Hoc Committee on Conventional Weapons*, it emerged that possible agreement could be reached on regulation of only three categories of conventional weapons: fragments not detectable by X-ray; landmines and booby-traps; and incendiary weapons.[231] In addition, a future discussion of small-calibre ammunition was also foreseen. But final agreement, even on this small number of conventional weapons, remained elusive and on 9 June 1977 the Diplomatic Conference decided to recommend to the General Assembly that a separate conference be convened to consider prohibitions or restrictions on the use of specific conventional weapons.[232]

1.2. The Negotiation of the 1980 Convention on Certain Conventional Weapons

In accordance with successive UN General Assembly resolutions,[233] preparatory conferences attended by some 85 States were held in August-September 1978 and March-April 1979 under the auspices of the United Nations. The *United Nations Conference on Prohibitions or Restrictions of Use of Certain Conventional Weapons Which May be Deemed to be Excessively Injurious or to Have Indiscriminate Effects* met for two sessions in Geneva, from

---

229 De Mulinen, F., "A propos de la Conférence de Lucerne et Lugano sur l'emploi de certaines armes conventionelles", *op. cit.*, p. 113.

230 Working Paper submitted by the Experts of France, the Netherlands and the United Kingdom, "Land Mines and Booby-Traps and Proposals for the Regulation of Their Use", Annex A2 (COLU/203), *Report on the 1976 Lugano Weapons Conference, op. cit.*, pp. 167-71. See Rogers, Lt.-Col. A.P.V., "A Commentary on the Protocol on Prohibitions or Restrictions on the Use of Mines, Booby-Traps and Other Devices", *Military Law and Law of War Review*, Vol. 26, 1987, p. 187.

231 Roach, Capt. J.A., "Certain Conventional Weapons Convention", *op. cit.*, pp. 12-13.

232 Resolution 22 (IV), Diplomatic Conference. See Roach, Capt. J.A., "Certain Conventional Weapons Convention", *op. cit.*, pp. 12-13. A number of delegations had pushed hard for the establishment of a permanent international weaponry review committee under 1977 Additional Protocol I, but this proposal too, was voted down, albeit only by a narrow margin. Fenrick, W.J., "The Conventional Weapons Convention: A modest but useful treaty", *International Review of the Red Cross*, November-December 1990, No. 279, p. 501.

233 UN General Assembly Resolutions 32/152 of 19 December 1977 and 33/70 of 14 December 1978. Resolution 32/152, which was adopted by 115 votes to 0, with 21 abstentions, including, once again, France, the UK, the US and the USSR, called for a UN Conference to be convened in 1979 with a preparatory conference to precede it 'with a view to reaching agreements on prohibitions or restrictions on the use of specific conventional weapons.'

10 to 28 September 1979,[234] and from 15 September to 10 October 1980.[235] Although controls on the use of landmines, especially remotely-delivered mines, were discussed at length, the most controversial issue continued to be the regulation of incendiary weapons, particularly napalm. A last-minute compromise negotiated with the US opened the way to the adoption of a new instrument of international law, hereinafter referred to as the Convention on Certain Conventional Weapons (CCW).

1.3. The Structure of the Convention

The structure of the Convention was an unusual one, comprising a *chapeau* Convention of 10 Articles, to which were annexed three Protocols. The idea, intended to allow flexibility in the future regulation of weapons, came from Mexico. At the end of the second preparatory conference, it had put forward an 'Outline of a General Treaty' whereby a series of optional protocol agreements would be annexed to an 'umbrella' agreement.[236] Following negotiations with a number of Western States, at the first session of the Conference proper, the Dutch and UK delegations jointly tabled a draft treaty reflecting this approach.[237]

In adhering to the Convention, States were obliged to accept at least two of the three annexed Protocols.[238] There had been a fear – which subsequently appears to have been unjustified[239] – that because of the relative redundancy of CCW Protocol I, which banned the use of a weapon no one believed in existence or even under development,[240] governments would be tempted to ratify just this Protocol so as to become party to the Convention.[241]

---

[234] For a brief report on the first session of the conference see Szasz, P., "The Conference on Excessively Injurious or Indiscriminate Weapons", *The American Journal of International Law*, Vol. 74, January 1980, pp. 212-5.

[235] See UN, *Summary of Negotiations*, *op. cit.*, pp. 5-18. In a precursor for subsequent difficulties, Roach notes that the chief negotiators in the Conference were arms control and disarmament specialists, most of whom had not been involved in the drafting of the 1977 Additional Protocols. He adds that the 'mixed lineage' of the CCW is well illustrated in its preamble, which combines four paragraphs on the principles of international humanitarian law followed by five paragraphs referring to wider issues, such as the need to end the arms race and a call for global disarmament. Roach, Capt. J.A., "Certain Conventional Weapons Convention", *op. cit.*, p. 14.

[236] See for instance Roach, Capt. J.A., "Certain Conventional Weapons Convention", *op. cit.* p. 13.

[237] *Ibid.*

[238] Article 4(3), CCW. According to Levie, the US had even proposed that adherence to *all* annexed Protocols should be mandatory. See Levie, H.S., "Prohibitions and Restrictions on the Use of Conventional Weapons", *St John's Law Review*, Vol. 68, Summer 1994, pp. 651-2.

[239] Of the 77 parties to the CCW as of end April 2000, only 11 had not accepted all three original Protocols. Benin, Colombia, El Salvador, Estonia, Jordan, Lithuania, Monaco, Peru, and Senegal were not bound by 1980 Protocol II (though Colombia, El Salvador, Lithuania, Monaco, Peru and Senegal had all consented to be bound by amended Protocol II); El Salvador and Senegal alone were not bound by Protocol I; and El Salvador, France, Israel, Monaco and the United States were not bound by 1980 Protocol III.

[240] 'Any weapon the primary effect of which is to injure by fragments which in the human body escape detection by X-rays.' Many weapons, of course, have such secondary effects.

[241] See for example Fenrick, W.J., "The Law of Armed Conflict: The CUSHIE Weapons Treaty", *Canadian Defence Quarterly*, Vol. 11, 1981, p. 27; Fenrick, W.J., "The Conventional Weapons Convention", *op. cit.*, p. 501.

1.4. The Scope and Applicability of the Convention[242]

Article 1 of the 1980 CCW provides that the Convention and its annexed Protocols apply 'in the situations referred to in Article 2 common to the Geneva Conventions of 12 August 1949 for the Protection of War Victims, including any situation described in paragraph 4 of Article 1 of Additional Protocol I to these Conventions.'

Article 2 common to the Four Geneva Conventions of 1949[243] in turn provides for application 'in addition to the provisions which shall be implemented in peacetime', to 'all cases of declared war or any other armed conflict' between two or more States Parties, 'even if the state of war is not recognised by one of them' and to 'all cases of partial or total occupation of the territory' of a State Party, 'even if the said occupation meets with no armed resistance'. Thus, Article 2 is limited to cases of inter-State conflict.

Article 1(4) of 1977 Additional Protocol I, however, extends the applicability of the CCW to certain internal armed conflicts 'in which peoples are fighting against colonial domination and alien occupation and against racist régimes in the exercise of their right of self-determination, as enshrined in the Charter of the United Nations and the Declaration on Principles of International Law concerning Friendly Relations and Co-operation among States in accordance with the Charter of the United Nations.' This broadening of application in 1977 Additional Protocol I is unwelcome and unfortunate insofar as it 'injects subjective and politically controversial standards into international humanitarian law and undermines the traditional distinction between international and non-international armed conflicts.'[244] So manifestly political is the language in Article 1(4) that it is doubtful that any armed conflict would ever be widely characterised as falling within its ambit, let alone by the State in question.[245] Its inclusion may also have deterred adherence to the Protocol.[246]

In the context of the 1980 CCW, Article 7(4) of the Convention clarifies that the extension of applicability of international armed conflict will occur in either of two situations. The first is where the State Party in which armed conflict is taking place is also a party to 1977 Additional Protocol I and the relevant authority of the 'national liberation movement' has formally undertaken to apply

242 For a detailed discussion of the scope and applicability of the 1980 CCW see Roach, Capt. J.A., "Certain Conventional Weapons Convention", *op. cit.*, pp. 3-61.

243 See for instance Geneva Convention Relative to the Protection of Civilian Persons in Time of War of 12 August 1949 (Geneva Convention IV).

244 Nash, M., "Contemporary Practice of the United States Relating to International Law", *The American Journal of International Law*, Vol. 88, October 1994, p. 752. Article 1(4) was designed to deal with specific conflicts, such as the de-colonialisation wars and the struggle against *apartheid* South Africa, and, apart, potentially, from the situation of the Palestinians, now appears increasingly redundant.

245 Even the ICRC Commentary, which tactfully refrains from criticising the paragraph, acknowledges that it gave rise to 'heated controversy'. *ICRC Commentary on the 1977 Additional Protocols*, p. 41.

246 See for instance Greenwood, C., "Scope of Application of Humanitarian Law", in Fleck, D. (ed.), *The Handbook of Humanitarian Law in Armed Conflicts, op. cit.*, p. 42.

the 1949 Geneva Conventions and 1977 Additional Protocol I.[247] The second is where the State Party in question is not a party to 1977 Additional Protocol I but the relevant authority 'accepts and applies'[248] the obligations of the 1949 Geneva Conventions and the CCW and annexed Protocols.[249]

The second of these two cases has been the object of critical comment since a State can be bound by obligations under the CCW even though it has not adhered to it.[250] Thus, one authority complained that it might 'render a State subject to a series of obligations without its express consent as formulated through signature and ratification of a treaty in force, and this in a highly sensitive area. In particular, the arrangement has implications in the field of recognition of non-State entities. It may well be that the net result will be to discourage adherence to the [CCW] (...) on the part of States that feel vulnerable.'[251] Yet, the point has also been made that the provision seeks to ensure a 'complete reciprocity of obligations' between the parties to an 'internationalised' armed conflict and prevents an authority purporting to represent a people fighting for self-determination from taking advantage of the Convention unless it had accepted and applied certain rules of warfare such as the humane treatment of prisoners of war and the protection of the civilian population.[252]

As a result of the controversy surrounding the provision as a whole, a number of States have entered a declaration or reservation with respect to the scope of the CCW. France, for instance, signed the Convention declaring that it would apply the Convention and the Protocols to 'all the armed conflicts referred to in Articles 2 and 3 common to the Geneva Conventions of 12 August 1949.' It thereby excludes the application of Article 1(4) of 1977 Additional Protocol I,[253] while expanding application overall to armed conflicts not of an international character. The US entered a similar declaration upon its ratification of the Convention and annexed Protocols I and II.[254] For its part, the ICRC regretted

247 In this case, the authority of the national liberation movement concerned should file a unilateral declaration of acceptance with the Swiss Federal Council in accordance with Article 96(3) of 1977 Additional Protocol I. Article 96(3) provides that such a declaration 'shall, upon its receipt by the depositary' bring into force for the authority immediately the 1949 Geneva Conventions and the 1977 Additional Protocol and that these instruments will be equally binding upon all Parties to the conflict. See Roach, Capt. J.A. "Certain Conventional Weapons Convention", *op. cit.*, p. 25.

248 Article 7(4)(b), 1980 CCW.

249 A proposal to allow such an authority to lodge a declaration of acceptance of the Convention with the UN Secretary-General was blocked by Israel, which regarded this as giving too much political recognition to liberation movements. *Ibid.*, pp. 19, 20-2.

250 See for example Shaw, M., "The United Nations Convention on Prohibitions or Restrictions on the Use of Certain Conventional Weapons, 1981", *op. cit.*, p. 115; Levie, H.S., "Prohibitions and Restrictions on the Use of Conventional Weapons." *op. cit.*, pp. 652-3.

251 Shaw, M., "The United Nations Convention on Prohibitions or Restrictions on the Use of Certain Conventional Weapons, 1981", *op. cit.*, p. 115.

252 Roach, Capt. J.A. "Certain Conventional Weapons Convention", *op. cit.*, pp. 18-19.

253 See Levie, H.S., "Prohibitions and Restrictions on the Use of Conventional Weapons", *op. cit.*, p. 650. Levie records that no party to the 1980 CCW has objected to the French reservation.

254 A similar reservation was entered by Israel upon ratification, with the additional qualification that application would be only to armed conflicts 'involving regular armed forces of States' and that Article 7(4) would have 'no effect'. The UK entered an understanding upon ratification that

the decision not to apply automatically the CCW and all annexed Protocols in conflicts of a non-international character and called upon all parties to conflict, whether or not they were bound by the relevant instruments and irrespective of the classification of the conflict, to observe their provisions 'because this is a humanitarian demand that transcends the strict limits of the law.'[255]

1.5. The Implementation of the Convention

As a result of substantial resistance to the establishment of a system of international verification of the CCW,[256] the only provision addressing its implementation merely requires States Parties to disseminate the Convention and its annexed Protocols 'as widely as possible'. Statements regretting the omission of verification procedures were made at signature by France,[257] Italy,[258] the US[259] and – rather surprisingly given its later stance – China.[260]

A US military lawyer has claimed that the absence of provisions for individual criminal responsibility for violations of the Convention and the annexed Protocols means that it is 'in this regard only partially a law of armed conflict treaty.'[261] Although the omission of such compliance measures is indeed regrettable, this view does not appear to be sustainable. Prior to the International Military Tribunal at Nuremberg, laws of war treaties did not contain such provisions, although the 1907 Hague Convention IV had decreed that States

it would not consider itself bound by a declaration made in the name of a national liberation movement unless it had expressly recognised that body as 'genuinely an authority' representing people engaged in an 'Article 1(4)-type' armed conflict. The specific intent of these declarations needs no clarification.

255 "ICRC appeal following the entry into force of the Convention on Prohibitions and Restrictions on the Use of Certain Conventional Weapons", *International Review of the Red Cross*, No. 238, January-February 1984, p. 30. See Aubert, M., "The International Committee of the Red Cross and the problem of excessively injurious or indiscriminate weapons", *International Review of the Red Cross*, November-December 1990, No. 279, pp. 493-4.

256 See Levie, H.S., "Prohibitions and Restrictions on the Use of Conventional Weapons", *op. cit.*, p. 654.

257 Upon signature of the 1980 CCW, France regretted that it had not been possible to reach agreement on verification and reserved the right to submit 'proposals aimed at filling that gap' at the first review conference of the Convention.

258 Italy declared upon signature its 'great regret' at the failure to include an article on the 'establishment of a consultative committee of experts competent to verify facts which might be alleged' as proposed by the then Federal Republic of Germany. In line with the statement by France, Italy also declared its intention to 'undertake active efforts' to fill the gap in the Convention.

259 'The United States strongly supported proposals (...) to include special procedures for dealing with compliance matters, and reserves the right to propose at a later date additional procedures and remedies, should this prove necessary, to deal with such problems.'

260 Upon signature of the 1980 CCW, China declared that 'it should be pointed out that the Convention fails to provide for supervision or verification of its clauses, thus weakening its binding force.' A decade later, however, during the review process of the CCW, China declared on a number of occasions that it would be 'premature' to include verification clauses – asserting that such inclusion would deter adherence.

261 Roach, Capt. J.A., "Certain Conventional Weapons Convention", *op. cit.*, p. 58.

were responsible for acts committed by their armed forces.[262] In fact, the absence of provisions laying down individual criminal responsibility can be largely attributed to the disarmament background of the treaty negotiators[263] and their consequent ignorance (or mistrust) of international humanitarian law and its modern compliance measures.[264]

1.6. THE ADOPTION AND ENTRY INTO FORCE OF THE CONVENTION

After its adoption by consensus on 10 October 1980 at the closing of the 1980 UN Weapons Conference, the Convention with its three annexed Protocols[265] was opened for signature for one year from 10 April 1981. International reaction to the new instrument was relatively subdued. Most attention focused on the continuing, if restricted, legality of the use of incendiary weapons, or the need to address the use of fuel-air explosives.[266] Consequently, little thought was given to the continuing threat posed by landmines, and the likelihood of a problem resulting from their continuing proliferation, especially in internal conflicts.

In the view of one military lawyer, the CCW would have a 'comparatively minor impact on the conduct of warfare' as it did 'not affect the use of war-winning weapons.'[267] In submitting the CCW for ratification on 12 May 1994, US President Clinton declared that the Convention constituted 'a modest but significant humanitarian effort to protect the victims of armed conflict from the effects of particular weapons.'[268] He further asserted that by becoming party to the Convention, the US would 'encourage the observance by other countries of restrictions on landmines and other weapons that US Armed Forces and those

[262] Article 3, 1907 Hague Convention IV Respecting the Laws and Customs of War on Land. See for example *Documents on the Laws of* War, p. 153.

[263] Roach, for example, points out that 'the most remarkable feature of CCW is that this "son of CDDH" [the Diplomatic Conference that negotiated and adopted the two 1977 Additional Protocols] was for the most part negotiated by arms control and disarmament personnel who had little or nothing to do with the development of the Additional Protocols.' Roach, Capt. J.A., "Certain Conventional Weapons Convention", *op. cit.*, p. 14. Indeed the disarmament background of representatives on many of the governmental delegations would also be manifest during the First Review Conference of the CCW and the subsequent negotiation of the Convention on the Prohibition of Anti-Personnel Mines.

[264] The 1949 Geneva Conventions and 1977 Additional Protocol I provide for compulsory universal jurisdiction for 'grave breaches' of the provisions. (See for example Article 146 of 1949 Geneva Convention IV and Article 85 of 1977 Additional Protocol I.) This strict form of jurisdiction, sometimes referred to by its Latin formulation *aut dedere aut iudicare*, obliges a State Party either to prosecute alleged offenders, irrespective of the territory on which the relevant acts took place, or to extradite them for prosecution.

[265] Protocol on Non-Detectable Fragments (Protocol I); Protocol on Prohibitions or Restrictions on the Use of Mines, Booby-Traps and Other Devices (Protocol II); and Protocol on Prohibitions or Restrictions on the Use of Incendiary Weapons (Protocol III). For the text of the CCW and its three annexed Protocols see *Documents on the Laws of War*, pp. 473-85.

[266] See for example Wulff, T., *Barriers Against Weapons, Development of Weapons and Restrictions on Their Use*, Swedish Red Cross, Stockholm, 1984, p. 51.

[267] Fenrick, W.J., "The Conventional Weapons Convention", *op. cit.*, pp. 508-9.

[268] Cited by Nash, M., "Contemporary Practice of the United States Relating to International Law", *op. cit.*, October 1994, p. 748.

of [its] (...) allies already observe as a matter of humanity, common sense and sound military doctrine.'[269]

A total of 51 States signed the Convention,[270] which subsequently entered into force on 2 December 1983, six months after the 20th State – Poland – deposited its instrument of ratification with the UN Secretary-General.[271] As of February 2001, only 84 States were party to the Convention, the most recent adherent being Nicaragua, which joined on 5 December 2000.[272]

1.7. Protocol II on Mines, Booby-Traps and Other Devices

1.7.1. The Historical Background to Protocol II[273]

According to one military lawyer, prior to the adoption of 1980 CCW, landmines and booby-traps were the 'neglected stepchildren' of modern international humanitarian law.[274] Yet, mines do have the distinction of being the only weapon specifically referred to in the 1949 Geneva Conventions. The Geneva Convention Relative to the Treatment of Prisoners of War (Geneva

---

269 *Ibid.*, p. 749.

270 Afghanistan, Argentina, Australia, Austria, Belarus, Belgium, Bulgaria, Canada, China, Cuba, Denmark, Ecuador, Egypt, Finland, France, Germany, Greece, Hungary, Iceland, India, Ireland, Italy, Japan, Liechtenstein, Luxembourg, Mexico, Mongolia, Morocco, the Netherlands, New Zealand, Nicaragua, Nigeria, Norway, Pakistan, the Philippines, Poland, Portugal, Romania, the Russian Federation (as the former USSR), Sierra Leone, Spain, Sudan, Sweden, Switzerland, Togo, Turkey, the UK, Ukraine, the US, Vietnam and Yugoslavia.

271 Article 5, 1980 CCW. Roach reports that the relatively high number was a compromise related to the review and amendment of the CCW. The Mexican original draft had required five ratifications to bring the Convention into force. Roach, Capt. J.A., "Certain Conventional Weapons Convention", *op. cit.*, p. 53. See also Sandoz, Y., "Prohibitions or Restrictions on the Use of Certain Conventional Weapons", *op. cit.*, pp. 8-9.

272 Argentina, Australia, Austria, Bangladesh, Belarus, Belgium, Benin, Bosnia-Herzegovina, Brazil, Bulgaria, Cambodia, Canada, Cape Verde, China, Colombia, Costa Rica, Croatia, Cuba, Cyprus, the Czech Republic, Denmark, Djibouti, Ecuador, El Salvador, Estonia, Finland, the Former Yugoslav Republic of Macedonia, France, Georgia, Germany, Greece, Guatemala, Holy See, Hungary, India, Ireland, Israel, Italy, Japan, Jordan, Lao People's Democratic Republic, Latvia, Lesotho, Liechtenstein, Lithuania, Luxembourg, Maldives, Malta, Mauritius, Mexico, Moldova, Monaco, Mongolia, the Netherlands, New Zealand, Nicaragua, Niger, Norway, Pakistan, Panama, Peru, the Philippines, Poland, Portugal, Romania, the Russian Federation, Senegal, Seychelles, Slovakia, Slovenia, South Africa, Spain, Sweden, Switzerland, Tajikistan, Togo, Tunisia, Uganda, Ukraine, the UK, Uruguay, the US, Uzbekistan, Yugoslavia. Yugoslavia succeeded to the Convention on 12 March 2001.

273 For greater detail on the negotiating history of Protocol II to the 1980 CCW from the 1974 Lucerne Weapons Conference to the adoption of the Protocol itself in 1980, see for example Rogers, Brig. A.P.V., "The Mines Protocol: Negotiating History", ICRC, *Report on the Symposium on Anti-Personnel Mines, Montreux, 21-23 April 1993*, ICRC, Geneva, 1993, pp. 227-65.

274 Carnahan, Lt.-Col. B.M., "The Law of Land Mine Warfare", *op. cit.*, p. 73. As authority for this 'neglect' he points to the existence of 1907 Hague Convention VIII Relative to the Laying of Automatic Submarine Contact Mines, which regulates the use of sea mines, and the fact that 1907 Hague Convention IV does not even mention landmines. For details of Hague Convention VIII see for instance Roberts, A. and Guelff, R., *Documents on the Laws of War*, 3rd edn., Oxford University Press, Oxford, UK, 2000, pp. 103-10.

Convention III) prohibited the compulsory use of POWs for mine clearance.[275] Moreover, the problem of remotely-delivered landmines had already been considered in the elaboration of the *1955 Draft Rules for the Protection of the Civilian Population from the Dangers of Indiscriminate Warfare.* According to Article 11 of the 1955 Draft Rules referred to above: 'The use of so-called delay-action projectiles is only authorised when their effects are limited to the objective itself.'[276]

The ICRC's commentary on the provision indicates that the intent was to control in particular delay-action projectiles, such as time-delay bombs and air-dropped landmines, and especially missiles used in 'strategic' bombing. With respect to manually-emplaced landmines, it was stated that a legal solution raised 'great difficulties' and the ICRC claimed that its study of the subject was 'not sufficiently advanced for it to propose a rule concerning it.'[277]

Yet, the revised *Draft Rules for the Limitation of the Dangers Incurred by the Civilian Population in Time of War* issued the following year, proposed that: 'If the parties to the conflict make use of mines, they are bound, without prejudice to the stipulations of the VIIIth Hague Convention of 1907, to chart the minefields. The charts shall be handed over, at the close of active hostilities, to the adverse Party, and also to all other authorities responsible for the safety of the population.'[278] Thus, although addressing the important issue of easing the task of post-conflict mine clearance, this suggested provision did not tackle the major problem of the potentially indiscriminate effects of landmines during prolonged conflict caused by their time-delay feature.

---

275 Article 52 provides in part that: 'Unless he be a volunteer, no prisoner of war may be employed on labour which is of an unhealthy or dangerous nature[.] (...) The removal of mines or similar devices shall be considered as dangerous labour.' The ICRC official commentary on this provision discusses the use of POWs for mine clearance during the Second World War, with respect to German POWs first in North Africa and later in France. The use of POWs for such activities was already – implicitly – prohibited under the 1929 Geneva Convention. See Pictet, J.S. (ed.), *Commentary, III Geneva Convention Relative to the Treatment of Prisoners of War*, ICRC, Geneva, 1960, pp. 277-8; *The History of Landmines*, p. 88.
Croll reports that after the end of the Second World War the French alone used up to 49,000 POWs for mine clearance and that across Europe between 8 and 17.5 per cent of all POW mine clearers were killed or injured in the period 1945-46. He notes that these deminers were given a strong incentive to ensure that clearance was total – they were required to march, shoulder to shoulder, across any area that had been cleared. *Ibid.*, p. 89. Their efforts were, however, successful: using mainly POW labour some 90 million mines had been cleared by 1947. *Ibid.*, p. 94.
For an interesting description of Sherman's use of prisoners of war to clear mines during the American Civil War and a discussion of its legality under current international humanitarian law see Robisch, T.G., "Would the Georgia Campaigns of the First Commander of the Modern Era Comply with Current Law of War Standards?", *Emory International Law Review*, Vol. 9, Fall 1995, pp. 493-4, 503.

276 Article 10(4), 1955 Draft Rules.

277 ICRC, *Draft Rules for the Protection of the Civilian Population from the Dangers of Indiscriminate Warfare*, ICRC, Geneva, June 1955, pp. 86-7.

278 Article 15 (*Safety measures and devices*). See ICRC, *Draft Rules for the Limitation of the Dangers Incurred by the Civilian Population in Time of War*, 2nd edn., ICRC, Geneva, April 1958, pp. 12-13 and 114-5. See also Roach, Capt. J.A., "Certain Conventional Weapons Convention", *op. cit.*, p. 7.

After a hiatus of more than a decade, landmines returned to the international legal agenda in the early 1970s; allegedly the 'sudden interest in restricting landmines and other "delayed action weapons" arose for both political and technical reasons. Politically, the rise of international terrorism in the 1960s and 1970s stimulated efforts to curb some of the terrorists' favourite weapons, booby-traps and time-bombs. On the technical side, the development of remotely-delivered mines caused new concern that "offensive" mines might be used indiscriminately.'[279] It was otherwise suggested that the new-found momentum was due to 'the well-publicised use of modern conventional weapons such as incendiary weapons, landmines, and small calibre high velocity bullets in the Indochina war.'[280]

The report of the 1973 ICRC Experts Meetings referred to landmines as weapons that 'may expose non-combatants to a grave and prolonged hazard'[281] and found that: 'Certain uses of anti-personnel mines (...) can lead to indiscriminate effects and injuries far in excess of what is required to put combatants out of action.'[282] The same report, however, included a controversial – and almost certainly inaccurate – assertion by one expert that in conventional warfare, casualties from mines and booby-traps had 'normally been quite low in proportion to casualties from other weapons. This applies to both combatants and non-combatants.'[283] With respect to guerrilla warfare, however, it was claimed that in one medical facility in a theatre of war characterised by guerrilla operations, nearly 20 per cent of the patients had been injured by mines and booby-traps.[284]

At the 1974 Lucerne Weapons Conference, one military expert claimed that 'fields of landmines were at present the most economical and effective artificial obstacle system that could be provided with conventional means.'[285] With specific reference to anti-personnel mines, several experts asserted that their primary value was 'to prevent the rapid clearing of anti-vehicle minefields; in this role they served to reduce the degree of surveillance and firepower necessary to defend the minefield.'[286] Other experts emphasised the humanitarian costs of landmines.

At the outset of the 1976 Lugano Weapons Conference France, the Netherlands and the UK introduced a specific proposal for the regulation of landmines and booby-traps.[287] The proposal contained draft provisions requiring that records of minefields containing more than 20 mines be made public upon the cessation of hostilities, that remotely-delivered mines should either be equipped with a neutralising mechanism or the area in which they were delivered be marked, and that certain (rather limited) protection be ensured for the civilian

279 Carnahan, Lt.-Col. B.M., "The Law of Land Mine Warfare", *op. cit.*, p. 75.
280 Roach, Capt. J.A., "Certain Conventional Weapons Convention", *op. cit.*, p. 6.
281 *Weapons that may Cause Unnecessary Suffering*, para. 58, pp. 24-5.
282 *Ibid.*, para. 247, p. 71.
283 *Ibid.*, para. 175, p. 53.
284 *Ibid.*, para. 245, p. 69.
285 *Report on the 1974 Lucerne Weapons Conference*, para. 230, p. 65.
286 *Ibid.*, para. 232, p. 66.
287 See *supra*.

population.[288] In introducing the proposal, one of the co-sponsors of the proposal claimed that the 1973 ICRC Experts Meetings had given little space to the subject of mines indicating 'a lack of interest quite out of proportion to the number and severity of military and civilian casualties caused by mines even after cessation of hostilities.'[289]

1.7.2. The Provisions of Protocol II

It has been asserted that Protocol II 'is a typical offspring of the arranged marriage between military necessity and humanitarian imperatives, a union which has produced the whole of international humanitarian law.'[290] It is also clear that the Protocol is based on the assumption that mines would be used responsibly and with discrimination by well-organised governmental armed forces.[291] Yet, in the two decades since its adoption, the employment of land-mines has been often indiscriminate, by armed opposition groups, and during internal armed conflicts – circumstances that tended to place that use *de jure* or *de facto* outside the purview of the 1980 CCW.[292] And although the ICRC has claimed that 'texts of this kind also carry great weight outside their official legal context,'[293] it was already obvious that the failure to apply formally the provisions of the Protocol to all armed conflicts represented a serious shortcoming in the legal regime.

A. Key Definitions

(i) Mine

Article 2 of Protocol II defines a mine as 'any munition placed under, on or near the ground or other surface area and designed to be detonated or exploded by the presence, proximity or contact of a person or vehicle.'[294] Thus, 'the

---

288 *Report on the 1976 Lugano Weapons Conference*, pp. 170-171.

289 *Ibid.*, pp. 51-2. Another expert said that he had been struck by the limited interest that had been shown in mines and booby-traps at the 1974 Lucerne Conference; 'these weapons caused more civilian casualties than any other conventional weapons.' *Ibid.*, p. 58.

290 Sandoz, Y., "Prohibitions or Restrictions on the Use of Certain Conventional Weapons", *op. cit.*, p. 13.

291 Writing in 1994, Marion Nash of the Office of the Legal Adviser of the US Department of State claimed that the Protocol was 'essentially a Western proposal,' and one that 'on the whole (...) basically codified the responsible practices which had already been adopted by the United States and other Western military forces to minimise civilian casualties from the use of these devices.' Nash, M., "Contemporary Practice of the United States Relating to International Law", *op. cit.*, 1994, p. 750.

292 In accordance with Article 1 of the *chapeau* Convention, Protocol II does not apply to 'armed conflicts not of an international character occurring in the territory of one of the High Contracting Parties.' Article 3 common to the four Geneva Conventions of 12 August 1949.

293 Sandoz, Y., "Prohibitions or Restrictions on the Use of Certain Conventional Weapons", *op. cit.*, p. 15.

294 Of note given the continuing concern about improvised explosive devices (see Introduction *supra* p. 3, footnote 18; see also *infra* Chapter 2 for details of the discussion of the definition of an anti-personnel mine under the Convention on the Prohibition of Anti-Personnel Mines) is the US's assertion that the definition applies 'whether a munition is designed for this purpose

critical defining characteristic of a mine is not its relationship to the ground or other surface area but rather its design function of being exploded by the presence, proximity or contact of a target, be that target a person or a vehicle.'[295] Accordingly, items of unexploded ordnance (UXO) – bombs, shells, grenades, and so on, that have been fired but which have failed to detonate upon impact – do not fall within the scope of the Protocol since UXO 'is a result of a malfunction of a munition; UXO is not "designed" in any sense, and, in particular, is not designed to be detonated by the presence, proximity or contact of a person.'[296] The Protocol includes no definition of anti-tank/anti-vehicle mines or anti-personnel mines[297] and therefore its provisions apply equally to all landmines, the only distinction being that between manually-emplaced and remotely-delivered mines.

(ii) Remotely-Delivered Mines

Remotely-delivered mines, otherwise known as 'scatterable' mines,[298] are defined as any mine 'delivered by artillery, rocket, mortar or similar means or dropped from an aircraft.'[299] Arriving at this definition, however, took considerable effort. The draft proposal mooted at the 1976 Lugano Weapons Conference had excluded mines delivered by artillery, rocket, mortar or similar means at less than 2,000 metres.[300] At the 1979-1980 UN Weapons Conference, a lower threshold of 1,000 metres was proposed.[301] The UK, in particular, was deter-

in the factory or adapted for this purpose in the field.' Nash, M., "Contemporary Practice of the United States Relating to International Law", *American Journal of International Law*, Vol. 91, 1997, p. 331.

Furthermore, as noted *infra* at p. 57, footnote 422, the US has subsequently tried to expand the definition of a booby-trap (see *infra*, p. 40), claiming that a trip-wired hand grenade should be considered as a booby-trap and not a mine. In the view of the author, this is not sustainable in all cases. Although it is sometimes difficult to distinguish between a mine and a booby-trap, the use, for example, of a trip-wired hand grenade *qua* a fragmentation mine on a path does not make the device a booby-trap. On the other hand, attaching the trip-wire to a door handle in a military barracks, for example, would, in the view of the author, fall squarely within the definition of a booby-trap.

295 Nash, M., "Contemporary Practice of the United States Relating to International Law", 1997, *op. cit.*, p. 331.

296 *Ibid.*

297 In discussing the draft proposal made at the 1976 Lugano Weapons Conference, one expert had called for a distinction to be made between anti-personnel and anti-tank minefields, 'the technical characteristics of which were very different.' *Report on the 1976 Lugano Weapons Conference*, para. 19, p. 59.

298 See *ibid.*, p. 168. For details of the development of scatterable mines see for example *The History of Landmines*, pp. 46-8.

299 Article 2(1), 1980 Protocol II. Thus, delayed action bombs that are dropped from aircraft and explode at a pre-determined time after impact are not covered by the Protocol. Carnahan, Lt.-Col. B. M., "The Law of Land Mine Warfare", *op. cit.*, p. 78.

300 *Report on the 1976 Lugano Weapons Conference*, p. 170. For the justification of the proposed threshold by one of the sponsors of the draft (presumably the UK), see pp. 50-1.

301 Rogers, Brig. A.P.V., "The Mines Protocol: Negotiating History", *op. cit.*, p. 232. See also De Mulinen, F., "A propos de la Conférence de Lucerne et Lugano sur l'emploi de certaines armes conventionelles", *op. cit.*, p. 126.

mined to protect its *Ranger* delivery system,[302] which scattered long-lived[303] anti-personnel mines over distances of several hundred metres.[304]

(iii) Booby-Traps

According to Article 2(2) of the Protocol, a booby-trap is 'any device or material which is designed, constructed or adapted to kill or injure and which functions unexpectedly when a person disturbs or approaches an apparently harmless object or performs an apparently safe act.' Accordingly, a landmine may be used as a booby-trap in certain circumstances.[305] On the other hand, given the requirement that the object be 'apparently harmless' and the act 'apparently safe', the suggestion of one authority that an anti-handling device on a landmine would fall within the definition of booby-trap must surely be wrong.[306] It is rather difficult to term mine clearance an 'apparently safe' act.

(iv) Military Objective

According to Article 2(4) of CCW Protocol II, '"Military objective" means, so far as objects are concerned, any object by its nature, location, purpose or use makes an effective contribution to military action and whose total or partial destruction, capture or neutralisation, in the circumstances ruling at the time, offers a definite military advantage.' The definition of military objective contained in Protocol II does not differ substantively from that contained in 1977 Additional Protocol I.[307] According to Lieutenant-Colonel Rogers, the inclusion of the word 'location' in the definition of military objective demonstrated that an area of land could be a military objective.[308] To confirm this position, upon ratification of the CCW and annexed Protocols, the Netherlands and the UK entered understandings that a specific area of land could also be a military objective if, because of its location, nature, purpose or use, its total or partial destruction, capture, or neutralisation in the circumstances ruling at the time offered a definite military advantage.[309]

---

302 Croll records that the Ranger scatterable mine system was introduced into the British armed forces in 1976. A vehicle-mounted system that could fire 1,296 plastic-cased anti-personnel mines a hundred metres, its main purpose was to cover an anti-tank minefield or create instant 'nuisance' minefields on demolition sites or roads. *The History of Landmines*, pp. 110-1.

303 That is, anti-personnel mines not fitted with any self-destructing or self-neutralising mechanism.

304 See Rogers, Lt.-Col. A.P.V., "A Commentary on the Protocol", *op. cit.*, p. 189; Gander, T.J., "Land mine warfare – the British position", *Jane's Defence Review*, Vol. 4, No. 6, 1983, pp. 597-607.

305 For instance, a mine rigged to detonate when an object placed on top of it, such as a rifle, is removed.

306 Levie, H.S., "Prohibitions and Restrictions on the Use of Conventional Weapons", *op. cit.*, p. 659, footnote 74. But see *Landmine Monitor Report 1999*, pp. 593-4.

307 For further discussion of the definition of a military objective see *infra* Chapter 3, p. 187, footnote 1301.

308 Rogers, Lt.-Col. A.P.V., "A Commentary on the Protocol", *op. cit.*, p. 190; Rogers, A.P.V., *Law on the Battlefield*, Manchester University Press, Manchester, UK, 1996, p. 38.

309 Interestingly, the US did not enter a understanding with respect to definition of military objective contained in the 1980 Protocol II, but in a 1996 report by then Secretary of State Warren Christopher on amended Protocol II, which was submitted with the US President's letter

B. Prohibitions and Restrictions on the Use of Mines

(i) General Prohibitions and Restrictions

According to Article 3 of the Protocol it is prohibited to 'direct'[310] landmines against[311] the civilian population or individual civilians or to use mines indiscriminately. Mines must be targeted against legitimate military objectives. In addition, 'all feasible precautions' must be taken to protect civilians from mines.[312] These provisions, which form the basis for the protection of the civilian population against mines, draw heavily on Articles 51 and 57 of 1977 Additional Protocol I and 'may be thought of as an adaptation of those Articles to the peculiarities of landmine warfare.'[313]

To preclude the possibility of allegations of war crimes being made against its commanders on the basis of knowledge gained in hindsight, when adhering to the CCW and its annexed Protocols, including 1980 Protocol II, Canada entered an understanding whereby the 'compliance of commanders and others responsible for planning, deciding upon, or executing attacks to which the Convention and its Protocols apply cannot be judged on the basis of information which subsequently comes to light but must be assessed on the basis of the information available to them at the time such actions were taken.'[314] Thus, for example, ordering the use of mines against a certain target that is in fact a civilian object will not constitute a war crime unless the commander knew, or should reasonably be expected to have known, that the target was not a legitimate military objective.

The use of manually-emplaced mines is prohibited 'in any city, town, village or other area containing a similar concentration of civilians' unless (a) combat between ground forces is taking place or appears imminent, or (b) either the mines are placed on or close to a military objective belonging to the enemy, or

---

of transmittal of the Protocol to the Senate for advice and consent to ratification, it proposed to do so when ratifying amended Protocol II. Marion Nash explains that this was the result of a new provision that prohibited treating several distinct military objectives in an area containing a concentration of civilians as a single military objective. Nash, M., "Contemporary Practice of the United States Relating to International Law", *op. cit.*, 1997, p. 336.

310 For a discussion on the appropriateness of the term 'to direct' in the case of mines see *infra* Chapter 3, pp. 139-41.

311 It appears that an error occurred in the version of the Convention originally issued by the UN. In Article 3(3)(a), it should read directed 'against' rather than 'at'. See Shaw, M., "The United Nations Convention on Prohibitions or Restrictions on the Use of Certain Conventional Weapons, 1981", *op. cit.*, p. 109, footnote.

312 Article 3(4), 1980 Protocol II. Feasible precautions 'are those precautions which are practicable or practically possible taking into account all circumstances ruling at the time, including humanitarian and military considerations.'

313 Carnahan, Lt.-Col. B.M., "The Law of Land Mine Warfare", *op. cit.*, p. 78. See also Rogers, Lt.-Col. A.P.V., "A Commentary on the Protocol", *op. cit.*, p. 192.

314 Similar understandings were entered by Israel and the UK.

measures are taken to protect civilians from their effects.[315] These exceptions remove much of the apparent force of the prohibition.[316]

Reaching agreement on the regulation of remotely-delivered mines was, however, far more challenging. These mines had already been the subject of animated discussion during the 1974 Lucerne Weapons Conference,[317] the 1976 Lugano Weapons Conference, and throughout the 1974-1977 Diplomatic Conference.[318] At the 1979-1980 UN Weapons Conference, a number of delegations argued forcefully, but unsuccessfully, in favour of a prohibition on the use of remotely-delivered mines.[319] Eventually a compromise was accepted whereby in addition to the general restrictions on the use of all mines,[320] remotely-delivered mines could only be used 'within an area which is itself a military objective or which contains military objectives' and must either be 'accurately recorded in accordance with Article 7(1)(a)'[321] or contain an 'effective neutralising mechanism'.[322] Although efforts were made to specify the

315 Article 4(2). The posting of warning signs or sentries, the issue of warnings or the erection of fences are given as specific examples of such measures. (Article 4(2)(b)). See Carnahan, Lt.-Col. B.M., "The Law of Land Mine Warfare", *op. cit.*, pp. 81-2; Levie, H.S., "Prohibitions and Restrictions on the Use of Conventional Weapons", *op. cit.*, p. 657. Levie suggests that the posting of warning signs and the issue of warnings are 'somewhat unrealistic' because of the loss of surprise vis-à-vis the enemy. On the other hand, a number of military commanders have suggested that advertising the location of minefields respects the accepted utility for mines, insofar as they are used to delay the enemy or to canalise them down a preferred route.

316 Carnahan, Lt.-Col. B.M., "The Law of Land Mine Warfare", *op. cit.*, p. 81. Attempts to make the exceptions cumulative rather than alternative were unsuccessful.

317 *Report on the 1974 Lucerne Weapons Conference*, paras. 234-40, pp. 66-8.

318 A working paper on conventional weapons submitted to the fourth session of the 1974-1977 Diplomatic Conference (CDDH/IV/201) by Algeria, Austria, Egypt, Lebanon, Mali, Mauritania, Mexico, Norway, Sudan, Sweden, Switzerland, Venezuela and Yugoslavia had included a proposal to prohibit the laying of anti-personnel mines by aircraft. See *Report on the 1976 Lugano Weapons Conference*, pp. 198-9. For a description of the problems caused by the helicopter laying of mines during the Falklands/Malvinas conflict see Gander, T.J., "The Underground World of the Land Mine", *Jane's Military Review 1983/4*, p. 63.

319 According to Stefan Oeter, debates on this issue during the 1980 UN Weapons Conference were 'fierce'. Oeter, S., "Methods and Means of Combat", Fleck, D., (ed.), *The Handbook of Humanitarian Law in Armed Conflicts*, *op. cit.*, p. 128.

320 See for instance Carnahan, Lt.-Col. B.M., "The Law of Land Mine Warfare", *op. cit.*, p. 80.

321 This wording is, as one of the drafters has readily admitted, clumsy and led to an unfortunate lack of clarity in a key provision. See Rogers, Col. A.P.V., "A Commentary on the Protocol", *op. cit.* pp. 194-5; Rogers, A.P.V., *Law on the Battlefield*, *op. cit.*, p. 150. Article 7(1)(a) requires that parties to a conflict record the location only of all *pre-planned* minefields laid by them. In fact, as Lieutenant-Colonel Rogers has pointed out on a number of occasions, the intention of the drafters was to ensure that recording be mandatory whenever remotely-delivered mines without an effective neutralising mechanism were used. See for instance Rogers, Col. A.P.V., "Mines, Booby-traps and other devices", *International Review of the Red Cross*, November-December 1990, No. 279, p. 528; UN, *Summary of Negotiations*, *op. cit.*, p.12. Thus, in Article III(10) of the ICRC/UN General Assembly Guidelines for Military Manuals and Instructions on the Protection of the Environment in Times of Armed Conflict, it is provided that: 'Any unrecorded laying of remotely delivered non-self-neutralising landmines is prohibited.' See for instance Roberts, A. and Guelff, R., *Documents on the Laws of War*, 3rd edn., *op. cit.*, p. 611.

322 Article 5, 1980 Protocol II.

maximum time limit for the operation of the neutralising mechanism,[323] Protocol II effectively leaves that decision to the user.[324]

Writing in 1990, one military lawyer suggested that, in practice, most remotely-delivered mines would be fitted with a neutralising mechanism which would cause the mine to explode after a certain period of time.[325] Given the refusal in 1996 by certain key States, such as China and the Russian Federation, to accept an immediate prohibition on the use of remotely-delivered long-lived anti-personnel mines,[326] this view is open to question. Moreover, a number of States were constrained to begin destruction of their stockpiles of PFM-1 remotely-delivered anti-personnel mines, since these were either not self-destructing or were not sufficiently reliable.[327]

Article 5(2) requires that 'effective advance warning' be given of 'any delivery or dropping of remotely delivered mines which may affect the civilian population, unless circumstances do not permit.' Among the circumstances that might not permit prior warning could be the need for surprise or the safety of the aircraft dropping the mines.[328] The absence of an obligation to warn the civilian population after remotely-delivered mines have been deployed is extremely regrettable, although it is suggested that this might be required by the general duty to take all feasible precautions to protect civilians[329] from the effects of all mines, booby-traps and other devices.[330] There is no evidence that this has ever been done in practice.

(ii) Recording of Mines and Mine Clearance

Although the effectiveness (or otherwise) of recording the location of landmines has obvious implications for post-conflict clearance, Protocol II only requires parties to the conflict to record all 'pre-planned minefields' and to

---

323 At the 1976 Lugano Weapons Conference, a number of experts had suggested that a neutralising mechanism on a remotely-delivered mine should activate no later than 24 hours after delivery. (*Report on the 1976 Lugano Weapons Conference*, p. 148.) This proposal was contested vigorously, as it would be 20 years later at the First CCW Review Conference.

324 The mechanism could be (a) 'self-actuating' and should either detonate or render inactive the mine 'when it is anticipated that the mine will no longer serve the military purpose for which it was placed in position' or (b) 'remotely-controlled' and designed to render harmless or destroy the mine when it 'no longer serves the military purpose for which it was placed in position.' (Article 5(1)(b), 1980 Protocol II). Thus, in the view of one military lawyer, this 'is a matter for professional military judgement and the appropriate period is likely to vary considerably from case to case depending on both tactical and humanitarian considerations.' Carnahan, Lt.-Col. B.M., "The Law of Land Mine Warfare", *op. cit.*, p. 89.

325 Fenrick, W.J., "The Conventional Weapons Convention", *op. cit.*, p. 505.

326 See below the provisions of amended Protocol II on 3 May 1996. Upon ratification of amended Protocol II in 1999 both China and Pakistan opted to take advantage of the possibility to delay respect for the requirement to ensure that all remotely-delivered anti-personnel mines were both self-destructing and self-deactivating for nine years from entry into force of the Protocol.

327 See *infra*, Chapters 2 and 3 with respect to Ukraine's destruction of PFM-1 anti-personnel mines.

328 Carnahan, Lt.-Col. B.M., "The Law of Land Mine Warfare", *op. cit.*, p. 80.

329 Article 3(4), Protocol II referred to *supra*.

330 See Rogers, Col. A.P.V., "Mines, Booby-traps and other devices", *op. cit.*, p. 528; Carnahan, Lt.-Col. B.M., "The Law of Land Mine Warfare", *op. cit.*, pp. 80-1.

'endeavour to ensure' the recording of all other minefields and mines laid by them.[331] The term 'pre-planned' is not defined in the Protocol and its definition remains the subject of contention, although it is generally agreed that plans for such a minefield must exist considerably in advance of its being laid.[332] Upon adhering to the CCW and annexed Protocols in 1994, Canada entered an understanding that the term *pre-planned* 'means that the position of the minefield in question should have been determined in advance so that an accurate record of the location of the minefield, when laid, can be made.' The Protocol does not require minefields to be marked although this would clearly have offered greater protection to the civilian population.[333]

At the 1976 Lugano Weapons Conference the basic proposal under consideration by the conference had been to record the location of all minefields containing more than 20 mines and, after the cessation of active hostilities, in the case of minefields in the territory of the enemy, their public disclosure.[334] This figure was not acceptable – some experts felt it was too high; others too low – and the notion of recording pre-planned minefields was introduced as a compromise.[335]

The practical difficulty of recording the location of remotely-delivered mines was obvious to all. In adhering to Protocol II, Canada and Israel entered an understanding that: 'Any obligation to record the location of remotely-delivered mines pursuant to Article 5(1)(a) refers to the location of minefields and not to the location of individual remotely-delivered mines.'

In addition, the Technical Annex, which sets out the procedure for recording, would seem to be merely hortatory. Thus, in its report on the negotiations the US declared that the provisions of the Protocol's Technical Annex, including those dealing with the issue of recording, 'are not mandatory or uniformly applicable in all circumstances', but only "guidelines", which are to be "taken into ac-

331 Article 7(1) and (2), Protocol II. Parties are only obliged to record all 'pre-planned' minefields laid by them.

332 See for instance Carnahan, Lt.-Col. B.M., "The Law of Land Mine Warfare", *op. cit.*, p. 84.

333 At the 1976 Lugano Weapons Conference, opinions were divided on whether minefields should be marked. A number of military experts felt that such an obligation would unnecessarily limit the effectiveness of minefields. See De Mulinen, F., "A propos de la Conférence de Lucerne et Lugano sur l'emploi de certaines armes conventionelles", p. 126; *Report on the 1976 Lugano Weapons Conference*, p. 148. Lieutenant-Colonel Rogers asserted that [f]or military reasons it would have been unrealistic bearing in mind the need for dummy and nuisance minefields as well as marked minefields. Rogers, Lt.-Col. A.P.V., "A Commentary on the Protocol", *op. cit.*, p. 193. Writing a few years later, Rogers claimed that 'defensive minefields laid when combat is not imminent are likely to be marked so as to comply with the requirement to take measures to protect civilians.' Rogers, Col. A.P.V., "Mines, Booby-traps and other devices", *op. cit.*, pp. 527-8.

334 "Land Mines and Booby-Traps and Proposals for the Regulation of Their Use", Working Paper submitted by the experts of France, the Netherlands and the United Kingdom, Annex A2, para. 2, *Report on the 1976 Lugano Weapons Conference*, p. 168.

335 De Mulinen, F., "A propos de la Conférence de Lucerne et Lugano sur l'emploi de certaines armes conventionelles", *op. cit.*, pp. 125-126. Lieutenant-Colonel Rogers claimed that it 'was suggested by one delegate, and not disputed, that the word implied more than mere conscious act on the part of the mine layer and involved a co-ordinated plan for the laying of defensive minefields.' Rogers, Lt.-Col. A.P.V., "A Commentary on the Protocol", *op. cit.*, p. 201.

count."[336] It has likewise been asserted that the 'minimum standards of recording' were laid down in a 'non-binding' Technical Annex.[337] This view is further supported by the absence of any reference to the Annex in the provisions of the Protocol.[338]

Parties to the Protocol are not formally obliged to clear or ensure the clearance of all landmines[339] once the conflict is over[340] only 'whenever possible, by mutual agreement,' to 'provide for the release of information concerning the location of minefields, mines and booby-traps, particularly in agreements governing the cessation of hostilities.'[341] Carnahan refers to Professor Schwarzenberger's 'castigation' of rules of this type as 'the most questionable variant of the rules of warfare' whose true purpose is not to 'safeguard the minimum standard of civilisation' but rather to 'cover up the inability or unwillingness to achieve this object.'[342]

C. The Implementation of the Protocol

As with the *chapeau* Convention,[343] 1980 Protocol II does not contain a system for promoting compliance with its provisions.[344] The indiscriminate use of landmines in an international or internationalised armed conflict would, however, violate the provisions of 1977 Additional Protocol I to the Geneva Conventions and, if constituting a grave breach of this Protocol, would be subject to compulsory universal jurisdiction.[345] Evidential and other difficulties, however, have contributed to a situation where prosecutions for the indiscriminate use of mines are extremely rare.

---

336 Cited by Levie, H.S., "Prohibitions and Restrictions on the Use of Conventional Weapons", *op. cit.*, p. 660.

337 Oeter, S., "Methods and Means of Combat", *op. cit.*, p. 131.

338 This view is probably correct, although it is certainly regrettable. Fortunately, it is not the case with respect to the Technical Annex of amended Protocol II, since the operative provisions in that Protocol make specific reference to obligations in the Technical Annex. See *infra* p. 45, footnote 450.

339 For a detailed discussion of the duty under general international law to exchange information regarding minefield location, provide technical assistance for and participate in the removal and destruction of mines, and compensate for any material and moral damage caused, see Partsch, K.J., "Remnants of war as a legal problem in the light of the Libyan case", *American Journal of International Law*, Vol. 78, No. 2, April 1984, pp. 386-401.

340 See Hampson, F., *The Long Shadow – Landmines and the Law of Armed Conflicts*, Papers in the Theory and Practice of Human Rights, No. 12, University of Essex, Colchester, January 1995, p. 15.

341 Article 7(3)(c), Protocol II. See Carnahan, Lt.-Col. B.M., "The Law of Land Mine Warfare", *op. cit.*, pp. 82-3.

342 Schwarzenberger, G., *International Law as Applied by International Courts and Tribunals*, Vol. II, Sweet & Maxwell, London, 1968, p. 11, cited by Carnahan, Lt.-Col. B.M., "The Law of Land Mine Warfare", *op. cit.*, pp. 82-3.

343 See *supra*.

344 Hampson, F., *The Long Shadow C Landmines and the Law of Armed Conflicts*, *op. cit.*, p. 16.

345 *Ibid.* See Article 85(3), 1977 Additional Protocol I; see also Article 146, Geneva Convention IV.

D. Entry into Force of the Protocol

Protocol II entered into force on 2 December 1983, at the same time as the Convention as a whole.[346] As of end March 2001, a total of 76 States were party to the Protocol.[347] Specific reservations to one or more of the provisions of Protocol II were made on ratification by Canada, Cyprus, Israel, the Netherlands, the United Kingdom, and the United States. Most of these related to an interpretation of the definition of military objective contained in the Protocol. The Holy See, however, declared that the provisions of the Protocol were inadequate and hoped that its accession to the Convention would offer support to every effort aimed at effectively banning anti-personnel mines.

1.8. The First Review Conference of the Convention on Certain Conventional Weapons

The 1980 CCW had made specific provision for future review of its provisions, including amendment of the *chapeau* Convention and existing annexed Protocols,[348] as well as the addition of new Protocols.[349] Although the possibility of future conferences of States Parties to discuss amendments and additions was generally agreed, a number of States, particularly the Soviet Union, wished to give the UN Committee on Disarmament (now the UN Conference on Disarmament) a predominant, if not exclusive, role in the negotiation of new protocols.[350] Article 8 of the CCW, which sets out in some detail the procedure to be

[346] In accordance with CCW Article 5(3).

[347] Argentina, Australia, Austria, Bangladesh, Belarus, Belgium, Bosnia-Herzegovina, Brazil, Bulgaria, Cambodia, Canada, Cape Verde, China, Colombia, Costa Rica, Croatia, Cuba, Cyprus, the Czech Republic, Denmark, Djibouti, Ecuador, El Salvador, Finland, France, Georgia, Germany, Greece, Guatemala, Holy See, Hungary, India, Ireland, Israel, Italy, Japan, Lao People's Democratic Republic, Latvia, Lesotho, Liechtenstein, Luxembourg, Maldives, Malta, Mauritius, Mexico, Moldova, Mongolia, the Netherlands, New Zealand, Niger, Norway, Pakistan, Panama, the Philippines, Poland, Portugal, Romania, the Russian Federation, Seychelles, Slovakia, Slovenia, South Africa, Spain, Sweden, Switzerland, the former Yugoslav Republic of Macedonia, Tajikistan, Togo, Tunisia, Uganda, Ukraine, the UK, Uruguay, the US, Uzbekistan, and Yugoslavia.

[348] 'Such a[n] [amendment or review] conference may agree upon amendments which shall be adopted and enter into force in the same manner as this Convention and the annexed Protocols, provided that amendments to this Convention may be adopted only by the High Contracting Parties and that amendments to a specific annexed Protocol may be adopted only by the High Contracting Parties which are bound by that Protocol.' Article 8(1)(b), 1980 CCW.

[349] 'At such [a review conference] consideration may also be given to any proposal for additional protocols relating to other categories of conventional weapons not covered by the existing annexed Protocols. All States represented at the conference may participate fully in such consideration. Any additional protocols shall be adopted in the same manner as this Convention, shall be annexed thereto and shall enter into force as provided in paragraphs 3 and 4 of Article 5 of this Convention.' Article 8(3)(b), 1980 CCW. The meaning of 'full participation' is subject to debate. It could, for example, be taken to mean a right to vote (as opposed to attendance as observer) rather than a right to veto. For a discussion of the difference in procedure for amendments to the CCW and existing Protocols and the adoption of a new Protocol see Roach, Capt. J.A., "Certain Conventional Weapons Convention", *op. cit.*, pp. 42-3.

[350] *Ibid.*, p. 39.

followed, was reportedly one of the most difficult to negotiate, principally because of the fear of a number of States, particularly Mexico and Sweden, that a revision of Protocol III on incendiary weapons would be needed because the provisions adopted would not be sufficiently far-reaching.[351]

It has been claimed that the detailed review and amendment mechanism contained in the CCW is 'more a product of the arms control rather than the humanitarian law treaties. Neither the 1949 Geneva Conventions nor any of the older treaties in the field of international humanitarian law applicable in armed conflict contain [a] revision procedure or review mechanism. The 1977 Additional Protocols are quite similar.'[352] On the other hand, arms control treaties provide a more detailed and restrictive review and amending process.'[353] Given the rapid progression of weapons technology, however, it was widely understood that a more flexible mechanism was appropriate. Yet once Article 8 was finally adopted, a number of Western delegations presciently predicted that a first review conference would not be held before the mid-1990s at the earliest.[354]

By the end of the 1980s, it was becoming increasingly evident that the norms established under 1980 Protocol II were not being widely respected in practice.[355] Whether this was due to the inherent qualities of anti-personnel mines, the limited scope of applicability of the Protocol, ignorance of the law, or a wilful disregard for the principles of humanity (or, more likely, a combination of all four), is a moot point. The many civilian casualties due to landmines, especially anti-personnel mines, in Afghanistan, Angola, Cambodia, Mozambique and, in the early 1990s in the conflicts of the former Soviet Union and the former Yugoslavia, were evidence of a problem spiralling out of control. In 1992, a coalition of six Western non-governmental organisations (NGOs) had come together to issue a joint call for the total prohibition of anti-personnel mines.[356] One of these six NGOs, Handicap International, encouraged the French government to call for a review of the 1980 CCW[357] and on 9 February 1993, the French government formally submitted a request to the UN Secretary-General to convene the First CCW Review Conference.

---

[351] Roach, Capt. J.A., "Certain Conventional Weapons Convention", *op. cit.*, pp. 38-9, citing a report of the US delegation.

[352] Article 97 (1) and (2), 1977 Additional Protocol I provides that:
'Any High Contracting Party may propose amendments to this Protocol. The text of any proposed amendment shall be communicated to the depositary, which shall decide, after consultation with all the High Contracting Parties, and the International Committee of the Red Cross, whether a conference should be convened to consider the proposed amendment. (...) The depositary shall invite to that conference all the High Contracting Parties as well as the Parties to the Conventions, whether or not they are signatories of this Protocol.'
A similar provision is to be found in Article 24, 1977 Additional Protocol II.

[353] Roach, Capt. J.A., "Certain Conventional Weapons Convention", *op. cit.*, p. 44.

[354] *Ibid.*, p. 40.

[355] Writing after the success of the Ottawa Process, Jody Williams and Steve Goose, two of the key figures in the International Campaign to Ban Landmines, described the CCW as a 'dismal failure in reducing the impact of mines on civilian populations.' Williams, J. and Goose, S., "The International Campaign to Ban Landmines", *op. cit.*, p. 26.

[356] See *supra* Introduction, pp. 16-19.

[357] France had already signalled its interest in a Review Conference to strengthen verification provisions upon its signature of the CCW. See *supra* p. 33, footnote 257.

On 16 December 1993, the UN General Assembly formally welcomed the request, encouraged the establishment of a group of governmental experts to prepare the review conference, and called upon 'the maximum number of States' to attend.[358] Six days later, the States Parties formally requested the UN Secretary-General to set up a group of governmental experts to consider among other things 'as a matter of priority' concrete proposals for amendments to Protocol II, and especially:

- *strengthening restrictions on the use of anti-personnel mines and, in particular, those without neutralising and self-destruction mechanisms;*
- *considering the establishment of a verification system for provisions of this Protocol;*
- *studying opportunities for broadening the scope of this Protocol to cover armed conflicts that are not of an international character.*[359]

In total, four meetings of the group of governmental experts were necessary to prepare the Review Conference, which proved unable to report before the end of 1994 as had been hoped because of the difficulty in reaching agreement.[360] The first session of the Review Conference was held in Vienna from 25 September to 13 October 1995.[361] As agreement on amendments to Protocol

[358] UN General Assembly Resolution 48/79, paras. 5-7.

[359] See *UN Doc. CCW/CONF.I/GE/4*, pp. 2-3.

[360] The group met from 28 February-4 March 1994, from 16-27 May 1994, from 8-19 August 1994, and from 9-20 January 1995. Altogether, representatives of 33 States Parties and 33 States non-parties to the CCW participated in the work of the Group. The States Parties represented were: Australia, Austria, Benin, Bulgaria, Canada, China, Croatia, Cuba, Cyprus, the Czech Republic, Denmark, Finland, France, Germany, Greece, Hungary, India, Japan, Latvia, Mexico, the Netherlands, New Zealand, Norway, Pakistan, Poland, the Russian Federation, Slovakia, Slovenia, Spain, Sweden, Switzerland, Tunisia and Ukraine. The States non-parties represented were: Afghanistan, Algeria, Angola, Argentina, Belgium, Brazil, Cambodia, Canada (which ratified the CCW on 24 June 1994), Chile, Colombia, Egypt, Ethiopia, Iran, Ireland, Israel, Italy, Jamaica, Jordan, Kenya, Kuwait, New Zealand (which ratified the CCW on 18 April 1994), Nicaragua, Oman, Peru, Portugal, Republic of Korea, Romania, South Africa, Spain (which ratified the CCW on 29 June 1994), the Syrian Arab Republic, Turkey, the United Kingdom, and the United States of America. In accordance with General Assembly resolution 48/79, the ICRC was invited to attend the group of governmental experts as an observer. The United Nations was subsequently invited to attend in the same capacity. Non-governmental organisations (NGOs), however, were excluded, with China effectively imposing a veto on their participation.

[361] Altogether representatives of 44 States Parties and 40 States non-parties to the CCW participated in the first session of the Review Conference. The States Parties represented were: Australia, Austria, Belarus, Belgium, Bosnia and Herzegovina, Bulgaria, Canada, China, Croatia, Cuba, Cyprus, the Czech Republic, Denmark, Ecuador, Finland, France, Germany, Greece, Hungary, India, Ireland, Israel, Italy, Japan, Latvia, Liechtenstein, Mexico, Mongolia, the Netherlands, New Zealand, Norway, Pakistan, Poland, the Russian Federation, Slovakia, Slovenia, Spain, Sweden, Switzerland, Tunisia, Ukraine, the United Kingdom, and the United States of America. The States non-parties represented were: Albania, Angola, Argentina, Bolivia, Brazil, Cambodia, Chile, Colombia, Egypt, Ethiopia, Gabon, Holy See, Iceland, Indonesia, Iran, Jordan, Libyan Arab Jamahiriya, Morocco, Mozambique, Nicaragua, Oman, Paraguay, Peru, the Philippines, Portugal, Republic of Korea, Republic of Moldova, Romania, Saudi Arabia, Singapore, South Africa, Sudan, Syrian Arab Republic, Thailand, Turkey, the United Republic of Tanzania, Venezuela, and Vietnam.

II proved impossible to achieve,[362] the Conference decided to continue its work at resumed sessions in Geneva from 15 to 19 January 1996[363] and from 22 April to 3 May 1996. Finally, on 3 May 1996, more than two years after discussions on amending the Protocol had begun, the States Parties to the 1980 CCW adopted by consensus an amended Protocol II.[364] In accordance with its *chapeau* Article 2,[365] amended Protocol II entered into force on 3 December 1998, six months after Lithuania became the 20th State Party to the CCW to declare its consent to be bound by the Protocol.[366] As of end April 2001, a total of 57 States had adhered to it.[367]

Reaction from the international community to the adoption of amended Protocol II was noticeably underwhelming in its praise.[368] The ICRC, which had called for the total prohibition of the production, stockpiling, transfer and use of anti-personnel mines prior to the first meeting of governmental experts in February 1994,[369] called the restrictions on the use of anti-personnel mines

---

362 UN General Assembly resolution 50/74, adopted on 12 December 1995, called upon States Parties to 'intensify their efforts in order to conclude negotiations on a strengthened Protocol II.'

363 At a meeting of military experts to resolve deadlock on the 'technical' aspects of the Protocol.

364 Protocol on Prohibitions or Restrictions on the Use of Mines, Booby-Traps and Other Devices as Amended on 3 May 1996 (Protocol II as amended on 3 May 1996), hereinafter, amended Protocol II. The two versions of the Protocol continue to co-exist even though Protocol II as amended has formally entered into force and it remains open to States to ratify the 1980 Protocol, or the amended Protocol II, or even both. See further Roberts, A. and Guelff, R., *Documents on the Laws of War*, 3rd edn., *op. cit.*, p. 518.

365 See *UN Doc. CCW/CONF.I/16 (Part I)*, p. 32.

366 In its press release 98/23 of 5 June 1998, the ICRC welcomed the forthcoming entry into force of the amended Protocol and declared that although it 'considers that adherence to the Ottawa treaty is a top priority, it continues to encourage States to ratify amended Protocol II because this text also restricts the use and transfer of landmines, anti-tank mines and other weapons not covered by the Ottawa treaty. The ICRC is particularly concerned about the potential consequences in humanitarian terms that would arise from the widespread and irresponsible use of remotely-delivered anti-tank mines. In addition, for those States not yet prepared to ban anti-personnel mines outright, Protocol II as amended represents a step forward compared with the original text adopted in 1980.' With respect to possible future regulation of anti-vehicle mines, see the ICRC contribution to Landmine Monitor, *Landmine Monitor Report 1999*, pp. 1007-8.

367 Argentina, Australia, Austria, Bangladesh, Belgium, Bosnia-Herzegovina, Brazil, Bulgaria, Cambodia, Canada, Cape Verde, China, Colombia, Costa Rica, the Czech Republic, Denmark, Ecuador, El Salvador, Estonia, Finland, France, Germany, Greece, Holy See, Hungary, India, Ireland, Israel, Italy, Japan, Jordan, Liechtenstein, Lithuania, Luxembourg, Maldives, Monaco, the Netherlands, New Zealand, Nicaragua, Norway, Pakistan, Panama, Peru, the Philippines, Portugal, Senegal, Seychelles, Slovakia, South Africa, Spain, Sweden, Switzerland, Tajikistan, Ukraine, the UK, Uruguay, and the US. In 1997, the year of the adoption of the Convention on the Prohibition of Anti-Personnel Mines, General Assembly Resolution 52/42 on the status of the 1980 CCW was adopted without a vote. Operative paragraph 2 of the resolution 'urgently calls upon all States that have not yet done so to take all measures to become parties, as soon as possible, to the Convention and its protocols, in particular to amended Protocol II, with a view to achieving the widest possible adherence to this instrument at an early date.'

368 Apart from the Swedish Ministry of Foreign Affairs, which, mindful that the Review Conference had been presided by the Swedish Ambassador, Johan Molander, declared the agreement a significant diplomatic success for Sweden. "La Suède se félicite sur l'accord sur les mines antipersonnel", *AFP*, Stockholm, 3 May 1996.

369 See *UN Doc. CCW/CONF.I/SR.2*, p. 17.

'woefully inadequate' and indicated that the Protocol alone was 'unlikely to significantly reduce the level of civilian landmine casualties.'[370] The UN Secretary-General, Boutros Boutros Ghali, said he was 'deeply disappointed' by the failure to agree a ban.[371] Jody Williams, the ICBL Co-ordinator, declared that the diplomatic success was a humanitarian failure.[372] According to Yves Sandoz, the ICRC's Director of International Law and Principles, the practice of consensus had ensured that an international humanitarian crisis was met with only the most modest and measured legal response.[373]

Indeed, if negotiations throughout the review process had been so laborious, this was in large part due to the decision of the group of governmental experts,[374] and subsequently the Review Conference,[375] to take all its decisions by consensus. The consensus rule allowed each State Party to the CCW an effective veto over any proposals, and there was little reluctance to take advantage of the opportunity this provided when any country thought that its own stock of landmines was in any way threatened. As one study on military law puts it:

> *'The simple and obvious fact is that nations if willing to resort to violence at all are reluctant to place limits on the kinds of violence they employ – especially on weapons that cause them to think that they have an advantage over potential foes. (...) Cobras would advocate the banning of hooves, claws, and cutting teeth but would denounce in the strongest terms a proposal to outlaw venom.'*[376]

In fact, the Preparatory Conference to the 1979-1980 UN Weapons Conference had itself failed to reach agreement on the rules for decision-making.[377] According to one expert: 'Decisions were reached on the basis of an unofficial, and undefined, consensus,'[378] although he also notes that a number of delegations repeatedly asserted that voting would be possible.[379] It will be extremely difficult to change the practice of adopting any amendments or new protocols by

370 Statement of Eric Roethlisberger, Vice-President of the ICRC, to the closing session of the First Review Conference of the 1980 CCW, 3 May 1996.

371 See Williams, F., "UN fails to agree outright ban on landmines", *Financial Times*, 4 May 1996.

372 See AFP wire release, *AFP-DL82*, 3 May 1996.

373 Sandoz, Y., *Anti-Personnel Mines will be Banned*, ICRC, Geneva, May 1996.

374 See *UN Doc. CCW/CONF.I/GE/23*, p. 59.

375 The draft rules of procedure for the Review Conference merely stated that decisions would be taken in accordance with Article 8 of the 1980 Convention. See *UN Doc. CCW/CONF.1/GE/CRP.53/Rev.1 as amended.*

376 Bishop, Jr., J.W., *Justice Under Fire, A Study of Military Law*, Charterhouse, New York 1974, p. 270. See Green, L.C., "What one may do in combat – Then and Now", Delissen, A.J.M. and Tanja, G.J., (eds.), *Humanitarian Law of Armed Conflict: Challenges Ahead*, Martinus Nijhoff Publishers, Dordrecht, 1991, p. 277.

377 Roach, Capt. J.A., "Certain Conventional Weapons Convention", *op. cit.*, p. 43.

378 Fenrick, W.J., "The Conventional Weapons Convention", *op. cit.*, p. 501.

379 Fenrick, W.J., "New Developments in the Law Concerning the Use of Conventional Weapons in Armed Conflict", *Canadian Yearbook of International Law*, Vol. 19, No. 19, 1981, p. 238, footnote 36. Roach, Capt. J.A., "Certain Conventional Weapons Convention", *op. cit.*, p. 43, reports that the US delegation believed that the treaty's language 'shall be adopted (...) in the same manner as this Convention and the annexed Protocols" meant by consensus 'and only by consensus'.

consensus[380] in future Review Conferences,[381] but this was a crucial issue in the negotiations leading up to the adoption of amended Protocol II. It was probably the key factor in spurring the 'Ottawa Process'[382] and thus ultimately a separate treaty prohibiting anti-personnel mines.[383]

Adherence to the CCW and its annexed Protocols continued to increase, however, notwithstanding the entry into force of the Convention on the Prohibition of Anti-Personnel Mines. In 1999, at the UN General Assembly, resolution 54/58, adopted without as vote, welcomed the entry into force of amended Protocol II and called for its universal adherence. Speaking at the Annual Meeting of States Parties in Geneva in December 1999, the UN Secretary-General appealed to all States that had not yet done so to take 'all measures to become parties to the Protocol as soon as possible.' As of May 2000, four of the five permanent members of the UN Security Council had adhered to both the 1980 CCW and amended Protocol II.[384] The fifth, the Russian Federation, was already party to the 1980 CCW and 1980 Protocol II, and although in May 2000 the Russian President, Vladimir Putin, had urged swift ratification of amended Protocol II, as of writing this had not yet been secured.[385]

---

380 At the first Annual Conference of States Parties of amended Protocol II, which took place in Geneva from 15-17 December 1999, the President of the Conference, Ambassador Johan Molander of Sweden, proposed draft Rules of Procedure that had been elaborated and discussed at a preparatory meeting in May 1999. Rule 29 stated *inter alia* that: 'The Conference shall conduct work and take decisions in accordance with established practice under the Convention.' It was further decided at the preparatory meeting that in connection with the draft rules of procedure, the Conference President would make the following statement: 'With regard to Rule 29 of the draft Rules of Procedure, it is affirmed that in the deliberations and negotiations relating to the Convention and its annexed Protocols, High Contracting Parties have proceeded on the basis of consensus and no decisions have been taken by vote.' See for instance "Procedural Report of the Preparatory Meeting of the States Parties to the Protocol on Prohibitions or Restrictions on the Use of Mines, Booby-traps and Other Devices as amended on 3 May 1996 annexed to the CCW", *UN Doc. CCW/AP.II/CONF.1/1* of 27 September 1999.

381 The Second CCW Review Conference is scheduled to take place in 2001, with a first, brief governmental expert meeting in December 2000.

382 So-called because of the venue of the October 1996 conference at which the Canadian Foreign Minister's call for the fast-track negotiation and signature of an anti-personnel mine ban treaty was made. See *infra* Chapter 2, pp. 77-79.

383 With respect to the negotiation of the 1980 CCW and original protocols, Fenrick declared that: 'While (...) [the consensus] approach enabled States to protect what they perceived as their legitimate security interests, it did not, in the final analysis, serve the best interests of humanitarian law because it enabled single States or small groups to block progress on issues where the great majority of participants were agreed. Unfortunately, the end result of consensus negotiations between States with widely divergent interests was a text which is not always easy to understand, at times attempts to paper over difficulties, and contains some unusual provisions designed to satisfy certain States that adopted extreme positions on certain issues.' Fenrick, W.J., "New Developments in the Law", *op. cit.*, pp. 238-9.

384 China, France, the UK, and the US.

385 See for instance "Putin urges ratification of landmine protocol", *AFP*, Moscow, 8 May 2000.

1.8.1. The Provisions of Amended Protocol II

A. The Scope of Amended Protocol II

(i) The Application to Internal Armed Conflicts

Since the majority of mines were being laid in the course of civil strife rather than inter-State armed conflicts, the need to extend the scope of Protocol II to cover conflicts not of an international character was obvious.[386] Fearing interference in their internal affairs, for much of the negotiations a number of developing countries were forceful in their opposition to such a measure.[387]

After some discussion, the decision was taken not to amend the scope article contained in the *chapeau* Convention.[388] Writing before the adoption of the amended Protocol one humanitarian lawyer had questioned whether the failure to amend the *chapeau* Convention might not leave the Protocol legally applicable only in international armed conflicts.[389] In discussion with the author in 1998, she outlined two possibilities. The first is that the scope of amended Protocol II is still regulated by the provisions of the Convention and therefore its apparent extension to non-international armed conflicts is not effective. The second, preferred option is that the scope of the Protocol is *prima facie* determined by the Convention's general provisions, but that it is possible to broaden the effect in one particular Protocol by express terms. This is supported by the need to adhere expressly to each of the Protocols and not just to the Convention as a whole. Such an approach undoubtedly reflects the intention of the drafters.[390] Indeed, it seems clear that the States Parties have implicitly overridden Article 1 of the *chapeau* Convention – at least one informal remark was made along those lines during the negotiations – but have carefully avoided

386 As noted above, the group of government experts had been specifically requested to address this issue. Efforts by a number of Western governments to extend the scope of the CCW, or at least Protocol II, to cover all circumstances, including armed conflicts and peacetime, were unsuccessful.

387 India was particularly vocal in objecting to such an extension arguing that it would have no impact on the behaviour of the 'real violators', that is to say non-State actors. Finally, under pressure, India and other major States from the Non-Aligned Movement agreed to allow a carefully drafted (and limited) extension of scope. Thus, Hingorani's assertion that India was one of the vocal supporters for extending the scope of the Convention to internal strifes [*sic*] is therefore a somewhat revisionist interpretation of the negotiations. Hingorani, R.C., "Land Mines: military weapon or menace?", *India Quarterly*, Vol. 52, Nos. 1-2, January-June 1996, p. 20.

388 In its report submitted to the Review Conference, the ICRC had declared that the 'most obvious way to extend the application of the 1980 Convention to non-international armed conflicts is by amendment to Article I of the Convention. Should this cause too much difficulty, another possibility is to create an optional protocol to this effect, or to introduce into the Convention an additional article which parties could accept by a declaration to that effect or, conversely, which would be applicable to parties unless they specifically opted out.' ICRC, "Report of the ICRC for the Review Conference of the 1980 UN Convention on Certain Conventional Weapons", *International Review of the Red Cross*, ICRC, Geneva, March-April 1994, p. 150.

389 Hampson, F., *The Long Shadow – Landmines and the Law of Armed Conflicts*, *op. cit.*, p. 18.

390 See Vienna Convention on the Law of Treaties, Articles 31 and 32.

opening the door to making all annexed Protocols applicable to non-international armed conflicts.[391]

With a number of key States not party to 1977 Additional Protocol II, and therefore unwilling to see a reference to that instrument, agreement was finally secured on the following provision:

> *'This Protocol shall apply, in addition to situations referred to in Article 1 of this Convention, to situations referred to in Article 3 common to the Geneva Conventions of 12 August 1949. This Protocol shall not apply to situations of internal disturbances and tensions, such as riots, isolated and sporadic acts of violence and other acts of a similar nature, as not being armed conflicts.[392] (...) In case of armed conflicts not of an international character occurring in the territory of one of the High Contracting Parties, each party to the conflict shall be bound to apply the prohibitions and restrictions of this Protocol.'*

Article 3 common to the 1949 Geneva Conventions provides that each Party to an armed conflict not of an international character occurring in the territory of one of the High Contracting Parties is bound to apply, as a minimum, a set of basic humanitarian obligations listed in the article. The issue of the legally applicability of international law to third parties (*i.e.*, in this case, armed opposition groups) has been hotly debated for many years both within and outside the realms of international humanitarian law.[393]

In his analysis of the status of rebels under the 1977 Additional Protocol II, Professor Cassese refers to the 'more widespread opinion that Article 3 [common to the 1949 Geneva Conventions] (...) is able to confer rights and impose obligations on insurgents because, as a consequence of the State's ratification, the treaty becomes part of domestic law[394] and therefore obliges all citizens, including rebels.'[395] As he affirms, an example of this view is to be found in the ICRC Commentary to the 1949 Geneva Conventions. In the commentary to Article 3 of the Second Geneva Convention it is stated that:

> *'The obligation resting on the Party to the conflict which represents established authority is not open to question. On the other hand, what justification is there for the obligation on the adverse Party to the*

---

391 Moreover, this approach has avoided the need to ratify a formal amendment to the Convention, which would be time-consuming and potentially confusing. It is likely, though, that the scope of the CCW (and thereby all annexed Protocols) will again be the subject of extensive debate at the Second CCW Review Conference.

392 Article 1(2), amended Protocol II. To assuage the concerns of certain countries, provisions were added to guarantee State sovereignty and non-interference in internal affairs. See Article 1(4), (5) and (6).

393 Even though the ICRC regularly points out that it poses little difficulty in practice. See for instance Hampson, F., *The Long Shadow – Landmines and the Law of Armed Conflicts*, *op. cit.*, p. 17.

394 In fact, national implementation of international legal obligations is necessary in many States to give effect to those obligations domestically.

395 Curiously, in the same article Cassese claims that it is 'undisputed that Article 3 is binding on and grants rights to insurgents.' Cassese, A., "The Status of Rebels under the 1977 Geneva Protocol on Non-International Armed Conflicts", *International and Comparative Law Quarterly*, Vol. 30, April 1981, p. 424.

conflict in revolt against the established authority? Some doubt has been expressed as to whether insurgents can be legally bound by a Convention which they themselves have not signed. The answer is provided in most national legislations [sic]; by the fact of ratification, an international Convention becomes part of law and is therefore binding upon all the individuals of that country. '[396]

Cassese asserts that this is a misconception of the relationship between international and domestic law since what is at stake is not whether rebels are subjects of domestic law, but their legal standing in international law. But the ICRC also uses the argument that if the leadership of the insurgents exercise effective authority, they are bound by the very fact that they claim to represent the country, or part of the country.[397] A leading commentator takes a similar view suggesting that: 'One possible answer is that dissident force as a political entity aspiring to governmental status in some part of the state affected may be taken as having *de facto* assumed certain quasi-international obligations which are owed by the state with which they are in conflict as if they were in the position of a successor state.'[398]

However, it is also pointed out that 'if the rationale is accepted as the basis of the "obligation" of dissident forces under Protocol II, it is difficult to see how the disclaimer of effect upon legal status can be taken entirely at face value.' The same authority proposes that the dissident forces be considered as having taken upon themselves *de facto* obligations originating upon the international plane, even though they do not (yet) enjoy *locus standi* upon that plane.[399]

Cassese prefers to analyse the issue based on the Vienna Convention on the Law of Treaties, and specifically its Articles 34-36, which lay down a two-fold test for a treaty to create either obligations or rights for a third party.[400] The first condition is that the contracting parties must have intended the treaty to grant such rights or impose such obligations on third parties. The second is that a third party must accept the rights or obligations. Whereas the first of these two tests will be easy to satisfy, the second will not, normally requiring a declaration or commitment from the part of the opposition forces. This has occurred in a number of conflicts, but by no means all.

(ii) Application to Peacetime

At the closing session of the Review Conference, Belgium made a statement on behalf of 24 other delegations, formally entered into the negotiating record, that certain provisions of the amended Protocol must be observed at all times.[401] At the same session, the US declared that this requirement included the provi-

---

396 Pictet, J. (ed.), *Commentary to the II Geneva Convention*, ICRC, Geneva, 1960, p. 34.

397 *Ibid*; Pictet, J. (ed.), *Commentary to the I Geneva Convention*, ICRC, Geneva, 1952, p. 51.

398 McCoubrey, H., *International Humanitarian Law, The Regulation of Armed Conflicts*, Dartmouth Publishing Co., UK, 1990, p. 174.

399 *Ibid.*

400 Cassese, A., "The Status of Rebels under the 1977 Geneva Protocol", *op. cit.*, p. 423.

401 See Nash, M., "Contemporary Practice of the United States Relating to International Law", *op. cit.*, 1997, p. 330.

sions regarding the recording, marking, monitoring and protection of areas containing mines; the provisions of Article 8 regarding transfers;[402] and the provisions of Articles 13 and 14 regarding consultation and compliance. This declaration was made part of the negotiating record and was not contested.[403] Upon formal adherence to amended Protocol II, a number of States have entered an understanding whereby the provisions 'which by their contents or nature may also be applied in peacetime, shall be observed at all times.'[404]

B. Key Definitions

(i) Mine and Remotely-Delivered Mine

Despite two small textual amendments in the definition of a mine under amended Protocol II,[405] there was no material change from the definition contained in 1980 Protocol II. In the case of remotely-delivered mines, however, a significant exception was introduced, largely at the behest of the UK, to exclude 'mines delivered from a land-based system[406] from less than 500 metres' provided that they complied with the specific restrictions on the use of manually-emplaced anti-personnel mines contained in Article 5[407] and 'other relevant Articles' of the Protocol.[408] Thus, the UK's *Ranger* system,[409] which had already been a factor in the negotiation of 1980 Protocol II, again became an indirect influence on the drafting of amended Protocol II as the anti-personnel mines distributed by *Ranger* could not easily be amended to comply with the requirements for self-destruction and self-deactivation.[410]

---

402 This is extremely important, otherwise States Parties would be free to transfer prohibited mines in all circumstances other than in a situation of ongoing armed conflict.

403 See Nash, M., "Contemporary Practice of the United States Relating to International Law", *op. cit.*, 1997, p. 330.

404 Austria, Belgium, Denmark, Finland, France, Germany, Ireland, Liechtenstein, South Africa, and Sweden. A similar declaration has also been made by Canada, Greece, Italy and the Netherlands. Pakistan, for its part, declared that the provisions of the Protocol must be observed at all times, depending on the circumstances but pointed out that 'for the purposes of interpretation the provisions of Article 1 take precedence over provisions or undertakings in any other article.' This refers implicitly to the provision in Article 1(4), which states that nothing in the Protocol shall affect the sovereignty of a State or the responsibility of the Government, by all legitimate means, to maintain or re-establish law and order in the State or to defend the national unity and territorial integrity of the State. This provision was included at the request of Pakistan in return for agreement not to block a consensus on the adoption of amended Protocol II.

405 Article 2(1), amended Protocol II.

406 Thus, under amended Protocol II, low-level helicopter deployment of mines still constitutes remote delivery.

407 See below, pp. 79-81.

408 Article 2(2), amended Protocol II.

409 For details of the *Ranger* system see Gander, T.J., "Land mine warfare – the British position", *op. cit*, pp. 597-607.

410 Ironically, on 27 January 1998, even before the entry into force of amended Protocol II, the UK announced that it was planning to destroy its stockpiles of anti-personnel mines, including those dispersed by the *Ranger* system, within two years. "UK unveils plans to destroy a million landmines", *Reuters*, London, 27 January 1998.

(ii) *Anti-Personnel Mine*

One of the most contentious issues during the negotiation of amended Protocol II was the definition of an anti-personnel mine.[411] In contrast to the 1980 Protocol which applied restrictions to all landmines, differentiating only between manually-emplaced and remotely-delivered mines, it was intended that specific restrictions be imposed on anti-personnel mines, which were justifiably regarded as the heart of the humanitarian crisis,[412] over and above the general restrictions to be imposed on all landmines. In its 1994 report to the review conference, the ICRC, hoping for agreement to prohibit the use of anti-personnel mines, had already warned of the importance of a careful definition to ensure responsibilities were not evaded.[413] But a number of States were keen to restrict the ambit of their obligations. As a consequence, during the final meeting of governmental experts, the word 'primarily' had been introduced into the proposed definition such that it now read:

> *"Anti-Personnel mine" means a mine primarily designed to be exploded by the presence, proximity or contact of a person and that will incapacitate, injure or kill one or more persons.*[414]

This reformulation was seemingly intended to protect anti-vehicle mines with anti-handling devices,[415] but it was feared that its vagueness could also exclude 'dual-purpose' mines, which were believed to be under development.[416] Upon the adoption of amended Protocol II, 20 mainly Western, States led by Germany declared that the inclusion of the word *primarily* in the definition of an anti-personnel mine was to ensure that 'mines designed to be detonated by the presence, proximity or contact of a vehicle as opposed to a person, that are equipped with anti-handling devices, are not considered anti-personnel mines as a result of being so equipped.'[417] The ICRC, on the other hand, declared its opinion that an anti-personnel mine 'must continue to be understood as any mine which is "designed to be exploded or detonated by the presence, proximity or

---

411 As already noted, no distinction was made in 1980 Protocol II between anti-personnel mines and other landmines (*e.g.*, anti-vehicle/anti-tank).

412 Though the ICRC is currently preparing a report on the humanitarian impact of anti-vehicle mines.

413 "Report of the ICRC for the Review Conference", *op. cit.*, p. 137.

414 Article 2(3), amended Protocol II.

415 See for example Nash, M., "Contemporary Practice of the United States Relating to International Law", *op. cit.*, 1997, p. 332. An anti-handling device operates to detonate the mine when it is disturbed. The aim is to prevent or impede the removal of the mine by enemy sappers.

416 According to a study commissioned by the ICRC: 'Trends are moving towards the increased use of *hybrid* mines which have both anti-personnel and anti-tank characteristics. Their dual effects are produced by surrounding the anti-tank warhead with a pre-formed frangible case, optimised to attack personnel. The fusing of such mines is also responsive to both vehicles and humans.' *Anti-Personnel Landmines, Friend or Foe?*, ICRC, Geneva, March 1996, para. 107, p. 59.

417 This position was confirmed by the declarations of Austria, Canada, Denmark, Finland, France, Germany, Greece, Ireland, Italy, the Netherlands, South Africa, Sweden and Switzerland upon adherence to amended Protocol II.

contact of a person" (...) whatever other functions the munition may also have.'[418]

Finally, the definition of anti-personnel mine included directional fragmentation mines when tripwire-activated, but excluded them when they were automatically detonated, *e.g.*, by remote control.[419] These mines, a common example of which is the 'Claymore', were invented following the Korean War[420] to defend against human-wave attacks.[421] When triggered, the mines spray hundreds of steel balls in a 60 degree arc over distances of up to several hundred metres. When used with a tripwire, their effects can be as indiscriminate as other victim-actuated mines but when command-detonated by remote control, they can more easily be 'directed' and hence (potentially) pose less of a threat to the civilian population.[422]

However, in ratifying amended Protocol II, the US declared its understanding that a trip-wired hand-grenade should be considered as a 'booby-trap' under Article 2(4) of the Protocol and not as a mine or anti-personnel mine. This must be considered as a reservation to the definition, and a dangerous one at that, since there is no practical distinction between a tripwire-activated anti-personnel mine and a tripwire-activated hand grenade, and the fact that it is adapted in the field does not preclude it falling within the definition of 'mine' and 'anti-personnel mine' laid down in Article 2 of the Protocol.[423]

(iii) Anti-Handling Device

For the first time, a definition of anti-handling device was included in amended Protocol II.[424] The definition referred to 'a device intended to protect a mine and which is part of, linked to, attached to or place under the mine and which activates when an attempt is made to tamper with the mine.'[425] Speaking to the first Annual Conference of States Parties to the Protocol in Geneva in December 1999, the ICBL declared that: 'Both Mine Ban Treaty and Protocol II adherents must acknowledge that anti-vehicle mines with anti-handling devices that act like anti-personnel mines are anti-personnel mines and should be subject to restrictions under Protocol II and to a ban under the Mine Ban Treaty.'[426]

[418] Herby, P., "Third Session of the Review Conference of States Parties to the 1980 United Nations Convention on Certain Conventional Weapons (CCW) – Geneva, 22 April-3 May 1996", *International Review of the Red Cross*, No. 312, May-June 1996, p. 366.

[419] In this case, they are classified as 'other devices'. See Article 2(5), amended Protocol II.

[420] See for instance *The History of Landmines*, p. 99.

[421] See *supra*, Introduction, p. 8.

[422] See for example Nash, M., "Contemporary Practice of the United States Relating to International Law", *op. cit.*, 1997, pp. 332-3.

[423] See *supra* pp. 38-9, footnote 294.

[424] As is seen in Chapter 2 *infra*, the definition of an anti-handling device contained in the Convention on the Prohibition of Anti-Personnel Mines differs materially from that contained in amended Protocol II.

[425] Article 2(14).

[426] ICBL Statement to the First Conference of States Parties to Amended Protocol II of the Convention on Conventional Weapons, Geneva, 15 December 1999.

The question also arises as to whether an anti-personnel mine attached to an anti-tank mine and set to detonate when the anti-tank mine is moved should be considered an anti-handling device. In ratifying amended Protocol II in 1999, Pakistan specifically declared that: 'In the context of the word "primarily", it is understood that such anti-tank mines which use anti-personnel mines as a fuse but do not explode on contact with a person are not anti-personnel mines.' This issue would have merited clarification during the second Annual Conference of High Contracting Parties, which took place at the UN in Geneva in December 2000.[427]

C. General Prohibitions

In the August 1994 session of the group of governmental experts, the representative of Estonia had tabled a proposal for a new Protocol IV prohibiting the use, development, manufacture, stockpiling and transfer of anti-personnel mines.[428] Subsequently, the Swedish delegation, on the express instructions of its Parliament (and without much enthusiasm), formally proposed a prohibition on the production, stockpiling, transfer and use of anti-personnel mines. There was little discussion of these proposals, however, and despite oral support from Mexico, the ICRC and the UN observers, most States then regarded the idea as little more than a flight of fancy. Ultimately, States Parties decided on four general prohibitions: three encompassing certain mines, booby-traps and other devices and the fourth addressing the indiscriminate use of these weapons. In addition, the use of two specific types of anti-personnel mine was specifically prohibited.

(i) Mines causing 'Superfluous Injury or Unnecessary Suffering'

Article 3(3) of amended Protocol II prohibited the use of any mine, booby-trap or other device which is designed or of a nature to cause superfluous injury or unnecessary suffering. According to the US, this provision makes it clear that mines are generally not so designed or of such a nature.[429] Thus, the assertion by one, somewhat eccentric, governmental representative at the first session of the CCW Review Conference in Vienna that all mines were 'obviously' of a nature to cause superfluous injury or unnecessary suffering was seemingly not made in full understanding of its legal consequences.

(ii) Mines Designed to be Detonated by Mine Detectors

Under Article 3(5) of amended Protocol II, it is prohibited to use mines, booby-traps or other devices that are specifically designed to be detonated by the

427 See *infra* p. 72.

428 Estonia has since changed its position on the issue and thus was not among the original signatories of the Convention on the Prohibition of Anti-Personnel Mines. See*infra* Chapter 2, pp. 155-6.

429 See Nash, M., "Contemporary Practice of the United States Relating to International Law", *op. cit.*, 1997, p. 335. This issue is discussed in greater depth in Chapter 3 *infra* p. 222, footnote 1503.

presence of electromagnetic mine detectors during normal use in detection operations. The US has pointed out that during the negotiations no State was claiming to use such devices.[430] However, in his speech accepting the 1997 Nobel Peace Prize on behalf of the ICBL, Rae McGrath referred to an incident in November 1997 when an experienced deminer was killed by an anti-tank mine fitted with a 'magnetic influence anti-handling device', which had been detonated by the presence of the deminer's own mine detector.[431] Not prohibited under Article 3(5), however, are tilt-rods[432] (a sort of vertical tripwire) that can be set off by the sweep of a mine detector.[433]

(iii) 'Long-Lived' Anti-Handling Devices on Self-Deactivating Mines

The issue of anti-handling devices[434] had been briefly discussed at the 1976 Lugano Weapons Conference, in the course of which one expert had advocated their prohibition with respect to all mines.[435] A discussion on this issue had already taken place during the negotiation of the original Protocol, with specific reference to remotely-delivered mines.[436] During the review process considerable effort had been made, particularly by mine clearance organisations, to prohibit anti-handling devices, which not only targeted enemy combat engineers but also threatened humanitarian deminers tasked with returning a mined area to civilian use after the end of an armed conflict. The Netherlands had proposed, without success, a prohibition on anti-handling devices on any anti-personnel mines.[437] The US proposed that anti-handling devices on 'long-lived' mines should be prohibited, but this proposal did not find consensus either.[438] Finally, it was agreed that the use would be prohibited of any self-deactivating mine – anti-vehicle and anti-personnel – equipped with an anti-handling device that could

430 *Ibid.*

431 McGrath, R., "A Matter of Justice and Humanity", *Nobel Lecture*, Oslo, 10 December 1997.

432 Croll claims that tilt rods were invented by the German armed forces during the Second World War: previously anti-tank mines were detonated by tank tracks, which represented only 20 per cent of their width. The 'kill ratio' was enhanced by the use of tilt rods as they detonated the mine when the rod was struck by the tank hull. *The History of Landmines*, p. 46.

433 Nash, M., "Contemporary Practice of the United States Relating to International Law", *op. cit.*, 1997, p. 335.

434 Again, Croll ascribes the invention of the anti-handling device to German armed forces a decade before the Second World War. Small fuzes were screwed into the mine casing and anchored to the ground, thus ensuring detonation if the mine were removed. *The History of Landmines*, p. 39.

435 *Report on the 1976 Lugano Weapons Conference*, p. 149.

436 See for example Rogers, Lt.-Col. A.P.V., "A Commentary on the Protocol", *op. cit.*, p. 198. The working group set up during the 1979-1980 UN Weapons Conference to draft the provision on recording the location of mines had discussed the particular need to record details of anti-handling devices. See Carnahan, Lt.-Col. B.M., "The Law of Land Mine Warfare", *op. cit.*, p. 82.

437 See the Background Paper submitted by the Netherlands delegation to the January 1996 session of the Review Conference, *UN Doc. CCW/CONF.I/CRP.5* of 18 January 1996.

438 Nash, M., "Contemporary Practice of the United States Relating to International Law", *op. cit.*, 1997, p. 335.

continue to function after the mine had self-deactivated (and thereby defeat the purpose of the self-deactivation).[439]

(iv) The Indiscriminate Use of Anti-Personnel Mines

In addition to the provisions of 1980 Protocol II, which remain unchanged, Article 3(9) of amended Protocol II provides that: 'Several clearly separated and distinct military objectives located in a city, town, village or other area containing a similar concentration of civilians or civilian objects are not to be treated as a single military objective.' The US was concerned that this provision, which is derived from Article 51(5)(a) of 1977 Additional Protocol I, would not only prohibit the indiscriminate shelling of (or, in the case of mines, the indiscriminate remote delivery of mines against) an entire city, town or village containing a number of separate military objectives,[440] but also the use of mines 'to deny enemy access to or use of an area containing civilians or civilian objects.'[441] Also vociferous in their opposition to the provision had been France, which claimed that aerial bombardment and remote delivery of mines should not be treated in the same way.

D. The Prohibition of Certain Anti-Personnel Mines

Given that a total prohibition of anti-personnel mines would not attract consensus, discussions in the review process focused on increased restrictions on the use of all anti-personnel mines and the prohibition of the particular types considered the greatest humanitarian threat. A number of Western States sought an end to the use of 'long-lived' anti-personnel mines, which undoubtedly represented the most serious existing danger to the civilian population, whether manually emplaced or remotely delivered. A number of developing countries, suspicious of the West's motives,[442] were reluctant to accept such a blanket ban for both military and economic reasons. The resulting provisions were thrashed out over the many weeks of intense and difficult negotiations spread over three years.

(i) 'Undetectable' Anti-Personnel Mines

Even prior to the adoption of amended Protocol II, it had been questioned whether the 'ad hoc' use of non-metallic anti-personnel mines[443] outside pre-

439 *Ibid.*

440 A principle that the US supports and regards as customary law. *Ibid.*, p. 336.

441 *Ibid.*

442 The feeling was widespread that a number of Western countries were trying to carve out a market for their producing companies, while prohibiting cheaper competition.

443 Croll cites claims that the responsibility for inventing plastic mines should be ascribed to Hitler himself, 'who in December 1943 ordered that a new mine should be made out of plastic. "The other day I was thinking if it wouldn't be possible to infest the minefields with other mines, as well as anti-personnel mines, to such an extent that even our own men can't pass these minefields, because they explode no matter who steps on them. These mines should be cased in plastic instead of metal."' *The History of Landmines*, p. 44, citing Gilbert, F., *Hitler Directs*

planned (and therefore generally unrecorded) minefields should still be regarded as lawful. Insofar as these mines are extremely difficult to detect using electromagnetic mine detectors,[444] especially in ferrous soils, such as are found in southern Africa, they become a permanent threat to the civilian population, a foreseeable consequence incompatible with the standards of responsible warfare.[445] The experience of the British armed forces in trying to demine the Falklands after the end of the conflict in 1982[446] demonstrated to all the advantages of having a minimum metal content in, at least, all anti-personnel mines. In fact, very few all-plastic mines exist, although the metal content may be no more than one-thirtieth of a gram.

The need to prohibit all 'undetectable' anti-personnel mines was widely agreed in principle,[447] although the practical details were harder to nail down, a key issue being the conversion of existing stocks. During the discussions in the Group of Governmental Experts, a number of proposals had been considered, from the simple (and rather toothless) requirement for all anti-personnel mines to have irremovable metallic elements in their construction,[448] to the requirement for a specific quantity of metal to be incorporated in the mine.[449] The UN Department for Humanitarian Affairs, the body then charged with overall responsibility for mine clearance within the UN system,[450] called for metal rings to be attached or incorporated to all anti-personnel mines since the shape of the metal as well as the quantity was a key factor in aiding detection.

Article 4, amended Protocol II simply states that: 'It is prohibited to use anti-personnel mines which are not detectable as specified in paragraph 2 of the Technical Annex.'[451] It was finally agreed that all anti-personnel mines produced after 1 January 1997 should 'incorporate in their construction a material or device that enables the mine to be detected by commonly-available technical mine detection equipment and provides a response signal equivalent to a signal

---

His War: the Secret Records of His Daily Military Conferences, Oxford University Press, New York, 1950, p. 82.

444 Croll reports that the mine detector was invented by a Lieutenant Kozacki, a Polish signals officer who escaped to France and then to Britain in 1940. A later version of his invention was still being used by the British Army as recently as 1995. *The History of Landmines*, pp. 54-5.

445 Oeter, S., "Methods and Means of Combat", *op. cit.*, pp. 132-3.

446 See for example Rogers, Col. A.P.V., "Mines, Booby-traps and other devices", *op. cit.*, p. 532. Gander, T.J., "Land mine warfare – the British position", *op. cit.*, p. 603.

447 Apart from the Chinese delegation, which argued that it was not necessary to make mines that self-destructed also detectable. A proposal by a number of Western nations to require all mines to be made detectable, including anti-vehicle/anti-tank mines, failed to attract consensus, but is likely to again be debated in the upcoming CCW Review Conference.

448 This would have had little or no practical impact on the problem and would have presumably required no change to stockpiles on the part of States Parties.

449 Both 6 and 8 grams were formally proposed. See *UN Doc. CCW/CONF.I/GE/23*, p. 92.

450 The responsibility now lies with the UN Mine Action Service, located within the UN Department for Peacekeeping Operations.

451 Thus, as already noted, in contrast with 1980 Protocol II, the Technical Annex of amended Protocol II is clearly legally binding.

from 8 grams or more of iron in a single coherent mass.'[452] A similar requirement was made with respect to mines produced before 1 January 1997, with the exception that as an alternative to incorporation of such material or device, it could be attached prior to emplacement, 'in a manner not easily removable'.[453] But to reach consensus on the issue, it was necessary to allow States the option of a long period of deferral with respect to pre-1997 stockpiles.[454] Thus, the Technical Annex provides that at the time of adherence to the amended Protocol, a State can declare that it will defer compliance with the requirement to use only 'detectable' anti-personnel mines for a period not exceeding nine years from the entry into force of the Protocol.[455] During this period such a State must, 'to the extent feasible', minimise the use of non-detectable anti-personnel mines.[456] Both China and Pakistan have opted to take advantage of the option to defer compliance for nine years, although according to the ICBL, '[a]s a result of the new restrictions in [amended] Protocol II of the Convention on Conventional Weapons (CCW), production of non-detectable mines by CCW States parties is stopping, which would include the Type 72 by China.'[457] Finland has reportedly begun destruction of its non-detectable anti-personnel mines.[458] Moreover, there were reports that both China[459] and Pakistan had already begun converting stocks of non-detectable anti-personnel mines to conform to the requirements of the Protocol.[460] The US, too, was said to have modified 670,000 M14 anti-personnel mines by attaching metal washers to make them detectable.[461]

A number of countries have announced destruction of anti-personnel mines not in conformity with amended Protocol II. In May 1999, the Czech Republic, for example, declared before the First Meeting of States Parties of the Convention on the Prohibition of Anti-Personnel Mines that by the end of 1997 it had destroyed 45,000 mines that 'did not meet the criteria' of the Protocol, even before its ratification.[462] Although precise details of the mines destroyed were

---

452 Article 4 and Technical Annex, Article 2(a). The US, for instance, declared that its M-14 anti-personnel blast mine did not meet the required metallic signature and that it would either be modified or destroyed. Nash, M., "Contemporary Practice of the United States Relating to International Law", *op. cit.*, 1997, p. 345.

453 Technical Annex, Article 2(b). The US suggests that this could be achieved 'through the use of durable clamps, wiring or special metallic adhesive tape that is designed to resist environmental deterioration.' Nash, M., "Contemporary Practice of the United States Relating to International Law", *op. cit.*, 1997, p. 337.

454 The ICBL estimates, for example, that China has stockpiles of 110 million mines and that Russia has between 60 and 70 million mines in stocks. *Landmine Monitor Report 1999*, pp. 11-12.

455 That is, until 3 December 2007.

456 Technical Annex, Article 2(c).

457 *Landmine Monitor Report 1999*, pp. 6, 458.

458 *Landmine Monitor Report 2000*, p. 812.

459 *Landmine Monitor Report 1999*, p. 481.

460 *Ibid.*, pp. 521, 523.

461 *Landmine Monitor Report 2000*, p. 314. India and South Korea are apparently doing the same. *Ibid.*, pp. 488, 498.

462 Statement by Mr Martin Palouš, Deputy Minister of Foreign Affairs and Head of the Delegation of the Czech Republic to the First Meeting of States Parties to the Ottawa Treaty, Maputo, 4 May 1999.

not given, it seems likely that these were mines that did not meet the detectability requirement under Article 4.

(ii) 'Long-Lived' Remotely-Delivered Anti-Personnel Mines

The war in Afghanistan had seen widespread use of 'long-lived' remotely-delivered mines, in particular the infamous PFM-1 'butterfly' anti-personnel mine scattered from aircraft. These devices had caused a large number of victims, especially children, who were attracted by their shape and colour. As a proposal by India in the Review Conference to prohibit all remotely-delivered anti-personnel mines did not attract wide support, let alone consensus, one of the key provisions of amended Protocol II was to require that all remotely-delivered anti-personnel mines must be fitted with both self-destruct[463] *and* back-up self-deactivation mechanisms.[464] At least 90 per cent[465] of all 'activated' remotely-delivered anti-personnel mines[466] must automatically detonate within 30 days of emplacement[467] and after 120 days the back-up self-deactivating mechanism must have ensured that no more than 1 in 1,000 of the mines originally laid are capable of functioning as a mine.[468]

This apparently strict requirement is nonetheless substantially weakened by the option of a nine-year period of deferral[469] beginning with entry into force of amended Protocol II (although the period of deferral applies only with respect to mines produced before the entry into force of the Protocol). During the period of deferral, States must minimise 'to the extent feasible' the use of all non-compliant anti-personnel mines and must at least comply with either the requirements for self-destruction or the requirements for self-deactivation.[470]

Upon ratification of the Protocol, China, India, Pakistan, and Ukraine elected to take advantage of the option to delay compliance. Ukraine, however, was reported to have destroyed more than 100,000 PFM-1 'butterfly' anti-personnel

463 As already noted, a self-destructing mine is programmed to detonate automatically after a pre-set period of time. See Article 2(10).

464 Article 5. Self-deactivation is normally the exhaustion of the battery powering the mine; it therefore renders the mine inert rather than harmless.

465 Until the final session of the Review Conference, the specification of a maximum 5 per cent failure rate for self-destruction had been under consideration.

466 That is, activated as opposed to dud. The percentage of dud mines to be expected under battlefield conditions – which should not be considered harmless – is not known.

467 Although, during the review process, a number of Western military commanders had indicated publicly and privately that, for tactical reasons, the self-destruct timer would normally be set at no more than 48 hours.

468 Technical Annex, Article 3(a). Article 8(2), however, prohibits with immediate effect the transfer of remotely-delivered anti-personnel mines that are not both self-destructing and self-deactivating. As the US has noted, this is tantamount to a prohibition on production as there is no economic utility in producing a mine that can neither be used nor transferred. Nash, M., "Contemporary Practice of the United States Relating to International Law", *op. cit.*, 1997, p. 340.

469 Russia sought a period of deferral of 15 years, China reportedly proposed 25 years.

470 Technical Annex, Article 3(c).

mines in March 1998, since they were not in compliance with the Protocol.[471] The Russian Federation was reportedly planning to destroy non-CCW compliant mines over an eight-year period from 1998-2005. In 1998, more than 500,000 such mines were destroyed.[472] In December 1999, however, a Russian official stated that destruction of all the non-CCW compliant mines would not be completed before 2010-2012.[473] However, it was alleged that during the second Chechen conflict in 1999, Russia again dropped quantities of 'butterfly' anti-personnel mines, including – by mistake – on neighbouring Georgia.[474]

E. Restrictions on the Use of Other Anti-Personnel Mines

(i) Manually-Emplaced 'Long-Lived' Anti-Personnel Mines

Despite the potential danger posed by remotely-delivered mines, in most mine-affected countries the greatest threat to the civilian population came from manually-emplaced 'long-lived' anti-personnel mines, which can remain active for many decades.[475] Citing the long-term need to protect their borders, a number of developing countries successfully opposed a proposal to equip all anti-personnel mines with a neutralising mechanism. It was therefore obvious that far-reaching restrictions would have to be imposed on the use of all manually-emplaced long-lived anti-personnel mines.[476]

Under Article 5 of amended Protocol II, all anti-personnel mines that are not equipped with both self-destructing and self-deactivating mechanisms to the same effectiveness as for remotely-delivered anti-personnel mines, must be 'placed within a perimeter-marked area which is monitored by military personnel and protected by fencing or other means, to ensure the effective exclusion of civilians from the area. The marking must be of a distinct and durable character and must at least be visible to a person who is about to enter the perimeter-marked area.'[477] All emplaced anti-personnel mines must be cleared before the area is abandoned, unless it is handed over to the armed forces of another State

471 *Landmine Monitor Report 1999*, p. 759. Landmine Monitor report in 2000 that Ukraine was planning to destroy stocks of more than 7 million PFM mines in order to meet the requirements of the Protocol. *Landmine Monitor Report 2000*, p. 785.

472 *Landmine Monitor Report 1999*, p. 809.

473 *Landmine Monitor Report 2000*, p. 839.

474 ICBL Statement to the First Conference of States Parties to Amended Protocol II of the Convention on Conventional Weapons, Geneva, 15 December 1999. See for instance "Russian helicopters drop mines near Chechen border with Georgia",*AP*, Tbilisi, Georgia, 17 November 1999.

475 Croll refers to a British report on the 'Engineer Lessons from the North Africa Campaign' in the Second World War in which it was suggested that the British should design a new form of mine capable of 'self-destroying after a certain period to avoid the need for lifting'. He points out that it would be more than four decades before any serious efforts were made in that direction. *The History of Landmines*, p. 65.

476 As already noted, all remotely-delivered anti-personnel mines had to be fitted with self-destruct and back-up self-deactivation mechanisms.

477 Article 5(2)(a).

that accepts the duties to maintain the required protections and subsequently clear the mines.[478]

Although superficially attractive, the requirements of Article 5 have three, probably fatal, flaws. First, a nine-year period of deferral from entry into force of amended Protocol II was allowed for anti-personnel mines used outside of marked areas as long as the use of non-compliant mines was 'to the extent feasible' minimised and such mines at least self-deactivated within 120 days.[479] Second, under Article 5(3), a party to a conflict is 'relieved from further compliance' with the obligation to mark, fence and monitor 'only if such compliance is not feasible due to forcible loss of control of the area as a result of enemy military action, including situations where direct enemy military action makes it impossible to comply.' The ICRC complained bitterly about this potential loophole, which was introduced following a proposal by the Russian delegation. Despite an oral (and therefore non-binding) statement made by Denmark and approved by the Russian delegation that 'situations where direct enemy military action makes it impossible to comply' does not entitle an army to ignore the duty to mark, fence and monitor simply because combat is taking place, this understanding is not legally binding.[480] Third, as a number of organisations warned, it was scarcely realistic to expect armed opposition groups fighting in internal armed conflicts to be willing or even able to comply with the requirements of Article 5.

Finally with respect to this Article, a specific exception to the duties to mark, fence and monitor was granted for directional fragmentation mines ('Claymore-type devices') used in tripwire-mode,[481] for periods of up to 72 hours where the mines are 'located in immediate proximity to the military unit that emplaced them' and 'the area is monitored by military personnel to ensure the effective exclusion of civilians.'[482]

(ii) Remotely-Delivered Anti-Vehicle Mines

Although most of the negotiations during the Review Conference focused on controlling anti-personnel mines, the danger posed by anti-vehicle/anti-tank mines, especially when remotely delivered, was also discussed.[483] The significance of the issue was given further impetus by the definition of anti-personnel mine contained in amended Protocol II, since it excluded anti-vehicle mines

---

[478] Article 5(2)(b).

[479] Technical Annex, Article 3(b) and (c).

[480] The seriousness of the commitment was subsequently brought into question by a proposal by the Russian Federation to allow a period of deferral of up to 15 years for the provisions relating to self-destructing anti-personnel mines. Seen in this light, the assertion by the US that in effect all use is prohibited of long-lived anti-personnel mines outside of marked, monitored and protected areas looks a little tenuous. See Nash, M., "Contemporary Practice of the United States Relating to International Law", *op. cit.*, 1997, p. 339.

[481] See "Report of the ICRC for the Review Conference", *op. cit.*, pp. 139-40. As already noted, when used in command-detonated mode, these weapons are classified under the Protocol as 'other devices'.

[482] Article 5(6).

[483] See *Landmine Monitor Report 1999*, pp. 1007-8 for ICRC proposals for future regulation of anti-vehicle mines under the CCW.

equipped with anti-handling devices.[484] Article 6(3) rather weakly requires that remotely delivered anti-vehicle mines should 'to the extent feasible' be equipped with an effective self-destruction or self-neutralisation mechanism and a back-up self-deactivation feature, 'which is designed so that the mine will no longer function as a mine when the mine no longer serves the military purpose for which it was placed in position.'

The awkward drafting of the provision mirrors the negotiating somersaults required for its adoption by consensus. It can even be argued that the inclusion of the phrase 'to the extent feasible' in the provision, combined with the declaration of China that this constituted no obligation to include any such mechanism,[485] represented a step backwards in protection from the 1980 Protocol II, which appeared to require either that the mines could be and were recorded, or that an effective self-neutralising mechanism was incorporated in the mine.[486] In addition, the final text represented a considerable weakening from the proposal contained in the Chairman's Text emanating from the Group of Governmental Experts, which required that all remotely-delivered mines be self-destructing.[487] The US intends once again to propose a similar obligation in the Second Review Conference of the CCW.[488]

F. Prohibitions and Restrictions on the Transfer of Anti-Personnel Mines

Article 1 of the Protocol on Blinding Laser Weapons (Protocol IV) adopted by the First CCW Review Conference on 13 October 1995 prohibited the transfer[489] as well as the use of laser weapons 'specifically designed to blind'. This was the first time that such a provision has been included in an international humanitarian law treaty, since, as noted in the Introduction, international humanitarian law has tended only to regulate the use of a weapon. Indeed, in its report prepared for the review conference at the request of the States Parties and submitted to the Group of Governmental Experts, the ICRC declared that as the CCW was a humanitarian law treaty, it could only address the regulation or

---

484 Initially during the review process the US had asserted that anti-vehicle mines equipped with anti-handling devices should be considered as anti-personnel mines given the threat they pose to the civilian population. The acute sensitivity of certain anti-handling devices on anti-vehicle mines being acquired by signatories to the Convention on the Prohibition of Anti-personnel Mines is giving increasing grounds for concern about the humanitarian implications of these weapons and continues to blur the distinction between anti-vehicle and anti-personnel mines. See *infra* Chapter 2, pp. 99-103.

485 See *UN Doc. CCW/CONF.I/SR.14*, p. 5.

486 See *supra*.

487 See *UN Doc. CCW/CONF.I/1*, Article 5. At the first Annual Conference of States Parties, a number of countries, *e.g.*, Canada and the US, indicated support for the adoption of such a provision in the Second CCW Review Conference to be held in 2001.

488 See for instance *Landmine Monitor Report 2000*, p. 334.

489 Although, in contrast to amended Protocol II, the term 'transfer' is not defined in Protocol IV. See *infra* Chapter 2, pp. 111-3 for discussion on the definition of transfer as contained in the Convention on the Prohibition of Anti-Personnel Mines.

prohibition of the *use* of certain types of mines.[490] The likely effectiveness of further constraints on use was, however, clearly open to question. Falk, for instance, suggested an '*indirect* approach, that is, trying to influence the availability and design of landmines and their post-combat clearance, rather than focus exclusively on what combatants do by way of deployment and use.'[491]

In fact, the provision regulating transfer was not as innovative as might first have appeared. During the negotiation of the 1925 Geneva Protocol on Gas and Bacteriological Warfare,[492] the United States proposed a provision 'to prohibit the export from [the] (...) territory of [States Parties] of any such asphyxiating, poisonous or other gases and all analogous liquids, intended or designed for use in connection with operations of war.'[493] Objections to the proposal appear to have been based on the impracticability of controlling the export of such chemicals, since they had many peaceful industrial uses, rather than any reticence to include such a provision in a law of war treaty.[494]

With respect to the transfer of mines, a number of States from both North and South had been reluctant to include transfer restrictions in the Protocol, which was viewed as a pure law of war agreement (and therefore one that regulated 'use' only), but by the time of the Review Conference even the most implacable of original opponents, China, had moved to declare its willingness to accept a provision banning the transfer of mines the use of which was prohibited by the Protocol.[495] Thus, under amended Protocol II, the transfer of all mines whose use was prohibited by the Protocol was prohibited with immediate effect,[496] whether

---

490 Although later in the report it declared merely that arms control measures would 'probably not be included'. ICRC, "Report of the ICRC for the Review Conference of the 1980 UN Convention on Certain Conventional Weapons", *International Review of the Red Cross*, ICRC, Geneva, March-April 1994, p. 142. See also Hampson, F., *The Long Shadow – Landmines and the Law of Armed Conflicts*, *op. cit.*, p. 22.

491 Falk, R., "Walking the Tightrope of International Humanitarian Law: Meeting the Challenge of Land Mines", in Cahill, K. (ed.), *Clearing the Fields, Solutions to the Global Land Mines Crisis*, Basic Books, US, 1995, pp. 72-3.

492 As noted above, the formal title of the instrument is the *Protocol for the Prohibition of the Use in War of Asphyxiating, Poisonous or Other Gases, and of Bacteriological Methods of Warfare.* For the text of the Protocol, see for example *Documents on the Laws of* War, pp. 139-40.

493 Baxter , R.R., and Burgenthal, T., "Legal Aspects of the Geneva Protocol of 1925", *American Journal of International Law*, Vol. 64, October 1970, p. 861. The Geneva Protocol was drafted at the *Conference for the Supervision of the International Trade in Arms and Ammunition and in Implements of War*, which was convened to consider the adoption of a comprehensive treaty relating to the arms trade.

494 *Ibid.*, p. 861.

495 See *UN Doc. CCW/CONF.I/SR.4*, p. 8. In a further gesture of goodwill, on 22 April 1996, China announced unilaterally that, pending the entry into force of amended Protocol II, it would implement a moratorium on its exports of anti-personnel mines not in conformity with the technical specifications on detectability, self-destruction and self-deactivation. See *UN Doc. CCW/CONF.I/12* of 22 April 1996.

496 Article 8(3) provided that all High Contracting Parties, pending the entry into force of the Protocol, 'will refrain from any actions that would be inconsistent' with the prohibition on the transfer of all prohibited mines. The US considers this to be only a 'political commitment.' Nash, M., "Contemporary Practice of the United States Relating to International Law", *op. cit.*, 1997, p. 341. According to Article 25(1) of the Vienna Convention on the Law of Treaties, however, [a] treaty or a part of a treaty is applied provisionally pending its entry into force if: (a) the treaty itself so provides; or (b) the negotiating States have in some other manner agreed.

or not a State opted to take advantage of the possibility to defer compliance with the prohibition on the *use* of certain anti-personnel mines.[497] This means that 'undetectable' anti-personnel mines, remotely-delivered anti-personnel mines without effective self-destruction and back-up self-deactivation mechanisms, and any mines designed to be detonated by electromagnetic mine detector could not be transferred from the date of entry into force, and possibly even the adoption, of amended Protocol II.

It also means that it would appear not to be lawful to transfer any such mines even for the purposes of training or for their destruction.[498] Thus, when ratifying amended Protocol II, Canada specifically reserved the right to transfer and use a small number of mines prohibited under the Protocol exclusively for training and testing purposes.

Furthermore, the transfer is prohibited of *any* mine 'to any recipient other than a State or a State agency authorised to receive such transfers.'[499] This prohibition is intended to starve armed opposition groups, often the worst violators of humanitarian norms, of access to mines. In late 1999, Canada asked for clarification of claims made on UK television that the State-owned Pakistan Ordnance Factories had offered anti-personnel mines for sale to a (fictitious) private company.[500]

With respect to the transfer of all other mines, booby-traps and other devices, under Article 8(1)(c), State Parties must 'exercise restraint' and, in particular, must not to transfer mines to a State that is not party to the Protocol unless that State 'agrees to apply' the Protocol. Some, including the ICRC, would have preferred a much stronger provision barring States not party to the Protocol from receiving mines in order to encourage adherence to the Protocol.[501]

---

497 Article 8(2).

498 Compare Article 3 of the Convention on the Prohibition of Anti-Personnel Mines, which has a specific exception for this eventuality. See *infra* pp. 81-2.

499 Article 8(1)(b), amended Protocol II.

500 Statement by Bob Lawson, Canadian Department of Foreign Affairs and International Trade, to the first Annual Conference of States Parties to Amended Protocol II, Geneva, 15 December 1999. See "Pakistan Ordnance Factories: Action Alert", E-mail correspondence from Liz Bernstein, ICBL Co-ordinator, on behalf of the UK Working group to Ban Landmines, 10 December 1999; see also ICBL Statement to the First Conference of States Parties to Amended Protocol II of the Convention on Conventional Weapons, Geneva, 15 December 1999; *Landmine Monitor Report 2000*, pp. 236, 523-5.

501 See Herby, P., "Third Session of the Review Conference", *op. cit.*, p. 364. The ICRC was also concerned that since many States had unilaterally adopted comprehensive moratoria on the export of anti-personnel mines, these restrictions could represent a step backwards and legitimise new export. In fact, subsequent events, in particular the adoption and entry into force of the Convention on the Prohibition of Anti-Personnel Mines, have meant that this has not occurred. Today, there is little or no export of anti-personnel mines being recorded. According to the ICBL, 'Landmine Monitor researchers have not identified a single significant shipment of anti-personnel mines from one nation to another in 1998 and early 1999. This does not mean that no anti-personnel mines have been transferred; there are great difficulties in tracking mine trade. But the findings (or lack thereof) are consistent with the observations of military specialists that in fact there have been no major mine shipments of anti-personnel mines dating back some four years.' *Landmine Monitor Report 1999*, p. 8.

G. The Recording and Removal of Landmines

Under amended Protocol II, the location of all mines, booby-traps and other devices[502] must be mapped and recorded in all circumstances.[503] As specified in Article 1(a) of the Technical Annex, a party laying mines manually must record the location, perimeter and extent of minefields and mined areas, including, where feasible, the location of every mine as well as its type, number, method of emplacement, type and lifetime of fuse, date and time of emplacement and anti-handling devices, if any.[504] In the case of remotely-delivered mines, the party is obliged to record the estimated location and area by co-ordinates of reference points (normally corner points) and 'when feasible' these must be marked on the ground. In addition, the total number and types of mines laid, the date and time of laying and the self-destruction time periods must also be recorded.[505]

Each party to a conflict is 'responsible' for all mines employed by it[506] and must clear all mines, mined areas and minefields in areas under its control 'without delay after the cessation of active hostilities' or to comply with the

---

502 That is, not just pre-planned minefields as was the case with 1980 Protocol II.

503 Article 9(1). This appears to be a great improvement on the more limited obligation contained in 1980 Protocol II, although, as the ICRC pointed out in 1994 in their report prepared for the review conference, 'one cannot place too much reliance on the duty to record for the following reasons:

(i) *in the light of past experience, even if there were an absolute rule that all minefields (...) had to be recorded without exception, it is unlikely that the rule would be generally respected, especially in non-international armed conflicts;*

(ii) *in the confusion of war, records frequently get lost;*

(iii) *the recording of minefields is less effective than is generally expected as mines (especially scattered ones) frequently move to quite different locations owing to rainfall (which can displace mines kilometres from their original position) and to the movement of the soil or sand.'*

"Report of the ICRC for the Review Conference", *op. cit.*, p. 144. The last of these three issues was well known as a result of the experience of the Second World War. Croll, for instance, refers to a statement by British Prime Minister Clement Atlee on 17 October 1945 in response to a question about the clearance of mines laid to protect British beaches: 'The location of mines is a difficult problem, particularly as many have been shifted by tides and soil movements[.] (...) I am afraid that complete clearance might take some time.' Indeed, Croll reports that full clearance of 338,500 mines was not complete until 1958. *The History of Landmines*, p. 85. See also *Landmine Monitor Report 1999*, pp. 478, 794; *Landmine Monitor Report 2000*, p. 899. In March 2000, following the floods in Mozambique, there was a widespread fear that many minefields had simply been washed into another location. See for instance Jeter, J., "Drifting mines pose new risk in Mozambique", *Washington Post*, 9 March 2000; Murphy, D.E., "Danger lurks below the surface in Mozambique", *Los Angeles Times*, 3 March 2000. One demining expert claimed that the floods had submerged about 100 of the more than 1,000 minefields that had been identified across Mozambique. See Myre, G., "Floodwaters uproot landmines from Mozambique's civil war", *Philadelphia Inquirer*, 11 March 2000. In December 2000, it was reported that landmines had been washed downstream into Malawi killing civilians even in the heart of the city of Blantyre. See "Southern Africa: IRIN News Briefs", *IRIN*, Johannesburg, 1 December 2000; see further *Landmine Monitor Report 2000*, pp. 65, 67, 68.

504 See Nash, M., "Contemporary Practice of the United States Relating to International Law", *op. cit.*; 1997, pp. 341-2.

505 Article 1(b), Technical Annex.

506 Article 3(2).

obligations to mark, fence and monitor a minefield containing long-lived anti-personnel mines.[507] This clear attribution of responsibility has been widely welcomed and represents a significant precedent that should form a basis for future law.[508] Furthermore, a party that has used mines in an area over which it no longer has, or has never had, control is obliged to provide technical and material assistance to the party now in control (to the extent that this is permitted by that party).[509]

H. The Implementation of Amended Protocol II

Amended Protocol II requires each State Party to take 'all appropriate steps, including legislative and other measures, to prevent and suppress violations' of the Protocol 'by persons or on territory under its jurisdiction or control.' These measures include the imposition of penal sanctions against persons who, in violating the Protocol, wilfully kill or cause serious injury to civilians.[510] In addition, the Protocol requires that armed forces of a State Party 'issue relevant military instructions and operating procedures and that armed forces personnel receive training commensurate with their duties and responsibilities to comply with the provisions of the Protocol.'[511] The suggestion by the ICRC that legal advisers required by Article 82 of 1977 Additional Protocol I should be specifically expected to give guidance on matters relating to the use of weapons was not included.[512]

507 Article 10(1) and (2). See also Articles 3(2) and 5. Marking and fencing, however, was no guarantee of safety as Jerry White, the future founder of the eponymous Landmine Survivors Network, found out to his cost in 1984: 'I was only four years old when Syrian soldiers, retreating during the 1967 Arab-Israeli War, laid Soviet-supplied mines in the Golan Heights. My mine waited silently in the ground for 17 years before it exploded under my right foot while I was hiking in an unmarked minefield. (...) All the talk about fencing and marking minefields is a distraction from the real problem: how to stop the proliferation of landmines. Even in a small, security-conscious state like Israel, fences break down, signs fade, fall, or are stolen, and mines shift.' White, J. and Rutherford, K., "The Role of the Landmine Survivors Network", in *To Walk Without Fear*, p. 100. Moreover, a survey conducted on the border minefields in Zimbabwe concluded that more than 90 per cent of the minefields' protective fencing had been removed by local people to use as materials around small patches of vegetable gardens or in the construction of cattle pens. See *Landmine Monitor Report 1999*, p. 102.

508 For example, with respect to the clearance of unexploded ordnance in general, and cluster bomblets in particular. See for instance ICRC, *Explosive Remnants of War, Cluster Bombs and Landmines in Kosovo*, ICRC, Geneva, August 2000.

509 Article 10(3).

510 Article 14(1) and (2). The attempts, first by the US and later by the UK, to include compulsory universal jurisdiction for 'grave breaches' (see *UN Doc. CCW/CONF.I/1*, Article 12(4)) or 'serious violations' of the Protocol foundered, particularly as a result of objections from the Russian delegation, perhaps mindful of the behaviour of Russian troops in Chechnya. When ratifying the Protocol, however, the US declared that it would 'not recognise the jurisdiction of any international tribunal to prosecute a United States citizen for a violation of the Protocol or the Convention on Conventional Weapons.'

511 Article 14(3).

512 "Report of the ICRC for the Review Conference", *op. cit.*, pp. 146-7.

The issue of verification of amended Protocol II led to some of the most heated of all the negotiations in the Review Conference.[513] As already mentioned, upon signature of the CCW in 1981, a number of States had already signalled their regret at the lack of verification measures in the Convention and its annexed Protocols and had indicated an intention to address that absence at the earliest opportunity.[514] The issue remained controversial throughout the review process, with many developing countries wishing to stress the value of technology transfer and universality of adherence rather than verification. Western States, on the other hand, claimed that the credibility of the CCW in general and its Protocol II in particular would be jeopardised without an adequate verification and compliance mechanism.[515] Thus, in his letter of transmittal to the Senate for advice and consent to ratification of amended Protocol II, US President Clinton affirmed that the agreement 'was not as strong as we would have preferred. In particular, its provisions on verification and compliance are not as rigorous as we had proposed. (...) We shall pursue these issues in the regular meetings that the amended Protocol provides for review of its operation.'[516]

The regular meetings to which the US President referred were all that remained of the Western group proposals for a detailed fact-finding and inter-State 'Verification Commission'.[517] States Parties to amended Protocol II are required to submit to the Depositary (the UN Secretary-General) annual reports on a number of issues related to the operation of the Protocol.[518] These reports are circulated to other States Parties in advance of the Annual Conference of State Parties,[519] the first of which took place at the UN in Geneva from 15-17 December 1999.

---

513 Or, as it was more tactfully expressed in the report of the group of governmental experts, 'there was no consensus on the issue.' See *UN Doc. CCW/CONF.1/GE/23*, p. 17.

514 See *supra*.

515 One document prepared by a Canadian expert and circulated to delegates at the 1994-95 Group of government experts on an informal basis typified this approach. Its central argument was that a revised CCW Convention would require an effective verification regime to provide all participating States with reasonable assurances that parties are in compliance. Latham, A., *Toward an Effective Verification Regime for the Convention on Certain Conventional Weapons: The Outline of an Incremental Approach*, Centre for Defence and Security Studies, Winnipeg, December 1994, p. ii.

516 Letter dated 7 January 1997, cited by Nash, M., "Contemporary Practice of the United States Relating to International Law", *op. cit.*, 1997, pp. 325-6.

517 See for instance *UN Doc. CCW/CONF.1.1*, Alternative C, Articles 10-11.

518 Specifically: dissemination of information on the Protocol to the armed forces and to the civilian population; mine clearance and rehabilitation programmes; steps taken to meet the technical requirements of the Protocol and any other relevant information pertaining thereto; legislation related to the Protocol; measures taken on international technical information exchange, on international co-operation on mine clearance, and on technical co-operation and assistance; and other relevant matters. See Article 13(4).

519 Article 13(1).

(i) The Annual Conferences of States Parties

The first Annual Conference of States Parties was, overall, a relatively low-key affair, in stark contrast to the Meetings of States Parties of the Convention on the Prohibition of Anti-Personnel Mines. Specifically, the work of the conference was to include: a review of the operation and status of the Protocol; discussion of issues arising from the annual State Party reports;[520] preparation for review conferences; and 'consideration of the development of technologies to protect civilians against indiscriminate effects of mines.'[521]

Ambassador Johan Molander, once again presiding over events, opened the Conference stating that the Protocol had been 'overshadowed by an inability to find global consensus on the total prohibition of one category of landmines.' The Canadian delegation expressed the hope that the two agreements [*i.e.*, amended Protocol II and the Convention on the Prohibition of Anti-Personnel Mines] would some day become one.[522] The ICBL, which was given the opportunity to address the Conference in plenary session, declared that:

> *'Today, the plain truth is that, with respect to anti-personnel mines, [amended] Protocol II is at best a half measure for those who believe they must continue to cling to this despicable weapon... While it has often been argued that this Protocol is more all-embracing of the international community, the facts prove otherwise. Not only does the Mine Ban Treaty have twice as many States Parties as amended Protocol II, but of the 44 States Parties to the amended Protocol, only five have NOT signed the Mine Ban Treaty: China, Finland, India, Pakistan, and the United States. In a very real sense, with respect to anti-personnel mines, amended Protocol II binds just those five nations.'*[523]

The Second Annual Conference, which took place in December 2000, was scarcely a more lively affair, although the ICBL declared that during 2000:

> *'it would appear that the protocol has not only failed to curtail use, but has also resulted in increased production of antipersonnel mines. Our findings during the past year include the following: Russia has continued to use antipersonnel mines in Chechnya, resulting in numerous civilian casualties; Israel used mines in south Lebanon prior to its withdrawal; those mines continue to take civilian casualties; India appears ready to expand its production of antipersonnel mines; it is designing new*

[520] Under Article 13(4), each State Party must provide the Depositary with an annual report on *any* (author's emphasis; *i.e.*, not necessarily all) of the following: dissemination to the armed forces and the civilian population; mine clearance and rehabilitation programmes; steps taken to comply with the technical requirements of the Protocol; legislation related to the Protocol; information exchange and international cooperation on mine clearance; and 'other relevant matters'.

[521] Article 13(3).

[522] Statement by Bob Lawson, Canadian Department of Foreign Affairs and International Trade, to the first Annual Conference of States Parties to Amended Protocol II, Geneva, 15 December 1999. Molander himself has cast serious doubt on such a possibility. See also Chapter 2 below, p. 97, footnote 660.

[523] ICBL Statement to the First Conference of States Parties to Amended Protocol II of the Convention on Conventional Weapons, Geneva, 15 December 1999.

detectable hand-laid AP mines, and also, for the first time, remotely delivered mines with self-destruct mechanisms; likewise, it appears Pakistan is engaged in new production of both hand-laid detectable mines and remotely delivered mines. Moreover, it appears that India, Pakistan, China, and perhaps some of the other Protocol II States Parties are opting to retain and modify their non-detectable mines instead of destroying them. Thus, some nations are keeping existing mines AND producing new ones in response to Protocol II, increasing the number of mines held throughout the world.[524]

1.9. The Second Review Conference of the Convention on Certain Conventional Weapons

Preparations for the Second CCW Review Conference began in Geneva on 14 December 2000 with a one-day-long preparatory committee. A number of proposals were tabled for consideration: on the extension of scope of the Convention, and a compliance mechanism for, as well as further amendment of, Protocol II to strengthen provisions relating to anti-vehicle mines (by the US); on cluster munitions and small calibre bullets (by the Swiss); and on the extension of scope and a new protocol on the explosive remnants of war (by the ICRC).

A second preparatory committee was held from 2-6 April 2001, at which (surprisingly) wide support was expressed for extending the scope of the Convention and for a new protocol governing the explosive remnants of war. Following limited enthusiasm for further changes to Protocol II, even in relation purely to anti-vehicle mines, the US announced the tabling of a revised proposal jointly with Denmark for a new protocol which would be "devoted to restrictions on the use and transfer of mines other than anti-personnel mines."[525] This appeared to meet the concerns of a number of delegations, although doubts remain as to its legality in accordance with Article 8(2)(a) of the CCW.[526]

The various proposals will be discussed further at an additional "intersessional" meeting from 27-31 August 2001 and then formally at the third preparatory committee between 24-28 September 2001. The Review Conference itself is scheduled to take placed from 11-21 December 2001. According to delegates, it is likely that agreement will be reached to extend the scope of the Convention and possibly to regulate anti-vehicle mines in a new protocol, and a formal mandate given for negotiations on a further protocol dealing with the

---

524 ICBL Statement to the Second Conference of States Parties to Amended Protocol II to the CCW, 11 December 2000.

525 Statement of Edward Cummings, Head of the US Delegation to the Second Preparatory Conference of the 2001 CCW Review Conference, Geneva, 4 April 2001.

526 "At any time after the entry into force of this Convention any High Contracting Party may propose additional protocols relating to *other categories of conventional weapons not covered by the existing annexed Protocols.*" (Author's emphasis).

explosive remnants of war during 2002.[527] Depending on the breadth of application,[528] negotiations for such a protocol may last months or even years.

1.10. Concluding Remarks

Writing in 1984, after the entry into force of 1980 Protocol II, one commentator declared that 'if is widely and conscientiously applied by all sides in future wars, the Protocol may meaningfully expand the protection of civilian populations in armed conflict.'[529] A more realistic view, however, is that 'the specific regulation of Protocol II constitutes nothing more than a concretisation of the basic principles of distinction and the prohibitions against "indiscriminate warfare" which were in any event applicable to mine warfare.'[530]

It is clear that both 1980 Protocol II and amended Protocol II are based on a belief in the fundamental legitimacy of mine warfare. It assumed – wrongly for the most part – that even under battlefield conditions, 'responsible' use could be made of a weapon that clearly has a greater inherent tendency to strike civilian or combatant without discrimination than most other conventional weapons. Even when directly applicable, the limited prohibitions and restrictions contained in 1980 Protocol II were, for the most part, disregarded, including by a number of the relatively few States Parties to it. Although during armed conflict such reliable statistics as do exist tend to demonstrate that more combatants than civilians are killed or wounded, once hostilities have ended, the civilian population bears by far the largest burden, both in terms of the numbers of victims, and indirectly as a result of the wider social and economic impact.

1980 Protocol II required that remotely-delivered mines either contained a neutralising mechanism or were recorded. In those instances in which the use of remotely-delivered mines has been alleged or attested (*e.g.*, the conflicts in Afghanistan, Angola,[531] Chechnya, Daghestan,[532] Georgia, and the Gulf War against Iraq), there has been little recording and few instances of the use of effective neutralising mechanisms. These inadequacies led to the requirement under amended Protocol II that all remotely-delivered anti-personnel mines (albeit with the exclusion of land-based systems such as Ranger, and anti-vehicle mines fitted with anti-handling devices) must contain effective self-destructing and self-deactivating mechanisms.

Amended Protocol II also attempted to address the root of the existing humanitarian crisis by prohibiting, albeit with a long period of deferral in the

---

527 See also Walker, S., "CCW 2nd PrepCom Report", e-mail correspondence, 15 April 2001. The Norwegian delegation delivered a statement on explosive remnants of war to the preparatory committee in which it declared that: "The CCW is a natural framework for such a new instrument. To launch a process on an issue which is highly relevant to the objectives of the Convention may also contribute to a much needed revitalisation of the Convention."

528 For instance, will it deal only with cluster bombs; with all aerially-delivered munitions; or even with all munitions?

529 Carnahan, Lt.-Col. B.M., "The Law of Land Mine Warfare", *op. cit.*, p. 94.

530 Oeter, S., "Methods and Means of Combat", *op. cit.*, pp. 125-6.

531 See for instance ICBL, *Landmine Monitor Report 1999, op. cit.*, p. 115.

532 See for instance "Sources Say Russian Air Force to Apologise to Georgia", *Moscow Interfax*, 17 August 1999.

case of the requirement for self-destruction, the use of long-lived anti-personnel mines outside marked, fenced and monitored areas. Following its adoption, the ICRC declared that amended Protocol II would indirectly promote the development and use of *new* weapons (*i.e.*, anti-personnel mines equipped with neutralising mechanisms), which would have precisely the same effects, at least in the short term. 'This is the first time that a humanitarian law instrument may have the effect of promoting the use of a new weapon.'[533]

Protocol II does prohibit the use (and transfer)[534] of 'undetectable' anti-personnel mines, though the provision allows States Parties to opt to defer compliance for up to nine years after entry into force of amended Protocol II, and the impact of this provision on the ground is likely to be negligible in the near future.[535] Likewise, the prohibition of the use (and transfer) of mines specifically designed to detonate under the magnetic influence of mine detectors is welcome, but this hardly addresses the central humanitarian problem. Finally, the definition of an anti-personnel mine rightly gives cause for concern. Although the declaration by Germany and the subsequent understandings made by a number of other countries at ratification are welcome, the exclusion of anti-vehicle mines with anti-handling devices is surely an error in humanitarian terms, the ambiguity in the definition notwithstanding.

In 1997, the US declared that the Protocol was 'an essential step forward in dealing with the problem of anti-personnel landmines (...) and an important precursor to the total prohibition of these weapons that the United States seeks.'[536] In fact, the failure of the First CCW Review Conference to address effectively the landmine problem was the catalyst, rather than the precursor, to the Ottawa Process and the Convention on the Prohibition of Anti-Personnel Mines.

It is unlikely, then, that the Second Review Conference of the 1980 CCW will result in further revisions of amended Protocol II, at least with respect to anti-personnel mines. Thus, for example, Brazil noted at the first Annual Conference of States Parties to amended Protocol II that:

> *'While we remain open-minded, we believe that care should be taken not to waste our scarce resources in an endless effort to revise the provisions*

[533] Herby, P., "Third Session of the Review Conference", *op. cit.*, p. 366, citing the statement of ICRC Vice-President Eric Roethlisberger at the closing session of the Review Conference. This view seems to have been, regrettably, rather prescient, with production of hi-tech mines seemingly initiated in India and possibly other countries. See *Landmine Monitor Report 2000*, p. 490.

[534] The inclusion of transfer in amended Protocol II and Protocol IV is welcome because it breaks down an artificial distinction that humanitarian law treaties only regulate use of weapons. Supply of weapons, particularly in the case of small arms such as landmines, can create demand, and the widespread availability of weapons, including to civilians, inevitably makes control of their use difficult, if not impossible.

[535] It is only when mine clearance organisations are able to clear a certain area containing anti-personnel mines (which may be years or even decades after they have been laid) that the humanitarian advantage will be felt. Until then, the brunt of the problem will continue to fall on civilians.

[536] Nash, M., "Contemporary Practice of the United States Relating to International Law", *op. cit.*, 1997, p. 325.

of the Amended Protocol II as far as anti-personnel landmines are concerned. While some provisions can be broadened, there would be little sense in engaging in an indefinite process of amendment, when, in our view, we should be aiming at the universalisation and effective implementation of the Ottawa Convention.'[537]

[537] *Statement by Ambassador Adhemar G. Bahadian, Geneva, 15 December 1999.*

CHAPTER 2
ANTI-PERSONNEL MINES ON THE BATTLEFIELD UNDER THE CONVENTION ON THE PROHIBITION OF ANTI-PERSONNEL MINES

2.1. INTRODUCTION

As the First Review Conference of the 1980 CCW closed in Geneva on 3 May 1996, there was widespread dismay at the limited strengthening of the restrictions on the use of mines that had been achieved within the framework of the UN review process. In particular, amended Protocol II fell far short of the total prohibition of anti-personnel mines[538] already supported by more than 40 States, prompted by continuing pressure from the ICBL and the ICRC. Keen to sustain the international momentum that might otherwise have slackened, at the closing plenary of the Review Conference the Canadian delegation announced that Canada would host a meeting of pro-ban States later in the year to discuss ways to move the international community towards the prohibition of anti-personnel mines.

That meeting, the 'International Strategy Conference: Towards a Global Ban on Anti-Personnel Mines',[539] was held in the Canadian capital, Ottawa, from 3 to 5 October 1996. A 'defining moment' occurred when the head of the French delegation chose to make a statement 'perfectly suited to a forum like the CD'[540] but 'most certainly not suitable for the Ottawa Conference, dominated as it was by pro-ban countries and NGOs. (...) Distilled to its essence, the French position boiled down to this: France was prepared to ban landmines, until it needed them. This position was typical of countries that did not want to be seen by their publics to be opposing a ban, but that also did not want an international agreement in the short (or even medium) term.'[541] The intervention provided Jody Williams, the ICBL Co-ordinator and self-professed practitioner of 'in-your-face-diplomacy', with the perfect opportunity to castigate France for its inherently contradictory position and thereby serve warning to other governments that prevarication would receive short shrift.[542]

Determined to maintain the initiative on the issue,[543] and fearful that it would otherwise become mired in the CD where the consensus rule hindered swift and effective action, the Canadians took a political decision. At its closing session, the host country's Foreign Minister, Lloyd Axworthy, stunned the governments present by issuing an invitation to return to Ottawa before the end of 1997 to

---

538 That is, a prohibition on production, stockpiling and transfer as well as on use.

539 Hereinafter, the *1996 Ottawa Strategy Conference.*

540 The UN Conference on Disarmament, hereinafter referred to as the CD.

541 Tomlin, B.W., "On a Fast Track to a Ban: The Canadian Policy Process", *To Walk Without Fear*, p. 201.

542 *Ibid.*

543 A leading Canadian diplomat was apparently concerned that Belgium would seize the initiative if Canada did not. See Tomlin, B.W., "On a Fast track to a Ban", *op. cit.*, pp. 202-3.

sign a treaty banning anti-personnel mines.[544] Only the UN Secretary-General and representatives of the ICBL and the ICRC had been informed of his intentions beforehand,[545] and it was by no means certain that the initiative would be successful. Indeed, at that stage only about 50 governments had publicly declared their support for a comprehensive, worldwide ban on anti-personnel mines,[546] and of these, by no means all were believed to be genuinely committed to attaining that objective in the short- to medium-term.[547]

The *Convention on the Prohibition of the Use, Stockpiling, Production and Transfer of Anti-Personnel Mines and on Their Destruction*,[548] was the result of a remarkable process of pressure from civil society combined by a bold political gamble on the part of Lloyd Axworthy and his Ministry – the Canadian Department for Foreign Affairs and International Trade.[549] Of more significance for international humanitarian law, the Ottawa process marked a return to the 'traditional' procedure for negotiating IHL, shedding the absolute requirement for consensus in favour of a unilateral initiative backed by the option of majority voting. It further demonstrated that the military utility of a weapon that has been

---

544 The idea of a negotiated ban treaty, however, was not new in itself. In July 1995, at the International Meeting on Demining, the chair, Erik Derycke, the Belgian Foreign Minister, declared in his introductory speech: 'My third appeal will request everyone to give more comprehensive thought to mines. It seems to me that the time has come for an initial examination of the timeliness of an international convention banning anti-personnel mines following the example *mutatis mutandis* of chemical and biological weapons.' Speech of Belgian Foreign Minister Eric Derycke, Chairman of the International Meeting on Demining, Geneva, 6 July 1995, cited by *Landmine Monitor Report 1999*, p. 534.

Austria had also floated the idea towards the end of the CCW Review Conference – they believed, somewhat over-optimistically, that such a treaty could be 'short, clear and simple'. See for instance Hajnoczi, T. *et al.*, "The Ban Treaty", in *To Walk Without Fear*, p. 292. In fact, it would be none of these.

545 See Tomlin, B.W., "On a Fast Track to a Ban", *op. cit.*, p. 205.

546 A total of 50 States were full participants at the 1996 Ottawa Strategy Conference, thereby signalling their support for a total ban on anti-personnel mines: Angola, Australia, Austria, Belgium, Bolivia, Bosnia and Herzegovina, Burkina Faso, Cambodia, Cameroon, Canada, Colombia, Croatia, Denmark, Ethiopia, Finland, France, Gabon, Germany, Greece, Guatemala, Guinea, Honduras, Hungary, Iceland, Iran, Ireland, Italy, Japan, Luxembourg, Mexico, Mozambique, the Netherlands, New Zealand, Nicaragua, Norway, Peru, the Philippines, Poland, Portugal, Slovakia, Slovenia, South Africa, Spain, Sweden, Switzerland, Trinidad and Tobago, the UK, Uruguay, the US, and Zimbabwe. A further 24 countries – Albania, Argentina, Armenia, the Bahamas, Benin, Bulgaria, Brazil, Brunei Darussalam, Chile, Cuba, the Czech Republic, Egypt, the Federal Republic of Yugoslavia, the Holy See, India, Israel, Malaysia, Morocco, Pakistan, the Republic of Korea, Romania, the Russian Federation, Rwanda, and Ukraine – attended the Conference as official observers.

547 Based on research conducted in late 1996, officials at the Canadian Department of Foreign Affairs and International Trade (DFAIT) had concluded that, given the right conditions, support for a Convention prohibiting anti-personnel mines could peak at somewhere over 100 States. Lawson, R. *et al.*, "The Ottawa Process and the International Movement to Ban Anti-Personnel Mines", *To Walk Without Fear*, p. 170.

548 As previously mentioned, this work generally uses the term 'Convention on the Prohibition of Anti-Personnel Mines'. The ICBL prefers to use the term 'Mine Ban Treaty', even though the Convention does not prohibit anti-vehicle mines. The ICRC tends to use the term 'Ottawa treaty'.

549 For a fascinating insight into the evolution of Canadian policy with regard to anti-personnel mines see Tomlin, B.W., "On a Fast Track to a Ban", *op. cit.*, pp. 185-211.

in almost universal use can be subjugated, in law at least, by humanitarian concerns backed by sufficient political will. Set within this wider context, this chapter considers the obligations of the Convention, assesses whether it is likely to be effective in stopping the wider use of anti-personnel mines on the battlefield, but also discusses its implications for the future development of international humanitarian law.

2.2. The Negotiation of the Convention on the Prohibition of Anti-Personnel Mines

Only a few weeks after the 1996 Ottawa Strategy Conference, the Austrian government formally circulated a first draft of a treaty banning anti-personnel mines.[550] The text was clearly inspired by the negotiations in the First CCW Review Conference and by disarmament law, especially the Convention on the Prohibition of the Development, Production, Stockpiling and Use of Chemical Weapons and on their Destruction, adopted in Paris on 13 January 1993.[551] It contained clear prohibitions of the development, production, stockpiling, transfer and use of anti-personnel mines – though it maintained the existing, controversial, definition of anti-personnel mines contained in amended Protocol II[552] – and required each State Party to destroy stockpiles within one year and to clear emplaced anti-personnel mines within five years of the Convention entering into force for that State.

In November 1996, Madeleine Albright, the US Ambassador to the United Nations, introduced a draft resolution into the UN General Assembly with 84 co-sponsors calling for the negotiation of a total prohibition of anti-personnel mines. The objective, in the words of US President Clinton, was 'to allow children to walk safely on the earth'.[553] In December 1996, the UN General

550 See for instance *Landmine Monitor Report 1999*, p. 526; Hajnoczi, T. *et al.*, "The Ban Treaty", *op. cit.*, pp. 292-5.

551 Hereinafter, this instrument will be referred to as the *Chemical Weapons Convention*. Austrian Ambassador Thomas Hajnoczi, one of the principal authors of the draft Convention on the Prohibition of Anti-Personnel Mines, declared afterwards that it was 'firmly rooted in international humanitarian law' but that it also contained 'important elements of disarmament law.' *Ibid.*, p. 296. See also Goose, S.D., "The Ottawa Process and the 1997 Mine Ban Treaty", *Yearbook of International Humanitarian Law*, Vol. 1, Asser Press, 1998, p. 271. Goose later asserts that the 'humanitarian nature of the treaty is reflected in the Preamble, which begins by declaring that States Parties are "[d]etermined to put an end to the suffering and casualties caused by anti-personnel mines" and concludes with "[b]asing themselves on the principle of international humanitarian law that the right of the parties to an armed conflict to choose methods or means of warfare is not unlimited, on the principle that prohibits the employment in armed conflicts of weapons, projectiles and materials and methods of warfare of a nature to cause superfluous injury or unnecessary suffering and on the principle that a distinction must be made between civilians and combatants."' *Ibid.*, pp. 279-80.

552 '"Anti-personnel mine" means a mine primarily designed to be exploded by the presence, proximity or contact of a person and that will incapacitate, injure or kill one or more persons.' See *supra* Chapter 1, pp. 56-7.

553 'UN Landmines: US proposes UN ban on anti-personnel mines', *Reuters*, New York, 4 November 1996. Albright, now the US Secretary of State, had been a major force in pushing US policy forward on the issue. See Wareham, M., "Rhetoric and Policy Realities in the United States", *To Walk Without Fear*, p. 223. Already in May 1996, the US had set out 'a concrete

Assembly adopted the proposed text as resolution 51/45S,[554] which urged States to 'pursue vigorously an effective, legally binding international agreement to ban the use, stockpiling, production and transfer of anti-personnel landmines with a view to completing the negotiation as soon as possible.'[555]

Following the successful adoption of the General Assembly resolution, a 'core group' of supportive governments from around the world began meeting informally to discuss how to push the process forward,[556] as Canada sought to mend the fences that had been broken by its 'cavalier' approach to international diplomacy.[557] The first of a series of governmental meetings was held in Vienna under the auspices of the Austrian Foreign Ministry from 12 to 14 February 1997 to enable States to exchange views on the content of a Convention prohibiting anti-personnel mines. The *Expert Meeting on the Text of a Convention to Ban Anti-Personnel Mines*,[558] which was attended by representatives of 111 governments, opened discussions on a number of key issues, particularly the virtues of an immediate versus a phased approach to a ban, the definition of an anti-personnel mine, verification, universality of adherence, and the choice of the negotiating forum.[559]

One option for the Convention, following the approach taken with the 1980 CCW, was to negotiate a *chapeau* Convention annexed to which would be four separate protocols each prohibiting, respectively, the production, stockpiling, transfer, and use of anti-personnel mines.[560] Such an approach would be more likely to attract adherence from States not willing to accept an immediate and

path to a global ban' on anti-personnel mines, although it appeared that the US was expecting that the ban would primarily affect mines held by other nations. See for instance 'US Announces Anti-Personnel Landmine Policy', *White House Fact Sheet*, Washington, 16 May 1996.

554 The resolution was supported by 157 States with no votes against and only 10 abstentions (Belarus, China, Cuba, Democratic Republic of Korea, Israel, Pakistan, Republic of Korea, Russian Federation, Syria, and Turkey). A Canadian academic, David Lenarcic, refers to an unsourced remark by China that the vote on the resolution was a 'beauty and popularity contest.' Lenarcic, D.A., *Knight-Errant? Canada and the Crusade to Ban Anti-Personnel Land Mines*, Contemporary Affairs Number 2, Irwin Publishing, Toronto, Canada, 1998, p. 28.

555 Conspicuous by its absence was a reference to the negotiating forum, specifically the CD, which could have dealt a potentially fatal blow to the Canadian initiative.

556 According to Canadian diplomats, the most frequently used metaphor was that of a train leaving the station. Those who were first on board would be welcome to help steer the train. Those who hesitated for too long might be forced to travel on the train to a destination chosen by others. Lawson, R. *et al.*, "The Ottawa Process and the International Movement to Ban Anti-Personnel Mines", *op. cit.*, p. 169.

557 See for example *ibid.*, p. 162; Cameron, M.A. *et al.*, "To Walk Without Fear", *To Walk Without Fear*, p. 6: Tomlin, B.W., "On a Fast Track to a Ban", *op. cit.*, pp. 204-6.

558 Hereinafter, the *Vienna Expert Meeting*.

559 The ICBL issued a press release in Vienna on 14 February 1997 setting out its view of the key elements of a 'ban treaty' as: (1) a comprehensive treaty banning use, production, stockpiling and trade of anti-personnel mines; (2) provisions for the destruction of stockpiles in a rapid fashion and a requirement for destruction of emplaced mines; (3) transparency measures requiring reporting of details of stockpiles and minefields. ICBL, "Mine Ban Closer to Reality", *Press release*, Vienna, 14 February 1997, cited by Goose, S.D., "The Ottawa Process and the 1997 Mine Ban Treaty", *op. cit.*, p. 275, footnote 9.

560 Lawson, R. *et al.*, "The Ottawa Process and the International Movement to Ban Anti-Personnel Mines", *op. cit.*, p. 163.

total prohibition of the weapons, but who might, for example, support a ban on their transfer.[561] At the Vienna Expert Meeting, a number of governments spoke in favour of such an approach, but there was much wider support for an immediate prohibition on new use, production, stockpiling, and transfer of anti-personnel mines, with only the destruction of existing stockpiles and the clearance of mines already deployed being subject to time delays.[562]

Both the ICBL and the ICRC emphasised the crucial importance of having an 'unambiguous' definition of anti-personnel mines, which omitted the word 'primarily' as contained in amended Protocol II. A substantial number of governments, though, appeared reluctant to change a definition previously negotiated at some length.

Verification was, as it had been in the context of the CCW, a thorny issue.[563] A number of, largely Western, governments felt that a prohibition without a monitoring and enforcement mechanism would be a toothless beast. The ICRC suggested that the best method would be to set up an independent mechanism to investigate credible reports of the use of anti-personnel mines following the entry into force of the new treaty, although it cautioned against allowing the issue to stand in the way of a clear norm prohibiting anti-personnel mines. It reminded States that although earlier norms of humanitarian law prohibiting the use of specific weapons had been enacted without provisions on verification, this had not prevented them from being very largely respected.[564] Not all governments were convinced, though, and it was clear that substantial negotiating time would have to be devoted to finding an approach acceptable to all;[565] Germany, a long-time enthusiast of verification, offered to host a meeting devoted to the issue.

---

561 A number of States, including Cuba, Sri Lanka, South Korea, and Ecuador, argued that anti-personnel mines were essential for self-defence and hence there should be certain exceptions to a total prohibition on use. See for instance Dolan, M. and Hunt, C., "Negotiating in the Ottawa Process: The New Multilateralism", *To Walk Without Fear*, p. 406. See also *Landmine Monitor Report 1999*, p. 314.

562 A number of States present felt that the one-year period for stockpile destruction contained in the first Austrian draft was too short. See for instance Dolan, M. and Hunt, C., "Negotiating in the Ottawa Process: The New Multilateralism", *op. cit.*, p. 406.

563 According to Dolan and Hunt, most of the debate at Vienna focused on the 'intrusive inspection regime' outlined in the draft; few States present expressed support for stringent verification measures for ensuring compliance. *Ibid.*, p. 406.

564 Statement of the ICRC to the Vienna Expert Meeting, 12 February 1997.

565 Throughout the process views were divided between those who regarded the instrument as one of humanitarian law demanding a minimum of verification, and others who saw the Convention as fundamentally a disarmament text needing a regime similar to that enshrined in other disarmament treaties, such as the Chemical Weapons Convention. Roberts and Guelff, for instance, acknowledge that there are humanitarian law elements to the Convention but seem to imply at one point that the Convention is primarily an arms control and disarmament agreement. Roberts, A. and Guelff, R., *Documents on the Laws of War*, 3rd edn., *op. cit.*, p. 37.
Austrian diplomats involved in the drafting of the Convention noted that at the Vienna Experts Meeting it had become clear that the issue of verification was 'potentially the most difficult one' and would need 'further and deeper consideration'. Hajnoczi, T. *et al.*, "The Ban Treaty", *op. cit.*, p. 301.

The issues of universality and the negotiating forum to be used were clearly closely linked. States that were ostensibly unwilling to accept an immediate and total prohibition of anti-personnel mines repeated the need for universality of adherence and recommended that the Conference on Disarmament be engaged to undertake the formal negotiations. The ICRC pointed out, however, that no major instrument of humanitarian law has attracted universal adherence from the outset.[566]

Following the Vienna Expert Meeting, and taking into account the comments made by the participants, the Austrian government revised its original draft treaty text and on 14 March 1997 issued its second draft of the *Convention on the Prohibition of the Use, Stockpiling, Production and Transfer of Anti-Personnel Mines and on their Destruction.* The title, and much of the text, would remain unchanged in the treaty ultimately adopted. The most notable amendment from the first draft was in the definition of an anti-personnel mine, from which the word 'primarily' had been removed[567] and a specific exemption added for anti-vehicle mines equipped with anti-handling devices.[568]

In accordance with its offer to organise a meeting on verification, on 24 and 25 April 1997 Germany hosted the International Expert Meeting on Possible Verification Measures to Ban Anti-Personnel Landmines. To stimulate debate on the topic, Germany had drafted an 'Options Paper for a possible verification scheme for a convention to ban anti-personnel landmines'. A total of 121 States were represented at the meeting, and views were again divided between States which affirmed that detailed verification was essential to ensure that any agreement was effective and others that followed an approach similar to that of the ICRC, arguing that the proposed agreement was essentially humanitarian in character and stressing the overriding importance of a clear norm prohibiting anti-personnel mines.[569] Austrian diplomats involved in the negotiation of the Convention noted afterwards that: 'While some progress was achieved, no convergence of minds was in sight. Having dodged this controversial issue in the second version, the final Austrian draft had to find a viable middle ground. After numerous consultations, Austria presented a compromise solution that did not satisfy any side fully, but was conceptually acceptable for everyone.'[570]

---

566 'Indeed, a number of States took decades to ratify the 1925 Geneva Gas Protocol, and in 1899 two of the major powers of the day voted against a prohibition of dumdum bullets. And yet the vast majority of States have observed the norms laid down by these agreements.' Statement of the ICRC to the Vienna Expert Meeting, 12 February 1997.

567 According to one diplomat closely involved in the process, the issue was raised at a meeting of the core group of States and no representative spoke in favour of its retention.

568 The language chosen was deliberately that used by Germany at the end of the First CCW Review Conference on behalf of more than 20 States to explain the meaning of the word *primarily* included in the definition of an anti-personnel mine in amended Protocol II to the 1980 CCW. See *supra* Chapter 1, p. 56.

569 Steve Goose, however, claims that 'the majority view that emerged was that a ban treaty is essentially a humanitarian law treaty and as such, should not require stringent and costly verification which are more appropriate to arms control treaties.' Goose, S.D., "The Ottawa Process and the 1997 Mine Ban Treaty", *op. cit.*, p. 275.

570 Hajnoczi, T. *et al.*, "The Ban Treaty", *op. cit.*, p. 301. But see *infra* p. 72, footnote 522, for the views of Ambassador Molander of Sweden.

With the third Austrian draft text widely accepted as a solid basis for the anti-personnel mine ban treaty, the task was now to pave the way for a Diplomatic Conference to formally negotiate and adopt it. From 24 to 27 June 1997, the Belgian government hosted the International Conference for a Global Ban on Anti-Personnel Mines,[571] the official follow-up to the 1996 Ottawa Strategy Conference. Its primary task was to adopt a declaration forwarding the third and final Austrian draft text for negotiation and adoption to the Diplomatic Conference that would be convened in Oslo in September 1997.[572] Out of the 156 States attending the Brussels Conference, a total of 97 signed the 'Brussels Declaration', which affirmed that the essential elements of a treaty to ban anti-personnel mines were:

- *a comprehensive ban on the use, stockpiling, production and transfer of anti-personnel mines;*
- *the destruction of all stockpiled and cleared anti-personnel mines; and*
- *international co-operation and assistance in the area of mine clearance in affected countries.*

In addition to forwarding the Austrian draft text to the Oslo Diplomatic Conference, States supporting the Brussels Declaration also reaffirmed the goal set by the Canadian Foreign Minister of signing the treaty in Ottawa before the end of 1997. Notable by their absence from the declaration were references to the importance of international support for assistance to mine victims and to an absolute duty to clear emplaced mines (the duty being only to destroy 'cleared' anti-personnel mines); the refusal to include the former enraged African governments; South Africa in particular.[573]

The Diplomatic Conference on an International Total Ban on Anti-Personnel Land Mines (the Oslo Diplomatic Conference), convened by Norway, opened in Oslo on 1 September 1997 and was scheduled to last a maximum of three weeks. The host country had already announced the draft Rules of Procedure at the end of the 1997 Brussels Conference. Reportedly modelled on those used in the negotiation of the 1977 Additional Protocols,[574] they provided for resolution of issues by a two-thirds majority vote in cases where consensus proved impossible. Only States that had formally supported the Brussels Declaration

[571] Hereinafter, the 1997 Brussels Conference.

[572] In a keynote speech to the Conference, Jody Williams, the ICBL Co-ordinator repeated the call of the ICBL for a comprehensive ban treaty with 'no exceptions, no reservations, no loopholes!' As one of the leading figures within ICBL notes, this phrase became a mantra during the negotiations of the treaty. See also Goose, S.D., "The Ottawa Process and the 1997 Mine Ban Treaty", *op. cit.*, p. 276.

[573] A joint statement by 12 landmine survivors present in Brussels called on governments to: 're-read the current draft of the treaty and consider how it appears to us landmine survivors. There is virtually nothing in it to urge governments to take responsibility for the victims. Yet people are bleeding and dying even as we speak. To this day, the real needs of mine-affected communities are not being addressed. Survivors remain an afterthought. Their numbers grow each day, but without your help they have little hope of ever receiving proper medical attention or rehabilitation.' White, J. and Rutherford, K., "The Role of the Landmine Survivors Network", *To Walk Without Fear*, p. 111.

[574] Although Canadian diplomats otherwise suggested that they were based on standard UN General Assembly rules of procedure. Lawson, R. *et al.*, "The Ottawa Process and the International Movement to Ban Anti-Personnel Mines", *op. cit.*, p. 176.

were officially recognised as participants in the Oslo Diplomatic Conference and therefore entitled to vote. All other States present were officially classed as observers, together with the ICBL,[575] the ICRC, and representatives of the UN. The stakes had been raised significantly two weeks prior to the Conference when the US announced its intention to support the Brussels Declaration and thereby to join the Ottawa process.[576] Subsequently, the US was joined by Japan and Poland.[577] In a letter from US Secretary of State, Madeleine Albright, to key Foreign Ministers, the US laid down five conditions as a prerequisite for the US's eventual signature of the treaty:

- *'a geographical exception for the use of mines in South Korea;*
- *a change in the definition of an anti-personnel mines to allow the US to continue to use its mixed anti-tank and anti-personnel 'munitions' systems;*
- *a transition period, either through entry into force requiring 60 countries, including all five permanent members of the Security Council and at least 75 per cent of historic producers and users of anti-personnel mines, or an optional nine-year deferral period for compliance with certain provisions;*
- *a strengthening of the verification regime; and*
- *a clause permitting a party to withdraw when its supreme national interests were threatened.'*[578]

At the opening of the Oslo Diplomatic Conference, delegates observed a minute's silence in memory of the late Princess of Wales who had died in a car

---

575 According to Steve Goose, the Oslo Diplomatic Conference was the first occasion on which NGOs were given official status in international negotiations of an arms control or humanitarian law treaty. See Goose, S.D., "The Ottawa Process and the 1997 Mine Ban Treaty", *op. cit.*, p. 278.

576 The White House announced on 18 August 1997 that the US would be a full participant in the negotiations at the Oslo Diplomatic Conference. See for instance "United States to Join Ottawa Process", *Statement by the Press Secretary*, Martha's Vineyard, Massachusetts, 18 September 1997. Not everyone, though, was enthralled by the announcement. Cecilia Tuttle, for instance, the Co-ordinator of the Canadian national NGO campaign, Mines Action Canada, asked rhetorically: 'It would be nice to have the US in, but do you kiss every frog, hoping it'll turn in to a prince?' See O'Neill, J., "US Joins Canada in drive to ban landmines", *Ottawa Citizen*, 19 August 1997, p. A7, cited by Dolan, M. and Hunt, C., "Negotiating in the Ottawa Process", *op. cit.*, p. 409.

577 France and the UK had joined the Ottawa process a few months before, both having been previously sceptical, if not downright critical, of the process. France, for example, had actively sought the establishment of an ad hoc committee within the Conference on Disarmament to negotiate, on a step-by-step basis, a global ban on anti-personnel mines. French Ambassador Joëlle Bourgeois declared that 'France preferred an efficient treaty, even if the result took time, to a hastily concluded but useless agreement.' See UN, 'Disarmament Conference hears further calls for bans on landmines and fissile materials, establishment of negotiating committee on nuclear disarmament', *Press release DCF/283*, Geneva, 23 January 1997.

578 Cited in ICBL, *Report on Activities: Diplomatic Conference on an International Total Ban on Anti-Personnel Landmines*, pp. 18-20; see also Lawson, R. *et al.*, "The Ottawa Process and the International Movement to Ban Anti-Personnel Mines", *op. cit.*, p. 177; Wareham, M., "Rhetoric and Policy Realities in the United States", *op. cit.*, p. 231.

crash in Paris the weekend before.[579] Ambassador Jakob Selebi of South Africa was formally elected the President of the Conference and he outlined his plans for the negotiations – a series of working groups, in parallel where necessary, no square brackets around text under discussion,[580] and all negotiations to be concluded by 17 September allowing time for the text to be checked in all languages.[581]

Ambassador Selebi offered the Provisional Rules of Procedure for adoption by the Conference. The most significant provision was Rule 35, which stated that: 'Decisions of the Conference on all matters of substance shall be taken by a two-thirds majority of the representatives present and voting.'[582] Only France intervened, stressing the importance of making every effort to achieve consensus. With this observation duly noted, the Rules of Procedure were formally adopted without objection thereby ensuring that the negotiations would not be held hostage to the objections of one State or a small group of States.[583]

---

579 As noted above in the Introduction, the Princess had drawn enormous media attention to the problem of landmines through her visits to Angola in January 1997 with the British Red Cross and then to Bosnia-Herzegovina with the Landmine Survivors Network in August 1998. See for instance "Clashes mar mines debate", *Guardian*, 11 July 1998; White, J. and Rutherford, K., "The Role of the Landmine Survivors Network", *op. cit.*, p. 1112.
But the issue of whether the Princess's death had altered the negotiations remains disputed. An unnamed member of the US delegation was reported as having stated that he did not know a single country that had changed its position because of Diana. Bonner, R., 'How a Group of Outsiders Moved Nations to Ban Landmines', *New York Times*, 20 September 1997. Steve Goose, the head of the ICBL delegation to the Oslo Diplomatic Conference, remarked that the tragedy did not shift the negotiating process or positions of governments in Oslo, though he suggested that the increased media attention might have made it 'that much more difficult for governments to seriously consider any changes that would affect the integrity of the mine ban treaty.' Goose, S.D., "The Ottawa Process and the 1997 Mine Ban Treaty",*op. cit.*, p. 278. Not so categorical were certain members of the British delegation, who grumbled privately that they were forced to negotiate 'with their hands tied behind their backs'.
More bizarrely, it was reported in late 1998 that US intelligence agencies held more than 1,000 pages of files on the late Princess, which they claimed could cause 'exceptionally grave damage to the national security' if made public. An expert on the US intelligence services mused that the US government might have been interested in her campaign against landmines. Ellison, M., "US has top secret files on Diana", *Guardian*, 10 December 1998, p. 7. In August 1999, however, it was reported that a US intelligence assessment had warned that the late Princess's campaign against landmines threatened to sour relations between the UK and the US. The same report claimed that disagreement between the British Foreign Office and the Ministry of Defence, which was more sympathetic to US concerns, led to a 'loophole' in the 1998 Landmines Act. "Emotional Warfare", *Guardian*, 27 August 1999, cited on the ICBL Website, <www.icbl.org>.

580 These brackets indicate that one or more States reserves its position with respect to the enclosed text.

581 It is difficult to overstate the importance of the role of Ambassador Selebi in ensuring the successful adoption of the Convention in Oslo. His blend of skilful and direct diplomacy combined with immense good humour made an intensely difficult task appear almost easy. See also Lawson, R. *et al.*, "The Ottawa Process and the International Movement to Ban Anti-Personnel Mines", *op. cit.*, p. 177.

582 Draft Rules of Procedure, Diplomatic Conference on a Convention on the Prohibition of the Use, Stockpiling, Production and Transfer of Anti-Personnel Mines and on Their Destruction, *APL/CRP.2*, Oslo, 1 September 1997.

583 See Goose, S.D., "The Ottawa Process and the 1997 Mine Ban Treaty", *op. cit.*, p. 278.

Negotiations during the Oslo Diplomatic Conference centred on the demands of the US for substantial changes in the draft Convention. The US came with a plethora of proposals, including an exception for use of mines in Korea to protect the Republic. Although the US came extremely close to persuading enough governments to support it, and even obtained a 24-hour suspension of the plenary at the eleventh hour,[584] the US was finally forced to admit defeat,[585] despite an astonishing volte-face by Canada.[586] The US's final negotiating position,[587] which in substance and effect hardly differed from its earlier positions, was for the definition of anti-personnel mines to exclude those contained in its anti-tank systems, to allow withdrawal from the treaty during armed conflict,[588] and to provide for a transition period of nine years before full compliance was required.[589]

With the US standing aside, the *Convention on the Prohibition of the Use, Stockpiling, Production and Transfer of Anti-Personnel Mines and on Their Destruction* was formally adopted on 18 September 1997. In seeking to justify

---

584 See for instance "US wins more time for landmines pact", *Financial Times*, 17 September 1997; Bonner, R., "New US Terms on Mine Ban Are Called Unacceptable", *New York Times*, 16 September 1997.

585 Although the precise sequence of events remains the subject of more rumour and conjecture, it appears that the steadfastness of a very small number of countries, including notably South Africa, was ultimately determinant.

586 Canadian Prime Minister, Jean Chrétien, attracted particular criticism from humanitarian organisations after he initiated intense diplomatic discussions 'to try to accommodate US misgivings over a total ban.' See for instance "US wins more time for landmines pact", *op. cit.*; Dolan, M. and Hunt, C., "Negotiating in the Ottawa Process", *op. cit.*, pp. 413-4. He was reported as having declared that some exceptions on use were acceptable because of 'technical elements of a military nature.' See for instance Warmington, V. and Tuttle, C., "The Canadian Campaign", *To Walk Without Fear* p. 57; Dolan, M. and Hunt, C., "Negotiating in the Ottawa Process", *op. cit.*, pp. 408-9. In a subsequent report for the Canadian government, released at the end of November 2000, it is asserted that the US badly mishandled the negotiations, but also notes that Canada now regrets not involving the US from the beginning. See for instance Pugliese, D., "How US bungled landmine talks", *Ottawa Citizen*, Ottawa, 1 December 2000.

587 The influential Republican Senator Jesse Helms (Chairman of the Senate Foreign Relations Committee) wrote to President Clinton calling for the US delegation to be recalled if other delegations failed to 'recognise that the US negotiation position in Oslo is our bottom line (...) not a starting point for debate.' Cited in Lawson, R. *et al.*, "The Ottawa Process and the International Movement to Ban Anti-Personnel Mines", *op. cit.*, p. 163.

588 This proposal, which would have effectively made the Convention only applicable in peacetime, was supported by a small number of States, including Australia, Brazil, Ecuador, Spain, the United Kingdom and Venezuela. See Dolan, M. and Hunt, C., "Negotiating in the Ottawa Process", *op. cit.*, p. 412; *Landmine Monitor Report 1999*, pp. 305, 312.

589 See for instance Dolan, M. and Hunt, C., "Negotiating in the Ottawa Process", *op. cit.*, p. 412. During the negotiations, the Financial Times, in an editorial, claimed that the US did 'have a point over Korea' and argued that other States should agree to exempt Korea from the rapid decommissioning provided for in the proposed treaty or, if that was unacceptable, to extend the decommissioning period more generally to get the US on board. *Financial Times*, 11 September 1997. Canadian diplomats have implied, undoubtedly accurately, that had the US negotiators been able to isolate the period of deferral from the definition of anti-personnel mines, their chances of success would have improved significantly. Lawson, R. *et al.*, "The Ottawa Process and the International Movement to Ban Anti-Personnel Mines", *op. cit.*, p. 178. Indeed, in the discussion on the US proposed exemption for Korea, Germany specifically indicated that some form of temporal exception could be envisaged.

the US rejection of the treaty, US President Clinton declared that 'there is a line I simply cannot cross and that line is the safety and security of our men and women in uniform.'[590] According to one US columnist: 'For serious countries facing serious risks (...) a land mine ban could be a fatal luxury. It is the safe and parasitic – those countries living comfortably behind the protection of others who act as their shield, their land mine – who do not need land mines. It is they who are leading the charge against those, like the Americans, who must calculate how many of their soldiers will die on the altar of yet another disarmament delusion.'[591]

Among humanitarian organisations, however, the reaction to the adoption of the treaty was one of euphoria. In its speech to the closing plenary of the Diplomatic Conference, the ICBL stated: 'We strongly support this treaty. Indeed, we believe it is a gift to the world. Governments have responded to the demands of civil society and have come together with unprecedented speed and produced a treaty that unambiguously bans all anti-personnel mines'.[592] The ICRC, in a rare display of emotion, 'wholeheartedly welcome[d] and endorse[d]' the treaty, and Louise Doswald-Beck, the head of the ICRC delegation to the Conference, described it as 'a victory for humanity'.[593] Many States, too, were positive. Slovenia, for instance, welcomed the fact that 'a new legal norm of human behaviour' had been established and Antigua and Barbuda eloquently declared its hope that 'the scourge of landmines will one day soon join the dustbin of plagues trashed by human perseverance and common sense.'

---

590 Gertz, B., "Clinton resisted pressure to join ban on landmines", *Washington Times*, 20 September 1997. Other analysts believed he would not go against the advice of the Chiefs of Staff, particularly given his 'war record'. On 6 October 1999, President Clinton stated that 'one of the biggest disappointments I've had as President, a bitter disappointment for me, is that I could not sign in good conscience the treaty banning landmines…' The White House, Office of the Press Secretary, Remarks by the President at Comprehensive Test Ban Treaty Event, 6 October 1999, cited in *Landmine Monitor Report 2000*, p. 333.
Politically, domestic reaction to the US position was mixed. The Washington Post claimed that accepting the proposed American exceptions, as well as the further exceptions from other parties that such a precedent would have provoked, would not have made it a 'bad' treaty. "The Mines Treaty and the US", *Washington Post*, 19 September 1997, p. A22. In addition, and somewhat uncharacteristically, the influential Chairman of the US Senate Foreign Relations Committee, Republican Senator Jesse Helms, declared that President Clinton deserved 'praise' for refusing to accept the Convention. "Helms praises Clinton Refusal to Accept Landmine Treaty", <http://www.usia.gov>.
In contrast, former US President Jimmy Carter described the decision as 'embarrassing' and Senator Patrick Leahy, a leader on the landmine issue in the Senate, condemned the lack of US leadership. Priest, D., "Mine Decision Boosts Clinton-Military Relations", *Washington Post*, 21 September 1997, p. A22; Leahy, Sen. P., "The Landmine Ban Treaty: 'A Lost Chance for US Leadership'", *Address to the US Senate*, 23 September 1997. For the background to Senator Leahy's involvement in the landmines issue, see for instance Wareham, M., "Rhetoric and Policy Realities in the United States", *op. cit.*, p. 213.

591 Krauthammer, C., "In Defence of Land Mines", *The Washington Post*, 12 September 1997, cited by Troxell, J.F., "Landmines: Why the Korea Exception Should Be the Rule", *Parameters*, Spring 2000.

592 See Goose, S.D., "The Ottawa Process and the 1997 Mine Ban Treaty", *op. cit.*, p. 271.

593 ICRC and the International Federation of Red Cross and Red Crescent Societies, *Press release*, Oslo, 17 September 1997.

Having initially had the courage to stick its head above the parapet, at the formal treaty signing conference in Ottawa from 3-4 December 1998[594] Canada swept up the plaudits.[595] Representative of government after government praised Canada's role in launching the 'Ottawa Process'. At the end of the Conference a 67-page report, *Agenda for Mine Action*, detailed pledges of more than US$500 million to the mine effort over a five-year period.[596] The same month, by resolution 52/38A, the UN General Assembly welcomed the conclusion of the Convention at Oslo and requested the Secretary-General to render the necessary assistance and provide such services as may be necessary to fulfil the tasks entrusted to him.[597]

2.3. Discussions in the UN Conference on Disarmament

The principal threat to the success of the Ottawa Process came from the UN's disarmament negotiation body, the CD,[598] to which a number of States had turned on the basis of its success in negotiating the text of the 1993 Chemical

594 In accordance with Article 15 of the Convention.

595 Not all Canadians, however, were enthusiastic about their government's seminal role in the so-called 'Ottawa process'. David Lenarcic, for example, asserted that: 'Canadian policy has apparently been grounded in a "the-ends-justify-the-means" mentality. But in this case the "means" include isolating Canada's closest friend and neighbour (without which no APL ban will fly), boxing into a corner one of its principal NATO partners (Turkey), and estranging fellow members of the Commonwealth (Bangladesh, India, Pakistan, Singapore, and Sri Lanka) and the Francophonie (Chad, Laos, Lebanon, Vietnam, and associate members Egypt and Morocco).' Lenarcic, D.A., *Knight-Errant? Canada and the Crusade to Ban Anti-Personnel Land Mines*, *op. cit.*, p. 72. Since this work was published, however, Bangladesh and Chad have both signed and ratified the Convention. A number of the other countries cited (though not all) have signalled their intention to join the Convention in the coming years.

596 Although questions were already being posed as to the way in which such huge sums would be disbursed (and indeed whether they could or would actually be disbursed). See also "Landmine Ban Treaty nears Entry into Force", *Geneva Reporter*, October-November 1998.

597 Resolution 52/38A of 9 December 1997 was adopted by 142 votes to 0 with 18 abstentions. The abstentions were: Azerbaijan, China, Cuba, Egypt, India, Iran, Israel, Kazakhstan, Mongolia, Morocco, Myanmar, Pakistan, the Republic of Korea, the Russian Federation, Syria, Tajikistan, Turkey, and the US.

598 See for instance Tomlin, B.W., "On a Fast Track to a Ban: The Canadian Policy Process", *op. cit.*, p. 202. See also Goose, S., "Anti-Personnel Mines and the Conference on Disarmament", ICBL, Washington, February 1999. It should, however, be noted that when the Belgian Foreign Minister first raised the possibility of an anti-personnel mine ban treaty in July 1995 he suggested entrusting the Conference on Disarmament 'with the preliminary studies of such a Convention.' Speech of Belgian Foreign Minister Eric Derycke, Chairman of the International Meeting on Demining, Geneva, 6 July 1995, cited by *Landmine Monitor Report 1999*, p. 534. The CD Member States are currently: Algeria, Argentina, Australia, Austria, Bangladesh, Belarus, Belgium, Brazil, Bulgaria, Cameroon, Canada, Chile, China, Colombia, Cuba, the Democratic People's Republic of Korea, the Democratic Republic of Congo, Ecuador, Egypt, Ethiopia, the Federal Republic of Yugoslavia, Finland, France, Germany, Hungary, India, Indonesia, Iran, Iraq, Ireland, Israel, Italy, Japan, Kazakhstan, Kenya, Malaysia, Mexico, Mongolia, Morocco, Myanmar, Netherlands, New Zealand, Nigeria, Norway, Pakistan, Peru, Poland, Republic of Korea, Romania, Russian Federation, Senegal, Slovakia, South Africa, Spain, Sri Lanka, Sweden, Switzerland, Syrian Arab Republic, Tunisia, Turkey, Ukraine, the UK, the US, Venezuela, Vietnam, and Zimbabwe.

Weapons Convention.[599] As Goose explains: 'The Conference on Disarmament is a forum for arms control and disarmament negotiations located in Geneva, Switzerland. It has 61 member states.[600] In the past it has focused on weapons of mass destruction. The Comprehensive Test Ban Treaty and the Chemical Weapons Convention were negotiated in the CD.'[601]

A number of countries, such as France, the UK and the US, undertook efforts to secure a mandate for negotiations on landmines within a disarmament context.[602] In response, Canada declared that: 'If it is the will of this body to pursue the issue of [anti-personnel] mines, we will not oppose it; but we will strongly oppose any initiative that does not reinforce or complement the work of the Ottawa Process or which delays the establishment of the urgently-needed norm against [anti-personnel] mines.'[603]

Discussions continued, but progress towards a mandate was impeded, on the one hand by committed supporters of the Ottawa Process, such as Mexico and South Africa, and on the other by States, such as Syria, which were implacably opposed to even discussing the possibility of a ban on anti-personnel mines. Indeed, the appointment of a Special Co-ordinator for Anti-Personnel Landmines, Australian Ambassador John Campbell, on 26 June 1997 was only possible due to the discreet departure of the Syrian Representative from the room while the vote was taken.[604] The task of the Special Co-ordinator was to try to find an agreed mandate that could form the basis for discussions. On 14 August 1997, the Special Co-ordinator declared that there was little point in the CD taking any decisions on a possible mandate until the outcome of the Ottawa process was known in December 1997.[605] He did, however, remind the Conference that he had proposed four possible mandates:

- *work to commence simultaneously on the various aspects of a ban – production, use, transfer, and stockpiling;*
- *step-by-step efforts toward a global ban;*
- *partial approach looking at export, import, transfers and verification; or*

599 Though the difference in context was startling. The use, or at least the first use, of chemical weapons in warfare had been prohibited for decades by the time the CD was entrusted with the task of negotiating their total prohibition. In stark contrast, only the use of a certain, limited types of anti-personnel mines had been prohibited by international agreement (amended Protocol II), and even these were subject to an optional nine-year deferral period for compliance.

600 Now 66, as listed *supra*.

601 Goose, S., "Anti-Personnel Mines and the Conference on Disarmament", *op. cit.*

602 See for instance Mannion, J., "US wants talks on landmine ban held in Geneva", *AFP*, Washington, 17 January 1997; UN Information Service, 'Disarmament Conference hears further calls for bans on landmines and fissile materials, establishment of negotiating committee non nuclear disarmament', *Press release DCF/283*, Geneva, 23 January 1997; "Britain calls for ban on landmine exports", *Financial Times*, 31 January 1997.

603 Nebehay, S., "UN Disarmament: Canada prefers landmines pact under own talks", *Reuters*, Geneva, 6 February 1997.

604 All decisions in the Conference on Disarmament are taken by consensus.

605 UN Information Service, "Disarmament Conference hears statements on anti-personnel landmines nuclear disarmament and fissile material cut-off", *Press release DCF/311*, Geneva, 15 August 1997.

- *the establishment of an ad hoc committee simply to review and discuss the global mines situation.*[606]

In September 1997, Mexico, Morocco and Syria blocked an attempt by Western nations to extend the mandate of the Special Co-ordinator, thereby requiring that a new appointment be made in 1998.[607] At the UN General Assembly the same year, a resolution entitled 'Contributions towards banning anti-personnel mines' invited the CD 'to intensify its efforts on the issue of anti-personnel landmines'.[608]

During 1998, the US again sought to initiate negotiations in the CD, this time opting for an agreement to ban transfers of anti-personnel mines as opposed to a comprehensive ban of the weapons.[609] In June 1998, the US secured Chinese support for its initiative, and the Sino-US Joint Presidential Statement on Landmines declaring that: 'China and the United States agree to actively pursue at the Conference on Disarmament the commencement of negotiations on an anti-personnel landmines transfer/export ban by supporting the prompt establishment of an Ad Hoc Committee.'[610] The ICBL notes, however, that as in 1997, the only progress made was in the appointment of a Special Co-ordinator (once more, Australian Ambassador John Campbell) to examine the possibility of further action. Attempts to secure agreement on the creation of an ad hoc committee to negotiate on mines were unsuccessful.[611]

In February 1999, 22 States[612] led by Bulgaria, called for the CD to re-appoint a Special Coordinator, 'with a view to the early establishment of an ad hoc committee' to negotiate an anti-personnel mine transfer ban.[613] A number of

---

606 *Ibid.*

607 Nebehay, S., "US blames non-aligned countries for arms deadlock", *Reuters European*, Geneva, 9 September 1997.

608 UN General Assembly resolution 52/38H of 9 December 1997, adopted by 147 votes to O with 15 abstentions (Benin, Botswana, Cuba, Eritrea, Indonesia, Kenya, Malawi, Mexico, Mozambique, Namibia, the Philippines, South Africa, Togo, Zambia, and Zimbabwe). In the General Assembly First Committee Eritrea and South Africa had actually opposed the adoption of the resolution, which was passed with 121 votes in favour and 19 abstentions.
On 3 December 1997, speaking in Ottawa at one of the Working Groups in the Mine Action Forum that accompanied the Treaty Signing Conference, France's Permanent Representative to the CD, Ambassador Joëlle Bourgeois, claimed that 'the criticisms levelled against the Conference do not withstand examination. The rule of consensus favours universalisation.' Bourgeois, J., *Universalisation of the Ottawa Process. Contribution of the Conference on Disarmament to the Elimination of Anti-Personnel Mines*, Ottawa, 3 December 1997, p. 1.

609 *Landmine Monitor Report 1999*, p. 321.

610 *Ibid.*, pp. 459-60. See further *Landmine Monitor Report 2000*, p. 335.

611 *Landmine Monitor Report 1999*, pp. 9, 321. The ICBL is opposed to 'any effort to negotiate a transfer ban, or any other anti-personnel mine-related measure in the CD, believing that, regardless of the intention, it could serve to undermine the establishment of the norm completely banning the weapons.' *Ibid.*, pp. 321-2; see also Goose, S., *Anti-Personnel Landmines and the Conference on Disarmament, op. cit.*

612 The 22 were: Argentina, Belgium, Bulgaria, Chile, Finland, France, Germany, Greece, Hungary, Italy, Japan, Poland, Romania, Russia, Slovakia, Spain, Turkey, Ukraine, the UK, the US, Venezuela. *Landmine Monitor Report 1999*, p. 9; see also pp. 753-4.

613 Statement by Bulgarian Ambassador Petko Draganov to the Conference on Disarmament, undated but February 1999, cited by *Landmine Monitor Report 1999*, p. 9; see also pp. 784-5.

other States were prepared to support the proposal, including, notably, Austria[614] and also Estonia.[615] In December 1999, Pakistan called for the States in the CD to 'explore (...) further measures which would advance the goal of the ultimate prohibition of [anti-personnel mines]' and expressed its continued support for negotiations of 'a universally accepted ban' on the weapons.[616]

At the First Meeting of States Parties of the Convention on the Prohibition of Anti-Personnel Mines in Maputo, a number of States made reference to the CD. Poland, for example, reiterated its support for a global ban on the transfer of anti-personnel mines 'that would take account of the security concerns of States' claiming that this would be 'a fitting theme' for the CD.[617] Likewise, Romania called for the success of the Ottawa Process to 'enhance discussions' on anti-personnel mines in the CD with a view to 'enabling a broader implementation of its final aim.'[618] Australia, too, continued to press the case for the CD, claiming that giving formal treaty status to the moratoria on transfer many States had in place would be a 'practical achievement – worth having in itself as well as being useful in keeping non-Ottawa countries engaged on the landmines issue.'[619]

Even a number of States Parties to the Convention supported the idea of negotiating a transfer ban in the CD.[620] Belgium, for instance, one of the core group of countries in the Ottawa process mirrored the views of a number of such States when it declared: 'Belgium's approach is inspired by a wish for integrity. We have always, from the very beginning of the Ottawa Process, expressed the desire to attend the two complementary processes. At the Disarmament Conference, there are countries which did not attend the Ottawa Process. Discussing these issues in different fora is one way to commit those countries towards the banning of anti-personnel landmines. But it remains clear that in our minds we will never agree with any initiative which should risk to weaken the Conven-

---

614 According to the ICBL, Austria supports all efforts that might contribute to the total elimination of anti-personnel mines worldwide, in all appropriate international fora, including the CD, providing these efforts are in support of and consistent with the Convention on the Prohibition of Anti-Personnel Mines. *Landmine Monitor Report 1999*, p. 528.

615 See *Landmine Monitor Report 1999*, p. 778.

616 *Landmine Monitor Report 2000*, p. 522.

617 Statement of Mr Zbigniew Szymanski, Director of the Department of the United Nations Political Affairs of the Republic of Poland, at the First Meeting of States Parties to the Convention on the Prohibition of the Use, Stockpiling, Production and Transfer of Anti-Personnel Mines and on their Destruction, Maputo, 4 May 1999. See also *Landmine Monitor Report 1999*, pp. 753-4.

618 Statement of Mr Valeriu Nicolae, Chargé d'affaires of Romania to the Republic of Mozambique, to the First Meeting of States Parties, undated, but May 1999.

619 Statement by John J. Griffin, Assistant Secretary, International Security Division, Department of Foreign Affairs and Trade, and Head of the Australian Delegation to the First Meeting of States Parties of the Ottawa Treaty. Australia also commended amended Protocol II to the 1980 CCW as 'a useful complement' to the Convention on the Prohibition of Anti-Personnel Mines. This view is shared by many, including the author, who see the CCW as an appropriate forum to tighten restrictions on, at least, anti-vehicle mines. See, for example, the position of Canada as reproduced in *Landmine Monitor Report 1999*, p. 225; Goose, S., "Anti-Personnel Mines and the Conference on Disarmament", *op. cit.*, pp. 5, 6.

620 See for instance *Landmine Monitor Report 2000*, pp. 606, 745.

tion.'[621] An attempt by France to pass a resolution in the UNGA supporting negotiations on a prohibition in 'all relevant fora' was a dismal failure; the proposed resolution was withdrawn following strong opposition.[622]

Opponents of using the CD as a forum for negotiations on landmines included Canada,[623] the ICBL,[624] New Zealand,[625] Norway,[626] and Switzerland.[627] New Zealand, for instance, a recent member of the Conference on Disarmament, has expressed a strong preference to promote the Convention on the Prohibition of Anti-Personnel Mines, not lesser measures through the CD, because of its belief that 'the best way to push forward is to continue to extend the Ottawa membership, not to develop new instruments that run the risk of diluting support for all mine control and elimination measures.'[628] This position is shared by the author; from a humanitarian point of view, there is precious little to be gained from a prolonged discussion in the CD and a proliferation of international instruments. The new norm has been set, and sooner or later it will become generally accepted, even if not universally respected. And with the CD in a current state of total gridlock, with each potential issue for negotiation inextricably tied up in linkages with the others, it is very hard to see any progress being made in the foreseeable future, particularly, but not only, with regard to anti-personnel mines.

In early 2000, a number of countries, led by Convention State Party Germany, called for the re-appointment of the Special Co-ordinator by the CD.[629] Yet, no progress was made on the issue in the CD in 2000.[630] Australia had already noted in March 2000 that it was 'prepared to consider alternative options

621 Statement by the Disarmament and Non-Proliferation Service of the Belgian Ministry of Foreign Affairs, 9 March 1999, cited by *Landmine Monitor Report 1999*, p. 540. For the position of Italy and Germany, see *Landmine Monitor Report 1999*, pp. 610-1, 716. France declared its belief that 'the opening of further negotiations in the Disarmament Conference, to deal first with the issue of mine transfers, would mark a definite step in the right direction and would help to dry up supply markets for anti-personnel mines.' Contribution by Mrs Bujon-Barre, Sub-Department for Chemical and Biological Disarmament and Control of Conventional Weapons, Ministry of Foreign Affairs, at the Symposium "For a World Without Mines", organised by Handicap International, Paris, 25 February 1999, cited by *Landmine Monitor Report 1999*, p. 590.

622 *Landmine Monitor Report 2000*, p. 636.

623 *Ibid.*, p. 239.

624 For detail of ICBL objections, see for instance Goose, S., "Anti-Personnel Mines and the Conference on Disarmament", *op. cit.*, pp. 2-5.

625 See for instance *Landmine Monitor Report 2000*, p. 417.

626 According to ICBL, Norway believes it is 'superfluous' to have a partial ban when there is already a total ban in place on anti-personnel mines. *Landmine Monitor Report 1999*, pp. 635-6.

627 Switzerland reportedly opposes tackling the subject of a transfer ban within the CD if the definition is not the same as that of the Convention on the Prohibition of Anti-Personnel Mines. *Landmine Monitor Report 1999*, p. 668.

628 Morton, G., New Zealand Ministry of Foreign Affairs and Trade, E-mail correspondence with Landmine Monitor researcher, 16 February 1999, cited by *Landmine Monitor Report 1999*, p. 370.

629 *Landmine Monitor Report 2000*, p. 606.

630 Thus, the CD closed its annual session on 21 September 2000 without even agreeing on a programme of work for the year. See for instance "Désarmement, La session annuelle se termine sans accord", *Tribune de Genève*, 22 September 2000, p. 34.

[towards a transfer ban] should the CD route prove unfeasible.'[631] It is not yet clear what these would be.

2.4. The Content of the Convention on the Prohibition of Anti-Personnel Mines

2.4.1. Scope and Application

According to Article 1(1) of the Convention, each State Party 'undertakes never under any circumstances' to use, develop, produce, otherwise acquire, stockpile, retain or transfer to anyone, directly or indirectly, anti-personnel mines. Although there is no specific clause on the scope of the Convention, the unequivocal nature of the obligation undertaken by States covers acts in times of peace and in situations of armed conflict, whether of an international or non-international character.[632] Thus, Steve Goose points out that without a scope article, the Convention is assumed to apply at all times, and notes that there 'are precedents for this approach, such as the Genocide Convention and the Convention on Environmental Modification.'[633]

The Convention does not specifically oblige non-State actors involved in armed conflict within the territory of a State Party to obey the proscriptions laid down by the Convention. Nevertheless, the Preamble refers to the 'principle of international humanitarian law that the right of the parties to an armed conflict to choose methods or means of warfare is not unlimited, on the principle that prohibits the employment in armed conflicts of weapons, projectiles and materials and methods of warfare of a nature to cause superfluous injury and unnecessary suffering and on the principle that a distinction must be made between civilians and combatants.'[634]

Colombia had proposed that the Convention apply 'in particular' to situations and to Parties mentioned in Article 3 common to the 1949 Geneva Conventions and the 1977 Additional Protocols but it was poorly drafted and gave the impression that the scope was actually being narrowed. At the formal adoption of the treaty, Colombia made a formal declaration of understanding that the obligations under the Convention 'apply equally to a State Party and to non-governmental entities in situations where such entities already have obligations under international humanitarian law. In the case of an armed conflict not of an international character in the territory of one of the States Parties, each party to the conflict shall be bound to respect, as a minimum, the general obligations of [the] Convention.' It further specified that the understanding 'shall not affect the legal status of the parties to the conflict.'[635] No State objected to this statement.

---

631 Statement cited in *Landmine Monitor Report 2000*, p. 374.

632 See for instance Roberts, A. and Guelff, R., *Documents on the Laws of War*, 3rd edn., *op. cit.*, pp. 25, 646; Swiss Federal Council, *Message concernant la Convention sur l'interdiction de l'emploi, du stockage, de la production et du transfert des mines antipersonnel et sur leur destruction*, *op. cit.*; Goose, S.D., "The Ottawa Process and the 1997 Mine Ban Treaty", *op. cit.*, p. 281.

633 *Ibid.*, footnote 14.

634 See also Hajnoczi, T. *et al.*, "The Ban Treaty", *op. cit.*, p. 306.

635 Final Declaration by Colombia, Oslo Diplomatic Conference 1-19 September 1997, *APL/CRP.5/Attach.16.*

Indeed, a number of NSAs reacted positively to the Convention on the Prohibition of Anti-Personnel Mines. In Afghanistan, for example, the Taliban[636] declared its strong support for the prohibition of landmines as the Convention was being signed by 121 States in Ottawa. Taliban 'Foreign Ministry' official Sattar Paktis declared in Kabul that: 'The policy of the Islamic Emirate of Afghanistan is that production, trade and stockpiling of mines should be banned. We strongly support its total eradication across the globe.'[637] The absence of any reference to use combined with recurring allegations that mines were being used gave rise to concern. But a year later, the Taliban's Supreme Leader, Mulla Mohammad Omer Akhund, declared that anyone who 'uses mines in personal, political or other disputes shall be punished according to Islamic principles.'[638] Omer explained that the Taliban had been unable to sign the treaty because the international community has not recognised the Taliban government and declared that: 'The Islamic Emirate of Afghanistan wants a total ban on manufacture, stockpiling, trade and use and it is ready to take part in its implementation.'[639]

Other NSAs[640] that have declared their support for a prohibition on the use of mines include the Sudan People's Liberation Movement,[641] the authorities of the self-styled Republic of Somaliland,[642] the Polisario Front/Sahrawi authorities in the Western Sahara,[643] and the Philippine National Democratic Front.[644]

---

636 The Taliban is the *de facto* government of Afghanistan, but so far, only three States have recognised the Taliban as the official representatives of Afghanistan: Pakistan, Saudi Arabia, and the United Arab Emirates. See for instance <http://www.rawa.org>.

637 Salahuddin, S., "Afghan Taliban Support Ban on Landmines", *Reuters*, Kabul, 3 December 1997. The Taliban had previously described the use of landmines as 'un-Islamic'. See for instance Chawla, S., "Diffusion of Landmines in Afghanistan", article distributed on the MGM Network, E-mail by Hendrik Ehlers, 13 October 2000.

638 "Afghan Anti-Landmines campaigners to monitor Taliban, Masood", *AFP Internationale*, 30 November 1998.

639 *Ibid.* See also *Landmine Monitor Report 2000*, p. 455.

640 See generally *Landmine Monitor Report 1999*, pp. 943-4; *Landmine Monitor Report 2000*, pp. 992-3.

641 "Resolution on the Problem Posed by the Proliferation of Anti-Personnel Mines in Liberated Parts of New Sudan", New Kush-Himan, 1 November 1996, cited by NSA Working Group, *Landmine Ban by Non State Actors*, undated, p. 10. Landmine Monitor reported in 2000 that the SPLA was 'believed' to have used anti-personnel mines between March 1999 and April 2000 despite this pledge. *Landmine Monitor Report 2000*, pp. 180, 182.

642 Somaliland issued an open letter to the Canadian Department of Foreign Affairs and International Trade indicating its willingness to sign the Ottawa Treaty in December 1997. See NSA Working Group, *Landmine Ban by Non State Actors*, *op. cit.* A representative of Somaliland was refused permission to address the First Meeting of States Parties in Maputo in May 1999. See for instance *FMSP Highlights*, 4 May 1999, prepared by the Media Liaison Team of the First Meeting of States Parties.

643 Sahrawi Ministry of Information, 1 March 1999, in *Western Sahara Weekly News*, Week 10, 7-13 March 1999; Declaration by the Polisario Representative, Barhim Mokhtar, to the ICBL Non-State Actors Working Group, telephone conversation, March 1999, cited in *Landmine Monitor Report 1999*, p. 944.

644 See "Comprehensive Agreement on Respect for Human Rights and International Humanitarian Law between the Government of the Republic of the Philippines and the National Democratic Front of the Philippines", signed in The Hague on 16 March 1998. See NSA Working Group, *Landmine Ban by Non State Actors*, *op. cit.*

On the other hand, mines continued to be used by certain NSAs, even in signatory States. In Cambodia on 11 October 1997, the day after the announcement of the awarding of the Nobel Peace Prize jointly to the ICBL and its Co-ordinator, the Khmer Rouge announced by radio that it had laid more mines in the north-west of the country. Four days later, in a further radio broadcast the Khmer Rouge again referred to landmines claiming that the Vietnamese occupying army in the 1980s had laid most of Cambodia's mines. Citing the UN Charter, the Khmer Rouge claimed that its forces had the right to use 'any type of weapon' to defend Cambodia's sovereignty from 'Vietnamese aggression'.[645]

In the Casamance province of Senegal, the separatist Movement of Democratic Forces of Casamance (MFDC) has been fighting for independence from Senegal since 1982, although the use of landmines has only been recorded since 1993.[646] Between June 1997 and January 1998, mines caused 32 deaths and a further 109 people suffered amputations.[647] According to one authority, the MFDC were split on their use of landmines, admitting in November 1997 that they were using them,[648] while their international representatives continued to deny it. In February 1998, following NGO pressure, the MFDC military wing in Casamance pledged not to use anti-personnel mines in their struggle against the government,[649] although reports of use continued into 2000.[650] Although an agreement was seemingly reached between the government and rebels in January 2000 to co-operate on a demining programme for the province, in March of the same year, as Senegal geared up for a Presidential election, authorities in the Casamance expressed concern that landmines could hamper the poll.[651]

Certainly it was regrettable that States chose not to apply the treaty specifically to armed opposition groups, especially given that international humanitarian law is no stranger to such applicability.[652] Sri Lanka, for instance, called for the ban to encompass the use of anti-personnel mines not only by the 'security forces' but also by 'terrorist groups'.[653] To respond to the concern, the ICBL Working Group on Non-State Actors sought to develop 'Geneva Call', a mechanism whereby non-state actors could formally deposit a declaration renouncing anti-personnel mine use with an independent organisation based in

---

645 "Nobel Prize: a bit of solace for the maimed", *Phnom Penh Post*, 24 October – 6 November 1997, p. 20.

646 Vines, A., "The Crisis of Anti-Personnel Mines", *To Walk Without Fear*, p. 131. See also *Landmine Monitor Report 1999*, p. 76, for the assertion that large-scale mine-laying by the MFDC began in August 1997.

647 Vines, A., "The Crisis of Anti-Personnel Mines", *op. cit.*, p. 131.

648 See *Landmine Monitor Report 1999*, p. 77.

649 Vines, A., "The Crisis of Anti-Personnel Mines", *op. cit.*, pp. 131-2; see also *Landmine Monitor Report 1999*, p. 77.

650 *Landmine Monitor Report 1999*, p. 77; *Landmine Monitor Report 2000*, p. 98.

651 See "Landmines in Senegal's Casamance Province worry authorities", *SAPA-AFP*, Ziguinchor, Senegal, 17 March 2000.

652 See *supra* Chapter 1, pp. 53-4.

653 Statement of Sri Lanka to the First Meeting of States Parties, Maputo, undated, but May 1999.

Geneva.[654] As of writing, it remains unclear whether such a mechanism is likely to be successful.[655]

Indeed, similar initiatives with respect to other instruments of international humanitarian law, particularly 1977 Protocol I, have not proved particularly effective. Moreover, attempts to involve NSAs in the development of the law have likewise made little headway. Pressure can undoubtedly be brought to bear on NSAs (many have fund-raising offices in Western countries), but governments have so far been reluctant to use political and financial pressure points in order to effectively change NSA behaviour on the battlefield. Speaking in late 1999, Canadian Foreign Minister, Lloyd Axworthy, declared that there was 'the need to find ways to address the challenges they [NSAs] raise. Two years after the Ottawa Convention, the role of these non-State actors, as participants in armed conflict or in perpetuating the new war economies, is the subject of growing scrutiny from the G8 to the UN.'[656]

2.4.2. Key Definitions

A. 'Anti-Personnel Mine' and 'Anti-Handling Device'

For obvious reasons, the definition of an anti-personnel mine, and the related definition of an anti-handling device, are crucial to the effectiveness of the Convention, and were therefore the subject of extensive – and animated – discussion throughout the Ottawa process. From the outset, humanitarian organisations were determined to strengthen the definition contained in amended Protocol II to the CCW. The ICRC, for example, declared that: 'All mines designed to kill or injure people are anti-personnel mines'[657] and at the Vienna Expert Meeting the ICRC produced an informal *Information Paper on Dual-Use Munitions*, which illustrated the attempted reclassification of anti-personnel mines that had already been occurring as a result, direct or indirect, of the word 'primarily'.[658]

As previously noted, the first Austrian draft treaty text merely repeated the Protocol II definition of an anti-personnel mine verbatim, but, following the

---

654 NSA Working Group, *Landmine Ban by Non State Actors*, undated, p. 8. See also UK Working Group on Landmines, "Armed Groups Asked to Commit to Landmine Ban", *Press release*, 31 March 2000.

655 A conference entitled "Engaging Non-State Actors in a Landmine Ban", held in Geneva on 24-25 March 2000, did little to dispel the widely-held view that the initiative has, so far at least, attracted little support among governments, or even the ICBL leadership. Moreover, a number of the NSAs that adhered to Geneva Call continued to use anti-personnel mines, seemingly without restriction. See for instance Landmine Monitor Report 2000, p. 426.

656 *Landmine Monitor Report 2000*, pp. 234-5.

657 ICRC, Landmines, Crucial Decisions in 1997, *ICRC Position Paper*, Geneva, January 1997, p. 4. For further details on this issue see for example the Statement of the ICRC to the Vienna Expert Meeting, 12 February 1997, pp. 1-2.

658 One example given was of an Italian-made mine described as a directional fragmentation *anti-personnel* mine in Jane's Military Vehicles and Logistics 1994-1995, but in August 1995 was described in a Jane's Special Report entitled Trends in Landmine Warfare as a directional *anti-vehicle* mine despite the fact that the actuating load needed to detonate the mine was between only 3-6 kg.

Vienna Expert Meeting, the second draft contained an amended definition, with the qualifier 'primarily' replaced with a specific exception for anti-vehicle mines equipped with anti-handling devices.[659] Prior to the Oslo Diplomatic Conference, Sweden proposed that the definition be amended to again include the word 'primarily' but it pressed this issue without conviction and surely in the knowledge that the argument for its inclusion had already been lost. Ambassador Molander, the President of the First CCW Review Conference, complained bitterly that departure from the definition contained in amended Protocol II would deter adherence to the Convention on the Prohibition of Anti-Personnel Mines[660] and create unnecessary confusion while only representing a slight improvement on the existing wording.[661]

In the Convention as adopted, it is provided that an anti-personnel mine is 'a mine designed to be exploded by the presence, proximity or contact of a person and that will incapacitate, injure or kill one or more persons. Mines designed to be detonated by the presence, proximity or contact of a vehicle as opposed to a person, that are equipped with anti-handling devices, are not considered anti-personnel mines as a result of being so equipped.'[662] An anti-handling device is defined as 'a device intended to protect a mine and which is part of, linked to, attached to or placed under the mine and which activates when an attempt is made to tamper with or otherwise intentionally disturb the mine.'[663]

There are four separate issues to be addressed here: the distinction between an anti-personnel mine and an anti-vehicle mine; the precise ambit of the definition of an anti-handling device and its consequences for arsenals around the world; the situation of so-called 'Claymore' mines; and the status of other weapons, such as booby-traps and improvised explosive devices (IEDs).

---

659 The terms of the clarification intentionally adopted exactly the same language as that used to clarify the meaning of the word primarily at the end of the CCW Review Conference. At the Vienna Expert Meeting, the ICRC declared that: 'Of particular concern to us are remotely-delivered anti-tank mines equipped with anti-handling devices[.] (...) Use of these weapons has the potential to recreate many of the humanitarian problems associated with traditional anti-personnel mines, with the exception that all victims will probably be killed.' *Statement of the ICRC to the Vienna Expert Meeting*, 12 February 1997, p. 2. The ICRC was well aware, however, as was the ICBL, that the prospects of achieving a prohibition that encompassed anti-tank mines equipped with anti-handling devices were extremely low.

660 See for instance Foreword by Ambassador Molander in Maresca, L. and Maslen, S. (eds.), *The Banning of Anti-Personnel Landmines*, *op. cit.*, p. xxv.

661 Thus Steve Goose notes that: 'Some now see it as problematic that two international instruments governing the use of mines have different definitions.' Goose, S.D., "The Ottawa Process and the 1997 Mine Ban Treaty", *op. cit.*, p. 281. Though given that the definition in the Convention on the Prohibition of Anti-Personnel Mines is simply that in amended Protocol II as interpreted by more than 20 governments and unchallenged by others, this should not necessarily be the case. Though see above the declaration by Pakistan with respect to the definition of an anti-handling device under amended Protocol II to the 1980 CCW, *supra* Chapter 1, p. 58. See also Gourley, S., "Towards the 'Smart' Mine", *Jane's Defence Weekly*, 19 July 2000, pp. 5-6. Gourley claims, wrongly in the view of the author, that: 'Essentially you can put just about anything within the confines of the Ottawa definition and say that it's banned because of Ottawa.'

662 Article 2(1).

663 Article 2(3).

B. Anti-Vehicle Mines

As already noted,[664] there is no international legal definition of what constitutes an anti-vehicle mine,[665] although it could be considered implicit in existing definitions of an anti-personnel mine. Thus, for instance, under Article 2(1) of the Convention on the Prohibition of Anti-Personnel Mines, a working definition could be 'mines designed to be detonated by the presence, proximity or contact of a vehicle as opposed to a person and which cannot be detonated by a person unless tampered with or otherwise intentionally disturbed.'[666]

In practice, however, determining whether devices fall within such a definition will be problematic since many modern anti-vehicle/anti-tank mines, even when not equipped with anti-handling devices, can detonate under relatively small amounts of pressure. Thus, for instance, in a letter to US Senator Patrick Leahy, US Air Force General Joseph Ralston declared that the minimum weight needed to detonate a US anti-tank mine was 290lb (approximately 130kg) but that foreign pressure-activated anti-tank mines could be triggered with only 200lb (just under 100kg).[667] Rae McGrath, the former director of the MAG, claimed that the Brazilian ACNMAE T1 anti-tank mine could be detonated by 60kg of pressure and that the NaMiBa anti-tank mine from the Czech Republic and Slovakia could be set off by only 2.2kg of pressure.[668]

Following consultations with military experts, the ICRC reported that a number of pressure activated anti-vehicle mines detonated with 50-100kg of pressure[669] and would explode under the weight of an adult who happened to step on it. The ICRC stated its opinion that 'any anti-vehicle mine which functions as an anti-personnel mine, that is, which is capable of being detonated "by the presence, proximity or contact of a person", is an anti-personnel mine and is prohibited by the [Convention on the Prohibition of Anti-Personnel Mines]. This is the case irrespective of the primary purpose for which the mine is intended to be used.'[670] It recommended that pressure-activated anti-vehicle fuses should not activate under less than 150kg of pressure.[671]

---

664 See *supra* Introduction, p. 3, footnote 17.

665 This term tends to be used instead of anti-tank mine as a more precise description of mines other than anti-personnel mines.

666 An alternative definition could be simply 'a mine other than an anti-personnel mine.'

667 Letter dated 19 June 1996.

668 McGrath, R., "Definitions and Anti-Handling Devices", *op. cit.* During the negotiations at the Oslo Diplomatic Conference, Australia declared its understanding that anti-tank mines configured as anti-personnel mines were covered by the definition of an anti-personnel mine and therefore prohibited. This understanding was not challenged by any delegation. Australia did not, however, repeat this understanding in writing upon ratification of the Convention.

669 But note the comments by a German deminer, Henrik Ehlers, that depending on the state of the mine and its fuzing system, in practice the minimum force can be 0kg. Ehlers, H., "Re: the crux of the AT biscuit", E-mail correspondence on the MGM Demining Network, 14 September 2000.

670 See *Landmine Monitor Report 1999*, p. 1007.

671 See *ibid.*, p. 1008. The ICBL has also expressed concern that the Convention does not define *anti-vehicle mine*. It believes that '[a]t the least, States Parties should agree on a minimum amount of pressure needed to explode a pressure-activated anti-vehicle mine.' *Landmine Monitor Report 2000*, p. 12.

C. Anti-Vehicle Mines Equipped with Anti-Handling Devices

One of the most difficult negotiations at the Oslo Diplomatic Conference surrounded the US's desire to exclude its mixed anti-tank and anti-personnel mine systems from the ambit of the Convention.[672] Robert Bell, Senior Director for Defence Policy and Arms Control at the US National Security Council, asserted that the anti-personnel mines contained in so-called mixed systems were in fact anti-handling devices[673] and as a consequence, the US delegation at the Diplomatic Conference called for a device intended to protect an anti-tank mine and placed 'near' the mine to be treated as an anti-handling device.[674] This reclassification, which was resisted by the Conference despite strong US pressure,[675] was even denounced by the extreme right-wing US think-tank, the Centre for Security Policy, which claimed that what needed to be adjusted was not the description of mixed systems 'but the policy that seemingly would result in the complete elimination of all such systems from the US arsenal.'[676]

---

672 See for instance Lawson, R. *et al.*, "The Ottawa Process and the International Movement to Ban Anti-Personnel Mines", *op. cit.*, 1998, p. 178. The ICBL condemned the US for seeking to exempt from the ban US GATOR, Volcano and MOPMS anti-personnel mines which the officials 'deceivingly' called 'explosive devices.' ICBL, "Campaign Criticises Deceptions in Clinton's Landmine Statement", *Press Release*, Oslo, Norway, 19 September 1997.

673 See also the verbatim report of a News Briefing on the issue by Kenneth Bacon of the US Department of Defense given on 16 September 1997, <http://www.defenselink.mil>.

674 This is also surprising given the US policy announced in May 1996 wherein it was stated that the right to use smart mines in conflict situations would only be retained until an international ban took effect. See Wareham, M., "Rhetoric and Policy Realities in the United States",*op. cit.*, pp. 225. Wareham also cites (at p. 235) the statement by the Secretary of State for Defense at the same time that the US was 'prepared to give up smart mines as part of an international agreement. And we believe that may be necessary to get the international agreement.' Moreover, also in 1996 the Chief Executive Officer of Alliant Technosystems, the major US mine manufacturer, reportedly declared that the Pentagon had requested the company to reconfigure its Volcano landmine system solely to an anti-tank capacity. *Landmine Monitor Report 1999*, pp. 323-4.

675 Pressure by the ICBL was extremely important in preventing a change in the definition. Each day, when delegates arrived at the Conference site, they were handed a slogan or a short message. One of these asked, "When is an anti-personnel mine not an anti-personnel mine?" and answered, "When it's American!". Another, relating to the US attempts to redefine an anti-handling device to include anti-personnel mines placed near anti-tank mines, declared that "Near is too far!".

676 Center for Security Policy, "Too Clever by Half: Bob Bell's Sophistry Must Not be Allowed to Jeopardise US Military's Ability To Use Landmines", *Decision Brief No 97-D 142*, Washington DC, 24 September 1997. However, in 1999, the Pentagon was apparently planning to produce a new landmine system combining existing ADAM anti-personnel mines with RAAM anti-tank mines in a single canister that would be delivered by artillery. The cost of combining 300,000 RAAM anti-tank mines with 1.2 million ADAM anti-personnel mines was estimated at US$193.7 million. *Landmine Monitor Report 1999*, p. 324. In a press release on 1 March 1999, Human Rights Watch declared that 'RADAM is the latest of a growing number of indicators that the Pentagon is not serious about the 2006 deadline, and that it is very unlikely to be met.' Human Rights Watch, "Historical Landmine Ban Treaty Takes Effect", *Press release*, Washington, 1 March 1999, cited in *Landmine Monitor Report 1999*, p. 327.
As for the GATOR mine system, according to the ICBL, the Netherlands imported 5,984 GATOR anti-personnel mines in 1991 in a US$14.58 million deal. The GATOR is an air-delivered, self-destructing anti-personnel mine that is packaged with anti-tank mines in a

Despite the refusal of delegates to accept the US proposed amendment to the definition of an anti-handling device, controversy still surrounds its precise meaning in the Convention; specifically with respect to the words 'tamper with or otherwise intentionally disturb'. An earlier proposal to add only the words 'or otherwise disturb'[677] was felt to be too broad in compass,[678] excluding, in the view of at last one delegation, 'a person stumbling over an anti-personnel mine deployed in a mixed munitions field.'[679] To reduce the potential dangers to civilians, the word 'intentionally' was added to the proposed definition.[680]

During the negotiations in Oslo, a number of delegations referred to the so-called 'doctrine of the innocent act', whereby a mine that could be detonated by the footfall of a passer-by, as opposed to a deliberate manipulation of the mine in some way,[681] would be considered as an anti-personnel mine.[682] This doctrine

cluster-bomb unit (CBU-89). The Dutch government had indicated that it was 'technically feasible and operationally sensible' to remove all anti-personnel mines from the GATOR system and replace them with anti-tank mines. After deliberation, however, it decided that the entire GATOR system, including both anti-tank and anti-personnel mines, would be destroyed. According to Landmine Monitor, 'recent conflicts, such as in Kosovo, have shown there is a decreased need for such area denial munitions.' *Landmine Monitor Report 2000*, p. 693.

677 Made by the UK. See Oslo Diplomatic Conference document *APL/CW.32*.

678 See for instance *Landmine Monitor Report 2000*, p. 10.

679 Hajnoczi, T. *et al.*, "The Ban Treaty", *op. cit.*, p. 298.

680 *Ibid.* See also Goose, S.D., "The Ottawa Process and the 1997 Mine Ban Treaty", *op. cit.*, pp. 281-2.

681 According to the ICBL, 'numerous' French anti-tank mines are capable of being protected by anti-lift devices. According to military literature, one such system comprises anti-lifting ignitors, which are designed to explode if the anti-tank mine is handled by army engineers. See *Landmine Monitor Report 1999*, p. 593.

682 See Goose, S.D., "The Ottawa Process and the 1997 Mine Ban Treaty", *op. cit.*, p. 282 and footnote 15. According to the ICBL, the diplomatic record of negotiations at the Oslo Diplomatic Conference shows that anti-vehicle mines equipped with anti-handling devices and that explode from innocent, unintentional acts by one or more persons, are considered as anti-personnel mines and are therefore illegal under the Convention. See *Landmine Monitor Report 1999*, pp. 621, and 590, footnote 12. The ICBL complained, for example, that the Swiss national legislation did not prohibit the use of anti-vehicle mines with anti-handling devices, even when such mines were detonated upon being unintentionally disturbed by an individual. *Ibid.*, p. 667. They also note the 'unambiguous' nature of the French position, as stated during its adoption of national legislation: 'A tank is a tool of war. There is no connection between anti-tank and anti-personnel mines. The removal of an anti-tank mine from the battlefield is obviously a military action.' *Ibid.*, p. 594.

would, for instance, make activation of anti-tank mines by breakwire,[683] tripwire or tilt rods[684] illegal under the Convention.[685]

According to Colin King, the editor of the renowned Jane's Mines and Mine Clearance, there is 'some ambiguity' over the use of magnetic-influence fuses in anti-tank mines.[686] Although in theory such a fuse requires the proximity of several tonnes of steel (*i.e.*, a heavy vehicle) to initiate detonation, it is alleged that even the slight movement of the mine within the earth's magnetic field can cause it to explode. Thus, it is claimed, surface-laid or scatterable anti-tank mines with such fuses could easily be triggered by the movement of an innocent party.[687] An example of such a sensitive mine is deployed by the Shielder[688] vehicle scatter-launched mine system, which was ordered by the British Ministry of Defence in December 1995. Although not *prima facie* falling within the ambit of an anti-handling device, the anti-tank mine contains a highly sensitive magnetic influence fuse. King, for example, claims that: 'A person stepping on it would set it off immediately.'[689] Likewise, the US, in its assessment of which mines would be prohibited by the Convention on the Prohibition of Anti-Personnel Mines, believed that its anti-tank mines equipped with magnetic influences fuzes or infrared sensors might fall within the definitions in Article 2, since they would detonate 'if picked up quickly or rotated'.[690]

Also prohibited by the Convention is the UK's 'HB876', a remotely-delivered mine contained within the JP233 airfield denial weapon, which is equipped with a seismic disturbance fuse. After considerable discussion, the UK reclassified the weapon as an anti-personnel mine in June 1998.[691] Landmine Monitor reported in 1999 that the UK would destroy their stocks of this weapon by 1 January 2000.[692] The weapons were duly transferred to Germany – as permitted by Article 3 – where destruction was completed on 19 October 1999.[693] Moreover, as a result of the Convention, the UK cancelled the *Future*

683 The UK, for instance, included one anti-vehicle mine in its stockpile destruction on the grounds that it was activated by breakwire and could therefore be detonated inadvertently by a person. *Landmine Monitor Report 2000*, p. 749.

684 A tilt rod is a thin flexible rod usually protruding from the top of the mine. In most cases, only a few kg of pressure on the tilt rod are necessary to detonate the mine. See for instance McGrath, R., "Definitions and Anti-Handling Devices", *Discussion Paper*, Mines Advisory Group, Cockermouth, UK, August 1997. Thus, Canada is destroying its M21 anti-vehicle mines, which were all fitted with tilt rod fuses. *Landmine Monitor Report 1999*, p. 231. In addition, in its assessment of the legality of its stockpile of anti-tank mines under the Convention, the US considers that two anti-tank mines equipped with tilt rods would be prohibited – since these will be exploded by a person 'as an unintended consequence' of their design. *Landmine Monitor Report 1999*, p. 326.

685 On this point see King, C., *Legislation and the Landmine, op. cit.*, p. 20.

686 *Ibid.*, p. 21.

687 *Ibid.*

688 The mine is laid by the US-made Volcano system. *Landmine Monitor Report 1999*, p. 685.

689 "Government spends £62 million on landmines", *Sunday Telegraph*, 5 April 1998. See also *Landmine Monitor Report 1999*, pp. 684, 685-6, 688.

690 See *Landmine Monitor Report 1999*, p. 326.

691 See King, C., *Legislation and the Landmine, op. cit.*, p. 21; McGrath, "Definitions and Anti-Handling Devices", *op. cit.*; *Landmine Monitor Report 1999*, p. 681.

692 *Landmine Monitor Report 1999*, p. 681.

693 *Landmine Monitor Report 2000*, p. 749.

Anti-Personnel Scatterable Mine (FAPSM) project, but in 1996, it had already ordered a replacement for the JP233, the *Conventional Armed Stand-Off Missile* (CASOM), which is due to enter into service in 2001.[694]

Canada is currently assessing the legality of its 'FFV 028' self-neutralising anti-vehicle mine, which has a highly sensitive magnetic-influence sensor,[695] though it reported to Landmine Monitor that its tests remained 'inconclusive.'[696] The Dutch, from whom the mines were transferred,[697] had reportedly concluded that the mines would not be lawful under the Convention on the Prohibition of Anti-Personnel Mines.[698]

Towards the end of 1999, the German Campaign to Ban Landmines wrote to the German Chancellor, Gerhard Schröder, claiming that the aerially-delivered MUSPA (Multi-fragments-active-passive) 'sub-munitions' were in fact anti-personnel mines. The weapons are deployed by a Tornado fighter plane and after hitting the ground detonate from the sound of a plane landing or of a motorised military unit. The German Campaign expressed doubts as to the acoustic detonation system and pointed out that the fragmentation effect suggested that personnel were also targeted.[699] Concern was heightened by the disclosure by Italy in its report under Article 7 of the Convention that its MUSPA mines fall within the ambit of the Convention.[700]

At the First Meeting of States Parties of the Convention in Maputo, the ICRC had already expressed its concern, 'that increased use of certain anti-handling devices will endanger civilian populations. Of specific concern are devices which will trigger the mine's detonation through the innocent passage of a person over or near the mine or through inadvertent or accidental contact with the mine itself. This threat is particularly serious with regard to remotely-delivered mines which lie on the ground. In such cases the anti-handling device can cause the anti-vehicle mine to function as an anti-personnel mine. A range of experts consulted by the ICRC believe that anti-handling devices can be designed in such a manner so as to limit the danger to innocent civilians. The ICRC calls upon all States to examine the technical characteristics of existing and proposed anti-handling devices and to ensure that they are designed so as to minimise the risks of detonation through inadvertent or accidental contact.'[701] The ICRC attached to its statement to the First Meeting of States Parties an

---

694 *Landmine Monitor Report 1999*, p. 681.

695 *Ibid.*, p. 232.

696 *Ibid.*

697 Although they were apparently manufactured by Bofors in Sweden. Mines Action Canada/Pax Christi Netherlands, E-mail correspondence with *Jane's Defence Weekly*, January 1998, cited by *Landmine Monitor Report 1999*, p. 232.

698 *Landmine Monitor Report 1999*, p. 232. Other mines which the ICBL believe 'may not be consistent' with the Convention on the Prohibition of Anti-Personnel Mines, are the German MUSPA, DM-39, and AT-2 mines. *Ibid.*, p. 621.

699 Hebel, S., "Berlin dodges the prohibition of mines", *Frankfurter Rundschau*, 22 November 1999, unofficial translation.

700 See *Landmine Monitor Report 2000*, p. 647.

701 Statement by Eric Roethlisberger, Vice-President, International Committee of the Red Cross, to the First Meeting of States Parties of the Convention on the Prohibition of Anti-Personnel Mines. See also *Landmine Monitor Report 1999*, pp. 1006-7.

information paper, which identified some of the anti-vehicle mines that caused its concern.[702] It further called upon States to ensure that tripwires, breakwires and tilt rods are not used as fusing mechanisms for anti-vehicle mines.[703]

In January 2000, at the Standing Committee of Experts (SCE) meeting on the Status and Implementation of the Convention, the ICBL asked States Parties to 'reconfirm that according to the definitions in the treaty, anti-vehicle mines (...) equipped with anti-handling devices (...) that function like anti-personnel mines – that explode from an unintentional act – are banned by the treaty.'[704] According to Steve Goose, Ireland, followed by Australia, Austria, Canada, Mexico, the Netherlands, Norway, South Africa, Switzerland, and the ICRC, confirmed this interpretation.[705] Ireland proposed the formation of an expert group to clarify which specific types of anti-handling devices, anti-vehicle mines and delivery methods are permissible and which are prohibited under the treaty. The co-chairs of the SCE working group on the Convention, Canada and South Africa, were tasked to carry out consultations on the possible creation of such an expert group.[706] According to Landmine Monitor, the UK publicly opposed the idea.[707]

D. Claymore Mines

Australia was – rightly – concerned to ensure that the diplomatic record of the negotiations in Oslo included an accepted understanding of the definition of an anti-personnel mine, and therefore the reach of the Convention. Thus, for example, the Australian representative declared his understanding that command-detonated fragmentation munitions[708] (otherwise generically known as 'Claymore' mines/devices) were not covered by the Convention.[709] This understanding was not challenged by any other delegation. When ratifying the

---

702 See ICRC, *Anti-Vehicle Mines Equipped with Anti-Handling Devices*, Information Paper, Geneva, April 1999.

703 See *Landmine Monitor Report 1999*, p. 1007. Japan, in its national implementing legislation for the Convention, includes no exception for anti-vehicle mines equipped with anti-handling devices. During the debate in the Diet, the Japanese Parliament, the government declared that any mine equipped with an anti-handling device will be considered illegal. Statement by Masatada Hirose, Bureau Chief, Machinery and Information Industries Bureau, Ministry of International Trade and Industry, Commerce and Industry Committee, House of Representatives Proceedings Report No. 6, p. 2, cited by *Landmine Monitor Report 1999*, p. 360.

704 E-mail correspondence from Liz Bernstein, ICBL Co-ordinator, 12 May 2000. See "Review of the General Status and Operation of the Convention", *UN Doc. APLC/MSP.2/2000/SCE5/1*, p. 2.

705 Report on Standing Committee of Experts Meeting on General Status and Operation of the Convention from Steve Goose, Human Rights Watch, contained in E-mail correspondence from Liz Bernstein, ICBL Co-ordinator, 20 January 2000.

706 *Ibid.*

707 *Landmine Monitor Report 2000*, p. 751.

708 As, for instance, South Africa had found, these Claymore-type mines actuated in remote-controlled mode were a good substitute for victim-actuated anti-personnel mines as they could be easily directed and obviated the need for painstaking mine clearance.

709 As Colin King points out, 'the difference between mines and booby-traps has never been adequately defined and sometimes the distinction becomes unclear.' King, C., *Legislation and the Landmine*, Jane's Intelligence Review, Special Report No 16, UK, November 1997, p. 18.

Convention, Australia repeated its understanding that the definition of 'anti-personnel mines' does not include 'command-detonated munitions'.[710]

Indeed, it is logical that these weapons, when activated by remote control,[711] do not fall within the ambit of the Convention as they are most certainly 'directed' and are not victim-actuated.[712] Indeed, in the view of one expert, 'Claymore'-type mines are 'probably the single most effective generic group' of landmines.[713] Thus, a number of States Parties, such as Australia,[714] Austria,[715] Canada,[716] Denmark,[717] Japan,[718] and Switzerland,[719] decided to maintain or convert to command-detonated mode only their stocks of the weapon.[720]

E. Other Weapons

There was also consideration of whether other weapons similar to anti-personnel mines fell within the ambit of the Convention. During the Oslo

---

[710] And note the observation by Sinclair that 'it is debatable' that uncontested interpretations given at a conference constitute an 'agreement' forming part of the 'context' of the treaty which is being concluded, although considerable weight should be attached to them. Sinclair, Sir I., *The Vienna Convention on the Law of Treaties*, 2nd edn., Manchester University Press, UK, 1984, p. 130.

[711] The Convention clearly prohibits their use in tripwire-activation mode. Equally, if reports are confirmed of Russian Claymore mines being fitted with a light sensitive detector as a fusing mechanism, these mines too would fall within the Convention definition. *Landmine Monitor Report 1999*, p. 806, citing an oral statement by Nagorny, M., Department of the Chief Commander of the Engineering Forces, Russian Ministry of Defence. The Landmine Monitor claims that there are 'grounds to believe' that such anti-personnel mines are still being produced in Russia. *Ibid.*

[712] See for instance *Landmine Monitor Report 1999*, p. 529.

[713] King, C., *Legislation and the Landmine, op. cit.*, p. 18.

[714] In September 1999, the Australian Defence Force confirmed that it had brought command-detonated Claymore mines to East Timor as part of its peacekeeping mission. See *Landmine Monitor Report 2000*, p. 376.

[715] See *Landmine Monitor Report 1999*, p. 529.

[716] According to the ICBL, Canada is now calling the device an 'area defence weapon'. *Ibid.*, pp. 226-7; 231-2. In February 2000, the Canadian Foreign Minister asked for clarification as to why Canadian peacekeepers in East Timor and Kosovo were equipped with Claymore 'mines'. CBC Radio, 14 February 2000. In response, the Canadian Defence Minister declared that: 'The Claymore equipment that they use is detonated by personnel behind it and operates similar to a shotgun. (...) This weapon is only used if there is someone behind it and they pull the trigger. It is not something that you lay in the ground. It is not a mine.' "Canadian Forces will continue to use remote-controlled mines", *Vancouver Sun*, 15 February 2000; see *Landmine Monitor Report 2000*, p. 243-4.

[717] Denmark now terms them 'sector charges'. *Landmine Monitor Report 1999*, p. 583.

[718] It was reported in January 1999 that Japan was replacing its anti-personnel mines with such remotely controlled devices. A representative of Japan's defence agency was quoted as saying: 'This is not a landmine. We are not even calling it a landmine.' *New Scientist*, Vol. 159, No. 2149, cited in "Calling the shots", *New Internationalist*, January/February 1999, p. 4.

[719] Switzerland calls them 'charges dirigées 96 légères'. The Swiss Campaign to Ban Landmines has apparently taken legal advice as to whether these '96 directional fragmentation explosives' are lawful under national Swiss legislation. *Landmine Monitor Report 1999*, p. 671.

[720] The ICBL also reports that the US no longer classifies Claymores as anti-personnel mines, but points out that the US has always used them in command-detonated move and never with a tripwire. *Landmine Monitor Report 1999*, p. 334.

Diplomatic Conference, Australia declared its understanding that booby-traps were not covered by the Convention[721] but that bounding anti-personnel mines, anti-tank mines configured as anti-personnel mines,[722] other munitions and improvised explosive devices[723] designed or adapted[724] to serve as anti-personnel mines were all both covered and accordingly prohibited. This understanding was not challenged by any delegation.

F. Summary

Despite a lack of clarity in certain aspects, the definition contained in the Convention on the Prohibition on Anti-Personnel Mines is, overall, a good one, as it encompasses those mines that are most dangerous to civilians. Based on evidence currently available, the author believes that all weapons 'designed, altered or intended' to serve as anti-personnel mines as defined in Article 2(1) are prohibited under the Convention on the Prohibition on Anti-Personnel Mines. This includes mines other than anti-personnel mines equipped with highly sensitive anti-handling devices that are detonated by the innocent act of a passer-by.

Claymore-type 'mines' are also prohibited unless used only in command-detonated mode. Unexploded ordnance, including cluster bomblets, are not covered by the Convention, nor are booby-traps *per se*, as long as they do not otherwise constitute anti-personnel mines. Despite the concerns of Ambassador Molander, the definitions contained in amended Protocol II and the Convention are broadly similar, although the use of an anti-personnel mine as a fusing mechanism for an anti-vehicle mine would not be permitted under the Convention. Finally, a clearer definition is required of what *in practical terms* constitute booby-traps and anti-vehicle mines.

---

721 As Colin King points out, 'the difference between mines and booby-traps has never been adequately defined and sometimes the distinction becomes unclear.' King, C., *Legislation and the Landmine*, Jane's Intelligence Review, Special Report No 16, UK, November 1997, p. 18. But see *supra* Chapter 1, p. 40.

722 Thus, for example, Canada's implementing legislation for the Convention uses the formula 'designed, altered or intended' in its definition of an anti-personnel mine. See for example *Landmine Monitor Report 1999*, p. 224, in which Mines Action Canada appears surprisingly critical of a formulation that appears to widen the ambit of the definition.

723 The ICBL shares the view that improvised explosive devices (IEDs) activated by a person are prohibited by the Convention on the Prohibition of Anti-Personnel Mines. *Landmine Monitor Report 1999*, p. 171. The ICBL gives as an example of use of these devices Sudan, and claims that both the government and the opposition Sudan People's Liberation Army (SPLA) 'have considerable knowledge in improvisation techniques'. They claim that IEDs 'may be assembled using cheap components such as "two wooden blades with a hinge, set over a detonator and explosive."' *Landmine Monitor Report 1999*, p. 171, citing Aleu, A.A., "Landmine Information Sudan", Operation Save Innocent Lives, Nairobi, 8 January 1999; see also *Landmine Monitor Report 2000*, pp. 182-3.

724 Somewhat surprisingly, the ICBL indicates that devices adapted to function as anti-personnel mines were not prohibited by the Convention on the Prohibition of Anti-Personnel Mines. See *Landmine Monitor Report 1999*, p. 667. In the view of the author, this is not correct, and that as the Australian delegate stated, these devices are indeed covered.

2.4.3. Prohibitions

Along with the definition of an anti-personnel mine, central to the Convention's potential effectiveness is the nature of core obligations and prohibitions; these are contained in Article 1 of the Convention. As will be seen, the apparent force and clarity of the article is somewhat diminished by other provisions in the Convention and by State interpretation, especially of Article 1(c).

Article 1 - General obligations

1. Each State Party undertakes never under any circumstances:

a) To use anti-personnel mines;

b) To develop, produce, otherwise acquire, stockpile, retain or transfer to anyone, directly or indirectly, anti-personnel mines;

c) To assist, encourage or induce, in any way, anyone to engage in any activity prohibited to a State Party under this Convention.

A. Prohibition on the Use of Anti-Personnel Mines

In order to stress the significance of the prohibition, the core obligation 'never under any circumstances to use anti-personnel mines', was separated from others in the Convention. The clarity of the undertaking recalled the language of the Chemical Weapons Convention.

At the 1997 Brussels Conference, a number of States had signalled their intentions to seek an exception to the general prohibitions 'in exceptional circumstances'. With a view to introducing exceptions to the core obligations, at the Oslo Diplomatic Conference it was proposed to change 'never' to 'not', but this was not accepted. In addition, Spain formally proposed an exception to the prohibition on use when supreme national interests were threatened.[725] It was not until the final day of the negotiations that this proposal was withdrawn and Spain declared its readiness to sign the Convention.[726]

Most discussion in Oslo, however, focused on the US 'demand' for a proposed geographical exception that would effectively allow the continued use of mines in South Korea. In presenting its draft text for inclusion as an exception in Article 3, the US claimed both that the situation was 'unique'[727] and that its acceptance by the other delegations was 'fundamental' to US support for the treaty.[728] The US was verbally supported by the Republic of Korea, which, attending the Diplomatic Conference as an observer, declared that mines were

---

725 It was reported that Spain had stockpiles of anti-personnel mines, which it intended to use in the event of an attack on Ceuta and Melilla, towns in Morocco under Spanish jurisdiction. See for instance *Landmine Monitor Report 1999*, p. 654.

726 See *ibid.*, p. 649.

727 For an enlightening, though controversial, discussion of the effectiveness of mines in defending South Korea, see for instance Gard, R., "The Military Utility of Anti-Personnel Mines", *To Walk Without Fear*, p. 150.

728 A journalist for the *Washington Post* reported that in Korea, 'military officials painted a scenario, with visual aids, of allied carnage that would occur if one million North Korean troops, unimpeded by mines, overran the Demilitarised Zone on the way to Seoul some 27 miles away. Priest, D., "Mine Decision Boosts Clinton-Military Relations'", *Washington Post*, 21 September 1997, p. A22. See also *infra* pp. 144-6.

needed to deter North Korean aggression[729] and to serve as a defensive barrier.[730] The South Korean representative claimed that mines laid near the Demilitarised Zone (DMZ) had not caused civilian casualties.[731]

Yet, of the full participants at the Oslo Diplomatic Conference, only Australia, Ecuador, Japan, Poland, Spain and Venezuela supported the US position, although Germany indicated that some kind of interim temporal exception could be envisaged. Summing up the debate, President Selebi declared that 'a significant, if not overwhelming number of States' would have considerable problems should exceptions be included in the treaty.

An authoritative commentary on the Chemical Weapons Convention points out that the wording 'emphasises the comprehensive and totally binding character of the prohibitions' giving the prohibitions 'a universal dimension, which means they extend to all activities of States Parties everywhere. The wording excludes any justification for such activity, whether for self-defence, in the case of attack with those weapons or in other exceptional circumstances.'[732]

Although the Convention does not define what constitutes 'use',[733] it is generally taken to mean the active laying of new anti-personnel mines. Thus, for example, the Canadian implementing legislation for the Ottawa Treaty, Bill C-22 of 1997, although not specifically defining use declares that 'no person shall (a) place an anti-personnel mine under, on or near the ground or other surface area with the intent to cause the explosion of the anti-personnel mine by the presence, proximity or contact of a person.'[734] Furthermore, upon ratification of the

---

[729] In an obvious piece of mischief-making, the North Korean Ambassador to the Russian Federation opposed the US calls for a geographical exemption for Korea declaring that: 'The position of the DPRK is that no region should be excluded from the zone of application of such a Convention.' "North Korea against Landmine Ban Exclusion", *Reuters*, Moscow, 14 September 1997.

[730] Not all military strategists were convinced by the overriding need for anti-personnel mines. In an editorial in *The Times* on 12 September 1997, it was pointed out that 'if any North-Korean assault were armour-led, it would be accompanied by mechanised mine-clearing devices against which anti-personnel mines are of no effect. And in more difficult terrain the North Koreans would use "human-wave" tactics in which mine casualties would simply be disregarded.' The editorial further mentioned that 'Western strategists are already looking at alternatives to mines. Spy satellites and drones could monitor frontiers, and air-blast bombs could be as deadly a deterrent to aggression.'

[731] A claim that subsequently seemed to be contradicted by a report from the South Korean Defence Ministry, which on 2 October 1997 declared that at least 35 people had been killed and 43 injured by landmines on the southern approaches to the DMZ in the preceding five years. Although the Defence Ministry did not disclose the number of civilians, the opposition legislator who had requested the report claimed that 29 of the victims were civilians, including some children. See "Border landmines kill 35 South Koreans: minister", *AFP*, 2 October 1997. The Landmine Monitor in 2000 then reported that the official records of the South Korean government indicated that there were 91 landmine victims in the DMZ between 1992 and 1999. *Landmine Monitor Report 2000*, p. 502; see also p. 503.

[732] Krutzsch, W. and Trapp, R., *A Commentary on the Chemical Weapons Convention, op. cit.*, pp. 12-13.

[733] Nor, for instance, does the 1993 Chemical Weapons Convention, though the time-delay feature of landmines makes the question more pertinent than with chemical weapons.

[734] Bill C-22, Clause 6(1).

Convention, Australia declared its understanding that, 'in relation to Article 1(a), the term "use" means the actual physical emplacement of anti-personnel mines and does not include receiving an indirect or incidental benefit from anti-personnel mines laid by another State or person.' This is a sensible interpretation of the term, although it may indirectly facilitate participation in joint operations with non-party States using anti-personnel mines. It means, therefore, that taking advantage of the emplacement of mines by another party would not seem to constitute use, nor even would the maintenance of fences around existing mines.[735]

There have been no confirmed instances of use by States party to the Convention, although a number of allegations have been made,[736] as well as against certain signatories. In accordance with Article 18 of the 1969 Vienna Convention on the Law of Treaties, signatory States are obliged to refrain from any actions that might frustrate the object and purpose of the treaty.[737] Given that the central objective of the Convention on the Prohibition of Anti-Personnel Mines is to prevent the use of anti-personnel mines,[738] new deployments of mines by treaty signatories clearly violate this obligation.[739] This point was stressed by a number of States at the First Meeting of States Parties to the Convention on the Prohibition of Anti-Personnel Mines, held in Maputo from 3-7 May 1999,[740] and the ICRC urged the meeting 'to send a clear message that anti-personnel mines are no longer an acceptable weapon of warfare and remind any signatory State using them that such use is contrary to the spirit and purpose of the [Convention].'[741]

735 Likewise, in adhering to amended Protocol II as amended, Canada declared its understanding that 'the maintenance of a minefield (...) would not be considered as a use of the mines contained therein.' This issue is of great relevance, for example, in the Demilitarised Zone between North and South Korea.

736 See in general *Landmine Monitor Report 2000*, pp. 4-5; see also p. 89, 90, 91, 113.

737 See for instance D'Amato, A., "Good Faith", *Encyclopaedia of International Law*, North Holland, Amsterdam, 1984, pp. 107-9.

738 The prohibition on the use of anti-personnel mines was and remains the centrepiece of the Convention, separated out from the other core obligations not to produce, transfer or stockpile.

739 In addition, the transfer of anti-personnel mines by a signatory to a non-party State to avoid the requirement to destroy stocks could also be considered unlawful. ICBL's Landmine Monitor declared that it had not found evidence of anti-personnel mine exports or imports by treaty signatories, although it noted that certain allegations in this sense had been made. *Landmine Monitor Report 1999*, p. 8. Indeed, the report had found no evidence of any 'significant shipment' of anti-personnel mines between States in 1998 or early 1999. *Ibid.*

740 See for instance Statement of Austria, delivered by Dr Benita Ferrero-Waldner, State Secretary for Foreign Affairs, to the First Meeting of States Parties, Maputo, 3 May 1999.

741 Statement by Eric Roethlisberger, Vice-President, International Committee of the Red Cross, to the First Meeting of States Parties of the Convention on the Prohibition of Anti-Personnel Mines. In Landmine Monitor, the ICBL also raised the concern of use of anti-personnel mines by ECOMOG, the regional peacekeeping force of the Economic Community of West African States (ECOWAS), which includes States that are signatories to the Convention on the Prohibition of Anti-Personnel Mines, declaring that the implications of this for a treaty signatory 'need to be explored'. *Landmine Monitor Report 1999*, p. 153.

Allegations of new use of anti-personnel mines by signatories have been made principally by the ICBL and some of its member organisations.[742] In the first of its flagship annual publications, the Landmine Monitor Report 1999 highlights 'apparent' use in 1998 by Angola,[743] Guinea-Bissau,[744] and Senegal[745] after these States had signed the treaty.[746]

The clearest violations have occurred in Angola.[747] Already at the end of 1998, four NGOs had published an open letter to the government and UNITA, calling upon both sides to stop using landmines, noting that in one province alone landmines had maimed or killed 66 people since June 1998.[748] In December of 1998, the European Union called upon the government, 'as a signatory of the Ottawa Convention,' and UNITA to cease mine laying activity immediately.[749] Reports of violations continued throughout 1999,[750] and in January 1999, South Africa suspended its assistance to Angolan demining

742 In welcoming the 40th ratification of the Convention, the International Campaign to Ban Landmines expressed 'grave concern about reports of continued mine laying in countries that had signed, but not yet ratified, the Convention. These countries included Angola, Cambodia, Senegal, and Sudan.' Ken Rutherford, Statement at Landmine Press Conference, UN, New York, 17 September 1998.

743 Angola has admitted new use of anti-personnel mines in an interview with Human Rights Watch in December 1999. The Speaker of the Angolan National Assembly (constitutionally the number two in the country) declared: 'It is war. We have the right to defend ourselves. Landmines are part of that right. Once Savimbi is defeated we will stop using landmines.' *Landmine Monitor Report 2000*, p. 129.

744 The allegations were denied, but Landmine Monitor 'stood by' them in its second annual report. See *Landmine Monitor Report 2000*, pp. 167, 168.

745 Most upset at the content of the Landmine Monitor report was Senegal, which declared itself astonished by the allegation made (and repeated in a speech to the First Meeting of States Parties). See *Statement of the International Campaign to Ban Landmines to the First Meeting of States Parties to the 1997 Mine Ban Treaty*, Maputo, Mozambique, p. 4. The allegations of use by Senegal concerned the conflict in Guinea-Bissau, allegations which Senegal 'categorically' rejected. *Statement made by the Senegalese Delegation following some allegations contained in the 1999 Report of ICBL (First Meeting of States Parties to the Convention on AP Landmines)*, Unofficial Translation, 5 May 1999.

746 *Landmine Monitor Report 1999*, pp. 3, 4, 74-5, 78-9, 153, 194, 195. In addition, the ICBL notes that allegations have been made against Rwanda, Uganda and Zimbabwe of use of anti-personnel mines in the Democratic Republic of Congo, though points out that all three governments have denied this. *Ibid.*, pp. 4, 72. In August 1998, police in Cambodia allegedly used mines in order to capture a murderer who had taken refuge in a forest. The man emerged from the forest, stepped on a mine, and the police shot him. *Ibid.*, p. 393.

747 For a summary of the situation see for instance "Angola: IRIN Focus on Angola's continued use of landmines", *IRIN*, 14 September 2000.

748 Jesuit Refugee Service, Mines Advisory Group, Medico International, and the Vietnam Veterans of America Foundation, "Landmines in Moxico Kill and maim 66 Persons since June: Open Letter to the Angolan Government and UNITA", Luena, November 1998, cited by *Landmine Monitor Report 1999*, p. 113.

749 EU, "Declaration by the Presidency on behalf of the European Union on Angola", Vienna, 28 December 1998, cited in *ibid.*, p. 114.

750 Reports asserted, for example, that both the Government and UNITA were laying 'hundreds, possibly thousands, of mines, in particular around Huambo, Cuito, Malange and Luena.' See for instance "Clearance work falters as Angolans lay more mines", *Guardian*, 17 July 1999; Editorial, *De-mining Debate*, South African Institute of International Affairs, Issue III, 29 November 1999.

operations because of the new laying of mines.[751] An Angolan delegation was 'apparently' present towards the end of the First Meeting of States Parties, but sought to avoid discussion of its use of anti-personnel mines.[752]

The year 2000 brought little respite for the war-weary population of the country.[753] In an article entitled "War-torn Angola in grip of fresh mine nightmare", a journalist for the British newspaper the *Sunday Telegraph* reported that: 'Both sides find landmines too useful to discard. UNITA deploys them to paralyse the road network and generate as much terror as possible in an attempt to destabilise the government.[754] The army uses mines to keep UNITA away from the main cities. Teams of Angolan demining engineers are on standby but have no budget. Oil earns the government at least £6.5 million a day,[755] but ministers probably see mine clearance as an aid to UNITA – even if the real beneficiaries would be their own civilians.'[756]

There were also unconfirmed reports of use by Angolan troops within Namibia[757] and Zambia.[758] According to a press release by the Namibian Campaign to Ban Landmines in April 2000: 'At least 13 separate mine incidents have occurred between December 1999 and March 2000 in areas that were virtually mine-free. All of these incidents are conveniently blamed on "UNITA bandits" by the Namibian authorities. However, circumstantial evidence suggests that Angolan troops, widely reported to be using mines in their fight against UNITA rebels inside Angola, may be using Namibian territory as a conduit and or storage for anti-personnel mines to be used against the rebels in the south-eastern parts of Angola. Namibian troops and Angolan forces have reportedly conducted joint military operations inside the Angolan territory in "hot pursuit" of suspected UNITA rebels there.'[759]

According to the UN's Integrated Regional Information Network (IRIN) for southern Africa, on 22 May 2000, five Angolans believed to belong to the country's armed forces appeared in court in Rundu, Namibia, reportedly charged with, *inter alia*, murder and attempted murder and possession of anti-personnel mines. It appears that the accused were members of Angolan Special Forces sent to combat UNITA operations in Namibia.[760]

---

751 See *Landmine Monitor Report 1999*, p. 114.

752 *Landmine Monitor Report 2000*, p. 129. In December 1999, at the first Annual Conference of States Parties to amended Protocol II of the 1980 CCW, the Angolan representative is reported to have admitted new use by his country of anti-personnel mine at the same time protesting that UNITA was using anti-personnel mines within the context of the ongoing conflict.

753 See for instance *Landmine Monitor Report 2000*, pp. 132-3.

754 Thus, it was reported that UNITA laid anti-personnel mines on paths that mothers had to use to bring their children for vaccination during a polio vaccination campaign. *Landmine Monitor Report 2000*, p. 133.

755 Equivalent to just under US$10 million.

756 Shukman, D., "War-torn Angola in grip of fresh mine 'nightmare'", *Sunday Telegraph*, 7 May 2000.

757 See generally *Landmine Monitor Report 2000*, p. 83.

758 See *ibid.*, pp. 191, 193.

759 Namibian Campaign to Ban Landmines, "Two maimed by landmine", *Press release*, Windhoek, Namibia, 4 April 2000.

760 "Namibia: Angolans face terror charges", *IRIN-SA*, Johannesburg, 24 May 2000.

In August 2000, in its second annual publication, ICBL's Landmine Monitor also alleged that Burundi, also a treaty signatory, had 'likely' laid anti-personnel mines on its border with Tanzania – seemingly to prevent an outflow of refugees and an inflow of Hutu rebel forces based in Tanzania.[761] It also claimed that Sudan was using anti-personnel mines in its ongoing conflict in the south of the country.[762]

B. The Prohibition on the Production of Anti-Personnel Mines

Although humanitarian law traditionally focuses on the use of a weapon,[763] given the proliferation of anti-personnel mines, the size of global stockpiles, and the ease of production, it was felt necessary to prohibit the production, stockpiling and transfer of the weapon as well as its use in order to prevent effectively the use of anti-personnel mines on the battlefield. The prohibition on the production of anti-personnel mines was immediate and unequivocal, with no exceptions whatsoever; accordingly, any production of anti-personnel mines or components intended for anti-personnel mines by a State party constitute a violation of the Convention. So far, there have been no reliable reports[764] of new or continued production of anti-personnel mines by a State party.[765]

C. The Prohibition on the Transfer of Anti-Personnel Mines

The prohibition on the transfer of anti-personnel mines was immediate; there is, however, a limited exception set out 'for the development of and training in mine detection, mine clearance, or mine destruction techniques'[766] and 'for the purpose of destruction.'[767] Although there is no maximum amount specified in the article, the amount 'shall not exceed the minimum number absolutely necessary for such purposes.'[768]

The definition of the term 'transfer' under the Convention has, however, proved troublesome. Article 2(4) provides that: '"Transfer" involves, in addition to the physical movement of anti-personnel mines into or from national territory, the transfer of title to and control over the mines, but does not involve the transfer of territory containing emplaced anti-personnel mines.' This definition is reproduced without change from the one contained in amended Protocol II.

The question arises, however, as to whether the requirements are cumulative or alternative. In other words, can physical movement of anti-personnel mines across a State constitute transfer or is it also necessary that the State in question receive title to the mines being moved? This is of particular concern in the case of US stockpiles, since if it were the former, any movement of mines from the stockpiles within a State Party would constitute a violation of the Convention.

---

761 *Landmine Monitor Report 2000*, pp. 152-3.

762 *Ibid.*, pp. 180, 184.

763 See *supra* Introduction, p. 2, footnote 5, and Chapter 1, pp. 66-8.

764 Though see US government allegations against Sudan. *Landmine Monitor Report 2000*, p. 182.

765 *Landmine Monitor Report 2000*, pp. 6-7.

766 Article 3(1).

767 Article 3(2).

768 Article 3(1). For a discussion of this provision in the context of stockpiles see *infra*, pp. 113-5.

Already, a number of governments have taken a narrow view of the definition, regarding the requirements as cumulative. Thus, for example, Norway apparently deems anti-personnel mines that are moved through or transferred into the country only as a Norwegian 'concern' if the transfer happens both physically and in terms of property rights.[769]

Yet, the general obligation under Article 1(b) is clear. Each State Party 'undertakes never under any circumstances' to transfer 'to anyone, directly or indirectly, anti-personnel mines.' The wording of the Article reflected that used in the Chemical Weapons Convention. In an authoritative commentary of the corresponding provision in that Convention, it was explained that, 'with regard to "*transfer*", the adjectives "directly or indirectly" are added to include also a transfer under participation of anyone else than the receiver. Since all obligations in this paragraph have a universal dimension, "transfer" requires an interpretation comprising different kinds of possible transfer: not only the transfer from a place under the jurisdiction of one State Party to a place under the jurisdiction of another State, but also the transfer of the ownership or possession of weapons inside or outside the territory of a State Party to anybody else, irrespective whether to a State, an organisation, an enterprise, a natural person, etc., is included in the prohibition.'[770]

The ICRC declared that 'permitting the transit of anti-personnel mines through the territory of a State Party would undermine the object and purpose of the [Convention] (...) and contradict its prohibition on assisting anyone in the stockpiling and use of anti-personnel mines. (...) The ICRC believes that permitting or assisting the transit of anti-personnel mines through the territory of a State Party, by provision of transport infrastructure or other means, constitutes assistance in the stockpiling of anti-personnel mines and is prohibited.'[771]

This view was shared[772] by France, Slovakia,[773] South Africa,[774] and also Denmark, which declared that: 'In accordance with Article 1 of the Ottawa Convention, Denmark cannot transfer to anyone, directly or indirectly, anti-personnel mines or allow anyone to do so on Danish territory. According to Article 3, physical movement (transfer) of anti-personnel mines are [*sic*] permitted if the purpose is the development of and training in mine detection, mine clearance, mine destruction techniques or if the purpose is destruction of anti-personnel mines.'[775] Likewise, Belgian, Spanish[776] and New Zealand[777]

---

769 *Landmine Monitor Report 1999*, p. 638.

770 Krutzsch, W. and Trapp, R., *A Commentary on the Chemical Weapons Convention*, *op. cit.*, pp. 13-14.

771 See *Landmine Monitor Report 1999*, pp. 1005-6.

772 See *Landmine Monitor Report 2000*, p. 14.

773 *Ibid.*, p. 713.

774 Report on Standing Committee of Experts Meeting on General Status and Operation of the Convention from Steve Goose, Human Rights Watch, contained in E-mail correspondence from Liz Bernstein, ICBL Co-ordinator, 20 January 2000.

775 Cited in *Landmine Monitor Report 1999*, p. 582.

776 Though, curiously, Spain does not appear to agree that transfer under the Convention includes transit. See *Landmine Monitor Report 2000*, p. 723.

777 *Landmine Monitor Report 2000*, pp. 417-8.

national legislation on anti-personnel mines prohibit the transit of another State's anti-personnel mine stockpiles across the national territory.[778]

On the other hand, Canada[779] and Germany agree with Norway that transit is permitted by the Convention.[780] The UK, for its part, declared that the issue of transit was 'being looked at carefully by legal advisers'.[781]

In the view of the author, although it is uncomfortable for a number of States, especially certain members of NATO, it seems clear that given the clarity of obligations set out in Article 1, any movement of foreign stockpiles of anti-personnel mines represents a violation of the Convention, except as provided by the terms of Article 3.

D. The Prohibition on the Stockpiling of Anti-Personnel Mines[782]

Article 3 of the Convention also provided two exceptions to the general prohibition on stockpiling of anti-personnel mines; the first, 'for the development of and training in mine detection, mine clearance, or mine destruction techniques'[783] and the second, to the time period for destruction laid down in Article 4.[784]

During the Oslo Diplomatic Conference, there was specific debate as to the maximum quantity of anti-personnel mines that could lawfully be retained 'for the development of and training in mine detection, mine clearance or mine destruction techniques', since the Convention merely stipulated that the amount 'shall not exceed the minimum number absolutely necessary for the above-mentioned purposes.'[785] A number of delegations, including Côte d'Ivoire, the Czech Republic, and Slovakia, with strong support from the ICBL,[786] were in favour of including a specific limit to the number of anti-personnel mines, but their efforts were not successful.

In Oslo, the ICBL was particularly concerned about the reported intention of Italy to retain a total of 100,000 mines for training purposes. Sayed Aqa, a deminer from Afghanistan, pointed out that in several years of mine clearance his organisation had used only a few hundred mines for training and he called on delegates to set a similar limit in the Convention. Although this position received only limited support in the hall, upon the adoption of the Convention, Germany led a number of States who declared that they would retain only a few

778 See Ayllón, L., "España insiste a EE. UU. para que destruya sus minas antipersonal", *ABC*, 2 November 1998, p. 23, cited by *ibid.*, p. 652; see also p. 546.

779 *Landmine Monitor Report 2000*, p. 241.

780 See *ibid.*, p. 14.

781 *Hansard*, 20 March 1998, col. 746, cited by *Landmine Monitor Report 1999*, p. 688.

782 Similar concerns arose with respect to the lawfulness under the Convention of US/NATO stockpiles held on the territory of States Parties. This issue is treated below during consideration of the obligation upon each State Party to destroy stockpiles under its jurisdiction or control within four years of entry into force of the Convention for that State.

783 Article 3(1).

784 Four years from entry into force of the Convention for each State Party.

785 Article 3(1).

786 See Goose, S.D., "The Ottawa Process and the 1997 Mine Ban Treaty", *op. cit.*, p. 282.

hundred or at most a few thousand mines for training purposes.[787] Although not tantamount to a formal understanding of the provision, its persuasive force was considerable and indeed Italy subsequently decided it would retain only 10,000 mines at most.[788]

In its formal report to the Depositary, Belgium reported that it had retained 6,240 M35 anti-personnel mines for training purposes and that it had transferred 11 further M35s to Netherlands for use by the Dutch armed forces in training.[789] Other States reported similar figures: Australia has decided to keep 10,000 anti-personnel mines,[790] Bosnia-Herzegovina 2,615,[791] Cambodia retains 'less than 1,000' anti-personnel mines for training purposes,[792] Canada 'a maximum of 2,000',[793] Croatia 17,500,[794] Denmark 4,962,[795] France 5,000,[796] Japan 15,000,[797] Luxembourg 1,500,[798] Mali 2,000,[799] the Netherlands 'around 5,000',[800] New Zealand O (nil),[801] Norway 'less than 100 units', although it had previously indicated 0 (nil),[802] Slovakia 'some 7,000',[803] South Africa a total of 18,000,[804] Spain 10,000,[805] Thailand, 15,600,[806] and the UK 'about 4,000'.[807]

---

787 See *ibid.*, footnote 16.

788 See Italian Chamber of Deputies, *Rules for the Ban of Anti-Personnel mines, Italian Law No 374 of 29 October 1997*, Occhetto, undated, p. 12. Following continuing pressure from the ICBL, this figure was reduced to 8,000 anti-personnel mines in the subsequent ratification bill for the Convention on the Prohibition of Anti-Personnel Mines. See *Landmine Monitor Report 1999*, pp. 728-9.

789 *Landmine Monitor Report 1999*, p. 546. See also Ministry of Foreign Affairs, Ministry of National Defence and General Department for Development Co-operation, *Belgium's Position Regarding Action Against Anti-Personnel Mines*, April 1999, Section I(2.2).

790 *Landmine Monitor Report 2000*, p. 375.

791 *Ibid.*, p. 590.

792 *Landmine Monitor Report 1999*, p. 392.

793 *Ibid.*, p. 233.

794 *Landmine Monitor Report 2000*, p. 609.

795 *Landmine Monitor Report 1999*, p. 583.

796 *Ibid.*, p. 600. See also "Plus de mines anti-personnel en France en 2001", *Reuters*, 25 February 1999, as corrected.

797 *Landmine Monitor Report 1999*, p. 363; *Landmine Monitor Report 2000*, p. 402. See also Munthit, K., "Japan PM vows Cambodia mine aid", *AP*, 12 January 2000.

798 *Landmine Monitor Report 1999*, p. 742.

799 Statement of Mali to the First Meeting of States Parties of the Ottawa Treaty, Maputo, 3-7 May 1999.

800 *Landmine Monitor Report 1999*, p. 751.

801 'No live anti-personnel mines are retained for operational or training purposes[.] (...) All mines being retained are either practice or inert and contain no explosives.' Lilley, Brig. C.W., Deputy Chief of General Staff, New Zealand Defence Force, Letter to Neil Mander, Convenor CALM, 23 February 1999, cited by *Landmine Monitor Report 1999*, p. 372. See further "Anti-Personnel Mines Retained for Training", *UN Doc. APLC/MSP.2/2000/INF.2* of 14 September 2000 submitted by New Zealand.

802 *Landmine Monitor Report 2000*, p. 701.

803 *Landmine Monitor Report 1999*, p. 647.

804 Five thousand 'high explosive' anti-personnel mines for research and development, and 13,000 for training in demining. *Landmine Monitor Report 1999*, p. 85. This number has subsequently been reduced. See *Landmine Monitor Report 2000*, p. 104.

805 *Landmine Monitor Report 1999*, p. 652.

806 *Landmine Monitor Report 2000*, p. 436.

807 *Landmine Monitor Report 1999*, p. 688; *Landmine Monitor Report 2000*, p. 749.

The ICBL continued to express concern as to the number of anti-personnel mines being retained by States Parties, especially where this exceeded 10,000. As a result, Croatia, Slovakia, and Thailand have reportedly offered to re-evaluate their training needs.[808] It further recommended that States Parties come to the May 2000 SCE working group meeting on the Convention with a statement about precisely how they have retained used mines thus far, and how they expect to use them in future;[809] the working group formally endorsed this call.[810] Ecuador has caused concern by declaring in its Article 7 report that it would keep more than 170,000 anti-personnel mines for training,[811] but at the May SCE meeting, it reported that this was 'a mistake' and promised that the true number would be forthcoming.[812]

E. Prohibition on Assisting, Encouraging or Inducing Others to Violate the Convention

The obligation upon States Parties in Article 1(1)(c) 'never under any circumstances (...) to assist, encourage or induce, in any way, anyone to engage in any activity prohibited to a State Party under this Convention' has proved the most controversial of all the provisions of the Convention so far; it has potentially significant ramifications for interoperability in NATO as well as other military operations.[813] To the best knowledge of the author, there was no open discussion of the issue during or prior to the Oslo Diplomatic Conference, yet since the adoption of the Convention, the precise meaning of the undertaking contained in Article 1(1)(c) has been widely debated.[814]

Upon ratification of the Convention Canada declared that 'in the context of operations, exercises or other military activity sanctioned by the United Nations or otherwise conducted in accordance with international law, the mere participation by the Canadian Forces, or individual Canadians, in operations, exercises or other military activity conducted in combination with the armed forces of States not party to the Convention which engage in activity prohibited under the

808 *Landmine Monitor Report 2000*, p. 10.

809 See *ibid.*, p. 242 for details of information subsequently provided by Canada.

810 E-mail correspondence from Liz Bernstein, ICBL Co-ordinator, 12 May 2000.

811 *Landmine Monitor Report 2000*, p. 264.

812 See *ibid.*, p. 10.

813 The US retains anti-personnel mines and reserves the right to use them in situations of armed conflict, including in the context of NATO operations. Such was the case, for instance, in Kosovo, although in fact no landmines, anti-vehicle or anti-personnel, were used in the NATO operations. See for instance ICRC, *Explosive Remnants of War, Cluster Bombs and Landmines in Kosovo*, ICRC, Geneva, August 2000, p. 17. Writing to the Acting Co-ordinator of the US Campaign to Ban Landmines in 1998, President Clinton declared that: 'We will also continue to work with our allies to resolve questions that have arisen concerning the Ottawa Convention's impact on NATO military plans and interoperability. We are engaged in close consultations with our allies on the questions in search of mutually satisfactory solutions that are consistent with NATO's military requirements, and, for those who are signatories, consistent with the Convention's provisions.' Letter to Ms Marissa Vitagliano, Co-ordinator of the US Campaign to Ban Landmines, 31 August 1998.

814 Thus, as Belgium rightly points out, there is no definition in the Convention of what constitutes 'assistance' under Article 1. See *Landmine Monitor Report 2000*, p. 580.

Convention would not, by itself, be considered to be assistance, encouragement or inducement in accordance with the meaning of those terms in article 1, paragraph 1 (c).' Similar declarations were subsequently made on ratification by Australia,[815] the Czech Republic and the UK;[816] it is alleged that Spain wished to make a similar declaration, but seemingly backed down in the face of public pressure.[817]

The formulation was reproduced from the Chemical Weapons Convention;[818] a commentary on the corresponding provision stated that it 'prohibits any action which contributes to prohibited activities.'[819] More specifically, assistance 'can be given by material or intellectual support (...) but also financial resources, technological-scientific know-how or provision of specialised personnel, military instructors, etc. to anybody who is resolved to commit such prohibited activity or by support in the concealment of such activities.'[820] The prohibition on 'encouraging or inducing' means 'contributing to the emergence of resolve of anybody to commit a prohibited activity by instigating, promising assistance, etc.'[821]

According to Austrian diplomats involved in drafting the original text of the Convention on the Prohibition of Anti-Personnel Mines, the provision 'obliges a State Party to omit any active support of third parties, whether other states or private persons, while those third parties are engaged in prohibited activities.'[822] Thus, Canada and the Netherlands are both reported as having declared that they could participate in joint operations in which anti-personnel mines were used,

---

815 'It is the understanding of the Australia that, in the context of operations, exercises or other military activity authorised by the United Nations or otherwise conducted in accordance with international law, the participation by the Australian Defence Force, or individual Australian citizens or residents, in such operations, exercises or other military activity, conducted in combination with the armed forces of States not party to the Convention which engage in activity prohibited under that Convention would not, by itself, be considered to be in violation of the Convention.'

816 'It is the understanding of the Government of the United Kingdom that the mere participation in the planning or execution of operations, exercises or other military activity by the United Kingdom's Armed Forces, or individual United Kingdom nationals, conducted in combination with the armed forces of States not party to the [said Convention], which engage in activity prohibited under that Convention, is not, by itself, assistance, encouragement or inducement for the purposes of Article 1, paragraph (c) of the Convention.'

817 See letter from Raul Romeva included in "News from Afghan and Spanish campaigns", E-mail correspondence from Liz Bernstein, ICBL Co-ordinator, 7 October 1998.

818 See Goose, S.D., "The Ottawa Process and the 1997 Mine Ban Treaty", *op. cit.*, p. 280. He asserts that the provision would prohibit, for example, the export of components for use in anti-personnel mines, and notes that the ICBL also believes that it prohibits the stockpiling of US anti-personnel mines in States Parties or the transit of US aircraft and ships carrying anti-personnel mines through States Parties. *Ibid.*, footnote 13.

819 Krutzsch, W. and Trapp, R., *A Commentary on the Chemical Weapons Convention*, *op. cit.*, p. 15.

820 *Ibid.*

821 *Ibid.*, p. 17. Krutzsch and Trapp report that similar provisions are to be found in other arms control and disarmament agreements, such as the Biological Weapons Convention and the Nuclear Non-Proliferation Treaty.

822 However, as justification for this assertion they cite Canada's declaration. Hajnoczi, T. *et al.*, "The Ban Treaty", *op. cit.*, p. 299.

but could not take part in planning for the use of mines, and if ordered to use mines, would not do so.[823]

According to one of the leading Canadian diplomats involved in the negotiation of the treaty: 'Canada's "understanding" was carefully researched and worded in an attempt to clarify a situation which is a reality for Canada – that as a member of a military alliance such as NATO, or as an active participant in UN-sanctioned operations, we may find ourselves engaging in military operations with an ally that is not signatory to the Convention. In short, we were simply attempting to indicate our perceptions of our obligations under the Convention under a set of specific circumstances. In this case our perception is that "the mere participation by the Canadian Forces, or individual Canadians" in such coalition operations would not be considered to be efforts to "assist, encourage or induce" others to engage in activities prohibited by the Convention. We believe that this is a realistic "perception of our obligations", which does not in any way undermine the core obligations of the Convention.'[824]

The author believes that the respective declarations made by Australia, Canada, the Czech Republic, and the UK[825] would appear to be lawful according to the terms of the Convention since, firstly, the provision in Article 1(2) does not include the word 'permit', which would certainly have covered participation in a joint enterprise, and, secondly, 'mere participation' or 'participation (...) by itself' is not an act that *per se* ostensibly contributes to the commission of prohibited activities. No State has so far objected to the declarations and the ICBL claims that the ICRC has no formal position on the legality of joint operations. Even the ICBL itself hedges its opinion on the issue declaring: 'At worst, the understanding could be interpreted to constitute a reservation to the treaty, and reservations are prohibited under Article 19. At best, the understanding goes against the spirit of a treaty aimed at an end to all possession and use of anti-personnel mines.'[826]

Of greater concern, however, is the declaration by Australia, of its understanding of the definition of the terms 'assist, encourage or induce':

> *'In Article 1(c) Australia will interpret the word "assist" to mean the actual and direct physical participation in any activity prohibited by the Convention but does not include permissible indirect support such as the provision of security for the personnel of a State not party to the Convention engaging in such activities, "encourage" to mean the actual request for the commission of any activity prohibited by the Convention, and "induce" to mean the active engagement in the offering of threats or incentives to obtain the commission of any activity prohibited by the Convention.'*

---

823 E-mail correspondence from Liz Bernstein, ICBL Co-ordinator, 12 May 2000.

824 E-mail, correspondence from Bob Lawson, Canadian Department of Foreign Affairs and International Trade, 15 March 1999, cited by *Landmine Monitor Report 1999*, p. 222.

825 In May 2000, the UK acknowledged that it had participated in 15 joint operations involving the use of anti-personnel mines over the previous three years, primarily in the Balkans, while stressing that in no case were UK forces responsible for their use. *Landmine Monitor Report 2000*, pp. 12, 745-6.

826 *Landmine Monitor Report 1999*, p. 222.

Sinclair notes that there 'are few topics in international law which have given rise to such extensive doctrinal dispute as the topic of treaty interpretation.'[827] Even the aim and goal of treaty interpretation are the subject of disagreement among publicists.[828] Article 31(1) of the Convention on the Law of Treaties provides that a treaty 'shall be interpreted in good faith in accordance with the ordinary meaning to be given to the terms of the treaty in their context and in the light of its object and purpose.'

According to Sinclair, the principle of good faith underlies the most fundamental of all norms – namely, the rule *pacta sunt servanda*.[829] He therefore concludes that if 'good faith' is required of the parties in relation to the observance of treaties, logic demands that 'good faith' be applied to the interpretation of treaties.[830] The second basic rule of interpretation is that of the ordinary meaning to be given to the terms of the treaty.[831] This meaning should, in principle, be the one that would be attributed to it at the time of the conclusion of the treaty.[832] In the present context, the terms assist,[833] induce[834] and encourage[835] have a clear definition, and, as already noted, have already been used with the same objectives in significant international disarmament treaties.

In the view of the author, the Australian interpretation of Article 1(c) is one restricting the effect of the Convention and thereby tantamount to a reservation (which is itself prohibited by Article 19 of the Convention).[836] According to the terms of the Australian declaration, an Australian soldier could lawfully participate in a joint planning meeting discussing the possible use of anti-personnel mines and muse aloud how great it would be if someone could plant some anti-personnel mines on a particular road and escape prosecution if a US soldier were subsequently to lay mines thereon. In one reading of the Australian understanding, an Australian soldier could also guard a convoy of anti-personnel mines being taken out for deployment.[837] Both of these actions clearly contribute actively to the commission of prohibited activities.[838]

---

827 Sinclair, Sir I., *The Vienna Convention on the Law of Treaties*, *op. cit.*, p. 114.

828 *Ibid.*

829 See also Cheng, B., *General Principles of Law as applied by International Courts and Tribunals*, Grotius Publications Limited, Cambridge, 1987, pp. 112-9.

830 Sinclair, Sir I., *The Vienna Convention on the Law of Treaties*, *op. cit.*, p. 119.

831 *Ibid.*, p. 121.

832 *Ibid.*, p. 124.

833 Defined by the 1993 New Shorter Oxford English Dictionary as 'to help' (someone to do something).

834 Likewise defined as 'to lead, persuade, influence'.

835 Likewise defined as to 'urge, incite, recommend or advise'.

836 See *infra*, pp. 158-60.

837 The Canadian military, for example, appears to make a distinction between 'normal assistance' provided to the armed forces 'as a whole' of a State Party that engages in activities prohibited by the Convention on the Prohibition of Anti-Personnel Mines (which could include the provision of fuel and security) and 'active assistance' in a prohibited activity. See Statutes of Canada, Chapter 33, An Act to implement the Convention on the Prohibition of the Use, Stockpiling, Production and Transfer of Anti-Personnel Mines and on their Destruction, Bill C-22, Assented to on 27 November 1997, Section 6(3)(d) and Fredenburg, Maj. P.W., "The Banning of the Antipersonnel Landmines", *Canadian Defense Quarterly*, Winter 1997, p. 9, footnote, cited by *Landmine Monitor Report 1999*, pp. 222-4.

838 In this regard, see for instance *Landmine Monitor Report 2000*, p. 418.

According to Article 31(3)(b) of the Convention on the Law of Treaties, also to be taken into account in treaty interpretation is 'any subsequent practice in the application of the treaty which establishes the agreement of the parties regarding its interpretation'.[839] In January 2000, the ICBL called upon States Parties to come to a common understanding as to what acts are and are not permitted under Article 1(c), in particular the definition of the term 'assist' as regards both the use of anti-personnel mines by non-signatories in joint operations with States Parties, and the stockpiling and transit of foreign anti-personnel mines.[840]

Although, as already noted, the US reserved the *right* to use anti-personnel mines in the NATO operations in Kosovo, they did not actually exercise this right. In the author's view, anti-personnel mines are unlikely to be used in the future by NATO forces. US military planners are well aware that the use of anti-personnel mines in such an operation, resulting in civilian deaths might well spell the immediate end of anti-personnel mines for US forces.[841] Moreover, with its gaze firmly fixed across the Atlantic, France has declared that it will 'refuse to agree to rules of engagement in any military operation calling for the use of anti-personnel mines.'[842]

2.4.4. Implementation of the Convention

A. The Destruction of Stockpiles

The Convention requires each State Party to 'destroy or ensure the destruction of all stockpiled anti-personnel mines it owns or possesses, or that are under its jurisdiction or control, as soon as possible but not later than four years after the entry into force of this Convention for that State Party.'[843]

As already noted, the time-frame set for the destruction of stockpiles in the original Austrian draft text had been one year from entry into force of the treaty

---

839 Though again note the caution by Sinclair that the 'value and significance of subsequent practice will naturally depend on the extent to which it is concordant, common and consistent[.] (...) A practice is a sequence of facts or acts and cannot in general be established by one isolated fact or act or even by several individual applications.' Sinclair, Sir I., *The Vienna Convention on the Law of Treaties*, *op. cit.*, p. 137.

840 *Landmine Monitor Report 2000*, pp. 13-14.

841 Similarly, the number of civilian casualties during and after the conflict in Kosovo that resulted from the use of cluster bombs may well be the spur to new international humanitarian law governing these weapons in 2001 or thereafter.

842 In June 1998, at the time of the vote on ratification of the Convention on the Prohibition of Anti-Personnel Mines by the French Parliament, the Minister of Defence declared: 'This law authorising ratification of the Mine Ban Treaty will make France the first permanent member of the UN Security Council to adhere to these standards. It indicates out determined willingness to arrive at a total and universal ban on anti-personnel mines. This same determination to see a total mine ban recently led France to declare before the Atlantic alliance that it would unreservedly enforce the Ottawa Treaty. France will prohibit the planned or actual use of anti-personnel mines in any military operation whatsoever by its military personnel. Furthermore, France will refuse to agree to rules of engagement in any military operations calling for the use of anti-personnel mines.' Speech by French Minister of Defence, Unabridged report of Parliamentary sessions of 25 June 1998, Official Journal of the French Republic, pp. 5402, 5403, cited by *Landmine Monitor Report 1999*, p. 587.

843 Article 4. See also Article 1(2).

for each State Party. Following comments by a number of States that this period was too short, the third draft text had extended the deadline to a more realistic three years. At the Diplomatic Conference, some States, especially from Latin America, called for the limit to be increased to five years.[844] To accommodate their concerns, the Conference settled on a deadline of four years from entry into force of the treaty for each State party.[845]

According to Austrian diplomats involved in drafting the Convention, although the terms 'jurisdiction' and 'control' have been used in other treaties, they have never been defined.[846] They assert, however, that there is an accepted understanding of them. However, given the decision by Australia to make a declaration upon ratification as to their meaning, this assertion must be open to question. According to Australia, the phrase *jurisdiction or control* 'is intended to mean within the sovereign territory of a State Party or over which it exercises legal responsibility by virtue of a United Nations mandate or arrangement with another State and the ownership or physical possession of anti-personnel mines, but does not include the temporary occupation of, or presence on, foreign territory where anti-personnel mines have been laid by other States or persons.'[847]

In the context of the Convention on the Prohibition of Anti-Personnel Mines, there are two specific issues to consider. The first is where a State has jurisdiction over its territory but is not in control of that area because of the existence and activities of an armed opposition group. Such is the situation, for example, in Georgia with respect to the breakaway Abkhaz republic, and this has been one of the key reasons advanced for Georgia's decision not to sign the treaty.

The other bone of contention is with respect to stockpiles of US mines held in NATO and other countries that have adhered to the Convention. Human Rights Watch obtained a confidential US State Department memorandum dated 6 February 1998 that contained an assessment of consultations with five of these States – Germany, Italy, Norway, Spain and the UK.[848] According to this memorandum: 'The talks were tough, on both sides[.] (...) In varying degrees – and with the exception of the Germans – our allies were insistent that they could not allow our mixed munitions to remain indefinitely, as this would put them in violation of the Convention[.] (...) Germany has stated that our anti-personnel mines can remain indefinitely.'[849] In August 2000, Landmine Monitor claimed

[844] Even five years would probably not be sufficient for certain States, notably China and the Russian Federation, which possess enormous stockpiles according to Landmine Monitor. (See for instance *Landmine Monitor Report 2000*, pp. 8-9.) A longer period might have been more in the medium-term interests of the Convention.

[845] See for instance Goose, S.D., "The Ottawa Process and the 1997 Mine Ban Treaty", *op. cit.*, pp. 282-3.

[846] Hajnoczi, T. *et al.*, "The Ban Treaty", *op. cit.*, pp. 299-300. The authors cite the examples of the Biological Weapons Convention, the Chemical Weapons Convention, amended Protocol II to the CCW, and the Comprehensive Nuclear Test Ban Treaty.

[847] This declaration applies also to the use of the phrase in Article 7(1)(b) and (c) relating to reporting obligations.

[848] *Ibid.*

[849] Department of State/PM memorandum, APL Consultations with NATO Basing Countries, 6 February 1998, cited by *ibid.*

that the US still had stockpiles of anti-personnel mines on the territory of at least five State Parties to the Convention: Germany,[850] Japan,[851] Norway, Qatar,[852] and the UK.[853] In addition, the US has stored anti-personnel mines in Greece, a signatory to the Convention, Kuwait, Saudi Arabia, the Republic of Korea, and Turkey.[854] Landmine Monitor further alleged that the US was planning to move stocks to Bahrain[855] and Oman.[856]

Germany argues that, according to the terms of the Status of Forces Agreement in force, weapons belonging to foreign forces stationed in Germany are not covered by German law and control.[857] Thus, in its national mine legislation, Germany provided the following interpretation of the obligation to destroy stockpiles of anti-personnel mines under the jurisdiction or control of a State party to the Convention on the Prohibition of Anti-Personnel Mines. 'Stocks from foreign armed forces do not come under the definition of Article 4 if they are not under (...) [the] authority and control of a State Party.'[858]

Spain, on the other hand, told the US to withdraw its stocks; the deadline for completion was fixed at 1 July 1999.[859] In Italy, national legislation already in force seemingly required that all NATO anti-personnel mines should have been handed over to specially-designated sites by 14 June 1998.[860] However, Article 6 of the bill for the ratification of the Convention specified that: 'The stocks of anti-personnel mines kept by the North Atlantic Treaty Organization (NATO) armed forces and located in the national territory at the time of the entry into force of the present bill, will remain under the control of pertaining commands until the term fixed for their destruction by Article 5 of Law No. 374 of 29 October 1997. If need be, these authorities can transfer the mines to any other suitable place for their custody.'[861] Italy reported, however, that all US stocks had been removed from its territory.[862]

850 According to Human Rights Watch, the US has more than 112,000 anti-personnel mines stored in Germany. *Landmine Monitor Report 2000*, p. 648.

851 *Landmine Monitor Report 2000*, p. 404.

852 *Ibid.*, p. 901.

853 *Ibid.*, p. 14. The UK, though, argued that the anti-personnel mines were not actually on the island but on a US warship anchored off Diego Garcia enjoying State immunity – and therefore outside the UK's jurisdiction and control. *Ibid.*, p. 753.

854 *Ibid.*, p. 341. See also "Group says at least 250 million landmines are stockpiled", *AP*, Geneva, 9 December 1999.

855 *Landmine Monitor Report 2000*, p. 918.

856 *Ibid.*, p. 342.

857 'Wie alle andern Waffen unterliegen auch die US Landminen aufgrund obiger Bestimmungen nicht det Kontrolle des Bundesrepublik Deutschland', Statement by the Federal Ministry of Defence in Bonn, 2 December 1997, cited by *Landmine Monitor Report 1999*, p. 621.

858 Bundesrat, Drucksache 34/98, Gesetzentwurf der Bundesregierung of 16 January 1998, <http://www.bundestag.de>, p. 28, cited in Landmine Monitor Report 1999, pp. 608-9; see also *Landmine Monitor Report 2000*, p. 649.

859 See *Landmine Monitor Report 1999*, pp. 653-4; *Landmine Monitor Report 2000*, p. 342.

860 *Landmine Monitor Report 1999*, p. 729.

861 *Ibid.*

862 *Landmine Monitor Report 2000*, p. 671.

Following intense US pressure,[863] in a letter to US Secretary of State Madeleine Albright, the Norwegian Foreign Minister declared that the US could keep its NATO mines in Norway, which were formally under Norwegian jurisdiction, until 2003 and that Norway's report on its stockpiles to the depositary under Article 7 would not include any reference to the number of mines held on behalf of NATO.[864]

Regarding the stockpiles of US anti-personnel mines in Japan, a representative of the Japanese Ministry of Foreign Affairs declared that: 'Under the treaty, the obligation as the state party is to undertake measures within the framework of its jurisdictional authority to cease or deter activities prohibited under the treaty[;] (...) thus it continues to be feasible for the US forces to retain any antipersonnel landmines withheld and stockpiled in the US bases in Japan[.] (...) [O]n the other hand, apart from treaty obligations, the policy of Japan is to terminate the use of landmines for defence purposes, and therefore, the government requested the US not to use, develop or produce landmines within Japanese territory.'[865]

At the First Meeting of State Parties, held in Maputo, Mozambique, from 3-7 May 1999, an informal discussion paper on stockpile destruction was circulated, which included brief consideration of the different means of destroying stockpiles. These were classified into three categories: detonation (the method used by Austria, South Africa and Switzerland, for example); disassembly, with partial recycling of components for industrial use (as Germany had done with its stock of anti-personnel mines) or what was termed new innovation/technology, the example given of Plasma Energy Pyrolysis.[866] It was noted that since these means of destruction involved case-specific considerations, such as cost analysis, impact assessment on the environment prior to and after destruction, the existence of industrial capacity, and the possibility of co-operation between the military and the private sector, there was no uniform approach that could be

[863] The US asked NATO nations to allow stockpiling of anti-personnel mines until 2003 and mixed systems including anti-personnel mines indefinitely. Myers, L., "US seeks to keep landmines", *Philadelphia Inquirer*, 1 March 1998; see also "NATO treads carefully on touchy landmines issue", *Reuters*, Brussels, 16 December 1997. The US even threatened to remove all its military equipment from the country if Norway insisted on the US removing all its mines. See for instance "New US European commander to visit Norway", *AFP*, Oslo, 5 December 1997.

[864] Letter from Norwegian Minister of Foreign Affairs, Knut Vollbaeck, to US Secretary of State, Madeleine Albright, 20 May 1998, cited in *Landmine Monitor Report 1999*, p. 639. See also *Landmine Monitor Report 2000*, p. 342. Thus, Norway's report to the Depositary submitted in accordance with Article 7 states: 'There are pre-stocked US mines on Norwegian territory. Due to previously concluded agreements, information on pre-stocked military material is not available for reporting.'

[865] Statement by Akio Suda, Deputy Director-General for Arms Control and Scientific Affairs, Foreign Policy Bureau, Ministry of Foreign Affairs, Commerce and Industry Committee, House of Representatives Proceedings Report No. 6, 25 September 1998, p. 2., cited in *Landmine Monitor Report 1999*, p. 360.

[866] "Stockpile Destruction: Discussion Points", undated, but May 1999. Plasma energy pyrolysis is a newly-developed technique for burning the explosive contained in a mine at a very high temperature without detonating the mine. The US is reported to be spending US$6.4 million in research and development funds to develop cryofracture methods – using extremely cold gas – for the destruction of anti-personnel mines. *Landmine Monitor Report 2000*, p. 344.

devised for all States Parties.[867] Particular concern arose as to the destruction of the so-called "Butterfly" PFM mine made by the Russian Federation because of its liquid explosive content. A two-day conference on the issue was held in Budapest at the beginning of February 2001.

Certainly, stockpile destruction was not cheap in absolute terms – Bulgaria, for instance, offered its competence in 'environmentally-friendly' disassembly to States Parties during their First Meeting in Maputo, at a cost ranging from US$2-4 per mine (depending on the model).[868] The Czech Republic talked of a cost of less than US$5 per mine for the destruction of its 230,000 anti-personnel mines.[869] Previously, a representative of the Austrian government had cited typical costs of stockpile destruction at about US$1 per mine,[870] with dismantling slightly more expensive at US$1.50.[871]

'To disarm', it has been said, 'is an irregular verb with no first person singular and only a future tense.'[872] Yet, a number of States Parties announced that they had completed the destruction of their anti-personnel mine stockpile well in advance of the timetable set down in the Convention.[873] Australia destroyed its stockpile of nearly 130,000 anti-personnel mines in five days in September 1999.[874] In November of the same year, Bosnia-Herzegovina completed destruction of its stockpiles of more than 450,000.[875] The following month, the ICBL's Landmine Monitor claimed that 17 signatories had already completed landmine destruction,[876] eradicating at least 10.3 million anti-personnel mines.[877] Belgium, for instance, destroyed 4,489 M35 anti-personnel mines, leaving only 6,240 such mines, which it declared it would keep for training in mine clearance.[878] In late December 1999, France announced it had

867 *Ibid.*

868 Republic of Bulgaria, *Technology for Safe and Ecologically clean Destruction of Stockpiled APLs through Disassembling*, Maputo, undated, but May 1999.

869 Statement by Mr Martin Palouš, Deputy Minister of Foreign Affairs and Head of the Delegation of the Czech Republic to the First Meeting of States Parties to the Ottawa Treaty, Maputo, 4 May 1999. The Deputy Minister announced that the process of destruction was expected to be completed by the year 2001.

870 Thus, in March 1998, a Pentagon report indicated that the total costs of destroying 3.3 million 'long-lived' mines would be US$3.3 million. Office of the Secretary of Defence, Annual Report to Congress on Use by Armed Forces of Antipersonnel Landmines, March 1998, p. iii, cited by *Landmine Monitor Report 1999*, p. 332.

871 Hajnoczi, T., Panel Presentation, "Toward a Ban: The Ottawa Treaty, An Overview" in ICBL, Regional Conference on Landmines, Budapest, Hungary, 26-28 March 1998, *ICBL Conference Report*, p. 51, cited by *Landmine Monitor Report 1999*, p. 352.

872 See for instance Editorial, *Financial Times*, 27 January 2000.

873 By May 2000, 21 States Parties had reportedly completed destruction of stocks, totalling some 10 million anti-personnel mines. *Landmine Monitor Report 2000*, p. 9.

874 *Ibid.*, pp. 372, 375.

875 *Ibid.*, p. 586.

876 Australia, Austria, Belgium, Canada, El Salvador, Germany, Guatemala, Hungary, Luxembourg, Mali, Namibia, New Zealand, Norway, the Philippines, South Africa, Switzerland, and the UK. See also "Group says at least 250 million landmines are stockpiled", *AP*, Geneva, 9 December 1999.

877 Landmine Monitor, "New Study reveals 250 million stockpiled landmines in 105 countries, 17 million destroyed to date", *Press release*, Geneva, 9 December 1999.

878 Report by Belgium to the Depositary under Article 7 of the Convention.

completed the destruction of its anti-personnel mine stockpile of more than one million anti-personnel mines;[879] Denmark also completed its stockpile destruction.[880] Mali declared at the First Meeting of States Parties that in addition to its destruction of its anti-personnel mine stocks it had also destroyed several thousand anti-tank mines.[881] By early 2001, Bulgaria, Malaysia, Spain and Zimbabwe had announced the completion of the destruction of their stockpiles.

In October 1999, the UK reported that the Royal Air Force (RAF) had completed the destruction of its last HB876 anti-personnel mine,[882] representing the total destruction of British anti-personnel mine stocks (apart from those retained for training purposes).[883] The British Army had already completed the destruction of its two million or so anti-personnel mines by early 1999. In a symbolic gesture, George Robertson, the then UK Secretary of State for Defence, handed over deactivated mines to a number of British NGOs declaring that: 'No British soldier will ever again lay an anti-personnel mine.'[884]

Other States advanced progressively in their destruction programme.[885] On 17 January 2000, Japan held a 'kick-off' demonstration of the destruction of stockpiled anti-personnel mines at the Air Self-Defence Force Base, about 500km south-west of Tokyo, and announced plans to destroy the remaining stockpiles before the end of February 2003, in accordance with its obligations under the Convention.[886] On 10 May 2000, Jordan announced on television that it had implemented the 'third stage' of the Armed Forces' plan to destroy all anti-personnel mines within four years by destroying a further 8,000 of the weapons in addition to the 12,552 already destroyed.[887] In May 2000, however, a Jordanian officer indicated that all anti-personnel mine stocks (totalling some 90,000) would be destroyed even earlier – by the end of 2001.[888] Similarly, on 14 February 2000, Yemen began the destruction of 10,000 anti-personnel mines,[889] said to be one-fifth of the total stockpile.[890] At the end of February

---

879 See for instance "France destroys anti-personnel landmines", *AP*, Paris, 21 December 1999. These included stockpiles in Djibouti, French Guyana, Côte d'Ivoire, and New Caledonia. *Landmine Monitor Report 2000*, p. 639. Five thousand anti-personnel mines were to be retained for developing detection equipment. See also "France: All Anti-personnel mines To Be Destroyed By December", *AFP*, Paris, 23 September 1999.

880 *Landmine Monitor Report 2000*, p. 629.

881 Statement of Mali to the First Meeting of States Parties of the Ottawa Treaty, Maputo, 3-7 May 1999. It decided, however, to preserve intact its stock of anti-tank mines equipped with anti-handling devices.

882 See also *Landmine Monitor Report 2000*, p. 749.

883 See for instance "Britain completes destruction of anti-personnel landmines", *AP*, London, 19 October 1999.

884 "Army's landmine stocks destroyed", *Times*, 23 February 1999.

885 According to Landmine Monitor, at the end of 1999, 27 signatories were in the process of completely eliminating anti-personnel mine stocks, destroying more than three million to date. Landmine Monitor, "New Study reveals 250 million stockpiled landmines in 105 countries, 17 million destroyed to date", *Press release*, Geneva, 9 December 1999.

886 Bernstein, L., *ICBL Landmines Update No 1*, 2 May 2000.

887 Jordan Television Channel 1, the official television station of the Jordanian government, news item, 10 May 2000, FBIS translated text.

888 *Landmine Monitor Report 2000*, p. 896.

889 *Landmine Monitor Report 1999*, p. 267.

890 UNOPS, "Yemen Begins Landmine Destruction", *Press release*, 24 February 2000.

2001, NATO announced it would assist Moldova in the destruction of "some 12,000 anti-personnel mines and other potentially dangerous munitions and military supplies."[891]

B. Mine Clearance

Article 5(1) of the Convention requires each State Party to destroy or ensure the destruction of all anti-personnel mines in mined areas under its jurisdiction or control,[892] as soon as possible but not later than 10 years after the entry into force of the Convention for it. In addition, while mine clearance is ongoing, each State Party is obliged to make 'every effort' to identify all areas under its jurisdiction or control in which anti-personnel mines are known or suspected to be emplaced and to perimeter-mark, monitor and protect by fencing or other means these areas, to ensure the effective exclusion of civilians.[893]

Previous drafts of the treaty had proposed that a distinction be made between minefields and mined areas, the view being that clearance of the former was far easier than of the latter as detailed maps tended to exist of minefields that had been laid. In fact, it soon became clear that the distinction was untenable and the term mined areas, defined as 'an area which is dangerous due to the presence or suspected presence of mines', was the only one retained in the treaty. Developing a proposal by the ICRC, the duty to clear emplaced anti-personnel mines was subject to a specific deadline of 10 years but provision was made for heavily mined countries to seek additional extensions of periods from the Meeting of States Parties not exceeding 10 years at a time.[894]

With the situation in the Falkland Islands specifically in mind, the UK had unsuccessfully sought an exception for areas 'not of humanitarian priority'.[895] In 1998, the Government reported to Parliament that 14,000 Argentinian mines remained uncleared[896] and one British anti-personnel mine remained unaccounted for on the Islands.[897] In November 1999, the government claimed there

---

891 "Safe Destruction of Anti-personnel Landmines and Munitions in Moldova", *NATO Press Release*, 27 February 2001.

892 Thus, the ICBL stated that the question of who is responsible for clearance in the buffer zone on Cyprus between the Greek and Turkish parts of the island remained 'outstanding'. *Landmine Monitor Report 1999*, p. 707.

893 Article 5(2).

894 Article 5(3)-(6).

895 The UK proposed the possibility of seeking the grant of an exemption by the other States Parties from the requirement to clear emplaced mines if:

a) the anti-personnel mines were not laid by the State Party;
b) the minefield is outside inhabited areas;
c) the risk of death or injury in leaving the minefield undisturbed is outweighed by the risks of clearing it; and
d) the costs of destroying the mines would be wholly disproportionate to the benefit.

See also *Landmine Monitor Report 1999*, p. 674.

896 See for instance Adkin, M., *Goose Green*, Orion, UK, 1994, p. 359.

897 *Hansard*, 28 April 1998, cols. 64-65. See generally *Landmine Monitor Report 1999*, pp. 342-344, 697. Other reports suggested variously that between 13,000 and 40,000 mines remained to be cleared. See for instance "Britain and Argentina in talks on ridding Falklands of landmines", *AFP Internationale*, 31 July 1998. The US Government Humanitarian Demining Program estimates the quantity of uncleared mines at 25,000 to 30,000.

were 16,600 mines remaining on the Islands.[898] Argentina had offered to help clear the mines but the UK government initially refused, claiming that this would violate national sovereignty (even though it was by then an obligation under amended Protocol II to the 1980 CCW).[899] By mid-1998, however, discussions were ongoing between the UK and Argentina on co-operation in mine clearance on the Islands, and on 17 November 1998, Argentina's representative told the UN General Assembly that Argentina and the UK had 'signed a declaration through which they agreed to work together on the evaluation (...) and costs of the removal of anti-personnel mines in the Malvinas Islands' and that the governments hoped to arrive soon at a Memorandum of Understanding describing the way in which the evaluation would be carried out.[900]

Upon ratification of the Convention, Argentina lodged a declaration reaffirming 'its rights of sovereignty over the Malvinas, South Georgia and South Sandwich and the surrounding maritime areas which form an integral part of the territory.' It also declared that since the 'Malvinas' were under 'illegal occupation' by the UK, Argentina was 'effectively prevented from having access to the anti-personnel mines (...) in order to fulfil the obligations undertaken in the (...) Convention.'

Other European States were also obliged to undertake mine clearance by virtue of their adherence to the Convention. For example, following allegations in the press in March 1998, France was forced to admit that Solenzara Air Base in the south of the island of Corsica was still protected by anti-personnel mines.[901] Clearance was finally completed on 28 May 1998, with delays ascribed to problems caused by flooding.[902]

As is well known, humanitarian mine clearance[903] is difficult, expensive,[904] and not without risk.[905] It is widely agreed that current mine clearance techniques are extremely slow, the technology having barely advanced since the 1940s.[906]

898 *Landmine Monitor Report 2000*, p. 368.

899 See for instance Scott, C., "Britain caught in minefield by Argentina clearance offer", *Sunday Times*, 12 July 1998.

900 *Landmine Monitor Report 1999*, p. 344. See further *Landmine Monitor Report 2000*, pp. 370-1.

901 *Libération*, 4 March 1998, cited by *Landmine Monitor Report 1999*, p. 600.

902 *Landmine Monitor Report 1999*, p. 600.

903 Otherwise known as humanitarian demining. The term *humanitarian* is used to distinguish it from military mine clearance, otherwise known as minefield breaching. As the military accept casualties as a reality of life, and speed is of the essence in their operations, military mine clearance does not normally expect to achieve more than 60-75 per cent clearance of a given mined area. Often channels will be opened in minefields using mechanised flails, explosive hoses, aerial bombardment, or fuel-air explosives. Humanitarian mine clearance, on the other hand, aims to return land to the civilian population and therefore anything less than 100 per cent clearance is unacceptable, notwithstanding the UN minimum success rate required contractually, which in the past has been a controversial 99.6 per cent.

904 For a thoughtful discussion of the issues surrounding mine clearance see for instance Hubert, D., "The Challenges of Humanitarian Mine Clearance", in *To Walk Without Fear*, pp. 314-35.

905 Although there is no reason for casualties if the clearance operation is well organised and the deminers are well trained, equipped and supervised. In this regard, see *Landmine Monitor Report 2000*, pp. 120, 126.

906 The mine detector was reportedly developed in 1941 by a Polish signals officer, Lieutenant Jozef Stanislaw Kozacki, who had escaped to Britain through France the previous year. The War Office had requested the manufacture of such a device as a result of the need to move or relay

Most mine clearance is done manually in lanes, with one or more individuals[907] using a mine detector and/or a metal prodder to locate each mine,[908] before a charge is placed to detonate it.[909] Vegetation must be cleared with extreme caution, as tripwires will otherwise detonate surface-laid or above-ground mines.[910] Mechanical forms of clearance, such as ploughs, rollers or flails, are also used in a number of countries, with varying degrees of success.[911]

---

minefields laid to protect Britain's beaches – the original emplacement had been so poor that 'entirely new methods of clearance, laying and accurate recording had to be devised.' The detector Lt. Kozacki produced saw service throughout the remainder of the Second World War and the British Army was still using a later version of the same device up to 1995. *The History of Landmines*, 1998, pp. 54-5, 59.

907 A number of mine clearance organisations use specially trained dogs as mine detectors since dogs having an excellent sense of smell and can detect the explosive contained in a mine. Others claim that dogs lose concentration quickly and that in a mixed field of anti-tank/anti-personnel mines, the dog will rush headlong towards the anti-tank mines. There seems to be widespread agreement, however, that dogs are excellent at quality assurance once a minefield is reported to have been successfully cleared. For a brief discussion of the use of dogs in mine clearance see for instance *The History of Landmines*, pp. 87-8, 139-40.
Detection techniques continue to be the subject of research and development, including, somewhat surpisingly, the use of bees, pigs, and rats to find anti-personnel mines. See for instance Coryell, G., "US combs the world for deadly mines", *Tampa Tribune*, 19 March 2000; "Rats train as landmine detectors, researchers say", *Reuters*, Brussels, 30 December 1999. More promising appears to be other work, including research around quadrapole resonance (QR). According to a company press release, QR applies 'a radio-frequency magnetic-field pulse at a frequency specific to individual explosive compounds[.] (...) The current QR prototype system detects metal, RDX, TNT, and Composition B, and is thus able to detect the vast majority of all landmines deployed throughout the world. Future systems are expected to be able to detect Tetryl as well. QR has the ability to operate in almost all soil conditions including saturated soils, as well as through water.' See for instance Bigelow, B.V., "San Diego business detects landmines with sensor", *San Diego Tribune*, 29 February 2000; InVision Technologies, "InVision Technologies receives US$4 million in additional funding for its landmine detection programme", *Press release*, Newark, California, 1 March 2000.
Astonishing claims of effectiveness in locating mines were also made by the Texan organisation, Loch Harris, which tested its ELF (Eliminate Landmines Forever) mine detector in Croatia in February 2000. One of those involved in its development described the device as 'a portable X-ray fluorescent-based, remote sensing optical instrument designed to provide direct, real-time discrimination and mapping of unknown landmines from stand-off distances of up to 30 metres.' See "ELF's field efficiency surprises Loch/ChemTech scientists", *PRNewswire*, Karlovac, Croatia, 14 February 2000. But there were suggestions that payments to a Croatian scientist involved in the test may have clouded its independence. See "Loch Harris bribed Scientist for ELF test", e-mail sent out on the MGM network, 11 July 2000; see also "ICBL letter to Loch Harris re ELF", e-mail correspondence from Liz Bernstein, ICBL Co-ordinator, 15 March 2000.

908 Mine clearance will obviously also destroy or render harmless other items of unexploded ordnance that litter the battlefield, such as shells or bombs.

909 Although the destruction of at least anti-personnel mines is often carried out *in situ*, a number of mine clearance operatives prefer to collect certain mines and destroy them *en masse* at the end of the day. See for instance Hubert, D., "The Challenges of Humanitarian Mine Clearance", *op. cit.*, p. 316.

910 *E.g.*, those placed in trees.

911 The efficiency and effectiveness of mechanical mine clearance depend on the machine and the country context. Certainly, some of the heaviest mine clearance machines are not appropriate for a number of developing countries as bridges are not sufficiently strong to bear their weight. See for instance Hubert, D., "The Challenges of Humanitarian Mine Clearance", *op. cit.*, p. 329; *The History of Landmines*, pp. 140-1. Yet, mechanical mine clearance is an increasingly present component of the mine clearer's 'toolkit'.

Although mine clearance operations are relatively expensive,[912] once the start-up expenses of a clearance operation have been subsumed, costs diminish rapidly in relation to the amount of area cleared.[913] Obvious risks remain, however, particularly as a result of the development of technologies, such as anti-handling or anti-lift devices, designed to endanger the work of a mine clearer, though it is claimed that: 'Surprisingly, the danger appears to be greatest where mines are encountered only infrequently, increasing the probability of lapses in concentration.'[914]

As Croll points out: 'In the closing years of the second millennium man is capable of exploring space but the technology for clearing minefields remains frustratingly primitive. There is a striking difference between the ease with which mines can be laid and the difficulty and the time it takes to clear them.'[915] He speaks for many deminers in asserting that: 'Despite the tedium and hazards of manual clearance, it remains the most flexible and effective technique.'[916]

C. International Co-operation and Assistance

For many developing countries a provision on international co-operation and assistance was an essential *quid pro quo* for their support for the treaty. It also recognised the reality of the landmines problem whereby the vast majority of mine-affected States badly needed outside help if they were effectively to tackle the problem.

For donor governments, there were advantages too. They were able to use their financial leverage to ensure adherence to the Convention by promising to channel all or much of their funding to States that had adhered to the treaty.[917] Norway, for instance, has declared that 'as a general rule' it will 'provide support to mine-related activities primarily in countries that have signed and ratified the Convention.'[918] Likewise, Belgium has stated that assistance in mine clearance 'may in principle only be granted *where the country asking for aid is a signatory of the Convention on the prohibition of anti-personnel mines and is*

912 Especially in developing countries when costs are compared with other rural development programmes – few countries can afford to spend US$700 million on mine clearance, as did Kuwait following the Gulf War. See for instance *After the Guns Fall Silent*, p. 261. Even then, Kuwait was not totally cleared. See *Landmine Monitor Report 2000*, p. 939.

913 See for example Hubert, D., "The Challenges of Humanitarian Mine Clearance", *op. cit.*, p. 330.

914 *Ibid.*, p. 317. See also *Landmine Monitor Report 2000*, pp. 1075-7.

915 Hubert, D., "The Challenges of Humanitarian Mine Clearance", *op. cit.*, p. 141.

916 *The History of Landmines*, p. 140. Seen in this light, the phrase 'years not decades' applied by the ICBL and Canadian Government to the challenge of global mine clearance appears, to the author at least, unnecessarily optimistic. See for instance Chair's Summary, Years Not Decades: Agenda for Mine Action II, Mine Action Co-ordination Workshop, Ottawa, Canada, 23-24 March 1998; *Landmine Monitor Report 1999*, p. 20.

917 A concern noted by those not planning to adhere to the Convention in the near future. Thus, for example, Lebanon declared at the Brussels Conference in June 1997 that 'a non-signatory State should not be deprived of any assistance in support of demining and other mine-related actions.' *Landmine Monitor Report 1999*, p. 892.

918 Statement by Ms Hilde F. Johnson, Minister of International Development and Human Rights, Royal Ministry of Foreign Affairs, Norway, to the First Meeting of States Parties, Maputo, 3-7 May 1999, p. 2.

implementing the Convention.'[919] In addition, 'in support of the efforts of Germany to establish a strong verification system within the treaty, German policy reserves the right to stop support for mine clearance and survivor assistance if a State does not sign the ban treaty or violates its treaty obligations.'[920]

Britain's Department for International Development (DFID) declared to ICBL's Landmine Monitor that it 'does not support government programmes in countries that are unwilling to sign up to the Ottawa Convention and continue to use anti-personnel landmines; in these countries DFID support is limited to humanitarian mine clearance in designated areas to reduce the immediate threat of loss of life or injury, provided that the laying of new mines ('re-mining') is not taking place locally at the same time.'[921] This appeared to be the approach favoured by the ICBL, which declared in a press release that 'civilian victims of landmines should not be further victimised because of a government's use of mines or failure to join the treaty. In such cases, the ICBL favours continued funding of NGOs operating in mine-affected areas, but not the governments.'[922]

Unfortunately, amid complaints of lack of resources being attributed to mine clearance,[923] a major scandal was breaking in Cambodia.[924] Rumours had been circulating for some time that all was not well with the Cambodian Mine Action Center (CMAC), the country's national co-ordinating body for mine action, and one of the oldest in existence. International auditors confirmed reports of fraud, mismanagement, nepotism and cases of priority being given to clearance of sites owned by officials, military officers and former Khmer Rouge guerrillas.[925] Donors issued 32 demands that had to be met before they would continue to fund the government programme.[926]

In February 2000, further problems arose as Canada withdrew its mine clearance advisers from the field when it found that Cambodian demining site managers were designating some mined areas as cleared – even after no work had been done.[927] Yet, at the beginning of April 2000, Cambodian leader, Hun Sen, claiming that CMAC had reformed, called for a speeding-up of interna-

---

919 Ministry of Foreign Affairs, Ministry of National Defence and General Department for Development Co-operation, *Belgium's Position Regarding Action Against Anti-Personnel Mines*, April 1999, Section III(2). (Original emphasis)

920 *Landmine Monitor Report 1999*, p. 607.

921 *Ibid.*, Appendices, p. 958.

922 See for instance Norwegian People's Aid, "Humanitarian Mine Action", Landmine Monitor Fact Sheet prepared for the Meeting of the Standing Committee of Experts on Mine Clearance, Geneva, 13-15 September 1999. See also ICBL, "Landmines Campaign Condemns Recent Use of the Weapon", *Press Release*, Geneva, 13 September 1999.

923 See for instance *Landmine Monitor Report 1999*, pp. 18-20.

924 See generally *Landmine Monitor Report 2000*, pp. 391-2.

925 The scandal was discussed by a number of speakers as Cambodia passed national legislation prohibiting the possession, use and trafficking of anti-personnel landmines. See for instance "Cambodia Gets Tough New Law Anti-Landmine Law", *AFP Internationale*, 28 April 1999. For an interesting overview of some of the donor responsibility for the problems with CMAC see Kyne, P., "Donors fiddle while CMAC burns", *Phnom Penh Post*, 3-16 March 2000.

926 See for instance Sheridan, M., "Scandal Continues To Tarnish Cambodian Agency", *Times*, 22 August 1999; Faulder, D., "An International Minefield, A Scandal blows up under the demining agency", *Asiaweek*, 17 September 1999, cited on ICBL Website, <www.icbl.org>.

927 See Fontaine, C., "Land Mine Agency won't stop work", *AP*, Phnom Penh, 23 February 2000.

tional aid to remove mines left by three decades of war.[928] In August 2000, the new Director-General of CMAC, a former Deputy Commander-in-Chief of the Cambodian armed forces, claimed that the organisation had carried out 85 per cent of what the auditors and donors had asked of it.[929] In September 2000, the Cambodian government announced the creation of a new institution to oversee the work of CMAC; it was far from certain that this would reassure donors sufficiently.[930] Thus, in October 2000, 70 per cent of CMAC's staff had to be laid off because of lack of funds.[931]

During the negotiations at the Oslo Diplomatic Conference, there was considerable discussion of the importance of including specific reference to the need of mine victims for 'social and economic reintegration' as well as for care and rehabilitation. After a lot of toing and froing between governments and the ICBL agreement was finally secured on its inclusion. On 19 November 1997 some of the leading NGOs within ICBL addressed a letter to major donor governments calling for US$3 billion over 10 years for 'a significant expansion of the number and quality of prosthetic workshops, as well as new programmes offering psychological, social and economic support to victims, their families and their communities.'[932] In fact, only a limited number of organisations were actively involved in operational support to mine victims, most notably the ICRC[933] and the French NGO, Handicap International. Moreover, discussions in international fora of assistance to mine victims varied from the theoretical and structural to the legislative, but rarely seemed to encompass concrete action at field level.[934]

Despite (or perhaps as a result of) the huge funding that has been allocated for mine action,[935] a number of governments are currently considering the cost-

928 Munthit, K., "Cambodia seeks land mine funds", *AP*, Kompong Chhnang, Cambodia, 2 April 2000.

929 Richardson, M., "In Cambodia, Mine-Clearing Group's Future Is In Doubt", *International Herald Tribune*, 21 August 2000.

930 "Cambodia Creates New Authority to Clear Landmines", *Oana-Kyodo*, Phnom Penh, 14 September 2000.

931 "Cambodia mining agency cuts staff", *AP*, Phnom Penh, 17 October 2000.

932 See for instance White, J. and Rutherford, K., "The Role of the Landmine Survivors Network", *op. cit.*, pp. 116 and 117, footnote 1.

933 At the First Meeting of States Parties in Maputo, the ICRC reported that in 1998 it had fitted artificial limbs to 7,000 mine victims. Statement by Eric Roethlisberger, Vice-President, International Committee of the Red Cross, to the First Meeting of States Parties of the Convention on the Prohibition of Anti-Personnel Mines.

934 A variety of documents emanated directly or indirectly from the Ottawa Process, but many seemed either divorced from reality or superfluous to real needs. See for instance "Mine Victim Assistance, Proposed Strategic Framework for Planning Integrated Mine Victim Assistance Programmes", *Working paper related to the Informal Consultations on International co-operation and assistance in accordance with Article 6 of the Convention on Victim assistance, social and economic reintegration and mine awareness*, 6 May 1999 (revised version); International Campaign to Ban Landmines, Working Group on Victim Assistance, *Guidelines for the Care and Rehabilitation of Survivors*, undated; Republic of Mozambique, *Strategic Framework for Mine and Other Trauma Victims Assistance*, Draft Document circulated during the First Meeting of States Parties.

935 Mine action is said to comprise five complementary 'pillars' or 'core components': mine survey, marking and clearance; mine victim assistance; mine awareness; mine stockpile destruction and mine ban advocacy. See for instance UNMAS homepage, <http://www.un.org>.

benefit of the discipline, especially as far as mine clearance is concerned. In late 1999, the UN Development Fund (UNDP) contracted the Geneva International Centre for Humanitarian Demining (GICHD) to undertake a study of socio-economic approaches to mine action programmes.[936]

D. National Legislation

In accordance with Article 9 of the Convention on the Prohibition of Anti-Personnel Mines, each State Party is required to take 'all appropriate legal, administrative and other measures, including the imposition of penal sanctions, to prevent and suppress any activity prohibited to a State Party under this Convention undertaken by persons or on territory under its jurisdiction or control.'[937]

The first draft Austrian text had contained a 'grave breaches' provision,[938] but unfortunately this was removed in the second draft text following resistance at the Vienna Experts Meeting and within the core group of countries formed to push the Ottawa Process forward.[939] Despite efforts by the ICRC and others to strengthen the provisions by including a modified form of compulsory universal jurisdiction, the proposed language before delegates at the Oslo Diplomatic Conference was the same as amended Protocol II. At the International Expert Meeting on Possible Verification Measures to Ban Anti-Personnel Landmines held in Bonn in April 1997, the ICRC had circulated an informal draft article on national implementation measures. Central to this draft was the following proposed provision:

> *'Each State Party shall search for all persons on its territory or under its jurisdiction or control, being nationals of a State party to this Convention, alleged to have used, or to have ordered the use of, anti-personnel mines, in violation of this Convention, regardless of the place where such acts were committed, and shall either bring such persons before its own courts or hand such persons over for trial to another State Party.'*

Switzerland, supported orally by Belgium, Colombia, Ghana, Mexico and Venezuela, introduced a proposal to extend the duty to prosecute individuals alleged to have violated the treaty to a national of other State Parties even if the offence was committed outside the State under whose jurisdiction the individual

---

936 The Study was published in March 2001.

937 In its national implementing legislation, Norway included a specific exemption from penal sanctions for foreigners, primarily military personnel, whose own country has not ratified the treaty. According to ICBL, Norway bases this exception on the inclusion of the word*appropriate* in Article 9 of the Convention on the Prohibition of Anti-Personnel Mines, claiming that 'a possible prosecution of allies [*i.e.*, the US] in such a situation cannot be seen as appropriate.' *Landmine Monitor Report 1999*, p. 635.

938 See *supra* Chapter 1, p. 70, footnote 510.

939 Hajnoczi, T. *et al.*, "The Ban Treaty", *op. cit.*, p. 306.

fell.[940] As had occurred in negotiations within the framework of the 1980 CCW and its review, the disarmament background of many of the delegates led either to their outright rejection of the proposal or to their suspicion that new legal ground was being broken. By the time the ICRC intervened in the discussion to remind delegates that there was nothing new about compulsory extraterritorial jurisdiction for war crimes the fate of the Swiss proposal was already sealed.

For most States Parties, implementing legislation is necessary to give effect at national level to the obligations undertaken by States at international level.[941] According to the ICRC, the provisions of Article 9 will entail 'for most States' the adoption of criminal legislation.[942] Excepted would be States that had already implemented a prohibition on anti-personnel mines in national legislation that was at least as wide in its ambit as the Convention on the Prohibition of Anti-

---

940 In its comments on the third draft Austrian text, the ICRC had called for the following measures to be included in the treaty:

'(a) *national penal sanctions for persons who develop, use, produce, acquire, stockpile, retain or transfer anti-personnel mines or who assist in the commission of such acts in violation of the Convention;*

(b) *a requirement to try or extradite nationals of States Parties alleged to have used, or to have ordered the use of, anti-personnel mines, regardless of the place of the offence;*

(c) *a requirement for Parties to undertake other legal or administrative measures necessary to prevent and suppress violations; and*

(d) *a provision on dissemination of the provisions of the Convention and related national law and administrative measures, so that these provisions become known to the armed forces and to the general population.*'

ICRC, Comments on the Third Austrian Draft (13/5/97) of the Convention on the Prohibition of Anti-Personnel Mines, *Informal Working Paper for the Oslo Negotiations*, Geneva, September 1997. Sweden, in its comments on the third draft Austrian text, had also proposed that the use of anti-personnel mines be considered as a 'grave breach' of the Convention.

941 See for instance *Landmine Monitor Report 2000*, p. 16; Verification and Research Training Information Centre (VERTIC), "Landmines in International Law: Ratification and National Implementation", *Landmine Monitor Report 1999*, Appendices, pp. 1042-4. The ICRC also pointed out the likelihood of the need for 'other regulatory measures such as changes in military doctrine and procedures, the notification of organisations and corporations involved in anti-personnel mine production and sale and instructions to the relevant ministries to rescind export licences which may involve anti-personnel mines.' ICRC, *Implementing the Ottawa Treaty: National Legislation*, ICRC, Geneva, April 1999.

942 ICRC, *Implementing the Ottawa Treaty*, *op. cit.*

Personnel Mines.[943] According to Landmine Monitor, 20 governments had reported that having enacted implementing legislation.[944]

In the UK and most other Commonwealth countries, for example, the conclusion and ratification of treaties are within the prerogative of the Head of State (the Crown or its equivalent). But, under the so-called transformation doctrine, treaties only become part of domestic law if an enabling Act of Parliament has been passed.[945] Thus, Uganda declared that under national law the Convention was merely persuasive and not binding until domestic legislation had been passed.[946]

In other countries, such as the US and many European States, certain 'self-executing' treaties[947] (or certain provisions contained within such treaties) that are adhered to by the executive, bind the courts without the need for any further specific act of incorporation into domestic law.[948] The inclusion of an article on national implementation might suggest that the Convention is not to be considered as self-executing; more significant is the implicit requirement for penal sanctions. Thus, with respect to the equivalent provision in amended Protocol II (Article 14), the US introduced national penal legislation to give effect to its provisions in domestic law.

Qatar, however, informed Landmine Monitor that by virtue of its ratification of the Convention the provisions had become 'part and parcel of the national laws of the State of Qatar.'[949] Likewise, in Mexico, no implementing legislation

---

943 Thus, for example, Austrian national legislation prohibiting anti-personnel mines, which predated the adoption and entry into force of the Convention, served also as its implementing legislation for the Convention without the need for further legislative measures. So did Belgium, which was the first State in the world to declare *de jure* a complete ban on anti-personnel mines. Belgian response to the Landmine Monitor questionnaire, *Landmine Monitor Report 1999*, p. 533.
In contrast, Spain's "Law Banning Anti-personnel Landmines as well as those Arms with similar Effects", Law 33/1998, does not include any penal sanctions. In an annex to the Law, it was stated that sanctions would be developed in subsequent implementing legislation. *Landmine Monitor Report 1999*, pp. 648-9. Landmine Monitor further reported that in the Netherlands, domestic implementation legislation was being prepared and would be considered as soon as the instruments of ratification had been deposited at the UN. *Ibid.*, p. 748. This latter act took place on 12 April 1999.

944 Austria, Australia, Belgium, Cambodia, Canada, the Czech Republic, France, Germany, Guatemala, Hungary, Italy, Japan, Luxemburg, Monaco, New Zealand, Nicaragua, Norway, Spain, Switzerland, and the UK. *Landmine Monitor Report 2000*, p. 15.

945 *Ibid.*, pp. 1042-3.

946 *Ibid.*, p. 113.

947 See for instance Vázquez, C.M., "The Four Doctrines of Self-Executing Treaties", *American Journal of International Law*, Vol. 89, No. 4, October 1995, pp. 695-723; Bleckmann, A., "Self-Executing Treaty Provisions", *Encyclopaedia of International Law*, North Holland, Amsterdam, 1984, pp. 414-7.

948 For a discussion of the monist and dualist doctrines of international law see for instance Lauterpacht, H., *International Law, A Treatise*, 7th edn., Longman, Green and Co., London, 1948, pp. 34-44. See also *Landmine Monitor Report 1999*, p. 1043.

949 Letter of H.E. Saad Mohamed Al-Kobaisi, Qatari Ambassador, to Landmine Monitor, 9 September 1999.

was adopted because once the Convention was promulgated and published in the Official Federal Gazette,[950] it became part of domestic law.[951]

Article 9 does not explicitly assume extraterritorial jurisdiction, though it is open for States Parties to implement such a provision in their national legislation, should they so wish.[952] Thus, according to the legislation adopted by Germany, extraterritorial offences 'count as offences irrespective of the national law of the scene of the crime (...) if the perpetrator is German.'[953]

In the UK, the ratification process was held up, ostensibly because of lack of parliamentary time,[954] but more probably because of concerns within the Ministry of Defence about the risk of British soldiers involved in multinational military operations being subject to allegations of, or even prosecutions for, war crimes.[955] Thus, for example, in an editorial in The *Times*, it was claimed that '[t]he partial nature of the Ottawa accord makes it imperative to safeguard British troops from the most obvious hazards arising from its inconsistencies.'[956] Accordingly, when faced with mounting public pressure to ratify the treaty before the anniversary of the death of the Princess of Wales, a bill was hastily tabled that provided for a maximum 14-year prison sentence for certain offences, yet included a 'shield against unreasonable prosecution' to British soldiers serving alongside forces from the United States.[957]

Particularly controversial was Clause 5 of the Bill, which provided a defence against prosecution if the accused were able to prove that:

'*(a) the conduct was in the course of, or for the purposes of, a military operation or the planning of a military operation;*

(b) the conduct was not the laying of an anti-personnel mine;

(c) at the time of the conduct he believed, on reasonable grounds, that the operation was or would be an operation to which this section applies; and

(d) he did not suspect, and had no grounds for suspecting, that the conduct related to the laying of anti-personnel mines in contravention of the Ottawa Convention.'[958]

---

950 This occurred on 21 August 1998. *Landmine Monitor Report 1999*, p. 261.

951 *Ibid.*

952 Hajnoczi, T. *et al.*, "The Ban Treaty", *op. cit.*, p. 306. See also Goose, S.D., "The Ottawa Process and the 1997 Mine Ban Treaty", *op. cit.*, p. 286.

953 *Bundesgesetzblatt Teil I*, No. 43, 9 July 1998, p. 1778, cited in *Landmine Monitor Report 1999*, p. 609.

954 See for instance *Landmine Monitor Report 1999*, p. 675.

955 The Secretary of State for Defence, George Robertson, reportedly insisted that the issue be resolved before legislation was enacted. He was concerned that British soldiers would be breaking the law if they were, for example, to escort convoys carrying landmines or were present at a planning meeting with a non-party State where the use of mines was discussed. See for instance Shrimsley, R., "Commons to sit on day off to ban landmines", *Daily Telegraph*, 26 June 1998.

956 *Times*, 13 July 1998. The Editorial Comment included a complaint that a 'long list of key countries' were not party to the Convention and asserted that it would lead to greater use of booby-traps.

957 Secretary of State for Foreign Affairs, Robin Cook, cited in Morrison, J., "Britain accused of watering down landmines ban", *Reuters*, London, 10 July 1998.

958 Clause 5(1), Landmines Bill.

Concerned by the potential loopholes opened up by the provision, the UK Working Group on Landmines called for ministerial assurances during the passage of the Bill through the House of Commons that Clause 5 did not permit the 'active participation' of British service personnel in prohibited activities in international military operations with a State not party to the Ottawa Convention.[959] The Conservative MP and former Home Secretary, Michael Howard, declared that the proposed legislation gave the Government 'full licence (...) to breach the Ottawa Convention.'[960] In response, the Secretary of State for Foreign Affairs, Robin Cook, firmly denied this, claiming – somewhat dubiously on a reading of the draft law – that the law 'prohibits British servicemen or any other British citizen from using, developing, producing, possessing or exporting a landmine. It also prevents them from assisting, encouraging or inducing anybody else from doing these things.'[961] But in a radio interview the Secretary of State was more cautious, declaring only that: 'The Landmines Bill does not allow British servicemen to actively participate in mine-laying operations, nor to assist, encourage or induce others to do so.'[962]

But even on this narrower formula, it still appears that the Landmines Bill (now the 1998 Landmines Act) is not in conformity with the Convention on the Prohibition of Anti-Personnel Mines since it seemingly excludes criminal responsibility for British soldiers involved in an international military operation as long as they do not actually lay mines. Thus, they may lawfully protect convoys containing US mines without committing a criminal act under UK law even though that surely constitutes assistance in a prohibited activity.[963]

Despite robust parliamentary debate in the House of Commons, the government pushed through the Landmines Bill unamended and deposited its instrument of ratification, together with a declaration similar to that made by Canada,[964] with the UN Secretary-General on 31 July 1998, becoming the 30th State to do so. It was not until a month later, however, that the Secretary of State for Defence, George Robertson, formally withdrew the emergency power that would give Ministers the right to allow the use of anti-personnel mines in the

959 Defined as a military operation that 'takes place wholly or mainly outside the United Kingdom', that 'involves the participation both of members of Her Majesty's Armed Forces and of members of the armed forces of a State other than the United Kingdom', and 'the operation is one in the course of which there is or may be some deployment of anti-personnel mines that are not parties to the Ottawa Convention, but in the course of which such mines are not to be laid in contravention of that Convention.' Landmines Bill, Clause 5(3).

960 See Morrison, J., "Britain accused of watering down landmines ban", *op. cit.*; "Clashes mar mines debate", *Guardian*, 11 July 1998.

961 *Ibid.*

962 Interview on the *Today Programme*, Radio 4, 10 July 1998. Indeed, the same day in the debate in the House of Commons that accompanied the adoption of the Landmines Bill, a Defence Minister declared that Clause 5 'enables United Kingdom service men and women to engage closely in the planning and conduct of an operation with those who may, lawfully for them, use anti-personnel mines.' *Hansard*, 10 July 1998, col. 1391, cited by *Landmine Monitor Report 1999*, p. 677.

963 This is seemingly supported by legal advice on the government's requirement for the exemption. See *Landmine Monitor Report 1999*, p. 678.

964 See *supra*.

event of an armed conflict involving the UK.[965] A Ministry of Defence Spokesman described it somewhat mysteriously as 'a brave decision.'[966]

The UK's legislation was first put to the test when the Police forwarded a file for investigation by UK Customs and Excise after allegations that British Aerospace was exporting the key explosive component of anti-personnel mines, RDX, to the US.[967] Then in September 1999 the Ministry of Defence was constrained to launch an investigation following claims that anti-personnel mines were put on sale by a Romanian company at a UK Government-backed arms fair.[968] The UK Working Group on Landmines called for 'all those responsible to be dealt with under the Landmines Act'.[969] In response, Romania claimed that the advertisement of anti-personnel mines had been 'a mistake'. 'We specify that, starting from 1990, these [anti-personnel mines] have not been delivered and there is no intention to offer for exportation [sic] any type of anti-personnel mines,' the Romanian Ministry of National Defence said. It added that those responsible for the error had been punished.[970] The UK Ministry of Defence Police passed a case file to the Crown Prosecution Service, which stated in February 2001 that the file was 'still open'.[971]

Thereafter, on 7 December 1999, Pakistan's High Commissioner in London was summoned to the UK Foreign and Commonwealth Office to explain the alleged involvement of a technical attaché to the Pakistan Embassy in the offer for sale of anti-personnel mines. In a letter of 11 December 1999, Pakistan Ordnance Factories claimed that the items offered for sale were 'not anti-personnel mines, but devices that can only be exploded manually by the installer/defender. These are not victim-actuated mines which are prohibited under the Amended Protocol II on landmines.'[972]

There was also controversy in Australia, where the Antipersonnel Mines Bill 1998 included the following provision in Part 2, Clause 7(3):

'Section 7(3) Subsection (1) does not apply to anything done by way of participation in operations, exercises or other military activities conducted in combination with an armed force that:

(a) is an armed force of a country that is not a party to the Convention, and

[965] See *Landmine Monitor Report 1999*, p. 678.

[966] "Loophole on mines to end", *Independent*, 31 July 1998.

[967] "Britain Sells Landmine Explosive to US Army", *Independent on Sunday*, 27 June 1999.

[968] See for instance "Landmines for sale claim", *Birmingham Post*, 18 September 1999, p. 6.

[969] See "Urgent action on Romania/UK", e-mail correspondence from Liz Bernstein, ICBL Co-ordinator, 27 September 1999.

[970] "Landmine advert 'a mistake'", *Daily Telegraph*, 20 September 1999. See also "Romanian Firm Denies Manufacturing Anti-Personnel Mines", *Bucharest Adevarul*, 21 September 1999, p. 14; "Romania Dismisses Army Officials Over Landmine Scandal", *Reuters*, Bucharest, 22 September 1999, all cited on ICBL website, <http://www.icbl.org>.

[971] See Donovan, P., "Anti-tank mines: bending, not breaking anti-landmine treaty", *The Guardian*, 13 February 2001; see also *Landmine Monitor Report 2000*, p. 783.

[972] See "Pakistan Ordnance Factories: Action Alert", E-mail correspondence from Liz Bernstein, ICBL Co-ordinator, on behalf of the UK Working group to Ban Landmines, 10 December 1999; see also *Landmine Monitor Report* 2000, p. 748; Evans, M., "Pakistani 'in deal for landmines'", *Times*, 7 December 1999.

(b) engages in an activity prohibited under the Convention.[973]

In response to concern about the ambit of this exclusion, the Australian Minister for Foreign Affairs issued a statement of clarification on the government's understanding:

'Clause 7(3) is not intended to be construed as a blanket decriminalisation of the activities listed in clause 7(1). There may be circumstances in which there are military operations carried out jointly with the armed forces of a country which is not a party to the convention. In the course of those operations, the armed forces of that country might engage in an activity which would be prohibited under the convention. Clause 7(3) provides that a person to whom the act applies will not be guilty of an offence merely by reason of participation in such combined exercises. However, that subclause does not provide a defence in circumstances where such a person actually carries out one of the prohibited acts in the course of those combined operations. In the event of a charge being laid, the prosecution would be required to prove that the actions alleged constituted an offence prohibited under clause 7(1). If the accused wished to rely on the exception of clause 7(3), he or she would need to produce evidence that suggests a reasonable possibility that the exception applies. If the accused is able to do this, it is for the prosecution to prove otherwise if the person is to be convicted.[974]

In a similar vein to its near neighbour, New Zealand's Anti-Personnel Mines Prohibition Act included a provision that allows a member of the armed forces 'in the course of his or her duties, to participate in operations, exercises, or other military activities with armed forces of a state not a party to the Convention that engage in conduct prohibited by Section 7(1), if that participation does not amount to active assistance in the prohibited conduct.'[975] Under the legislation, engaging in prohibited activity is made an offence punishable by up to seven years' imprisonment or a fine not exceeding NZ$500,000.[976]

In sum, the legislative provision in the Convention is disappointingly weak. The lack of even a modified grave breaches provision sets a poor precedent for the future implementation of international humanitarian law. Notwithstanding these lacunae, national implementing legislation remains important, including in countries where civilians as well as soldiers are involving in laying anti-personnel mines. Sadly, as the ICRC has found, a substantial number of

---

973 Cited by *Landmine Monitor Report 1999*, p. 349.

974 The Honourable Alexander Downer, Minister for Foreign Affairs, Speech to the Australian House of Representatives (*Hansard*, pp. 624-5), 26 November 1998, cited by *Landmine Monitor Report 1999*, pp. 349-50. Downer added for the parliamentary record that 'the Australian Defence Force doctrinal and operation manuals will be amended to comply with the prohibitions contained in the bill, including the interpretation of clause 7(1) and (3)' and noted that 'Australia's compliance with the provisions of the convention will also be subject to the transparency measures in article 7 of the convention.' Downer defended the necessity for clause 7(3) and named the non-signatory country that Australia would need to conduct joint military operations as 'its traditional defence ally', the US.

975 Cited by *Landmine Monitor Report 1999*, p. 371.

976 Approximately US$250,000. *Ibid.*, p. 370.

countries have not yet enacted the necessary legislation to give effect at domestic level to obligations under the four 1949 Geneva Conventions.

2.4.5. Adoption and Entry into force

A. Signature

In accordance with Article 15, signature of the Convention was possible until its entry into force on 1 March 1999.[977] At the formal signing ceremony held in Ottawa from 3-4 December 1997, a total of 121 States signed the Convention,[978] an achievement described by Canadian Prime Minister Jean Chrétien, as 'without precedent or parallel in either international disarmament or international humanitarian law.'[979] Further notable signatories included Ukraine, which, according to the ICBL, possesses the world's fifth largest stockpile of anti-personnel mines.[980] Ukraine signed the Convention on 24 February 1999,[981] becoming the 133rd and last State to do so.[982]

---

977 In the view of the author, removing the possibility of signing the Convention after its entry into force was a tactical mistake, since it forces those still outside the Convention (*i.e.*, those most reticent to embrace a total prohibition on anti-personnel mines) to accede directly to it if they wish to support legislatively a ban on the weapons. It would have been preferable to have left the Convention open for signature indefinitely since States with huge stockpiles, such as Belarus, China and Russia, could signal their intention to become States Parties, accept through signature an obligation to cease using anti-personnel mines, but not be obliged to destroy all stockpiles within the relatively short time-frame of four years from the date of entry into force.

978 In total, 150 governments attended the Conference. See for instance Canadian Department of Foreign Affairs and International Trade, "A Global Ban on Landmines", Fact Sheet, undated.

979 See Lawson, R. *et al.*, "The Ottawa Process and the International Movement to Ban Anti-Personnel Mines", *op. cit.*, p. 181.

980 President Leonid Kuchma claimed that Ukraine had a stock of 7 million anti-personnel mines. See "Canada to help Ukraine on landmine ban, international loans", *AFP International*, 27 January 1999. The ICBL, citing Canadian government information, claimed that the figure was actually 10.1 million. *Landmine Monitor Report 1999*, p. 759; see also *Landmine Monitor Report 2000*, p. 786.

981 As an inducement to join the treaty, Canada had offered financial assistance to Ukraine in the destruction of its stockpiles (and help in securing a further loan for Ukraine from the European Bank of Reconstruction and Development to complete two reactors to replace the stricken Chernobyl nuclear power plant). The cost of stockpile destruction was estimated at US$10 million; the proposed loan by the EBRD amounted to some US$200 million. In welcoming the Ukrainian decision, Canadian Prime Minister Jean Chrétien declared, somewhat hyperbolically: 'If seven million mines are destroyed (millions of) children, women and men will not suffer any more.' See "Canada to help Ukraine on landmine ban, international loans", *op. cit.*

982 Albania, Algeria, Andorra, Angola, Antigua and Barbuda, Argentina, Australia, Austria, Bahamas, Bangladesh, Barbados, Belgium, Belize, Benin, Bolivia, Bosnia and Herzegovina, Botswana, Brazil, Brunei Darussalam, Bulgaria, Burkina Faso, Burundi, Cambodia, Cameroon, Canada, Cape Verde, Chad, Chile, Colombia, Cook Islands, Costa Rica, Côte d'Ivoire, Croatia, Cyprus, Czech Republic, Denmark, Djibouti, Dominica, Dominican Republic, Ecuador, El Salvador, Ethiopia, Fiji, France, Gabon, Gambia, Germany, Ghana, Greece, Grenada, Guatemala, Guinea, Guinea-Bissau, Guyana, Haiti, Holy See, Honduras, Hungary, Iceland, Indonesia, Ireland, Italy, Jamaica, Japan, Jordan, Kenya, Lesotho, Liechtenstein, Lithuania, Luxembourg, Madagascar, Malawi, Malaysia, the Maldives, Mali, Malta, Marshall Islands, Mauritania, Mauritius, Mexico, Monaco, Mozambique, Namibia, the Netherlands, New Zealand, Nicaragua, Niger, Niue, Norway, Panama, Paraguay, Peru, Philippines, Poland, Portugal, Qatar, Republic

B. Entry Into Force

The number of ratifications needed to trigger entry into force of the treaty was the subject of some debate at the Oslo Diplomatic Conference. The original draft Austrian text, as well as the third draft submitted to the Oslo Diplomatic Conference, had proposed 40 as the threshold needed. Prior to the formal negotiations in Oslo, the ICRC, pointing out that the Geneva Conventions needed only 2 ratifications and the CCW required 20,[983] declared its desire for only a very small number of ratifications to trigger entry into force. Sweden, on the other hand, wanted 65[984] (as in the 1992 Chemical Weapons Convention), and the US wanted 75, to include all 5 Permanent Members of the Security Council and 75 per cent of historic mine producers and users. After the Diplomatic Conference had heard a variety of proposals, both higher and lower than the limit proposed, it was finally agreed that the number should remain at 40.[985]

Thus, according to Article 17(1) of the Convention, it would enter into force 'on the first day of the sixth month after the month in which the 40th instrument of ratification, acceptance, approval or accession' was deposited with the UN Secretary-General.[986] The requisite level of adherence was achieved in record time,[987] and on 16 September 1998 Burkina Faso becoming the 40th State to adhere to the treaty, a little under a year since its adoption.[988] The Convention

of Moldova, Romania, Rwanda, Saint Kitts and Nevis, Saint Lucia, Saint Vincent and the Grenadines, Samoa, San Marino, Sao Tomé and Principé, Senegal, Seychelles, Sierra Leone, Slovakia, Slovenia, Solomon Islands, South Africa, Spain, Sudan, Suriname, Swaziland, Sweden, Switzerland, Thailand, Togo, Trinidad and Tobago, Tunisia, Turkmenistan, Uganda, Ukraine, the United Kingdom, United Republic of Tanzania, Uruguay, Vanuatu, Venezuela, Yemen, Zambia, and Zimbabwe.

983 ICRC, Comments on the Third Austrian Draft (13/5/97) of the Convention on the Prohibition of Anti-Personnel Mines, *Informal Working Paper for the Oslo Negotiations*, Geneva, September 1997.

984 A proposal 'which was certainly not viewed by the ICBL as "ban friendly"'. *Landmine Monitor Report 1999*, p. 656. Indeed, Landmine Monitor remarks that despite its national position, Sweden was a surprisingly lukewarm participant in the Ottawa Process. *Ibid.*

985 According to Article 16 it is also possible to accede directly to the Convention or to approve or accept rather than ratify signature. See *Landmine Monitor Report 1999*, pp. 1040-1. The Netherlands accepted the Convention; Japan and Slovakia both approved it.

986 According to Article 21, the Secretary-General was designated as the Depositary of the Convention.

987 ICBL, for instance, believes that this represents the fastest entry into force of any major treaty ever. *Landmine Monitor Report 1999*, p. 2.

988 In welcoming the 40th ratification of the treaty, the ICRC President, Cornelio Sommaruga, declared that it was 'especially encouraging that mine-affected countries on three continents, including Bosnia and Herzegovina, Croatia, Mozambique, Yemen, and Zimbabwe, are among the first 40 countries to ratify.' He further asserted that: 'The challenge ahead is actual implementation of the treaty. (...) Real success will be measured in terms of fewer victims, the replanting of fertile farmland, and the resumption of normal life in communities plagued by landmines.' ICRC, *Press release No 98/34*, Geneva, 17 September 1998. According to ICBL Ambassador, Jody Williams: 'This accomplishment underscores the urgency of dealing with the global landmine crisis and the strength of the new international standard against this insidious weapon.' ICBL, "Landmine Treaty Ratified by Forty Countries in Record time", *Press release*, Dublin, 17 September 1998.

entered into force as binding international law on the first 40 States Parties on 1 March 1999. At a ceremony in Geneva, the UN Secretary-General, Kofi Annan, declared it 'a day few could have predicted and whose import to the millions whose lives or limbs may be saved and from these barbarous weapons cannot be overestimated.'[989] On 21 July 2000, Mauritania became the 100th State to adhere to the Convention,[990] and by mid-April 2001, a total of 111 States had deposited their instruments of ratification or accession,[991] the latest to adhere being Kenya, Romania, Tanzania, and Zambia.

C. Ratification by Signatories

Not all the Convention signatories, however, were equally committed to early ratification, although some were apparently unaware of the legal consequences that resulted from signature.[992] Lithuania, for instance, made a formal declaration upon signature whereby it 'subscribed to the principles enshrined within the Convention' but stated that ratification would take place as soon as 'relevant conditions relating to the implementation of its provisions are fulfilled.'[993] It was allegedly unwilling to ratify the treaty while close, heavily-armed neighbours, remained outside its purview.[994] Thus, a month before signing the treaty an official from the Lithuanian Ministry of Defence stated:

> *'Lithuania recognises that anti-personnel mines are a barbaric arm and shall be eliminated from the arsenals. At the same time Lithuania is just*

---

989 See for instance UN, "Secretary-General Rings Peace Bell to Mark Occasion of Entry Into Force of Ottawa Convention Banning Anti-Personnel Mines", *Press release SG/SM/6909*, 1 March 1999; see also Brown, P., "Landmines banned but threats stay", *Guardian*, 2 March 1999.

990 See for instance "Mauritania Marks 100th Ratification of the Mine Ban Treaty", *Africa News Service*, Nouakchott, 27 July 2000.

991 Albania, Andorra, Antigua and Barbuda, Argentina, Australia, Austria, the Bahamas, Bangladesh, Barbados, Belgium, Belize, Benin, Bolivia, Bosnia-Herzegovina, Botswana, Brazil, Bulgaria, Burkina Faso, Cambodia, Canada, Chad, Colombia, Costa Rica, Croatia, the Czech Republic, Denmark, Djibouti, Dominica, Ecuador, El Salvador, Equatorial Guinea (by accession), Fiji, Former Yugoslav Republic of Macedonia (by accession), France, Gabon, Germany, Grenada, Guatemala, Guinea, Holy See, Honduras, Hungary, Iceland, Ireland, Italy, Jamaica, Japan (by acceptance), Jordan, Kenya, Kiribati (by accession), Lesotho, Liberia (by accession), Liechtenstein, Luxembourg, Madagascar, Malawi, Malaysia, Maldives, Mali, Mauritius, Mexico, Moldova, Monaco, Mozambique, Namibia, the Netherlands (by acceptance), New Zealand, Nicaragua, Niger, Niue, Norway, Panama, Paraguay, Peru, the Philippines, Portugal, Qatar, Romania, Saint Kitts and Nevis, Saint Lucia, Samoa, San Marino, Senegal, the Seychelles, Slovakia (by approval), Slovenia, Solomon Islands, South Africa, Spain, Swaziland, Sweden, Switzerland, Tajikistan (by accession), Tanzania, Thailand, Togo, Trinidad and Tobago, Tunisia, Turkmenistan, Uganda, the United Kingdom, Venezuela, Yemen, Zambia, and Zimbabwe.

992 See *supra*, p. 79 *et seq.*

993 See *Landmine Monitor Report 1999*, pp. 709, 737. In September 1998, President Valdas Adamkus had informed the UN General Assembly that ratification of the Convention was the 'long-term goal' of Lithuania; its signature took place on 26 February 1999. *Ibid.*, p. 737. Cyprus made a similar declaration. See *Landmine Monitor Report 2000*, p. 761.

994 Though see also *Landmine Monitor Report 2000*, p. 766. Greece had previously made a similar declaration though it appears that agreement had been reached with Turkey to adhere simultaneously to the Convention. See for instance "Excellent news: Turkey and Greece!", e-mail correspondence from Liz Bernstein, 7 April 2001.

now forming its army, and mines obtained during the first years of independence cannot be destroyed only for support of ideas. At this time safe storage and use is secured by corresponding measures taken by Lithuanian armed forces. There are technical problems to get all the documents relevant to the landmine issue, including translation into Lithuanian. The negative attitude of neighbours (Belarus, Russia) towards the ban is also to be taken into account. Lithuania has neighbours who have said they will ratify only after all Security Council members have joined the ban. Today it is hard to refuse of [sic] the tactical use of landmines, since it forms a significant part of the Lithuanian defence potential (which is small anyway). There is a long time period needed to replace anti-personnel mines with other weapon systems, retraining of ground force personnel for the use of such other weapon systems, and revision of military doctrine. [995]

Other signatories had likewise declared an unwillingness to ratify in the immediate future. Poland, for instance, which had also signed the Convention with some reluctance, declared that it would only implement the Convention when it became 'truly universal with the participation of all major powers as well as the countries of [its] region.' And in addition to entertaining reservations about NATO implications and the cost of destroying stockpiles, Poland would first have to find an alternative to anti-personnel mines.[996] This stance was repeated in early 2000, when Poland's position came under scrutiny from the ICBL.[997] The Chairman of the Sejm Commission for National Defence declared that: 'Our strategy provides for the use of anti-personnel mines. We can hardly relinquish them when other states keep using them. The fighting in Chechnya has shown what an important role mines can play.'[998]

D. Non-signatories

Despite the extremely high level of signatories to the Convention, more than 50 States, including the world's leading military powers, chose to remain outside. The reasons varied, though tended mostly to fall within one of three categories: a) the perceived military utility of anti-personnel mines and lack of available alternatives[999] (undoubtedly the primary reason); b) the cost of

995 Telephone conversation and interview with Andrius Krivas, Lithuanian Ministry of Defence, Vilnius, 20 January 1999, cited by *Landmine Monitor Report 1999*, p. 738.

996 Statement at Budapest Conference by Mr. Kazimierz Tomaszewski, Senior Counsellor to the Minister for Foreign Affairs, Ministry of Foreign Affairs, Poland, 26-28 March 1998, cited by *Landmine Monitor Report 1999*, p. 753.

997 See generally *Landmine Monitor Report 2000*, p. 778.

998 Wronski, P., "Poland said unlikely to ban landmines before US", *Gazeta Wyborcza*, Warsaw, 7 March 2000.

999 As well as, in a number of instances, the desire to use anti-personnel mines to protect borders against smugglers and immigrants.

destruction of existing stockpiles;[1000] and c) the lack of universal support for the Convention.[1001]

(i) Africa

In Africa, support for the Convention is extremely solid, with only the Central African Republic, Congo (Brazzaville), the Democratic Republic of Congo, Egypt, Eritrea, Libya, Morocco, Nigeria, and the collapsed State of Somalia outside the purview of the Convention.[1002]

The Central African Republic, a State currently traversing a period of great insecurity, especially in rural areas and the eastern region,[1003] has remained relatively silent on the question of adherence to the Convention. In an interview with a researcher for the Landmine Monitor report, its Ambassador to Belgium declared that the Central African Republic supported a partial ban on anti-personnel mines negotiated through the CD.[1004] When questioned again in July 2000, an official from the Ministry of Foreign Affairs declared that he knew nothing about the Convention and since the country had no landmines it was not of interest.[1005]

In Congo-Brazzaville, foreign diplomats have explained that the politico-military crisis that has gripped the country since the outbreak of the 1997 civil war, has pushed the issue down the political agenda.[1006] The ICBL also muses that Congolese President Denis Sassou Nguesso may be reluctant to relinquish the weapon under the present circumstances.[1007] Certainly both sides used landmines widely in the 1997 civil war,[1008] indeed, the French government became sufficiently alarmed to warn publicly against the use of the weapon.[1009] In December 1999, Congo voted in favour of the UN General Assembly resolution supporting the Convention, one of 18 non-signatories to do so.[1010] Then in July 2000, Congo was reported to have ratified the Convention and to have begun steps to destroy its stockpile of anti-personnel mines.[1011]

Congo's neighbour, the Democratic Republic of Congo (DRC),[1012] has also seen regular use of anti-personnel mines. In addition to use by rebel armed

---

1000 Although, as Ukraine has demonstrated, signature of the Convention could also bring financial benefits.

1001 Notwithstanding the potentially circular nature of the argument.

1002 Of these, in December 1999, Congo, Eritrea and Nigeria all voted in favour of UN General Assembly resolution 54/545B supporting the Convention; Egypt, Libya, and Morocco all abstained.

1003 *Landmine Monitor Report 1999*, p. 187.

1004 *Ibid.*

1005 *Landmine Monitor Report 2000*, p. 196.

1006 *Landmine Monitor Report 1999*, p. 188.

1007 *Ibid.*

1008 *Ibid.*, pp. 189-91.

1009 "France warns against the use of landmines in Congo", *AFP*, 11 September 1997, cited by *Landmine Monitor Report 1999*, p. 189.

1010 See for instance "UNGA 54/54B Resolution Clarification", E-mail correspondence from Mary Wareham, Human Rights Watch, 10 March 2000.

1011 *Landmine Monitor Report 2000*, p. 197.

1012 Formerly known as Zaire.

groups in the east of the country, it appears likely that this includes governmental armed forces, though there is no confirmation of this.[1013]

Egypt has been the most vocal African opponent of the Convention, claiming, for example, that the Convention does not take into account 'the legitimate security and defence concerns of States, particularly those with extensive territorial borders' which need anti-personnel mines to protect against terrorist attacks and drug traffickers.[1014] Egypt has also complained at the 'lack of financial and technical incentives' in the Convention to help the country deal with its landmine problem.[1015] In 1999, Egypt abstained from the General Assembly resolution supporting the Convention. Their opposition continued in 2000, including in a regional conference in Cairo hosted by the Arab League, in which ICBL accused Egypt of 'manipulation of the final declaration'.[1016] The ICBL also asserted that Egypt continued to produce anti-personnel mines, a charge that an unnamed foreign affairs official denied.[1017]

Other major African States outside the Convention are Libya[1018] and Morocco, both of which are alleged to have used mines in the past.[1019] According to the Landmine Monitor report, in its war against the Polisario Front in Western Sahara, Morocco has protected 'berms' (mounds of earth piled two to three metres high) with 'extensive' use of anti-tank and anti-personnel mines.[1020] However, in its formal statement to the First Meeting of States Parties of the Convention, Morocco claimed that it had done no more than 'postpone' its signature of the Convention because of the situation in the south of the country.[1021] Nigeria is likely to accede in the near future.[1022]

1013 See *Landmine Monitor Report 1999*, pp. 192-5; *Landmine Monitor Report 2000*, pp. 198-9.

1014 Statement of Egypt to the Brussels Conference as reported in *Landmine Monitor Report 1999*, p. 876.

1015 In April 2000 at a regional meeting on landmines held in Cairo, Mary Wareham, a Senior Researcher of Human Rights Watch, referred to this issue in the following terms: 'Throughout this meeting, we listened as Egypt pleaded over and over again for international assistance to deal with its mine problem[.] (...) Egypt frequently raises the need for funding for clearance of mines laid in its Western desert but neglects to discuss mines it has laid in the Suez and Sinai[,] which also hurt and maim innocent civilians. As long as Egypt refuses to join the ban treaty, no donors will be willing to donate to the Government's mine clearance efforts.' ICBL, "ICBL deplores continued obstruction of the ban on anti-personnel mines in Egypt", *Press release*, Cairo, 11 April 2000. The previous month, however, it had been reported that with the help of the US, Egypt expected to clear all its landmines by 2005. See Coryell, G., "US combs the world for deadly mines", *Tampa Tribune*, 19 March 2000.

1016 "Egypt under fire over anti-personnel mine policy", *Reuters*, Cairo, 11 April 2000. See also ICBL, "ICBL deplores continued obstruction of the ban on anti-personnel mines in Egypt", *Press release*, Cairo, 11 April 2000.

1017 *Ibid.* See *Landmine Monitor Report 2000*, pp. 919-21.

1018 See *Landmine Monitor Report 1999*, p. 899; *Landmine Monitor Report 2000*, pp. 950-1.

1019 See for instance "Mines by the million threaten North Africa, Conference told", *AFP Internationale*, 26 January 1999.

1020 *Landmine Monitor Report 1999*, p. 902.

1021 See also *Landmine Monitor Report 2000*, p. 954.

1022 *Ibid.*, p. 209.

(ii) The Americas

In the Americas, the Convention has been well supported, with signatures by all States from the region except Cuba and the US. In explaining its decision not to sign, a representative of the Ministry of Foreign Affairs declared that Cuba 'cannot be attached to any international agreement prohibiting the use of anti-personnel mines whilst she is under the threats and hostility of the United States of America' and that 'the use of this type of mine is a vital need for Cuba's national security in our conception of the Peoples' War, aimed to reject, neutralise, resist and annihilate the aggressor'.[1023] The representative further pointed out that Cuba was only using anti-personnel mines in the area around the US Naval Base at Guantanamo, and asserted that, 'if one day the [US] changes its present dangerous decision of destroying the Cuban revolution, that day there will be no more need of our landmines.'[1024]

Having been firmly defeated in its efforts to amend the Convention at the Oslo Diplomatic Conference, the US was, unsurprisingly, only an observer at the Treaty Signing Conference in Ottawa. In a letter dated 18 April 2000 addressed to Mr David Warshaw, the manager of a US company that has not yet renounced the manufacture of anti-personnel mines, a researcher for the Arms Division of Human Rights Watch summarised US policy in the following manner:

- *The US will ban the use of anti-personnel mines, except those in mixed munitions, in 2003 everywhere except for Korea.*
- *The US intends to develop alternatives to anti-personnel mines by 2006.*
- *The US will sign the Mine Ban Treaty by 2006 if such alternatives are identified and fielded.*
- *The stockpile of antipersonnel mines was permanently capped in January 1997.*
- *The Department of Defense has destroyed over 3 million anti-personnel mines and is developing plans to demilitarise the rest of its inventory to meet the President's goals.*
- *The export of anti-personnel landmines is banned and the Department of State will not issue export licenses for anti-personnel mine production technology or related defence services.*[1025]

In exchange for an agreement not to force through domestic legislation prohibiting the use of anti-personnel mines outside of international borders and demilitarised zones for one year in 1999,[1026] US National Security Adviser

[1023] Cited in *Landmine Monitor Report 1999*, p. 313.

[1024] *Ibid.*, p. 314; see also *Landmine Monitor Report 2000*, p. 329.

[1025] Letter from Mark A. Hiznay to Mr David Warshaw, Manager of Corporate Communications, General Electric Company, Fairfield, US, 18 April 2000. See e-mail correspondence from Liz Bernstein, ICBL Co-ordinator, 5 May 2000.

[1026] The 1999 Leahy Use Amendment, sponsored by Senator Patrick Leahy of Vermont, was passed as part of the 1997 Defence Authorisation Bill. The Administration was apparently concerned that the moratorium on use, even with the exceptions included, would prevent US forces using anti-personnel mines between the DMZ and Seoul. According to Assistant Secretary of Defense, Kenneth Bacon, an alternative strategy to the use of landmines would require 17,000 additional troops, 350 additional tanks, 410 additional Bradley Fighting Vehicles, 24 additional helicopters

Sandy Berger formally stated in a letter to Senator Leahy that the US would end the use of landmines outside Korea by 2003[1027] and hope to sign the treaty in 2006,[1028] but only if the Pentagon had found an alternative weapon.[1029] In May 1999, at the First Meeting of States Parties of the Convention in Maputo, the United States President, Bill Clinton, sent a message declaring once more his hope that the US would sign the treaty by 2006. Of course, by the time he had sent the message, it was already too late for signature[1030] and accordingly the US will be obliged either to remain outside the treaty or to accede to its provisions directly. The US abstained from the 1999 UN General Assembly resolution supporting the Convention.[1031]

The search for alternatives appeared, strangely, to include new mixed systems, even though these were clearly prohibited by the treaty. In early 1999, the Pentagon was seeking nearly US$50 million for an artillery shell, the Remote Area Denial Artillery Munition (RADAM),[1032] which would disperse both anti-

---

and 144 other aircraft. Bacon, K., News briefing, 5 May 1998. See also "'Korea Exception' keeps us out of Ottawa Treaty", *AFP Internationale*, 26 February 1999.

1027 As the Convention entered into force on 1 March 1999, it was reported that Senator Leahy and Representatives Lane Evans and Jack Quinn would present legislation to cut off funding by 2003 for any activity inconsistent with the treaty, and adopt a moratorium on the production of mines. "US Lawmakers Push for Landmine Treaty Compliance", *Fox News Online*, 2 March 1999.

1028 See *Landmine Monitor Report 1999*, pp. 318-9; Price, R., "Compliance with International Norms and the Mines Taboo", *To Walk Without Fear*, p. 346.

1029 See for instance Wolffe, R., "Landmines – US proposal on treaty", *The Financial Times*, 25 May 1998; Myers, S.L., "Clinton Agrees to Land-Mine Ban, But Not Yet", *New York Times*, 22 May 1998. In October 1997, one US military official said that the Pentagon was 'working very feverishly' to honour the deadlines set by President Clinton for developing alternatives to anti-personnel mines. Ellis, S., "Army General says most landmines will be banned by 2003", *Washington File*, Washington, 30 October 1997. Concern was expressed, though, that since the US no longer considered the anti-personnel mines contained in their mixed anti-armour systems as anti-personnel mines, no efforts would be made to find alternatives. See for instance Seffers, G.I., "Pentagon Plan for Mixed System Draws Criticism", *Defense News*, Canada, 3-9 November 1997.

In response to remarks at the Conference by US Special Representative for Global Humanitarian Demining, Karl Inderfurth, that the US would join the treaty by 2006 'if we are able to develop alternatives to mixed munition systems and there is nothing promising available right now', US Senator Patrick Leahy declared: 'If the use of anti-personnel mines near anti-tank mines is what prevents the United States from signing the treaty then solve it. We run a little Rover around on mars. If we can do that, we can solve this problem. If the Pentagon had spent the past three years since the President first called for a worldwide ban really trying to solve the problem rather than to keep from having to solve it, the United States might have been able to show the leadership on this issue that the world needs and, frankly, the world wants.' Leahy, *Congressional Record*, 23 September 1997, cited by Wareham, M., "Rhetoric and Policy Realities in the United States", *op. cit.*, p. 238.

1030 According to the provisions of Article 15 of the Convention.

1031 See "UNGA 54/54B Resolution Clarification", E-mail correspondence from Mary Wareham, Human Rights Watch, 10 March 2000. Senator Bill Bradley, who challenged Al Gore unsuccessfully for the Democratic Presidential nomination, was the only one of the four main US Presidential candidates to call for swift US accession to the treaty. See for instance article by Jeff Zeleny, *Des Moines Register*, 7 January 2000; "Bradley supports Ottawa Treaty banning landmines, Gore, Administration still lag behind", *Arms Trade Insider*, No. 26, 19 January 2000.

1032 For details of RADAM see *Landmine Monitor Report 1999*, pp. 324-5.

tank and anti-personnel mines.[1033] The Pentagon claimed, somewhat disingenuously, that putting anti-personnel mines and anti-tank mines in a single shell moved it closer to President Clinton's pledge to end the use of 'pure' anti-personnel mines by 2003 outside Korea.[1034] Another possible replacement for non-self-destructing anti-personnel mines was a bounding anti-personnel weapon that is normally command-detonated (and therefore legal under the Convention) but which contains a battlefield override system, turning the weapon into a (victim-activated) anti-personnel mine 'precisely the type of weapon the US has said for years must be banned worldwide.'[1035]

Also under research is an "intelligent" anti-vehicle mine that can leap 30 feet into the air and fill gaps left by minefield clearance operations. The researcher at the heart of the project based his development on observing grasshoppers.[1036] A third research track seeks to develop alternatives to the mixed systems, such as GATOR.[1037] In total, the Pentagon expects to spend US$300 million on research and development and US$500 million on procurement for weapons to enable it to adhere to the Convention in 2006.[1038]

As President Clinton left power in January 2001, he deferred further action on alternatives to anti-personnel mines to his successor, George Bush.[1039] Pressure began to mount from the US army to include the battlefield override system even though it would preclude accession to the Ottawa Convention, and the Pentagon noted that 2006 was 'an objective, not a deadline'.[1040] Further, in March 2001, a report by the National Research Council found that new technologies under development could replace some, but not all,[1041] of US anti-personnel landmines by 2006, although it recommended halting production of the RADAM system.[1042]

1033 On 25 May 1999, the Senate Appropriations Committee struck funding for RADAM from the Fiscal Year 2000 budget, but on 30 July 1999, the House Appropriations Committee moved to support financially RADAM development as requested by the Pentagon. Subsequently, both the House and Senate approved the conference report of the congressional Committee, which provides US$8 million for RADAM. E-mail communication from Liz Bernstein, ICBL Co-ordinator, 21 October 1999. See also Human Rights Watch, "New US mines would violate treaty", *Press release*, Washington, 7 April 2000.

1034 See for instance "'Korea Exception' keeps us out of Ottawa Treaty", *AFP Internationale*, 26 February 1999; *Landmine Monitor Report 1999*, pp. 319, 324-5.

1035 Human Rights Watch, "New US mines would violate treaty", *op. cit.*; see also *Landmine Monitor Report 2000*, pp. 338-40.

1036 Uhlig, R., "Landmine armed with hopping foot can rearrange itself", *Daily Telegraph*, 28 September 2000; *Landmine Monitor Report 2000*, p. 340.

1037 *Landmine Monitor Report 2000*, p. 340.

1038 *Ibid.*, p. 336.

1039 See for instance "Anti-personnel landmine decisions deferred", *US Department of Defence News Release No. 029-01*, 19 January 2001.

1040 See for instance Strohm, C., "Bush Administration Faces Decisions on Land Mine Programs, Treaty", *Inside The Army*, Vol. 13, No. 5, p. 1.

1041 Specifically, a replacement would not be ready for the US mixed systems.

1042 See National Research Council, *Copies of Alternative Technologies to Replace Antipersonnel Landmines*, National Academy Press, Washington DC, March 2001.

(iii) Asia

Adherence in Asia and the Middle East remains extremely low, with key military powers such as China, India, and Pakistan, among others, all non-signatories. In Central Asia, Afghanistan, one of the world's most mine-affected countries, has not signed the Convention, despite the Taliban having expressed support for it on a number of occasions and at the highest level.[1043] Reports of new use of anti-personnel mines by all sides have, however, continued.[1044]

Elsewhere in Central Asia, of the five republics, only Tajikistan[1045] and Turkmenistan have adhered to the Convention on the Prohibition of Anti-Personnel Mines. Kazakhstan voted for UN General Assembly resolution 51/45S, but was one of 18 countries which abstained from the 1997 vote on resolution 52/38A supporting the December treaty signing, and was one of 19 nations which abstained from the 1998 vote on resolution 53/77 encouraging early adherence to the Convention.[1046] In a letter addressed to an NGO in April 2000, the government declared that 'joining the treaty in the close future is problematic, primarily because the treaty obliges complete and immediate destruction of landmines which are used in Kazakhstan for defensive purposes only, to protect considerable parts of its long border.'[1047]

An unknown quantity of anti-personnel mines laid during the time of the Soviet Union remain on the Kyrgyz-China border.[1048] The perceived need to maintain those minefields may be the reason Kyrgyzstan has not signed the ban treaty.[1049] However, Kyrgyzstan has recently begun discussions with China on how to clear the border minefields between the two countries.[1050] There have also been reports of the use of landmines, apparently anti-vehicle mines, by rebel forces.[1051]

Little is known about Uzbekistan's policy towards anti-personnel mines. In June 1997, at a regional conference on landmines in Turkmenistan, the Uzbekistan representative stated only that the government was carefully studying the issue.[1052] In December 1999, it abstained from the UN General

---

1043 See *supra*; *Landmine Monitor Report 1999*, pp. 433-4. As noted *supra*, the Taliban has been recognised as the legitimate government of Afghanistan by only a handful of States. *Ibid.*, p. 433.

1044 The ousted Rabbani government has admitted to Landmine Monitor that it is still using anti-personnel mines, justifying it as a legitimate and useful weapon, though it has also alleged that the Taliban continue to deploy anti-personnel mines. *Landmine Monitor Report 1999*, p. 436.

1045 Tajikistan voted in favour of 1996 UN General Assembly resolution 51/45S, but was one of 18 countries which abstained from the 1997 resolution 52/38A. In the past, both the government and the United Tajik Opposition (UTO) have laid anti-personnel mines, with media reports suggesting continuing use as recently as November 1998, despite the signature by both sides of a peace accord. *Landmine Monitor Report 1999*, pp. 815-6.

1046 *Ibid.*, pp. 796-7.

1047 *Landmine Monitor Report 2000*, p. 826.

1048 See *ibid.*, pp. 828-9.

1049 *Landmine Monitor Report 1999*, p. 798.

1050 Correspondence from ICRC official, Tashkent, 13 January 1999, cited by *ibid.*

1051 See for instance "Kyrgyz APC Hits Rebel Landmine; One Dead, Two Injured", *ITAR-TASS*, Moscow, 20 September 1999.

1052 *Ibid.*, p. 825.

Assembly resolution supporting the Convention on the Prohibition of Anti-Personnel Mines.[1053] Uzbekistan is reported to have mined its borders with Kyrgyzstan[1054] and Tajikistan.[1055]

In South and East Asia, the People's Republic of China, which according to the ICBL is one of the world's biggest producers and exporters of anti-personnel mines,[1056] has been one of the most vigorous opponents to the Convention on the Prohibition of Anti-Personnel Mines,[1057] although it appeared that the adoption and signature of the treaty spurred renewed landmine clearance operations within China on the border with Vietnam[1058] and, significantly, China has endorsed the ultimate objective of a total ban on anti-personnel mines.[1059] Thus, the 1998 Defence White Paper declares that:

China has all along attached great importance to the problem of threat to innocent people caused by the indiscriminate use of anti-personnel landmines (APLs). It is in favour of imposing proper and rational restrictions on the use and transfer of APLs in a bid to achieve the ultimate objective of comprehensive prohibition of such landmines

---

1053 See for instance "UNGA 54/54B Resolution Clarification", E-mail correspondence from Mary Wareham, Human Rights Watch, 10 March 2000.

1054 *Landmine Monitor Report 2000*, pp. 851, 852.

1055 "Uzbekistan Mines Border with Tajikistan", *Radio Free Europe/Radio Liberty Newsline*, Vol. 4, No. 193, Part I, Prague, 5 October 2000.

1056 *Landmine Monitor Report 1999*, p. 454.

1057 '[W]hile China agrees with the humanitarian efforts of the international community to keep the indiscriminate use of landmines from harming the innocent, the method of disregarding varying national conditions, overstating the humanitarian aspect, and absolutely denying the military value of landmines, to propose the all-out banning of anti-personnel mines, is neither comprehensive nor reasonable.' Chinese Ambassador to the UN Conference on Disarmament, cited by Lenarcic, D. A., *Knight-Errant? Canada and the Crusade to Ban Anti-Personnel Land Mines*, *op. cit.*, p. 28.
Furthermore, it appeared that memories ran deep for in 1996, China's Ambassador for Disarmament Affairs claimed before the General Assembly's First Committee that: 'The Chinese people have not forgotten how landmines, during the eight long years of war against the invasion of Japanese fascists, raised havoc among the invaders, thus playing an important role in China's triumph in the war.' "China Opposes Total Ban on Landmines", *Reuters*, New York, 18 October 1996.

1058 See for instance "Chinese soldier dies in demining operation on Vietnam border", *AFP*, Beijing, 26 May 1998; "China clears mines along Vietnam border", *AP*, Beijing, 1 December 1997. The clearance operations began on 28 November just days before the formal signing of the Ottawa treaty. At the First Meeting of States Parties, China reported that this demining operation had cleared more than 1 million landmines and explosive devices, covering an area of 129.5 km², and it estimated that by the end of the century, China would have completely solved the threat caused to innocent civilians by uncleared landmines within its borders. Statement by Ambassador Shao Guanfu, Head of the Chinese Observer Delegation to the First Meeting of States Parties, Maputo, 4 May 1999, pp. 2-3. See also "China clears minefields", *Financial Times*, 23 February 199, p. 6.

1059 Though Landmine Monitor notes that 'while treaty advocates might see these as encouraging developments, Chinese officials state that there has been no pro-ban evolution in Chinese policy, and that the Chinese position has always been consistent.' Landmine Monitor Tokyo telephone interview with a Chinese official, 26 February 1999, cited in *Landmine Monitor Report 1999*, p. 457. In fact, in informal discussions with the author in 1997, a Chinese military expert acknowledged that support for the ultimate objective of a total prohibition of anti-personnel mines represented a significant change in Chinese policy towards the issue.

through a phased approach. In the meantime, the Chinese government maintains that, in addressing the problem of APLs, consideration should be given to both humanitarian concern and the legitimate defence requirements of sovereign states.[1060]

In December 1997, the head of the Chinese observer delegation to the Treaty Signing Conference declared that '[b]efore an alternative of [anti-personnel mines] (...) is found, the Chinese army must reserve the right to use [anti-personnel mines] on its own soil so as to form defensive capability.'[1061] Eighteen months later, at the First Meeting of States Parties in Maputo, the Chinese representative made the following remarks:

The Chinese Government shares the humanitarian concerns by the international community on anti-personnel landmines, and supports the international humanitarian efforts in eliminating the casualties caused by anti-personnel landmines to innocent civilians. (...)

To some countries, especially the developing ones, anti-personnel landmines, as a defensive weapon, is [sic] still an important military means for safeguarding national sovereignty and preventing foreign invasion. Under the present situation, when international conflicts prop [sic] up here and there, and foreign interference is on the rise, anti-personnel landmines are still of important practical significance for countries like China, who lack advanced defensive weapons, to defend their national sovereignty and territorial integrity. It should be pointed out that the present rampant gunboat policy towards the developing countries is of no help to the goal of a global ban on anti-personnel landmines.[1062]

India, although likewise endorsing the objective of the eventual elimination of anti-personnel mines, has been critical of the Ottawa Process itself.[1063] The Indian Government's position on anti-personnel mines was spelled out in the Ministry of External Affairs 1998 Annual Report to the Parliament:

India remains committed to the goal of the eventual elimination of landmines and supports a phased approach towards attaining the objective of a non-discriminatory and universal ban on anti-personnel landmines. In the meanwhile, the responsible use of mines should be permitted for the long-term defence of borders, perimeters and peripheries of states. India has closely watched the developments within the 'fast-track' Ottawa Process. India is convinced that a global, effective and

---

1060 "White Paper: China's National Defense", Information Office of the State Council, People's Republic of China, 27 July 1998, cited by *Landmine Monitor Report 1999*, p. 455.

1061 Krishnaswami, S., "A minefield ahead of Canada", *Hindu*, New Delhi, 6 December 1997. See also "China's Position on APL", Statement submitted by Mr. Song Rong Hua, Second Secretary of the Embassy of the People's Republic of China in Japan at the 3rd NGO Tokyo Conference on AP mines organised by Association to Aid Refugees, Japan held on 28-29 November 1998 in Tokyo; *Landmine Monitor Report 1999*, p. 455.

1062 Statement by Ambassador Shao Guanfu, Head of the Chinese Observer Delegation to the First Meeting of States Parties, Maputo, 4 May 1999, pp. 1-2. China abstained from the 1999 General Assembly resolution supporting the Convention on the Prohibition of Anti-Personnel Mines.

1063 *Landmine Monitor Report 1999*, p. 463.

lasting solution to the problem of anti-personnel landmines requires sustained international co-operation in all relevant fora and enhanced international assistance for care and rehabilitation of mine victims. India is concerned about the humanitarian tragedy caused by the indiscriminate export and irresponsible use of anti-personnel landmines especially in internal conflicts. A consensus that would prohibit such transfers and use of these weapons in internal conflicts, coupled with increasing attention to the humanitarian issues of demining and rehabilitation of mine victims would go a long way in addressing the problem. India remains flexible on the issue of forum for negotiations and believes that availability of non-lethal technologies to perform the legitimate defensive role of landmines will help accelerate their complete elimination.[1064]

Both the Democratic People's Republic of Korea (DPRK) and the Republic of Korea (ROK) have remained outside the Convention,[1065] and are unlikely to join until a solution is found to the problems on the peninsula.[1066] The DPRK, in a rare discussion of the issue, has recognised the humanitarian dimensions of the problem, though has affirmed that the 'complicated security situation' made it impossible to join 'at this juncture'.[1067]

As the ICBL reports, the ROK asserts that mines are needed both as a deterrent, and for their combat value. 'The use of anti-personnel landmines on the Korean peninsula has been an essential element in deterring the possible aggression. It has helped prevent the recurrence of another devastating war[.] (...) Mining along the north-south invasion routes would work to slow down and break up a North Korean attack[.] (...) Minefields have been an indispensable component of our defensive barrier system. (...) Anti-Personnel landmines have thus served as a powerful deterrent to military adventurism in Korea and will continue to do so.'[1068] It was estimated by a ruling party lawmaker of the ROK

1064 Ministry of External Affairs, *Annual Report 1997-98*, p. 92. Similar language is found in Ministry of Defence, *Annual Report 1997-98*, p. 6. *Landmine Monitor Report 1999*, p. 465. See also *Landmine Monitor Report 2000*, pp. 488-9.

1065 Though, as previously noted, during the negotiation of the Convention the DPRK declared that no geographical exemption should be made for Korea. See above p. 130, footnote 171; see also *Sankei Newspaper*, Jiji Press, Geneva, 15 September 1997, cited by *Landmine Monitor Report 1999*, p. 471.

1066 Though in 1996, Mr. Lee Yang Ho, a former ROK Minister of National Defence, suggested that North and South Korea should get rid of their landmines jointly. Response to the National Defence Committee of the National Assembly, 6 August 1996. *Landmine Monitor Report 1999*, pp. 475-6.

1067 *Ibid.*, pp. 471-2; see also *Landmine Monitor Report 2000*, p. 496.

1068 ROK Foreign Ministry statement, "Banning Antipersonnel Landmine: Republic of Korea's Security Situation Must Be Given Special Consideration", undated but 1997, cited by *Landmine Monitor Report 1999*, p. 475. The ICBL, on the other hand, has argued that: 'While the geopolitical situation in Korea may be unique, the requirement for and impact of the use of AP mines is not. (...) The case cannot be made that only in Korea does the military utility of anti-personnel mines outweigh the humanitarian costs.' ICBL Statement to Oslo Diplomatic Conference, "Say No to the US Demand for a Korea Exception", September 1997. In support of this position, they cite several former commanders of joint US-ROK forces in South Korea, who have stated that anti-personnel mines can be safely eliminated from the ROK. See for instance ICBL, "Report on Activities, Diplomatic Conference on an International Total Ban on

that removing the one million landmines on the southern side of the border would cost US$10 billion and prove one of the most difficult demining operations in history.[1069]

Indeed, as relations with North Korea thawed, the implementation of an agreement to reconnect the inter-Korean rail link and the construction of an adjacent highway was confronted by the threat of landmines.[1070] The Ministry estimated that some 100,000 mines would need to be removed in the operation.[1071]

Laos has not signed the Convention despite having been among the first governments to call publicly for an immediate, comprehensive ban on anti-personnel mines in a statement delivered to the 1994 UN General Assembly.[1072] A high-ranking official from the Ministry of Foreign Affairs has claimed that the main reason for Laos not to sign the Convention was its concern that it would not be able to meet the deadline laid down for destruction of mines in the ground.[1073] Other sources have suggested that Laos will not join until China and Vietnam do,[1074] and that landmines still represent an 'economically viable' option for the defence of poor countries.[1075]

Mongolia has given a mixed reaction to the Convention on the Prohibition of Anti-Personnel Mines, having abstained from the vote in the UN General Assembly supporting the signing of the Convention in December 1997,[1076] while supporting the relevant resolution the following year urging adherence to it.[1077] In April 2000, the Minister of External Relations declared that Mongolia had adopted a 'phased approach towards the prohibition of anti-personnel mines' but was 'supportive of the noble objective of banning landmines' and was 'seeking ways and means to accede as early as possible' to the Convention.[1078]

Myanmar has continued to oppose the Convention, claiming that 'the real problem lies in indiscriminate use of anti-personnel landmines and the export and trade in these weapons[.] (...) We should effectively address these real issues, rather than reach out for an indiscriminate and all-encompassing total ban

---

Antipersonnel Landmines", November 1997, cited in *Landmine Monitor Report 1999*, p. 475.

1069 "$77– Needed to Strip Korean 'Belt of Death'", *South China Morning Post*, 30 October 1998. In September 1999, it was reported that clearance would take place every year through to 2003 of the 75,000 landmines 'installed (...) in the rear areas (...) for security'. "Over 1.12 Million Landmines Laid Throughout ROK", *Yonhap*, Seoul, 28 September 1999.

1070 Seok-jae, K., "Public Attention Focused on Safety of Soldiers in Mine-Clearing Work", *Korea Herald*, 19 September 2000.

1071 *Ibid.*

1072 See *Landmine Monitor Report 1999*, p. 482.

1073 "Logistics Prevent Laos from Signing Mine Pact", *Bangkok Post*, 30 June 1998, cited by *Landmine Monitor Report 1999*, p. 482. Though as the Landmine Monitor duly notes, the official claimed, inaccurately, that the deadline was four years, which applied to stockpiled anti-personnel mines. *Ibid.*

1074 In this regard, Vietnam's position on the Convention appears to be shifting. In early 1999, one government official declared that Vietnam's acceptance of the treaty 'was a matter of time, not of principle.' *Landmine Monitor Report 2000*, p. 540.

1075 *Landmine Monitor Report 1999*, p. 482.

1076 UN General Assembly resolution 52/38A.

1077 UN General Assembly resolution 53/77.

1078 *Landmine Monitor Report 2000*, pp. 513-4.

on anti-personnel landmines.'[1079] According to interviews with government and opposition commanders, both sides use anti-personnel mines and use is even increasing.[1080] A news report in January 1999, for instance, claimed that Government troops had admitted laying 7,000 mines since August 1998 at one section along the Thai border to deter an expected incursion by an opposition armed faction.[1081] Landmine Monitor estimated that there were as many as 1,500 new mine victims in 1999.[1082]

Surprisingly, Nepal was not among the treaty signatories, since there is no evidence that it has ever used, produced, stockpiled or transferred anti-personnel mines. In 2000, however, the Nepali Prime Minister directed the Foreign Ministry to accelerate the signing process and in early 2001 a government minister declared that Nepal was 'positive towards signing on [sic] this treaty'.[1083] Neighbouring Bhutan also did not sign the Convention, despite supporting relevant General Assembly resolutions in 1996, 1997, and 1998.[1084] In December 1999, both voted in favour of the UN General Assembly resolution supporting the Convention.[1085]

Pakistan has been a strong defender of anti-personnel mines, allegedly believing that they will be needed both for possible future conflicts with India and for the situation in Jammu and Kashmir.[1086] At least some observers feel that, in the absence of 'viable alternatives' the prospects of Pakistan changing its position are fairly poor.[1087] In 2000, Landmine Monitor reported that Pakistan had stockpiles of at least 6 million, much larger than had previously been thought.[1088] Singapore has also reserved the right to use anti-personnel mines for 'legitimate self-defence purposes'. It did, though, support UN General Assembly resolutions 53/77 and 54/54B.[1089]

At the Vienna Expert Meeting in February 1997, Sri Lanka was one of only four out of the 111 governments attending, which spoke openly of the continued

[1079] U Ohn Gyaw, Minister for Foreign Affairs of the Union of Myanmar, Statement to the 52nd Session of the UN General Assembly, New York, 26 September 1997, cited by *Landmine Monitor Report 1999*, p. 444. See also "UNGA 54/54B Resolution Clarification", E-mail correspondence from Mary Wareham, Human Rights Watch, 10 March 2000; *Landmine Monitor Report 2000*, p. 468.

[1080] *Landmine Monitor Report 1999*, p. 446.

[1081] "Burmese Troops Said Plant Mines Along Thai Border", *Phuchatkan*, 14 January 1999, cited in *ibid.*, p. 446.

[1082] *Landmine Monitor Report 2000*, p. 468.

[1083] "Nepal hosts South Asian landmine-monitoring meeting", *Kathmandu Post*, 30 January 2001.

[1084] See *Landmine Monitor Report 1999*, p. 443.

[1085] See for instance "UNGA 54/54B Resolution Clarification", E-mail correspondence from Mary Wareham, Human Rights Watch, 10 March 2000; see also *Landmine Monitor Report 2000*, pp. 518-9.

[1086] *Landmine Monitor Report 1999*, p. 494.

[1087] Banerjee, D., Co-Director, Institute of Peace and Conflict Studies, New Delhi, *South Asian Regional Survey*, prepared for Landmine Monitor, p. 25, cited in *Landmine Monitor Report 1999*, pp. 494-5. For an overview of the situation in South Asia and possible steps forward see ICRC, "South Asia Regional Seminar on Landmines", Wadduwa, Sri Lanka, 18-20 August 1999, Summary Report.

[1088] *Landmine Monitor Report 2000*, p. 521.

[1089] *Landmine Monitor Report 1999*, p. 503; *Landmine Monitor Report 2000*, p. 530.

need to use anti-personnel mines.[1090] It has since, however, endorsed General Assembly resolutions of 1996, 1997, 1998 and 1999 supporting a ban on anti-personnel mines, and at the First Meeting of States Parties of the Convention Sri Lanka welcomed 'in principle' a comprehensive ban on anti-personnel mines on humanitarian grounds and claimed that were it not for the ongoing conflict against the LTTE, 'a small group of terrorists',[1091] Sri Lanka would have been 'among the first group of member countries' who had ratified it.[1092] The Sri Lankan representative reaffirmed, however, its need to use anti-personnel mines to defend security establishments.[1093]

In the Middle East, only Jordan, Qatar and Yemen have ratified the Convention – all the other States of the region remain outside the treaty. Iran was one of 50 full participants at the International Strategy Conference in Ottawa in 1996, but did not sign the Convention believing that the 'particular security concerns of states should be effectively addressed.'[1094] Iran has abstained from both the 1998 and 1999 General Assembly resolutions supporting the Convention, though is reportedly in need of demining assistance.[1095] According to the ICBL, Iraq is both a producer and an exporter of anti-personnel mines and is the only known mine exporter in the world that has not instituted an export ban or moratorium, or at least made a policy declaration of no current export.[1096] Iraq became a member of the Conference on Disarmament in 1996 and the following year the Iraqi Ambassador to the UN urged the CD to launch negotiations on a global landmine ban.[1097]

According to the Landmine Monitor report, Israel has used anti-personnel mines 'extensively in combat (...) and for border protection'.[1098] Attending the treaty signing conference in Ottawa as an observer, an Israeli Ambassador, David Sultan, stated: 'Due to our unique situation in the Middle East involving an ongoing threat of hostilities as well as terrorist threats (...) we are still obliged to maintain anti-personnel landmines as necessary for self-defence[.] (...) Israel, regrettably, is unable to sign the treaty until effective alternative measures are available to ensure the protection of civilians threatened on a daily basis by terrorists and to ensure the protection of Israeli forces operating in areas of

---

1090 *Landmine Monitor Report 1999*, p. 508.

1091 Though as of writing this small group of terrorists appeared close to retaking the entire Jaffna peninsula.

1092 Statement of Sri Lanka to the First Meeting of States Parties, undated but May 1999. See also *Landmine Monitor Report 1999*, pp. 507-8.

1093 In this light, it is surprising that the Sri Lankan security forces are not able to forego anti-personnel mines in favour of remotely-controlled Claymores – lawful under the terms of the Convention on the Prohibition of Anti-Personnel Mines – as a more discriminate, and potentially more effective, means of defending military bases. But see *Landmine Monitor Report 2000*, pp. 532-5, wherein an early accession to the Convention appears unlikely.

1094 Statement by Ambassador of the Islamic Republic of Iran at the Treaty Signing Conference in Ottawa, 1-4 December 1997, cited in *Landmine Monitor Report 1999*, p. 883.

1095 UNMAS was planning an assessment mission to Iran in 2000. See UNMAS website, <http://www.un.org>.

1096 *Landmine Monitor Report 1999*, p. 886.

1097 *Ibid.*

1098 *Ibid.*, p. 889.

armed conflict.'[1099] Israel abstained from General Assembly resolutions in 1996, 1997, 1998 and 1999 supporting the prohibition of anti-personnel mines and adherence to the Convention.

Kuwait came to the Oslo negotiations in September as a full participant, not an observer, and voted for the 1997 General Assembly resolution supporting the December treaty signing. According to the UN mines database, Kuwait has said that it does not have a stockpile of anti-personnel mines, and in 1996 stated that it would not use anti-personnel mines, with certain unidentified exceptions.[1100]

According to its Ministry of Foreign Affairs, 'Lebanon agrees to and appreciates all noble principles and objectives of the Ottawa Mine Ban Treaty. However, Lebanon did not sign the Treaty due to the Israeli occupation of West Bekaa and South Lebanon. Israel is still laying landmines in South Lebanon.'[1101] In December 1999, however, Lebanon became the first ever State to vote against a UN General Assembly resolution supporting the Convention.[1102] It is not yet clear what motivated this unprecedented ste[1103]p. Lebanon's position on the Convention seemingly remained unchanged despite Israel's withdrawal from South Lebanon in the summer of 2000. Syria has been a strong defender of the continued need for anti-personnel mines, declaring that they represent an important weapon of defence against Israel, and that accordingly it is unable to sign the Convention.[1104]

(iv) Europe

In Europe, every European Union country with the exception of Finland is either signatory or party to the Convention and Turkey is the only NATO member State apart from the US that has not signed or ratified.[1105] Other European States outside the Convention include Armenia and Azerbaijan, Belarus, the Federal Republic of Yugoslavia, Georgia, and the Russian Federation.

Armenia is believed to have used anti-personnel mines in its conflict with Azerbaijan,[1106] though at the Treaty Signing Conference in Ottawa in December 1997, Armenia was surprisingly positive about the Convention declaring: 'Notwithstanding its security considerations, Armenia nevertheless believes that

---

1099 *Ibid.*, pp. 887-8.

1100 *Ibid.*, pp. 890, 891.

1101 *Ibid.*, p. 892.

1102 See for instance "UNGA 54/54B Resolution Clarification", E-mail correspondence from Mary Wareham, Human Rights Watch, 10 March 2000.

1103 See *Landmine Monitor Report 2000*, p. 944. Following the Israeli withdrawal from south Lebanon, it is likely that substantial mine clearance will be required. Only a few days afterwards it was reported that two young girls had been killed and seven other people, including four children, injured when a mine exploded in the former occupied zone. "Liban-Sud: Fillettes tuées par l'explosion d'une mine", *Le Temps*, 29 May 2000.

1104 *Landmine Monitor Report 1999*, pp. 907, 908. See also "UNGA 54/54B Resolution Clarification", *op. cit.*

1105 Although, as mentioned above, there are signs that Turkey may soon accede to the Convention simultaneous with Greece's ratification of its signature.

1106 *Ibid.*, p. 763.

the human and social costs of anti-personnel landmines far outweigh their military significance[.] (...) Armenia supports the Convention, and is ready to take measures consistent with the provisions of the treaty[.] (...) Armenia's full participation in the Convention is contingent upon a similar level of political commitment by other parties in the region to adhere to the treaty and comply with its regime.'[1107] Thus, it is believed that Armenia is unlikely to sign the Convention until Azerbaijan does,[1108] although it was one of 18 non-signatory States to vote in favour of the UN General Assembly resolution supporting the Convention in 1999.[1109] And Azerbaijan, which according to the UN continues to use anti-personnel mines, has shown little enthusiasm for the Convention on the Prohibition of Anti-Personnel Mines.[1110]

Belarus remains seemingly on the fringes of the Convention, declaring that the reason they cannot adhere to it is purely financial – the result of a huge stockpile of anti-personnel mines[1111] left over from the former Soviet Union.[1112] At an international workshop on humanitarian demining and mine stockpile elimination in Minsk from 6-7 March 2000, participants were informed among other things that:

- *the Republic of Belarus supports the goal of prohibiting use, stockpiling, production and transfer of anti-personnel mines;*
- *the Republic of Belarus does not produce anti-personnel mines;*
- *in 1995 the Republic of Belarus signed a moratorium on the export of anti-personnel landmines which now enjoys a de-facto international recognition; it has been extended by Belarus to the end of 2002;*
- *the Republic of Belarus faces a severe problem of eliminating a huge stockpile of anti-personnel landmines left in the country after the break-up of the Soviet Union;*
- *the Republic of Belarus will consider becoming a Party to the Convention on the Prohibition of the Use, Stockpiling, Production and Transfer of Anti-Personnel Mines and on their Destruction after demining and stockpile elimination activities with international financial and technological assistance has been provided.*[1113]

In March 2000, Belarussian officials reaffirmed their commitment to a total prohibition of anti-personnel mines as soon as the assistance necessary to destroy existing stockpiles is provided.[1114]

1107 *Ibid.*, p. 762.

1108 See *ibid.*, p. 762; see also *Landmine Monitor Report 2000*, pp. 791-2.

1109 See for instance "UNGA 54/54B Resolution Clarification", E-mail correspondence from Mary Wareham, Human Rights Watch, 10 March 2000.

1110 *Landmine Monitor Report 1999*, p. 764. See also *Landmine Monitor Report 2000*, p. 799.

1111 *Landmine Monitor Report 1999*, p. 772. The precise number of anti-personnel mines is not known – the government has acknowledged that it holds 'millions' and that it would cost 'tens of millions of dollars' to destroy them.

1112 *Ibid.*, p. 769.

1113 Chairman's Summary, International Workshop on Humanitarian Demining and Mine Stockpile Elimination, Minsk, Belarus, 6-7 March 2000.

1114 *Landmine Monitor Report 2000*, p. 804.

Of the three Baltic States, only Lithuania has signed the Convention. Estonia, which in the intergovernmental group of experts convened to prepare the first Review Conference of the 1980 CCW had actually proposed the adoption of a fourth protocol banning anti-personnel mines,[1115] now declares that it must have alternatives to the weapon before it can support a total prohibition. At the same time, it affirms that it currently possesses only a small quantity of anti-personnel mines – not exceeding that allowed for training purposes under the Convention.[1116] It did, though, vote in favour of the 1999 UN General Assembly resolution supporting the Convention,[1117] and recently adhered to the 1980 CCW. Estonia continues to prefer the negotiation of a prohibition on anti-personnel mines through the CD.[1118]

Latvia, too, remains outside the Convention, though in 1998 a Foreign Ministry official declared that: 'Latvia looks forward to joining the Ottawa Convention in the nearest possible future. However, due to the very limited resources of military equipment and material forces available to the Latvian military, we must first seek suitable and cost-effective alternatives[;] (...) the problem of alternatives (...) is, in fact, the sole obstacle on our way to join the Ottawa process.'[1119] In 1999, during the 54th session of the UN General Assembly, Latvia abstained in the First Committee vote on the Convention, but then changed to voting in favour in the final vote.[1120]

Finland is now the only Western European country not to have signed the Convention, and according to the ICBL it seems 'increasingly uncomfortable to be in that position.'[1121] Finland has the European Union's only border with Russia and the memories of the Second World War still run deep among Finns. In December 1997, a government working group concluded that Finland should take steps to replace its landmine arsenal and it was suggested that if efforts to do so started in 2001 Finland could be ready to sign the treaty by 2006.[1122] In December 1999, it reiterated its goal of adhering to the Convention in 2006 and replacing its stock of anti-personnel mines by 2010.[1123] At the same time, Finland has been a strident supporter of negotiations in the CD,[1124] although it

[1115] See *supra* Chapter 1, p. 43.

[1116] *Landmine Monitor Report 1999*, p. 779.

[1117] See for instance "UNGA 54/54B Resolution Clarification", E-mail correspondence from Mary Wareham, Human Rights Watch, 10 March 2000.

[1118] *Landmine Monitor Report 2000*, p. 811.

[1119] Statement of Mr. Ingemars Biseneiks, Security Policy Division, Ministry of Foreign Affairs of Latvia, to the Budapest Regional Conference on Antipersonnel Landmines, 26-28 March 1998, cited by *Landmine Monitor Report 1999*, p. 799.

[1120] See for instance "UNGA 54/54B Resolution Clarification", E-mail correspondence from Mary Wareham, Human Rights Watch, 10 March 2000. See further *Landmine Monitor Report 2000*, pp. 829-30.

[1121] Indeed, as President of the European Union in the latter half of 1999, Finland found itself in the position of having to deliver a warm tribute to the Convention on behalf of the EU to the UN General Assembly in October 1999. See Statement of Finland on behalf of the European Union to the First Committee of the UN General Assembly, New York, 11 October 1999.

[1122] "Finland Considers Steps to Phase out Landmines", *Reuters*, Helsinki, 16 December 1997.

[1123] See *Landmine Monitor Report 2000*, p. 813.

[1124] See *Landmine Monitor Report 1999*, pp. 784-5.

did vote in favour of the 1999 UN General Assembly resolution supporting the Convention.[1125]

In 1999, more mines were planted on the territory of the Federal Republic of Yugoslavia than anywhere else in Europe.[1126] As tensions mounted in Kosovo, Yugoslav soldiers planted more and more mines along the border with Albania and the Former Yugoslav Republic of Macedonia in a vain attempt to prevent infiltration by the Kosovo Liberation Army. A number of newspapers incorrectly reported that Yugoslavia had been among the 123 signatories to the Convention on the Prohibition of Anti-Personnel Mines.[1127] One newspaper report cited unnamed Serb military sources as having declared that mines were 'a regrettable necessity' given the inaccessible nature of the boundary between Albania and Montenegro.[1128] It is not yet known whether the change of regime in Belgrade will affect Yugoslav policy on anti-personnel mines.

Georgia came close to signing the Convention at the official signing in Ottawa in December 1997, but decided against this at the last minute claiming that it could not fulfil its obligations to clear mines and destroy stockpiles in Abkhazia, since the region was not under its control, and that it lacked the financial resources necessary to implement the Convention.[1129] During a visit to Georgia in February 1999 by ICBL Ambassador Jody Williams, President Shevardnadze stated his intention to sign the ban treaty and indicated that the Georgian Council of National Security was discussing the issue.[1130] Despite subsequently agreeing with the Russian Federation to mine its own borders to prevent Chechen infiltration, in December 1999 Georgia had voted in favour of UN General Assembly resolution 54/54B supporting the Convention.[1131] In March 2000, the Ministry of Defence cited additional reasons for not signing the Convention: (1) Russian forces stationed on Georgian territory have 'great amounts of landmines'; (2) none of the States in the region had signed; and (3) Russia continued to lay mines on Georgian territory.[1132]

The Russian Federation did not sign the treaty although former Russian President Boris Yeltsin made a number of declarations promising that Russia would adhere to the treaty at an unspecified future date, an assurance repeated

---

1125 See for instance "UNGA 54/54B Resolution Clarification", E-mail correspondence from Mary Wareham, Human Rights Watch, 10 March 2000.

1126 See for instance "War in the Balkans: A deadly crop of mines is sown in Kosovo: Weapons of power", *Independent*, 19 April 1999; "Landmine ban is defied on border", *Times*, 10 February 1999.

1127 Thus, the report in *Independent* of April 1999 that the Federal Republic of Yugoslavia had signed the Convention was incorrect. See also "Landmine ban is defied on border", *Times*, 10 February 1999; "War in the Balkans: A deadly crop of mines is sown in Kosovo: Weapons of power", *op. cit.* Although in 1998, at a regional conference in Budapest the Yugoslav representative had given positive signals of the possibility of future adherence to the Convention, this never resulted in signature.

1128 "Landmine ban is defied on border", *Times*, 10 February 1999.

1129 See *Landmine Monitor Report 1999*, p. 792.

1130 *Ibid.*

1131 See for instance "UNGA 54/54B Resolution Clarification", E-mail correspondence from Mary Wareham, Human Rights Watch, 10 March 2000.

1132 *Landmine Monitor Report 2000*, p. 822.

by senior officials from the Ministries of Defence and Foreign Affairs.[1133] On 1 March 1999, the date of entry into force of the Convention, Russian Foreign Minister Igor Ivanov declared that Russia would sign the Convention 'at a reasonable time in the future' which 'will be determined mostly by the need for solving technical, financial and other tasks related to liquidation of anti-personnel landmines, preparation for their functional replacement with account for national security interests.'[1134] Russia has also announced the destruction of more than 500,000 anti-personnel mines and an end to the production of blast anti-personnel mines.[1135] A government press release in March 2000 spoke of the policy 'aimed at banning of landmines' and indicated Russia's impending adherence to amended Protocol II to the CCW.[1136]

Turkey, which in the past has made considerable use of anti-personnel mines,[1137] refused to sign the Convention due to its conflict with the PKK and security concerns related to its neighbours.[1138] But in December 1999, Turkey was one of 18 non-signatories to vote in favour of the UN General Assembly resolution supporting the Convention.[1139] The same month, in a meeting with members of the ICBL in Geneva, Turkish officials had indicated their hope to adhere to the Convention in two or three years' time, assuming the security situation did not deteriorate.[1140]

E. Reservations

Article 19 of the Convention provides that the articles of the Convention 'shall not be subject to reservations.' However, the difficulty in applying this provision is in determining what does or does not constitute a reservation. Article 2(1)(d) of the 1969 Vienna Convention on the Law of Treaties, defines a reservation as 'a unilateral statement, however phrased or named, made by a State when signing, ratifying, accepting, approving or acceding to a treaty,

[1133] See for instance "Minefields Will Remain in Russia for Long", *Izvestia*, 14 October 1997. Adam Nizhelovsky, deputy commander-in-chief of Russia's military engineers declared that: 'The time-frame is simply unacceptable for financial and technical reasons.' Heritage, T., "Russia rebuffs calls to sign landmines treaty", *Reuters European*, Moscow, 27 May 1998. See also *Landmine Monitor Report 1999*, pp. 802-3.

[1134] Polishchuk, *ITAR-TASS*, 1 March 1999. One scholar notably described the effort to decode the promise to sign 'within a reasonable future time frame' as like trying to nail jelly to a wall. Lenarcic, D.A., *Knight-Errant? Canada and the Crusade to Ban Anti-Personnel Land Mines*, *op. cit.*, p. 29.

[1135] See "Nobel laureate targets Russia in anti-landmine drive", *AFP*, Moscow, 27 May 1998; *Landmine Monitor Report 1999*, pp. 802-3. See also Lawson, R. *et al.*, "The Ottawa Process and the International Movement to Ban Anti-Personnel Mines", *op. cit.*, p. 163.

[1136] *Landmine Monitor Report 2000*, p. 833.

[1137] *Landmine Monitor Report 1999*, pp. 821-3.

[1138] *Ibid.* See also "Official Explains Turkish Position on Ottawa Agreement", *Ankara Anatolia*, 15 October 1998.

[1139] See for instance "UNGA 54/54B Resolution Clarification", E-mail correspondence from Mary Wareham, Human Rights Watch, 10 March 2000.

[1140] *Landmine Monitor Report 2000*, p. 847.

whereby it purports to exclude or to modify the legal effect of certain provisions of the treaty in their application to that State.'[1141]

According to Sinclair, prior to the conclusion of the Convention on the Law of Treaties, doctrine was divided as to whether interpretive declarations should be considered as reservations.[1142] He approves, however, the following statement by Fitzmaurice, which is particularly relevant to the Convention on the Prohibition of Anti-Personnel Mines:

> *'[G]overnments not infrequently make declarations in which they do not say they will not carry out, or will only partly carry out, a certain provision – but make statements of intention, or say how they understand or propose to interpret or apply the provision, either generally or in certain events. Whether this will amount strictly to an actual reservation or not will depend on whether, by way of special interpretation, the party concerned is really purporting, so far as its own obligations are concerned, to alter the substantive content or application of the provision affected; or whether the statement is truly interpretational, and merely clarifies some obscurity, or makes explicit something that in the clause is only implicit. Thus, the use of the term 'reservation' is not conclusive in either sense.*[1143]

In addition to the discussion of the 'understandings' made upon ratification by Australia, Canada, the Czech Republic, and the UK,[1144] the question also arises of application to territory. The Netherlands, for instance, approved its signature of the Convention on the Prohibition of Anti-Personnel Mines 'for the Kingdom in Europe' only, despite having non-metropolitan territories.[1145] The question, as phrased by Sir Ian Sinclair, is the following: 'What is the rule of international law which applies when a treaty is silent on its territorial application?'

Once again, prior to the adoption of the Convention on the Law of Treaties, expert opinion as to the answer was divided. According to Article 29 as adopted (*Territorial scope of treaties*): 'Unless a different intention appears from the treaty or is otherwise established, a treaty is binding upon each party in respect of its entire territory.'[1146] This formula is clearly a flexible one, and indeed, the UK among others has made a declaration on the territorial effect of ratification on a number of occasions. Yet, as Sinclair points out: 'There are certain treaties, principally in the field of disarmament or humanitarian law, which are clearly

---

1141 See Sinclair, Sir I., *The Vienna Convention on the Law of Treaties*, *op. cit.*, p. 51 *et seq.*

1142 *Ibid.*, p. 52.

1143 Fitzmaurice, "Law and Procedure of the International Court of Justice, 1951-4: Treaty interpretation and other treaty points", *British Yearbook of International Law*, Vol. 33 (1957), p. 273, cited by Sinclair, Sir I., *The Vienna Convention on the Law of Treaties*, *op. cit.*, p. 53.

1144 Note that in accordance with UN General Assembly resolution 1452(XIV) of 7 December 1959, the UN Secretary-General in his capacity as depositary was instructed to accept reservations or objections to reservations without taking any position as to their legal consequences, a matter left to the States concerned. Bindschedler, R.L., "Treaties, Reservations" *Encyclopaedia of International Law*, North Holland, Amsterdam, 1984, p. 497.

1145 For example, the Netherlands Antilles and Aruba, located in the Caribbean.

1146 Sinclair, Sir I., *The Vienna Convention on the Law of Treaties*, *op. cit.*, p. 89.

intended to be world-wide in their application. It is arguable that the nature of such treaties would preclude the making of a reservation designed to limit their territorial application.'[1147]

The Convention on the Prohibition of Anti-Personnel Mines is clearly one such treaty, and accordingly any attempt to limit the territorial application of the Convention should *prima facie* be considered tantamount to a reservation, although no lack of good faith should be inferred from the Dutch decision.[1148] Thus, in March 2000, officials from the Portuguese Ministry of Foreign Affairs declared that the military base on Terceira Island in the Atlantic Azores Islands belonged to the US but was under Portuguese sovereignty 'so the Treaty of Ottawa should apply to the base.'[1149]

F. Provisional Application

According to Article 18 of the Convention, any State may at the time of its ratification, acceptance, approval or accession, declare that it will apply provisionally Article 1(1) of the Convention pending its entry into force. Article 18 was the brainchild of Belgium[1150] and was largely intended to ensure early entry into force of obligations pending the entry into force of the treaty as a whole.[1151] Delegates at the Oslo Diplomatic Conference watered down to a voluntary basis the suggested wording, which proposed compulsory provisional application. As of end April 2000, five States – Austria, Mauritius, South Africa, Sweden, and Switzerland – had made the requisite declaration at the time of adherence.

G. Withdrawal

Article 20 provides for the possibility to each State Party to withdraw from the Convention, giving notice of the withdrawal to all other States Parties, to the depositary and to the United Nations Security Council.[1152] The instrument of withdrawal must include a full explanation of the reasons motivating it.[1153] According to Article 20(3): 'Such withdrawal shall only take effect six months

---

1147 *Ibid.*, p. 91.

1148 Though Sinclair notes that this general rule does not apply 'in special circumstances', such as when a State is not in a position to implement the provisions in a named territory. *Ibid.*, pp. 110-1, endnote 37. It is the author's view, for example, that Georgia could lawfully make such a declaration with respect to Abkhazia were it to accede to the Convention. Apart from the inconvenience for the Netherlands in securing approval for ratification from a number of non-metropolitan countries, it is not known what special circumstances might justify their limiting territorial application.

1149 *Landmine Monitor Report 2000*, p. 708.

1150 See for instance *Landmine Monitor Report 1999*, p. 533.

1151 For a brief discussion of the rather peculiar argument that this provision might in some way undermine the obligation of signatories not to act contract to the object and purpose of the treaty (under Article 18, Vienna Convention on the Law of Treaties), see Goose, S.D., "The Ottawa Process and the 1997 Mine Ban Treaty", *op. cit.*, p. 288.

1152 Article 20(2).

1153 *Ibid.*

after the receipt of the instrument of withdrawal by the Depositary. If, however, on the expiry of that six-month period, the withdrawing State Party is engaged in an armed conflict, the withdrawal shall not take effect before the end of the armed conflict.'

There was considerable discussion in Oslo of the possibility to withdraw from the Convention in exceptional circumstances (which basically meant armed conflict). As mentioned above, the US had proposed the right to withdraw from the treaty when a State's supreme national interests were under threat. A number of other States called for the right to withdraw upon six month's notice even during an armed conflict, and Brazil had sought to limit the restriction on withdrawal to a situation where the State seeking to withdraw was involved in an armed conflict against another State Party. Although the right to withdraw was reduced from the proposed 12 months to six months, the crucial clause prohibiting effective withdrawal during an armed conflict was retained.[1154]

There were reports in early 2000 that Tajikistan was considering withdrawing from the Convention, due to an evaluation of the consequences of clearing minefields along the Tajik-Afghan border.[1155]

H. Amendments

Under Article 13 of the Convention, any State Party may propose the holding of an Amendment Conference to consider amendments to the provisions of the treaty. If a majority of State Parties support the proposal to convene the Conference, the UN Secretary-General will do so in his capacity as depositary, normally immediately following an annual Meeting of States Parties or a Review Conference. Amendments are to be adopted by a two-thirds majority of States voting and will enter into force for States having ratified the amendments on the day of deposit of the instrument, once a simple majority of States Parties have notified the depositary of their consent to be bound by it.

According to Steve Goose, the ICBL intends to address four main areas of concern with the Convention during the Annual Meetings of States Parties, the Review Conference and any Amendment Conference:

- *anti-vehicle mines equipped with anti-handling devices;*[1156]
- *the retention of mines for training purposes;*
- *the lack of a binding requirement for provision of assistance to mine victims;*
- *the 'failure' to include specific language regarding application to non-State actors.*[1157]

1154 See Goose, S.D., "The Ottawa Process and the 1997 Mine Ban Treaty", *op. cit.*, p. 288.

1155 *Landmine Monitor Report 2000*, p. 741.

1156 *On this point see also Atwood, D.C., "Implementing Ottawa", op. cit., p. 10.*

1157 Goose, S.D., "The Ottawa Process and the 1997 Mine Ban Treaty", *op. cit.*, p. 289. David Atwood also claims that the modest compliance mechanisms of the Convention represent a potential limitation of the Convention. Atwood, D.C., "Implementing Ottawa", *op. cit.*, p. 5.

I. Review Conference of States Parties

Article 12 provides for the convening of a Review Conference five years after the entry into force of the treaty – accordingly, this will take place in 2004. The first Review Conference is likely to be a detailed assessment of the effectiveness of the treaty in tackling the global landmine threat as a whole.

2.4.6. Promoting Compliance

A. Transparency measures

In accordance with Article 7(1) of the Convention, no later than 180 days after its entry into force for the respective State, each State Party is obliged to submit an initial report to the depositary detailing a number of issues, including: its national implementation measures; the number of anti-personnel mines stockpiled; 'to the extent possible', the location of all mined areas containing anti-personnel mines under its jurisdiction or control;[1158] the quantity of anti-personnel mines retained for training in mine clearance; and the progress of stockpile destruction. A similar report must then be filed annually.[1159]

These reporting duties are quite far-reaching and will require considerable effort on the part of States to comply with the requirements. Indeed, at the Oslo Diplomatic Conference there was some discussion of allowing a State Party one full year rather than six months after entry into force for the submission of the reports. This was not, however, accepted and thus the first 40 ratifying States were due to submit their first report no later than 27 August 1999.[1160]

To ensure consistent quality and assist punctuality of submission, at the First Meeting of States Parties of the Convention, a proposed reporting format was presented by Austria.[1161] Nonetheless, by early March 2000, 34 States were late in submitting their reports.[1162] At the January 2000 SCE working group meeting on the Convention, the ICBL complained about the lack of timely reporting

1158 At the First Meeting of States Parties of the Convention, Jordan declared that 'like other delegations', they were still hoping for a common agreement over the meaning of the term 'location' contained in Article 7(1)(c). Statement by Prince Zeid Bin Ra'Ad, Head of Delegation to the First Meeting of States Parties, Maputo, 3 May 1999, p. 1.

1159 Article 7(2).

1160 This concerned the following governments: Andorra, Austria, the Bahamas, Belgium, Belize, Benin, Bolivia, Bosnia-Herzegovina, Bulgaria, Burkina Faso, Canada, Croatia, Denmark, Djibouti, Equatorial Guinea. Fiji, the Former Yugoslav Republic of Macedonia, France, Germany, Grenada, Holy See, Honduras, Hungary, Ireland, Jamaica, Japan, Malawi, Mali, Mauritius, Mexico, Mozambique, Namibia, Niue, Norway, Peru, Samoa, San Marino, Senegal, South Africa, Switzerland, Trinidad and Tobago, Turkmenistan, the United Kingdom, Yemen, and Zimbabwe.

1161 See Annex II to the "Final Report", *UN Doc. APLC/MSP.1/1999/1*, of 20 May 1999.

1162 Andorra, Bahamas, Barbados, Bosnia-Herzegovina, Burkina Faso, Costa Rica, Djibouti, Dominica, El Salvador, Equatorial Guinea, Grenada, Guatemala, Guinea, Jamaica, Lesotho, Malawi, Mali, Mauritius, Monaco, Mozambique, Namibia, Nicaragua, Niger, Panama, Paraguay, Peru, Qatar, St Kitts and Nevis, Samoa, San Marino, Solomon Islands, Trinidad and Tobago, Turkmenistan, and Uganda. "Reporting Update No. 7", E-mail correspondence from Mary Wareham, Human Rights Watch, 8 March 2000.

under Article 7, claiming that only about half of the States required to do so had filed their reports, and that of these, some were incomplete.[1163]

B. The Compliance Mechanism

At the Oslo Diplomatic Conference, the Canadian delegation was given the task as a 'Friend of the Chair' of resolving the tricky issue of a compliance mechanism for the Convention.[1164] According to one authoritative view, the result is 'a mix of the disarmament model of an intrusive verification regime and the international humanitarian law model of a fact-finding mechanism.'[1165] The central issue of dispute, which touched on the sensitive domain of State sovereignty, was whether a fact-finding mission could visit a country that had been accused of violating the Convention only with,[1166] or even without,[1167] its consent.[1168] The provision that was finally adopted allows for a formal exchange of information between State Parties in instances where a violation of the Convention is alleged, but also allows fact-finding to take place if such exchange does not satisfactorily resolve the situation.[1169]

The clearest explanation of what is a long and intricate provision was given by the Austrian diplomats largely responsible for its elaboration.[1170] They break down the process conveniently into five stages. The *first stage* is a request from one or more States Parties ('the requesting State') for information regarding allegations of non-compliance.[1171] The 'requested State Party' has 28 days to respond to these allegations.

The *second stage* follows in the event of a failure by the 'requested State Party' to respond satisfactorily (or at all) to the allegations. The requesting State or States may then refer the matter to the next Meeting of States Parties[1172] or call for a Special Meeting of States Parties. A Special Meeting would be convened if one-third of the States Parties agree (within 14 days).[1173]

The *third stage* is the meeting itself, at which a decision can be taken to authorise a fact-finding mission[1174] by simple majority of those present and voting (though every effort must be taken to reach a decision by consensus).[1175]

1163 E-mail correspondence from Liz Bernstein, ICBL Co-ordinator, 12 May 2000; see further *Landmine Monitor Report 2000*, pp. 14-15.

1164 Hajnoczi, T. *et al.*, "The Ban Treaty", *op. cit.*, p. 301.

1165 *Ibid.* See also Goose, S.D., "The Ottawa Process and the 1997 Mine Ban Treaty", *op. cit.*, p. 289.

1166 The proposal of Mexico, see *APL/CW.6.*

1167 The proposal of Germany, see *APL/CW. 24* and *APL/CW. 25.*

1168 Hajnoczi, T. *et al.*, "The Ban Treaty", *op. cit.*, p. 301.

1169 See *ibid.*, p. 302.

1170 *Ibid.*, pp. 302-3. This section is adapted from their helpful description of the operation of the compliance mechanism. See also Goose, S.D., "The Ottawa Process and the 1997 Mine Ban Treaty", *op. cit.*, p. 285.

1171 Article 8(2).

1172 Article 8(3).

1173 Article 8(5).

1174 Article 8(8).

1175 Article 8(6).

A requested State Party may also invite such a mission at any stage without the need for a specific decision to be taken.[1176]

The fact-finding mission itself is the *fourth stage* in the process. The mission shall consist of up to nine experts drawn from a list submitted by States Parties and held by the UN Secretary-General.[1177] The Secretary-General is responsible for nominating the members of the mission, after consultation with the requested State Party.[1178] That State has the right to withhold access to certain areas for reasons of security, but if it does so, must make every reasonable effort to demonstrate through alternative means its compliance with the Convention.[1179] In the absence of consent, the mission may remain in the territory of the requested State Party for no more than 14 days, including a maximum of seven days at any one site.[1180]

The *fifth stage* in the process (and the final one) is the review of information collected by the fact-finding mission, which is to report to the Meeting of States Parties through the Secretary-General.[1181] If the mission finds that the requested State Party has not complied with the Convention, the Meeting 'may suggest to the States Parties concerned ways and means to further clarify or resolve the matter under consideration, including the initiation of appropriate procedures in conformity with international law.'[1182] The Meeting must make every effort to reach decisions by consensus, but if this is not possible, they will be taken by a two-thirds majority of States Parties present and voting.[1183]

Within this seemingly complex and bureaucratic procedure for 'facilitation and clarification of compliance', the key issue remains the possibility of sending fact-finding missions to a State accused of having violated the treaty, without the need for that State's consent or approval. Such verification measures continue to be controversial, pitting the sensitivity of developing nations against the Western disarmament specialists, and were the subject of long negotiation during the Diplomatic Conference. Early in the Ottawa Process the ICRC, fearful that this issue could be used by a small number of States to block the establishment of the norm, had called on States 'not to permit verification to stand in the way of an absolute prohibition on the use, production, stockpiling and transfer' of the weapon.[1184]

The final result is something of a mish-mash, although, as the Swiss Federal Council has observed, the mechanism is fairly similar to those found in traditional disarmament texts, for example, Article IX of the 1993 Chemical Weap-

[1176] Article 8(8).
[1177] Article 8(9).
[1178] Article 8(10).
[1179] Article 8(14).
[1180] Article 8(15).
[1181] Article 8(17).
[1182] Article 8(19).
[1183] Article 8(20).
[1184] Statement of the ICRC to the Vienna Expert Meeting, 12 February 1997, p. 3. They were careful to declare their support at the same time for the 'maximum possible verification' of the treaty.

ons Convention.[1185] It is, however rather unlikely that it will be frequently used,[1186] since the mere proposal for the convening of such a procedure would inevitably be seen as a diplomatically hostile gesture, and especially unlikely that it will be used in the next few years for fear of deterring adherence to the Convention. Yet, those closely involved in the drafting regard the result as a 'remarkable achievement' since it goes well beyond provisions accepted in the 1949 Geneva Conventions or their Additional Protocols of 1977, and claim that by its very existence it serves to encourage compliance.[1187]

In January 2000, at the SCE working group meeting on the Convention, the ICBL stressed the need to 'urgently' put in place the structures and methodology necessary to carry out Article 8 on compliance, and called upon States to use the possibility of calling for clarification regarding possible violations 'whenever appropriate, and not to only use it in the most dire situations.'[1188] The co-chairs of the working group agreed to co-ordinate a group of interested states to produce a document aimed at 'operationalising' Article 8.[1189]

The second annual Landmine Monitor report, published in August 2000, called upon States Parties to make detailed requests for clarification from Rwanda, Uganda, and Zimbabwe as to their alleged use of anti-personnel mines in the Democratic Republic of Congo. 'Even if those States Parties have not used anti-personnel mines themselves, they may have engaged in co-operative military action with armed forces that have laid anti-personnel mines, which could also constitute a treaty violation.'[1190]

C. Annual Meetings of States Parties

Annual Meetings of States Parties shall be held until at least the first Review Conference in accordance with Article 11. The Meetings are tasked to consider the operation and status of the Convention; issues arising from reports submitted; international co-operation and assistance; mine clearance technologies; compliance issues; and requests for extensions to the requirement to clear all mined areas within 10 years of entry into force of the Convention for a given State Party. This broad agenda is in line with the more co-operative form of

1185 Swiss Federal Council, *Message concernant la Convention sur l'interdiction de l'emploi, du stockage, de la production et du transfert des mines antipersonnel et sur leur destruction*, Bern, January 1998.

1186 A fact acknowledged even by those closely involved in the drafting. See Hajnoczi, T. *et al.*, "The Ban Treaty", *op. cit.*, p. 304.

1187 *Ibid.* Ambassador Molander of Sweden, on the other hand, the President of the First CCW Review Conference, criticised the compliance mechanism as he feared that it would deter adherence to the Convention. See for instance Foreword by Ambassador Molander in Maresca, L. and Maslen, S. (eds.), *The Banning of Anti-Personnel Landmines*, p. xxv. In fact, this issue has never been raised by any State that has not signed or adhered to it, though it may be a factor that will be taken into account when deciding at a future date whether to join or not. See for instance Goose, S.D., "The Ottawa Process and the 1997 Mine Ban Treaty", *op. cit.*, p. 289.

1188 E-mail correspondence from Liz Bernstein, ICBL Co-ordinator, 12 May 2000.

1189 *Ibid.*

1190 *Landmine Monitor Report 2000*, pp. 5, 198, 200.

implementation likely to promote compliance with the treaty, particularly given that NGOs have direct access to the proceedings.

Following the adoption of UN General Assembly Resolution 53/77 of 12 January 1999,[1191] the first Annual Meeting of States Parties took place in Maputo, Mozambique, from 3-7 May 1999.[1192] Some 1,000 delegates[1193] gathered for the five-day conference,[1194] which was opened by the Mozambican President, Joaquim Chissano,[1195] determined, in the words of one State Party, 'to eliminate one of the most ferocious arms that exists'.[1196]

Rules of procedure were adopted requiring the presence of 30 States Parties for a quorum,[1197] and decisions on all matters of substance were to be taken by a two-thirds majority of the representatives of States Parties present and voting.[1198]

No requests were made pursuant to Article 5 (requests for extensions to the requirement to clear all mined areas within 10 years) or Article 8 (compliance issues) at the Meeting. Indeed, one of the major outcomes of the First Meeting of States Parties was the decision to hold inter-sessional working groups (Standing Committees of Experts) on a range of key themes.[1199] It was decided that the Geneva International Centre for Humanitarian Demining, opened by the Swiss government in 1998, would serve as the secretariat for these working

1191 The Resolution was passed with 20 abstentions – Azerbaijan, China, Cuba, Egypt, India, Iran, Israel, Libya, marshall Islands (despite its signature of the Convention), Micronesia, Morocco, Myanmar, Pakistan, Russian Federation, Syria, Tajikistan, the US, and Vietnam. Its operative paragraph 6 invited all States Parties to the First Meeting of States Parties and, in accordance with Article 11(4) of the Convention, States not parties to the Convention, as well as the United Nations, other relevant international organisations or institutions, regional organisations, the International Committee of the Red Cross and relevant non-governmental organisations to attend the Meeting as observers in accordance with the agreed rules of procedure. See*Landmine Monitor Report 1999*, p. 1057.

1192 There were at that time 55 States Parties to the Ottawa Treaty.

1193 A total of 43 States Parties were represented in Maputo, together with 18 that had ratified but for which the Convention had not yet entered into force, and 47 States not party to the Convention.

1194 The cost of which was estimated to be a rather staggering US$1.85 million. See "Estimated Costs for Convening the First Meeting of States Parties to the Convention on the Prohibition of the Use, Stockpiling, Production and Transfer of Anti-Personnel Mines and on Their Destruction", *UN Doc. APLC/MSP.1/1999/L.5*, 30 April 1999.

1195 See for instance "International Landmines Conference opens in Maputo",*AFP Internationale*, 3 May 1999.

1196 Statement of the Holy See to the First Meeting of States Parties (Statement corrected on 5 May 1999).

1197 See "Draft Rules of Procedure", *UN Doc. APLC/MSP.1/1999/L.3*, 22 March 1999, Rule 15.

1198 *Ibid.*, Rule 16. Rule 18 clarified that an abstention did not count as a vote for these purposes.

1199 Mine clearance; Victim assistance, socio-economic reintegration and mine awareness; Stockpile destruction; Technologies for mine action; and General status and operation of the Convention. See "Final Report", *UN Doc. APLC/MSP.1/1999/1*, of 20 May 1999. The idea for the intersessional working groups apparently came from Steffan Kongstad, a canny Norwegian diplomat determined to find ways to keep the momentum of the Ottawa process going. See also Atwood, D.C., "Implementing Ottawa", *op. cit.*, pp. 8-9. See also *Landmine Monitor Report 2000*, pp. 32, 984.

groups.[1200] Moreover, Switzerland also announced at the First Meeting of States Parties its readiness to host the Second Meeting of States Parties in Geneva in the year 2000,[1201] an offer accepted by the Conference.[1202]

The Meeting ended with a formal declaration by States Parties by which they voiced their 'outrage at the unabated use of anti-personnel mines in conflicts around the world.'[1203] It went on: 'To those who continue to use, develop, produce, otherwise acquire, stockpile, retain and transfer these weapons: cease now, and join us in this task.'[1204] But the declaration was especially strong on the signatories – presumably with a particular eye on Angola – that continued to use anti-personnel mines. 'To those few signatories who continue to use these weapons, this is a violation of the object and purpose of the Convention that you solemnly signed. We call upon you to respect and implement your commitments.' And in a thinly veiled warning it continued: 'Our assistance and co-operation will flow primarily to those who have foresworn the use of these weapons forever.'

The second Annual Meeting of States Parties, which took place in Geneva from 11-15 September 2000, was a relatively low-key affair,[1205] most notable for the President, Ambassador Steffan Kongstad, effectively throwing the US Special Representative for Humanitarian Demining, Donald Steinberg, out of the room as the US had refused to pay the costs of being an observer. Steinberg was forced to watch from the public gallery and reportedly returned home early. The major decisions of the Meeting were to reduce the number of SCE meetings and groups and to change their name to merely *Standing Committees*.[1206] From now on, there are only four Standing Committees: Mine Clearance and Related Technologies; Victim Assistance, Socio-Economic Reintegration and Mine Awareness; Stockpile Destruction; and General Status and Operation of the Convention.[1207]

1200 For the view of the ICBL regarding the SCE working groups see for instance "Intersessional Update No 6", E-mail correspondence from Susan B. Walker, ICBL Government Relations Liaison, 28 April 2000.

1201 Statement of Switzerland to the First Meeting of States Parties delivered by Ambassador Erwin Hoffer, Head of the Swiss Delegation.

1202 The Final Report of the First Meeting of States Parties announced that the Second Meeting of States Parties would take place in Geneva from 11-15 September 2000. See "Final Report", *UN Doc. APLC/MSP.1/1999/1*, of 20 May 1999. This was included in the draft General Assembly resolution on the Convention, A/C.1/54/L.2, introduced into the GA First Committee by Mozambique in October 1999 with 85 co-sponsors, including four non-signatories: Comoros, Liberia, Nepal, and Nigeria. (Liberia has since acceded to the Convention.) Speaking in January 2000, the ICBL recommended that the third Annual Meeting of States Parties in 2001 be again held in a mine-affected State Party. E-mail correspondence from Liz Bernstein, ICBL Co-ordinator, 12 May 2000.

1203 Maputo Declaration, 7 May 1999. See also "Ottawa Convention Landmine Conference outraged by continued use", *AFP Internationale*, 7 May 1999.

1204 *Ibid.*

1205 It was also considerably cheaper than the first Annual Meeting held in Maputo, with estimated costs of some US$450,000. See *UN Doc. APLC/MSP.2/2000/L.4.*

1206 See "President's Paper on Revisions to the Intersessional Work Programme", *UN Doc. APLC/MSP.2/2000/L.5.*

1207 *Ibid.*, p. 5.

The third Annual Meeting of States Parties will take place in Managua from 18-21 September 2001. A total of 143 States supported General Assembly resolution 55/33V on the Implementation of the Convention that, *inter alia,* requested the UN Secretary-General to make the necessary preparations for the Meeting.[1208]

D. Landmine Monitor

Concerned that a State-based regime intended to ensure respect of the treaty's provisions would not be adequate to the task, and encouraged by Canada and others, NGOs began discussions to establish a 'civil-society-based reporting network for monitoring nations' compliance with the Mine Ban Treaty.'[1209] After a number of preparatory meetings, it was decided that this network would take the format of an annual report on the global landmines situation, with State-by-State analysis, and not limited to signatories or parties to the Convention on the Prohibition of Anti-Personnel Mines.

The first of these annual reports, co-ordinated by Human Rights Watch, was issued in early May 1999, just prior to the First Meeting of States Parties of the Convention. According to its own description:

> *'Landmine Monitor is an unprecedented initiative by the International Campaign to Ban Landmines (ICBL) to monitor implementation of and compliance with the 1997 Mine Ban Treaty, and more generally to assess the efforts of the international community to resolve the landmines crisis. It is the first time that non-governmental organisations are coming together in a co-ordinated, systematic and sustained way to monitor a humanitarian law or disarmament treaty, and to regularly document progress and problems. The main elements of the Landmine Monitor system are a global reporting network, a central database, and an annual report[.] (...) It should be understood that Landmine Monitor is not a technical verification system or a formal inspection regime. It is an effort by civil society to hold governments accountable to the obligations that they have taken on with regard to anti-personnel mines; this is done through extensive collection, analysis and distribution of information that is publicly available.* '[1210]

The *Landmine Monitor Report 1999* is, especially given the time constraints in producing it, a remarkable piece of work. Although country reports – inevitably – vary in quality (and size), the overall impression is the establishment of a fairly comprehensive, and certainly essential, standard by which all States and non-State actors will be judged.[1211] The second annual report, also

---

1208 No States voted against the resolution and 22 countries – an increase of two on the previous year – abstained, including treaty signatory the Marshall Islands.

1209 The idea was first raised by the Canadian Foreign Minister, Lloyd Axworthy, during his visit to the NGO Forum running in parallel with the Oslo Diplomatic Conference.

1210 "About Landmine Monitor", *Landmine Monitor Report 1999.*

1211 It is to be expected that the report will improve year by year. The Monitor itself acknowledges that 'this ambitious report has its shortcomings. It is to be viewed as a work in progress, a system that will be continuously updated, corrected and improved. We welcome comments,

referred to extensively in this work, was published in August 2000, and formally launched prior to the second Annual Meeting of States Parties. It has already become the frame of reference for the success (or otherwise) of the Convention and its implementation. It was generally well received, although it includes a statement from Switzerland (referring to the 1999 report) that 'the report makes it difficult to distinguish factual information provided by the governments of the member States from the evaluations of the authors,'[1212] and that some non-signatory States might be dissuaded from adhering to the Convention.[1213]

Landmine Monitor Report 2001 is due to be published around the middle of September, just prior to the Third Meeting of States Parties in Managua.

2.5. Conclusion

In concluding this chapter, two separate issues should be considered: whether the Convention effectively prohibits the use of anti-personnel mines; and the possible implications of the Ottawa process for the future of international humanitarian law.

2.5.1. Does the Convention Effectively Prohibit the Use of Anti-Personnel Mines?

Speaking on the third day of the Oslo Diplomatic Conference, UN Secretary-General Kofi Annan, reminding delegates that the first UN peacekeeper to die was as a result of a landmine explosion in the Middle East, called anti-personnel mines 'weapons of the past and a symbol of shame'. In a similar vein, an editorial in the *Hindustan Times* on 24 September 1998 claimed that: 'Without much fanfare, the world quietly became that much safer a place to live in last week when the anti-personnel landmine (...) treaty became international law at the United Nations.' It further asserted that the Convention 'certainly provides undisputed legal and moral principles which a State or an armed group can ignore only at the cost of acquiring pariah status in the civilised world.'[1214]

On the other hand, a Canadian defence analyst repeated the views of a number of sceptics and opponents of the anti-personnel mine ban[1215] when he suggested that the treaty 'amounts to little more than a pact among the virtuous.'[1216] It is therefore appropriate to consider whether the Convention on

---

clarifications, and corrections from governments and others, in the spirit of dialogue and in the search for accurate and reliable information on a difficult subject.' *Ibid.*

1212 *Landmine Monitor Report 2000*, p. 736.

1213 This is unlikely in the view of the author given that the position and policy of all States are described in the report.

1214 "A life-saving treaty", *Hindustan Times*, 24 September 1998.

1215 For example, former British Army bomb-disposal officer Paul Jefferson who was wounded by a landmine in Kuwait in 1991 while engaged in mine clearance declared that a mine ban would not work and declared at the same time that even if it did work, it would not start to reduce casualties for 15 years. Jefferson, P., "The landmine ban is worse than useless", *Guardian*, 19 September 1997.

1216 Lenarcic, D.A., *Knight-Errant? Canada and the Crusade to Ban Anti-Personnel Land Mines*, *op. cit.*, p. 27.

the Prohibition of Anti-Personnel Mines does in fact prohibit anti-personnel mines, both in law and in practice.

A. The Reach of the Convention

Although a scope article would have reinforced the obligations contained in the Convention, it is clear that it applies at all times and in all circumstances, including peacetime as well as armed conflict. Despite a lack of clarity in certain aspects, the definition contained in the Convention on the Prohibition on Anti-Personnel Mines is, overall, a good one as it encompasses those mines that are most dangerous to civilians. Thus, the Convention prohibits both long-lived 'dumb' and self-destructing 'smart' anti-personnel mines. To have done otherwise, would have been to divide North and South and effectively destroy the putative agreement, but this is nonetheless an impressive achievement.

Based on evidence currently available, the author believes that all weapons 'designed, altered or intended' to serve as anti-personnel mines as defined in Article 2(1) are prohibited under the Convention on the Prohibition on Anti-Personnel Mines. This includes mines other than anti-personnel mines equipped with highly sensitive anti-handling devices that are detonated by the innocent act of a passer-by.[1217] Claymore 'mines' are also prohibited unless used only in command-detonated mode. Unexploded ordnance, including cluster bomblets,[1218] are not covered by the Convention, nor are booby-traps. But a clearer definition is required of what *in practice* constitute booby-traps and anti-vehicle mines (especially the minimum weight needed to detonate an anti-vehicle mine); an Annual Meeting of States Parties should address this issue at the earliest possible opportunity.

Despite expressed concerns, the definitions contained in amended Protocol II and the Convention are broadly similar, although Pakistan's declaration with respect to the word 'primarily' in the definition in amended Protocol II would not be acceptable under the Convention, as the use of all anti-personnel mines are prohibited, even as the fuzing mechanism of an anti-vehicle mine.

With respect to the prohibition on assisting, inciting and encouraging others to commit prohibited activities, the picture is less rosy. Although the respective declarations made by Australia, Canada, the Czech Republic, and the UK would appear to be lawful according to the terms of the Convention, they do go against its spirit. On the other hand, Australia's interpretation of Article 1(c) is one that effectively restricts the ambit of the Convention and thereby tantamount to a reservation; a violation of Article 19.

The obligation to enact implementing legislation at national level contained in the Convention is disappointingly weak. The lack of even a modified grave

1217 But as anti-vehicle mines are being equipped with increasingly sensitive anti-handling devices, great care will be needed to ensure that, in practice, the fuzing mechanisms used to protect anti-tank mines do not lead to future humanitarian problems.

1218 The ICBL decided that it would not, as a body, address cluster bomblets but that national campaigns and member organisations could do so of their own accord. *Landmine Monitor Report 2000*, p. 997.

breaches provision sets a poor precedent for the future implementation of international humanitarian law. Notwithstanding these lacunae, national implementing legislation remains important, including in countries where civilians as well as soldiers are involving in laying anti-personnel mines. Sadly, as the ICRC has found, a substantial number of countries have not yet enacted the necessary legislation to give effect at domestic level to obligations under the four 1949 Geneva Conventions.

With respect to universality of adherence, according to one commentator, 'the glass is more than half full.'[1219] But although more than two-thirds of the world's States have signed the Convention and more than half have ratified or acceded to it, it is rightly pointed out that a substantial number of key States remain outside its purview.[1220] Certainly of great concern is the claim that no less than 90 per cent of the world's estimated anti-personnel landmine stockpiles of 250 million mines are in the possession of non-signatory States.[1221]

In 1996, the then US Secretary of State Warren Christopher noted that anti-personnel mines 'probably kill more children than soldiers', expressed American 'determination to eliminate these deadly instruments of terror', and claimed that 'an international ban on landmines cannot happen without American leadership'.[1222] Although some consider the absence of key States in the negotiation and adoption of the Convention on the Prohibition of Anti-Personnel Mines as a major failing, as the ICRC pointed out at the Vienna Expert Meeting in February 1997: 'None of the major instruments of humanitarian law has attracted universal adherence from the outset. Indeed in the case of dumdum bullets two of the major powers of the day voted against a prohibition.[1223] And yet the vast majority of States have respected the norms created by these agreements.'[1224] Likewise, Price points out that the poison taboo took hundreds of years to consolidate in Renaissance Europe, and even though the chemical weapons' taboo has been 'rather successful', it too does not enjoy universal support.[1225]

Indeed, it seems likely that despite its prevarication, the US will join the Convention within the coming decade, a decision that will almost inevitably result in further adherence, for example by Finland and Turkey, probably Belarus and the Russian Federation, and possibly India and Pakistan. Retired US

1219 Atwood, D.C., "Implementing Ottawa", *op. cit.*, p. 4.

1220 As Richard Price remarks, for example, the Convention has been criticised for being a 'feel-good treaty' due to the fact that States containing well over half the world's population that are also key military powers, are not party to it. But he also points out that while support for the ban is not universal, the vast majority of anti-personnel mine victims have not been in the hold-out countries, and in contrast to norms contained in human rights treaties, the Convention has support 'where it needs it most – in countries where the pernicious effects of the now-deviant practice have been most prevalent.' See Price, R., "Compliance with International Norms and the Mines Taboo", *To Walk Without Fear*, p. 346.

1221 "Report on the Informal Consultations on stockpile destruction in accordance with Article 4", undated document circulated at the First Meeting of States Parties.

1222 Gard, R., "The Military Utility of Anti-Personnel Mines", *op. cit.*, p. 147.

1223 The UK and the US.

1224 Statement of the ICRC to the Vienna Expert Meeting, 12 February 1997, p. 4.

1225 Price, R., "Compliance with International Norms and the Mines Taboo", *op. cit.*, p. 347.

General Robert Gard recalled the parallels between the US reaction to the Geneva Gas Protocol of 1925 and its reaction to the Convention on the Prohibition of Anti-Personnel Mines:

> *'Although now there is nearly universal agreement, even among US military professionals, that the use of chemical weapons should be prohibited, representatives of the US War Department, the Pentagon of its day, argued that chemicals were one of the most effective weapons ever known, decisive in offensive operations; that it would not be possible to prevent the use in war of a weapon that is militarily effective; and that the treaty was impractical, unenforceable, and ineffective.'*[1226]

Moreover, as Human Rights Watch has pointed out, while some States in the Middle East and North Africa – it cites Egypt, Iran, Iraq, Israel, Libya and Syria – are 'very hostile' to a prohibition on anti-personnel mines, nearly every one has expressed support for a ban at some point in the future.[1227] China, possibly the most significant and the most obdurate of the 'hold-outs' has, in the view of the author at least, already come a long way in its landmine policy, and will continue to feel increasing pressure to bring itself into line with other countries. Within a decade or so, and with these key States on board, universality of at least the norm against use on the battlefield, if not the Convention itself, will probably be assured. In the words of Belgium:

> *'The process of universalisation is a success. The accession of so many States in such an unbelievably short time can but be interpreted in one way: an international standard has been set that can no longer be ignored or circumvented.'*[1228]

B. The Implementation of the Convention

Hand in hand with universality of adherence goes respect for the core norm created by the Convention on the Prohibition of Anti-Personnel Mines[1229] – the prohibition of deployment of anti-personnel mines on the battlefield. It is against this benchmark that the Convention must be judged. The signs so far are mixed. There is no evidence that States Parties have deliberately violated the core provisions of the Convention – and clearly attested and fairly widespread use of anti-personnel mines by governmental armed forces has only been recorded in

1226 Gard, R., "The Military Utility of Anti-Personnel Mines", *op. cit.*, p. 139, footnote omitted. Later in his thoughtful article, General Gard cites Secretary of State Madeleine Albright, who in attempting to sell the Chemical Weapons Convention to a sceptical Congress, stressed 'the imperative of American leadership[.] (...) I believe that if the United States joins the CWC most other nations will too[.] (...) But the problem States will never accept a prohibition of chemical weapons if America stays out, keeps them company and gives them cover.' Albright, M.K., *Prepared Statement before the Senate Foreign Relations Committee*, 8 April 1997, cited by Gard, R., "The Military Utility of Anti-Personnel Mines", *op. cit.*, p. 147.

1227 See *Landmine Monitor Report 1999*, p. 1031.

1228 *Landmine Monitor Report 2000, p. 1002.*

1229 According to Steve Goose of the ICBL, the Convention 'codifies the illegal status of anti-personnel mines and is establishing the new international norm that any use or possession of anti-personnel mines is unacceptable.' Goose, S.D., "The Ottawa Process and the 1997 Mine Ban Treaty", *op. cit.*, p. 291.

the case of Angola, which has since ratified the Convention – even though allegations have been made against other signatories and parties.

According to Landmine Monitor Report 1999, '*nowhere* in the world in 1998 and early 1999 were mines being laid on a very large scale and sustained basis. This is arguably attributable mainly to the global movement to ban the weapon and the stigmatisation of its use. It is not a reflection of a decrease in global warfare, or of the development of a new weapon system to replace the anti-personnel mine in the arsenals of governments or guerrilla groups.'[1230]

Yet substantial deployments continued during 1999 in a number of States, most notably the Russian Federation (Chechnya). In August 1999, for example, the Russian Air Force was forced to apologise to Georgia for mistakenly dropping landmines on Georgian territory while on a bombing run to Daghestan. An official from the Ministry of Defence declared that the mines 'missed their target by a few dozen kilometres due to error.'[1231] Yet, only a few months later, plans were being discussed to mine Russia's border with neighbouring Georgia, with a view to interdicting Chechen supply routes.[1232] In early 2000, both Russian Federation forces and Chechen guerrillas used tens of thousands, possibly hundreds of thousands of anti-personnel mines. On 23 April 2000, the federal troops command had reportedly claimed that Grozny had been cleared of mines, with more than 177,000 explosive devices and rounds of ammunition being rendered harmless,[1233] yet, military officials complained that rebels, still hiding in the ruins of Grozny, were planting new mines every night.[1234] And local Russian authorities had admitted that they were continuing to lay mines around Grozny's factories and power plants – ostensibly 'to stop a plague of

[1230] Landmine Monitor believes it likely that during the period December 1997 to March 1999, there was new use of anti-personnel mines in the following: *Africa* – Angola: government and rebels; Djibouti: rebels; Guinea-Bissau: government, rebels, Senegalese forces; Somalia: various factions ; Uganda: rebels; *The Americas* – Colombia: various rebel groups ; *Asia-Pacific* – Afghanistan: opposition forces; Myanmar: government and various rebel groups; Sri Lanka: government and rebels; *Europe/Central Asia* – Georgia: partisans (in Abkhazia); Turkey: government and rebels; Federal Republic of Yugoslavia: government and rebels; *Middle East/North Africa* – Lebanon: Israel and non-state actors in occupied south Lebanon. There have also been frequent allegations of new mine use in this period in: (1) Democratic Republic of Congo by government, rebels, and foreign armies (Angola, Rwanda, Uganda, Zimbabwe); (2) Eritrea by government forces; (3) Sudan by government and rebels; (4) Afghanistan by Taliban; (5) Georgia by Abkhazian partisans; and (6) Tajikistan by rebels. *Landmine Monitor Report 1999*, pp. 3-4. See also *Landmine Monitor Report 2000*, pp. 1, 3, 5, 6.

[1231] "Sources Say Russian Air Force to Apologise to Georgia", *Moscow Interfax*, 17 August 1999.

[1232] See for instance Igorev, A. and Dvali, G., "Minefields will separate Russia from Georgia", *ITAR-TASS*, Moscow, 9 April 2000. On 12 May 2000, the ICBL issued a press release and a copy of a letter to the Russian President, Vladimir Putin, dispatched the previous day, wherein it called for plans to mine the border with Georgia to be abandoned and for the Russian armed forces to halt the use of anti-personnel mines in Chechnya. E-mail correspondence from Liz Bernstein, ICBL Co-ordinator, 12 May 2000.

[1233] Allenova, O., "Walk round Grozny; Chechen capital still full of mines", *Moscow Kommersant*, 25 April 2000. A report by the RIA news agency on 23 April cited 120,000 explosive devices having been defused. "Russia says shattered Grozny free of mines", *Reuters*, Moscow, 23 April 2000.

[1234] "Russia says shattered Grozny free of mines", *Reuters*, Moscow, 23 April 2000.

looting by their own troops', according to the city's new mayor.[1235] In early March 2001, a Russian Lieutenant-General stated that Interior Ministry engineering units had laid 210 minefields and set more than 43 km of non-explosive barrages to cover troop positions in Chechnya.[1236]

In the conflict between Eritrea and Ethiopia, which intensified in spring 2000, considerable numbers of landmines, including anti-personnel mines, were apparently used.[1237] This surely includes Eritrean forces (Eritrea is a non-signatory); it is not known if Ethiopian forces also resorted to the use of landmines (Ethiopia is a signatory to the Convention.)[1238] The upsurge of violence in Sri Lanka between government forces and the armed opposition group, the LTTE, seemingly resulted in substantial numbers of anti-personnel mines and improvised explosive devices being used.[1239] Another conflict that has seen the use of anti-personnel mines is the ongoing struggle in the Democratic Republic of Congo.[1240] On the other hand, the brutal violence in Sierra Leone has probably not included a widespread use of landmines.[1241]

Yet, despite considerable ongoing use of anti-personnel mines, Alex Vines has rightly pointed out that '[r]ebel forces and governments know that using landmines is publicly abhorred. Five years ago,[1242] few governments and most rebel groups would ever have been divided about using anti-personnel landmines.'[1243] Indeed, in March 1997, a company from Pakistan displayed anti-personnel mines at an arms fair in Abu Dhabi but was forced to remove them because of the reaction from the floor – such is the extent of the stigmatisation of the weapon.[1244]

A political scientist, Richard Price, gave this view on the effectiveness of the Ottawa norm:

> *'The criticism that the norm cannot prevent the use of anti-personnel landmines (and is therefore not worthwhile) is both true and trivial. Laws prohibiting murder do not prevent murder from occurring, but no one suggests we therefore ought to do away with such laws. Immanuel Kant observed that laws are not for angels or devils, for the former need not be deterred by laws, while the latter will violate them regardless. Laws,*

[1235] Whittell, G., "Grozny is mined to stop troops looting", *Times*, 13 May 2000.

[1236] "Interior Ministry Engineers Set 210 Minefields in Chechnya", AVN, Moscow, 2 March 2001.

[1237] See *Landmine Monitor Report 2000*, p. 203; see also Turner, M., "Battle goes on as Eritrea cedes ground", *Financial Times*, 27-28 May 2000, p. 3.

[1238] See *Landmine Monitor Report 2000*, p. 205.

[1239] See for instance Harrison, F., "Sri Lanka landmine deaths high", BBC, Colombo, 4 April 2001.

[1240] *Ibid.*, pp. 198-201.

[1241] The landmine problem in Sierra Leone, despite decades of conflict, is almost insignificant (although a quantity of unexploded ordnance remains). A UN assessment mission that visited the country in early 2000 called for the creation of limited mine and UXO clearance capacity within the peacekeeping operation but did not see the need for a national mine awareness programme. See UNMAS homepage, <http://www.un.org>; see also See *Landmine Monitor Report 2000*, pp. 175-6, 178.

[1242] Vines was writing in 1998.

[1243] Vines, A., "The Crisis of Anti-Personnel Mines", *To Walk Without Fear*, p. 133.

[1244] Chakmakjianm H., "Arms industry shows off latest technology in war on mines", *AFP*, Abu Dhabi, 20 March 1997.

for Kant, were aimed primarily at those in between who occasionally are tempted to cross the line, but who are susceptible to the variety of costs of social sanction, from shame to punishment. Similarly, it would be misguided, indeed, to measure the success of the landmines taboo by its immediate ability to prevent any use of anti-personnel mines by those most desperate to use them under any circumstances. (...) Initially it would be appropriate to gauge a successful level of compliance with the norm according to its contribution to ameliorating the problem it was designed to solve – 26,000 casualties per year. Without a norm prohibiting the use of anti-personnel mines, demining efforts would be but a Sisyphean exercise.'[1245]

2.5.2. *The Implications for International Humanitarian Law of the Ottawa Process*

A Canadian diplomat involved at the heart of the Ottawa Process described it as 'an extraordinary exploration of new forms of multilateral diplomacy in the post-Cold War era.'[1246] According to the Chair of the Senate Foreign Relations Committee in the Philippines, 'small countries (...) could make a difference in international affairs and the success of the Ottawa Process was a humbling experience for big powers such as the US which bitterly opposed it.'[1247] In its speech to the closing plenary of the Diplomatic Conference, the ICBL stated: 'Together, we have shown that there can be a new way of conducting international diplomacy in the post-Cold War period. This accomplishment is perhaps as important as the treaty itself.'[1248]

Rather more coolly, two specialists in arms control suggested that the Ottawa approach, defined by Professor Jozef Goldblat as 'specialised open-ended negotiating conferences, to be convened by countries interested in, or directly affected by various arms control measures',[1249] might illustrate the future structure of global arms control negotiations.[1250] They went on to point out that: 'Globally, the Ottawa fast-track approach has highlighted the inflexibility and subsequent slow movement of forums, such as the CD, which will have implications for the evolution of multilateral arms control negotiations.'[1251]

1245 Price, R., "Compliance with International Norms and the Mines Taboo", *op. cit.*, p. 350.

1246 Lawson, R., "Towards a New Multilateralism: Canada and the Landmine Ban", *Behind the Headlines*, Vol. 54, No. 4 (1997), p. 18, cited by Dolan, M. and Hunt, C., "Negotiating in the Ottawa Process", *op. cit.*, p. 396.

1247 See *Landmine Monitor Report 2000*, p. 424.

1248 See Goose, S.D., "The Ottawa Process and the 1997 Mine Ban Treaty", *op. cit.*, p. 271.

1249 Goldblat, J., "The CD on the Brink", *Disarmament Diplomacy*, No. 18, September 1997, p. 2.

1250 Naidoo, V. and McMillin, P., "Towards Ottawa: A Total Ban Treaty on Anti-Personnel Landmines", *ISS Paper No 26*, Small Arms Programme ISS South Africa, November 1997, p. 5. Two other initiatives have taken heart from the Ottawa Process – the attempts to regulate small arms and the effort to prohibit nuclear weapons.

1251 *Ibid.*, p. 6. Thus, for example, a proposed Convention to criminalise under international law biological and chemical weapons was not intended to be submitted to the Conference on Disarmament for discussion – the authors, a group of noted academics, ventured that a group of States could submit a resolution to the UN General Assembly directly, referring a draft to the

Notable also was the close involvement of non-governmental organisations (NGOs) in the Ottawa Process. The CCW Review Conference had been largely closed to NGOs, particularly as a result of Chinese opposition. However, the Preamble to the Convention duly recognises the crucial role played by NGOs and the ICRC in the Ottawa Process:

'Stressing the role of public conscience in furthering the principles of humanity as evidenced by the call for a total ban of anti-personnel mines and recognising the efforts to that end undertaken by the International Red Cross and Red Crescent Movement, the International Campaign to Ban Landmines and numerous other non-governmental organisations around the world... '[1252]

But perhaps of greatest note is the fact that the Ottawa Process marks a return to the traditional method of adopting international humanitarian law – one State leading a process that results in the adoption of an international legal treaty, if necessary by a vote.[1253] In this regard, the concern has been expressed in some quarters that the Convention on the Prohibition of Anti-Personnel Mines will sound the death knell for the 1980 CCW, which still follows a consensus approach to multilateral negotiation.[1254] In the author's view this is unfounded as the next (Second) Review Conference of the CCW will have the opportunity

GA's Sixth Committee for negotiation, adoption and opening for signature. See for instance "A Draft Convention to Prohibit Biological and Chemical Weapons Under International Criminal Law", *The CBW Conventions Bulletin*, No. 42, December 1998.

1252 Not everyone, though, was equally enthusiastic about the role of NGOs in the development of international humanitarian law. See for instance Lynch Jr., Maj.-Gen. J.D., "Landmines, Lies, And Other Phenomena", *op. cit.*, p. 44. According to one commentator: 'The United States (...) should guard against losing control of the national security policy agenda to NGOs and their associated special interests.' Troxell, J.F., "Landmines: Why the Korea Exception Should Be the Rule", *op. cit.*, p. 83.
For its part, the ICBL has stated that: 'In awarding the ICBL the 1997 Nobel Peace Prize, the Norwegian Nobel Committee was recognizing more than our work to help transform a mine ban from "a vision to a feasible reality." The Committee also sought to recognize the new model of diplomacy forged through the Ottawa Process, whereby civil society has worked in open partnership with governments to address a global crisis of concern to all. (...) The ICBL has never sought to replace governments; but through the Ottawa Process, the contributions of civil society to the resolution of issues of concern have been rightly acknowledged. This openness and cooperation has carried over into issues such as child soldiers and small arms. Yet, in this forum, we again revert to an old model in which some governments wish to conduct the business of the people behind closed doors. The ICBL is invited to participate in this Conference only in the plenary sessions. Even though we are barred from other participation, we invite and strongly encourage delegations this week to meet with us to discuss why they must retain mines and to hear our views on how they can move forward to embrace the global norm to eliminate anti-personnel landmines.' ICBL Statement to the First Conference of States Parties to Amended Protocol II of the 1980 CCW, Geneva, 15 December 1999.

1253 Although no vote was taken in Oslo, the possibility ensured that negotiations were not drawn out, or blocked by one or more States intent on wrecking the process.

1254 The incompatibility between amended Protocol II (which allows the continued use of landmines) and the Ottawa Treaty is not a legal problem. Reference can be made to Article 30(3) and (4) of the Vienna Convention on the Law of Treaties. Moreover, Article 2 of the CCW declares that: 'Nothing in this Convention or annexed Protocols shall be interpreted as detracting from other obligations imposed upon the High Contracting Parties by international humanitarian law applicable in armed conflict.'

to regulate or reinforce the regulation of the use of a number of conventional weapons, including anti-tank mines,[1255] unexploded cluster bombs and other unexploded ordnance, naval mines, fuel-air explosives, small calibre ammunition, and possibly the new generation of 'non-lethal' weapons. How the States Parties respond to these challenges will determine the future of the CCW, not the adoption of one treaty on one specific conventional arms issue.[1256]

[1255] Colin King thinks it may be inevitable that international attention will now turn to the legitimacy of anti-tank mines. King, C., *Legislation and the Landmine, op. cit.*, p. 22. See for instance the position of the ICRC with regard to anti-vehicle mines as set out in the appendices to Landmine Monitor. *Landmine Monitor Report 1999*, pp. 1007-8.

[1256] Though it is true that adherence to amended Protocol II has been slightly affected by the adoption of the Convention. Mexico, for instance, does not intended to ratify the Protocol as it views it as being surpassed by the Convention on the Prohibition of Anti-Personnel Mines, and too limited in comparison. See *Landmine Monitor Report 1999*, p. 262. Likewise, Yemen stated that it would not ratify amended Protocol II as it would 'diminish' the role of the Convention. See *Landmine Monitor Report 2000*, p. 904.

CHAPTER 3
ANTI-PERSONNEL MINES ON THE BATTLEFIELD UNDER CUSTOMARY INTERNATIONAL HUMANITARIAN LAW

3.1. INTRODUCTION

Notwithstanding the rapid adoption and entry into force of the Convention on the Prohibition of Anti-Personnel Mines, and its already impressive number of signatories and States Parties, a significant minority of major military powers remain outside its purview. This chapter, therefore, assesses how customary international humanitarian law regulates the use of anti-personnel mines, aside from the conventional prohibitions and restrictions discussed in the preceding two chapters.

According to the Statute of the International Court of Justice (ICJ), international custom 'as evidence of a general practice accepted as law'[1257] is one of the primary sources of international law, along with international conventions and general principles of law.[1258] To determine custom, it is necessary to identify 'a general recognition among States of a certain practice as obligatory'.[1259] The key elements permitting such a determination are: duration; uniformity and consistency of practice; generality of practice; and *opinio juris sive necessitas*.[1260]

It is asserted that no particular duration is required provided the consistency and generality of practice are proved[1261] (although obviously a long duration of practice will be evidence of consistency and generality). Thus, the view expressed in 'older publications (...) that customary law presupposes that the origins of a rule are hidden in the dark of history, that a rule must exist from "time immemorial" (...) is no longer valid.'[1262]

1257 Meron, however, claims that general practice demonstrates custom and not vice versa, and points out that Paragraph 102(2) of the Third Restatement of the Foreign Relations Law of the United States of 1987 provides, 'more accurately', that customary international law 'results from a general and consistent practice of States which is followed by them from a sense of legal obligation.' Meron, T., *Human Rights and Humanitarian Norms as Customary Law*, Clarendon Press, Oxford, UK, 1991, p. 3.

1258 Article 38(1).

1259 Brierly, *The Law of Nations*, 6th edn. by Sir Humphrey Waldock, 1963, p. 61, cited by Brownlie, I., *Principles of Public International Law*, 4th edn., Clarendon Press, Oxford, UK, 1990, p. 4.

1260 Brownlie, I., *Principles of Public International Law*, *op. cit.*, p. 4. In the Advisory Opinion on the Legality of the Threat or Use of Nuclear Weapons of 8 July 1986, (hereinafter the *Nuclear Weapons Case*), the International Court of Justice referred with approval to its dictum in the 1985 Continental Shelf Case that the substance of [customary] (...) law must be 'looked for primarily in the actual practice and *opinio juris* of States.' *Continental Shelf (Libyan Arab Jamahiriya/Malta), Judgement, ICJ Reports 1985*, p. 29, para. 27.

1261 *Ibid.*, p. 5.

1262 Stoll, J., "Customary International Law", *Encyclopaedia of International Law*. Stoll cites as evidence the judgement of the ICJ in the North Sea Continental Shelf Case:
'Although the passage of only a short period of time is not necessarily, or of itself, a bar to the formation of a new rule of customary international law on the basis of what was originally a purely conventional rule, an indispensable requirement would be that within

It is asserted that practice must be substantially, though not completely, uniform.[1263] So, for example, in the *Nicaragua Case*, the ICJ declared that: 'In order to deduce the existence of customary rules, the Court deems it sufficient that the conduct of States should, in general, be consistent with such rules, and that instances of State conduct inconsistent with a given rule should generally have been treated as breaches of that rule, not as indications of the recognition of a new rule.'[1264]

The requisite *opinio juris* equates to a 'conception that the practice is required by, or consistent with, prevailing international law'.[1265] In the *North Sea Continental Shelf Cases*, the ICJ discussed in some detail the requirements for customary law, including *opinio juris*. According to the Court:

> *'Not only must the acts concerned amount to a settled practice, but they must also be such, or be carried out in such a way, as to be evidence of a belief that this practice is rendered obligatory by the existence of a rule of law requiring it. The need for such a belief, i.e., the existence of a subjective element, is implicit in the very notion of the opinio juris sive necessitas. The States concerned must therefore feel that they are conforming to what amounts to a legal obligation. The frequency, or even habitual character of the acts is not in itself enough. There are many international acts, e.g., in the field of ceremonial and protocol, which are performed almost invariably, but which are motivated only by considerations of courtesy, convenience or tradition, and not by any sense of legal duty.'*[1266]

In many cases, the ICJ has been willing to assume the existence of an *opinio juris* on the basis of evidence of a general practice, a consensus in the literature, or the previous determinations of the Court or other international tribunals.

---

the period in question, short though it may be, State practice, including that of States whose interests are specially affected, should have been both expansive and virtually uniform in the sense of the provision invoked; and should moreover have occurred in a way as to show a general recognition that a rule of law or legal obligation is involved.'

ICJ Reports 1969, p. 43. In *US* v. *Von Leeb*, the Nuremberg Tribunal concluded that the 1929 Geneva Convention on the Protection of Prisoners of War had become customary law (and was therefore binding on Germany) even though it had been adopted only 12 years before the alleged violations took place. Benesch, S. *et al.*, "International Customary Law and Anti-Personnel Landmines: Emergence of a New Customary Norm", *Landmine Monitor Report 1999*, p. 1032.

1263 Brownlie, I., *Principles of Public International Law*, *op. cit.*, p. 6.

1264 *ICJ Reports 1986*, p. 98, para. 186. Previously, in the *Asylum Case* between Peru and Colombia, the Court referred to the need for a 'constant and uniform usage, accepted as law'. See *ICJ Reports 1950*, p. 266. Although the case concerned local custom, the requirement was generally regarded as being also applicable to general international custom. See Harris, D.J., *Cases and Materials on International Law*, 4th edn., Sweet and Maxwell, London, 1991, p. 27. See also Benesch, S. *et al.*, "International Customary Law and Anti-Personnel Landmines", *op. cit.*, pp. 1026, 1027.

1265 Hudson (ed.), *International Legislation*, quoted in Briggs, *The Law of Nations: Cases, Documents and Notes*, 2nd edn., 1952, p. 25. See also Clark, R.S., "Treaty and Custom", Boisson de Chazournes, L. *et al.* (eds.), *International Law, the International Court of Justice and Nuclear Weapons*, *op. cit.*, pp. 176-8.

1266 At para. 77. See Harris, D.J., *Cases and Materials on International Law*, *op. cit.*, p. 42. See also Benesch, S. *et al.*, "International Customary Law and Anti-Personnel Landmines", *op. cit.*, p. 1024.

However, in a significant minority of cases the Court has called for positive evidence in the practice of States.[1267]

It has also been noted, however, that '[m]any judges, scholars and legal practitioners say that *opinio juris* should be more important than practice in the formation of custom. These jurists argue that a rule need not be universally followed before it can be anointed as an international customary norm – it just has to be universally, or generally defended[.] (...) Both the International Court of Justice and the International Criminal Tribunal for the Former Yugoslavia (...) have used this view of *opinio juris* in major recent decisions on the formation of international custom. In both cases, the courts held that custom had crystallised, based on evidence of *opinio juris*, not practice.'[1268]

Within the realm of international humanitarian law, it has proved far easier to discern general customary rules governing the use of weapons than to find agreement on their application to specific weapons.[1269] In the 1996 *Nuclear Weapons Advisory Opinion*, the ICJ had occasion to pronounce on these customary norms. Whereas its application of the principles to nuclear weapons was not universally welcomed or approved, its identification of general custom does not appear to be contested.[1270]

> *'The cardinal principles contained in the texts constituting the fabric of humanitarian law are the following. The first is aimed at the protection of the civilian population and civilian objects and establishes the distinction between combatants and non-combatants; States must never make civilians the object of attack and must consequently never use weapons that are incapable of distinguishing between civilian and military targets. According to the second principle, it is prohibited to cause unnecessary suffering to combatants: it is accordingly prohibited*

1267 Brownlie, I., *Principles of Public International Law*, *op. cit.*, p. 7. See also Benesch, S. *et al.*, "International Customary Law and Anti-Personnel Landmines", *op. cit.*, p. 1025.

1268 Benesch, S. *et al.*, "International Customary Law and Anti-Personnel Landmines", *op. cit.*, pp. 1027, 1028.

1269 See for instance Cassese, A., "The Means of Warfare: The Present and the Emerging Law", pp. 152-3. According to Baxter, in the case of the laws of war, military manuals provide 'telling evidence' of the practice of States. Baxter, R.R., "Multilateral Treaties as Evidence of Customary International Law", *British Yearbook of International Law*, Vol. 41, No. 275, (1965-66), pp. 282-3, cited by Meron, T., "The Continuing Role of Custom in the Formation of International Humanitarian Law", Editorial Comment in *The American Journal of International Law*, Vol. 90, No. 238, April 1996, p. 241.

1270 Though see the sharp criticisms of the ICJ's approach to international humanitarian law in Condorelli, L., "Le droit international humanitaire, ou de l'exploration par la cour d'une *terra* à peu près *incognita* pour elle", in Boisson de Chazournes, L. *et al.* (eds.), *International Law, the International Court of Justice and Nuclear Weapons*, *op. cit.*, pp. 229-46. In his conclusion (p. 245), Condorelli remarks for instance:

> *'A mon sens, le bilan d'ensemble, concernant l'évaluation de l'avis du point de vue du DIH [droit international humanitaire], est franchement négatif. Certes, ce chapitre du droit international a fait l'objet pour la première fois d'une ample reconnaissance par la C.I.J., qui en a mis en valeur de façon heureuse certains traits importants. mais les défauts de l'avis, toujours du point de vue du DIH, sont graves et prépondérants: on dirait que la Cour, s'aventurant pour la première fois dans l'exploration en profondeur d'un territoire peu connu, n'a pas su prendre les mesures nécessaires pour mener son expédition sans risquer d'en endommager sérieusement l'équilibre général.'*

to use weapons causing them such harm or uselessly aggravating their suffering. In application of that second principle, States do not have unlimited freedom of choice of means in the weapons they use.[1271]

The Court would likewise refer, in relation to these principles, to the Martens Clause, which was first included in the Hague Convention II with Respect to the Laws and Customs of War on Land of 1899 and which has proved to be an effective means of addressing the rapid evolution of military technology[.] (...)

In conformity with the aforementioned principles, humanitarian law, at a very early stage, prohibited certain types of weapons either because of their indiscriminate effect on combatants and civilians or because of the unnecessary suffering caused to combatants, that is to say, a harm greater than that unavoidable to achieve legitimate military objectives. (...)

[T]hese fundamental rules are to be observed by all States whether or not they have ratified the Conventions that contain them, because they constitute intransgressible[1272] *principles of international customary law.'*[1273]

Despite this seemingly impressive corpus of customary international law,[1274] its effectiveness in prohibiting the use of specific weapons is disappointing.[1275] Greenwood, for example, points out that the record of the 20th Century in prohibiting weapons based on customary principles 'is not particularly impressive'. Apart from the prohibitions on chemical and biological weapons and anti-personnel landmines, 'treaty law has added little to the general principles.' He recalls that a 1973 survey of the law on weaponry by the United Nations Secretariat cited bayonets or lances with barbs, irregular shaped bullets and projectiles filled with glass as examples of weapons considered outlawed by the

1271 In the view of the author, the Court was unnecessarily limited in the application of the principle as formulated that 'States do not have unlimited freedom of choice in the weapons they use.' This basic principle should apply to indiscriminate weapons.

1272 For discussion of the meaning to be attributed to this term, in particular with respect to peremptory norms of international law, see Werksman, J. and Khalastchi, R., "Nuclear weapons and *jus cogens*: peremptory norms and justice pre-empted?" Boisson de Chazournes, L. *et al.* (eds.), *International Law, the International Court of Justice and Nuclear Weapons, op. cit.*, pp. 183, 195-6; Condorelli, L., "Le droit international humanitaire", *op. cit.*, pp. 234-5.

1273 *Nuclear Weapons Case*, paras. 78 and 79.

1274 Though see Condorelli, L., "Le droit international humanitaire", *op. cit.*, pp. 236-7.

1275 According to Cassese: 'The principal advantage of general principles lies in their covering vast categories of weapons. They do not affect only those agencies of destruction existing at the time when they were laid down, but can work also with respect to future means of combat. Consequently, they have a continuing force of expansion and a reach that can broaden with the passage of time. Two elements, however, go hand in hand to erode the value of general principles. First, they are couched in very vague terms; accordingly they do not amount to safe standards of conduct but are susceptible to divergent interpretations. Their implementation calls for the existence of international bodies capable of verifying impartially whether a given weapon falls within their prohibitory scope, and of enforcing them. It is common knowledge that at present such bodies do not exist in the international society. This is precisely the second element eroding the normative force of the principles under consideration.' Cassese, A., "The Means of Warfare: The Present and the Emerging Law", *op. cit.*, p. 147.

unnecessary suffering principle.[1276] 'Scarcely standard weapons at the beginning of the twentieth century, these were museum pieces by its end. Similarly, leading text books still refer to the unnecessary suffering principle as meaning that "cannons must not be loaded with chain shot, crossbar shot, red-hot balls and the like".[1277] Such examples suggest that the law is firmly rooted in the nineteenth century.'[1278]

3.1.1. Basic Rules Governing the Use of Weapons on the Battlefield

According to 1977 Additional Protocol I: 'In any armed conflict, the right of the parties to the conflict to choose methods or means of warfare[1279] is not unlimited.'[1280] This rather awkwardly phrased rule,[1281] a version of which first appeared in 1874 in the Brussels Declaration of the Laws and Customs of War,[1282] is nonetheless fundamental to customary international humanitarian law as it applies to the use of weapons.[1283] A party to a conflict is not free to use any weapon it wishes, nor in a manner of its own choosing; legal restraint is thus

---

1276 "Respect for Human Rights in Armed Conflicts: Existing Rules of International Law concerning the Prohibition or Restriction on the Use of Specific Weapons", *UN Doc. A/9215*, 1973, Vol. I, p. 204.

1277 Lauterpacht, H., *Oppenheim's International Law*, 7th edn., 1952, Vol. II, p. 34, cited by Greenwood, C., *Humanitarian Law and Laws of War*, Preliminary Report for the Centennial of the First International Peace Conference, London, March 1999, p. 40.

1278 Greenwood, C., *Humanitarian Law and Laws of War*, *op. cit.*, p. 40.

1279 The term 'means of warfare' refers to weaponry; 'methods of warfare' are tactics and the manner of use of weaponry. See for instance Verri, P., *Dictionary of the International Law of Armed Conflict*, ICRC, Geneva, 1992, p. 126.

1280 Article 35(1).

1281 See for example Cassese, who complains that the provisions of Article 35 'do not clarify previous law, but merely restate it with all its ambiguities.' Cassese, A., "The Geneva Protocols of 1977 on the Humanitarian Law of Armed Conflict and Customary International Law", *UCLA Pacific Basin Law Journal*, Spring and Fall 1984, Vol. 3, Nos. 1 and 2, p. 76.

1282 In 1874, the Russian Tsar, prompted by the famous Russian lawyer Fedor de Martens, convened an international conference on the law of land warfare, which brought together 15 nations to draft a legally binding code of the law of war based on the Lieber Code, a list of the laws of war to be applied in the United States Civil War. The conference adopted a draft *Declaration of the Laws and Customs of War*, which, although it never entered into legal force, was influential in the subsequent development of the law of war. The Declaration included a statement that 'the laws of war do not recognise in belligerents an unlimited power in the adoption of means of injuring the enemy.' Robblee Jr., Capt. P.A., "The Legitimacy of Modern Conventional Weaponry", *The Military Law and Law of War Review*, Vol. XVI, No. 4, 1977, p. 407.
The rule was later repeated in a similar form ('The right of belligerents to adopt means of injuring the enemy is not unlimited.') in Article 22 of the Regulations Respecting the Laws and Customs of War on Land annexed to the 1907 Hague Convention IV. The Convention as a whole was recognised to be declaratory of customary law by the International Military Tribunal in Nuremberg in 1948. See for instance *Documents on the Laws of War*, pp. 43-4. It was subsequently reaffirmed on a number of occasions, including in 1968 by the United Nations General Assembly in its Resolution 2444 (XXIII). See for instance Kalshoven, F., *Constraints on the Waging of War*, 2nd edn., ICRC, Geneva, 1991, p. 29.

1283 Kalshoven, for instance, points out that the general principle has been identified 'with some justification' as the foundation of the entire humanitarian law of armed conflict. See Kalshoven, F., *Constraints on the Waging of War, op. cit.*, p. 29. See also Oeter, S., "Methods and Means of Combat", *op. cit.*, p. 112.

imposed by customary and conventional international law.[1284] The rule, as it is set out in 1977 Additional Protocol I, is widely regarded as being declaratory of customary international law.[1285]

The general principle contained in Article 35(1) is a reminder that 'violence is permitted only in so far as it serves the specific purpose of subduing the enemy.'[1286] What this means in practice is that, 'a line must be drawn between action accepted as "necessary" in the harsh exigencies of warfare and that which violates basic principles of moderation.'[1287] Hence, the 'law of war is itself a compromise between unbridled license, on the one hand, and on the other, the absolute demands of humanity, which if carried to a logical extreme, would proscribe war altogether[.] (...) Stated in other terms, the law seeks to limit the measures of war to those activities which produce suffering out of all proportion to the military advantage to be gained.'[1288]

1284 Notwithstanding his concern as to its ambiguities, the rule, according to Cassese, at least as it was phrased in Article 22 of the Hague Regulations, 'must be construed to the effect that it (...) excludes the inference that weapons which are not prohibited by the Hague Regulations are *ipso facto* allowed. Such weapons are banned or permitted according to whether or not they are prohibited by *other* rules of international law.' Cassese, A., "Means of Warfare", *op. cit.*, p. 144. The ICRC Commentary on the 1977 Additional Protocols concludes that the rule as a whole 'implies principally the obligation to respect the rules of international law applicable in case of armed conflict.' Sandoz, Y., *et al.*, (eds.), *Commentary on the Additional Protocols of 8 June 1977 to the Geneva Conventions of 12 August 1949*, ICRC/Martinus Nijhoff, Geneva, 1987, p. 399. Hereinafter, this work will be referred to as the *ICRC Commentary of the 1977 Additional Protocols*.

1285 See for example Meron, T., *Human Rights and Humanitarian Norms as Customary Law*, *op. cit.*, p. 64; Oeter, S., "Methods and Means of Combat", *op. cit.*, p. 112; *ICRC Commentary of the 1977 Additional Protocols*, p. 390; Cassese, A., "The Geneva Protocols of 1977 on the Humanitarian Law of Armed Conflict and Customary International Law", *op. cit.*, p. 76. Indeed, in the Nuclear Weapons Case, the ICJ referred to the many humanitarian law instruments and stated that: 'All this shows that the conduct of military operations is governed by a body of legal prescriptions. This is so because "the right of belligerents to adopt means of injuring the enemy is not unlimited" as stated in Article 22 of the 1907 Hague Regulations relating to the laws and customs of war on land.' *Nuclear Weapons Advisory Opinion*, para. 77.

1286 Blix, H., "Means and Methods of Combat", in *op. cit.*, p. 136. Blix attributes this doctrine to the 'rationalism and humanitarianism which pervaded the enlightenment and the teachings of Jean-Jacques Rousseau, one of the inspirers of the laws of war, [which] required that no suffering be inflicted, no injury caused, and no destruction or damage brought about which was not necessary for the sole legitimate purpose of overcoming the enemy.' *Ibid.*, pp. 136-7.

1287 McCoubrey, H. and White, N.D., *International Law and Armed Conflict*, Dartmouth Publishing Co., Aldershot, UK, 1992, p. 226.

1288 Baxter, R.R., "The Geneva Conventions of 1949", *Naval War College Review*, Vol. 9, 1956, p. 59. See Robblee Jr., Capt. P.A., "The Legitimacy of Modern Conventional Weaponry", *op. cit.*, p. 412. One authority, however, has gone further to assert that as a result of the precarious balancing act between military necessity and humanitarian concerns, 'from among several available means of achieving a legitimate military aim, should be chosen those which inflicted least suffering, injury, destruction or damage. It is said, for example, that if an enemy soldier can be placed *hors de combat* by being taken prisoner he should not be injured; if he can be disabled, he should not be killed, and if he can be neutralised by light injury, he should not be severely wounded.' Blix, H., "Means and Methods of Combat", in *op. cit.*, p. 137. If this were true, it would imply a duty upon a commander to use the most accurate weapons at his disposal. Blix concedes, however, that 'this reasoning obviously cannot be so rigorously applied as to oblige a soldier in the heat of battle to aim only at non-vital parts of the enemy's body'. For a brief discussion of the issue see Baxter, R.R., "Criteria of the Prohibition of Weapons in

Thus, an understanding of the doctrine of military necessity is integral to an appreciation of the development of international humanitarian law.[1289] According to one widely-cited definition: 'Military necessity is an urgent need, admitting of no delay, for the taking by a commander, of measures which are indispensable for forcing as quickly as possible the complete surrender of the enemy by means of regulated violence, and which are not forbidden by the laws and customs of war.'[1290]

Earlier in this century a number of commentators, especially from Germany, had claimed that the doctrine of *Kriegsraison* entitled belligerents to override the considerations of humanity and the law of war where militarily necessary.[1291] The potential ramifications of such a doctrine are obvious.[1292] Its existence was, however, roundly rejected by the judgements of the Nuremberg war crimes tribunals that followed the end of the Second World War, and this rejection has been confirmed by subsequent legal writings.[1293] According to the ICRC: 'One can and should consider this theory discredited. It is totally incompatible with

International Law", in Ehmke, H. *et al.* (eds.), *Festschrift für Ulrich Scheuner zum 70. Geburtstag*, Duncker & Humblot, Berlin, 1973, p. 49.

1289 It has been suggested that military necessity has been the fundamental concept underlying all humanitarian rules on methods and means of warfare since the bloody excesses of the Thirty Years War. Oeter, S., "Methods and Means of Combat", in *op. cit.*, p. 106. 'According to the traditional approach, only the use of those weapons and means of combat (...) necessary to attain the military purposes of war, purposes based on the ultimate goal of overpowering the enemy armed forces, is permitted.'

1290 Downey, W., "The Law of War and Military Necessity", *American Journal of International Law*, Vol. 47, 1953, p. 254. In his judgement of military necessity as recognized by international law, Jean Pictet declared: 'Military necessity admits of all direct destruction of life or limb of armed enemies, and of other persons whose destruction in incidentally unavoidable in the armed contests of the war. (...) Military necessity does not admit of cruelty, that is the infliction of suffering for the sake of suffering or for revenge, not of maiming or wounding except in fight[.] (...) It does not admit the use of poison in any way, nor the wanton devastation of a district. It admits of deception, but disclaims acts of perfidy and in general military necessity does not include any act of hostility which makes the return to peace unnecessarily difficult.' Pictet, J., "International Humanitarian Law", *International Review of the Red Cross*, Vol. 6, 1966, p. 466. See also Rauch, E., "Le concept de nécessité militaire dans le droit de la guerre", *Military Law and Law of War Review*, 1980, p. 209 *et seq.*; McCoubrey, H., "The nature of the modern doctrine of military necessity", *Military Law and Law of War Review*, 1991, p. 215 *et seq.*; Rogers, A.P.V., *Law on the Battlefield*, *op. cit.*, pp. 3-6.

1291 See for instance Robblee Jr., Capt. P.A., "The Legitimacy of Modern Conventional Weaponry", *op. cit.*, p. 414; Fenrick, Lt.-Col. W.J., "New Developments in the Law Concerning the Use of Conventional Weapons in Armed Conflict", *Canadian Yearbook of International Law*, Vol. 19, No. 19, 1981, p. 230. For the historical background to the issue see Best, G., *Humanity in Warfare*, Columbia University Press, New York, 1980, p. 170 *et seq.*

1292 See for instance Green, L., *The Contemporary Law of Armed Conflict*, Manchester University Press, Manchester, UK, 1993, p. 118.

1293 *ICRC Commentary on the 1977 Additional Protocols*, p. 391. See for instance Green, L., *The Contemporary Law of Armed Conflict*, *op. cit.*, pp. 118-9; see also Greenwood, C., "*Jus ad bellum* and *jus in bello* in the *Nuclear Weapons* Advisory Opinion", Boisson de Chazournes, L. *et al.* (eds.), *International Law, the International Court of Justice and Nuclear Weapons*, *op. cit.*, pp. 263-4; Gardam, J., "Necessity and proportionality in *jus ad bellum* and *jus ad bello*", *ibid.*, pp. 281-2.

the wording of Article 35, paragraph 1, and with the very existence of the Protocol.'[1294]

3.1.2. Criteria to Assess the Legality of the Use of Anti-Personnel Mines

Given that there are limits to what constitute lawful acts in warfare, irrespective of the military situation, a number of principles (or, more accurately perhaps, prohibitions)[1295] follow more or less logically, against which the legality of the use of anti-personnel mines can be tested.

The 1868 St Petersburg Declaration provided *inter alia* that 'the only legitimate object which States should endeavour to accomplish during war is to weaken the military forces of the enemy.' Thus, it is readily concluded that parties to a conflict should distinguish between military objectives on the one hand, and civilians and civilian objects on the other, and limit their attacks to the former – the principle of distinction. It follows from this that at least the use of weapons *incapable*[1296] of being used 'discriminately' is prohibited.[1297]

The St Petersburg Declaration also included an assertion that 'this object would be exceeded by the employment of arms which uselessly aggravate the sufferings of disabled men, or render their death inevitable' and that 'the employment of such arms would, therefore, be contrary to the laws of humanity'. On this premise is founded the prohibition on the use of weapons of a nature to cause unnecessary suffering.[1298] Thus, integral to the principle of unnecessary suffering (a certain level of suffering is thus by definition 'necessary') is a balance between military utility and humanitarian costs.

A similar balance, this time involving the protection of civilians as opposed to combatants, is inherent in the principle of proportionality, which seeks to prevent excessive injury to civilians even when an attack is not, by itself, indiscriminate. The protection of the environment, including in situations of armed conflict, has become a major issue in international law over the past few years. Given the longevity of anti-personnel mines, it is necessary to assess how far international humanitarian law controls battlefield weapons that can affect the environment (in its widest sense) many years after the fighting has ended.

1294 *ICRC Commentary on the 1977 Additional Protocols*, p. 391.

1295 See on this point Greenwood, C., "*Jus ad bellum* and *jus in bello* in the *Nuclear Weapons* Advisory Opinion" *op. cit.*, p. 251.

1296 The precise ambit of this prohibition, which is discussed further below, is crucial to an assessment of the legality of anti-personnel mines, since, in the view of the author, these are weapons that are *capable* of discriminate use, but which are typically, even 'irresistibly' (to paraphrase the military historian Geoffrey Best), used indiscriminately. See Best, G., *Humanity in Warfare*, *op. cit.*, p. 159.

1297 According to Cassese, for instance: 'The prohibition of "blind" weapons is a natural consequence as well as a significant specification of the general principle forbidding any attack on non-military objectives.' Cassese, A., "The Geneva Protocols of 1977 on the Humanitarian Law of Armed Conflict and Customary International Law", *op. cit.*, p. 84. As already noted, in the *Nuclear Weapons Advisory Opinion*, the ICJ declared that: 'States must never make civilians the object of attack and must consequently never use weapons that are incapable of distinguishing between civilian and military targets.'

1298 For the text of the St Petersburg Declaration see for instance *Documents on the Laws of War*, pp. 29-30.

The final criterion by which the legality of the use of anti-personnel mines will be tested is that flowing from the 'principles of humanity and the dictates of the public conscience' – the so-called Martens Clause.[1299] As in the case of the Ottawa Process, public pressure can play an integral role in the success of such an initiative. This chapter will not, however, address the issue of perfidy, since this refers to 'acts misleading the adverse party into the belief that there is a situation affording protection under international law' – not the case with anti-personnel mines.[1300]

3.2. Anti-Personnel Mines and the Principle of Distinction

3.2.1. The Principle of Distinction and Conventional Weapons

According to Article 48, one of the basic rules of 1977 Additional Protocol I: 'In order to ensure respect for and protection of the civilian population and civilian objects, the Parties to the conflict shall at all times distinguish between the civilian population and combatants and civilian objects and military objectives and accordingly shall direct their operations only against military objectives.'[1301]

The principle of distinction – the duty to 'distinguish' between military targets and civilians and civilian objects – is central to the protection afforded to civilians by international humanitarian law. Indeed, '[t]he prohibition of indiscriminate warfare probably constitutes the most important expression of the principle of "limited warfare." It is both the greatest consequence of and a modification of the fundamental orientation of warfare towards the requirements

---

1299 See above judgement in the *Nuclear Weapons Advisory Opinion.*

1300 Oeter, S., "Methods and Means of Combat", *op. cit.*, p. 200. It is codified in Article 37(1), 1977 Additional Protocol I, and is widely regarded as a customary prohibition when so phrased.

1301 1294 Military objectives are defined elsewhere in the Protocol. According to Article 52(2): 'Attacks shall be strictly limited to military objectives. In so far as objects are concerned, military objectives are limited to those objects which by their nature, location, purpose or use make an effective contribution to military action and whose total or partial destruction, capture or neutralization, in the circumstances ruling at the time, offers a definite military advantage.' According to one view, the inclusion of the word 'location' in the definition demonstrated that an area of land could be a military objective. Rogers, Lt.-Col. A.P.V., "A Commentary on the Protocol on Prohibitions or Restrictions on the Use of Mines, Booby-Traps and Other Devices", *Military Law and Law of War Review*, Vol. 26, 1987, p. 190; Rogers, A.P.V., *Law on the Battlefield, op. cit.*, p. 38.
It appears likely that this definition set out in Article 52 has become customary law. According to a report cited by Meron, an expert who conducted a detailed study of the Protocols for the US Joint Chiefs of Staff found that the definition of a military objective included in Protocol I 'was deemed "almost certainly" to embody rules of customary law.' In addition, Meron points out that the definition has been included in US military manuals even though the US has not ratified Protocol I. Meron, T., *Human Rights and Humanitarian Norms as Customary Law, op. cit.*, p. 64; see also Cassese, A., "The Geneva Protocols of 1977 on the Humanitarian Law of Armed Conflict and Customary International Law", *op. cit.*, p. 89. It was reproduced with only minor semantic changes in Article 2 of Protocol II to the 1980 CCW, a definition subsequently made applicable also in internal armed conflicts. In its assessment of the definition contained in amended Protocol II to the 1980 CCW, the US referred to it as a 'well-settled understanding of the term.' Nash, M., "Contemporary Practice of the United States Relating to International Law", *op. cit.*, 1997, pp. 331-2.

of "military necessity."'[1302] In the application of the principle to weapons, it is now generally accepted that customary international law prohibits the use of indiscriminate weapons both in international and in internal armed conflict,[1303] that is, weapons that are incapable of 'distinguishing' between military objectives and civilians and civilian objects.[1304]

1302 Oeter, S., "Methods and Means of Warfare", *op. cit.*, p. 118. According to the *ICRC Commentary on the 1977 Additional Protocols* (at p. 598), it is the 'foundation on which the codification of the laws and customs of war rests. (...) The entire system established in The Hague in 1899 and 1907 [footnote omitted] and in Geneva from 1864 to 1977 [footnote omitted] is founded on this rule of customary law.' It is also a norm that has been recognised for thousands of years. See for instance Singh, N., "Armed conflicts and humanitarian laws of ancient India", in Swinarski, C. (ed.), *Studies and essays on international humanitarian law and Red Cross principles*, ICRC/Martinus Nijhoff, Geneva/The Hague, 1984, p. 534; Solf, W.A., "Protection of Civilians Against the Effects of Hostilities Under Customary International Law and Under Protocol I", *The American University Journal of International Law and Policy*, Vol. 1, Summer 1996, p. 118. See also Oeter, S., "Methods and Means of Combat", *op. cit.*, pp. 105-13.

1303 Although efforts to include general prohibitions on the use of weapons in 1977 Additional Protocol II were unsuccessful, the *Tadic Case* before the Appeals Chamber of the International Tribunal for the Prosecution of Persons Responsible for Serious Violations of International Humanitarian Law Committed in the Territory of Former Yugoslavia since 1991, clearly identified the protection of civilians against hostilities, in particular from indiscriminate attacks, as a customary rule governing internal armed conflict. *Prosecutor* v. *Tadic, Case No. IT-94-1-AR72*, Appeal on Jurisdiction, 2 October 1995, (hereinafter the *Tadic Case*), pp. 67-68, para. 127, cited by Meron, "The Continuing Role of Custom in the Formation of International Humanitarian Law", Editorial Comment in *The American Journal of International Law*, Vol. 90, No. 238, April 1996, p. 242.
As Greenwood points out, '[t]he law of armed conflict (...) contains very few provisions on the conduct of hostilities themselves,' but one of the striking exceptions to this general reality is Article 13 of 1977 Additional Protocol II, which declares that 'the civilian population as such, as well as individual civilians, shall not be the object of attack.' Greenwood, C., *Humanitarian Law and Laws of War, op. cit.*, p. 63. Greenwood notes, however, that the absence in the Protocol of a definition of the civilian population is a 'significant and damaging omission, since the distinction between civilians and combatants tends to be more difficult to draw in an internal conflict.'

1304 According to the *Nuclear Weapons Advisory Opinion*, as cited *supra*: 'States must never make civilians the object of attack and must consequently never use weapons that are incapable of distinguishing between civilian and military targets.' In 1969, the Institute of International Law at its session in Edinburgh adopted a set of resolutions, including an assertion that: 'Existing international law prohibits the use of all weapons which, by their nature, affect indiscriminately both military objectives and non-military objects, or both armed forces and civilian populations. In particular, it prohibits the use of weapons the destructive effect of which is so great that it cannot be limited to specific military objectives or is otherwise uncontrollable (self-generating weapons), as well as of "blind" weapons.' See Fenrick, Lt.-Col. W.J., "New Developments in the Law Concerning the Use of Conventional Weapons in Armed Conflict", *op. cit.*, pp. 231-2, citing Schindler, D. and Toman, J., *The Laws of Armed Conflict*, Martinus Nijhoff, Geneva, 1973, pp. 95-6. A prohibition on indiscriminate weapons also has historical antecedents. The use of 'hyper-destructive weapons' was prohibited by the Indian Book of Manu as they would have caused indiscriminate loss of life, particularly when the enemy had not used such weapons. See Singh, N., "Armed conflicts and humanitarian laws of ancient India", in Swinarski, C. (ed.), *Studies and essays on international humanitarian law and Red Cross principles, op. cit.*, p. 532.

The prohibition on inherently indiscriminate weapons[1305] has been codified in Article 51(4) of 1977 Additional Protocol I, which provides that: 'Indiscriminate attacks are prohibited. Indiscriminate attacks are (...) (b) those which employ a method or means of combat which cannot be directed at a specific military objective.'[1306]

According to the ICRC Commentary on the provision, the weapons covered are 'primarily long-range missiles which cannot be aimed exactly at the objective. The V2 rockets used at the end of the Second World War are an example of this.'[1307] It has also been suggested that Scud missiles, used extensively by Iraq during the Gulf War of 1990-91, fall within this prohibition.[1308] Baxter, writing before the adoption of the Additional Protocols, appeared to suggest that chemical and bacteriological warfare had been prohibited by treaty not only because they caused unnecessary suffering, but also because they had indiscriminate effects.[1309]

But even the ambit of what constitutes indiscriminate use is the subject of continued debate. During the 1974 Lucerne Weapons Conference, the UK submitted a paper in which it argued that it would be wrong to seek to ban certain weapons 'merely on the ground that they had been used indiscriminately in the past' and asserted instead that the solution should be 'a sensible restric-

---

1305 Article 8(2)(b)(xx) of the 1998 Rome Statute of the International Criminal Court provides for the Court's jurisdiction over the use, in international armed conflicts only, of 'weapons, projectiles and material and methods of warfare (...) which are inherently indiscriminate in violation of the international law of armed conflict, provided that such weapons, projectiles and material and methods of warfare are the subject of a comprehensive prohibition and are included in an annex to this Statute, by an amendment in accordance with the relevant provisions set forth in articles 121 and 123.' See for example Roberts, A. and Guelff, R., *Documents on the Laws of War*, 3rd edn., *op. cit.*, p. 678.
But note the issue raised by Cassese as to whether a weapon is considered indiscriminate for the mere fact of not being selective (*i.e.* capable of hitting combatants only) or because it can entail civilian losses that are out of proportion to the military advantage gained through the use of the weapon. Cassese, A., "The Means of Warfare", *op. cit.*, p. 148.

1306 The US considers that the prohibition on indiscriminate attacks is already part of customary law applicable to all weapons. Nash, M., "Contemporary Practice of the United States Relating to International Law" *op. cit.*, 1997, p. 336. A violation of Article 51 that results in civilian deaths or serious injuries is treated as a grave breach subject to compulsory universal jurisdiction.

1307 At p. 621. See also Cassese, A., "Means of Warfare", *op. cit.*, p. 146. Cassese cites the late British Prime Minister, Winston Churchill, who in a statement made in the House of Commons on 6 July 1944, said: 'A very high proportion of these casualties I have mentioned (...) have fallen upon London, which presents to the enemy (...) a target 18 miles wide by over 20 miles deep. It is, therefore, the unique target of the world for the use of a weapon of such proved inaccuracy. The flying bomb is a weapon literally and essentially indiscriminate in its nature, purpose and effect.' *Keesing's Contemporary Archives*, 1943-45, pp. 6536-7.

1308 See for instance Rogers, A.P.V., *Law on the Battlefield*, *op. cit.*, p. 20; Oeter, S., "Methods and Means of Combat", *op. cit.*, p. 175.

1309 'However, it must not be forgotten that chemical and bacteriological warfare fall under the prohibition of the Geneva Protocol not only because they cause unnecessary suffering, but also because they can be highly unpredictable in their effects, affecting the force using them and civilians as well as enemy personnel. That unpredictability both called for and facilitated the interdiction of the treaty.' Baxter, R.R., "Criteria of the Prohibition of Weapons in International Law", *op. cit.*, p. 48. See also Cassese, A., "The Means of Warfare", *op. cit.*, p. 151.

tion' on the method of use.[1310] Other experts, however, claimed that not only inherently indiscriminate weapons but also those 'whose normal or typical use would be one which had indiscriminate effects' would have to be considered indiscriminate weapons.[1311] An attempted compromise whereby 'those weapons ought to be regarded as indiscriminate which, having regard to their effects in time or space, cannot be employed with sufficient or predictable accuracy against the chosen target' foundered on the inherently subjective notion of 'accuracy'.[1312]

3.2.2. Application of the Principle to Anti-Personnel Mines

Although Additional Protocol I prohibits the use of means of combat which cannot be 'directed' at a specific military objective, Fenrick doubted whether the Protocol applies to landmines.[1313] He did, however, note that 'some writers have argued that, as landmines are used to neutralise territory, they come within the scope of the indiscriminate attack rule of Article 51.'[1314] Thus, in its official commentary on the provision in Article 51, the ICRC points out that the use of land (and sea) mines 'raises some problems'[1315] since 'the question may arise at what point the use of mines constitutes an attack[.] (...) Is it when the mine is laid, when it is armed, when a person is endangered by it, or when it finally explodes?'[1316]

Moreover, Fenrick declared that the definition of indiscriminate use contained in Protocol II to the 1980 CCW (which effectively reproduces the key provisions of Article 51 of 1977 Additional Protocol I) 'may provide the basis for legal arguments favouring the intrinsic illegality of mine warfare in the future because it is difficult to argue that a mine is "directed" at anything.'[1317] Indeed,

---

1310 *Report on the 1974 Lucerne Weapons Conference*, para. 31.

1311 See for example Kalshoven, F., "The Conference of Government Experts on the Use of Certain Conventional Weapons, Lucerne, 24 September to 18 October 1974", *op. cit.*, p. 90-1.

1312 *Report on the 1974 Lucerne Weapons Conference*, para. 31. See Kalshoven, F., "The Conference of Government Experts on the Use of Certain Conventional Weapons, Lucerne, 24 September to 18 October 1974", *op. cit.*, pp. 91-2.

1313 See Fenrick, Lt.-Col. W.J., "New Developments in the Law Concerning the Use of Conventional Weapons in Armed Conflict", *op. cit.*, p. 243. Fenrick cites the argument that since a landmine is detonated 'when certain persons or objects approach it' it is 'nonsensical to refer to a landmine as something which "attacks" a person or object.' *Ibid.*, p. 244. This approach is not convincing. The fact that these are time-delay weapons that are – usually – victim-activated, does not preclude the use of a mine being tantamount to an attack.

1314 *Ibid.*, pp. 243-4.

1315 Para. 1959, p. 621.

1316 The ICRC records that the participants at the meeting of the International Society of Military Law and the Law of War (Lausanne, 1982) conceded that from the legal point of view the use of mines constituted an attack in the sense of the Protocol when a person was directly endangered by such a mine. Para. 1960, p. 622.

1317 Fenrick, Lt.-Col. W J., "New Developments in the Law Concerning the Use of Conventional Weapons in Armed Conflict", *op. cit.*, p. 244. Writing in 1959, Professor Morris Greenspan distinguished between a 'defensive' use of mines (to protect a position or to delay pursuit by the enemy) and an 'offensive' use, 'for instance, when laid by a raiding force in enemy territory, since generally there would be no way of ensuring that they would not injure or ill persons and destroy vehicles protected by the law from attack. Mines used in this fashion are indiscriminate

at the 1974 Lucerne Weapons Conference a number of experts felt that mines were indiscriminate by their very nature, 'though other experts contested this'.[1318] It was suggested, correctly in the view of the author, that marking of 'mine deposits' and the application of reliable self-destruct devices could mitigate the indiscriminate effects.[1319]

But if manually-emplaced mines are potentially indiscriminate, the dangers are all the more acute in the case of remotely-delivered mines.[1320] According to Human Rights Watch, for example: 'Air dispersion, in particular, leads to lack of accuracy in placement. Almost inevitably, a certain number of air-delivered mines are dropped outside target areas.'[1321] Thus, a Gulf War veteran reported that he was 'struck by the fact that US minefields were unmarked; that no minefield maps were available; that the US could not even provide a general area description of where the mines were supposed to have landed, let alone where they actually did.'[1322]

Already during the preparatory conferences for the 1977 Additional Protocols specific concerns had been expressed as to the potential indiscriminateness

---

in their effects, and may as easily explode under a civilian, an ambulance, or a civilian passenger train, as under a soldier, a tank, or a train carrying troops.' Greenspan, M., *The Modern Law of Land Warfare*, University of California Press, Berkeley and Los Angeles, 1959, p. 363. This view is, however, no longer valid as technological developments, such as remotely-delivered mines, have rendered such a distinction obsolete.

1318 *Report on the 1974 Lucerne Weapons Conference*, para. 248. See Kalshoven, F., "The Conference of Government Experts on the Use of Certain Conventional Weapons, Lucerne, 24 September to 18 October 1974", *op. cit.*, p. 98.

1319 *Report on the 1974 Lucerne Weapons Conference*, para. 248.

1320 A remotely-delivered mine is defined under Protocol II to the 1980 CCW as a mine 'not directly emplaced but delivered by artillery, missile, rocket, mortar, or similar means, or dropped from an aircraft.' Excluded from the legal definition, however, are mines delivered from a land-based system from less than 500 metres provided that they are accurately marked and civilian protection can be reliably maintained. Nash, M., "Contemporary Practice of the United States Relating to International Law", *op. cit.*, 1997, pp. 331-2.
According to a study on the military effectiveness of anti-personnel mines commissioned by the ICRC: 'Mines can now be delivered to any area of the battlefield within rocket or gun range, that is up to 40 km from the launch point. Those delivered by aircraft can be deployed at even greater ranges. The only limitation on the use of such **"remotely-delivered" mines** will therefore be the ability and range of delivery systems and of remote sensor equipment, such as intelligence-collecting satellites or drones, to detect concentrations of enemy forces which will justify their use.' *Anti-Personnel Landmines: Friend or Foe, A Study of the Military Use and Effectiveness of Anti-Personnel Mines*, ICRC, Geneva, 1996, (hereinafter, *ICRC Military Study*), p. 54.

1321 *A Deadly Legacy*, p. 27. Later, at p. 278, however, it is acknowledged that the experience of the 1980s has shown that the use of remotely-delivered mines 'has not become as widespread as had been feared'. But it points out that 'the failure to ban remotely-delivered mines has had terrible consequences in Afghanistan, where vast areas of land were saturated with mines delivered from the air, and in Indochina during US involvement there.' Considerable numbers of remotely-delivered anti-personnel mines are believed to have been dropped on Chechnya, both during the conflict in 1995-1996, and in the fighting in 1999 and 2000.

1322 E-mail correspondence to Human Rights Watch from Timothy Connolly, former Principal Deputy Assistant Secretary of Defense for Special Operations and Low Intensity Conflict, who served with the 82nd Airborne Division, 3 March 1997, cited in *Landmine Monitor Report 1999*, pp. 335-6.

of remotely-delivered mines,[1323] especially those dropped by aircraft. One opponent of a prohibition on the weapons asserted that the humanitarian concerns could be 'adequately satisfied' by including self-destruct mechanisms, thereby removing the danger to the civilian population.[1324] Indeed, during the revision of Protocol II to the 1980 CCW a number of States, especially from the West, proposed the incorporation of self-destruct devices as the way to prevent excessive civilian casualties due to mines. According to one US military expert, US smart mines are programmed to self-destruct in up to 15 days, with an estimated 90-95 per cent reliability. The remaining 5-10 per cent deactivate by exhaustion of their batteries within 90 days, with a claimed combined reliability of 99.9 per cent.[1325]

Yet, technical theory does not necessarily correspond to practical reality.[1326] Retired US General Robert Gard points out that 'mistakes in air speed, dropping height, and fuze settings add to the failure rate of the activating mechanisms of these weapons.' As an example, he refers to the report by a US clearance contractor in Kuwait cited in the *ICRC Military Study* that some 1,700 mines equipped with self-destruct fuses in the Gulf War failed to self-destruct within the time specified in their design.[1327] A mine clearance expert commenting on the situation after the end of the war remarked that: 'One alarming feature of scatterable systems in general and their self-destruct systems in particular was

---

1323 Remotely-delivered mines are generally regarded as having been developed during the Vietnam War, initially being delivered in huge numbers by aircraft. See for instance *A Deadly Legacy*, p. 17. But according to one authority, during the Second World War German forces developed, but used only infrequently, an air-dropped scatterable mine system known as *Spreng Dickenwend 2 Kg* (SD2), or, on account of its winged appearance, 'butterfly bombs'. Apparently, Italian forces also used a similar device. *The History of Landmines*, pp. 47-8 and 57-8.

1324 Robblee Jr., Capt. P.A., "The Legitimacy of Modern Conventional Weaponry", *op. cit.*, p. 434. He stressed the 'undeniable military utility' of scatterable mines in restricting enemy movement on the battlefield, both defensively and offensively, with little drain on combat troop strength. On the other hand, a consultant for the State Department has acknowledged that remotely-delivered mines posed 'particular hazards to civilians, in part because their location cannot be marked as accurately as mines placed by hand or by mechanical mine layers and in part because, emplaced from long distances, it is often difficult to ensure that civilians are excluded from areas containing such mines.' Nash, M., "Contemporary Practice of the United States Relating to International Law", *op. cit.*, 1997, p. 331.

1325 Gard, R., "The Military Utility of Anti-Personnel Mines", *op. cit.*, pp. 145-6.

1326 According to retired-Brigadier-General Patrick Blagden, a reason for the high failure level of self-destruct systems is that the manufacturers' dud rates are calculated on the basis of the design reliability of the *component parts* of the munition, whereas in reality the munition is only part of a system which includes human operators, and it is here that reliability expectations become most suspect. *ICRC Military Study*, p. 57. Thus, the ICRC, in its official commentary on Article 36 of 1977 Additional Protocol I (*ICRC Commentary on the 1977 Additional Protocols*, p. 426), declares that the purchaser of a weapon 'should not blindly depend on the attitude of the seller or the manufacturer, but should proceed itself to evaluate the use of the weapon in question with regard to the provisions of the Protocol or any other rule of international law which applies to it.'

1327 CMS Environmental Inc., Tampa, Florida, cited in *ICRC Military Study*, p. 57.

their failure rate. The presence of GATOR mines[1328] across the Kuwaiti desert was highly apparent after the war and an estimated 10 per cent of all these mines did not self-destruct – 56 mines from each of the hundreds of units dropped.'[1329]

Furthermore, the military utility of remotely-delivered mines has even been doubted. According to the *ICRC Military Study*: 'When the precise location of enemy forces can be determined, the relevance of remotely-delivered mines must be questioned; one could probably achieve more kills with conventional artillery or air support. Thus the better the intelligence the less the need for remotely-delivered mines; and the worse the intelligence the more their use will tend to be widespread[1330] or indiscriminate.'[1331] However, the ICRC also cites an 'authoritative' report by Jane's Information Group in London that 'the future is probably linked to the remote/airborne delivery of mines over large distances' and that 'the old style hand or mechanical emplacement is far too slow for present day realities.'[1332]

According to Human Rights Watch: 'Remotely-delivered and manually-emplaced mines (...) share basic problems intrinsic to mine warfare: both cause egregious injuries, long-term devastation, and operate on the same delayed-action principles which render them implicitly indiscriminate weapons[.] (...) Thus, in the view of the Arms Project and Physicians for Human Rights, remotely-delivered mines should not be treated differently than manually emplaced mines: to conform to existing customary humanitarian law, the use of either type of mine must be banned.'[1333]

3.2.3. Conclusion

In the view of the author, although customary international law prohibits the use of inherently indiscriminate weapons, anti-personnel mines do not fall within this category. Certainly, anti-personnel mines are an immensely difficult weapon to 'direct' accurately against their target. Even when the greatest care is taken to ensure that civilians are not caught up in a mine blast, there is still no guarantee that civilians will not be injured.[1334] And regrettably, instances of

---

1328 The GATOR system delivered by the US Air Force is made up of canisters, each containing 72 anti-tank and 22 anti-personnel mines; some 600 mines can be spread over a wide area in a single sortie. Gard, R., "The Military Utility of Anti-Personnel Mines", *op. cit.*, p. 142. See *supra* footnote 666.

1329 *The History of Landmines*, p. 121.

1330 This view is not universally held, however. One authority suggests that increasing sophistication of mines will lead to smaller numbers being laid, pointing out that in the 1940s 2,000 anti-tank mines were needed per mile of front, by the 1970s the figure was 1,000, by 1980 it was 500, and today only 20 mines are required to cover the same mile. *The History of Landmines*, p. 144.

1331 *ICRC Military Study*, p. 55.

1332 *Trends in Land Mine Warfare*, Special Report, Jane's Information Group, London, July 1995, pp. 5-6, cited by *ICRC Military Study*, p. 54.

1333 *A Deadly Legacy*, p. 281.

1334 For instance, environmental factors, including the weather, can intervene to change the location of mines. As the ICRC points out: 'With heavy rain or melting snow mines can be washed into streams and may migrate many kilometres from their original point of emplacement.' *ICRC Military Study*, pp. 57-8. For the example of Georgia, and specifically the Inguri river, see

parties to the conflict taking the necessary care are relatively few and far between.[1335] In the view of the author, however, a set of clear conditions for 'responsible' use could ensure that loss of life and limb to civilians is reduced to a minimum. Thus, for example, one authority suggests that traditional minefields laid without 'customary precautions (*i.e.*, unrecorded, unmarked, and not designed to destroy themselves within a reasonable time) are difficult to imagine as compatible with Article 51(4)(b) of 1977 Additional Protocol I.'[1336] The fact that these precautions are not followed in practice is tantamount to indiscriminate use of anti-personnel mines and fully justifies efforts to prohibit them, but does not constitute grounds for a legal determination that they are indiscriminate weapons *per se*.

Remotely-delivered mines, whether anti-tank or anti-personnel, could more easily be considered inherently indiscriminate, especially if they do not have effective self-destruct mechanisms incorporated, but here the analogy with a bombing raid is instructive. Indiscriminate bombing is certainly prohibited, but as long as bombs are, and can be, directed towards a specific military objective, the bombs themselves cannot be considered as inherently indiscriminate. The specific time-delay feature of landmines, however, particularly when distributed over long distances or dropped from great height, demands additional protection, including very short periods for self-destruction, measured in hours not days, to ensure that their effects are not indiscriminate.[1337]

3.3. Anti-Personnel Mines and the Principle of Proportionality

3.3.1. Introduction

The principle of proportionality involves a balancing of the advantage to be expected from a military attack against its humanitarian consequences.[1338] In this, there is an obvious corollary with the balance between the principles of

Landmine Monitor Report 1999, p. 794. In relation to Mozambique, see *supra* footnote 503.

1335 Indeed, an assessment of future trends in landmine warfare predicted that nuisance mining (military parlance for indiscriminate mine-laying) might well be the future: 'The traditional view of a well-laid minefield, properly recorded, is not the norm and mines are often laid indiscriminately[.] (...) This latter practice can be termed "nuisance mining" and is certainly taught formally to British Army engineers[.] (...) With the constricted urbanised terrain of North-West Europe, can we not perhaps anticipate a much wider use of nuisance mining, particularly in conjunction with fighting in built-up areas?' Wyatt, Maj. (ret.) J.R., "Land mine warfare, Recent lessons and future trends", *International Defense Review*, November 1989, p. 1502.

1336 Oeter, S., "Methods and Means of Combat", *op. cit.*, p. 176, citing also Solf, W.A., in Bothe, M. *et al.*, *New Rules for Victims of Armed Conflicts*, The Hague, 1982, p. 305.

1337 In turn, it is not unreasonable to require that, given the high rate of duds, bombs, especially cluster bomblets, should also incorporate a fail-safe mechanism intended to ensure that unexploded ordnance does not pose a post-use danger to civilians. The humanitarian situation in Kosovo following prolonged NATO bombing in 1999 is instructive in this regard. See for instance ICRC, *Explosive Remnants of War, Cluster Bombs and Landmines in Kosovo*, *op. cit.*

1338 See for instance Rogers, A.P.V., *Law on the Battlefield*, *op. cit.*, p. 14, citing Krüger-Spengel, F., "Le concept de proportionalité dans le droit de la guerre", *Military Law and Law of War Review*, 1980, p. 179.

military necessity and humanity.[1339] Most commentators, however, including the present one, see the principle of proportionality as a sub-category of the principle of distinction.[1340] Such an approach is also reflected in the codification of the principle in 1977 Additional Protocol I. Thus, Article 51(5)(2), which deals with the protection of the civilian population, provides that 'an attack which may be expected[1341] to cause incidental loss of civilian life, injury to civilians, damage to civilian objects, or a combination thereof, which would be

1339 The principle of proportionality has also been described as the principle of economy of force, which 'prescribes that in the use of armed force as an instrument of national policy no greater force should be employed than is necessary to achieve the objectives toward which it is directed; or, stated in another way, the dimensions of military force should be proportionate to the value of the objectives at stake.' Osgood, R., *Limited War: the Challenge to American Strategy*, 1957, p. 4, cited by Robblee Jr., Capt. P.A., "The Legitimacy of Modern Conventional Weaponry", *op. cit.*, p. 413. It is suggested that the distinction between the principles of economy of force and proportionality is that the former limits violence in war for reasons of logistics and the latter does so for reasons of humanity. See Robblee Jr., Capt. P.A., "The Legitimacy of Modern Conventional Weaponry", *op. cit.*, pp. 413-4 and accompanying footnotes.
Another commentator, however, sees the distinction as being fundamental, arguing that 'the law of war and the economy of means principle are diametrically opposed, since these two categories of thought and action have different purposes. Whereas the military principle aims at limiting a belligerent's own losses (in men, material, resources and money), the law of war (...) aims at limiting the losses and damage inflicted on the enemy.' Meyrowitz, H., "The Principle of Superfluous Injury or Unnecessary Suffering, From the Declaration of St Petersburg of 1868 to Additional Protocol I of 1977", in *International Review of the Red Cross*, March-April 1994, No. 299, p. 111.

1340 See for instance Cassese, A., "The Means of Warfare", *op. cit.*, p. 146, who states that the rule of proportionality represents an 'important development and specification of the general principle on the distinction to be made between civilians and combatants.' This approach also has an historical basis. According to Solf, for instance: 'The principle of discrimination prescribed the immunity of the innocent from direct attack[.] (...) Realising that collateral casualties among the innocent must be expected, theologians recognised the rule of "double effect", distinguishing intended killing of combatants from unintended, accidental killing of civilians. [footnote omitted] The latter is excusable. But what about a situation where it is expected that there will be accidental killings? [Francisco de] Vitoria concludes: "[I]t is never right to slay the guiltless, even as an indirect and unintended result, except when there is no other means of carrying on the operations of a just war. [footnote omitted] (...) For if little effect upon the ultimate issue of the war is to be expected from the storming of a fortress or fortified town wherein are many innocent folk, it would not be right, for the purpose of assailing a few guilty, to slay the many innocent by (...) means likely to overwhelm indifferently both innocent and guilty."' Solf, W., "Protection of Civilians Against the Effects of Hostilities Under Customary International Law and Under Protocol I", *op. cit.*, p. 119 and footnote 16, citing De Vitoria, F., *De Indis et de Iure Belli Relectiones*, Transln. Bate, J. in 1917 of 1696 edition, p. 179. According to Gardam: 'As with rules proscribing the infliction of unnecessary suffering or superfluous injury on combatants, the requirement that armed conflict be conducted in a way that does not involve disproportionate civilian casualties is derived from the precept that the only legitimate object of war is to weaken the military forces of the enemy.' Gardam, J., "Necessity and proportionality in *jus ad bellum* and *jus ad bello*" Boisson de Chazournes, L. *et al.* (eds.), *International Law, the International Court of Justice and Nuclear Weapons*, *op. cit.*, p. 283.

1341 Cassese was particularly scathing about this formulation, pointing out that it is a subjective judgement and not an objective standard. Cassese, A., "The Means of Warfare", *op. cit.*, p. 156. See also Oeter, S., "Methods and Means of Combat", *op. cit.*, p. 179.

excessive in relation to the concrete and direct military advantage anticipated'[1342] is to be considered indiscriminate.

Similarly Article 57, which deals with precautions in attack, requires that those who plan or decide upon an attack shall 'refrain from deciding to launch any attack which may be expected to cause incidental loss of civilian life, injury to civilians, damage to civilian objects, or a combination thereof, which would be excessive in relation to the concrete and directly military advantage anticipated.'[1343] It further requires that 'an attack shall be cancelled or suspended if it becomes apparent that the objective is not a military one or is subject to special protection or that the attack may be expected to cause incidental loss of civilian life, injury to civilians, damage to civilian objects, or a combination thereof, which would be excessive in relation to the concrete and direct military advantage anticipated.'[1344]

Thus: 'The use of means and methods of warfare may be illegal, even if collateral damage to the civilian population and civilian goods could be justified in principle by reference to "military necessity", on the grounds that such damage is unavoidable in mounting an effective attack on a military objective in the centre of the operation. Manifestly disproportionate collateral damage

---

1342 Fenrick cites the initial ICRC draft provision, which stated in part:
'The employment of means of combat, and any methods which strike or affect indiscriminately the civilian population and combatants, or civilian objects and military objectives, are prohibited. In particular it is forbidden: (...)
(b) To launch attacks which may be expected to entail incidental losses among the civilian population and cause the destruction of civilian objects to an extent disproportionate to the direct and substantial military advantage anticipated.'
Fenrick, Lt.-Col. W.J., "The Rule of Proportionality and Protocol I in Conventional Warfare", *op. cit.*, p. 103. Fenrick (*ibid.*, at p. 104) goes on to claim that the US, in supporting the ICRC proposal, added that it was a codification of existing international law. Though note Oeter's observation that proportionality has been 'a point of a fierce controversy. It was debated to what extent Article 51(4)(c) of 1977 Additional Protocol I refers to an established principle of proportionality.' Oeter, S., "Methods and Means of Combat", *op. cit.*, p. 176.

1343 In ratifying 1977 Additional Protocol I, a number of States, including Australia, Belgium, Canada, Germany, Italy the Netherlands, New Zealand, Spain, and the UK, declared that the military advantage anticipated from an attack is intended to refer to the advantage anticipated from the attack as a whole and not only from isolated or particular parts of the attack.

1344 Although there is little dispute about the customary nature of the principle in international armed conflicts, it is far from certain that the rule of proportionality applies to internal armed conflicts. Hampson, for instance, declares that while the principles of distinction, proportionality and the prohibition or weapons causing superfluous injury or unnecessary suffering 'certainly apply in international [armed] conflicts[,] (...) [i]t is less clear to what extent they apply to conflicts not of an international character.' Hampson, F., *Anti-Personnel Mines and the Law: The Legal Background*, Paper presented to the NGO Conference on Anti-Personnel Mines, London, 24-26 May 1993, p. 4. None was included in the 1998 Rome Statute of the International Criminal Court. And as Greenwood points out, 1977 Additional Protocol II does not incorporate the principle of proportionality. Greenwood, C., *Humanitarian Law and Laws of War*, *op. cit.*, p. 64. This is despite the fact that a specific article on the proportionality principle was discussed in detail before the Diplomatic Conference that adopted the Protocol. For the text of the proposal see for instance Cassese, A., "The Means of Warfare", *op. cit.*, p. 159.

inflicted in order to achieve operational objectives will result in the action being deemed an (illicit) form of indiscriminate warfare.'[1345]

In the mid-1970s, as the relevant provisions were being drafted, Cassese was already criticising the proportionality rule for being 'vague' and 'full of holes'.[1346] He referred to Baxter's contention that it 'calls for comparing two things for which there is no standard of comparison. Is one, for example, compelled to think in terms of a certain number of casualties as justified in the gaining of a specified number of yards?'[1347] He did acknowledge, however, that it does provide a standard 'for at least the most glaring cases'.[1348]

There are, though, additional problems in applying the principle to anti-personnel mines. As Human Rights Watch has rightly pointed out, 'a field commander contemplating the use of a non-delayed-action weapon can make a legitimate calculation regarding its military utility compared to humanitarian risk by carefully surveying the situation at the time he proposes to use the weapon; he can make a reasonable determination, for example, as to whether there are civilians immediately in the area who might suffer harm. In the context of landmine use, however, such a calculation is essentially irrelevant, because it cannot deal with future dangers caused by unexploded, uncleared mines.'[1349] With this in mind, an understanding of the downstream effects of anti-personnel mines, as opposed to their perceived military utility, is even more important if a commander is to make a reasonably informed decision as to the legality of the use of anti-personnel mines.

1345 Oeter, S., "Methods and Means of Combat", *op. cit.*, p. 119. According to the US Army Field Manual on the Law of Land Warfare, 'proportionality' means that the 'loss of life and damage must not be out of proportion to the military advantage to be gained' by the conduct of a military operation. Cited by Gard, R., "The Military Utility of Anti-Personnel Mines", *op. cit.*, p. 136.

1346 Cassese, A., "Means of Warfare", *op. cit.*, p. 147. With regard to the final formulation, the ICRC conceded that it is 'by no means as clear as it might have been' but declares that 'in the circumstances it seems a reasonable compromise between conflicting interests and a praiseworthy attempt to impose some restrictions in the domain where arbitrary behaviour has existed too often.' *ICRC Commentary on the 1977 Additional Protocols*, p. 685.

1347 Baxter, R.R., "Criteria of the Prohibition of Weapons in International Law", *op. cit.*, pp. 48-9, cited by Cassese, A., "Means of Warfare", *op. cit.*, p. 146.

1348 *Ibid.*, p. 147. Indeed, there have been specific instances where the customary rule has clearly avoided excessive civilian casualties. Rogers cites an interesting example from the Vietnam War (Rogers, A.P.V., *Law on the Battlefield, op. cit.*, p. 15): 'Parks describes a US air attack, during the Vietnam War in 1972, on a hydro-electric plant at Lang Chi. It was estimated to supply up to 75 per cent of Hanoi's industrial and defence needs. On the other hand, it was thought that if the dam at the site were breached, as many as 23,000 civilians could die, presumably in the resultant floods. President Nixon's military advisers said that if laser-guided bombs were used there was a 90 per cent chance of the mission being accomplished without breaching the dam. On that basis, the President authorised the attack, which successfully destroyed the electricity generating plant without breaching the dam. [Parks, "Air war and the law of war", *Air Force Law Review*, 1990, pp. 168-9.] This seems to be a good example of the proportionality principle at work.'

1349 *A Deadly Legacy*, p. 272, footnote 30.

3.2.2. The Humanitarian Impact of Anti-Personnel Mines

It was the sharply increasing number of amputees, particularly in Afghanistan and Cambodia, which first alerted field workers to the specific dangers caused by anti-personnel mines. But with its seminal study on the wider socio-economic impact of mines in Cambodia in 1991,[1350] the Boston-based NGO, Physicians for Human Rights, and Asia Watch, a division of Human Rights Watch, identified the longer-term consequences of anti-personnel mines that set them apart from other conventional weapons.[1351] Not only were the effects of anti-personnel mines savage on the unfortunate individuals caught up in the blast or hit by the fragments, the consequences of their use also affected the society, the economy and the environment.

A. The Impact on the Individual

Although the precise number of men, women and children killed or maimed each year by anti-personnel mines is unknown,[1352] it certainly runs into many thousands.[1353] At least in post-conflict situations,[1354] the victims of anti-personnel mines are almost invariably the poorest and most vulnerable members of society.[1355] 'It is the subsistence farmer, nomads and their herds, and fleeing refugees and the displaced who are often most affected. Economic necessity – bare survival – forces people to enter known mined areas in search of food and water, to graze livestock, to grow food, cut wood, or gather thatch to sell for building materials.[1356] Moreover, those people who live and work among

---

1350 Asia Watch and Physicians for Human Rights, *Land Mines in Cambodia: The Coward's War*, HRW & PHR, New York, September 1991.

1351 Thus, in September 1997, when the Finnish Prime Minister, Paavo Lipponen, railed against the comprehensive prohibition of anti-personnel mines being negotiated in Oslo, asking 'Why aren't they proposing a ban on Kalashnikovs? They are killing more people – have killed more people', he was clearing neglecting the wider humanitarian argument against anti-personnel mines. See *Landmine Monitor Report 1999*, pp. 783-4.

1352 See *supra* Introduction.

1353 The ICRC's database of war-wounded, which records treatment in ICRC hospitals and by ICRC surgical teams, recorded that between 1985 and 1995, of a total of 140,000 patients no fewer than 30,000 were victims of landmines. *The Worldwide Epidemic of Landmine Injuries*, *op. cit.*, p. 2.

1354 See for instance the situation in Bosnia-Herzegovina, *Landmine Monitor Report 1999*, p. 566.

1355 Contrary to what had been expected, the most comprehensive socio-economic impact study yet conducted found that the 'overwhelming majority' of mine victims were adult males. *After the Guns Fall Silent*, p. 9. This finding was subsequently supported, in the case of Afghanistan at least, by research indicating that 81.5 per cent of mine victims were adult males. See Mine Clearance Planning Agency, *Socio-Economic Impact Study of Mine Action Operations Afghanistan*, Interim Report, United Nations Mine Action Programme for Afghanistan, October 1998, p. 12. Likewise, in Bosnia-Herzegovina, women represent only 10 per cent of mine casualties even after the end of the war.

1356 As an example, a report by the United Nations Integrated Regional Information Network (IRIN) on the situation in Angola contained the following information: 'The basis of the local economy in the besieged, government-held central highlands city of Kuito is a simple but vital commodity – firewood[.] (...) It is collected almost exclusively by women who are forced to trek up to 40 km in a day, dodging UNITA rebels and minefields that ring this city crammed with some

landmines are very often the same people who rely most on their physical fitness for work and who can least afford the care necessary to treat landmines.'[1357]

The injuries caused by anti-personnel mines are typically severe, and in the case of a blast mine, invariably cause traumatic amputation of the leg of the person detonating it.[1358] As many as 85 per cent of all amputations performed in ICRC hospitals are for victims of landmines. 'The doctors, nurses and orthopaedic technicians of the ICRC have witnessed and recorded the human voices behind the cries of pain, and the inhumane consequences of what can only be described as a man-made public health catastrophe and a worldwide epidemic.'[1359]

For mine victims, especially amputees, life tends to be harsh.[1360] In addition to the daily pain they must endure comes the realisation that they are likely to remain a burden on their family and community, unable to work or earn money as they did before.[1361] In a survey of mine victims in Afghanistan, 40 per cent of those interviewed claimed that they had lost their jobs and were currently without work and a further quarter had been forced to accept other, less-well-paid employment.[1362]

B. The Socio-Economic Impact of Anti-Personnel Mines

If the consequences of anti-personnel mines for the individual are dramatic, so too is the wider socio-economic impact. The loss of fertile agricultural land and access to water points are among the most serious effects for rural developing communities,[1363] but the mining of schools and hospitals also has acute social and economic effects. In a speech by Queen Noor of Jordan in 1998, she declared that 'about 10 per cent of (...) [the Jordanian] population lives in areas still dangerous and economically unproductive because of landmines. Scarce

---

70,000 internally displaced people[.] (...) Maria Naneli, 52, is one of the unlucky ones. Last week, collecting firewood 30 km outside Kuito, she detonated a mine and lost her right foot. "It was my first time in the area," she told IRIN. "I stepped off the path and into the bush." (...) Still trying to come to terms with her injury in a ward in Kuito hospital she said: "If I wasn't so hungry I would have stayed at home."' "Angola: Women bear the brunt of war", *IRIN – Southern Africa*, 26 July 1999.

1357 *After the Guns Fall Silent*, p. 8.

1358 By no means all landmine victims suffer amputation, either traumatic or surgical, however. The ICRC recorded in 1995 that just under 30 per cent of landmine patients in the ICRC database underwent an amputation. *The Worldwide Epidemic of Landmine Injuries*, *op. cit.*, p. 5.

1359 *Ibid.*, p. 2.

1360 Amputees experience sensations ranging from a stabbing feeling, pins and needles, shooting (like electrical shocks), cramping, crushing, and burning. Wartan, S.W. *et al.*, "Phantom pain and sensation among British veteran amputees", *British Journal of Anaesthesia*, Vol. 78, No. 6, 1997, p. 652, cited by Cameron, M. *et al.*, "To Walk Without Fear", *To Walk Without Fear*, p. 4.

1361 See further Cameron, M. *et al.*, "To Walk Without Fear", *op. cit.*, p. 4.

1362 Mine Clearance Planning Agency, *Socio-Economic Impact Study of Mine Action Operations Afghanistan*, Interim Report, *op. cit.*, p. 21.

1363 A study in Afghanistan found that 223 km^2 of productive agricultural land had been mined resulting in a loss of US$137.7 million over 10 years. Mine Clearance Planning Agency, *Socio-Economic Impact Study of Mine Action Operations Afghanistan*, Interim Report, *op. cit.*, p. 13.

agricultural lands and some of the most beautiful and sacred landscapes in Jordan, especially in the Jordan River Valley, remain scarred and forbidden because of the danger of mines.'[1364] Further, anti-personnel mines have exacerbated the impact of drought because mine-affected roads have impeded the movement of domestic foodstuffs and hampered food relief.[1365]

According to Roberts and Williams: 'Countries with a minimal infrastructure (...) are particularly vulnerable to landmine use. Dams and electrical installations have been mined, which can seriously reduce the ability of a nation to produce the power necessary for reconstruction. Transportation systems have been mined, interrupting the movement of people and the flow of goods and services. Market systems have been seriously disrupted or abandoned because farmers and herders have been unable to move over mined roads and footpaths to bring their produce to market.'[1366]

The economic effects of anti-personnel mines have even included a potential threat to tourism. In Zimbabwe, for instance, the Victoria Falls are reportedly ringed by some 66,000 anti-personnel mines – tourists pass through cleared paths in the minefields. Further expansion of the Victoria Falls was also hampered because the town's sewage system could be expanded to cope with increased tourist demand, resulting in frequent spillages and raw effluent flowing into the Zambezi river.[1367] However, in July 1998, Zimbabwean troops working with the US army began clearing mines in the area.[1368] By April 2000, the clearance programme had 'unearthed' 26,000 landmines, opening large tracts of land in Victoria Falls to tourism and other tracts in the Zambezi valley for resettlement.[1369] Elsewhere in the country it was reported that some Zim$5 million per year was being lost because mature timber could not be cut down in the Eastern Highlands due to the presence of anti-personnel mines.[1370]

C. The Impact on the Environment

In 1995, the United Nations, repeating the view expressed by the US State Department,[1371] declared that mines were 'one of the most widespread, lethal and long-lasting forms of pollution' the world has ever known.[1372] The environmental

[1364] Cited in *Landmine Monitor Report 1999*, p. 851.

[1365] *After the Guns Fall Silent*, p. 6.

[1366] *Ibid.*

[1367] Rupiah, M., *Deadly Legacy: Landmines in Zimbabwe*, *op. cit.*

[1368] "Zimbabwe begins clearing landmines from prime resort town", *AFP Internationale*, 26 July 1998.

[1369] Chigodo, T., "Military clearing programme traces some 26,000 landmines", *All Africa News Agency*, Harare, 17 April 2000.

[1370] See *Landmine Monitor Report 1999*, p. 110.

[1371] See US Department of State, *Hidden Killers: The Global Problem with Uncleared Landmines*, Washington DC, 1993.

[1372] "Assistance in Mine Clearance", Report of the Secretary-General, *UN Doc. A/49/357*, 6 September 1995, p. 7. In this vein, one sapper from the Angolan Armed Forces admitted in October 1996 admitted, 'I hate mines. They destroy the lives of Angolans on a daily basis and make our country poorer. They are the worst sort of environmental pollution you can find.' Human Rights Watch, *Still Killing: Landmines in Southern Africa*, Human Rights Watch, New York, 1997, pp. 2-3, cited by Vines, A., "The Crisis of Anti-Personnel Mines", *op. cit.*, p. 128.

impact of landmines had already been recognised at the end of the 1970s.[1373] On 5 December 1980, the UN General Assembly adopted Resolution 3571 entitled 'Problem of Remnants of War' in which it acknowledged that 'the presence of material remnants of war, particularly mines, on the territories of certain developing countries seriously impedes their development efforts and entails loss of life and property.'[1374] Large-scale use of anti-personnel mines drives rural populations onto increasingly fragile, marginal lands, furthering the land's rapid degradation, or into the cities thereby contributing to overcrowding, unemployment and other urban problems.[1375]

The presence of uncleared anti-personnel mines has also facilitated the spread of disease. In Zimbabwe, for instance, the border minefields have become a haven for tsetse flies.[1376] They have also been acknowledged as contributing to the 'serious breakdown in animal disease control with outbreaks of tick-bone and foot and mouth occurring in border regions. An estimated one million cattle were affected.'[1377]

The widespread use of anti-personnel mines has also accelerated deforestation since communities may be constrained to sell forest-land in order to buy sufficient food. This can, in turn, affect marshlands and watertables, which have an impact on fish and other wildlife.[1378] Thus, in Zimbabwe, since 1980, it is reported that '9,084 cattle have been reported killed in minefields, representing a loss of income. Many people have been injured trying to save or retrieve livestock that has strayed into minefields. Cattle are not just food for these people – they play a critical social and economic function. A cow represents family wealth, insurance against periods of hardship, and a form of payment for rituals, such as marriages. The loss of cattle is therefore very significant.'[1379]

In addition, as Roberts and Williams have pointed out: 'Landmines have also threatened the already fragile environments of some rare animals, such as the snow leopard in Afghanistan – which is already in danger of extinction. In Africa, elephants and other animals have been killed or maimed by landmines[1380] after national parks have been used as military bases. One of the few remaining

---

1373 See for instance *ICRC Commentary on the 1977 Additional Protocols*, p. 411.

1374 *A Deadly Legacy*, p. 310-312. It is extremely hard to accept, however, the claim made by the authors that 'there is consensus at least that landmine use may be expected to cause environmental damage that is severe, long-lasting, and widespread.' According to one leading military lawyer: 'Other commentators have referred to the UN General Assembly resolution on the remnants of war and stress that such remnants may constitute significant environmental degradation. This argument is not always valid. Unexploded munitions cannot damage the environment unless they contain toxic chemicals or heavy metals. They may make areas inaccessible or unusable, but that may even encourage the growth of the natural vegetation.' Rogers, A.P.V., *Law on the Battlefield*, *op. cit.*, p. 118.

1375 *After the Guns Fall Silent*, p. 11.

1376 Human Rights Watch, *Still Killing: Landmines in Southern Africa*, *op. cit.*, p. 159. See also *Landmine Monitor Report 1999*, p. 110.

1377 Cited in *Landmine Monitor Report 1999*, p. 103.

1378 *Ibid.*

1379 Rupiah, M., *Deadly Legacy: Landmines in Zimbabwe*, Southern Africa Political and Economic Series, Harare, 1998, cited by Vines, A., "The Crisis of Anti-Personnel Mines", *op cit.*, p. 128.

1380 See also Vines, A., "The Crisis of Anti-Personnel Mines", *op. cit.*, p. 130; "Hunted Elephants", <http://www.dsk.de/mgm.>.

male silver-backed gorillas fell victim to landmines.'[1381] In addition, mines on the India-China border are killing endangered animals like the Tibetan gazelle, Tibetan wild ass, blue sheep, alpine musk deer and the snow leopard.[1382] In Cambodia, poachers are reportedly using mines to kill tigers.[1383]

The traumatic amputation of a elephant's foot on the Thai-Myanmar border in August 1999 made headlines around the world. Four months after surgery on her shattered leg which had required a crane and 'enough anaesthetic to flatten 70 humans', Motola was recovering well and preparations were being made to fit a prosthesis.[1384] But as one journalist noted, though, it only made headlines because her trainer took her to a special elephant hospital in northern Thailand. 'Countless other hapless, smaller beasts die unremarked in the wild.'[1385]

There are also potential environmental consequences from the destruction of large numbers of stockpiled or cleared anti-personnel mines. According to Ukraine, for instance, its own experience in stockpile destruction of PFM-1 anti-personnel mines has shown that the pollution of the environment exceeds by hundreds or more times the permissible norms and standards of pollution.[1386] The main pollutants are aluminium oxide, lead residues, and hydrocyanic acid, resulting from the liquid explosive content of the scatterable mines.[1387]

3.3.3. The Military Utility of Anti-Personnel Mines

To date, there has been relatively little debate as to the – substantial – military utility of anti-tank/anti-vehicle mines.[1388] The utility of anti-personnel mines, on the other hand, has increasingly been questioned,[1389] where once it was

1381 *Ibid.*

1382 Peck, G., "Animals and Land Mines", *AP*, Bangkok, 7 May 2000; see also *Landmine Monitor Report 2000*, p. 488.

1383 *Ibid.*

1384 "Four months after surgery, Thai elephant maimed by landmine in good health", *AP*, Lampang, Thailand, 28 December 1999.

1385 Peck, G., "Animals and Land Mines", *op. cit.*; see also *Landmine Monitor Report 2000*, p. 479.

1386 See *Landmine Monitor Report 2000*, pp. 786-7.

1387 *Ibid.*, p. 787. Belarus faces a similar problem with its PFM-1 stockpiles. *Ibid.*, p. 806.

1388 See *supra* Introduction, p. 11. Thus, for example, Chinese military doctrine in 1980 praised the defensive effectiveness of anti-vehicle/anti-tank mines in rather quaint, ideological terms: 'In the aggressive war, the imperialists and all their running dogs will surely use numerous technical equipment such as tanks, armoured cars, etc. to launch an offensive by a mobile surprise attack at high speed. Therefore (...) the employment of vast numbers of mines will remain to be one of the important means of struggling against the enemy.' Cited in *The History of Landmines*, p. 126.

1389 Though note the view of the Netherlands which, as recently as 1995, claimed that there was a continuing military need for anti-personnel mines, and South Africa, which in 1997 produced a paper suggesting that 'anyone doubting the effectiveness of (...) an anti-personnel minefield, should try it sometime.' *Landmine Monitor Report 1999*, pp. 747, 83, respectively. The Landmine Monitor reports that Canada is currently developing an operational research study in computer modelling, to demonstrate the limited military utility of anti-personnel mines. *Ibid.*, p. 228; see also *Landmine Monitor Report 2000*, p. 240.

undisputed that they were essential weapons of war.[1390] In 1997, at a regional seminar in Budapest, the Director of Military Engineering of the Canadian armed forces set out seven principal functions for anti-personnel mines:

- *to provide early warning;*
- *to protect anti-tank mines;*
- *to delay or canalise enemy forces;*
- *to provide economy of force in close terrain;*
- *to inflict casualties on enemy personnel;*
- *to deny use of terrain; and*
- *to provide close protection of defenders.*[1391]

But the situation most usually cited as the justification for the continued possession and use of anti-personnel mines is the case of those countries that, by reason of geography, are forced to defend long borders against potential aggressors. This represented the core of objections to a prohibition by China, Finland, India,[1392] Russia,[1393] and the US (in the specific case of South Korea). One study on the military utility of anti-personnel mines, for example, concludes that while they are useful in static defensive situations, they are of marginal utility in a defence that also employs tactical offensive operations.[1394]

1390 Croll, for instance, cites the view of many experts at an ICRC-hosted meeting of military experts in 1994 that 'mines were an indispensable defence weapon in time of war and their banning would be undesirable or impossible in practical terms, but that some action should be taken to reduce the risks posed to civilians.' *The History of Landmines*, p. 134.
According to Croll, 'Soviet defensive philosophy was profoundly shaped by the German invasion of the Soviet Union in 1941. Mines played a significant role in halting the Germans and henceforth they were considered indispensable for defence. By the mid-1970s Warsaw Pact forces had over fifty different types of mine in their inventories. Most were fairly simple devices, cheap to manufacture and easy to use, even by soldiers with limited training. [footnote omitted] In addition to the creation of barrier minefields in front of an enemy, it was standard practice for Soviet forces to protect the perimeters of airfields, barracks, bridges and other potential targets with a belt of anti-personnel mines – a practice they exported to developing countries.' *The History of Landmines*, pp. 125-6. Likewise, the US Army Field Manual, updated to take account of the lessons of the Korean War, stated that: 'Mines are among the best artificial obstacles – they are portable, installed relatively easily, and constitute a hazard to the enemy; however, large-scale employment of mines requires considerable time, manpower, and logistical effort. Mines delay and canalise enemy movement, lower the enemy's will to fight, and cause fear of sudden and unexpected casualties.' *Ibid.*, p. 101.

1391 Colonel E. Fitch, *Presentation to the ICRC Seminar on the Humanitarian Impact and Military Utility of Anti-Personnel Mines*, Budapest, 26-28 March 1998. See also Gard, R., "The Military Utility of Anti-Personnel Mines", *op. cit.*, p. 141; Hewish, M. and Pengelley, R., "In search of a successor to the anti-personnel landmine, Non-lethal weapons, precision weapons and close surveillance", *Jane's International Defense Review*, March 1998, p. 30.

1392 See for instance *Landmine Monitor Report 1999*, pp. 464-5, 468.

1393 Though their use of mines in Chechnya and Daghestan clearly goes far beyond this limited alleged military need. See for instance *Landmine Monitor Report 1999*, p. 845.

1394 Gard, R., "The Military Utility of Anti-Personnel Mines", *op. cit.*, pp. 140-1, citing Institute for Defence Analyses (IDA), "The Military Utility of Landmines: Implications for Arms Control", *Document D-1559*, June 1994, p. 69. According to Croll, in the latter half of 1968, 57 per cent of all casualties in the US 1st Marine Division were attributed to mines and booby-traps. *The History of Landmines*, p. 106, citing US Department of State, *Hidden Killers, The Global Landmine Crisis*, Office of International Security and Peacekeeping Operations, Washington, 1994, p. 7. Many of these were US-made mines. For details see for instance *Landmine Monitor Report 1999*, p. 335.

Both sides used landmines in large numbers during the 1991-1992 Gulf War, particularly the Iraqis – as barriers to the allied advance. One authority claims that the Iraqis laid around two million mines,[1395] most in well-organised fields that were often fenced. The minefields were covered with fire[1396] and the overall defence was developed in considerable depth, although it is suggested that the minefields themselves were probably not sufficiently wide.[1397] Despite the fact that the minefields were breached by the Coalition forces in about two hours,[1398] Croll alleges that barrier minefields still have a role to play in defence arguing that 'mines, even in Kuwait, added to the strain of war – additional fear was created, movement was inhibited, and extra *matériel*, training and co-ordination were required. Although ultimately peripheral to the Gulf War, barrier minefields were the only means of enhancing defence available to the Iraqis.'[1399]

Other authorities, however, question the effectiveness of barrier minefields. In one study of the use of anti-personnel mines in conflicts in southern Africa it was claimed that there were 'few, if any, examples where anti-personnel mines have provided significant or lasting military advantages. In Mozambique, during the 1977-92 war Renamo quickly breached government minefields. In Angola, government mine belts around the main towns did not stop UNITA from capturing several of them. In the 1960s and 1970s, saboteurs simply shovelled their way across the minefield protecting the Kariba power station in Rhodesia, did their damage and left.[1400] In 1988, South Africa scrapped plans to build a 30 km-long minefield along Namibia's northern border in part because it determined that such a barrier would only delay any potential invasion by some 30 minutes.[1401]

Peacekeeping forces have seemingly used anti-personnel mines in the past,[1402] although at least in the case of the United Nations, this is no longer

1395 The *ICRC Military Study* (at pp. 37-8), on the other hand, refers to nine million mines being laid, a considerable discrepancy! See *supra* Introduction, footnote 83.

1396 According to one authority, 'to be effective, minefields should be covered by fire. The Canadian armed forces have carried out some very interesting computer studies on this aspect, which showed quite conclusively that the effectiveness of a minefield was enhanced, particularly when covered by direct fire. A synergistic effect was achieved by the mines and direct-fire weapons as the vehicles slowed down or bunched.' Wyatt, Maj., (ret.) J.R., "Land mine warfare, Recent lessons and future trends", *op. cit.*, p.1500. It should be noted that this paper refers to both anti-tank/anti-vehicle and anti-personnel mines. See also McManners, H., *The Scars of War*, Harpers Collins, London, 1993, p. 179.

1397 *The History of Landmines*, p. 118.

1398 The *ICRC Military Study*, pp. 37-38. On the other hand, it has been noted that the mining of beaches by the Iraqi forces did prevent an amphibious assault by US Marines. Gard, R., "The Military Utility of Anti-Personnel Mines", *op. cit.*, p. 142.

1399 *The History of Landmines*, p. 121.

1400 ICRC Military Study, p. 30.

1401 Human Rights Watch, *Still Killing: Landmines in Southern Africa*, *op. cit.*, p. 110. Vines, A., "The Crisis of Anti-Personnel Mines", *op. cit.*, p. 127. Note also the remarks of a Royal Engineer during the Falklands Conflict: 'minefields should not be too big a hindrance to the advance. Mines are terrifying things but their aim is to demoralise rather than hinder[.] (...) You need thousands of them to stop an advance.' Cited in McManners, Capt. H., *Falklands Commando*, William Kimber, London, 1984, p. 220.

1402 See for instance the case of France. *Landmine Monitor Report 1999*, p. 601.

permissible. The Secretary-General's Bulletin on the 'Observance by United Nations forces of international humanitarian law' provides, *inter alia*, that: 'The use of certain conventional weapons, such as (...) anti-personnel mines (...) is prohibited.'[1403]

The military utility of remotely-delivered mines demands additional consideration. According to Jane's 'the future is probably linked to the remote/airborne delivery of mines over large distances' and that 'the old style hand or mechanical emplacement is far too slow for present day realities.'[1404] As far as the Coalition use of scatterable mines in the Gulf War is concerned, Gard indicates that it 'appears unlikely' that the deployment of remotely-delivered mines was necessary to deter a counter-attack by Iraqi forces on the flank of the US VIIth Corps and that there is 'stronger evidence' that the use of mixed mine systems actually impeded the manoeuvrability of Coalition troops.[1405] He refers to a 'follow-up report' of the 1st Infantry Division, which expressed 'grave concern about minefields created by US weapons.'[1406]

Yet one consideration of the issue refers also the utility of mines before the allied advance. An alleged agreement with Saudi Arabian officials not to use anti-personnel mines 'did not apply to special operations patrol actions in the desert behind Iraqi lines. The patrols were tasked to find Iraqi Scud missile-launching sites and stop the launchings. Retired Army General Carl Stiner, then-Commander-in-Chief, US Special Operations Command, cited the use of Claymore mines and self-destructing CBU-87 GATOR mines for "night defensive purposes". His thoughts were echoed by retired Army General Wayne Downing (...) who (...) added that the GATOR mines were "highly effective" and "paralysed Iraqi movement to Scud launch sites."'[1407]

Anti-personnel mines continue to play a role also in internal armed conflicts, as the conflict in the breakaway Russian Republic of Chechnya has demonstrated. Both sides have used landmines and booby-traps extensively,[1408] with the Russian forces scoring a major victory when they tricked the rebels into leaving Grozny and heading straight into a minefield. Several hundred fighters were apparently killed or wounded; including rebel commander Shamil Basayev.[1409]

1403 Section 6.2, *UN Doc. ST/SGB/1993/13* of 6 August 1999. A report in the Washington Times in May 2000 claimed that the UN in New York wanted the Pentagon to supply 1,200 anti-tank mines 'for protection against rampaging rebels'. A US government official reportedly declared that: 'The UN appears to be coming around to understand the importance we attach to protecting our troops in the field with land mines.' Gertz, B. and Scarborough, R., "Inside the ring", *Washington Times*, 12 May 2000. Four days later, however, the same newspaper printed a letter from the Spokesman for the UN Secretary-General, Fred Eckhard, in which the allegations were denied. Eckhard declared that the columnists 'can be assured that their premise is correct that the "United Nations remains a bastion of political opposition to landmines."' Eckhard, F., "Landmines not part of UN Peacekeeping Operations", Letter, *Washington Times*, 16 May 2000.

1404 *Trends in Land Mine Warfare*, Special Report, Jane's Information Group, London, July 1995, pp. 5-6, cited by *ICRC Military Study*, p. 54.

1405 Gard, R., "The Military Utility of Anti-Personnel Mines", *op. cit.*, p. 142.

1406 Report cited by Arkin, W.M., "Treaty Barriers are within US, not in Korean fields", *San Jose Mercury News*, 20 September 1997, p. 7P.

1407 Lynch Jr., Maj.-Gen. J.D., "Landmines, Lies and Other Phenomena", *op. cit.*

1408 See *Landmine Monitor Report 2000*, pp. 839-42.

1409 *Ibid.*, pp. 840-1.

In one account of the incident, a Chechen fighter said: 'I saw dreadful things during fighting in Grozny but that massacre was beyond comparison. We had to walk on our dead comrades to avoid stepping on unexploded mines.'[1410]

A. Alternatives to Anti-Personnel Mines

Important in any discussion of proportionality is the availability of alternatives that can perform the military task as effectively but without an equivalent humanitarian impact.[1411] There are doctrinal and weapons alternatives to using anti-personnel mines in combat,[1412] although it is widely agreed by military authorities that no other single weapon or tactic can fulfil as successfully the military tasks that anti-personnel mines do.[1413]

Colonel Fitch asserted that once redundancies were eliminated, the list of tasks performed by anti-personnel mines could be reduced to a fundamental two: early warning/surveillance; and the threat of casualties. To replace the former, he cited the possibility of seismic, acoustic or electrical field sensors coupled with cameras and remotely-controlled area-denial systems. These have an advantage over landmines because, being passive sensors, they alert the defender without the intruder knowing that he has been detected.[1414] In addition, he points out that in being programmed to alert the defender, such sensors would overcome the ever-present danger that soldiers quickly become bored when conducting long-term surveillance, a risk reinforced by the use of minefields to protect positions.[1415]

1410 *Ibid.*, p. 869.

1411 Though if a weapon is illegal, there is no requirement that there be a suitable (in terms of military needs) alternative.

1412 For some of the alternatives available or being developed see generally Gard Jr., R.G., "Alternatives to Anti-personnel Mines", Vietnam Veterans Monograph Series, Vol. 1, No. 1, Spring 1999, Washington, and specifically pp. 22-3.

1413 See for instance *Landmine Monitor Report 1999*, p. 227.

1414 Though a mine can be nonetheless effective, as is noted by a Sergeant McCullum with respect to the attack on Mount Longdon during the Falklands Conflict: 'The silent attack worked well – until a lad trod on a mine and woke them all up. Then all hell broke loose. We were caught in open ground, stuck while – Company took lots of casualties. We couldn't fire because nobody knew what was happening, or where anybody else was.' Cited by McManners, H., *The Scars of War*, Harpers Collins, London, 1993, p. 173.

1415 Colonel E. Fitch, *Presentation to the ICRC Seminar on the Humanitarian Impact and Military Utility of Anti-Personnel Mines, op. cit.*

With respect to the threat of casualties,[1416] there are currently two major alternatives: the use of directional fragmentation 'Claymore-type' mines,[1417] which were first developed by the US following human-wave attacks during the Korean War, or air-delivered fragmenting bombs, such as under development in the Swedish armed forces.[1418] The protection of anti-tank mines can be effectively carried out by the incorporation of anti-handling devices, intended to prevent unauthorised removal.[1419] As noted *supra*, the US is seeking to develop further alternatives.[1420]

Thus, for instance, Japan is reported to be developing an alternative weapon system to anti-personnel mines. The 'Anti-Personnel Obstacle System' combines sensor and remote control, and is detonated by manual command so that civilians are not targeted indiscriminately.[1421] In contrast, the US has been sceptical at various times about finding alternatives to all anti-personnel mines by the deadline set by the US of 2006. Pentagon officials are variously reported as declaring that '2006 is a hard date to achieve' and 'we have not been real successful in identifying concepts'.[1422] Criticising the Pentagon's focus only on material solutions, Human Rights Watch recommended in April 2000 that non-material solutions, such as changes in doctrine and tactics, should be actively explored.[1423] It noted that: 'Many military experts believe that alternatives to anti-personnel mines already exist, as evidenced by the fact that 137 countries have signed the ban treaty, including every NATO ally except Turkey.'[1424]

1416 According to McManners, for instance, for 'infantrymen, mines are particularly frightening. Whereas anti-tank mines explode only under the weight of a heavy vehicle, anti-personnel mines are intended for people, and to maim rather than kill. A crippled soldier, screaming out in agony for help is far more of a burden than a dead one, both emotionally to his comrades and logistically to the medical system. The flash and blast of the explosion can also temporarily blind those nearby and perforate eardrums. The blast "de-gloves" the boots, trousers and flesh from feet and legs, sometimes leaving the bones intact.' McManners, H., *The Scars of War*, *op. cit.*, p. 265.

1417 According to Dr Smith, both Austria and Norway renounced the use of anti-personnel mines and opted instead to rely on command-detonated Claymore-type mines, which fall outside the definition of an anti-personnel mine because they are not victim-activated. The Dutch military adopted a 'more studied' position, deciding to use Claymore-type mines to protect observation posts and installations and anti-tank mines, including scatterable mines, to provide obstacles. In addition, anti-personnel mines would no longer be used in cluster bombs: according to Dr Smith, the Netherlands was the first country to take this step. Smith, Dr. C., (ed.), *The Military Utility of Landmines......?*, North-South Defence and Security Programme, Centre for Defence Studies, King's College, University of London, June 1996, p. 99, pp. 103-4.

1418 Hewish, M. and Pengelley, R., "In search of a successor to the anti-personnel landmine", *op. cit.*, p. 33. For details of US research, see above Chapter 2, pp. 145-6.

1419 The Dutch, for instance, are considering importing scatterable anti-tank mines equipped with anti-handling devices. See *Landmine Monitor Report 1999*, p. 749. Though note the concern expressed by the ICRC with respect to such mines; see *ibid.*, p. 1002.

1420 See *supra* pp 145-6.

1421 Statement by Director of Planning and Programming Division of the Japanese National Defense Agency, cited in *Landmine Monitor Report 1999*, p. 361.

1422 Cited in *Landmine Monitor Report 1999*, pp. 326, 327-8.

1423 Human Rights Watch, "New US mines would violate treaty", *Press release*, Washington, 7 April 2000.

1424 *Ibid.*

Likewise, an Australian government document from 1998 reported: 'Anti-Personnel mines represent a significant tactical capability that has had a well-established place in (...) Australian Defence Force plans for the conduct of military operations. Finding alternatives will involve a costly research and development effort. As alternative technology does not exist and is some years away, the ADF for this period could face an increased risk of casualties, especially if deployed overseas, and a potentially reduced capacity for coalition operations in certain circumstances.'[1425] Norway, for its part, reported that it was seeking alternatives to substitute for the combat effect that anti-personnel mines represented but was not currently engaged in developing such alternatives. 'Norway is monitoring international developments in this arena.'[1426]

3.3.4. Conclusion

The principle of proportionality involves a balancing of the advantage to be expected from a military attack against its humanitarian consequences. Thus, in the words of Oeter, the use of means and methods of warfare may be illegal, even if collateral damage to the civilian population and civilian goods could be justified in principle by reference to 'military necessity', on the grounds that such damage is unavoidable in mounting an effective attack on a military objective in the centre of the operation. Manifestly disproportionate collateral damage inflicted in order to achieve operational objectives will result in the action being deemed an (illicit) form of indiscriminate warfare.

It is not possible to argue convincingly that anti-personnel mines have no military utility whatsoever.[1427] On the other hand, the claim by certain military authorities that this was an indispensable weapon of high military value[1428] does not seem to be borne out by the evidence. It is claimed, for instance, that although anti-personnel mines are low cost their effectiveness is also low while their humanitarian cost is high.[1429] Indeed, at the signing of the Convention on the Prohibition of Anti-Personnel Mines in Ottawa in December 1997, the Malaysian Ambassador declared that: 'The landmines problem is first and foremost a humanitarian problem. Malaysia is firm in its conviction that the humanitarian impact of anti-personnel mines far outweighs their military utility and economics.'[1430]

1425 See *Landmine Monitor Report 1999*, p. 347.

1426 *Ibid.*, p. 637.

1427 Neither the ICRC study, nor the study conducted by Dr Smith of the Centre for Defence Studies, came to this conclusion. According to Dr Smith, 'it is extremely difficult to counter the claim that anti-tank mines and anti-personnel mines have a military utility.' Smith, Dr. C. (ed.), *The Military Utility of Landmines......?*, *op. cit.*, p. 98.

1428 According to one expert, for example, 'it is inconceivable that any modern army could operate effectively in a high intensity conflict without recourse to a very large number of mines of all types.' Heyman, Maj. C., *Trends in Landmine Warfare*, Jane's Information Group, Coulden, 1995, p. 7, cited in *The History of Landmines*, p. 152.

1429 He notes, however, that anti-tank mines have the reverse relationship to anti-personnel mines: high military utility and low humanitarian effect. Colonel E. Fitch, *Presentation to the ICRC Seminar on the Humanitarian Impact and Military Utility of Anti-Personnel Mines, op. cit.*

1430 Cited in *Landmine Monitor Report 1999*, p. 412.

The *ICRC Military Study* concluded that anti-personnel mines had 'little or no effect on the outcome of hostilities' and even that they had a 'limited effect on unprotected infantry'.[1431] Moreover, in 'order to use them responsibly, anti-personnel mines have to be included as a part of a properly laid, marked and recorded anti-tank minefield. If they are used any other way, in pursuit denial, or to prevent occupation and in a general nuisance mode, for example, responsible use is almost impossible. The use of anti-personnel mines with (...) self-destructing/self-neutralising mechanisms may be considered less irresponsible but serious risks to civilians remain.'[1432]

The risks to civilians are especially high in internal armed conflicts – a sad reality to which the people of Angola and Cambodia, among others, can testify. According to Dr Smith, for instance: 'If anti-personnel mines have a debatable utility when used in tandem with anti-tank mines, they really come into their own when used in low intensity conflicts. In Afghanistan, Viet Nam, Sri Lanka, El Salvador and throughout Africa the anti-personnel mine had a devastating impact upon both soldiers and civilian mixed up in low intensity conflicts. Anti-personnel mines laid by irregular forces can be very valuable as a way of affecting morale and terrorising civilians in the battle for hearts and minds.'[1433] In the view of the author, in many, if not most situations of internal conflict, the use of anti-personnel mines may be expected to be disproportionate to the objective sought, especially in the case of long-lived mines. It is by no means certain, however, that the principle of proportionality applies in such situations.

[1431] But note Croll's assertion that: 'Where the infantry are, so too will there be a need for anti-personnel mines.' *The History of Landmines*, p. 146.

[1432] Smith, Dr. C. (ed.), *The Military Utility of Landmines......?*, *op. cit.*, p. 99, referring to "Anti-Personnel Mines", Appendix 38, *Memorandum by General Sir Hugh Beach to the Foreign Affairs Select Committee*, (HMSO, 1995), pp. 383-5.

[1433] Smith, Dr. C., (ed.), *The Military Utility of Landmines.......?*, *op. cit.*, p. 101. See also Vines, A., "The Crisis of Anti-Personnel Mines", *op. cit.*, p. 127.

3.4. ANTI-PERSONNEL MINES AND 'SUPERFLUOUS INJURY OR UNNECESSARY SUFFERING'

3.4.1. Introduction

The prohibition of the use of weapons causing *maux superflus*[1434] dates back to the 19th Century[1435] and possibly before.[1436] Its most recent codification is to be found in 1977 Additional Protocol I, wherein it is prohibited 'to employ weapons, projectiles and material and methods of warfare of a nature to cause superfluous injury or unnecessary suffering.'[1437]

1434 In Article 23(e) of the Regulations annexed to 1899 Hague Convention II Respecting the Laws and Customs of War on Land, it was prohibited in the authentic French original text to employ arms 'propres à causer des maux superflus.' The phrase *maux superflus* was rendered in the English translation of Article 23(e) of the 1899 Hague Regulations as *superfluous injury*. The equivalent translation of the 1907 Regulations, on the other hand, declared that it was 'especially forbidden (...) [t]o employ arms, projectiles or material calculated to cause unnecessary suffering'. This almost exactly mirrored the formulation in the 1874 Brussels Declaration, which had purported to outlaw 'the employment of arms, projectiles or material calculated to cause unnecessary suffering.' Article 13(e), *Project of an International Declaration concerning the Laws and Customs of War*, Brussels, 27 August 1874. See for instance Schindler, D. and Toman, J., *The Laws of Armed Conflicts*, *op. cit.*, pp. 22-34.
1977 Additional Protocol I included both concepts: *unnecessary suffering* and *superfluous injury*, the latter of which is felt to better render the French with its notion of a more objective criterion than *suffering* capable of being measured. See for example Robblee Jr., Capt. P.A., "The Legitimacy of Modern Conventional Weaponry", *op. cit.*, p. 416; Kalshoven, F., "The Conference of Government Experts on the Use of Certain Conventional Weapons, Lucerne, 24 September to 18 October 1974", *op. cit.*, p. 90; Blix, H., "Means and Methods of Combat", *op. cit.*, p. 138. In any event, it seems clear that this combined rendition has entered the realm of customary international law, although the *Nuclear Weapons Advisory Opinion* only refers specifically to 'unnecessary suffering'. See for instance Robblee Jr., Capt. P.A., "The Legitimacy of Modern Conventional Weaponry", *op. cit.*, p. 416.

1435 In the 1868 St Petersburg Declaration, which outlawed the use of explosive projectiles under 400 g in weight, States accepted that 'the only legitimate object which States should endeavour to accomplish during war is to weaken the military forces of the enemy,' and that 'this object would be exceeded by the employment of arms which uselessly aggravate the sufferings of disabled men, or render their death inevitable.' See for instance *Documents on the Laws of War*, pp. 29-31.

1436 Oeter, S., "Methods and Means of Combat", *op. cit.*, p. 113. Thus, in Ancient India the Book of Manu had declared unlawful arrows with hooked spikes, which after entering human flesh would be difficult to remove. See Singh, N., "Armed conflicts and humanitarian laws of ancient India", in Swinarski, C. (ed.), *Studies and essays on international humanitarian law and Red Cross principles*, *op. cit.*, p. 532.

1437 Article 35(2).

It is generally agreed that the obligation not to use weapons causing[1438] superfluous injury or unnecessary suffering forms part of customary law.[1439] Thus, States negotiating the 1980 CCW based the Convention 'on the principle of international law that (...) prohibits the employment in armed conflicts of weapons, projectiles and materials and methods of warfare of a nature to cause superfluous injury or unnecessary suffering.'[1440] Similarly, the ICJ clearly identified the principle as one of the customary norms of international humanitarian law.[1441]

It is not, however, certain that the prohibition applies to internal armed conflicts.[1442] Indeed the 1998 Rome Statute of the International Criminal Court

1438 There has been considerable discussion of whether the customary standard involves a subjective element of malice '*calculated* to cause unnecessary suffering' or, as in the 1907 Hague IV Regulations, the more objective '*of a nature* to cause unnecessary suffering'. The French authentic original text 'propres à causer' is more accurately rendered by an objective standard. See for example Blix, H., "Means and Methods of Combat", *op. cit.*, p. 138. Experts at the 1974 Lucerne Weapons Conference supported this view.
Moreover, the objective formulation was included in the preamble to the 1980 CCW. See for instance *Documents on the Laws of War*, pp. 52, footnote 3, and 473. Yet despite the pleadings of the ICRC, during the First Review Conference of the 1980 CCW the controversy was sustained, at least with respect to mines, booby-traps and other devices, by the inclusion of the introductory 'designed to' as well as 'of a nature to' cause superfluous injury and unnecessary suffering. Article 3 of amended Protocol II. See *supra* Chapter 1, p. 58, footnote 429.

1439 See for instance Carnahan, B.M., "Unnecessary Suffering, The Red Cross and Tactical Laser Weapons", *Loyola of Los Angeles International and Comparative Law Journal*, Vol. 18, September 1996, p. 711. Carnahan cites as evidence the report of the UN Secretary-General on the proposed Statute of the International Tribunal for the Prosecution of Persons Responsible for Serious Violations of International Humanitarian Law Committed in the Territory of the Former Yugoslavia ("Report of the Secretary-General Pursuant to Paragraph 2 of the Security Council Resolution 808", *UN Doc. S/25704*, 1993) and the Statute of the Tribunal accepted by the Security Council. (See *International Legal Materials*, Vol. 32, 1993, p. 1192.) Unfortunately, the relevant provision, contained in Article 3(a) of the Statute, uses the formula 'weapons calculated to cause unnecessary suffering'.

1440 Preambular paragraph to the 1980 Convention on Conventional Weapons.

1441 'The cardinal principles contained in the texts constituting the fabric of humanitarian law are the following[.] (...) According to the second principle, it is prohibited to cause unnecessary suffering to combatants: it is accordingly prohibited to use weapons causing them such harm or uselessly aggravating their suffering. In application of that second principle, States do not have unlimited freedom of choice of means in the weapons they use.' *Nuclear Weapons Advisory Opinion*, para. 78.

1442 In its draft of 1977 Additional Protocol II, the ICRC proposed to extend to internal armed conflict the general principles governing the use of weapons that were ultimately included in Additional Protocol I. In particular, Article 20(2) of the draft provided that: 'It is forbidden to employ weapons, projectiles, substances, methods and means which uselessly aggravate the sufferings of disabled adversaries or render their death inevitable in all circumstances.' Cited in Cassese, A., "The Means of Warfare", *op. cit.*, p. 159. Cassese claimed that the 'general tendency' of the drafting Committee in the Diplomatic Conference was to 'accept its substance'. In the Conference itself, only Saudi Arabia objected, pointing out – somewhat speciously – that no State would ever want to kill its own citizens.
Sadly, the proposal was not included in the Protocol finally adopted, as a number of developing countries led by Pakistan gutted its content, unwilling to accept oversight of its 'internal affairs'. Despite this reality Meyrowitz claims that: 'It is important to assert that the principle of superfluous injury or unnecessary suffering is equally applicable to international *and* non-international armed conflicts, with no need to distinguish between conflicts coming within the provisions of Article 3 common to the four Geneva Conventions and conflicts having reached

includes in its list of acts committed in the course of an international armed conflict over which the Court is to have jurisdiction '[e]mploying weapons, projectiles and material and methods of warfare which are of a nature to cause superfluous injury or unnecessary suffering';[1443] no similar jurisdiction is stipulated where the acts took place in an internal armed conflict.

Writing before the adoption of 1977 Additional Protocol I, one authority had termed the equivalent provision contained in the Hague Regulations[1444] as 'one of the most unclear and controversial rules of warfare.'[1445] There is certainly no consensus in the literature as to the precise ambit of the prohibition of the use of means of warfare of a nature to cause superfluous injury[1446] or unnecessary suffering[1447], nor how it is be applied to specific weapons.[1448] Moreover, the

---

the level defined in Article 1 of Protocol II thereto. Such applicability is imperative, we believe, for fundamental reasons of humanity.'

Such a belief, however, does not constitute valid international law. More realistically, Greenwood, has pointed out that the 'logic behind the unnecessary suffering principle (...) is equally applicable to internal conflicts' and has called for it to be specifically agreed that the principle also applies in such situations. Greenwood, C., *Humanitarian Law and Laws of War*, *op. cit.*, p. 64. He declared that there was 'good reason to apply to internal armed conflicts more of the provisions and methods of warfare which apply in international conflicts. As the Appeals Chamber of the International Criminal Tribunal of the Former Yugoslavia has said: "elementary considerations of humanity and common sense make it preposterous that the use by States of weapons prohibited in armed conflicts by themselves be allowed when States try to put down rebellion by their own nationals on their own territory. What is inhumane, and consequently proscribed, in international wars, cannot but be inhumane and inadmissible in civil strife."' *Ibid.*, citing *Tadic Case, op. cit.*, para. 119.

1443 Article 8(2)(b)(xx), 1998 Rome Statute of the International Criminal Court. See for instance Roberts, A. and Guelff, R., *Documents on the Laws of War*, 3rd edn., *op. cit.*, p. 678.

1444 Article 23(e).

1445 Cassese, A., "Weapons Causing Unnecessary Suffering: Are they prohibited?", *Rivista di Diritto Internazionale*, Vol. LVIII, 1975.

1446 According to Oeter, the term *superfluous injury* 'implicitly clarifies what should properly constitute the decisive criterion of proportionality. Injuries can only be *superfluous* either if they are justified by any requirement of military necessity or if the injuries normally caused by the weapon or projectile are manifestly disproportionate to the military advantage reasonably expected from the use of the weapon. The first will only rarely be the case, since the intended injuring effect generally serves a military goal, namely the neutralisation of enemy combatants or military material. The second condition will only be fulfilled if the weapons is at least relatively superfluous – which requires a comparative judgement as to how much suffering weapons cause and whether alternative military means could achieve the same results with less suffering.' Oeter, S., "Methods and Means of Combat", *op. cit.*, p. 115.

1447 Kalshoven, declares that suffering is 'unnecessary' when it is not justified by the military utility of a given weapon, either because such utility is entirely lacking or at best negligible, or 'because in weighing utility against suffering the scale dips to the latter side and, in so doing, to prohibition.' Kalshoven, F., *Constraints on the Waging of War*, *op. cit.*, pp. 29-30. Oeter, however, claims that it is 'much more difficult to find an adequate description of the effects of weaponry which are intended to be outlawed by the choice of that wording.' Citing Bretton, he asserts that the notion of *suffering* is not quantifiable under a medical perspective, for it is defined according to psychological criteria. Oeter, S., "Methods and Means of Combat", *op. cit.*, p. 115, citing Bretton, "Principes humanitaires et impératifs militaires dans le domaine des armes classiques à travers le droit international actuel", in *Société Française pour le Droit International, Colloque de Montpellier sur le droit international et les armes*, 1983, p. 39.

1448 According to Oeter, 'the prohibition of *maux superflus* is characterised by a particularly complex mixture of very definite prohibitions of certain specific categories of arms on [the] one hand, and a rather abstract prohibition of means of warfare which cause unnecessary sufferings

ICRC Commentary is unusually obscure in its treatment of the subject.[1449] According to a number of States, the principle of superfluous injury or unnecessary suffering embodies the purpose of the principles of military necessity and humanity, requiring a finding that the suffering or destruction caused by the use of a given weapon is 'plainly excessive or disproportionate to the military advantage reasonably expected to be gained from its use' for the weapon to be declared unlawful.[1450] Thus, Greenwood has stated that:

> *'While it is difficult to point to any weapon with real military utility which it is generally agreed has been outlawed by the unnecessary suffering principle, it must be remembered that this principle requires a balancing of the military advantage which may result from the use of a weapon with the degree of injury and suffering which it is likely to cause. As a Japanese court has stated, "the use of a certain weapon, great as*

---

on the other; the relationship between these two sets of rules is far from clear. How far the definite prohibitions are only specific expressions or materialisations of the general prohibitory provision, and to what extent they are, to the contrary, constitutive developments of a merely political programme envisaged in Article 23(e) [of the] Hague Regulations, is a question which still needs careful consideration.' Oeter, S., "Methods and Means of Combat", *op. cit.*, p. 114.

1449 It remarks for instance, that: 'The concept of superfluous injury or unnecessary suffering, its objective effect on the victim (severity of the injury, intensity of the suffering), and its relation to military necessity (rendering the enemy *hors de combat*) are not interpreted in a consistent and generally accepted manner. This concept continues to be the basis on which judgement is formed, but debates have shown its relative and imprecise character.' *ICRC Commentary on the 1977 Additional Protocols*, pp. 409-10. The *Fundamental rules of international humanitarian law applicable in armed conflicts*, published in Geneva in 1979 by the ICRC and the League of Red Cross Societies (now the International Federation of Red Cross and Red Crescent Societies), sought to demystify the concepts by rephrasing them as 'unnecessary losses' or 'excessive suffering'. The document points out clearly, however, that the roles 'are not vested with the authority of an international legal instrument and are not intended to take the place of the treaties in force. Their sole purpose is to facilitate the dissemination of knowledge of international humanitarian law.'

1450 See for instance Robblee Jr., Capt. P.A., "The Legitimacy of Modern Conventional Weaponry", *op. cit.*, p. 415; Oeter, S., "Methods and Means of Combat", *op. cit.*, p. 114. Colonel David Hughes-Morgan, speaking on behalf of the United Kingdom at the 1974 Lucerne Weapons Conference, declared that 'a weapon which in practice is found inevitably to cause injury or suffering disproportionate to its military effectiveness would be held to contravene this prohibition.' Hughes-Morgan, Col. Sir D., "Legal Criteria for the Restriction of Use of Categories of Conventional Weapons", *Paper presented to the Lucerne Weapons Conference*, p. 6, cited by Robblee Jr., Capt. P.A., "The Legitimacy of Modern Conventional Weaponry", *op. cit.*, p. 418.

This opinion was mirrored by the US delegation to the 1974 Lucerne Weapons Conference, which declared that 'the "necessity" of the suffering must be judged in relation to the military utility of the weapon.' *Resort to War and Armed Force*, 1974 Digest 1, p. 707, quoted by Carnahan, B.M., "Unnecessary Suffering, The Red Cross and Tactical Laser Weapons", *op. cit.*, p. 712. According to McDougal and Feliciano: 'All war instruments are "cruel" and "inhuman" in the sense that they cause destruction and human suffering. It is not, however, the simple fact of destruction, nor even the amount thereof, that is relevant in the appraisal of such instruments; it is rather the needlessness, the superfluity of harm, the gross imbalance between the military result and the incidental injury that is commonly regarded as decisive of illegitimacy. (...) [The principle of unnecessary suffering prohibits] gratuitous violence which serves no military end [and] the infliction of suffering which serves no useful military purpose.' McDougal, M.S. and Feliciano, F.P., *Law and Minimum World Public Order*, US, 1961, p. 616.

its inhuman result may be, need not be prohibited by international law if it has a great military effect." '[1451]

There is also dispute, though, as to the object of protection of the prohibition. The minority of opinion believes that the principle is not limited to combatants,[1452] and may even include physical objects. Henri Meyrowitz, for example, basing his argument on the 1868 St Petersburg Declaration and the term 'maux' in the original authentic French version of 1899 Hague Convention II, argues that it includes the idea of superfluous deaths.[1453] Certainly, neither the text of Article 35(2) of 1977 Additional Protocol I, nor that of Article 36 of the same Protocol, refers solely to means or methods of warfare directed against combatants.[1454] Human Rights Watch, in its 1993 legal analysis of landmines, also points out that the principle was codified in 1977 Additional Protocol I without specific reference to combatants.[1455] It further declares that 'because the material treated here tends not to distinguish combatants and civilians with regard to the rules against superfluous injury or unnecessary suffering, this chapter does not make the distinction, and assumes that the weighing of military and humanitarian considerations must also take into account the humanitarian impact on civilians.'[1456]

A more convincing view, however, is that the principle is 'intended to protect soldiers and other personnel taking a direct part in hostilities, rather than civilians or other non-combatants. In the course of combat operations, it is, in principle, legitimate to deliberately injure or kill persons taking a direct part in hostilities. The rule against weapons causing unnecessary suffering or superfluous injury is a limit on means used to accomplish this legitimate injury and killing.'[1457] This view is supported by the judgment in the *Nuclear Weapons Advisory Opinion*, which refers to the 'cardinal principle' that 'it is prohibited to cause unnecessary suffering to combatants: it is accordingly prohibited to use weapons causing them such harm or uselessly aggravating their suffering.'[1458]

3.4.2. Criteria for the Assessment of 'Superfluous Injury or Unnecessary Suffering'

According to Kalshoven, the rule on unnecessary suffering appears 'too vague to permit a great many practical results. Apart from the case that States

1451 Greenwood, C., *Humanitarian Law and Laws of War, op. cit.*, p. 41.

1452 See for instance Gardam, J., "Necessity and proportionality in *jus ad bellum* and *jus ad bello*", Boisson de Chazournes, L. *et al.* (eds.), *International Law, the International Court of Justice and Nuclear Weapons, op. cit.*, p. 292.

1453 Meyrowitz, H., "The Principle of Superfluous Injury or Unnecessary Suffering, From the Declaration of St Petersburg of 1868 to Additional Protocol I of 1977", in *International Review of the Red Cross*, March-April 1994, No. 299, pp. 104-5.

1454 *Ibid.*, p. 105.

1455 *A Deadly Legacy*, p. 268, footnote 19.

1456 *Ibid.*

1457 Carnahan, B.M., "Unnecessary Suffering, The Red Cross and Tactical Laser Weapons", *op. cit.*, pp. 711-2. See also Fenrick, Lt.-Col. W.J., "New Developments in the Law Concerning the Use of Conventional Weapons in Armed Conflict", *op. cit.*, p. 231.

1458 *Nuclear Weapons Advisory Opinion*, para. 78.

expressly agree to forbid employment of a specified weapon (...) they will not lightly decide to discard a weapon, once admitted into their arsenals, on the ground that it is said to cause unnecessary suffering.'[1459] Fenrick, for example, affirms that a weapon causes unnecessary suffering 'when in practice it inevitably causes injury or suffering disproportionate to its military effectiveness. In determining the military effectiveness of a weapon, one looks at the primary purpose for which it was designed.'[1460] He concedes, however, that this approach 'clearly leaves considerable scope for differences of opinion based upon value judgements.'[1461]

Writing in the same vein, Robblee claims that 'in the final analysis (...) the best test of which weapons contravene the criterion of unnecessary suffering is the practice of States.'[1462] According to the United States Manual of Land Warfare, for instance: 'What weapons cause unnecessary suffering can only be determined in light of the practice of States in refraining from the use of a given weapon because it is believed to have that effect.'[1463]

In contrast, Swedish experts to the 1974 Lucerne Weapons Conference urged the consideration of such humanitarian factors as medical effects, degree of disability, risk of death, overburdening of medical resources, and public opinion in determining the admissibility of conventional weapons in warfare.[1464] Yet, according to one authority, 'as the Lucerne Weapons Conference amply demonstrated, a paucity of definitive technical data presently exists to establish the degree of suffering or indiscriminateness that a given weapon might inflict. Therefore, until more is known about the actual effects of weapons, proposals to modify the rules of war regulating weaponry are singularly without the

---

1459 Kalshoven, *Constraints on the Waging of War*, *op., cit.*, p. 30. According to Baxter, however, 'speaking in general terms, the popular prejudice against weapons which cause "unnecessary suffering" is less strong when the weapon is used against military personnel than it is when the weapon is directed against civilians or used in such a way that civilians as well as military personnel might be affected.' Baxter, R.R., "Criteria of the Prohibition of Weapons in International Law", *op. cit.*, p. 47.

1460 Fenrick, Lt.-Col. W.J., "New Developments in the Law Concerning the Use of Conventional Weapons in Armed Conflict", *op. cit.*, pp. 233-4.

1461 *Ibid.*, p. 234.

1462 Robblee Jr., Capt. P.A., "The Legitimacy of Modern Conventional Weaponry",*op. cit.*, p. 418. See also Kalshoven, F., "Laws of War" *Encyclopaedia of Public International Law*, North-Holland Publishing Co., Amsterdam, 1982, p. 318.

1463 Department of the Army Field Manual FM 27-10, *The Law of Land Warfare*, Department of the Army, Washington DC, July 1956, para. 34. See for example Blix, H., "Means and Methods of Combat", *op. cit.*, p. 140.

1464 See Kalshoven, F., "The Conference of Government Experts on the Use of Certain Conventional Weapons, Lucerne, 24 September to 18 October 1974", *op. cit.*, pp. 89-90. Scott remarks that during the 1974 Lucerne Weapons Conference 'a number of physicians met together to discuss the concept of "suffering" and to consider whether it could be defined or quantified in some scientific way. They agreed that it could not whereas "injury" probably could. It was suggested that "injury" should be substituted for "suffering" in the legal discussions that followed. However, the legal experts agreed that "suffering" was a valid concept, even if the physicians found it hard to quantify.' Scott, R., "Unnecessary Suffering? A Medical View", Meyer, M.A. (ed.), *Armed Conflict and the New Law: Aspects of the 1977 Geneva Protocols and the 1981 Weapons Convention*, British Institute of International and Comparative Law, London, 1989, p. 277.

necessary capacity to garner the shared interpretation of the States whose weapons they would seek to regulate. Without agreement as to that which was to be prohibited, binding law could not result.'[1465]

To seek to address this lacuna in knowledge, the ICRC has undertaken in-depth research into the medical effects of weapons with a view to developing objective medical criteria by which to judge the relative injury and suffering inflicted by any given weapon. According to Dr Robin Coupland, who masterminded the SIrUS project:[1466]

> *'A review of data from military medical sources, who know the number of fatalities in the field, shows how little the mortality has changed since World War II. The proportion of wounded who die in the field varies between 18 per cent and 22 per cent (...) Likewise the proportion of all casualties who die after reaching a medical facility varies between about 2.5 per cent and 4.5 per cent (...) This gives a baseline proportion of deaths among casualties that has been accepted by military and political leaders as a consequence of wars waged in this period of history.'*[1467]

He then goes on to propose that objective judgement of superfluous injury or unnecessary suffering could be made on the basis of a weapon that results in, *inter alia*:

> '1. *A field mortality of more than 25 per cent of all casualties.*
> 2. *A hospital mortality more than 7 per cent in a medical facility adequately equipped with basic and non-specialised facilities.'*

However, the SIrUS project criteria have been criticised by military lawyers for failing to take into account the military utility of the weapon.[1468] Greenwood, for instance, praises the criteria and the medical study on which they are based as being 'of considerable value in helping to show how the balancing act required by the unnecessary suffering principle can be made more precise and less anecdotal than at present.' At the same time he points out that 'the fact that a particular weapon meets one of these criteria is not, in itself, sufficient to brand it unlawful without consideration of the military advantages which that weapon may offer[.] (...) Moreover, the report only considers the "medical" or "humanitarian" side of the balance. Greater precision is also needed in determining what are the relevant factors to be taken into account on the military side of the equation.'[1469] Likewise, as a US diplomat has pointed out:

> *'The difficulty of coming to an objective conclusion [on the legality of a weapon] is compounded by the fact that "military effectiveness" cannot be measured simply in terms of battlefield casualties but must also take into account such factors as the destruction or neutralisation of military material, restriction of movement, interdiction of lines of communication*

1465 Robblee Jr., Capt. P.A., "The Legitimacy of Modern Conventional Weaponry", *op. cit.*, p. 436.

1466 The acronym stands, appropriately enough, for 'superfluous injury or unnecessary suffering'.

1467 Coupland, Dr. R.M., "The effect of weapons: defining superfluous injury or unnecessary suffering", *Medicine and Global Survival*, Vol. 3, 1 March 1996, available on ICRC Website: <http://www.icrc.org>.

1468 See for instance Carnahan, B.M., "Unnecessary Suffering, The Red Cross and Tactical Laser Weapons", *op. cit.*, pp. 731-2.

1469 Greenwood, C., *Humanitarian Law and Laws of War*, *op. cit.*, p. 43.

and effects on morale,[1470] *command and control, stamina and cohesion of opposing forces, effectiveness against particular targets, availability of alternate weapons, cost, and the security of the troops involved.* '[1471]

With a view to overcoming these objections, the ICRC convened a meeting of governmental experts in Geneva in early 1999. As a result of the discussions, the ICRC suggested that '[i]n determining whether a proposed weapon, by its design, causes effects on health which may constitute "superfluous injury or unnecessary suffering[.]"(…) States take into account the health-based criteria proposed (...) on the basis of work carried out by a group of medical experts in "The SIrUS Project" and endorsed by a number of medical associations.'[1472] At the 27th International Red Cross Conference in Geneva in November 1999, delegates agreed only to 'analyse the extent' to which SirUS might help them determine which weapons breached international humanitarian law. To date, only Australia has declared publicly that it will take the criteria into account when reviewing the legality of weapons.[1473]

3.4.3. *Weapons Causing Superfluous Injury or Unnecessary Suffering*

In determining the application of the principle to anti-personnel mines, it is necessary to consider historical precedent. A number of weapons have ostensibly been prohibited because they cause superfluous injury or unnecessary suffering, beginning with exploding bullets in 1868.

A. Exploding Bullets

According to the 1868 St Petersburg Declaration: 'The Contracting Parties engage mutually to renounce, in case of war among themselves, the employment by their military or naval troops of any projectile of a weight below 400 grammes, which is either explosive or charged with fulminating or inflammable substances.'

The use of explosive projectiles as artillery munition had already been long established and was perceived to be militarily necessary. Their use against infantry, however, was seen to be avoidable in military terms, and therefore

---

[1470] The issue of morale is particularly relevant in the case of the anti-personnel mine, where the psychological impact on enemy soldiers is often said to be the most potent effect of the weapon. See for example McManners, H., *The Scars of War*, *op. cit.*, p. 316. Though note Carnahan's assertion that: 'Terror induced by the frightfulness of wounds has never been considered a military benefit in assessing the legitimacy of weapons, and this approach should continue.' Carnahan, B.M., "Unnecessary Suffering, The Red Cross and Tactical Laser Weapons",*op. cit.*, p. 730. Ms Doswald-Beck of the ICRC has also pointed out that 'the terror value of a certain weapon is not a factor that can be validly taken into account when making an assessment of the military utility of a weapon for the purpose of this rule.' Doswald-Beck, L. (ed.), *Blinding Weapons*, ICRC, Geneva, 1993, p. 331.

[1471] *Resort to War and Armed Force*, 1974 Digest 1, p. 708, cited by Carnahan, B.M., "Unnecessary Suffering, The Red Cross and Tactical Laser Weapons", *op. cit.*, pp. 713-4.

[1472] Point 19, Draft Plan of Action of the 1999 International Conference of the Red Cross and Red Crescent.

[1473] Edwards, R., "Humane Killing", *New Scientist*, 4 December 1999.

superfluous.[1474] The weight limit of 400 grammes set in the St Petersburg Declaration was, however, 'set rather arbitrarily; artillery projectiles of the time were considerably heavier, whereas infantry munitions were much lighter than 400 grammes. (...) The absolute weight limit set in 1868 should therefore not be taken too strictly.'[1475]

B. Expanding Bullets

In the 1890s, the British were engaged in fighting tribesmen of the Indian North-West Frontier. The military expressed concern about the stopping power of the .303 calibre Mark II high-velocity bullet being used in the new Lee-Mitford rifle.[1476] While endeavouring to produce a potent bullet, Captain Clay of the ammunition factory at Dum Dum (near Calcutta) found that by slitting the nickel casing of the bullet, the lead filling spread in the wound and effectively halted the incoming soldier. It also aggravated the wound very considerably.[1477]

The *Declaration (IV, 3) Concerning Expanding Bullets*, adopted at the First Hague Peace Conference of 1899, prohibited the use of 'bullets which expand or flatten easily in the human body, such as bullets with a hard envelope which does not entirely cover the core or is pierced with incisions.'[1478] The prohibition

[1474] Oeter, S., "Methods and Means of Combat", *op. cit.*, p. 122, citing Kalshoven, F., "Arms, Armaments and International Law", *Recueil des Cours* 191 (1985 II), pp. 205-8 and 212-3.
[1475] Oeter, S., "Methods and Means of Combat", *op. cit.*, p. 122.
[1476] O'Connell, R.L., *Of Arms and Men*, Oxford University Press, Oxford, UK, 1990, p. 232.
[1477] Ffoulkes, C.J., *Arms and Armament*, Harrap & Co., London, 1945, p. 69.
[1478] See *Documents on the Laws of War*, p. 40.

was adopted despite objections from Great Britain[1479] and the US,[1480] two of the leading military powers of the day.[1481]

It is widely agreed that the prohibition on the use of dumdum bullets has achieved the level of customary international law applicable to all States.[1482] But the application of this principle to modern bullets remains problematic.[1483] Efforts to outlaw in the 1980 Convention on Certain Conventional Weapons certain small calibre ammunition producing analogous effects to the dumdum

---

1479 It has been claimed that Great Britain objected to the proposed prohibition on the grounds that the dumdum bullet did not expand in such a manner as to create wounds of exceptional cruelty and that, in fact, the wounds were less severe than those produced by certain rifles which had been in use. *Documents on the Laws of War*, p. 40. However, Sir John Ardagh, one of the British representatives at the 1899 Hague Peace Conference, claimed that the enemies encountered in the colonies were not to be equated with signatories of the St Petersburg Declaration, nor should they be treated as such:

[T]here is a difference in war between civilised nations and that against savages. If, in the former, a soldier is wounded by a small projectile, he is taken away in the ambulance, but the savage, although run through two or three times, does not cease to advance (...) For this reason the English delegate demands the liberty of employing projectiles of sufficient efficacy against savage races.

Cited in Scott, J.B., *The Proceedings of the Hague Peace Conferences: the Conference of 1899*, Oxford University Press, New York, 1920, pp. 286-7. See also O'Connell, *Of Arms and Men*, *op. cit.*, p. 232; Kalshoven, F., "The soldier and his golf clubs", in Swinarski, C. (ed.), *Studies and essays on international humanitarian law and Red Cross principles in honour of Jean Pictet*, *op. cit.*, p. 375.

Moreover, that Great Britain realised that the dumdum was not likely to be acceptable to the international community is suggested by the fact that it conducted experiments with a view to producing a more humane but equally effective bullet. This had already been achieved in 1897, at least to a certain extent, with the development of the Mark III bullet. Ffoulkes, C.J., *Arms and Armament*, *op. cit.*, p. 69.

1480 The US's objections allegedly included an assertion that since the bullet was being used by the British Army any condemnation should follow from real evidence of its effects rather than from implication drawn from its design. See *Documents on the Laws of War*, p. 39. Carnahan, however, suggests that the motivation for the US objection was that they were about to put them to use in the Philippines. Carnahan, B.M., "Unnecessary Suffering, The Red Cross and Tactical Laser Weapons", *op. cit.*, p. 719.

1481 According to one authority, the decision that expanding bullets caused unnecessary suffering resulted from the fact that they actually had little military value (even Great Britain and the US were only intending to use them against 'savages' not in armed conflict) and yet inflicted severe injuries on their victims. Carnahan, B.M., "Unnecessary Suffering, The Red Cross and Tactical Laser Weapons", *op. cit.*, p. 721.

1482 Thus, Article 8(2)(b)(xix) of the 1998 Rome Statute of the International Criminal Court provides that the Court will have jurisdiction over the use of expanding bullets as a war crime committed in the course of an international armed conflict. See for instance Roberts, A. and Guelff, R., *Documents on the Laws of War*, 3rd edn., *op. cit.*, pp. 63, 677.

It had already been asserted in the 1970s that a customary prohibition had resulted from the practice of States in the First World War in refraining from their use. Robblee Jr., Capt. P.A., "The Legitimacy of Modern Conventional Weaponry", *op. cit.*, p. 442, footnote 70. In addition, as has been noted, Britain had acceded to the Declaration in 1907, and the US had formally declared it would abide by its terms. Carnahan, B.M., "Unnecessary Suffering, The Red Cross and Tactical Laser Weapons", *op. cit.*, p. 720. For an interesting discussion of allegations of violations of the use of dumdum bullets in the First World War see Stockholm International Peace Research Institute, *Working Papers on International Law and the Prohibition of Unnecessary Injury*, SIPRI, Stockholm, 1974.

1483 See for instance Oeter, S., "Methods and Means of Combat", *op. cit.*, p. 123.

bullet failed,[1484] as did those in the First Review Conference of the Convention, which ended in May 1996.

Cassese refers to a statement made by the Dutch delegate to the 1868 negotiations, who proposed the prohibition which was subsequently laid down in the Declaration on expanding bullets (and who was also the Rapporteur of the Sub-Commission entrusted with drafting the Declaration):

> *'The dumdum bullet whose point is very soft, whose projectile covering is very hard, and whose interior is formed of a softer substance, makes, by exploding at the slightest resistance, enormous ravages in the body, its entrance being very small, but its exit very large. It is sufficient to disable an armed man for the rest of the campaign and such ravages are not necessary.'*[1485]

On this basis, Cassese argues that weapons causing 'incurable wounds', namely wounds remaining unhealed even after the cessation of war, are unlawful, while weapons are permitted that disable combatants for the (foreseeable) length of belligerent hostilities.[1486] He goes on to claim that 'what is important is the inevitability or the high degree of probability for a weapon to incapacitate men with lasting effects. Ordinary bullets have among their possible effects the one consisting in disabling an enemy for the rest of his life; but this is neither the typical nor the usual effect. If on the contrary a weapon by its very nature produces the normal effect of putting men out of action for a period largely exceeding the length of a war, that weapon could be regarded as illegal.'[1487] If true, this statement would have a profound impact on the legality of at least buried blast anti-personnel mines, since traumatic, or at least surgical, amputation invariably results to the person who triggers such mines.

C. Chemical and Bacteriological Warfare

According to Oeter, the 'bans on the use of poisonous gases as a means of warfare provided for by the Geneva Gas Protocol of 1925 and the Biological Weapons Convention of 1972 were further steps on the war to a total ban on the use of certain particularly barbaric weapons.'[1488] It is suggested by some[1489] that the prohibition on the use of poison gas rests on the customary prohibition against poisoned weapons, which according to one commentator dates back to at least the late Middle Ages.[1490] Thus, according to one commentator: 'When

---

1484 See *Documents on the Laws of War*, p. 471.

1485 Cassese's emphasis. The quotation is taken from Scott, J.B. (ed.), *Proceedings of The Hague Peace Conference 1899*, *op. cit.*, p. 286.

1486 Cassese, A., "Weapons causing unnecessary suffering: Are they prohibited?", *op. cit.*, p. 18.

1487 *Ibid.*

1488 1481 Oeter, S., "Methods and Means of Combat", *op. cit.*, p. 114.

1489 Cassese, however, claimed that the prohibition on bacteriological weapons was due to their indiscriminate nature. See also *ICRC Commentary on the 1977 Additional Protocols*, *op. cit.*, p. 623.

1490 Carnahan, B.M., "Unnecessary Suffering, The Red Cross and Tactical Laser Weapons", *op. cit.*, p. 714 citing Meron, T., *Henry's Wars and Shakespeare's Laws*, 1993, p. 116, and Khadduri, M., *War and Peace in the Law of Islam*, 1955, p. 104.

some of the later persistent gases of World War I (...) settled in the mud holes and sometimes streams and wells of no-man's land, the similarity to the outlawed poisoning of wells was instant legal linkage to the century-old ban on such actions.'[1491]

Referring to 1899 Hague Declaration Concerning Asphyxiating Gases, which purported to prohibit the use of projectiles whose sole object was to diffuse asphyxiating gases,[1492] it is suggested that the agreement was derived from the general principles of customary international law prohibiting the use of poison and materials causing unnecessary suffering.[1493]

D. Non-Detectable Fragments

The Protocol on Non-Detectable Fragments (Protocol I) annexed to the 1980 Convention on Certain Conventional Weapons provides that: 'It is prohibited to use any weapon the primary effect of which is to injure by fragments which in the human body escape detection by X-rays.' This beguilingly simple provision was adopted by consensus and without too much difficulty since no one was thought to be either manufacturing or planning to manufacture such a weapon. Weapons with such secondary effects, such as plastic mines, are not covered by the prohibition.[1494]

E. Blinding Laser Weapons

Prior to the adoption in October 1995 of Protocol IV to the 1980 CCW, one authority had claimed that the 'practical significance' of the prohibition on the use of weapons causing superfluous injury or unnecessary suffering was demonstrated by the 'continuing discussion on the legality of laser guns, a new weapon which can cause blindness.' It was thus asserted that there were 'convincing arguments that such laser weapons could be useful in a military conflict, but they are also claimed to cause "superfluous injury" in the sense of aggravated suffering not justified by corresponding advantages in neutralising enemy combatants.'[1495]

According to the ICRC: 'Blinding as a method of warfare is a superfluous injury and a cause of unnecessary suffering, both of which are prohibited under existing international humanitarian law.'[1496] A retired US military lawyer, though, vigorously asserts that the ICRC 'is wrong as a matter of law and (...) blinding as a method of warfare, particularly with a laser weapon, does not

---

1491 Hammond Jr., J.W., *Poison Gas, The Myths Versus Reality*, Greenwood Press, Westport, US, 1999, p. xi.

1492 And was therefore an – albeit unsuccessful – precursor to the 1925 Geneva Gas Protocol.

1493 Roberts, A. and Guelff, R., *Documents on the Laws of War*, 3rd edn., *op. cit.*, p. 59.

1494 1487 See for instance Oeter, S., "Methods and Means of Combat", *op. cit.*, p. 124.

1495 1488 *Ibid.*, p. 116.

1496 ICRC, *Blinding Weapons*, Campaign leaflet, ICRC, Geneva, 1995, p. 7, quoted by Carnahan, B.M., "Unnecessary Suffering, The Red Cross and Tactical Laser Weapons", *op. cit.*, p. 705.

violate existing international law norms.'[1497] However, the same authority accepts that the blinding laser rifle offers a military value that 'appears marginal at best. Even if such weapons needlessly blind only a few combatants, it will be difficult to argue that their suffering was militarily necessary.'[1498]

3.4.4. The Application of the Principle to Anti-Personnel Mines

On the basis of application of the principle to specific weapons since 1868, the following conclusions have been drawn:

'(1) *An otherwise effective weapon becomes unlawful when it is deliberately altered for the purpose of increasing the suffering it inflicts. Examples include poisoned bullets and barbed bayonets.*

(2) *A new weapon or method of warfare may inflict unnecessary suffering if its military advantages are marginal, temporary or otherwise vastly disproportionate to the anticipated increase in suffering. The dumdum bullet is an example.*

(3) *The legality of a weapon may change depending on technological and military developments. Small calibre explosives or incendiary ammunition in air warfare are examples of weapons whose status change according to technological developments.*

(4) *A weapon may not be deliberately selected for the suffering that it inflicts when other, equally effective means are readily available. Examples include projectiles filled with glass or non-detectable fragments.* '[1499]

Anti-personnel mines *per se* do not fit into any of these four categories. And yet, the suffering that they inflict is acute. According to then ICRC President Dr Cornelio Sommaruga:

'If a person steps on a buried anti-personnel mine, his or her foot or leg is blown off. The force of the blast drives earth, grass, the vaporized mine case and portions of the victim's shoe and foot upwards into the tissues of the other leg, buttocks, genitals, arms and sometimes the eyes. With those mines which have a larger volume of explosive, death may be inevitable. If the wounded person gets to hospital and if the hospital has the necessary facilities and expertise (both of which are rare in mine affected countries) he or she will require several operations, will stay in hospital four weeks at least and will require a safe blood transfusion. Awaiting the survivor is permanent and severe disability with all the social, psychological and economic implications of being an amputee. Mines are designed to produce these effects. Likewise, fragmentation mines, which can propel hundreds of metal fragments into a person at

---

[1497] Carnahan, B.M., "Unnecessary Suffering, The Red Cross and Tactical Laser Weapons",*op. cit.*, p. 708. Sweden had proposed a prohibition on blinding as a method of warfare. A protocol including this assertion was not, however, adopted. The US objected strongly, arguing that it would lay the ground for false war crimes charges.

[1498] Carnahan, B.M., "Unnecessary Suffering, The Red Cross and Tactical Laser Weapons",*op. cit.*, p. 730.

[1499] 1492 *Ibid.*, p. 722.

waist height, are designed to inflict very severe wounds. "Very severe" means tearing the person apart, or, for the one who triggers the mine, death (...) Would not most people, including soldiers, describe the effects of mines described above as superfluous and excessive to the military need? '[1500]

Yet, a leading humanitarian lawyer has raised the question of whether a weapon that has been used for ages without attracting such a complaint can be found to violate the prohibition on weapons causing superfluous injury or unnecessary suffering (the implication being that the criteria or standards for assessing superfluous injury or unnecessary suffering have changed, rather than the weapon).[1501] Likewise, the ICRC in its official commentary of Article 36 of 1977 Additional Protocol I points out that 'it cannot be expected that States will introduce specific prohibitions on the basis of general principles, when such prohibitions could be considered as an *a posteriori* condemnation of prior use of such weapons.'[1502]

According to the US, the fact that amended Protocol II to the 1980 CCW prohibits the use of mines, booby-traps or other devices which are designed or of a nature to cause superfluous injury or unnecessary suffering 'implicitly' makes clear that they are not, *per se,* of such a nature.[1503] The US does, however, consider that a mine filled with shards of glass would come under the prohibition 'because the shards would be undetectable by X-ray in the victim's body, and this would cause suffering that would be wholly unnecessary for its military purpose.'[1504]

Dr Robin Coupland of the ICRC, however, points out that: 'Buried or "point detonating" anti-personnel mines are the only conventional weapons which cause specific and severe injury resulting in specific and permanent disability. The treatment of the injury requires, on average, twice as many operations and four times as many blood transfusions as injury from other weapons.'[1505]

3.4.5. Conclusion

The principle against the use of weapons that inflict superfluous injury or unnecessary suffering is, in the view of the author, intended to protect combatants rather than civilians, who are protected under other customary principles of international humanitarian law. Although it is obviously lawful to target a soldier in a situation of armed conflict, the use of weapons that needlessly aggravate or

---

1500 Sommaruga, C., "Does the nature of mine injuries also justify a total ban?", UN, *Landmines,* Vol. 1.4, September 1996, p. 11.

1501 1494 Hampson, F., letter to the author, 19 March 1997. Though, as Ms Hampson points out, the definition of cruel, inhuman and degrading treatment under international human rights law has shifted over time.

1502 *ICRC Commentary on the 1977 Additional Protocols,* p. 427.

1503 Nash, M., "Contemporary Practice of the United States Relating to International Law", *op. cit.,* 1997, p. 334.

1504 *Ibid.,* p. 335.

1505 Coupland, Dr. R.M., "Abhorrent weapons and 'superfluous injury or unnecessary suffering': from field surgery to law", *British Medical Journal,* Vol. 315, 29 November 1997, p. 1450. He points out, though, that this 'is a surgeon's view.'

inflict gratuitous suffering is prohibited. This view is supported by the judgment in the *Nuclear Weapons Advisory Opinion*, which refers to the 'cardinal principle' that 'it is prohibited to cause unnecessary suffering to combatants: it is accordingly prohibited to use weapons causing them such harm or uselessly aggravating their suffering.'[1506]

Buried blast anti-personnel mines contain considerably more explosive than is necessary to render a soldier who detonates them *hors de combat*. They are specifically designed to cause traumatic amputation of, at least, the foot and lower leg. It is thus hard to see what military purpose is achieved by deliberately inflicting life-long disability on the soldier, when wounding him less severely would still take him out of the battle and demand serious medical attention. It is hard to avoid the conclusion seemingly reached by the ICRC that such buried blast anti-personnel mines, at least with the level of explosive they generally contain[1507] are indeed 'of a nature' to cause superfluous injury or unnecessary suffering.[1508]

3.5. Environmental Protection

Environmental protection is one of the fastest growing areas of international law,[1509] a reaction to man's proliferating ability to threaten and undermine his own surroundings.[1510] Until the discussion in the 1996 Advisory Opinion of the International Court of Justice regarding the threat or use of nuclear weapons, however, the impact of this development in the context of international humanitarian law had been far less significant.[1511]

1506 *Nuclear Weapons Advisory Opinion*, para. 78.

1507 Thus, as Croll has pointed out: 'A smaller explosive charge is cheaper and provides other economies for manufacturers, such as a requirement for less casing material. For defending armies, smaller mines require less transport and they are easier to bury and to conceal.' *The History of Landmines*, p. 43.

1508 In the case of fragmentation anti-personnel mines, on the other hand, such a conclusion is not possible to draw. The effect of such mines is similar to an explosion from a standard grenade, the legality of use of which is hardly contested.

1509 The Stockholm Conference of June 1972 on the Human Environment is regarded as being seminal in this regard, and, in particular, the Declaration on the Human Environment adopted by the Conference. See for instance Clark, R.S., "Treaty and Custom", Boisson de Chazournes, L. *et al.* (eds.), *International Law, the International Court of Justice and Nuclear Weapons*, *op. cit.*, pp. 178-9.
On the other hand, the definition of what is encompassed by the term *environment* has been the subject of some dispute. For example, in relation to the negotiation of the 1977 Additional Protocol I, discussed below, the ICRC 'had considered that the concept of the environment was extremely vague, and in the absence of a satisfactory definition, had deemed it best to avoid introducing it into the draft.' ICRC Commentary on the 1977 Additional Protocols, *op. cit.*, p. 413, footnote 96. Though compare this assertion with their commentary on Article 55, also dealing with the protection of the environment.

1510 See for instance Starke, J.G., *Introduction to International Law*, 10th edn., Butterworths, London, 1989, p. 401.

1511 See Greenwood, C., "*Jus ad bellum* and *jus in bello* in the *Nuclear Weapons Advisory Opinion*" *op. cit.*, pp. 256-7; Brown Weiss, E., "Opening the door to the environment and to future generations", Boisson de Chazournes, L. *et al.* (eds.), *International Law, the International Court of Justice and Nuclear Weapons*, *op. cit.*, pp. 338-53. See also Antoine, P., "International

As mentioned *supra*, the ICJ has declared that States taking part in armed conflict had a duty 'to take environmental considerations into account in assessing what is necessary and proportionate in the pursuit of legitimate military objectives.'[1512]

3.5.1. 1977 Additional Protocol I

The treaty provisions of humanitarian law most directly relevant to the protection of the environment against the use of conventional weaponry are to be found in 1977 Additional Protocol I,[1513] and particularly its Articles 35 and 55.[1514] Article 35(3), one of the 'basic rules' applicable to methods and means of warfare[1515] prohibits the use of 'methods or means of warfare which are intended, or may be expected, to cause widespread, long-term and severe damage to the natural environment.'

One commentator describes the Protocol as 'a turning point in the history of environmental protection in time of armed conflict'.[1516] Yet according to another, it was customary law and general environmental treaties, rather than the

---

humanitarian law and the protection of the environment in time of armed conflict", *International Review of the Red Cross*, ICRC, Geneva, p. 517 *et seq*.

According to Richard Falk: 'In describing "existing law" on this topic one is beset by complexity, which is itself part of the unsatisfactory character of the present international law of environmental protection in wartime[.] (...) The legal norms that exist are scattered, and are either very general and vague, as well as subject to "military necessity" exceptions, or more specific and relevant, but not directed at prevailing belligerent practices of the sort most likely to generate environmental harm. Furthermore, the status and relevance of principles of customary international law are quite indefinite, as is the related matter of whether treaty norms reflect and embody customary norms[.] (...) [I]f general norms are treated as authoritative, then almost all environmentally harmful belligerent practices are illegal; if general norms are ignored, then almost nothing is prohibited.' Falk, R., "The Environmental Law of War: an Introduction", p. 79. See also Oeter, "Methods and Means of Combat", *op. cit.*, p. 114 *et seq*.

1512 *Nuclear Weapons Advisory Opinion*, para. 30.

1513 1506 Though note must be made of the UN Convention on the Prohibition of Military or any Other Hostile Use of Environmental Modification Techniques (hereinafter, the Enmod Convention), adopted by the UN General Assembly in 1976, and which entered into force on 5 October 1978. According to the ICRC, the Convention sought to prevent the use of environmental modification techniques as weapons in themselves by prohibiting the deliberate manipulation of natural processes in order to change 'the dynamics, composition or structure of the Earth, including its biota, lithosphere, hydrosphere and atmosphere, or of outer space.' *ICRC Commentary on the 1977 Additional Protocols*, p. 415, citing Article II of the Enmod Convention.

1514 Although as has been pointed out, other customary and conventional law regulating the means and methods of warfare, including the use of poison or the destruction of property not required by military necessity, could also be relevant. See for example *Documents on the Laws of War*, p. 378; Falk, R., "The Environmental Law of War: an Introduction", *op. cit.*, p. 94. Indeed, during the Gulf War against Iraq in 1991, the US was forced to rely on Article 23(g) of 1907 Hague Convention IV to condemn Iraq's setting fire to the Kuwaiti oil wells, the US not being party to 1977 Additional Protocol I.

1515 Philippe Antoine claims that the inclusion of this paragraph in an article on basic rules implies that the protection of the environment in time of international armed conflict should be given priority in the conduct of hostilities. Antoine, P., "International humanitarian law and the protection of the environment in time of armed conflict", *op. cit.*, p. 521.

1516 *Ibid.*, p. 520.

Protocol, which motivated the ICJ to make its determination.[1517] Certainly the US and a number of other, especially, Western countries, do not regard Article 35(3) as forming part of customary law.[1518]

In its official commentary on Article 35(3), the ICRC refers specifically to the danger of landmines and booby-traps, which 'have in some cases been scattered in astronomical quantities in certain theatres of war',[1519] pointing out at the same time that the threat posed to the environment 'is not limited to the period of hostilities.'[1520] Notwithstanding the status of the provision under customary law, in order to assess the legality of the use of anti-personnel mines under Article 35(3), it is necessary to discuss the meaning of the terms 'widespread, long-term and severe damage'.[1521] The same phrasing was used in the 1977 Enmod Convention. Yet whereas in that case an interpretive agreement specified the meaning of the terms in the context of the Convention,[1522] in the 1977 Additional Protocol there is only some guidance from the *Travaux préparatoires*, although it seems clear that for the purposes of the Protocol the meanings are different to those in the Convention.[1523] Thus, '[i]t is much more difficult to give an exact interpretation of the terms used in the Protocol, since its provisions protect the natural environment as such as are therefore less specific (...) However, it is generally understood that "widespread" implies an

[1517] See Greenwood, Prof. C., "The Advisory Opinion on nuclear weapons and the contribution of the International Court to international humanitarian law", *International Review of the Red Cross*, No. 316 (January-February 1997), ICRC, Geneva, p. 69. Professor Greenwood affirms that paragraph 30 of the Opinion 'is, in fact, quite close to the view expressed in the 1995 edition of the *United States Naval Commander's Handbook*, para. 8.1.3.' *Ibid.*, at footnote 16.

[1518] See for instance Meron, T., *Human Rights and Humanitarian Norms as Customary Law*, *op. cit.*, p. 66. Cassese refers to the declaration of West Germany that it had joined the consensus of Article 35 with the understanding that paragraphs 1 and 2 reaffirm customary international law, while paragraph 3 is an important new contribution in times of international armed conflict. See Cassese, A., "The Geneva Protocols of 1977 on the Humanitarian Law of Armed Conflict and Customary International Law", *op. cit.*, p. 76.

[1519] See *ICRC Commentary on the 1977 Additional Protocols*, p. 411.

[1520] *Ibid.*

[1521] According to Rogers, Articles 35 and 55 'only come into play once the military planner has surmounted two hurdles: first, that the object to be attacked is a military objective and, secondly, that the rule of proportionality will not be violated. After that he must have regard to the specific rules on environmental protection. It is likely, though, that if the environmental damage is going to be widespread, long-term and severe, the military planner may well fall at the second hurdle in any event.' Rogers, A.P.V., *Law on the Battlefield*, *op. cit.*, p. 112.

[1522] The Conference of the Committee on Disarmament (CCD) that negotiated the treaty text submitted with it a set of Understandings to the General Assembly. The Understanding relating to Article 1 stated the following: 'It is the understanding of the Committee that, for the purposes of this Convention, the terms, "widespread", "long-lasting" and "severe" shall be interpreted as follows: (a) "widespread": encompassing an area on the scale of several hundred square kilometres; (b) "long-lasting": lasting for a period of months, or approximately a season; (c) "severe": involving serious or significant disruption or harm to human life, natural and economic resources or other assets.' See for example *Documents on the Laws of War*, pp. 377-8.

[1523] See Momtaz, D., "Le recours à l'arme nucléaire et la protection de l'environnement: l'apport de la Cour internationale de Justice", Boisson de Chazournes, L. *et al.* (eds.), *International Law, the International Court of Justice and Nuclear Weapons*, *op. cit.*, pp. 355-74. See also, in relation to Article 55 (which uses the same terminology), *ICRC Commentary on the 1977 Additional Protocols*, p. 664.

area of less than several hundred square kilometres, "long-term" refers to ten years or more and "severe" involves "damage as would be likely to prejudice, over a long term, the continued survival of the civilian population or would risk causing it major health problems."'[1524]

Prima facie, anti-personnel landmines might appear in certain instances to fulfil at least two of the three criteria.[1525] They certainly endanger the survival of the civilian population when used in fertile agricultural land in rural developing communities, and can render useless huge swathes of land.[1526] Whether, though, the damage lasts for a decade or more obviously depends on whether the mines are – or can be – cleared.[1527] It should be borne in mind, however, that mines and unexploded ordnance left over from the First as well as the Second World War are still being cleared from a number of European countries. These still cause a few dozen deaths each year, largely to farmers. However, the report of the Rapporteur of the drafting committee responsible for the text (known rather quaintly as 'Biotope') seemed to suggest that such damage lay outside the scope of the Protocol:

> *'Others referred to battlefield destruction in France in the First World War as being outside the scope of the prohibition[.] (...) It appeared to be a widely shared assumption that battlefield damage incidental to conventional warfare would not normally be proscribed by this provision.'*

Article 55 of the Protocol, entitled 'Protection of the natural environment',[1528] also addressed the use of means of warfare and their impact on the environment in the following terms:

> '1. *Care shall be taken in warfare to protect the natural environment against widespread, long-term and severe damage. This protection includes a prohibition of the use of methods or means of warfare which are intended or may be expected to cause such damage to*

[1524] Antoine, P., "International humanitarian law and the protection of the environment in time of armed conflict", *op. cit.*, p. 526. At a debate on humanitarian law and the environment at the Sixth Committee of the UN General Assembly during the Gulf War the ICRC called for 'concerted interpretation' of what constituted 'widespread, long-term and severe damage' to the environment. See Bloom, S. *et al* (eds.), *Hidden Casualties, Environmental, Health and Political Consequences of the Persian Gulf War*, Earthscan, London, 1994, p. 307.

[1525] It should be noted that these requirements are cumulative, not, as in the Enmod Convention, alternatives.

[1526] See for example *After the Guns Fall Silent.*

[1527] As we have seen in Chapter 2 *supra* above, mine clearance may be expensive in terms of financial or human cost. For the illuminating position with regard to Kuwait see *Landmine Monitor Report 1999*, pp. 891, 892.

[1528] According to the ICRC: 'The concept of the natural environment should be understood in the widest sense to cover the biological environment in which a population is living. It does not consist merely of the objects indispensable to survival mentioned in Article 54 (*Protection of objects indispensable to the survival of the civilian population*) – foodstuffs, agricultural areas, drinking water, livestock – but also includes forests and other vegetation mentioned in the Convention of 10 October 1980 on Prohibitions or Restrictions on the Use of Certain Conventional Weapons, (...) as well as fauna, flora and other biological or climatic elements.' *ICRC Commentary on the 1977 Additional Protocols*, p. 662.

the natural environment and thereby to prejudice the health or survival of the population.

2. *Attacks against the natural environment by way of reprisals are prohibited.'*

The ICRC, while accepting that Articles 35(3) and 55 'overlap to some extent, and their tenor is similar', claim that they do not duplicate each other. In the author's view, this claim is difficult to sustain. The normative content is to all intents and purposes the same. At the Drafting Committee stage the UK delegation made its feelings known in relation to Article 35(3):

'We regard this paragraph as otiose repetition of Article 48 bis [which would become Article 55 in the final text] and would have preferred that paragraph 3 not be included in this Article. We consider that it is basically in order to protect the civilians living in the environment that the environment itself is to be protected against attack. Hence the provision on protection of the environment is in our view rightly placed in the section on protection of civilians. Now that Article 33 [which would become Article 35 in the final text] has been adopted with paragraph 3, we shall interpret that paragraph in the same way as Article 48 bis, which in our view is a fuller and more satisfactory formulation.'[1529]

The difference between the two Articles had been more marked at an earlier drafting stage. The ICRC itself had not included any provision specifically protecting the environment in its draft Protocol, but the Australian delegation had put forward a proposal at the 1974 Diplomatic Conference by which it was 'forbidden to despoil the natural environment as a technique of warfare.' A breach of this provision, which included the prohibition on attacks against the natural environment by way of reprisals that found its way into the final text, was to constitute a grave breach of the Protocol.[1530]

3.5.2. Applicability to Internal Armed Conflict

It is probably in internal armed conflict that the impact on the environment has been most acute. The commonplace use of anti-personnel mines to deny sustenance to the civilian population in a situation where, even when the conflict is over, the capacity to clear mines is limited, invariably means that the damage to the environment will be widespread, long-term and severe. However, no such legal protection as that afforded by Articles 35(3) and 55 of 1977 Additional Protocol I was included in the second 1977 Additional Protocol Relating to the Protection of Victims of Non-International Armed Conflicts.[1531] In addition,

1529 O.R. VI, p. 118, *CDDH/SR.39*, Annex, cited by *ICRC Commentary on the 1977 Additional Protocols*, p. 1341.

1530 See for example Antoine, P., "International humanitarian law and the protection of the environment in time of armed conflict", *op. cit.*, p. 524. Antoine cites another author, Bretton, as suggesting that the motivation for the proposed article was the French nuclear testing which was taking place at the time in the Pacific.

1531 At the debate in the UN General Assembly referred to above, the ICRC called for attention to be paid to the protection of the environment in non-international conflicts. See Bloom, S.*et al* (eds.), *Hidden Casualties, Environmental, Health and Political Consequences of the Persian Gulf War, op. cit.*, p. 307.

there is no evidence of a general customary rule protecting the environment against excessively damaging means and methods of warfare.

3.5.3. Conclusion

In the view of the author, despite the development of environmental law, the provisions attributing legal protection to the environment in times of armed conflict contained in 1977 Additional Protocol I have not yet attained the status of customary international law. Moreover, given the high threshold contained in them, it is not surprising that one leading commentator has asserted that: 'Articles 35(3) and 55 will not impose any significant limitation on combatants waging conventional warfare.'[1532]

One author states categorically, though without justifying his assertion, that mines, booby-traps and other devices 'are not of a nature to cause widespread, long-lasting and severe damage to the environment' although he concedes that 'they can nevertheless be harmful to it in many ways.'[1533] Indeed, although environmental considerations must certainly be taken into account when using anti-personnel mines on the battlefield, it is extremely hard to accept the claim made by Human Rights Watch that 'there is consensus at least that landmine use may be expected to cause environmental damage that is severe, long-lasting, and widespread.'[1534] Finally, further research into the environmental impact of anti-personnel mines and unexploded ordnance would certainly be worthwhile.

3.6. The Laws of Humanity and the Dictates of the Public Conscience

3.6.1. The Martens Clause

The Martens Clause was named after the Russian jurist Fedor Fedorovitch Martens[1535] who was instrumental in drafting the text of the Clause and ensuring its adoption.[1536] It first appeared in the Preamble to 1899 Hague Convention IV as a response to a dispute at the 1899 Peace Conference on the status of civilians who took up arms against an occupying force,[1537] although it is more often its inclusion – unchanged – in the Preamble to 1907 Hague Convention IV that is cited in the literature. The paragraph reads as follows:

1532 Bothe, M. *et al.*, *New Rules for Victims of Armed Conflicts, Commentary on the Two 1977 Additional Protocols Additional to the Geneva Conventions of 1949*, 1982, p. 345, para 2.3, cited by Baker, B., "Legal Protections for the Environment in Times of Armed Conflict", *Virginia Journal of International Law*, No. 33 (Winter 1993), p. 370.

1533 Antoine, P., "International humanitarian law and the protection of the environment in time of armed conflict", *op. cit.*, p. 528.

1534 *A Deadly Legacy*, pp. 310-2.

1535 1528 For background on the adoption of the clause and the life and work of Martens see for instance Pustogarov, V., "Fyodor Fyodorovich Martens (1845-1909) – A Humanist of Modern Times", *International Review of the Red Cross (IRRC)*, No. 312 (May-June 1996), Geneva, pp. 300-14; and Best, G., *Humanity in Warfare*, *op. cit.*, pp. 163-6.

1536 See for instance Best, *G., Humanity in Warfare*, *op. cit.*, p. 165.

1537 See *ibid.*, p. 164; and Ticehurst, R., "The Martens Clause and the Laws of Armed Conflict", *International Review of the Red Cross*, No. 317 (March-April 1997), Geneva, p. 125 *et seq.*

'Until a more complete code of the laws of war has been issued, the high contracting Parties deem it expedient to declare that, in cases not included in the Regulations adopted by them, the inhabitants and the belligerents remain under the protection and the rule of the principles of the law of nations, as they result from the usages established among civilised peoples, from the laws of humanity, and the dictates of the public conscience.'

Although adopted unanimously at the two respective Hague Peace Conferences,[1538] since the clause was not included in the main body of the Convention its status as customary law was never as clear as that of the provisions of the Convention and the annexed Regulations. It was, however, included in the clause on denunciation common to the four 1949 Geneva Conventions[1539] and then as Article 1(2) of 1977 Additional Protocol I,[1540] with only slight amendments.[1541]

According to one commentator, the primary importance of the Martens clause is that it disproves the claim sometimes made that anything that is not specifically prohibited by international humanitarian law is *ipso facto* lawful.[1542] Two views of the clause can be distinguished: a broader one that claims that weapons thought to be contrary to the principle of humanity as conceived by the general public were prohibited;[1543] the other, narrower, view held that a weapon was prohibited once it could be shown that the influence of public opinion 'had resulted in the introduction of a new principle of customary international law denying the legitimacy of a particular weapon in war'.[1544] According to another

1538 See for example *ICRC Commentary on the 1977 Additional Protocols*, p. 38.

1539 For instance Article 63 of the *Geneva Convention for the Amelioration of the Condition of the Wounded and Sick in Armed Forces in the Field of 12 August 1949* states *inter alia* that: 'The denunciation shall have effect only in respect of the denouncing Power. It shall in no way impair the obligations which the Parties to the conflict shall remain bound to fulfil by virtue of the principles of the law of nations, as they result from the usages established among civilized peoples, from the laws of humanity and the dictates of the public conscience.'

1540 In its official commentary on the article, the ICRC claimed that the Martens clause applies independently of participation in the treaties containing it, though without giving overt justification for this assertion. See *ICRC Commentary on the 1977 Additional Protocols*, p. 39.

1541 'In cases not covered by this Protocol or by any other international agreements, civilians and combatants remain under the protection and authority of the principles of international law derived from established custom, from the principles of humanity and from the dictates of public conscience.'

1542 Robblee Jr., Capt. P.A., "The Legitimacy of Modern Conventional Weaponry", *op. cit.*, p. 415.

1543 Professor Greenwood, for example, states that it is 'not clear (...) whether the Martens Clause (...) introduces into humanitarian law a rule that all weapons and means of warfare are to be judged against the standard of the "public conscience" even if their use does not contravene the specific rules of customary international law such as the unnecessary suffering principle.' He personally rejects the possibility as being 'impracticable' since 'the public conscience' is too vague a concept to be used as the basis for a separate rule of law and has attracted little support. Greenwood, C., "Historical Development and Legal Basis", *op. cit.*, p. 28. Greenwood's view is shared by the author.

1544 *Ibid.*, pp. 421-2. As Robblee asserts, 'the fundamental difficulty with accepting the public opinion criterion is that it is more appropriate as a political consideration than as an independent legal criterion regulating weaponry.' See also Kalshoven, F., "The Conference of Government Experts on the Use of Certain Conventional Weapons, Lucerne, 24 September to 18 October

view: 'The Martens Clause is important, because it confirms the persistence of customary international law in relation to belligerent practices not covered by treaty norms, and extends the law of war to States that have failed to accede to recent developments in treaty law. The true relevance of this purported applicability of customary norms depends on the existence of a forum or tribunal that can offer authoritative interpretations of contested practices.'[1545]

Ticehurst, reiterating that there is no accepted interpretation of the Martens Clause, cites the view of Professor Greenwood that the Clause merely serves as a reminder that customary international law continues to apply after the adoption of a treaty norm.[1546] He refers to the *Nuclear Weapons Advisory Opinion*, in which judgment it was merely stated, rather unsatisfactorily and without justifying the assertion, that the Martens Clause had 'proved to be an effective means of addressing the rapid evolution of military technology.'[1547]

3.6.2. Applicability to Internal Armed Conflicts

According to Miyazaki, '[t]he Martens Clause plays an important role particularly in non-international armed conflicts'[1548] because of the absence of extensive legal regulation as is the case with international armed conflicts. In contrast to 1977 Additional Protocol I, 1977 Additional Protocol II applicable to high intensity internal armed conflicts contained a truncated form of the Martens Clause and in the Preamble, not an operative provision.

> *'Recalling that, in cases not covered by the law in force, the human person remains under the protection of the principles of humanity and the dictates of the public conscience.'*

In its official commentary the ICRC explained that the different wording 'takes into account the specific nature of non-international armed conflicts[.] (...) If a case is "not covered by the law in force", whether this is because the parties do not consider themselves to be bound by common Article 3, or are not bound by Protocol II, this does not mean that anything is permitted.'[1549]

1974", *op. cit.*, pp. 92-3; and Greenwood, C., "Historical Development and Legal Basis", *op. cit.*, p. 28.

1545 Falk, R., "The Environmental Law of War: an Introduction", *op. cit.*, p. 84.

1546 Ticehurst, R., "The Martens Clause and the Laws of Armed Conflict", *op. cit.*, p. 126. Greenwood adds that the Clause also serves as a statement of the factors that are likely to lead States to adopt a ban on a particular weapon or means of warfare. Greenwood, "Historical Development and Legal Basis", *op. cit.*, p. 28.

1547 Opinion, para. 78. Rather ironically given the origin of the Clause, the Russian Federation had argued in its submission to the Court that as a complete code of the laws of war was formulated in 1949 and 1977, the Martens Clause was now redundant. Russian Federation, written submission on the Opinion requested by the General Assembly, p. 13, cited by Ticehurst, R., "The Martens Clause and the Laws of Armed Conflict", *op. cit.*, p. 127.

1548 1541 Miyazaki, S., "The Martens Clause and international humanitarian law", in Swinarski, C. (ed.), *Studies and essays on international humanitarian law and Red Cross principles, op. cit.*, p. 439.

1549 *ICRC Commentary on the 1977 Additional Protocols*, p. 1341. The ICRC sought to justify the omission of reference to established custom on the basis that the regulation of non-international armed conflicts was too recent a matter for State practice to have developed. Given recent jurisprudence in this area, this is extremely unfortunate. Indeed, the commentary goes on to

3.6.3. Conclusion

In the view of the author, the Martens Clause plays two roles: the first, in reminding combatants that merely because there is no applicable law to certain behaviour or at certain times, that does not mean that there are no constraints that apply. Unfortunately, such a clause is likely to have negligible impact in practice. The second role, of more relevance to the present case, is in testing the legality of the use of weaponry that is not already regulated under existing humanitarian law.

Thus, for example, the applicability of the Martens Clause is one of the arguments that may be used in seeking to prohibit the use of cluster bombs in populated areas.[1550] This is lawful under existing international humanitarian law (obviously as long as they are aimed at a military objective) but the reality of their use by NATO in the conflict against the Federal Republic of Yugoslavia is that they can malfunction and cause significant civilian casualties, both during and after conflict. This concern led to the presumed Executive Directive by the White House in mid-May 1999 prohibiting their further use in the conflict by US forces (although the RAF continued to deploy the weapons.)[1551]

Public opinion played a key role in ensuring the successful adoption of the Convention on the Prohibition of Anti-Personnel Mines. It did not per se make anti-personnel mines illegal although it has made it much harder politically to be seen using them. Indeed, according to the President of the First CCW Review Conference:

> *'In a setting which excluded a number of major mine-using and mine-producing countries, some hundred states were able to translate their understanding of the "dictates of public conscience" in the words of the Martens clause, into a treaty text banning anti-personnel landmines.'*[1552]

It seems obvious that in the future development of international humanitarian law with respect to weapons, the 'laws of humanity' and the 'dictates of the public conscience' will continue to have a role to play, at least in standard setting.

3.7. The Convention on the Prohibition of Anti-Personnel Mines

The principle that customary law can develop from the provisions of treaties is set out in the 1969 Vienna Convention on the Law of Treaties: 'Nothing (...) precludes a rule set forth in a treaty from becoming binding upon a third State as a customary rule of international law.'[1553] Also in 1969, the ICJ, in its judgement in the *North Sea Continental Shelf Cases*, declared that a treaty

contradict the implication both that customary law does not apply in internal armed conflicts, and that no such customary rules have yet developed.

1550 See for instance Human Rights Watch, *Civilian Deaths in the Federal Republic of Yugoslavia*, HRW, Washington, May 1999.

1551 See for instance ICRC, *Explosive Remnants of War, Cluster Bombs and Landmines in Kosovo*, ICRC, Geneva, August 2000.

1552 Maresca, L. and Maslen, S. (eds.), *The Banning of Anti-Personnel Landmines*, *op. cit.*, p. xxiv.

1553 Article 38, 1969 Vienna Convention on the Law of Treaties.

provision "while only conventional or contractual has since passed into the general *corpus* of international law, and is now accepted as such by the *opinio juris*, so as to have become binding even for countries which have never, and do not, become parties to the Convention. There is no doubt that this process is a perfectly possible one and does from time to time occur: it constitutes indeed one of the recognised methods by which new rules of customary international law may be formed."[1554]

In the *North Sea Continental Shelf Cases*, the ICJ laid down three requirements which had to be met if a treaty provision which was substantially innovative was to be deemed to have become binding as part as general law: the provision must be a norm-creating character; State practice, particularly that of States whose interests are specially affected, must indicate a widespread acceptance of the principle; and that practice must be based upon *opinio juris*. According to Greenwood, 'this test suggests that an innovative provision in a treaty can only be regarded as having passed into custom if there is convincing evidence of widespread State practice applying the principle enshrined in that provision in circumstances where the treaty itself was not applicable and the States concerned appear to have treated the principle as binding in customary law.'[1555] Nevertheless, in the *Nicaragua Case*, the Court, while quoting with approval its earlier judgement above cited, adopted in practice "a far less rigorous approach, holding that numerous provisions in multilateral conventions – including common Articles 1 and 3 of the 1949 Conventions – has become part of customary law although the Judgement contains no examination of the State practice upon which such conclusions should have been based if the approach in the [*North Sea Continental Shelf Cases*] has indeed been followed."[1556]

It is claimed that treaties dealing with the conduct of war have been particularly susceptible to becoming customary law. In this regard, it is widely acknowledged by authors and States alike that many provisions of the Geneva Conventions and Additional Protocols of 1977 have been elevated to the status of customary international law.[1557] Thus, in the *Nicaragua Case*, where the question of the customary character of the Geneva Conventions was central because the multilateral treaty reservation made by the US appeared to preclude the ICJ from applying these Conventions as treaties, the Court did not hesitate to apply certain provisions of the Geneva Conventions as customary rules.

1554 *North Sea Continental Shelf Cases*, *ICJ Reports*, 1969, para. 71, p. 42. In this case, the Court concluded that Article 6 of the Geneva Convention of 1958 on the Continental Shelf was not a generator of custom.

1555 Greenwood, C., "Customary Law Status of the 1977 Geneva Protocols", Delissen, A.J.M. & Tanja, G.J. (eds.), *Humanitarian Law of Armed Conflict. Essays in Honour of F. Kalshoven*, Martinus Nijhoff, Dordrecht, The Netherlands, 1991, pp. 97-8.

1556 *Ibid.*, p. 98. For criticism of the Court's approach see Meron, T., "The Geneva Conventions as Customary Law", *American Journal of International Law*, Vol. 81, 1987, pp. 351-8; and Charney, J., "Customary International Law in the Nicaragua Judgement on the Merits", *Hague Yearbook of International Law*, Vol. 16, 1988.

1557 See for instance Meron, T., "The Geneva Conventions as Customary Law", *op. cit.*, pp. 351-8; Greenwood, C., "Customary Law Status of the 1977 Geneva Protocols", *op. cit.*

The Court focused on two common articles of the Geneva Conventions (Articles 1 and 3) as 'specific expression' of 'the general principles of humanitarian law.'[1558] With regard to Article 1 common to the 1949 Geneva Conventions, the Court concluded that 'there is an obligation on the United States Government, in the terms of Article 1 of the Geneva Conventions, to 'respect' the Conventions and even to "ensure respect" for them "in all circumstances", since such an obligation does not derive only from the Conventions themselves, but from the general principles of humanitarian law to which the Conventions merely give specific expression. The United States is thus under an obligation not to encourage persons or groups engaged in the conflict in Nicaragua to act in violation of the provisions of Article 3 common to the four 1949 Geneva Conventions.'[1559]

The Court's method in the *Nicaragua Case* is of general interest in determining the relationship between custom and treaty.[1560] As Meron has noted, the Court's discussion of the Geneva Conventions is remarkable for its total failure to inquire whether *opinio juris* and practice support the crystallisation of Articles 1 and 3 into customary law. Indeed, doubts about the Court's position regarding Article 1 and 3 were expressed by judges Sir Robert Jennings and Roberto Ago. For it has been justly pointed out that, "the parties to the Geneva Conventions have built a poor record of compliance with the norms stated in Article 3 and evidence of practice by non parties is lacking."[1561]

In the *Nuclear Weapons Advisory Opinion*, the ICJ, like the Nuremberg Tribunal that followed World War II, avoided any explicit discussion of the process by which treaty obligations become customary obligations in its response to the General Assembly, although it certainly agreed that such transformations can occur. Referring to the Hague and Geneva Conventions (and perhaps more widely to other humanitarian law treaties), and treating them as custom, the Court made vague references to a 'broad accession' and the 'extent of the accession'.[1562] Accordingly, breadth of accession is a factor that must surely be relevant to customary status[1563] but the Court's analysis is, in the view of one authority, 'ultimately as unsatisfactory as the Nuremberg Tribunal.'[1564] The strongest reference to the matter is a quotation made by the Court, with obvious approval, of a statement of the Secretary General in respect of offences

[1558] *ICJ Reports 1986*, para. 220, p. 114.

[1559] *Ibid.*

[1560] Meron, T., "The Geneva Conventions as Customary Law", *op. cit.*, p. 351.

[1561] *Ibid.*, pp. 357-8.

[1562] *ICJ Reports 1996*, paras. 79 and 82. In paragraph 82, the Court refers as well to "the fact that the denunciation clauses that existed in the codification instruments have never been used." According to one comment, "perhaps this is a factor relevant to whether the obligations have become customary ones, and thus not subject to unilateral denunciation." See Clark, R.S., "Treaty and Custom", Boisson de Chazournes, L. & Sands, P., *International Law, the International Court of Justice and Nuclear Weapons, op. cit.*, p. 175, note 15.

[1563] Refer on this point to the *North Sea Continental Sea Shelf Cases* stating that "a very widespread and representative participation in the Convention might suffice of itself, provided that it included that of States whose interests were specially affected." *ICJ Reports 1969*, para. 73.

[1564] Clark, R.S., "Treaty and Custom", *op. cit.*, p. 175.

proposed in Articles 2 to 5 of the Statute of the International Tribunal for the Former Yugoslavia Tribunal:

> *"In the view of the Secretary-General, the application of the principle nullum crimen sin lege requires that the international tribunal should apply rules of international humanitarian law which are beyond doubt part of customary law[.] (...) The part of conventional international law which has beyond doubt become part of customary law is the law applicable in armed conflict as embodied in: the Geneva Conventions of 12 August 1949 for the Protection of War Victims; the Hague Convention (IV) Respecting the Laws and Customs of War on Land and the Regulations annexed thereto of 18 October 1907; the Convention on the Prevention and Punishment of the Crime of Genocide of 9 December 1948; and the Charter of the International Military Tribunal of 8 August 1945."*[1565]

In the view of the author, however, even the core provision of the Convention on the Prohibition of Anti-Personnel Mines against use of anti-personnel mines, let alone the Convention as a whole, has not yet attained the status of customary law. There are too many major military States outside the Convention that may justifiably consider themselves 'specially affected' by its provisions and which purport to reserve the right to use the weapons, albeit under restricted circumstances. That said, however, a number of these: Belarus, Georgia, the Russian Federation, Turkey, and the US, for instance, have all indicated their willingness to consider adherence within the coming years. Other key States, such as China and India have expressed support for a phased approach towards the total prohibition of anti-personnel mines. In addition, as noted *supra*, violations by signatories or parties to the Convention have been relatively small in number and extent.

3.8. The ICRC Customary Law Study[1566]

In December 1995 the 26th International Conference of the Red Cross and Red Crescent endorsed a recommendation by the 1995 Intergovernmental Group of Experts for the Protection for War Victims that: "the ICRC be invited to prepare, with the assistance of experts in IHL [international humanitarian law] representing various geographical regions and different legal systems, and in consultation with experts from governments and international organisations, a report on customary rules of IHL applicable in international and non-interna-

---

1565 Report of the Secretary-General pursuant to paragraph 2 of Security Council Resolution 808(1993) with which he introduced the Statute of the International Tribunal for the Prosecution of Persons Responsible for Serious Violations of International Humanitarian Law Committed in the Territory of the Former Yugoslavia since 1991, paras. 33-5, quoted in the *Nuclear Weapons Advisory Opinion*, para. 81.

1566 This section is largely adapted from Henckaerts, J.-M., "Study on customary rules of international humanitarian law: Purpose, coverage and methodology", *International Review of the Red Cross*, No. 835, 1 September 1999, pp. 660-8, and is supplemented by the results of discussions between the author and, the head of the ICRC's Legal Division, which is responsible for the drafting of the Study.

tional armed conflicts, and to circulate the report to States and competent international bodies."[1567] As a consequence, the ICRC has since been preparing and drafting the most comprehensive study of customary rules of international humanitarian law ever undertaken.

For research purposes the study has been divided into six parts:

- *principle of distinction;*
- *methods of warfare;*
- *use of weapons;*
- *specific protection regimes;*
- *treatment of persons and human rights law applicable in armed conflict; and*
- *accountability and implementation.*

In accordance with the elements of customary law, the ICRC has commissioned or conducted research into both national and international sources reflecting State practice (*usus*)[1568] and/or legal opinion (*opinio juris*).

As regards national sources, since it would have been practically impossible to carry out research in every country, a selection was made of some 50 countries whose national source material was researched by one or more national researchers at the invitation of the ICRC. These 50 countries were selected by an overall Study Steering Committee[1569] on the basis of geographic representation as well as on the basis of recent experience with armed conflict. In the end, national reports were prepared concerning nine countries in Africa, eleven in the Americas, nine in Asia, twelve in Europe, and nine in the Middle East. Significant practice of other countries was identified through research into international sources and ICRC archives.

The sources of State practice and legal opinion collected by the national researchers include diplomatic correspondence, policy statements (both to national and to international bodies), opinions of official legal advisers, police manuals, military manuals, orders to armed and security forces, military communiqués during war, executive decisions and practices, legislation, judicial decisions, government responses and comments when making reservations to treaties or when refusing to adopt, sign, or ratify a treaty, official government

[1567] Resolution 1 of the 26th International Conference of the Red Cross and Red Crescent (Geneva, 1995).

[1568] In general, research for the study has focused on State practice during the last twenty years, although as noted *supra*, customary international law can emerge in an even shorter period of time.

[1569] The members of the Steering Committee are Georges Abi-Saab, Graduate Institute of International Studies, Geneva; Salah El-Din Amer, Faculty of Law, Cairo University; Ove Bring, Faculty of Law, University of Stockholm; Eric David, Centre de droit international, Université Libre de Bruxelles; John Dugard, Faculty of Law, University of Leiden; Florentino Feliciano, Appelate Body, World Trade Organization, Geneva; Horst Fischer, Institute for International Peacekeeping Law and Humanitarian Law, Ruhr-University, Bochum; Françoise Hampson, Department of Law, University of Essex, Colchester (UK); Theodor Meron, School of Law, New York University; Djamchid Momtaz, Faculty of Law, Tehran University; Milan Sahovic, Center for Human Rights, Belgrade; Raúl Emilio Vinuesa, Faculty of Law, University of Buenos Aires.

responses to NGO allegations and to international organisations, and, if necessary, press releases.[1570]

International practice is reflected in a variety of sources: resolutions adopted in the framework of the United Nations (in particular the Security Council, the General Assembly, and the Commission on Human Rights), United Nations *ad hoc* investigations, the work of the International Law Commission and comments it elicited from governments, the work of the Sixth Committee of the UN General Assembly, reports of the Secretary-General, thematic and country-specific procedures of the UN Commission on Human Rights, reporting procedures before the Human Rights Committee under the International Covenant on Civil and Political Rights, the *travaux préparatoires* of treaties, the practice of international organisations, the findings of specialised institutes, State submissions to international and regional courts, international court decisions, and press releases and NGO statements if needed.

The various findings of the different studies have since been consolidated and comprehensive documents revised, following input from government and other experts. It is now expected that the ICRC will publish the final Study documents in 2001 or even later. Although it would not be appropriate to second-guess the ultimate findings of the ICRC Customary Law Study, on the basis of discussions with the relevant ICRC experts, it seems most unlikely that the study will conclude that a prohibition on the use of anti-personnel mines has already crystallised as a norm of customary international law. It does, though, recognise the trend in that direction and may discern the existence of a customary norm in favour of the eventual elimination of the weapons.

[1570] Press releases were only used as a barometer of public opinion (in relation to the Martens Clause) in relation to certain serious and important events, not as a source for the determination of customary rules of international law.

4. CONCLUDING REMARKS

It has been claimed that the law on the battlefield stands at the 'vanishing point' of the law of war. Accordingly, this work has sought to consider not only the legality under international humanitarian law of the use in armed conflict of anti-personnel mines, but also the prospects for that law being respected in practice – on the battlefield.

4.1. The Development and Use of Anti-Personnel Mines

The invention of these 'infernal machines' is usually attributed to a Confederate Officer during the American Civil War. The first casualties of these early anti-personnel mines were reported on 4 May 1862; even some of the Confederate troops thought them 'barbaric' and the officer's commander forbade their further use, declaring them neither a 'proper nor effective method of war'. Yet, despite concerns on both sides, the weapons continued to be used. In a salutary indication of the problems that would subsequently be confronted as a result of the use of anti-personnel mines on the battlefield, in 1960 five landmines from the Civil War era were recovered in Alabama: nearly 100 years after they were laid, the powder was still quite dangerous.

Largely as a result of the static trench warfare in which the machine gun ruled supreme, anti-personnel mines were not extensively deployed on the battlefield in Europe during the First World War. In the Second World War, however, tens of millions of landmines, both anti-personnel and anti-tank, were used by all parties. One particular German-made anti-personnel mine was said to be 'probably the most feared device encountered by Allied troops in World War Two.'

The Vietnam War saw the first widespread use of remotely-delivered or 'scatterable' mines by US forces seeking to stop the flow of men and material from North to South Vietnam through Laos and Cambodia. Aerially-delivered anti-personnel mines had a number of obvious advantages of their manually-emplaced counterparts: they could be deployed rapidly, required little logistic support, and could be laid deep within enemy-held territory, causing disruption in troops movements and supply lines, all with minimal risk to the air-crews. But at the same time, they represented a substantial danger to advances by friendly forces, and a huge post-conflict threat to the civilian population.

Yet, while mine technology advanced rapidly, the typical use of landmines remained of 'long-lived'[1571] manually-emplaced anti-personnel mines in internal armed conflicts by both government armed forces and armed opposition groups. In Angola, Cambodia, Ethiopia, Mozambique, Nicaragua, Iraq, Somalia, Sudan and many other countries, mines were used to terrorise civilians and control their movements. And as the Soviet Union crumbled, bitter conflicts in the Caucasus

[1571] That is, without any self-destruct or self-neutralisation mechanism incorporated. Such mines are sometimes referred to as "dumb" mines. Self-destruct mechanisms are, as the name suggests, automatically functioning devices incorporated into the mine that cause it to explode after a pre-set period of time; self-neutralisation uses a chemical process to render the mine inert.

and the former Yugoslavia, which included some of the world's leading landmine producers, saw widespread use of anti-personnel mines. Half a century on from the appalling destruction inflicted by the Second World War, battlefields in Europe were once more littered with explosive remnants of war.

4.2. The Legality of Anti-Personnel Mines on the Battlefield under International Humanitarian Law

4.2.1. Customary International Humanitarian Law

Customary rules of warfare are part of the very first rules of international law. Yet, history has demonstrated the limitations of customary prohibitions in controlling the use of certain particularly injurious weapons. The basic rule of modern customary international humanitarian law is reproduced in 1977 Additional Protocol I whereby it is stated that: 'In any armed conflict, the right of the parties to the conflict to choose methods or means of warfare is not unlimited.' Thus, a party to a conflict is not free to use any weapon it wishes, nor in a manner of its own choosing; legal restraint is thus imposed by customary and conventional international law.

Although customary international law prohibits the use of inherently indiscriminate weapons – weapons that are incapable of being directed accurately against a military objective –, anti-personnel mines do not fall within this category. Certainly, anti-personnel mines may have indiscriminate effects: even when the greatest care is taken to ensure that civilians are not caught up in a mine blast, there is still no guarantee that civilians will not be injured. And regrettably, instances of parties to the conflict taking the necessary care are relatively few and far between. Yet, a set of clear conditions for 'responsible' (*i.e.*, lawful) use do exist and could ensure that collateral loss of life and limb to civilians is reduced to a minimum. Anti-personnel mines should be marked and fenced, their use carefully recorded, and, in the case of remotely-delivered mines, should self-destruct quickly after deployment on the battlefield. The fact that these 'customary precautions' have been honoured more in the breach than the observance represents indiscriminate use of anti-personnel mines and fully justifies their prohibition, but does not constitute grounds for a legal determination that they are indiscriminate weapons *per se*.

The principle of proportionality involves a balancing of the advantage to be expected from a military attack against its humanitarian consequences. Thus, the use of means and methods of warfare may be illegal, even if collateral damage to the civilian population and civilian goods could be justified in principle by reference to 'military necessity', on the grounds that such damage is unavoidable in mounting an effective attack on a military objective in the centre of the operation. Manifestly disproportionate collateral damage inflicted in order to achieve operational objectives will result in the action being deemed an (illicit) form of indiscriminate warfare.

It is not possible to argue convincingly that anti-personnel mines have no military utility whatsoever. On the other hand, the claim by certain military authorities that this is an indispensable weapon of high military value does not seem to be borne out by the evidence. It is rightly claimed that although anti-personnel mines are low cost their effectiveness is also low while their humanitarian cost is high. Risks to civilians are especially prevalent in internal armed conflicts – a sad reality to which the people of Angola and Cambodia, among many others, can testify. In many, if not most situations of internal conflict, the use of anti-personnel mines may be expected to be disproportionate to the objective sought, especially in the case of long-lived mines. It is by no means certain, however, that the principle of proportionality applies in such situations.

The legal rule operating against the use of weapons that are of a nature to cause superfluous injury or unnecessary suffering is intended to protect combatants rather than civilians. Although it is obviously lawful to target a soldier in a situation of armed conflict, the use of weapons that needlessly aggravate or inflict gratuitous suffering is prohibited. Buried 'blast' anti-personnel mines contain considerably more explosive than is necessary to render a soldier who detonates them *hors de combat.* They are specifically designed to cause traumatic amputation of, at least, the foot – the only widely used conventional weapon to deliberately inflict permanent disability on its victim. It is thus hard to see what military purpose is achieved by deliberately inflicting life-long disability on the soldier, when wounding him less severely would still take him out of the battle, divert other soldiers, and demand serious medical attention. It would seem, therefore, that such buried blast anti-personnel mines are indeed 'of a nature' to cause superfluous injury or unnecessary suffering.

Despite the rapid and extensive development of international environmental law, the provisions attributing legal protection to the environment in times of armed conflict contained in 1977 Additional Protocol I have not yet attained the status of customary international law. Even were it otherwise, given the high threshold contained in them, they would not prohibit the use of anti-personnel mines on the basis of damage to the environment.

The 'Martens Clause' performs two functions: the first, in reminding combatants that merely because there is no applicable law to certain behaviour or at certain times, that does not mean that there are no constraints that apply. The second role is in testing the legality of the use of weaponry that is not already regulated under existing humanitarian law. Neither has particular relevance to anti-personnel mines, although public opinion played a key role in ensuring the successful adoption of the Convention on the Prohibition of Anti-Personnel Mines. And, in the view of the author, in large part as a result of the Convention, a customary prohibition on the use on the battlefield of anti-personnel mines is now clearly *de lege ferenda.* No State can now claim persistent objector status to this new norm of international humanitarian law.

4.2.2. Conventional International Humanitarian Law

It was not until the latter half of the 19th Century that a written international agreement first prohibited a specific weapon or war. And despite widespread use in World War II, it was not until 1980 that States finally adopted international legislation specifically restricting the use of landmines. The 1980 Convention on Certain Conventional Weapons (1980 CCW), including an annexed Protocol

II that regulated anti-personnel mines, was greeted with little fanfare. The Protocol as it stood did little more than apply existing general customary rules to mine warfare. Moreover, it proved unable to prevent the continuing indiscriminate use, and effects, of the weapon.

Following general agreement that Protocol II was too weak and that its scope of application should be extended to include internal armed conflicts, a Review Conference of the 1980 CCW was convened and, in May 1996, adopted an amended, and somewhat strengthened Protocol. Amended Protocol II attempted to address the root of the existing humanitarian crisis by prohibiting, albeit with a long period of deferral in the case of the requirement for self-destruction, the use of long-lived anti-personnel mines outside marked, fenced and monitored areas. It does prohibit the use (and transfer) of 'undetectable' anti-personnel mines, though the provision allows States Parties to opt to defer compliance for up to nine years after entry into force of amended Protocol II, and the impact of this provision on the ground is likely to be negligible in the near future.

It is clear that both 1980 Protocol II and amended Protocol II are based on a belief in the fundamental legitimacy of mine warfare. It assumed – wrongly for the most part – that even under battlefield conditions, 'responsible' use could be made of a weapon that clearly has a greater inherent tendency to strike civilian or combatant without discrimination than most other conventional weapons. Even when directly applicable, the limited prohibitions and restrictions contained in 1980 Protocol II were, for the most part, disregarded, including by a number of the relatively few States Parties to it. Consensus negotiations had ensured a lowest common denominator that was inadequate to confront the growing humanitarian crisis. Indeed, the failure of the First CCW Review Conference to address effectively the landmine problem was the catalyst, rather than the precursor, to the Ottawa Process and the Convention on the Prohibition of Anti-Personnel Mines.

The Convention on the Prohibition of Anti-Personnel Mines prohibits the use, production, transfer and stockpiling of anti-personnel mines. It prohibits both long-lived 'dumb' and self-destructing 'smart' anti-personnel mines. Although there is a certain lack of clarity as to the ambit of the definition of the weapons, the author believes that all weapons 'designed, altered or intended' to serve as anti-personnel mines as defined in Article 2(1) are prohibited under the Convention on the Prohibition on Anti-personnel Mines. This includes mines other than anti-personnel mines equipped with highly sensitive anti-handling devices that are detonated by the innocent act of a passer-by. Claymore 'mines' are also prohibited, unless used only in command-detonated mode. Unexploded ordnance, including cluster bomblets, are not covered by the Convention, nor are booby-traps. But a clearer definition is required of what in practice constitute booby-traps and anti-vehicle mines (especially the minimum weight needed to detonate an anti-vehicle mine); an Annual Meeting of States Parties to the Convention should address this issue at the earliest possible opportunity.

The obligation to enact implementing legislation at national level contained in the Convention is disappointingly weak. The lack of even a modified 'grave breaches' provision sets a poor precedent for the future implementation of international humanitarian law. Notwithstanding these lacunae, national implementing legislation remains important, including in countries where civilians as well as soldiers are involving in laying anti-personnel mines. Sadly, as the ICRC has found, a substantial number of countries have not yet enacted the necessary legislation to give effect at domestic level to obligations under the four 1949 Geneva Conventions.

With respect to universality of adherence to the Convention, 'the glass is more than half full.' But although some two-thirds of the world's States have signed the Convention and more than half have ratified it, it is rightly pointed out that a substantial number of key States remain outside its purview. Certainly of great concern is the claim by the International Campaign to Ban Landmines' *Landmine Monitor* that no less than 90 per cent of the world's estimated anti-personnel landmine stockpiles of 250 million mines are in the possession of non-signatory States.

Yet, although the absence of key States in the negotiation and adoption of the Convention on the Prohibition of Anti-Personnel Mines is regarded by some as a major failing, it is not fatal to the Convention's effectiveness. Moreover, it seems likely that despite prevarication, most major 'hold-out' States will join the Convention within the decade, or at least prohibit or severely restrict the use of anti-personnel mines. Thus, within the next few years, universality of at least the norm against the use of anti-personnel mines on the battlefield, if not the Convention itself, will probably be assured.

Hand in hand with universality of adherence goes respect for the norm created by the Convention on the Prohibition of Anti-Personnel Mines – the essence of the treaty, which is a prohibition of deployment on the battlefield. It is against this benchmark that the Convention must be judged. The signs so far are mixed. There is little evidence that States Parties have deliberately violated the core provisions of the Convention and clearly attested and fairly widespread use of anti-personnel mines by governmental armed forces has only been recorded in the case of Angola, a signatory, even though allegations have been made against other signatories and parties.

Yet, substantial deployments continued during 1999 and 2000 in a number of States, notably in the conflict between Eritrea and Ethiopia, in Kosovo and, within the Russian Federation, in and around Chechnya. The use of anti-personnel mines worldwide may be down – but it is not yet out.

4.3. The Implications for International Humanitarian Law of the Ottawa Process

In terms of lessons from the Ottawa Process, perhaps the most significant is that it marks a return to the traditional method of adopting international humanitarian law – one State leading a process that leads to the adoption of a treaty, if necessary by a vote. In this respect, the international community shortly faces another test. In December 2001, will be convened the Second Review Conference of the 1980 Convention on Conventional Weapons. The measures that the Conference ultimately adopts will clearly indicate what future role the United Nations should be given in the development of international humanitarian law and whether the Ottawa Process will mark the start of a new trend in the negotiation of international humanitarian law.

In sum, this work should have demonstrated that although the situation is grim, there is still hope for international humanitarian law, and there should be optimism that, with the requisite political will, certain particularly pernicious weapons can be controlled. That such legal regulation is not universal or universally successful does not undermine the rationale for its existence, just as the existence of crime does not negate the need for criminal law. In the words of Bill Fenrick: 'The advances made in the law of armed conflict are marginal, but real nevertheless. Marginal forward movements are probably the best that can be expected when humanitarian interests clash with military necessity at the vanishing point of law.'[1572]

[1572] Fenrick, W.J., "New Developments in the Law Concerning the Use of Conventional Weapons in Armed Conflict", *Canadian Yeaook of International Law*, Vol. 19, No. 19, 1981, p. 256.

5. BIBLIOGRAPHY

5.1. PUBLICATIONS

Adkin, M., *Goose Green*, Orion, UK, 1994.

Africa Watch, *Landmines in Angola*, New York, 1993

African Rights and Mines Advisory Group, *Violent Deeds Live On – Landmines in Somalia and Somaliland*, London, 1993.

Amar, G., *Deux Ans sur les mines*, La Nef de Paris Editions, undated.

Ambrose, S.E., *D-Day June 6, 1944: The Climactic Battle of World War II*, Simon & Schuster, New York, 1994.

Americas Watch, *Landmines in El Salvador and Nicaragua: The Civilian Victims*, Human Rights Watch, New York, December 1986.

Asia Watch and Physicians for Human Rights, *Land Mines in Cambodia. The Coward's War*, US, 1991.

Bailey, S.D., *Prohibitions and Restraints in War*, Oxford University Press, UK, 1972.

Balladore-Pallieri, *Diritto bellico*, 2nd edn., Milan, 1954.

Best, G., *War and Law Since 1945*, Clarendon Press, Oxford, 1994.

Best, G., *Humanity in Warfare*, Columbia University Press, New York, 1980.

Bilton, M. and Sim, K., *Four Hours in My Lai. A War Crime and its Aftermath*, Penguin, UK, 1992.

Bishop Jr., J.W., *Justice Under Fire. A Study of Military Law*, Charterhouse, New York, 1974.

Bloom, S. *et al* (eds.), *Hidden Casualties. Environmental, Health and Political Consequences of the Persian Gulf War*, Earthscan, London, 1994.

Boisson de Chazournes, L. *et al.* (eds.), *International Law, the International Court of Justice and Nuclear Weapons*, Cambridge University Press, Cambridge, UK, 1999.

Bothe, M. et al., *New Rules for Victims of Armed Conflicts. Commentary on the Two 1977 Additional Protocols Additional to the Geneva Conventions of 1949*, 1982.

Bottagliero, I., *120 Million Landmines Deployed Worldwide: Fact or Fiction*, Fondation Pro Victimis Geneva, UK, 2000.

Brasseys Inc., *Mine Warfare on Land*, London, March 1986.

Brierly, *The Law of Nations*, 6th edn. by Sir Humphrey Waldock, 1963.

Briggs, *The Law of Nations: Cases, Documents and Notes*, 2nd edn., 1952.

Brownlie, I., *Principles of Public International Law*, 4th edn., Clarendon Press, Oxford, 1990.

Brownlie, I., *Principles of Public International Law*, 5th edn., Clarendon Press, Oxford, 1998.

Cahill, K. (ed.), *Clearing the Fields. Solutions to the Global Land Mines Crisis*, Basic Books, US, 1995.

Cahill, K. (ed.), *A framework for survival: health, human rights and humanitarian assistance in conflicts and disasters*, Basic Books and the Council on Foreign Relations, New York, 1993.

Cameron, M.A. *et al.*, (eds.), *To Walk without Fear. The Global Movement to Ban Landmines*, Oxford University Press, Toronto, 1998.

Carell, P. *The Foxes of the Desert*, Transln. Savill, M., Bantam Books, US, 1967.

Cheng, B., *General Principles of Law as applied by International Courts and Tribunals*, Grotius Publications Limited, Cambridge, UK, 1987.

Croll, M., *The History of Landmines*, Leo Cooper, UK, 1998.

David, E., *Principes de droit des conflits armés*, Bruylant, Brussels, 1994.

Davies, P., *The War of the Mines: Cambodia, Landmines and the Impoverishment of a Nation*, Pluto Press, Colorado, 1994.

de la Billière, General Sir P., *Storm Command. A Personal Account of the Gulf War*, Harpers Collins Publishers, London, 1995.

De Mulinen, F., *Handbook on the Law of War for Armed Forces*, ICRC, Geneva, 1987.

Doswald-Beck, L. (ed.), *Blinding Weapons. Reports of the meetings of experts convened by the International Committee of the Red Cross on Battlefield Laser Weapons 1989-1991*, ICRC, Geneva, 1993.

Draft Rules for the Protection of the Civilian Population from the Dangers of Indiscriminate Warfare, ICRC, Geneva, June 1955.

Dupuy, T.N. (ed.), *The International Military and Defence Encyclopaedia*, Vol. 4, Brassey's, London, 1993.

Ffoulkes, C.J., *Arms and Armament*, Harrap & Co., London, 1945.

Field-Marshal Viscount Montgomery of Alamein, *The History of Warfare*, World Publishing Company, Cleveland, 1968.

Fleck, D. (ed.), *The Handbook of Humanitarian Law in Armed Conflicts*, Oxford University Press, US, 1995.

Foss, C.F. and Gander, T.J., *Jane's Military Vehicles and Logistics*, 15th edn., 1994-5, United Kingdom, 1994.

Garner, J.W., *International Law and the World War*, London, 1920.

Gilbert, F., *Hitler Directs His War: the Secret Records of His Daily Military Conferences*, Oxford University Press, New York, 1950.

Greenspan, M., *The Modern Law of Land Warfare*, University of California Press, Berkeley and Los Angeles, 1959.

Hammond Jr., J.W., *Poison Gas, The Myths Versus Reality*, Greenwood Press, Westport, 1999.

Handicap International, *Landmines in Vietnam, The Coward's War*, Brussels, 1996.

Harber, D., *Improvised Land Mines: Their Employment and Destructive Capabilities*, Paladin Press, 1992.

Harris, D.J., *Cases and Materials on International Law*, 4th edn., Sweet & Maxwell, London, 1991.

Harris, D.J., *Cases and Materials on International Law*, 5th edn., Sweet & Maxwell, London, 1998.

Healy, M., *Kursk 1943, The Tide Turns in the East*, Osprey Military Campaign Series No 16.

Heyde, *International Law, Chiefly as Interpreted and Applied by the United States*, 2nd edn., 1945, Vol. 3.

Human Rights Watch, *Landmines in Mozambique*, New York, 1994.

Human Rights Watch Arms Project, *Still Killing: Landmines in Southern Africa*, US, 1997.

Human Rights Watch and Physicians for Human Rights, *Landmines, A Deadly Legacy*, HRW, New York, October 1993.

ICBL, *Landmine Monitor Report 1999, Toward a Mine-Free World*, Human Rights Watch, Washington DC, April 1999.

ICBL, *Landmine Monitor Report 2000, Toward a Mine-Free World*, Human Rights Watch, Washington DC, August 2000.

ICRC, *Draft Rules for the Limitation of the Dangers Incurred by the Civilian Population in Time of War*, 2nd edn., ICRC, Geneva, April 1958.

ICRC, *Final Record concerning the Draft Rules for the Limitation of the Dangers Incurred by the Civilian Population in Time of War*, ICRC, Geneva, April 1958.

ICRC, *Anti-Personnel Landmines: Friend or Foe, A Study of the Military Use and Effectiveness of Anti-Personnel Mines*, ICRC, Geneva, 1996.

ICRC, *Weapons that may cause unnecessary suffering or have indiscriminate effects. Report of the work of experts*, ICRC, Geneva, 1973.

ICRC, *Report on the Conference of Government Experts on the Use of Certain Conventional Weapons (Lucerne, 24 September – 18 October 1974)*, ICRC, Geneva, 1975.

ICRC, *Report on the Conference of Government Experts on the Use of Certain Conventional Weapons, Second Session (Lugano, 28 January – 26 February 1976)*, ICRC, Geneva, 1976.

ICRC, *Fundamental rules of international humanitarian law applicable in armed conflicts*, International Committee of the Red Cross and the League of Red Cross Societies, Geneva, 1979.

ICRC, *International Law Concerning the Conduct of Hostilities, Collection of Hague Conventions and Some Other Treaties*, ICRC, Geneva, 1989.

ICRC, *Anti-Personnel mines in Central America*, ICRC, Geneva, February 1996.

ICRC, *Seminario Regional Sobre Minas Terrestras Antipersonel, El Desminado y La Rehabilitación*, ICRC, Guatemala, 1997.

Jackson, R., *High-Tech Warfare, The Weaponry Explained*, Headline Book Publishing, London, 1991.

Johnson, J.T., *Can Modern War Be Just?*, Yale University Press, New Haven and London, 1984.

Kalshoven, F., *Constraints on the Waging of War*, 2nd edn., ICRC, Geneva, 1991.

Khadduri, M., *War and Peace in the Law of Islam*, 1955.

King, C. (ed.), *Jane's Mines and Mine Clearance 1997-1998*, Jane's, UK, 1998.

Kirk, J. and Young, R., *Great Weapons of World War II*, 1961.

Krutzsch, W. & Trapp, R., *A Commentary on the Chemical Weapons Convention*, Martinus Nijhoff, Dordrecht, 1994.

Lauterpacht, H., *International Law, A Treatise*, 7th edn., Longman, Green and Co., London, 1948.

Lauterpacht, H., *Oppenheim's International Law*, 7th edn., 1952, Vol. II.

Leckie, R., *Okinawa, The Last Battle of World War II*, Viking, US, 1995.

Lenarcic, D.A., *Knight-Errant? Canada and the Crusade to Ban Anti-Personnel Land Mines*, Contemporary Affairs Number 2, Irwin Publishing, Toronto, Canada, 1998.

Lewer, N. and Schofield, S., *Non-Lethal Weapons: A Fatal Attraction? Military Strategies and Technologies for 21st-Century Conflict*, Zed Books, London and New Jersey, 1997.

Maley, W., (ed.), *Dealing with Mines, Strategies for Peacekeepers, Aid Agencies and the International Community*, Australian Defence Studies Centre, Canberra, 1994.

Maresca, L. and Maslen, S. (eds.), *The Banning of Anti-Personnel Landmines, The Work of the International Committee of the Red Cross 1955-1999*, Cambridge University Press, Cambridge, UK, October 2000.

McCoubrey, H., and White, N.D., *International Law and Armed Conflict*, Dartmouth Publishing Co., Aldershot, 1992.

McCoubrey, H., *International Humanitarian Law, The Regulation of Armed Conflicts*, Dartmouth Publishing Co., UK, 1990.

McManners, H., *The Scars of War*, Harpers Collins, London, 1993.

Meron, T., *Henry's Wars and Shakespeare's Laws*, 1993.

Meron, T., *Human Rights and Humanitarian Norms as Customary Law*, Clarendon Press, Oxford, 1991.

Middle East Watch, *Hidden Death: Land Mines and Civilian Casualties in Iraqi Kurdistan*, HRW, New York, 1992.

National Research Council, *Copies of Alternative Technologies to Replace Antipersonnel Landmines*, National Academy Press, Washington DC, March 2001. *The New Oxford Dictionary of English*, Clarendon Press, Oxford, UK, 1998.

O'Connell, R.L., *Of Arms and Men*, Oxford University Press, Oxford, 1990.

Oman, C., *The Art of War in the Middle Ages, Volume One: 378-1278AD*, Greenhill, London, 1991.

Pakenham-Walsh, Maj.-Gen. R.P., *The History of the Corps of Royal Engineers*, Vol. X, Institute of Royal Engineers, Chatham, 1986.

Parker, G. (ed.), *The Cambridge Illustrated History of Warfare, The Triumph of the West*, Cambridge University Press, Cambridge, UK, 1995.

Perry, M.F., *Infernal Machines, The Story of Confederate Submarine and Mine Warfare*, Louisiana State University Press, Baton Rouge, US, 1985.

Phillipson, C., *International Law and Custom of Ancient Greece and Rome*, Macmillan & Co., 1911.

Physicians for Human Rights, *Hidden Enemies: Land Mines in Northern Somalia*, Boston, November 1992.

Pictet, J.S. (ed.), *Commentary, III Geneva Convention Relative to the Treatment of Prisoners of War*, ICRC, Geneva, 1960.

Prokosch, E., *The Technology of Killing, A Military and Political History of Antipersonnel Weapons*, Zed Books, London and New Jersey, 1995.

Reisman, W.M., and Antoniou, C.T. (eds.), *The Laws of War, A Comprehensive Collection of Primary Documents on International Laws governing Armed Conflict*, Vintage Books, New York, 1994.

Roberts, A. and Guelff, R. (eds.), *Documents on the Laws of War*, 3rd edn., Oxford University Press, Oxford, UK, 2000.

Roberts, A. and Guelff, R. (eds.), *Documents on the Laws of War*, 2nd edn., Clarendon Press, Oxford, UK, 1989.

Roberts, S. and Williams, J., *After the Guns Fall Silent, The Enduring Legacy of Landmines*, Vietnam Veterans of America Foundation, Washington DC, 1995.

Rupiah, M., *Deadly Legacy: Landmines in Zimbabwe*, Southern Africa Political and Economic Series, Harare, 1998.

Sandoz, Y. *et al.* (eds.), *Commentary on the Additional Protocols of 8 June 1977 to the Geneva Conventions of 12 August 1949*, ICRC/Martinus Nijhoff, Geneva, 1987.

Sandoz, Y., *Des armes interdites en droit de la guerre*, Thesis presented to Neuchâtel University, Imprimerie Grounauer, Geneva, 1975.

Schindler, D. and Toman, J., *The Laws of Armed Conflicts*, Martinus Nijhoff, The Netherlands, 1988.

School of Military Engineering, *The Work of the Royal Engineers in the European War 1914-19*, SME, Chatham, UK, 1924.

Schwarzenberger, G., *International Law as Applied by International Courts and Tribunals*, Vol. II, Sweet & Maxwell, London, 1968.

Schwarzkopf, N., and Petre, P. (ed.), *It Doesn't Take A Hero*, Mass Market Paperbacks, US, 1992.

Scott, J.B. (ed.), *The Hague Conventions and Declarations of 1899 and 1907*, 3rd edn., Oxford University Press, New York, 1918.

Scott, J.B., *The Proceedings of the Hague Peace Conferences: the Conference of 1899*, Oxford University Press, New York, 1920.

Sherman, W.T., *Memoirs of William T. Sherman*, Appleton & Co., US, 1875.

Sinclair, Sir I., *The Vienna Convention on the Law of Treaties*, 2nd edn., Manchester University Press, 1984.

Sloan, Lt.-Col. C.E.E., *Mine Warfare on Land*, Brassey's, London, 1986.

Solf, W.A. and Roach, J.A., *Index of International Humanitarian Law*, ICRC, Geneva, 1992.

Starke, J.G., *Introduction to International Law*, 10th edn., Butterworths, London, 1989.

Stockholm International Peace Research Institute, *Anti-Personnel Weapons*, Taylor & Francis, London, 1978.

Stockholm International Peace Research Institute, *The Law of War and Dubious Weapons*, Almqvist & Wiskell International, Stockholm, 1976.

Stone, J., *Legal Controls of International Conflict*, 2nd edn., Maitland Publications, Sydney, 1954.

Strupp-Schlochauer, *Wörterbuch des Völkerrechts*, Vol. 2, Berlin, 1960-1962.

Swinarski, C. (ed.), *Studies and essays on international humanitarian law and Red Cross principles*, ICRC/Martinus Nijhoff, Geneva/The Hague, 1984.

United States Department of State, *Hidden Killers: the Global Problem with Uncleared Landmines, a Report on International Demining*, Washington DC, 1993.

United States Department of State, *Hidden Killers: the Global Landmine Crisis*, Washington DC, 1994.

Verri, P., *Dictionary of the International Law of Armed Conflict*, ICRC, Geneva, 1992.

Westing, A.H. (ed.), *Explosive remnants of war: mitigating the environmental effects*, SIPRI & UNEP, London, 1985.

Wulff, T., *Barriers Against Weapons, Development of Weapons and Restrictions on Their Use*, Swedish Red Cross, Stockholm, 1984.

Würkner-Theis, G., *Fernverlegte Minen und humanitäres Völkerrecht*, Peter Lang, Frankfurt am main, 1990.

Zatylkin, B.V., *The Occupation of Sapper*, Dosaaf SSR, Moscow, 1978.

5.2. Articles, Monographs, Reports, and Statements

"A Draft Convention to Prohibit Biological and Chemical Weapons Under International Criminal Law", *The CBW Conventions Bulletin*, No. 42, December 1998.

Abdel Salam, A.A., *The Effects of the Second World War Remnants on the Economic Development in Libya*, Paper submitted to the Symposium on Material Remnants of the Second World War on Libyan Soil, UNITAR, Geneva, 28 April – 1 May 1981.

Akehurst, "Custom as a Source of International Law", *British Yearbook of International Law*, Vol. XLVII, 1974-5.

Albright, M.K., *Prepared Statement before the Senate Foreign Relations Committee*, 8 April 1997.

Alder, "Modern Land Mine Warfare", *Armada International*, Vol. 6, 1980.

Aldrich, G.H., *Establishing Legal Norms Through Multilateral Negotiation – The Laws of War*, Report submitted to a Geneva Conference of International Lawyers, 1977.

Aldrich, G.H., *Report of the United States Delegation to the Diplomatic Conference on the Reaffirmation and Development of International Humanitarian Law Applicable in Armed Conflicts*, Report submitted to the US Secretary of State, 8 September 1977.

Aleu, A.A., "Landmine Information Sudan", Operation Save Innocent Lives, Nairobi, 8 January 1999.

Andersson, N., da Sousa, C.P., Paredes, S., "Social cost of land mines in four countries: Afghanistan, Bosnia, Cambodia and Mozambique", *British Medical Journal*, 16 September 1995, Vol. 311.

"Anti-Personnel Mines", Appendix 38, *Memorandum by General Sir Hugh Beach to the Foreign Affairs Select Committee*, (HMSO, 1995).

Antoine, P., "International humanitarian law and the protection of the environment in time of armed conflict", *International Review of the Red Cross*, ICRC, Geneva.

Araujo, R.J., "Anti-Personnel Mines and Peremptory Norms of International Law: Argument and Catalyst", *Vanderbilt Journal of Transnational Law*, Vol. 30, January 1997.

Arkin, W.M., "Treaty Barriers are within US, not in Korean fields", *San Jose Mercury News*, 20 September 1997.

Ary, Maj. V.A., "Concluding Hostilities: Humanitarian Provisions in Cease-Fire Agreements", *Military Law Review*, Vol. 148, Spring 1995.

Atwood, D.C., "Implementing Ottawa: Continuity and Change in the Roles of NGOs in the Struggle to Eliminate Anti-Personnel Landmines and Overcome their Effects", UNIDIR, *Disarmament Review*, No. 4, 1999.

Aubert, M., "The International Committee of the Red Cross and the problem of excessively injurious or indiscriminate weapons", *International Review of the Red Cross*, November-December 1990, No. 279.

Background Paper submitted by the Netherlands delegation to the January 1996 session of the Review Conference, *UN Doc. CCW/CONF.I/CRP.5* of 18 January 1996.

Baker, B., "Legal Protections for the Environment in Times of Armed Conflict", *Virginia Journal of International Law*, No. 33 (Winter 1993).

Basso, Dr. L., *Advisory Opinion*, Paper submitted to the Symposium on Material Remnants of the Second World War on Libyan Soil, UNITAR, Geneva, 28 April – 1 May 1981.

Baxter, R.R. and Burgenthal, T., "Legal Aspects of the Geneva Protocol of 1925", *American Journal of International Law*, Vol. 64, October 1970.

Baxter, R.R., "Multilateral Treaties as Evidence of Customary International Law", *British Yearbook of International Law*, Vol. 41, No. 275, (1965-66).

Baxter, R.R., "Criteria of the Prohibition of Weapons in International Law", Ehmke, H. *et al.* (eds.), *Festschrift für Ulrich Scheuner zum 70. Geburtstag*, Duncker & Humblot, Berlin, 1973.

Belgian Ministry of Foreign Affairs, Ministry of National Defence and General Department for Development Cooperation, *Belgium's Position Regarding Action Against Anti-Personnel Mines*, Brussels, April 1999.

Biddle, S.D., and Klare, J., "Military Utility and the Control of Land Mines", *UNIDIR Newsletter*, Nos. 28/29, 12.94/05.95.

Bindschedler, R. L., "Treaties, Reservations", *Encyclopaedia of International Law*, North Holland, Amsterdam, 1984.

Blagden, P.M., "Mine Clearance", *UNIDIR Newsletter*, Nos. 28/29, 12.94/05.95.

Blagden, P., *New Technologies for Humanitarian Demining*, Presentation to the Tokyo Conference on Mine Clearance and Victim Assistance, March 1997.

Bleckmann, A., "Self-Executing Treaty Provisions", *Encyclopaedia of International Law*, North Holland, Amsterdam, 1984.

Blischchenko, Dr. I.P., *The Legal Basis of Claims for Damage to the Environment Resulting from Military Action*, Paper submitted to the Symposium on Material Remnants of the Second World War on Libyan Soil, UNITAR, Geneva, 28 April – 1 May 1981.

Blix, H., "Means and Methods of Combat", UNESCO, *International Dimensions of International Humanitarian Law*, Henry Dunant Institute, Geneva, 1988.

Blix, H., "Current Efforts to Prohibit the Use of Certain Conventional Weapons", *Instant Research on Peace and Violence*, Vol. IV, No. 1.

Bond, J.E., "Internal Conflict and Article Three of the Geneva Conventions", *Denver Law Journal*, Vol. 48, No. 2, 1971.

Bothe, M., *The Protection of the Environment in Times of Armed Conflict: Legal Rules, Uncertainty, Deficiencies and Possible Developments*, Revised paper submitted to the meeting of experts convened by the Government of Canada, Ottawa, July 10-12 1992.

Bourgeois, J., *Universalisation of the Ottawa Process, Contribution of the Conference on Disarmament to the Elimination of Anti-Personnel Mines*, Ottawa, 3 December 1997.

Boutros-Ghali, B., "The Land Mine Crisis: A Humanitarian Disaster", *Foreign Affairs*, Vol. 73, No. 5, September/October 1994.

Boutros-Ghali, B., *Message to the Symposium, Clearing the Fields: Solutions to the Land Mine Crisis*, New York, 29 April 1994.

Bretton, "Principes humanitaires et impératifs militaires dans le domaine des armes classiques à travers le droit international actuel", *Société Française pour le Droit International, Colloque de Montpellier – le droit international et les armes*, 1983.
Brown, B.L., "The Proportionality Principle in the Humanitarian Law of Warfare: Recent Efforts at Codification", *Cornell International Law Journal*, Vol. 10, 1976.
Bulletin of Peace Proposals, "Arms Control Agreements and Humanitarian Laws of War", *Bulletin of Peace Proposals*, Vol. 17, Nos. 3/4, 1986.
Canadian Department of Foreign Affairs and International Trade, "A Global Ban on Landmines", Fact Sheet, undated.
Cantrell, C.L., "Civilian Protection in Internal Armed Conflicts: The Second Diplomatic Conference", *Texas International Law Journal*, Vol. 11, 1976.
Carnahan, B.M. and Robertson, M., "The Protocol on 'Blinding Laser Weapons': A New Direction for International Humanitarian Law", *American Journal of International Law*, Vol. 90, July 1996.
Carnahan, B.M., "Unnecessary Suffering, the Red Cross and Tactical Laser Weapons", *Loyola of Los Angeles International and Comparative Law Journal*, Vol. 18, September 1996.
Carnahan, Lt.-Col. B.M., "The Law of Land Mine Warfare: Protocol II to the United Nations Convention on Certain Conventional Weapons", *Military Law Review*, Vol. 105, Summer 1984.
Cassese, A., "The Status of Rebels under the 1977 Geneva Protocol on Non-International Armed Conflicts", *International and Comparative Law Quarterly*, Vol. 30, April 1981.
Cassese, A., "The Geneva Protocols of 1977 on the Humanitarian Law of Armed Conflict and Customary International Law", *UCLA Pacific Basin Law Journal*, Spring and Fall 1984, Vol. 3, Nos. 1 & 2.
Cassese, A., "Weapons causing unnecessary suffering. Are they prohibited?", *Rivista di Diritto Internazionale*, Vol. 48, 1975.
Cassese, A., "Means of Warfare, The Present and Emerging Law", *Revue Belge de Droit International*, Vol. XII, 1976.
Cauderay, G.C., "Anti-Personnel Mines", *International Review of the Red Cross*, No. 295, July-August 1993, Geneva.
Center for Security Policy, "Too Clever by Half: Bob Bell's Sophistry Must Not be Allowed to Jeopardise US Military's Ability To Use Landmines", *Decision Brief No 97-D 142*, Washington DC, 24 September 1997.
Cestac, R., *The Technical Aspects Related to Material Remnants of War in Libyan Battlefields*, Paper submitted to the Symposium on Material Remnants of the Second World War on Libyan Soil, UNITAR, Geneva, 28 April – 1 May 1981.
Ceva, L., *The Influence of Mines and Minefields in the North African Campaign of 1940-1943*, Paper presented to the Symposium on Material Remnants of the Second World War on Libyan Soil, Geneva, 28 April – 1 May 1981.
Chair's Summary, *Years Not Decades: Agenda for Mine Action II*, Mine Action Coordination Workshop, Ottawa, Canada, 23-24 March 1998.
Chairman's Summary, International Workshop on Humanitarian Demining and Mine Stockpile Elimination, Minsk, Belarus, 6-7 March 2000.
Charney, J., "Customary International Law in the Nicaragua Judgement on the Merits", *Hague Yearbook of International Law*, Vol. 16, 1988.
Chawla, S., "Diffusion of Landmines in Afghanistan", article distributed on the MGM Network, E-mail by Hendrik Ehlers, 13 October 2000.
"China's Position on APL", Statement submitted by Mr. Song Rong Hua, Second Secretary of the Embassy of the People's Republic of China in Japan at the 3rd NGO Tokyo Conference on AP mines organized by Association to Aid Refugees, Japan held on 28-29 November 1998 in Tokyo.
Colonel E. Fitch, *Presentation to the ICRC Seminar on the Humanitarian Impact and Military Utility of Anti-Personnel Mines*, Budapest, 26-28 March 1998.
Conference of Government Experts on the Use of Certain Conventional Weapons (Lugano, 28.1 – 26.2.1976), Report, ICRC, Geneva, 1976.
Conference of Government Experts on the Use of Certain Conventional Weapons (Lucerne, 24.9 – 18.10.1974), Report, ICRC, Geneva, 1975.
Cornish, P., *Anti-Personnel Mines, Controlling the Plague of 'Butterflies'*, Royal Institute for International Affairs, London, 1994.

Coupland, Dr. R.M., "The effect of weapons: defining superfluous injury or unnecessary suffering", *Medicine and Global Survival*, Vol. 3, 1 March 1996.

Coupland, Dr. R.M. (ed.), *The SIrUS Project, Towards a determination of which weapons cause 'superfluous injury or unnecessary suffering'*, ICRC, Geneva, 1997.

Coupland, Dr. R.M., *Assistance for Victims of Anti-Personnel Mines: Needs, Constraints and Strategy*, ICRC, Geneva, June 1997.

Coupland, Dr. R.M., *The effects of weapons: surgical challenge and medical dilemma*, The Prestigious Lecture, Royal College of Surgeons of Edinburgh, 6 October 1995.

Coupland, Dr. R.M., "Abhorrent weapons and 'superfluous injury or unnecessary suffering': from field surgery to law", *British Medical Journal*, Vol. 315, 29 November 1997.

D'Amato, A., "Good Faith", *Encyclopaedia of International Law*, North Holland, Amsterdam, 1984.

David, E., "The Opinion of the International Court of Justice on the legality of the use of nuclear weapons", *International Review of the Red Cross*, January-February 1997.

Davies, P., "Mines and Unexploded Ordnance in Cambodia and Laos: Understanding the Costs", Kumar, K. (ed.), *Rebuilding Societies After Civil War, Critical Roles for International Assistance*, Lynne Rienner, US, 1997.

De Mulinen, F., "A propos de la Conférence de Lucerne et Lugano sur l'emploi de certaines armes conventionelles", *Annales d'études internationales 1977, Droit humanitaire et protection de l'homme*, Vol. 8.

De Albuquerque, C., *La guerre après la guerre: le droit international et les limites à l'utilisation de mines antipersonnel*, Mémoire pour l'obtention du Diplôme d'Etudes supérieures en relations internationales, Geneva, October 1996.

Department of the Army Field Manual FM 27-10, *The Law of Land Warfare*, Department of the Army, Washington DC, July 1956.

DHA Factsheet on Manufacturing and Trade, New York, 1996.

Dörmann, K., "The first Review Conference to the 1980 Convention on Prohibitions or Restrictions on the Use of Certain Conventional Weapons Which May Be Deemed to be Excessively Injurious or to Have Indiscriminate Effects: a story of failure?", *Humanitäres Völkerrecht*, Vol. 8, No. 4, 1995.

Doswald-Beck, L., "International humanitarian law and the Advisory of the International Court on the legality of the threat or use of nuclear weapons", *International Review of the Red Cross*, January-February 1997.

Doswald-Beck, L. and Cauderay, G.C., "The development of new anti-personnel weapons", *International Review of the Red Cross*, November-December 1990, No. 279.

Doswald-Beck, L. and Herby, P., "Land Mines: A Critical Examination of Existing Legal Instruments", *UNIDIR Newsletter*, No. 28/29, 12.94/05.95.

Doswald-Beck, L., "New Protocol on Blinding Laser Weapons", *International Review of the Red Cross*, May-June 1996.

Downey, Jr., W.G., "The Law of War and Military Necessity", *American Journal of International Law*, Vol. 47, 1953.

Draft Rules of Procedure, Diplomatic Conference on a Convention on the Prohibition of the Use, Stockpiling, Production and Transfer of Anti-Personnel Mines and on Their Destruction, *APL/CRP.2*, Oslo, 1 September 1997.

Draper, G.I.A.D., "The Emerging Law of Weapons Restraint", *Survival*, International Institute for Strategic Studies, January/February 1997.

Duval-Destin, M., "La lutte contre les mines: un élément clé pour la résolution des crises futures", *L'Armement*, Vol. 40, December 1993.

Editorial, *De-mining Debate*, South African Institute of International Affairs, Issue III, 29 November 1999.

Edwards, R., "Humane Killing", *New Scientist*, 4 December 1999.

Ekberg, P.J., "Remotely Delivered Landmines and International Law", *Columbia Journal of Transnational Law*, Vol. 33, 1995.

El-Saghir, K., *The Damage of the Second World War Remnants and Their Effects on Agriculture and Agricultural Development in The Libyan Arab Social People's Jamahiriya*, Paper submitted to the Symposium on Material Remnants of the Second World War on Libyan Soil, UNITAR, Geneva, 28 April – 1 May 1981.

Elliot, G., "Mine Clearance in Cambodia", *Discussion Document*, South African Institute of International Affairs, undated but 2000.

Enderberg, Lt.-Col. B., *The Disposal of Material Remnants of Wars*, Paper submitted to the Symposium on Material Remnants of the Second World War on Libyan Soil, UNITAR, Geneva, 28 April – 1 May 1981.

Engineer Agency for Resource Inventories, *Landmine and Countermine Warfare, Korea, 1950-54*, Vol. 5.

EU, "Declaration by the Presidency on behalf of the European Union on Angola", Vienna, 28 December 1998.

Falk, R., "The Environmental Law of War: An Introduction", Plant, G. (ed.), *Environmental Protection and the Law of War: A 'Fifth Geneva' Convention on the Protection of the Environment in Time of Armed Conflict*, Belhaven Press, London and New York, 1992.

Farer, T.J., "Illicit Means for the Conduct of Armed Conflicts", *Revue de droit pénal militaire et du droit de la guerre*, Vol. XII, No. 2, 1973.

Faulkner, F., "Anti-Personnel landmines: a necessary evil?", *International Relations*, Vol. XIII, No. 4, April 1997.

Fenrick, W.J., "The Conventional Weapons Convention: A modest but useful treaty", *International Review of the Red Cross*, November-December 1990, No. 279.

Fenrick, W.J., "New Developments in the Law Concerning the Use of Conventional Weapons in Armed Conflict", *Canadian Yearbook of International Law*, Vol. 19, No. 19, 1981.

Fenrick, W.J., "The Law of Armed Conflict: The CUSHIE Weapons Treaty", *Canadian Defence Quarterly*, Vol. 11, 1981.

Fenrick, W.J., "The Rule of Proportionality and Protocol I in Conventional Warfare", *Military Law Review*, Vol. 98, 1982.

Final Declaration by Colombia, Oslo Diplomatic Conference 1-19 September 1997, *APL/CRP.5/Attach.16*.

Fitzmaurice, "Law and Procedure of the International Court of Justice, 1951-4: Treaty interpretation and other treaty points", *British Yearbook of International Law*, Vol. 33 (1957).

Fredenburg, Maj. P.W., "The Banning of the Antipersonnel Landmines", *Canadian Defense Quarterly*, Winter 1997.

Ganado, Prof. J.M., *Some Reflections on Certain Private Law Principles and an Exposition of the Dispute Concerning War Remnants in Malta*, Paper submitted to the Symposium on Material Remnants of the Second World War on Libyan Soil, UNITAR, Geneva, 28 April – 1 May 1981.

Gander, T.J., "Land mine warfare – the British position", *Jane's Defence Review*, Vol. 4, No. 6, 1983.

Gander, T.J., "The Underground World of the Land Mine", *Jane's Military Review 1983/4*.

Gard, R., "Ban Land Mines Save Lives", *Defense News*, 25-31 August 1997.

Gard Jr., R.G., "Alternatives to Anti-Personnel Mines", Vietnam Veterans Monograph Series, Vol. 1, No. 1, Spring 1999, Washington.

Gasser, H.P., "For Better Protection of the Natural Environment in Armed Conflict: A Proposal for Action", *The American Journal of International Law*, Vol. 89, July 1995.

Goose, S.D., "The Ottawa Process and the 1997 Mine Ban Treaty", *Yearbook of International Humanitarian Law*, Vol. 1, Asser Press, 1998.

Goose, S., "The Economics of Land Mines", *UNIDIR Newsletter*, Nos. 28/29, 12.94/05.95.

Gourley, S., "Towards the 'Smart' Mine", *Jane's Defence Weekly*, 19 July 2000.

Gowdey, D., "The Land Mine Crisis: The Humanitarian Dimension", *UNIDIR Newsletter*, Nos. 28/29, 12.94/05.95.

Green, L.C., "What one may do in combat – Then and Now", Delissen, A.J.M. and Tanja, G.J., (eds.), *Humanitarian Law of Armed Conflict: Challenges Ahead*, Martinus Nijhoff Publishers, Dordrecht, 1991.

Green, L.C., "The Environment and the Law of Conventional Warfare", *Canadian Yearbook of International Law*, Vol. 29, 1991.

Greenwood, C., "Humanitarian Law and Laws of War", *Centennial of the First International Peace Conference, Preliminary Report*, June 1998.

Greenwood, C., "The Advisory Opinion on nuclear weapons and the contribution of the International Court to international humanitarian law", *International Review of the Red Cross*, No. 316 (January-February 1997), ICRC, Geneva.

Greenwood, C., "Customary Law Status of the 1977 Geneva Protocols", Delissen, A.J.M. & Tanja, G.J. (eds.), *Humanitarian Law of Armed Conflict. Essays in Honour of F. Kalshoven*, Martinus Nijhoff, Dordrecht, The Netherlands, 1991.

Greville (RL), Brig. P.J., *Why Australia Should Not Ratify the New Law of War*, Working Paper No. 175, Australian National University Strategic and Defence Studies Centre, Canberra, January 1989.

Guthrie, R., "The Chemical Weapons Convention: a Guide", Poole, J.B. and Guthrie, R. (eds.), *Verification 1993, Peacekeeping, Arms Control and the Environment*, Brassey's/Vertic, UK, 1993.

Herczegh, G., "La protection de l'environnement naturel et le droit humanitaire", Swinarski, C. (ed.), *Studies and essays on international humanitarian law and Red Cross principles in honour of Jean Pictet*, International Committee of the Red Cross and Martinus Nijhoff Publishers, Geneva and The Hague, 1984.

Hajnoczi, T., Panel Presentation, "Toward a Ban: The Ottawa Treaty, An Overview", in ICBL, Regional Conference on Landmines, Budapest, Hungary, 26-28 March 1998, *ICBL Conference Report*.

Hampson, F., *Anti-Personnel Mines and the Law: The Legal Background*, Paper presented to the NGO Conference on Anti-Personnel Mines, London, 24-26 May 1993.

Hampson, F., *The Long Shadow C Landmines and the Law of Armed Conflicts*, Papers in the Theory and Practice of Human Rights, No. 12, University of Essex, Colchester, January 1995.

Herby, P., "Third Session of the Review Conference of States Parties to the 1980 United Nations Convention on Certain Conventional Weapons (CCW) – Geneva, 22 April-3 May 1996", *International Review of the Red Cross*, No. 312, May-June 1996.

Hewish, M. and Pengelley, R., "In search of a successor to the anti-personnel landmine, Non-lethal weapons, precision weapons and close surveillance", *Jane's International Defense Review*, March 1998.

Heyman, C., *Trends in Land Mine Warfare*, Jane's Information group, UK, August 1995.

Hinge, A., "Mine Warfare in Australia's first line of defence", *Canberra Papers on Strategy and Defence*, Australian National University, Canberra, 1992.

Hingorani, R.C., "Land Mines: military weapon or menace?", *India Quarterly*, Vol. 52, Nos. 1-2, January-June 1996.

Huber, M., "Quelques considérations sur une révision éventuelle des Conventions de La Haye relatives à la guerre", *International Review of the Red Cross*, 1955, Vol. 2.

Hughes-Morgan, Col. Sir D., *Legal Criteria for the Restriction of Use of Categories of Conventional Weapons*, Paper presented to the Lucerne Weapons Conference.

Hughes-Morgan, Brig. Sir D., "The protection of the civilian population in international armed conflicts; general aspects", *Lecture given to the International Symposium of the Netherlands Red Cross on the Protocols of 1977 additional to the Conventions of Geneva of 1949*, The Hague, 25-26 September 1978.

Human Rights Watch Arms Project and Vietnam Veterans of America Foundation, *In Its Own Words, The US Army and Antipersonnel Mines in the Korean and Vietnam Wars*, Washington, July 1997.

Human Rights Watch, *Landmines in International Law: Why is a Complete Ban Required?*, Memorandum, 4 March 1994.

Human Rights Watch Arms Project, *Killers in the Commonwealth: Antipersonnel Landmine Policies of the Commonwealth Nations*, US, October 1997.

ICBL Working Group on Victim Assistance, *Guidelines for the Care and Rehabilitation of Survivors*, undated but 1999.

ICBL, *Report on Activities, Review Conference of the Convention on Conventional Weapons, 2nd resumed session*, Geneva, undated.

ICBL Statement to the First Conference of States Parties to Amended Protocol II of the Convention on Certain Conventional Weapons, Geneva, 15 December 1999.

ICBL Statement to Oslo Diplomatic Conference, "Say No to the US Demand for a Korea Exception", September 1997.

ICBL, "Report on Activities, Diplomatic Conference on an International Total Ban on Antipersonnel Landmines", November 1997.

ICBL, campaign leaflet, Human Rights Watch, Washington, March 1999.

ICBL, *Report on Activities: Diplomatic Conference on an International Total Ban on Anti-Personnel Landmines.*

ICBL Mine Action Working Group, "Statement of Facts", ICBL, 1998.

"ICRC appeal following the entry into force of the Convention on Prohibitions and Restrictions on the Use of Certain Conventional Weapons", *International Review of the Red Cross*, No. 238, January-February 1984.

ICRC, "The International Committee of the Red Cross and Disarmament", *International Review of the Red Cross*, March-April 1978.

ICRC, "'Review Conference of the 1980 United Nations Convention on Prohibitions or Restrictions on the Use of Certain Conventional Weapons', The Issues, The ICRC's position", *International Review of the Red Cross*, July-August 1995, No. 307.

ICRC, "Report of the ICRC for the Review Conference of the 1980 UN Convention on Certain Conventional Weapons", *International Review of the Red Cross*, ICRC, Geneva, March-April 1994.

ICRC, *Implementing the Ottawa Treaty: National Legislation*, ICRC, Geneva, April 1999.

ICRC, *Blinding Weapons*, Campaign leaflet, ICRC, Geneva, 1995.

ICRC, *Report on the Symposium on Anti-Personnel Mines, Montreux, 21-23 April 1993*, ICRC, Geneva, 1993.

ICRC, *Explosive Remnants of War, Cluster Bombs and Landmines in Kosovo*, ICRC, Geneva, August 2000.

ICRC, *Anti-Vehicle Mines Equipped with Anti-Handling Devices*, Information Paper, Geneva, April 1999.

ICRC, "Summary Report", South Asia Regional Seminar on Landmines, Wadduwa, Sri Lanka, 18-20 August 1999.

ICRC, *The worldwide epidemic of landmine injuries: The ICRC's health oriented approach*, ICRC, Geneva, 1995.

ICRC, *A Silent Menace: Landmines in Bosnia and Herzegovina*, ICRC/UNHCR, Geneva, March 1998.

ICRC, Landmines, Crucial Decisions in 1997, *ICRC Position Paper*, Geneva, January 1997.

ICRC, Comments on the Third Austrian Draft (13/5/97) of the Convention on the Prohibition of Anti-Personnel Mines, *Informal Working Paper for the Oslo Negotiations*, Geneva, September 1997.

ICRC Newsletter, ICRC Sri Lanka, No. 2, December 1997, <http://www.icrc.org>.

Institute for Defence Analyses (IDA), "The Military Utility of Landmines: Implications for Arms Control", *Document D-1559*, June 1994.

International Federation of Red Cross and Red Crescent Societies, *Assistance to Victims of Anti-Personnel Mines, A Federation Discussion Paper*, Geneva, 1993.

Italian Chamber of Deputies, *Rules for the Ban of Anti-Personnel mines, Italian Law No 374 of 29 October 1997*, Occhetto, undated.

Jesuit Refugee Service, Mines Advisory Group, Medico International, and the Vietnam Veterans of America Foundation, "Landmines in Moxico Kill and maim 66 Persons since June: Open Letter to the Angolan Government and UNITA", Luena, November 1998.

Kakar, F., *Direct and Indirect Consequences of Landmines on Public Health*, World Health Organization, Geneva, July 1995.

Kalshoven, F., "The Conventional Weapons Convention: Underlying Legal Principles", *International Review of the Red Cross*, 1990, No. 279.

Kalshoven, F., "Conventional Weaponry: The Law from St Petersburg to Lucerne and Beyond", Meyer, M.A. (ed.), *Armed Conflict and the New Law: Aspects of the 1977 Geneva Protocols and the 1981 Weapons Convention*, British Institute of International and Comparative Law, London, 1989.

Kalshoven, F., "Reaffirmation and Development of International Humanitarian Law Applicable in Armed Conflicts: The Diplomatic Conference, Geneva, 1974-77, Part II", *Netherlands Yearbook of International Law*, Vol. 9, 1978.

Kalshoven, F., "Arms, Armaments and International Law", *Recueil des Cours* 191 (1985 II).

Kalshoven, F., "The Conference of Government Experts on the Use of Certain Conventional Weapons, Lucerne, 24 September to 18 October 1974", *Netherlands Yearbook of International Law*, Vol. VI, 1975.

Kalshoven, F., "Reaffirmation and Development of International Humanitarian Law Applicable in Armed Conflicts: The Diplomatic Conference, Geneva, 1974-77, Part I: Combatants and Civilians", *Netherlands Yearbook of International Law*, Vol. 8, 1977.

Kalshoven, F., "Conventional Weaponry: The Law from St Petersburg to Lucerne and Beyond", Meyer, M.A. (ed.), *Armed Conflict and the New Law: Aspects of the 1977 Geneva Protocols and the 1981 Weapons Convention*, British Institute of International and Comparative Law, London, 1989.

Kalshoven, F., "Laws of War" *Encyclopaedia of Public International Law*, North-Holland Publishing Co., Amsterdam, 1982.

Kalshoven, F., "The Conventional Weapons Convention: Underlying Legal Principles", *International Review of the Red Cross*, 1990, No. 279.

Ken Rutherford, Statement at Landmine Press Conference, United Nations, New York, 17 September 1998.

King, C., *Legislation and the Landmine*, Jane's Intelligence Review, Special Report No 16, UK, November 1997.

Krepon, M., "Weapons Potentially Inhumane: The Case of Cluster Bombs", *Foreign Affairs*, Vol. 52, April 1974.

Külür, M.C., *Attitudes of International and Regional Organisations Towards the Material Remnants of War with Special Reference to the Effects of War Remnants in Libyan Arab Jamahiriya*, Paper submitted to the Symposium on Material Remnants of the Second World War on Libyan Soil, UNITAR, Geneva, 28 April – 1 May 1981.

Kussbach, E., "Internationale Bemühungen um die Beschränkung des Einsatzes bestimmter konventioneller Waffen", *Österreichische Zeitschrift für öffentliches Recht und Völkerrecht*, Vol. 28, 1977.

Latham, A., *Toward an Effective Verification Regime for the Convention on Certain Conventional Weapons: The Outline of an Incremental Approach*, Centre for Defence and Security Studies, Winnipeg, December 1994.

Lauterpacht, H., "The Problem of the Revision of the Law of War", *British Yearbook of International Law*, Vol. 29, 1952.

Leahy, Sen. P., "The Landmine Ban Treaty: 'A Lost Chance for US Leadership'", *Address to the US Senate*, 23 September 1997.

Letter from Mark A. Hiznay to Mr David Warshaw, Manager of Corporate Communications, General Electric Company, Fairfield, US, 18 April 2000.

Letter from Norwegian Minister of Foreign Affairs, Knut Vollbaeck, to US Secretary of State, Madeleine Albright, 20 May 1998.

Letter from H.E. Saad Mohamed Al-Kobaisi, Qatari Ambassador, to Landmine Monitor, 9 September 1999.

Letter from US President William Jefferson Clinton to Ms Marissa Vitagliano, Coordinator of the US Campaign to Ban Landmines, 31 August 1998.

Levie, H.S., "Prohibitions and Restrictions on the Use of Conventional Weapons", *St John's Law Review*, Vol. 68, Summer 1994.

Levie, H.S., "The Falklands Crisis and the Laws of War", Coll, A.R., and Arend, A.C. (eds.), *The Falklands War: Lessons for Strategy, Diplomacy and International Law*, 1985.

Li Ping, X., "The Latest Hot Topic in the Field of International Arms Control – Landmines", *International Prospect*, Shanghai, August 1997.

Libyan Institute of Diplomatic Studies, *Study of the Financial Aspects of the problem of Second World War Remnants on Libyan Soil*, Paper submitted to the Symposium on Material Remnants of the Second World War on Libyan Soil, UNITAR, Geneva, 28 April – 1 May 1981.

Lightfoot, P.J., "Landmine Review Conference: Will the Revised Landmine Protocol Protect Civilians?", *Fordham International Law Journal*, Vol. 18.

Liko, K., "Die genfer Waffenprotokolle 1980, Das Ergebnis des UN-Waffenkonferenz aus militärischer Sicht", *Österreiches Militärischer Zeitschrift*, Vol. 2, 1981.

Lilley, Brig. C.W., Deputy Chief of General Staff, New Zealand Defence Force, Letter to Neil Mander, Convenor CALM, 23 February 1999.

Lord, J., "Legal Restraints in the Use of Landmines: Humanitarian and Environmental Crisis", *California Western International Law Journal*, Vol. 25, Spring 1995.

Lynch Jr., Maj.-Gen. J.D., "Landmines, Lies, And Other Phenomena", *Proceedings (US Naval Institute)*, May 1998.

MacInnis, J.A., *Humanitarian Mine Clearance, Focus of Technology, An Opinion*, Presentation to the Tokyo Conference on Mine Clearance and Victim Assistance, March 1997.

Macintosh, J., *The Role of Confidence Building in the Convention on Certain Conventional Weapons*, Canadian Security Research Inc., Ontario, 15 December 1994.

Mahmoud, Dr. M.A., *The Problem of the War Remnants in the Light of General Principles of Law, with special reference to the Libyan case*, Paper submitted to the Symposium on Material Remnants of the Second World War on Libyan Soil, UNITAR, Geneva, 28 April – 1 May 1981.

Malinverni, G., "Armes conventionnelles modernes et droit international", *L'Annuaire suisse de droit international*, Vol. XXX, 1974.

Matheson, M.J., "The Revision of the Mines Protocol", *The American Journal of International Law*, Vol. 91, January 1997.

Matheson, M.J., "New landmine protocol is vital step towards ban", *Arms Control Today*, July 1996.

McCalister-Smith, P., "Protection of the Civilian Population and the Prohibition of Starvation as a Method of Warfare", *International Review of the Red Cross*, September – October 1991, No. 284.

McCall Jr., J.H., "Blinded by the Light: International Law and the Legality of Anti-Optic Laser Weapons", *Cornell International Law Journal*, Vol. 30, 1997.

McCall Jr., J.H., "Infernal Machines and Hidden Death: International Law and Limits on the Indiscriminate Use of Land Mine Warfare", *Georgia Journal of International and Comparative Law*, Vol. 24, Fall 1994.

McCormack, T.L.H., "A *non liquet* on nuclear weapons, The ICJ avoids the application of general principles of international humanitarian law", *International Review of the Red Cross*, January-February 1997, pp. 76-91.

McGrath, R., *Landmines and Proportionality, Balancing the Scales*, undated, <http://www.oneworld.org/landmines/rae_lecture.html>.

McGrath, R., *'Safe Mines' and Sub-Munitions*, Information Paper for the 2nd International NGO Conference on Landmines, May 1994.

McGrath, R., "Definitions and Anti-Handling Devices", *Discussion Paper*, Mines Advisory Group, Cockermouth, UK, August 1997.

McGrath, R., "A Matter of Justice and Humanity", *Nobel Lecture*, Oslo, 10 December 1997.

McNeill, J.H., "The International Court of Justice Advisory Opinion in the *Nuclear Weapons Cases*, A first appraisal", *International Review of the Red Cross*, January-February 1997.

Médecins Sans Frontières, *Living in a Minefield, An MSF Report on the Mine Problem in Afghanistan*, MSF, May 1997.

Medical Educational Trust, *Health and Environmental Effects of Military Activities*, London, March 1993 (revised).

Meron, T., "International Criminalisation of Internal Atrocities", *American Journal of International Law*, Vol. 89, July 1995.

Meron, T., "The Continuing Role of Custom in the Formation of International Humanitarian Law", Editorial Comment, *American Journal of International Law*, Vol. 90, No. 238, April 1996.

Meron, T., "The Time has Come for the United States to Ratify Geneva Protocol I", *American Journal of International Law*, Vol. 88, October 1994.

Meron, T., "The Geneva Conventions as Customary Law", *American Journal of International Law*, Vol. 81, 1987.

Meyrowitz, H., "The Principle of Superfluous Injury or Unnecessary Suffering, From the Declaration of St Petersburg of 1868 to Additional Protocol I of 1977", *International Review of the Red Cross*, March-April 1994, No. 299.

Miggiani, Dr. M.A., *War Remnants: The Establishment of Liability*, Paper submitted to the Symposium on Material Remnants of the Second World War on Libyan Soil, UNITAR, Geneva, 28 April – 1 May 1981.

Miggiani, Dr. M.A., *The After Effects of War Waste Left by Belligerent States During the Second World War on the Libyan Soil*, Paper submitted to the Symposium on Material Remnants of the Second World War on Libyan Soil, UNITAR, Geneva, 28 April – 1 May 1981.

Mine Clearance Planning Agency, *Socio-Economic Impact Study of Mine Action Operations Afghanistan*, Interim Report, United Nations Mine Action Programme for Afghanistan, October 1998.

"Mine Victim Assistance, Proposed Strategic Framework for Planning Integrated Mine Victim Assistance Programmes", *Working paper related to the Informal Consultations on International cooperation and assistance in accordance with Article 6 of the Convention on Victim assistance, social and economic reintegration and mine awareness*, 6 May 1999 (revised version).

Molander, J., "Strengthening International Humanitarian Law: The Review Conference of the 1980 Conventional Weapons Convention", *UNIDIR Newsletter*, Nos. 28/29, 12.94/05.95.

Münsch, F., "History of the Laws of War", *Encyclopaedia of Public International Law*, Vol. 4, North Holland, Amsterdam.

Naidoo, V. and McMillin, P., "Towards Ottawa: A Total Ban Treaty on Anti-Personnel Landmines", *ISS Paper No 26*, Small Arms Programme ISS South Africa, November 1997.

Nash, M., "Contemporary Practice of the United States Relating to International Law", *American Journal of International Law*, Vol. 91, April 1997.

Nash, M., "Contemporary Practice of the United States Relating to International Law", *American Journal of International Law*, Vol. 88, October 1994.

Norwegian People's Aid, "Humanitarian Mine Action", Landmine Monitor Fact Sheet prepared for the Meeting of the Standing Committee of Experts on Mine Clearance, Geneva, 13-15 September 1999.

O'Brien, "Biological-Chemical Warfare and International Law of War", *Georgetown Law Review*, Vol. 51.

Obradovic, Dr. K., *Le Désarmement et le Droit des Conflits Armés, Que faire?*, Paper submitted to the Vth Round Table on Current Problems in International Humanitarian Law, San Remo, 6-9 September 1978.

Office of the Under Secretary of Defense for Policy of the Government of the United States, *Report to the Secretary of Defense on the Status of DoD's Implementation of the U.S. Policy on Anti-Personnel Landmines*, May 1997.

Parks, "Air war and the law of war", *Air Force Law Review*, 1990.

Parlow, A., "Towards a global ban on landmines", *International Review of the Red Cross*, July-August 1995, No. 307.

Parlow. A., "Banning land mines", *Human Rights Quarterly*, Vol. 16, No. 4, November 1994.

Partsch, Dr. K.J., *Juridical Foundation of the Obligation to Co-operate*, Paper submitted to the Symposium on Material Remnants of the Second World War on Libyan Soil, UNITAR, Geneva, 28 April – 1 May 1981.

Partsch, K.J., "Remnants of war as a legal problem in the light of the Libyan case", *American Journal of International Law*, Vol. 78, No. 2, April 1984.

Peters, A., "Landmines in the 21st century", *International Relations*, Vol. XIII, No. 2, August 1996.

Peters, A., "Blinding Laser Weapons: New Limits on the Technology of Warfare", *Loyola of Los Angeles International and Comparative Law Journal*, Vol. 18, 1996.

Petrarca, A.H., "An Impetus of Human Wreckage: The 1996 Amended Landmine Protocol", *California Western International Law Journal*, Vol. 27, Fall 1996.

Plant, G., "Environmental Damage and the Laws of War: Points Addressed to Military Lawyers", Fox, H., and Meyer, M.A. (eds.), *Armed Conflict and the New Law*, Vol. II, 1992.

Prokosch, E., "The Swiss draft Protocol on Small-Calibre Weapon Systems, Bringing the dumdum ban (1899) up to date", *International Review of the Red Cross*, July-August 1995, No. 307.

Pustogarov, V., "Fyodor Fyodorovich Martens (1845-1909) – A Humanist of Modern Times", *International Review of the Red Cross (IRRC)*, May-June 1996, No. 312, Geneva.

Rauch, E., "The protection of the civilian population in international armed conflicts and the use of landmines", *German Yearbook of International Law*, Vol. 24, 1981.

Rauch, E., "Intervention", *Military Law and Law of War Review*, Vol. 26, 1987.

Refugee Studies Programme, *Mine Warfare: An Aid Issue*, Refugee Participation Network 9, UK, August 1990.

Republic of Bulgaria, *Technology for Safe and Ecologically clean Destruction of Stockpiled APLs through Disassembling*, Maputo, undated, but May 1999.

Republic of Mozambique, *Strategic Framework for Mine and Other Trauma Victims Assistance*, Draft Document circulated during the First Meeting of States Parties of the Convention on the Prohibition of Anti-Personnel Mines.

Roach, Capt. J.A., "Certain Conventional Weapons Convention: Arms Control or Humanitarian Law", *Military Law Review*, Vol. 105, Summer 1984.

Robblee Jr., Capt. P.A., "The Legitimacy of Modern Conventional Weaponry", *The Military Law and Law of War Review*, Vol. XVI, No. 4, 1977.

Robisch, T.G., "Would the Georgia Campaigns of the First Commander of the Modern Era Comply with Current Law of War Standards?", *Emory International Law Review*, Vol. 9, Fall 1995.

Rogers, Col. A.P.V., "Mines, Booby-traps and other devices", *International Review of the Red Cross*, November-December 1990, No. 279.

Rogers, Lt.-Col. A.P.V., "A Commentary on the Protocol on Prohibitions or Restrictions on the Use of Mines, Booby-Traps and Other Devices", *Military Law and Law of War Review*, Vol. 26, 1987.

Rogers, A.P.V., *Law on the Battlefield*, Manchester University Press, Manchester, UK, 1996.

ROK Foreign Ministry statement, "Banning Antipersonnel Landmine: Republic of Korea's Security Situation Must Be Given Special Consideration", undated but 1997.

Ross, M.A., "Environmental Warfare and the Persian Gulf War: Possible Remedies to Combat Intentional Destruction of the Environment", *Dickson Law Review*, Vol. 10, 1992.

Saddigh, Dr. A.M.A., *The Prejudices caused by Remnants of War and the Legitimacy of the Libyan Claim in Reparation*, Paper submitted to the Symposium on Material Remnants of the Second World War on Libyan Soil, UNITAR, Geneva, 28 April – 1 May 1981.

Sandoz, Y., *Anti-Personnel Mines will be Banned*, ICRC, Geneva, May 1996.

Sandoz, Y., *The International Committee of the Red Cross as guardian of international humanitarian law*, ICRC, Geneva, March 1998.

Sandoz, Y., "Prohibitions or Restrictions on the Use of Certain Conventional Weapons", *International Review of the Red Cross*, January-February 1981.

Sandoz, Y., "Unlawful damage in armed conflicts and redress under international humanitarian law", *International Review of the Red Cross*, Vol. 131, 1982.

Sandoz, Y., *Unlawful Damage in Armed Conflicts and Reparation Therefore Under International Humanitarian Law*, Paper submitted to the Symposium on Material Remnants of the Second World War on Libyan Soil, UNITAR, Geneva, 28 April – 1 May 1981.

Sands, P.J., "The Environment, Community and International Law", *Harvard Law Journal*, Vol. 30, 1989.

Santos, S., "Report on the South Asia Regional Seminar on Landmines", ICBL Working Group on Non-State Actors, Quezon, the Philippines, 22 August 1999.

Schneck, W., "Desert Storm Countermine Improvisations", *Engineer*, July 1992.

Schwarzenberger, G., *Self-Defence under the Charter of the United Nations and the Use of Prohibited Weapons*, Report to the 50th Conference of the International Law Association (Brussels, 1962), International Law Association Report, 1962.

Scott, R., "Unnecessary Suffering? – A Medical View", Meyer, M.A. (ed.), *Armed Conflict and the New Law: Aspects of the 1977 Geneva Protocols and the 1981 Weapons Convention*, British Institute of International and Comparative Law, London, 1989.

Shaw, M., "The United Nations Convention on Prohibitions or Restrictions on the Use of Certain Conventional Weapons, 1981", *Review of International Studies*, Vol. 9, No. 2, 1983.

Sheehan, E., and Croll, M., *Landmine Casualties in Mozambique*, Report, Halo Trust, Maputo, 1993.

Smith, Dr. C. (ed.), *The Military Utility of Landmines......?*, North-South Defence and Security Programme, Centre for Defence Studies, King's College, University of London, June 1996.

Smith, N.B., "A Plea for the Total Ban of Land Mines By International Treaty", *Loyola of Los Angeles International and Comparative Law Journal*, Vol. 17, April 1995.

Solf, W.A., "Protection of Civilians Against the Effects of Hostilities Under Customary International Law and Under Protocol I", *The American University Journal of International Law and Policy*, Vol. 1, Summer 1996.

Sommaruga, C., "Does the nature of mine injuries also justify a total ban?", *Landmines, Demining News from the United Nations*, Vol. 1.4, September 1996.

Sommaruga, C., *Humanitarian Aspects – An Integrated and Co-ordinated Approach*, Statement of the President of the ICRC to the International for the Total Prohibition of Anti-Personnel Mines, Brussels, 26 June 1997.

Statement of Ambassador of the Islamic Republic of Iran at the Treaty Signing Conference in Ottawa, 1-4 December 1997.

Statement of Mali to the First Meeting of States Parties of the Convention on the Prohibition of Anti-Personnel Mines, Maputo, 3-7 May 1999.

Statement of Eric Roethlisberger, Vice-President, International Committee of the Red Cross, to the First Meeting of States Parties of the Convention on the Prohibition of Anti-Personnel Mines.

Statement of Jadranko Prlic, Minister of Foreign Affairs of Bosnia and Herzegovina, to the First Meeting of States Parties of the Convention on the Prohibition of Anti-Personnel Mines, Maputo, 3 May 1999.

Statement of Sri Lanka to the First Meeting of States Parties of the Convention on the Prohibition of Anti-Personnel Mines, Maputo, undated, but May 1999.

Statement of Ieng Mouly, the Chairman of the Governing Council of the Cambodian Mine Action Center, to the First Meeting of States Parties of the Convention on the Prohibition of Anti-Personnel Mines, Maputo, May 1999.

Statement of Ambassador Shao Guanfu, Head of the Chinese Observer Delegation to the First Meeting of States Parties of the Convention on the Prohibition of Anti-Personnel Mines, Maputo, 4 May 1999.

Statement of John J. Griffin, Assistant Secretary, International Security Division, Department of Foreign Affairs and Trade, and Head of the Australian Delegation to the First Meeting of States Parties of the Convention on the Prohibition of Anti-Personnel Mines.

Statement of Mr Zbigniew Szymanski, Director of the Department of the United Nations Political Affairs of the Republic of Poland, at the First Meeting of States Parties to the Convention on the Prohibition of Anti-Personnel Mines, Maputo, 4 May 1999.

Statement of the Holy See to the First Meeting of States Parties of the Convention on the Prohibition of Anti-Personnel Mines (Statement corrected on 5 May 1999).

Statement of Switzerland to the First Meeting of States Parties of the Convention on the Prohibition of Anti-Personnel Mines delivered by Ambassador Erwin Hofer, Head of the Swiss Delegation, Maputo.

Statement of Finland on behalf of the European Union to the First Committee of the UN General Assembly, New York, 11 October 1999.

Statement of the ICRC to the Vienna Expert Meeting, 12 February 1997.

Statement of Belgian Foreign Minister Eric Derycke, Chairman of the International Meeting on Demining, Geneva, 6 July 1995.

Statement of Prince Zeid Bin Ra'Ad, Head of Jordanian Delegation to the First Meeting of States Parties of the Convention on the Prohibition of Anti-Personnel Mines, Maputo, 3 May 1999.

Statement of Mr Valeriu Nicolae, Chargé d'affaires of Romania to the Republic of Mozambique to the First Meeting of States Parties of the Convention on the Prohibition of Anti-Personnel Mines, Maputo, undated, but May 1999.

Statement of Dr Benita Ferrero-Waldner, Austrian State Secretary for Foreign Affairs, to the First Meeting of States Parties of the Convention on the Prohibition of Anti-Personnel Mines, Maputo, 3 May 1999.

Statement of Bulgarian Ambassador Petko Draganov to the Conference on Disarmament, Geneva, undated but February 1999.

Statement by Mr Martin Palouš, Deputy Minister of Foreign Affairs and Head of the Delegation of the Czech Republic to the First Meeting of States Parties to the Convention on the Prohibition of Anti-Personnel Mines, Maputo, 4 May 1999.

Statement by Ambassador Shao Guanfu, Head of the Chinese Observer Delegation to the First Meeting of States Parties, Maputo, 4 May 1999.

Statement at Budapest Conference by Mr. Kazimierz Tomaszewski, Senior Counselor to the Minister for Foreign Affairs, Ministry of Foreign Affairs, Poland, 26-28 March 1998.

Statement of the Disarmament and Non-Proliferation Service of the Belgian Ministry of Foreign Affairs, 9 March 1999.

Statement of Akio Suda, Deputy Director-General for Arms Control and Scientific Affairs, Foreign Policy Bureau, Japanese Ministry of Foreign Affairs, Commerce and Industry Committee, House of Representatives Proceedings Report No. 6, 25 September 1998.

Statement of Edward Cummings, Head of the US Delegation to the Second Preparatory Conference of the 2001 CCW Review Conference, Geneva, 4 April 2001.

Statement of Ingemars Biseneiks, Security Policy Division, Ministry of Foreign Affairs of Latvia, to the Budapest Regional Conference on Antipersonnel Landmines, 26-28 March 1998.

Statement of Rudolf Joó, Deputy State Secretary of the Ministry of Foreign Affairs of the Republic of Hungary at the First Meeting of the States Parties of the Convention on the Prohibition of Anti-Personnel Mines, Maputo, 4 May 1999.

Statement of the Senegalese Delegation following some allegations contained in the 1999 Report of ICBL (First Meeting of States Parties to the Convention on AP Landmines), Unofficial Translation, 5 May 1999.

Statement of Eric Roethlisberger, Vice-President of the ICRC, to the closing session of the First Review Conference of the 1980 CCW, 3 May 1996.

Statement of Hilde F. Johnson, Minister of International Development and Human Rights, Royal Ministry of Foreign Affairs, Norway, to the First Meeting of States Parties, Maputo, 3-7 May 1999.

Statement of the International Campaign to Ban Landmines to the First Meeting of States Parties to the 1997 Mine Ban Treaty, Maputo, Mozambique, May 1999.

Statement of Martin Palouš, Deputy Minister of Foreign Affairs and Head of the Delegation of the Czech Republic to the First Meeting of States Parties of the Convention on the Prohibition of Anti-Personnel Mines, Maputo, 4 May 1999.

Statutes of Canada, Chapter 33, An Act to implement the Convention on the Prohibition of the Use, Stockpiling, Production and Transfer of Anti-Personnel Mines and on their Destruction, Bill C-22, Assented to on 27 November 1997.

"Statutes of the International Committee of the Red Cross", *International Review of the Red Cross*, No. 324, 1 September 1998.

Stern, J.E., "All's Well that Ends Well? Verification and the CWC", Poole, J.B., & Guthrie, R. (eds.), *Verification 1993, Peacekeeping, Arms Control and the Environment*, Brassey's/Vertic, UK, 1993.

Stockholm International Peace Research Institute, *Working Papers on International Law and the Prohibition of Unnecessary Injury, SIPRI*, Stockholm, undated.

Stockholm International Peace Research Institute, *The US Rules of Engagement in Vietnam as they Relate to the Use of Certain Specific Weapons: A brief survey and analysis, SIPRI*, Stockholm, 1976.

Strong, J.M., "Blinding Laser Weapons and Protocol IV: Obscuring the Humanitarian Vision", *Dickson Journal of International Law*, Vol. 15, Fall 1996.

Svensson, U., *Statement*, Paper submitted to the Symposium on Material Remnants of the Second World War on Libyan Soil, UNITAR, Geneva, 28 April – 1 May 1981.

Swiss Federal Council, *Message concernant la Convention sur l'interdiction de l'emploi, du stockage, de la production et du transfert des mines antipersonnel et sur leur destruction*, Bern, January 1998.

Szasz, P., "The Conference on Excessively Injurious or Indiscriminate Weapons", *American Journal of International Law*, Vol. 74, January 1980.

Ticehurst, R., "The Martens Clause and the Laws of Armed Conflict", *International Review of the Red Cross*, March-April 1997, No. 317, ICRC, Geneva.

U Ohn Gyaw, Minister for Foreign Affairs of the Union of Myanmar, Statement to the 52nd Session of the UN General Assembly, New York, 26 September 1997.

UNICEF, *Anti-Personnel Mines. A Scourge on Children*, UNICEF New York, 1994.

United Kingdom Foreign and Commonwealth Office, "British Policy on Anti-Personnel Landmines", *FCO On-Line Briefing Paper*, http://www.fco.gov.uk, June 1997.

US Defense Intelligence Agency and US Army Foreign Science and Technology Center, *Landmine Warfare – Trends and Projections*, DST-1160S-019-92, December 1992.

Van Minh, T., *Un exemple de réglement du problème des restes matériels et des destructions de la guerre: L'accord de Paris sur le Vietnam*, Paper submitted to the Symposium on Material Remnants of the Second World War on Libyan Soil, UNITAR, Geneva, 28 April – 1 May 1981.

Vázquez, C.M., "The Four Doctrines of Self-Executing Treaties", *American Journal of International Law*, Vol. 89, No. 4, October 1995.

Wartan, S.W. *et al.*, "Phantom pain and sensation among British veteran amputees", *British Journal of Anaesthesia*, Vol. 78, No. 6, 1997.

Western European Union, *La lutte contre la prolifération des mines antipersonnel*, Report presented on behalf of the Commission on Defence to the 43rd session of the Assembly, 13 May 1997.

Wiebe, V. and Peachey, T., *Drop Today, Kill Tomorrow, Cluster Munitions as Inhumane and Indiscriminate Weapons*, United States, December 1997.

Williams, J., "Landmines and measures to eliminate them", *The International Review of the Red Cross*, No. 305, July-August 1995.

Wyatt, Maj. (ret.) J.D.R., "Land mine warfare, recent lessons and future trends", *International Defense Review*, Vol. 22, No. 1, 1989.

Zillman, D.N., A book review of Dycus, S., *A Review of National Defense and the Environment, George Washington Law Review*, Vol. 65, January 1997.

5.3. UNITED NATIONS DOCUMENTS, RESOLUTIONS AND JUDICIAL DECISIONS

"Assistance in Mine Clearance", Report of the Secretary-General, issued as *UN Doc. A/49/357* on 6 September 1994.

Continental Shelf (Libyan Arab Jamahiriya/Malta), Judgement, ICJ Reports 1985.

"Estimated Costs for Convening the First Meeting of States Parties to the Convention on the Prohibition of the Use, Stockpiling, Production and Transfer of Anti-Personnel Mines and on Their Destruction", *UN Doc. APLC/MSP.1/1999/L.5*, 30 April 1999.

"President's Paper on Revisions to the Intersessional Work Programme", *UN Doc. APLC/MSP.2/2000/L.5.*

Prosecutor v. *Tadic, Case No. IT-94-1-AR72*, Appeal on Jurisdiction before the Appeals Chamber of the International Tribunal for the Prosecution of Persons Responsible for Serious Violations of International Humanitarian Law Committed in the Territory of Former Yugoslavia, 2 October 1995.

Report of the Secretary-General on the proposed Statute of the International Tribunal for the Prosecution of Persons Responsible for Serious Violations of International Humanitarian Law Committed in the Territory of the Former Yugoslavia ("Report of the Secretary-General Pursuant to Paragraph 2 of the Security Council Resolution 808", *UN Doc. S/25704*, 1993.

Resolution XXIII, "Human rights in armed conflicts" of 12 May 1968 of the International Conference on Human Rights, Tehran, 22 April to 13 May 1968, *UN Doc. A/CONF.32/41.*

"Respect for Human Rights in Armed Conflicts: Existing Rules of International Law concerning the Prohibition or Restriction on the Use of Specific Weapons", *UN Doc. A/9215*, 1973, Vol. I.

UN General Assembly ordinary resolution 3076 (XXVIII) of 6 December 1973.

UN General Assembly ordinary resolution 32/152 of 19 December 1977.

UN General Assembly ordinary resolution 33/70 of 14 December 1978.

UN General Assembly ordinary resolution 48/75K of 16 December 1993.

UN General Assembly ordinary resolution 48/79.

UN General Assembly ordinary resolution 51/45S.

UN General Assembly ordinary resolution 52/38A.

UN General Assembly ordinary resolution 52/38H of 9 December 1997.

UN General Assembly ordinary resolution 53/77.

UN General Assembly ordinary resolution 54/545B.

UN, "Summary of Negotiations Leading to the Conclusion of the Convention on Prohibitions or Restrictions on the Use of Certain Conventional Weapons Which May Be Deemed to Be Excessively Injurious or to Have Indiscriminate Effects and of Subsequent Developments Related to the Convention", *UN Doc. CCW/CONF.I/GE/5*, 6 May 1994.

UN, "Review Conference of the States Parties to the Convention on Prohibitions or Restrictions on the Use of Certain Conventional Weapons Which May Be Deemed to Be Excessively Injurious or to Have Indiscriminate Effects, Final Document, Part I, Final Report of the Conference", *UN Doc. CCW/CONF.1/16 (Part I)*, Geneva, 1996.

UN, "Review Conference of the States Parties to the Convention on Prohibitions or Restrictions on the Use of Certain Conventional Weapons Which May Be Deemed to be Excessively Injurious or to Have Indiscriminate Effects, Final Document, Part II, Documents and Summary Records of the Conference", *UN Doc. CCW/CONF.1/16 (Part II)*, Geneva, 1996.

UN, "Summary of Negotiations Leading to the Conclusion of the Convention on Prohibitions or Restrictions on the Use of Certain Conventional Weapons Which May Be Deemed to Be Excessively Injurious or to Have Indiscriminate Effects and of Subsequent Developments Related to the Convention", *UN Doc. CCW/CONF.I/GE/5* of 6 May 1994.

UN, *International Tribunal for the Prosecution of Persons Responsible for Serious Violations of International Humanitarian Law Committed in the Territory of the Former Yugoslavia since 1991, Basic Documents*, United Nations, 1995.

UN, "Final Act of the International Conference on Human Rights, Teheran, 22 April to 13 May 1968", *UN Doc. A/CONF.32/41.*

UN Environment Programme, *A Rapid Assessment of the Impacts of the Iraq-Kuwait Conflict on Terrestrial Ecosystems, Part I, Iraq*, September 1991.

UN Environment Programme, *A Rapid Assessment of the Impacts of the Iraq-Kuwait Conflict on Terrestrial Ecosystems, Part II, Kuwait*, September 1991.

UN General Assembly, "Final Report of the United Nations Conference on Prohibitions or Restrictions on the Use of Certain Conventional Weapons Which May Be Deemed to Be Excessively Injurious or to Have Indiscriminate Effects", *UN Doc. A/CONF.95/15*, 27 October 1980.

UN General Assembly, "Report of the Secretary-General of the United Nations on Napalm and Other Incendiary Weapons and All Aspects of their Possible Use", *UN Doc. A/8803/Rev.1.*

UN General Assembly, "Report of the Secretary-General of the United Nations, United Nations Environment Programme: Material remnants of wars and their effect on the environment", *UN Doc. A/32/137*, 27 July 1977.

5.4. Press Articles and Releases

"600-Year-Old Mines Unearthed in Inner Mongolia", *Xinhua Press Agency*, Hohhot, Mongolia, 11 April 2001.

"$77– Needed to Strip Korean 'Belt of Death'", *South China Morning Post*, 30 October 1998.

"Afghan Anti-Landmines campaigners to monitor Taliban, Masood", *AFP Internationale*, 30 November 1998.

Alford, P., "Cambodia's landmine myths exploded", *The Australian*, 3 June 2000, <http://www.news.com.au.>

"A life-saving treaty", *Hindustan Times*, 24 September 1998.

Allenova, O., "A Walk round Grozny; Chechen capital still full of mines", *Moscow Kommersant*, 25 April 2000.

"Angola: Women bear the brunt of war", *IRIN – Southern Africa*, 26 July 1999.

"Anti-personnel landmine decisions deferred", *US Department of Defence News Release No. 029-01*, 19 January 2001.

"Army's landmine stocks destroyed", *Times*, 23 February 1999.

Ayllón, L., "España insiste a EE. UU. para que destruya sus minas antipersonal", *ABC*, 2 November 1998.

"Ban the mine", leader in *The Economist*, 25 December 1993-7 January 1994.

Bernstein, L., *ICBL Landmines Update No 1*, 2 May 2000.

Bigelow, B.V., "San Diego business detects landmines with sensor", *San Diego Tribune*, 29 February 2000.

Bonner, R., "New US Terms on Mine Ban Are Called Unacceptable", *New York Times*, 16 September 1997.

Boulet-Gercourt, P., "Mines Antipersonnel: L'Amérique zigzague", *Le Nouvel Observateur*, 9-15 October 1997.

"Border landmines kill 35 South Koreans: minister", *AFP*, 2 October 1997.

"Bradley supports Ottawa Treaty banning landmines, Gore, Administration still lag behind", *Arms Trade Insider*, No. 26, 19 January 2000.

"Brazilian Police probe alleged landmine use by landowners", *AFP Internationale*, 20 March 1999.

"Britain and Argentina in talks on ridding Falklands of landmines", *AFP Internationale*, 31 July 1998.

"Britain completes destruction of anti-personnel landmines", *AP*, London, 19 October 1999.

"Britain Sells Landmine Explosive to US Army", *Independent on Sunday*, 27 June 1999.

"Britain calls for ban on landmine exports", *Financial Times*, 31 January 1997.

Brown, P., "Landmines banned but threats stay", *Guardian*, 2 March 1999.

"Bulgaria-Turkey Ratify Agreement On Landmines", <http://www.unfoundation.org>, 15 March 2000.

Bundesrat, *Drucksache 34/98, Gesetzentwurf der Bundesregierung*, 16 January 1998, <http://www.bundestag.de>.

"Burmese Troops Said Plant Mines Along Thai Border", *Phuchatkan*, 14 January 1999.

"Calling the shots", *New Internationalist*, January/February 1999.

"Cambodia mining agency cuts staff", *AP*, Phnom Penh, 17 October 2000.
"Cambodia Gets Tough New Law Anti-Landmine Law", *AFP Internationale*, 28 April 1999.
"Canada to help Ukraine on landmine ban, international loans", *AFP International*, 27 January 1999.
"Canada dismisses UN bid to ban landmine use", *Reuters European*, 17 February 1997.
"Canadian Forces will continue to use remote-controlled mines", *Vancouver Sun*, 15 February 2000.
Chakmakjianm H., "Arms industry shows off latest technology in war on mines", *AFP*, Abu Dhabi, 20 March 1997.
Chauveau, L., "Déminage, La 'poêle à frire' du future", *L'Express*, 1 July 1999.
Chazan, G., "Dumped World War II Shells", *Daily Telegraph*, 8 October 2000.
"Chemical Weapons Destruction Complete on Johnston Atoll", *Press Release No. 715-00*, Office of the Assistant Secretary of Defense (Public Affairs), Washington DC, 30 November 2000.
Chigodo, T., "Military clearing programme traces some 26,000 landmines", *All Africa News Agency*, Harare, 17 April 2000.
"Chile rejects Bolivian Charges about Mines", *Reuters*, 30 September 1997.
"China clears minefields", *Financial Times*, 23 February 1999.
"China Opposes Total Ban on Landmines", *Reuters*, New York, 18 October 1996.
"China clears mines along Vietnam border", *AP*, Beijing, 1 December 1997.
"Chinese soldier dies in demining operation on Vietnam border", *AFP*, Beijing, 26 May 1998.
"Clashes mar mines debate", *Guardian*, 11 July 1998.
"Clearance work falters as Angolans lay more mines", *Guardian*, 17 July 1999.
"CMAC recovering from scandal – Chairman", *AP*, Phnom Penh, 3 December 1999.
"Compliance with the Ottawa Convention", *Tiempo Digital*, Honduras, 3 March 2000, unofficial translation.
Constable, P., "Afghan minefields go to the dogs", *Washington Post*, 6 March 2000.
Coryell, G., "US combs the world for deadly mines", *Tampa Tribune*, 19 March 2000.
Croll, M., "Wrong turning in a minefield: Diana was wrong", *Independent*, 20 August 1998.
"Désarmement, La session annuelle se termine sans accord", *Tribune de Genève*, 22 September 2000.
Eckhard, F., "Landmines not part of UN Peacekeeping Operations", Letter, *Washington Times*, 16 May 2000.
"Egypt to Ask WWII Rivals to Clear Landmines", *Xinhua*, Cairo, 20 October 1997.
"Egypt under fire over anti-personnel mine policy", *Reuters*, Cairo, 11 April 2000.
"Egypt's landmines are old and hard to locate in The Devil's Garden", *Arabic News*, 9 October 1997.
"ELF's field efficiency surprises Loch/ChemTech scientists", *PRNewswire*, Karlovac, Croatia, 14 February 2000.
Ellis, S., "Army General says most landmines will be banned by 2003", *Washington File*, Washington, 30 October 1997.
Ellison, M., "US has top secret files on Diana", *Guardian*, 10 December 1998.
"Emotional Warfare", *Guardian*, 27 August 1999.
Evans, M., "Pakistani 'in deal for landmines'", *Times*, 7 December 1999.
Farrell, S., "Serb pupils learnt tactics of terror", *Times*, 29 June 1999.
Faulder, D., "An International Minefield, A Scandal blows up under the demining agency", *Asiaweek*, 17 September 1999.
"Finland Considers Steps to Phase out Landmines", *Reuters*, Helsinki, 16 December 1997.
Flynn, M., "Politisches Minenfeld", *Der Überblick*, No. 2, 1999.
Fontaine, C., "Land Mine Agency won't stop work", *AP*, Phnom Penh, 23 February 2000.
"Four months after surgery, Thai elephant maimed by landmine in good health", *AP*, Lampang, Thailand, 28 December 1999.
"Four deaths in blast show risk to refugees", *Irish Times*, 22 June 1999.
"France: All Anti-Personnel mines To Be Destroyed By December", *AFP*, Paris, 23 September 1999.
"France warns against the use of landmines in Congo", *AFP*, 11 September 1997.
"France destroys anti-personnel landmines", *AP*, Paris, 21 December 1999.
"German KFOR Soldiers Injured Through Mine, Two Flown Out", *AND*, Berlin/Heidelberg, 23 September 1999.
"German Soldiers Wounded in Kosovo Minefield", *Reuters*, Pristina, 23 September 1999.
Gertz, B., "Clinton resisted pressure to join ban on landmines", *Washington Times*, 20 September 1997.

Gertz, B. and Scarborough, R., "Inside the ring", *Washington Times*, 12 May 2000.
Goldblat, J., "The CD on the Brink", *Disarmament Diplomacy*, No. 18, September 1997.
"Government spends £62 million on landmines", *Sunday Telegraph*, 5 April 1998.
Graham, B., "US Dispatches Team To Discuss Mine Treaty", *Washington Post*, 17 August 1997.
"Group says at least 250 million landmines are stockpiled", *AP*, Geneva, 9 December 1999.
Harrison, F., "Sri Lanka landmine deaths high", BBC, Colombo, 4 April 2001.
Hebel, S., "Berlin dodges the prohibition of mines", *Frankfurter Rundschau*, 22 November 1999, unofficial translation.
"Helms praises Clinton Refusal to Accept Landmine Treaty", <http://www.usia.gov>.
Heritage, T., "Russia rebuffs calls to sign landmines treaty", *Reuters European*, Moscow, 27 May 1998.
Highlights of the Noon Briefing by Fred Eckhard, Spokesman for the Secretary-General, UN Headquarters New York, 1 March 2000, <http://www.un.org>.
"Hold Off On Hollow-Point Bullets", Editorial, *New York Times*, 7 March 1997.
Human Rights Watch, "New US mines would violate treaty", *Press release*, Washington, 7 April 2000.
Human Rights Watch, "Historical Landmine Ban Treaty Takes Effect", *Press release*, Washington, 1 March 1999.
ICBL, "ICBL deplores continued obstruction of the ban on anti-personnel mines in Egypt", *Press release*, Cairo, 11 April 2000.
ICBL, "Landmine Treaty Ratified by Forty Countries in Record time", *Press release*, Dublin, 17 September 1998.
ICBL, "Landmines Campaign Condemns Recent Use of the Weapon", *Press release*, Geneva, 13 September 1999.
ICBL, "Campaign Criticises Deceptions in Clinton's Landmine Statement", *Press release*, Oslo, Norway, 19 September 1997.
ICBL, "Mine Ban Closer to Reality", *Press release*, Vienna, 14 February 1997.
ICBL, "Mine Ban Treaty Enters Into Force – ICBL Praises Progress, Condemns Users", *Press release*, Oslo, 1 March 1999.
ICRC, *Statement of the ICRC to the International Meeting of Experts on the Possible Verification of a Comprehensive International Treaty Prohibiting Anti-Personnel Landmines*, ICRC, Bonn, 24-25 April 1997.
Igorev, A. and Dvali, G., "Minefields will separate Russia from Georgia", *ITAR-TASS*, Moscow, 9 April 2000.
"Interior Ministry Engineers Set 210 Minefields in Chechnya", AVN, Moscow, 2 March 2001.
International Committee of the Red Cross and the International Federation of Red Cross and Red Crescent Societies, *Press release*, Oslo, 17 September 1997.
"International Landmines Conference opens in Maputo", *AFP Internationale*, 3 May 1999.
InVision Technologies, "InVision Technologies receives $4 million in additional funding for its landmine detection programme", *Press release*, Newark, California, 1 March 2000.
Jefferson, P., "The landmine ban is worse than useless", *Guardian*, 19 September 1997.
Jefferson, P., "A Political Minefield", *Wall Street Journal*, 15 October 1997.
"'Korea Exception' keeps us out Ottawa Treaty", *AFP Internationale*, 26 February 1999.
Krauthammer, C., "In Defense of Land Mines", *Washington Post*, 12 September 1997.
Krishnaswami, S., "A minefield ahead of Canada", *Hindu*, New Delhi, 6 December 1997.
Kyne, P., "Donors fiddle while CMAC burns", *Phnom Penh Post*, 3-16 March 2000.
"Kyrgyz APC Hits Rebel Landmine; One Dead, Two Injured", *ITAR-TASS*, Moscow, 20 September 1999.
Landmine Monitor, "New Study reveals 250 million stockpiled landmines in 105 countries, 17 million destroyed to date", *Press release*, Geneva, 9 December 1999.
"La Suède se félicite sur l'accord sur les mines antipersonnel", *AFP*, Stockholm, 3 May 1996.
"La France va renoncer 'solennellement' à l'emploi des mines anti-personnel", *AFP*, 2 October 1996.
"Land Mine Victims Urge Clinton to Sign Pact", *Reuters*, 1 March 2000.
"Landmine advert 'a mistake'", *Daily Telegraph*, 20 September 1999.
"Landmine numbers 'hugely exaggerated'", *Sunday Telegraph*, 29 November 1998.
"Landmine Ban Treaty nears Entry into Force", *Geneva Reporter*, October-November 1998.
"Landmine ban is defied on border", *Times*, 10 February 1999.

"Landmines for sale claim", *Birmingham Post*, 18 September 1999.
"Landmines in Senegal's Casamance Province worry authorities",*SAPA-AFP*, Ziguinchor, Senegal, 17 March 2000.
"Le Canada va détruire les deux-tiers de son stock de mines anti-personnel",*AFP*, 2 October 1996.
"Logistics Prevent Laos from Signing Mine Pact", *Bangkok Post*, 30 June 1998.
"Loophole on mines to end", *Independent*, 31 July 1998.
Mahende, E., "A Look At The Impending Anti-Personnel Mines Ban",*Pan-African News Agency*, 14 August 1997.
Mannion, J., "US wants talks on landmine ban held in Geneva",*AFP*, Washington, 17 January 1997.
"Mauritania Marks 100th Ratification of the Mine Ban Treaty", *Africa News Service*, Nouakchott, 27 July 2000.
Morrison, J., "Britain accused of watering down landmines ban", *Reuters*, London, 10 July 1998.
"Minefields Will Remain in Russia for Long Time", *Izvestia*, 14 October 1997.
"Mines by the million threaten North Africa, Conference told", *AFP Internationale*, 26 January 1999.
Munthit, K., "Japan PM vows Cambodia mine aid", *AP*, 12 January 2000.
Munthit, K., "Cambodia seeks land mine funds",*AP*, Kompong Chhnang, Cambodia, 2 April 2000.
Mydans, S., "Pushed From the Land and the Trees", *New York Times*, 6 April 2000.
Myers, L., "US seeks to keep landmines", *Philadelphia Inquirer*, 1 March 1998.
Myers, S.L., "Clinton Agrees to Land-Mine Ban, But Not Yet", *New York Times*, 22 May 1998.
Namibian Campaign to Ban Landmines, "Two maimed by landmine", *Press release*, Windhoek, Namibia, 4 April 2000.
"NATO treads carefully on touchy landmines issue", *Reuters*, Brussels, 16 December 1997.
Nebehay, S., "UN Disarmament: Canada prefers landmines pact under own talks",*Reuters*, Geneva, 6 February 1997.
Nebehay, S., "US blames non-aligned countries for arms deadlock", *Reuters European*, Geneva, 9 September 1997.
"Nepal hosts South Asian landmine-monitoring meeting", *Kathmandu Post*, 30 January 2001.
News Briefing by Kenneth Bacon of the US Department of Defense, 16 September 1997, <http://www.defenselink.mil>.
Ngqiyaza, B., "Landmines: UN figures exaggerated, group says", *Johannesburg Business Day*, 4 May 2000.
"New US European commander to visit Norway",*AFP*, Oslo, 5 December 1997.
"Nobel Prize: a bit of solace for the maimed", *Phnom Penh Post*, 24 October – 6 November 1997.
"Nobel laureate targets Russia in anti-landmine drive",*AFP*, Moscow, 27 May 1998.
"North Korea against Landmine Ban Exclusion", *Reuters*, Moscow, 14 September 1997.
O'Neill, J., "US Joins Canada in drive to ban landmines", *Ottawa Citizen*, 19 August 1997.
"Official Explains Turkish Position on Ottawa Agreement",*Ankara Anatolia*, 15 October 1998.
"Only 30 Years: Cambodia's Landmines", *Economist*, 7 November 1998.
"Ottawa Convention Landmine Conference outraged by continued use",*AFP Internationale*, 7 May 1999.
"Over 1.12 Million Landmines Laid Throughout ROK", *Yonhap*, Seoul, 28 September 1999.
Peck, G., "Animals and Land Mines", *AP*, Bangkok, 7 May 2000.
"Plus de mines anti-personnel en France en 2001", *Reuters*, 25 February 1999, as amended.
"Press Conference on Anti-Personnel Mine Convention", 1 March 2000.
Priest, D., "Mine Decision Boosts Clinton-Military Relations", *Washington Post*, 21 September 1997.
Pugliese, D., "How US bungled landmine talks", *Ottawa Citizen*, Ottawa, 1 December 2000.
"Rats train as landmine detectors, researchers say", *Reuters*, Brussels, 30 December 1999.
"Remarks by the US President on Land Mines", *Press release*, Office of the Press Secretary, Washington, 17 September 1997.
"Resolution on the Problem Posed by the Proliferation of Anti-Personnel Mines in Liberated Parts of New Sudan", *New Kush-Himan*, 1 November 1996.
Richardson, M., "In Cambodia, Mine-Clearing Group's Future Is In Doubt", *International Herald Tribune*, 21 August 2000.
"Ridding the world of land mines", *Chicago Tribune*, 27 November 1999.
"Romania Dismisses Army Officials Over Landmine Scandal", *Reuters*, Bucharest, 22 September 1999.

"Romanian Firm Denies Manufacturing Anti-Personnel Mines", *Bucharest Adevarul*, 21 September 1999.
"Russia signals new readiness to ban anti-personnel mines", *AFP*, 14 February 1997.
"Russia says shattered Grozny free of mines", *Reuters*, Moscow, 23 April 2000.
"Safe Destruction of Anti-personnel Landmines and Munitions in Moldova", *NATO Press Release*, 27 February 2001.
Salahuddin, S., "Afghan Taliban Support Ban on Landmines", *Reuters*, Kabul, 3 December 1997.
"Scandal-ridden Cambodian demining agency faces huge job cuts: PM", *AFP*, Kampong Chhnang, Cambodia, 2 April 2000.
Scott, C., "Britain caught in minefield by Argentina clearance offer", *Sunday Times*, 12 July 1998.
"Secretary-General Rings Peace Bell to Mark Occasion of Entry Into Force of Ottawa Convention Banning Anti-Personnel Mines", *UN Press Release SG/SM/6909*, 1 March 1999.
Seffers, G.I., "Pentagon Plan for Mixed System Draws Criticism", *Defense News*, Canada, 3-9 November 1997.
Seok-jae, K., "DMZ mine clearing Deadline Questioned", *Korea Herald*, 29 August 2000.
Seok-jae, K., "Public Attention Focused on Safety of Soldiers in Mine-Clearing Work", *Korea Herald*, 19 September 2000.
"Seven dead in Philippine hostilities", *Electronic Telegraph*, International news update, 23 April 2000.
Shapley, T., "Clinton's cruel decision on land mines risks too many lives", *Seattle Post-Intelligencer*, 17 April 2000.
Sheridan, M., "Scandal Continues To Tarnish Cambodian Agency", *Times*, 22 August 1999.
Shrimsley, R., "Commons to sit on day off to ban landmines", *Daily Telegraph*, 26 June 1998.
Shukman, D., "War-torn Angola in grip of fresh mine 'nightmare'", *Sunday Telegraph*, 7 May 2000.
"Sources Say Russian Air Force to Apologise to Georgia", *Moscow Interfax*, 17 August 1999.
"Southern Africa: IRIN News Briefs", *IRIN*, Johannesburg, 1 December 2000.
Strohm, C., "Bush Administration Faces Decisions on Land Mine Programs, Treaty", *Inside The Army*, Vol. 13, No. 5.
"The Mines Treaty and the US", *Washington Post*, 19 September 1997.
Troxell, J.F., "Landmines: Why the Korea Exception Should Be the Rule", *Parameters*, Spring 2000.
Uhlig, R., "Landmine armed with hopping foot can rearrange itself", *Daily Telegraph*, 28 September 2000.
"UK unveils plans to destroy a million landmines", *Reuters*, London, 27 January 1998.
UK Working Group on Landmines, "Armed Groups Asked to Commit to Landmine Ban", *Press release*, 31 March 2000.
UN Information Service, "Disarmament Conference hears statements on anti-personnel landmines nuclear disarmament and fissile material cut-off", *Press release DCF/311*, Geneva, 15 August 1997.
UN Information Service, "Disarmament Conference hears further calls for bans on landmines and fissile materials, establishment of negotiating committee non nuclear disarmament", *Press release DCF/283*, Geneva, 23 January 1997.
UNOPS, "Yemen Begins Landmine Destruction", *Press release*, 24 February 2000.
"UN Landmines: US proposes UN ban on anti-personnel mines", *Reuters*, New York, 4 November 1996.
"UN Chief, Australian minister urge landmines ban", *Reuters*, 30 January 1997.
"United States to Join Ottawa Process", *Statement by the Press Secretary*, Martha's Vineyard, Massachusetts, 18 September 1997.
"US atoll destroying super-mines, ending North Pacific operations", *AFP*, Auckland, 5 October 2000.
"US Announces Anti-Personnel Landmine Policy", *White House Fact Sheet*, Washington, 16 May 1996.
"US wins more time for landmines pact", *Financial Times*, 17 September 1997.
"US Lawmakers Push for Landmine Treaty Compliance", *Fox News Online*, 2 March 1999.
"Uzbekistan Mines Border with Tajikistan", *Radio Free Europe/Radio Liberty Newsline*, Vol. 4, No. 193, Part I, Prague, 5 October 2000.
"War in the Balkans: A deadly crop of mines is sown in Kosovo: Weapons of power", *Independent*, 19 April 1999.

Webster, D., "One Leg, One Life at a Time", *New York Times Magazine*, 23 January 1994.
"White Paper: China's National Defense", Information Office of the State Council, People's Republic of China, 27 July 1998.
Whittell, G., "Grozny is mined to stop troops looting", *Times*, 13 May 2000.
"Wie alle andern Waffen unterliegen auch die US Landminen aufgrund obiger Bestimmungen nicht det Kontrolle des Bundesrepublik Deutschland", Statement by the Federal Ministry of Defence in Bonn, 2 December 1997.
Williams, F., "UN fails to agree outright ban on landmines", *Financial Times*, 4 May 1996.
Windrem, R., "How bad is the problem?", *NBC News*, 17 September 1997.
Wolffe, R., "Landmines – US proposal on treaty", *Financial Times*, 25 May 1998.
"World War II mine explodes in Ukraine, killing three children", *AP*, Kiev, 8 August 1997.
Wronski, P., "Poland said unlikely to ban landmines before US", *Gazeta Wyborcza*, Warsaw, 7 March 2000.
"Youngsters given lessons in how to make landmines", *Scotsman*, 29 June 1999.
"Zimbabwe begins clearing landmines from prime resort town", *AFP Internationale*, 26 July 1998.

5.5. E-MAIL CORRESPONDENCE AND WEBSITES

"Hunted Elephants", <http://www.dsk.de/mgm.>.
"ICBL letter to Loch Harris re ELF", e-mail correspondence from Liz Bernstein, ICBL Co-ordinator, 15 March 2000.
"Urgent action on Romania/UK", e-mail correspondence from Liz Bernstein, ICBL Co-ordinator, 27 September 1999.
"Intersessional Update No 6", e-mail correspondence from Susan B. Walker, ICBL Government Relations Liaison, 28 April 2000.
"Pakistan Ordnance Factories: Action Alert", e-mail correspondence from Liz Bernstein, ICBL Co-ordinator, on behalf of the UK Working Group to Ban Landmines, 10 December 1999.
"Reporting Update No. 7", e-mail correspondence from Mary Wareham, Human Rights Watch, 8 March 2000.
"UNGA 54/54B Resolution Clarification", e-mail correspondence from Mary Wareham, Human Rights Watch, 10 March 2000.
International Committee of the Red Cross, <http://www.icbl.org>.
International Campaign to Ban Landmines, <http://www.icbl.org>.
Letter from Raul Romeva included in "News from Afghan and Spanish campaigns", e-mail correspondence from Liz Bernstein, Co-ordinator ICBL, 7 October 1998.
Report on Standing Committee of Experts Meeting on General Status and Operation of the Convention from Steve Goose, Human Rights Watch, in e-mail correspondence from Liz Bernstein, ICBL Co-ordinator, 20 January 2000.
Walker, S., "CCW 2nd PrepCom Report", e-mail correspondence, 15 April 2001.

6. APPENDICES

6.1. Declaration Renouncing the Use, in Time of War, of Certain Explosive Projectiles

Saint Petersburg, 29 November – 11 December 1868

On the proposition of the Imperial Cabinet of Russia, an International Military Commission having assembled at St. Petersburg in order to examine the expediency of forbidding the use of certain projectiles in time of war between civilized nations, and that Commission having by common agreement fixed the technical limits at which the necessities of war ought to yield to the requirements of humanity, the Undersigned are authorized by the orders of their Governments to declare as follows:

Considering:

That the progress of civilization should have the effect of alleviating as much as possible the calamities of war;

That the only legitimate object which States should endeavour to accomplish during war is to weaken the military forces of the enemy;

That for this purpose it is sufficient to disable the greatest possible number of men;

That this object would be exceeded by the employment of arms which uselessly aggravate the sufferings of disabled men, or render their death inevitable;

That the employment of such arms would, therefore, be contrary to the laws of humanity;

The Contracting Parties engage mutually to renounce, in case of war among themselves, the employment by their military or naval troops of any projectile of a weight below 400 grammes, which is either explosive or charged with fulminating or inflammable substances.

They will invite all the States which have not taken part in the deliberations of the International Military Commission assembled at St. Petersburg by sending Delegates thereto, to accede to the present engagement.

This engagement is compulsory only upon the Contracting or Acceding Parties thereto in case of war between two or more of themselves; it is not applicable to non-Contracting Parties, or Parties who shall not have acceded to it.

It will also cease to be compulsory from the moment when, in a war between Contracting or Acceding Parties, a non-Contracting Party or a non-Acceding Party shall join one of the belligerents.

The Contracting or Acceding Parties reserve to themselves to come hereafter to an understanding whenever a precise proposition shall be drawn up in view of future improvements which science may effect in the armament of troops, in order to maintain the principles which they have established, and to conciliate the necessities of war with the laws of humanity. (...)

6.2. Project of an International Declaration Concerning the Laws and Customs of War

Brussels, 27 August 1874

Means of injuring the enemy

Article 12

The laws of war do not recognize in belligerents an unlimited power in the adoption of means of injuring the enemy.

Article 13

According to this principle are especially forbidden:

(a) Employment of poison or poisoned weapons;
(b) Murder by treachery of individuals belonging to the hostile nation or army;
(c) Murder of an enemy who, having laid down his arms or having no longer means of defence, has surrendered at discretion;
(d) The declaration that no quarter will be given;
(e) The employment of arms, projectiles or material calculated to cause unnecessary suffering, as well as the use of projectiles prohibited by the Declaration of St. Petersburg of 1868;
(f) Making improper use of a flag of truce, of the national flag or of the military insignia and uniform of the enemy, as well as the distinctive badges of the Geneva Convention;
(g) Any destruction or seizure of the enemy's property that is not imperatively demanded by the necessity of war.

6.3. Convention (II) with Respect to the Laws and Customs of War on Land and its Annex: Regulations Concerning the Laws and Customs of War on Land

The Hague, 29 July 1899

Considering that, while seeking means to preserve peace and prevent armed conflicts among nations, it is likewise necessary to have regard to cases where an appeal to arms may be caused by events which their solicitude could not avert;

Animated by the desire to serve, even in this extreme hypothesis, the interests of humanity and the ever increasing requirements of civilization;

Thinking it important, with this object, to revise the laws and general customs of war, either with the view of defining them more precisely or of laying down certain limits for the purpose of modifying their severity as far as possible;

Inspired by these views which are enjoined at the present day, as they were twenty-five years ago at the time of the Brussels Conference in 1874, by a wise and generous foresight;

Have, in this spirit, adopted a great number of provisions, the object of which is to define and govern the usages of war on land.

In view of the High Contracting Parties, these provisions, the wording of which has been inspired by the desire to diminish the evils of war so far as military necessities permit, are destined to serve as general rules of conduct for belligerents in their relations with each other and with populations.

It has not, however, been possible to agree forthwith on provisions embracing all the circumstances which occur in practice.

On the other hand, it could not be intended by the High Contracting Parties that the cases not provided for should, for want of a written provision, be left to the arbitrary judgment of the military commanders.

Until a more complete code of the laws of war is issued, the High Contracting Parties think it right to declare that in cases not included in the Regulations adopted by them, populations and belligerents remain under the protection and empire of the principles of international law, as they result from the usages established between civilized nations, from the laws of humanity, and the requirements of the public conscience;

They declare that it is in this sense especially that Articles 1 and 2 of the Regulations adopted must be understood;
The High Contracting Parties, desiring to conclude a Convention to this effect, have appointed as their Plenipotentiaries, to wit:(Here follow the names of Plenipotentiaries)Who, after communication of their full powers, found in good and due form, have agreed on the following:

Article 1

The High Contracting Parties shall issue instructions to their armed land forces, which shall be in conformity with the 'Regulations respecting the laws and customs of war on land' annexed to the present Convention.

Article 2

The provisions contained in the Regulations mentioned in Article 1 are only binding on the Contracting Powers, in case of war between two or more of them. These provisions shall cease to be binding from the time when, in a war between Contracting Powers, a non-Contracting Power joins one of the belligerents.

Article 3

The present Convention shall be ratified as speedily as possible. The ratifications shall be deposited at The Hague. A procès-verbal shall be drawn up recording the receipt of each ratification, and a copy, duly certified, shall be sent through the diplomatic channel, to all the Contracting Powers.

Article 4

Non-Signatory Powers are allowed to adhere to the present Convention. For this purpose they must make their adhesion known to the Contracting Powers by means of a written notification, addressed to the Netherlands Government, and by it communicated to all the other Contracting Powers.

Article 5

In the event of one of the High Contracting Parties denouncing the present Convention, such denunciation would not take effect until a year after the written notification made to the Netherlands Government, and by it at once communicated to all the other Contracting Powers. This denunciation shall affect only the notifying Power. In faith of which the Plenipotentiaries have signed the present Convention and affixed their seals thereto.

Done at The Hague 29 July 1899, in a single copy, which shall be kept in the archives of the Netherlands Government, and copies of which, duly certified, shall be delivered to the Contracting Powers through the diplomatic channel.

(Here follow signatures)

6.3.1. Annex to the Convention Regulations Respecting the Laws and Customs of War on Land

Section II

On Hostilities
Chapter 1

On means of injuring the enemy, sieges, and bombardments

Article 22

The right of belligerents to adopt means of injuring the enemy is not unlimited.

Article 23

Besides the prohibitions provided by special Conventions, it is especially prohibited:
(a) To employ poison or poisoned arms;
(b) To kill or wound treacherously individuals belonging to the hostile nation or army;
(c) To kill or wound an enemy who, having laid down arms, or having no longer means of defence, has surrendered at discretion;
(d) To declare that no quarter will be given;
(e) To employ arms, projectiles, or material of a nature to cause superfluous injury;
(f) To make improper use of a flag of truce, the national flag or military ensigns and uniform of the enemy, as well as the distinctive badges of the Geneva Convention;
(g) To destroy or seize the enemy's property, unless such destruction or seizure be imperatively demanded by the necessities of war.

6.4. DECLARATION (IV, 3) CONCERNING EXPANDING BULLETS

The Hague, 29 July 1899

The undersigned, Plenipotentiaries of the Powers represented at the International Peace Conference at The Hague, duly authorized to that effect by their Governments, inspired by the sentiments which found expression in the Declaration of St. Petersburg of 29 November (11 December) 1868,

Declare as follows:

The Contracting Parties agree to abstain from the use of bullets which expand or flatten easily in the human body, such as bullets with a hard envelope which does not entirely cover the core or is pierced with incisions.

The present Declaration is only binding for the Contracting Powers in the case of a war between two or more of them.

It shall cease to be binding from the time when, in a war between the Contracting Powers, one of the belligerents is joined by a non-Contracting Power.

The present Declaration shall be ratified as soon as possible.

The ratification shall be deposited at The Hague.

A procès-verbal shall be drawn up on the receipt of each ratification, a copy of which, duly certified, shall be sent through the diplomatic channel to all the Contracting Powers.

The non-Signatory Powers may adhere to the present Declaration. For this purpose they must make their adhesion known to the Contracting Powers by means of a written notification addressed to the Netherlands Government, and by it communicated to all the other Contracting Powers.

In the event of one of the High Contracting Parties denouncing the present Declaration, such denunciation shall not take effect until a year after the notification made in writing to the Netherlands Government, and forthwith communicated by it to all the other Contracting Powers.

This denunciation shall only affect the notifying Power.

In faith of which the Plenipotentiaries have signed the present Declaration, and have affixed their seals thereto.

Done at The Hague, 29 July 1899, in a single copy, which shall be kept in the archives of the Netherlands Government, and copies of which, duly certified, shall be sent through the diplomatic channel to the Contracting Powers.

6.5. Convention (IV) Respecting the Laws and Customs of War on Land and its Annex: Regulations Concerning the Laws and Customs of War on Land

The Hague, 18 October 1907

6.5.1. Annex to the Convention Regulations Respecting the Laws and Customs of War on Land

Section II
Hostilities

Chapter I
Means of injuring the enemy, sieges, and bombardments

Article 22

The right of belligerents to adopt means of injuring the enemy is not unlimited. Article 23

In addition to the prohibitions provided by special Conventions, it is especially forbidden:

(a) To employ poison or poisoned weapons;
(b) To kill or wound treacherously individuals belonging to the hostile nation or army;
(c) To kill or wound an enemy who, having laid down his arms, or having no longer means of defence, has surrendered at discretion;
(d) To declare that no quarter will be given;
(e) To employ arms, projectiles, or material calculated to cause unnecessary suffering;
(f) To make improper use of a flag of truce, of the national flag or of the military insignia and uniform of the enemy, as well as the distinctive badges of the Geneva Convention;
(g) To destroy or seize the enemy's property, unless such destruction or seizure be imperatively demanded by the necessities of war;
(h) To declare abolished, suspended, or inadmissible in a court of law the rights and actions of the nationals of the hostile party. A belligerent is likewise forbidden to compel the nationals of the hostile party to take part in the operations of war directed against their own country, even if they were in the belligerent's service before the commencement of the war.

6.6. Convention (VIII) Relative to the Laying of Automatic Submarine Contact Mines

The Hague, 18 October 1907

Inspired by the principle of the freedom of sea routes, the common highway of all nations;

Seeing that, although the existing position of affairs makes it impossible to forbid the employment of automatic submarine contact mines, it is nevertheless desirable to restrict and regulate their employment in order to mitigate the severity of war and to ensure, as far as possible, to peaceful navigation the security to which it is entitled, despite the existence of war;

Until such time as it is found possible to formulate rules on the subject which shall ensure to the interests involved all the guarantees desirable;

Have resolved to conclude a Convention for this purpose, and have appointed the following as their Plenipotentiaries: (Here follow the names of Plenipotentiaries)

Who, after having deposited their full powers, found in good and due form, have agreed upon the following provisions:

Article 1

It is forbidden:

1. To lay unanchored automatic contact mines, except when they are so constructed as to become harmless one hour at most after the person who laid them ceases to control them;
2. To lay anchored automatic contact mines which do not become harmless as soon as they have broken loose from their moorings;
3. To use torpedoes which do not become harmless when they have missed their mark.

Article 2

It is forbidden to lay automatic contact mines off the coast and ports of the enemy, with the sole object of intercepting commercial shipping.

Article 3

When anchored automatic contact mines are employed, every possible precaution must be taken for the security of peaceful shipping.

The belligerents undertake to do their utmost to render these mines harmless within a limited time, and, should they cease to be under surveillance, to notify the danger zones as soon as military exigencies permit, by a notice addressed to ship owners, which must also be communicated to the Governments through the diplomatic channel.

Article 4

Neutral Powers which lay automatic contact mines off their coasts must observe the same rules and take the same precautions as are imposed on belligerents.

The neutral Power must inform ship owners, by a notice issued in advance, where automatic contact mines have been laid. This notice must be communicated at once to the Governments through the diplomatic channel.

Article 5

At the close of the war, the Contracting Powers undertake to do their utmost to remove the mines which they have laid, each Power removing its own mines.

As regards anchored automatic contact mines laid by one of the belligerents off the coast of the other, their position must be notified to the other party by the Power which laid them, and each Power must proceed with the least possible delay to remove the mines in its own waters.

Article 6

The Contracting Powers which do not at present own perfected mines of the pattern contemplated in the present Convention, and which, consequently, could not at present carry out the rules laid down in Articles 1 and 3, undertake to convert the matériel of their mines as soon as possible, so as to bring it into conformity with the foregoing requirements.

Article 7

The provisions of the present Convention do not apply except between Contracting Powers, and then only if all the belligerents are parties to the Convention.

Article 8

The present Convention shall be ratified as soon as possible.

The ratifications shall be deposited at The Hague.

The first deposit of ratifications shall be recorded in a procès-verbal signed by the representatives of the Powers which take part therein and by the Netherlands Minister for Foreign Affairs.

The subsequent deposits of ratifications shall be made by means of a written notification addressed to the Netherlands Government and accompanied by the instrument of ratification.

A duly certified copy of the procès-verbal relative to the first deposit of ratifications, of the notifications mentioned in the preceding paragraph, as well as of the instruments of ratification, shall be at once sent, by the Netherlands Government, through the diplomatic channel, to the Powers invited to the Second Peace Conference, as well as to the other Powers which have adhered to the Convention. In the cases contemplated in the preceding paragraph, the said Government shall inform them at the same time of the date on which it has received the notification.

Article 9

Non-Signatory Powers may adhere to the present Convention.

The Power which desires to adhere notifies in writing its intention to the Netherlands Government, transmitting to it the act of adhesion, which shall be deposited in the archives of the said Government.

This Government shall at once transmit to all the other Powers a duly certified copy of the notification as well as of the act of adhesion, stating the date on which it received the notification.

Article 10

The present Convention shall come into force, in the case of the Powers which were a party to the first deposit of ratifications, sixty days after the date of the procès-verbal of this deposit, and, in the case of the Powers which ratify subsequently or adhere, sixty days after the notification of their ratification or of their adhesion has been received by the Netherlands Government.

Article 11

The present Convention shall remain in force for seven years, dating from the sixtieth day after the date of the first deposit of ratifications.

Unless denounced, it shall continue in force after the expiration of this period.

The denunciation shall be notified in writing to the Netherlands Government, which shall at once communicate a duly certified copy of the notification to all the Powers, informing them of the date on which it was received.

The denunciation shall only have effect in regard to the notifying Power, and six months after the notification has reached the Netherlands Government.

Article 12

The Contracting Powers undertake to reopen the question of the employment of automatic contact mines six months before the expiration of the period contemplated in the first paragraph of the preceding article, in the event of the question not having been already reopened and settled by the Third Peace Conference.

If the Contracting Powers conclude a fresh Convention relative to the employment of mines, the present Convention shall cease to be applicable from the moment it comes into force.

Article 13

A register kept by the Netherlands Ministry for Foreign Affairs shall give the date of the deposit of ratifications made in virtue of Article 8, paragraphs 3 and 4, as well as the date on which the notifications of adhesion (Article 9, paragraph 2) or of denunciation (Article 11, paragraph 3) have been received.

Each Contracting Power is entitled to have access to this register and to be supplied with duly certified extracts from it.

In faith whereof the Plenipotentiaries have appended their signatures to the present Convention.

Done at The Hague, 18 October 1907, in a single copy, which shall remain deposited in the archives of the Netherlands Government, and duly certified copies of which shall be sent, through the diplomatic channel, to the Powers which have been invited to the Second Peace Conference.

(Here follow signatures)

6.7. Convention Relative to the Treatment of Prisoners of War

Geneva, 27 July 1929

Part III
Captivity

Section III
Work of Prisoners of War

Chapter 3
Prohibited work

Article 31

Work done by prisoners of war shall have no direct connection with the operations of the war. In particular, it is forbidden to employ prisoners in the manufacture or transport of arms or munitions of any kind, or on the transport of material destined for combatant units.

In the event of violation of the provisions of the preceding paragraph, prisoners are at liberty, after performing or commencing to perform the order, to have their complaints presented through the intermediary of the prisoners' representatives whose functions are described in Articles 43 and 44, or, in the absence of a prisoners' representative, through the intermediary of the representatives of the protecting Power.

Article 32

It is forbidden to employ prisoners of war on unhealthy or dangerous work. Conditions of work shall not be rendered more arduous by disciplinary measures.

6.8. Convention (III) Relative to the Treatment of Prisoners of War

Geneva, 12 August 1949

Article 52

Unless he be a volunteer, no prisoner of war may be employed on labour which is of an unhealthy or dangerous nature.

No prisoner of war shall be assigned to labour which would be looked upon as humiliating for a member of the Detaining Power's own forces.

The removal of mines or similar devices shall be considered as dangerous labour.

6.9. DRAFT RULES FOR THE LIMITATION OF THE DANGERS INCURRED BY THE CIVILIAN POPULATION IN TIME OF WAR

International Committee of the Red Cross, 1956

Chapter IV: Weapons with Uncontrollable Effects

Prohibited methods of warfare

Article 14

Without prejudice to the present or future prohibition of certain specific weapons, the use is prohibited of weapons whose harmful effects – resulting in particular from the dissemination of incendiary, chemical, bacteriological, radioactive or other agents – could spread to an unforeseen degree or escape, either in space or in time, from the control of those who employ them, thus endangering the civilian population.

This prohibition also applies to delayed-action weapons, the dangerous effects of which are liable to be felt by the civilian population.

Safety measures and devices

Article 15

If the Parties to the conflict make use of mines, they are bound, without prejudice to the stipulations of the VIIIth Hague Convention of 1907, to chart the minefields. The charts shall be handed over, at the close of active hostilities, to the adverse Party, and also to all other authorities responsible for the safety of the population.

Without prejudice to the precautions specified under Article 9, weapons capable of causing serious damage to the civilian population shall, so far as possible, be equipped with a safety device which renders them harmless when they escape from the control of those who employ them.

6.10. 'Human Rights in Armed Conflicts' Resolution XXIII Adopted by the International Conference on Human Rights

Teheran, 12 May 1968

The International Conference on Human Rights,

Considering that peace is the underlying condition for the full observance of human rights and war is their negation,

Believing that the purpose of the United Nations Organization is to prevent all conflicts and to institute an effective system for the peaceful settlement of disputes,

Observing that nevertheless armed conflicts continue to plague humanity,

Considering, also, that the widespread violence and brutality of our times, including massacres, summary executions, tortures, inhuman treatment of prisoners, killing of civilians in armed conflicts and the use of chemical and biological means of warfare, including napalm bombing, erode human rights land engender counter-brutality,

Convinced that even during the periods of armed conflict, humanitarian principles must prevail,

Noting that the provisions of the Hague Conventions of 1899 and 1907 were intended to be only a first step in the provision of a code prohibiting or limiting the use of certain methods of warfare and that they were adopted at a time when the present means and methods of warfare did not exist,

Considering that the provisions of the Geneva Protocol of 1925 prohibiting the use of 'asphyxiating, poisonous or other gases and of all analogous liquids materials and devices' have not been universally accepted or applied and may need a revision in the light of modern development,

Considering further that the Red Cross Geneva Conventions of 1949 are not sufficiently broad in scope to cover all armed conflicts,

Noting that States parties to the Red Cross Geneva Conventions sometimes fail to appreciate their responsibility to take steps to ensure the respect of these humanitarian rules in all circumstances by other States, even if they are not themselves directly involved in an armed conflict,

Noting also that minority racist or colonial régimes which refuse to comply with the decisions of the United Nations and the principles of the Universal Declaration of Human Rights frequently resort to executions and inhuman treatment of those who struggle against such régimes and considering that such persons should be protected against inhuman or brutal treatment and also that such persons if detained should be treated as prisoners of war or political prisoners under international law,

1. *Requests* the General Assembly to invite the Secretary-General to study:

(a) Steps which could be taken to secure the better application of existing humanitarian international conventions and rules in all armed conflicts;
(b) The need for additional humanitarian international conventions or for possible revision of existing Conventions to ensure the better protection of civilians, prisoners and combatants in all armed conflicts and the prohibition and limitation of the use of certain methods and means of warfare;

2. *Requests* the Secretary-General, after consultation with the International Committee of the Red Cross, to draw the attention of all States members of the United Nations system to the existing rules of international law on the subject and urge them, pending the adoption of new rules of international law relating to armed conflicts, to ensure that in all armed conflicts the inhabitants and belligerents

are protected in accordance with 'the principles of the law of nations derived from the usages established among civilized peoples, from the laws of humanity and from the dictates of the public conscience;'

3. *Calls* on all States which have not yet done so to become parties to the Hague Conventions of 1899 and 1907, the Geneva Protocol of 1925, and the Geneva Conventions of 1949.

6.11. Respect for Human Rights in Armed Conflicts Resolution 2444 (XXIII) of the United Nations General Assembly

19 December 1968

The General Assembly,

Recognizing the necessity of applying basic humanitarian principles in all armed conflicts,

Taking note of resolution XXIII on human rights in armed conflicts, adopted on 12 May 1968 by the International Conference on Human Rights,

Affirming that the provisions of that resolution need to be implemented effectively as soon as possible,

1. *Affirms* resolution XXVIII of the XXth International Conference of the Red Cross held at Vienna in 1965, which laid down, inter alia, the following principles for observance by all governmental and other authorities responsible for action in armed conflicts:

(a) That the right of the parties to a conflict to adopt means of injuring the enemy is not unlimited;
(b) That it is prohibited to launch attacks against the civilian populations as such;
(c) That distinction must be made at all times between persons taking part in the hostilities and members of the civilian population to the effect that the latter be spared as much as possible;

2. *Invites* the Secretary-General, in consultation with the International Committee of the Red Cross and other appropriate international organizations, to study:

(a) Steps which could be taken to secure the better application of existing humanitarian international conventions and rules in all armed conflicts;

(b) The need for additional humanitarian international conventions or for other appropriate legal instruments to ensure the better protection of civilians, prisoners and combatants in all armed conflicts and the prohibition and limitation of the use of certain methods and means of warfare;

3. *Requests* the Secretary-General to take all other necessary steps to give effect to the provisions of the present resolution and to report to the General Assembly at its twenty-fourth session on the steps he has taken;

4. *Further requests* Member States to extend all possible assistance to the Secretary-General in the preparation of the study requested in paragraph 2 above;

5. *Calls upon* all States which have not yet done so to become parties to the Hague Conventions of 1899 and 1907, the Geneva Protocol of 1925 and the Geneva Conventions of 1949.

6.12. RESOLUTIONS OF THE DIPLOMATIC CONFERENCE OF GENEVA OF 1974-1977

Resolution 22 – Follow-up Regarding Prohibition Or Restriction of Use of Certain Conventional Weapons

The Diplomatic Conference on the Reaffirmation and Development of International Humanitarian Law Applicable in Armed Conflicts, Geneva, 1974-1977

Having met at Geneva for four sessions, in 1974, 1975, 1976 and 1977, and having adopted new humanitarian rules relating to armed conflicts and methods and means of warfare,

Convinced that the suffering of the civilian population and combatants could be significantly reduced if agreements can be attained on the prohibition or restriction for humanitarian reasons of the use of specific conventional weapons, including any which may be deemed to be excessively injurious or to have indiscriminate effects,

Recalling that the issue of prohibitions or restrictions for humanitarian reasons of the use of specific conventional weapons has been the subject of substantive discussion in the Ad Hoc Committee on Conventional Weapons of the Conference at all its four sessions, and at the Conferences of Government Experts held under the auspices of the International Committee of the Red Cross in 1974 at Lucerne and in 1976 at Lugano,

Recalling, in this connection, discussions and relevant resolutions of the General Assembly of the United Nations and appeals made by several Heads of State and Government,

Having concluded, from these discussions, that agreement exists on the desirability of prohibiting the use of conventional weapons, the primary effect of which is to injure by fragments not detectable by X-ray, and that there is a wide area of agreement with regard to land-mines and booby-traps,

Having also devoted efforts to the further narrowing down of divergent views on the desirability of prohibiting or restricting the use of incendiary weapons, including napalm,

Having also considered the effects of the use of other conventional weapons, such as small calibre projectiles and certain blast and fragmentation weapons, and having begun the consideration of the possibility of prohibiting or restricting the use of such weapons,

Recognizing that it is important that this work continue and be pursued with the urgency required by evident humanitarian considerations,

Believing that further work should both build upon the areas of agreement thus far identified and include the search for further areas of agreement and should, in each case, seek the broadest possible agreement,

1. *Resolves* to send the report of the Ad Hoc Committee and the proposals presented in that Committee to the Governments of States represented at the Conference and to the Secretary-General of the United Nations;

2. *Requests* that serious and early consideration be given to these documents and to the reports of the Conferences of Government Experts of Lucerne and Lugano;

3. *Recommends* that a Conference of Governments should be convened not later than 1979 with a view to reaching:(a) agreements on prohibitions or restrictions on the use of specific conventional weapons including those which may be deemed to be excessively injurious or have indiscriminate effects, taking into account humanitarian and military considerations; and (b) agreement on a mechanism for the review of any such agreements and for the consideration of proposals for further such agreements;

4. *Urges* that consultations be undertaken prior to the consideration of this question at the thirty-second session of the United Nations General Assembly for the purpose of reaching agreement on the steps to be taken in preparation for the Conference;

5. *Recommends* that a consultative meeting of all interested Governments be convened during September/October 1977 for this purpose;

6. *Recommends* further that the States participating in these consultations should consider inter alia the establishment of a Preparatory Committee which would seek to establish the best possible basis for theachievement at the Conference of agreements as envisaged in this resolution;

7. *Invites* the General Assembly of the United Nations at its thirty-second session, in the light of the results of the consultations undertaken pursuant to paragraph 4 of this resolution, to take any further action that may be necessary for the holding of the Conference in 1979.

Fifty-seventh plenary meeting
9 June 1977

6.13. Resolution on Small-Calibre Weapon Systems

Geneva, 28 September 1979

The United Nations Conference on Prohibitions or Restrictions of Use of Certain Conventional Weapons,

Recalling United Nations General Assembly resolution 32/152 of 19 December 1977,

Aware of the continuous development of small-calibre weapon systems (*i.e.*, arms and projectiles),

Anxious to prevent an unnecessary increase of the injurious effects of such weapon systems,

Recalling the agreement embodied in The Hague Declaration of 29 July 1899, to abstain, in international armed conflict, from the use of bullets which expand or flatten easily in the human body,

Convinced that it is desirable to establish accurately the wounding effects of current and new generations of small calibre weapon systems including the various parameters that affect the energy transfer and the wounding mechanism of such systems,

1. *Takes note* with appreciation of the intensive research carried out nationally and internationally in the area of wound ballistics, in particular relating to small-calibre weapon systems, as documented during the Conference;

2. *Considers* that this research and the international discussion on the subject has led to an increased understanding of the wounding effects of small-calibre weapon systems and of the parameters involved;

3. *Believes* that such research, including testing of small-calibre weapon systems, should be continued with a view to developing standardized assessment methodology relative to ballistic parameters and medical effects of such systems;

4. *Invites* Governments to carry out further research, jointly or individually on the wounding effects of small-calibre weapon systems and to communicate, where possible, their findings and conclusions;

5. *Welcomes* the announcement that an international scientific symposium on wound ballistics will be held in Gothenburg, Sweden, in late 1980 or in 1981, and hopes that the results of the symposium will be made available to the United Nations Disarmament Commission, the Committee on Disarmament and other interested fora;

6. *Appeals* to all Governments to exercise the utmost care in the development of small-calibre weapon systems, so as to avoid an unnecessary escalation of the injurious effects of such systems.

6.14. Convention on Prohibitions or Restrictions on the Use of Certain Conventional Weapons which may be Deemed to be Excessively Injurious or to have Indiscriminate Effects

Geneva, 10 October 1980

The High Contracting Parties,

Recalling that every State has the duty, in conformity with the Charter of the United Nations, to refrain in its international relations from the threat or use of force against the sovereignty, territorial integrity or political independence of any State, or in any other manner inconsistent with the purposes of the United Nations.

Further recalling the general principle of the protection of the civilian population against the effects of hostilities,

Basing themselves on the principle of international law that the right of the parties to an armed conflict to choose methods or means of warfare is not unlimited, and on the principle that prohibits the employment in armed conflicts of weapons, projectiles and material and methods of warfare of a nature to cause superfluous injury or unnecessary suffering,

Also recalling that it is prohibited to employ methods or means of warfare which are intended, or may be expected, to cause widespread, long-term and severe damage to the natural environment,

Confirming their determination that in cases not covered by this Convention and its annexed Protocols or by other international agreements, the civilian population and the combatants shall at all times remain under the protection and authority of the principles of international law derived from established custom, from the principles of humanity and from the dictates of public conscience,

Desiring to contribute to international détente, the ending of the arms race and the building of confidence among States, and hence to the realization of the aspiration of all peoples to live in peace,

Recognizing the importance of pursuing every effort which may contribute to progress towards general and complete disarmament under strict and effective international control,

Reaffirming the need to continue the codification and progressive development of the rules of international law applicable in armed conflict,

Wishing to prohibit or restrict further the use of certain conventional weapons and believing that the positive results achieved in this area may facilitate the main talks on disarmament with a view to putting an end to the production, stockpiling and proliferation of such weapons,

Emphasizing the desirability that all States become parties to this Convention and its annexed Protocols, especially the militarily significant States,

Bearing in mind that the General Assembly of the United Nations and the United Nations Disarmament Commission may decide to examine the question of a possible broadening of the scope of the prohibitions and restrictions contained in this Convention and its annexed Protocols,

Further bearing in mind that the Committee on Disarmament may decide to consider the question of adopting further measures to prohibit or restrict the use of certain conventional weapons,

Have agreed as follows:

Article 1
Scope of application

This Convention and its annexed Protocols shall apply in the situations referred to in Article 2 common to the Geneva Conventions of 12 August 1949 for the Protection of War Victims, including any situation described in paragraph 4 of Article 1 of Additional Protocol I to these Conventions.

Article 2
Relations with other international agreements

Nothing in this Convention or its annexed Protocols shall be interpreted as detracting from other obligations imposed upon the High Contracting Parties by international humanitarian law applicable in armed conflict.

Article 3
Signature

This Convention shall be open for signature by all States at United Nations Headquarters in New York for a period of twelve months from 10 April 1981.

Article 4
Ratification, acceptance, approval or accession

1. This Convention is subject to ratification, acceptance or approval by the Signatories. Any State which has not signed this Convention may accede to it.

2. The instruments of ratification, acceptance, approval or accession shall be deposited with the Depositary.

3. Expressions of consent to be bound by any of the Protocols annexed to this Convention shall be optional for each State, provided that at the time of the deposit of its instrument of ratification, acceptance or approval of this Convention or of accession thereto, that State shall notify the Depositary of its consent to be bound by any two or more of these Protocols.

4. At any time after the deposit of its instrument of ratification, acceptance or approval of this Convention or of accession thereto, a State may notify the Depositary of its consent to be bound by any annexed Protocol by which it is not already bound.

5. Any Protocol by which a High Contracting Party is bound shall for that Party form an integral part of this Convention.

Article 5
Entry into force

1. This Convention shall enter into force six months after the date of deposit of the twentieth instrument of ratification, acceptance, approval or accession.

2. For any State which deposits its instrument of ratification, acceptance, approval or accession after the date of the deposit of the twentieth instrument of ratification, acceptance, approval or accession, this Convention shall enter into force six months after the date on which that State has deposited its instrument of ratification, acceptance, approval or accession.

3. Each of the Protocols annexed to this Convention shall enter into force six months after the date by which twenty States have notified their consent to be bound by it in accordance with paragraph 3 or 4 of Article 4 of this Convention.

4. For any State which notifies its consent to be bound by a Protocol annexed to this Convention after the date by which twenty States have notified their consent to be bound by it, the Protocol shall enter into force six months after the date on which that State has notified its consent so to be bound.

Article 6
Dissemination

The High Contracting Parties undertake, in time of peace as in time of armed conflict, to disseminate this Convention and those of its annexed Protocols by which they are bound as widely as possible in their respective countries and, in particular, to include the study thereof in their programmes of military instruction, so that those instruments may become known to their armed forces.

Article 7
Treaty relations upon entry into force of this Convention

1. When one of the parties to a conflict is not bound by an annexed Protocol, the parties bound by this Convention and that annexed Protocol shall remain bound by them in their mutual relations.

2. Any High Contracting Party shall be bound by this Convention and any Protocol annexed thereto which is in force for it, in any situation contemplated by Article 1, in relation to any State which is not a party to this Convention or bound by the relevant annexed Protocol, if the latter accepts and applies this Convention or the relevant Protocol, and so notifies the Depositary.

3. The Depositary shall immediately inform the High Contracting Parties concerned of any notification received under paragraph 2 of this Article.

4. This Convention, and the annexed Protocols by which a High Contracting Party is bound, shall apply with respect to an armed conflict against that High Contracting Party of the type referred to in Article 1, paragraph 4, of Additional Protocol I to the Geneva Conventions of 12 August 1949 for the Protection of War Victims: (a) where the High Contracting Party is also a party to Additional Protocol I and an authority referred to in Article 96, paragraph 3, of that Protocol has undertaken to apply the Geneva Conventions and Additional Protocol I in accordance with Article 96, paragraph 3, of the said Protocol, and undertakes to apply this Convention and the relevant annexed Protocols in relation to that conflict; or (b) where the High Contracting Party is not a party to Additional Protocol I and an authority of the type referred to in subparagraph (a) above accepts and applies the obligations of the Geneva Conventions and of this Convention and the relevant annexed Protocols in relation to that conflict. Such an acceptance and application shall have in relation to that conflict the following effects:

(i) the Geneva Conventions and this Convention and its relevant annexed Protocols are brought into force for the parties to the conflict with immediate effect;
(ii) the said authority assumes the same rights and obligations as those which have been assumed by a High Contracting Party to the Geneva Conventions, this Convention and its relevant annexed Protocols; and
(iii) the Geneva Conventions, this Convention and its relevant annexed Protocols are equally binding upon all parties to the conflict.

The High Contracting Party and the authority may also agree to accept and apply the obligations of Additional Protocol I to the Geneva Conventions on a reciprocal basis.

Article 8
Review and amendments

1. (a) At any time after the entry into force of this Convention any High Contracting Party may propose amendments to this Convention or any annexed Protocol by which it is bound. Any proposal for an amendment shall be communicated to the Depositary, who shall notify it to all the High Contracting Parties and shall seek their views on whether a conference should be convened to consider the proposal. If a majority, that shall not be less than eighteen of the High Contracting

Parties so agree, he shall promptly convene a conference to which all High Contracting Parties shall be invited. States not parties to this Convention shall be invited to the conference as observers.
(b) Such a conference may agree upon amendments which shall be adopted and shall enter into force in the same manner as this Convention and the annexed Protocols, provided that amendments to this Convention may be adopted only by the High Contracting Parties and that amendments to a specific annexed Protocol may be adopted only by the High Contracting Parties which are bound by that Protocol.

2. (a) At any time after the entry into force of this Convention any High Contracting Party may propose additional protocols relating to other categories of conventional weapons not covered by the existing annexed Protocols. Any such proposal for an additional protocol shall be communicated to the Depositary, who shall notify it to all the High Contracting Parties in accordance with subparagraph 1 (a) of this Article. If a majority, that shall not be less than eighteen of the High Contracting Parties so agree, the Depositary shall promptly convene a conference to which all States shall be invited.

(b) Such a conference may agree, with the full participation of all States represented at the conference, upon additional protocols which shall be adopted in the same manner as this Convention, shall be annexed thereto and shall enter into force as provided in paragraphs 3 and 4 of Article 5 of this Convention.3. (a) If, after a period of ten years following the entry into force of this Convention, no conference has been convened in accordance with subparagraph 1 (a) or 2 (a) of this Article, any High Contracting Party may request the Depositary to convene a conference to which all High Contracting Parties shall be invited to review the scope and operation of this Convention and the Protocols annexed thereto and to consider any proposal for amendments of this Convention or of the existing Protocols. States not parties to this Convention shall be invited as observers to the conference. The conference may agree upon amendments which shall be adopted and enter into force in accordance with subparagraph 1 (b) above.

(c) At such conference consideration may also be given to any proposal for additional protocols relating to other categories of conventional weapons not covered by the existing annexed Protocols. All States represented at the conference may participate fully in such consideration. Any additional protocols shall be adopted in the same manner as this Convention, shall be annexed thereto and shall enter into force as provided in paragraphs 3 and 4 of Article 5 of this Convention.
(d) Such a conference may consider whether provision should be made for the convening of a further conference at the request of any High Contracting Party if, after a similar period to that referred to in subparagraph 3 (a) of this Article, no conference has been convened in accordance with subparagraph 1 (a) or 2 (a) of this Article.

Article 9
Denunciation

1. Any High Contracting Party may denounce this Convention or any of its annexed Protocols by so notifying the Depositary.

2. Any such denunciation shall only take effect one year after receipt by the Depositary of the notification of denunciation. If, however, on the expiry of that year the denouncing High Contracting Party is engaged in one of the situations referred to in Article 1, the Party shall continue to be bound by the obligations of this Convention and of the relevant annexed Protocols until the end of the armed conflict or occupation and, in any case, until the termination of operations connected with the final release, repatriation or re-establishment of the person protected by the rules of international law applicable in armed conflict, and in the case of any annexed Protocol containing provisions concerning situations in which peace-keeping, observation or similar functions are performed by United Nations forces or missions in the area concerned, until the termination of those functions.

3. Any denunciation of this Convention shall be considered as also applying to all annexed Protocols by which the denouncing High Contracting Party is bound.

4. Any denunciation shall have effect only in respect of the denouncing High Contracting Party.

5. Any denunciation shall not affect the obligations already incurred, by reason of an armed conflict, under this Convention and its annexed Protocols by such denouncing High Contracting Party in respect of any act committed before this denunciation becomes effective.

Article 10
Depositary

1. The Secretary-General of the United Nations shall be the Depositary of this Convention and of its annexed Protocols.
2. In addition to his usual functions, the Depositary shall inform all States of:

(a) signatures affixed to this Convention under Article 3;
(b) deposits of instruments of ratification, acceptance or approval of or accession to this Convention deposited under Article 4;
(c) notifications of consent to be bound by annexed Protocols under Article 4;
(d) the dates of entry into force of this Convention and of each of its annexed Protocols under Article 5; and
(e) notifications of denunciation received under article 9, and their effective date.

Article 11
Authentic texts

The original of this Convention with the annexed Protocols, of which the Arabic, Chinese, English, French, Russian and Spanish texts are equally authentic, shall be deposited with the Depositary, who shall transmit certified true copies thereof to all States.

6.14.1. Protocol on Non-Detectable Fragments (Protocol I)

Geneva, 10 October 1980

It is prohibited to use any weapon the primary effect of which is to injure by fragments which in the human body escape detection by X-rays.

6.14.2. Protocol on Prohibitions or Restrictions on the Use of Mines, Booby-Traps and Other Devices (Protocol II)

Geneva, 10 October 1980

Article 1
Material scope of application

This Protocol relates to the use on land of the mines, booby-traps and other devices defined herein, including mines laid to interdict beaches, waterway crossings or river crossings, but does not apply to the use of anti-ship mines at sea or in inland waterways.

Article 2
Definitions

For the purpose of this Protocol:

1. 'mine' means any munition placed under, on or near the ground or other surface area and designed to be detonated or exploded by the presence, proximity or contact of a person or vehicle, and "remotely delivered mine" means any mine so defined delivered by artillery, rocket, mortar or similar means or dropped from an aircraft.

2. 'Booby-trap' means any device or material which is designed, constructed or adapted to kill or injure and which functions unexpectedly when a person disturbs or approaches an apparently harmless object or performs an apparently safe act.

3. 'Other devices' means manually-emplaced munitions and devices designed to kill, injure or damage and which are actuated by remote control or automatically after a lapse of time.

4. 'Military objective' means, so far as objects are concerned, any object which by its nature, location, purpose or use makes an effective contribution to military action and whose total or partial destruction, capture or neutralization, in the circumstances ruling at the time, offers a definite military advantage.

5. 'Civilian objects' are all objects which are not military objectives as defined in paragraph 4.

6. 'Recording' means a physical, administrative and technical operation designed to obtain, for the purpose of registration in the official records, all available information facilitating the location of minefields, mines and booby-traps.

Article 3
General restrictions on the use of mines, booby-traps and other devices

1. This Article applies to: (a) mines (b) booby-traps; and (c) other devices.

2. It is prohibited in all circumstances to direct weapons to which this Article applies, either in offence, defence or by way of reprisals, against the civilian population as such or against individual civilians.

3. The indiscriminate use of weapons to which this Article applies is prohibited. Indiscriminate use is any placement of such weapons:

(a) which is not on, or directed against, a military objective; or
(b) which employs a method or means of delivery which cannot be directed at a specific military objective; or
(c) which may be expected to cause incidental loss of civilian life, injury to civilians, damage to civilian objects, or a combination thereof, which would be excessive in relation to the concrete and direct military advantage anticipated.

4. All feasible precautions shall be taken to protect civilians from the effects of weapons to which this Article applies. Feasible precautions are those precautions which are practicable or practically possible taking into account all circumstances ruling at the time, including humanitarian and military considerations.

Article 4
Restrictions on the use of mines other than remotely delivered mines, booby-traps and other devices in populated areas

1. This Article applies to: (a) mines other than remotely delivered mines; (b) booby-traps; and (c) other devices.

2. It is prohibited to use weapons to which this Article applies in any city, town, village or other area containing a similar concentration of civilians in which combat between ground forces is not taking place or does not appear to be imminent, unless either:

(a) they are placed on or in the close vicinity of a military objective belonging to or under the control of an adverse party; or
(b) measures are taken to protect civilians from their effects, for example, the posting of warning signs, the posting of sentries, the issue of warnings or the provision of fences.

Article 5
Restrictions on the use of remotely delivered mines

1. The use of remotely delivered mines is prohibited unless such mines are only used within an area which is itself a military objective or which contains military objectives, and unless:

(a) their location can be accurately recorded in accordance with Article 7(1)(a); or
(b) an effective neutralizing mechanism is used on each such mine, that is to say, a self-actuating mechanism which is designed to render a mine harmless or cause it to destroy itself when it is anticipated that the mine will no longer serve the military purpose for which it was placed in position, or a remotely-controlled mechanism which is designed to render harmless or destroy a mine when the mine no longer serves the military purpose for which it was placed in position.

2. Effective advance warning shall be given of any delivery or dropping of remotely delivered mines which may affect the civilian population, unless circumstances do not permit.

Article 6
Prohibition on the use of certain booby-traps

1. Without prejudice to the rules of international law applicable in armed conflict relating to treachery and perfidy, it is prohibited in all circumstances to use:

(a) any booby-trap in the form of an apparently harmless portable object which is specifically designed and constructed to contain explosive material and to detonate when it is disturbed or approached, or

(b) booby-traps which are in any way attached to or associated with:
  (i) internationally recognized protective emblems, signs or signals;
  (ii) sick, wounded or dead persons;
  (iii) burial or cremation sites or graves;
  (iv) medical facilities, medical equipment, medical supplies or medical transportation;
  (v) children's toys or other portable objects or products specially designed for the feeding, health, hygiene, clothing or education of children;
  (vi) food or drink;
  (vii) kitchen utensils or appliances except in military establishments, military locations or military supply depots;
  (viii) objects clearly of a religious nature;
  (ix) historic monuments, works of art or places or worship which constitute the cultural or spiritual heritage of peoples;
  (x) animals or their carcasses.

2. It is prohibited in all circumstances to use any booby-trap which is designed to cause superfluous injury or unnecessary suffering.

Article 7
Recording and publication of the location of minefields, mines and booby-traps

1. The parties to a conflict shall record the location of:

(a) all pre-planned minefields laid by them; and
(b) all areas in which they have made large-scale and pre-planned use of booby-traps.

2. The parties shall endeavour to ensure the recording of the location of all other minefields, mines and booby-traps which they have laid or placed in position.

3. All such records shall be retained by the parties who shall:

(a) immediately after the cessation of active hostilities:
  (i) take all necessary and appropriate measures, including the use of such records, to protect civilians from the effects of minefields, mines and booby-traps; and either,
  (ii) in cases where the forces of neither party are in the territory of the adverse party, make available to each other and to the Secretary-General of the United Nations all information in their possession concerning the location of minefields, mines and booby-traps in the territory of the adverse party; or
  (iii) once complete withdrawal of the forces of the parties from the territory of the adverse party has taken place, make available to the adverse party and to the Secretary-General of the United Nations all information in their possession concerning the location of minefields, mines and booby traps in the territory of the adverse party;
(b) when a United Nations force or mission performs functions in any area, make available to the authority mentioned in Article 8 such information as is required by that Article;
(c) whenever possible, by mutual agreement, provide for the release of information concerning the location of minefields, mines and booby traps, particularly in agreements governing the cessation of hostilities.

Article 8
Protection of United Nations forces and missions from the effects of minefields, mines and booby-traps

1. When a United Nations force or mission performs functions of peacekeeping, observation or similar functions in any area, each party to the conflict shall, if requested by the head of the United Nations force or mission in that area, as far as it is able:

(a) remove or render harmless all mines or booby traps in that area;
(b) take such measures as may be necessary to protect the force or mission from the effects of minefields, mines and booby traps while carrying out its duties; and
(c) make available to the head of the United Nations force or mission in that area, all information in the party's possession concerning the location of minefields, mines and booby traps in that area.

2. When a United Nations fact-finding mission performs functions in any area, any party to the conflict concerned shall provide protection to that mission except where, because of the size of such mission, it cannot adequately provide such protection. In that case it shall make available to the head of the mission the information in its possession concerning the location of minefields, mines and booby-traps in that area.

Article 9
International co-operation in the removal of minefields, mines and booby-traps

After the cessation of active hostilities, the parties shall endeavour to reach agreement, both among themselves and, where appropriate, with other States and with international organizations, on the provision of information and technical and material assistance – including, in appropriate circumstances, joint operations – necessary to remove or otherwise render ineffective minefields, mines and booby-traps placed in position during the conflict.

A. Technical Annex to the Protocol on Prohibitions or Restrictions on the Use of Mines, Booby-Traps and Other Devices (Protocol II)

(i) Guidelines on recording

Whenever an obligation for the recording of the location of minefields, mines and booby traps arises under the Protocol, the following guidelines shall be taken into account.

1. With regard to pre-planned minefields and large-scale and pre-planned use of booby traps:

(a) maps, diagrams or other records should be made in such a way as to indicate the extent of the minefield or booby-trapped area; and

(b) the location of the minefield or booby-trapped area should be specified by relation to the co-ordinates of a single reference point and by the estimated dimensions of the area containing mines and booby traps in relation to that single reference point.

2. With regard to other minefields, mines and booby-traps laid or placed in position: In so far as possible, the relevant information specified in paragraph 1 above should be recorded so as to enable the areas containing minefields, mines and booby traps to be identified.

6.14.3. Protocol on Prohibitions or Restrictions on the Use of Incendiary Weapons (Protocol III)

Geneva, 10 October 1980

Article 1
Definitions

For the purpose of this Protocol:

1. 'Incendiary weapon' means any weapon or munition which is primarily designed to set fire to objects or to cause burn injury to persons through the action of flame, heat, or combination thereof, produced by a chemical reaction of a substance delivered on the target.

(a) Incendiary weapons can take the form of, for example, flame throwers, fougasses, shells, rockets, grenades, mines, bombs and other containers of incendiary substances.

(b) Incendiary weapons do not include:

(i) Munitions which may have incidental incendiary effects, such as illuminants, tracers, smoke or signalling systems;

(ii) Munitions designed to combine penetration, blast or fragmentation effects with an additional incendiary effect, such as armour-piercing projectiles, fragmentation shells, explosive bombs and similar combined-effects munitions in which the incendiary effect is not specifically designed to cause burn injury to persons, but to be used against military objectives, such as armoured vehicles, aircraft and installations or facilities.

2. 'Concentration of civilians' means any concentration of civilians, be it permanent or temporary, such as in inhabited parts of cities, or inhabited towns or villages, or as in camps or columns of refugees or evacuees, or groups of nomads.

3. 'Military objective' means, so far as objects are concerned, any object which by its nature, location, purpose or use makes an effective contribution to military action and whose total or partial destruction, capture or neutralization, in the circumstances ruling at the time, offers a definite military advantage.

4. 'Civilian objects' are all objects which are not military objectives as defined in paragraph 3.

5. 'Feasible precautions' are those precautions which are practicable or practically possible taking into account all circumstances ruling at the time, including humanitarian and military considerations.

Article 2
Protection of civilians and civilian objects

1. It is prohibited in all circumstances to make the civilian population as such, individual civilians or civilian objects the object of attack by incendiary weapons.

2. It is prohibited in all circumstances to make any military objective located within a concentration of civilians the object of attack by air-delivered incendiary weapons.

3. It is further prohibited to make any military objective located within a concentration of civilians the object of attack by means of incendiary weapons other than air-delivered incendiary weapons, except when such military objective is clearly separated from the concentration of civilians and all feasible precautions are taken with a view to limiting the incendiary effects to the military objective and to avoiding, and in any event to minimizing, incidental loss of civilian life, injury to civilians and damage to civilian objects.

4. It is prohibited to make forests or other kinds of plant cover the object of attack by incendiary weapons except when such natural elements are used to cover, conceal or camouflage combatants or other military objectives, or are themselves military objectives.

6.14.4. Protocol on Blinding Laser Weapons (Protocol IV)

13 October 1995

Article 1

It is prohibited to employ laser weapons specifically designed, as their sole combat function or as one of their combat functions, to cause permanent blindness to unenhanced vision, that is to the naked eye or to the eye with corrective eyesight devices. The High Contracting Parties shall not transfer such weapons to any State or non-State entity.

Article 2

In the employment of laser systems, the High Contracting Parties shall take all feasible precautions to avoid the incidence of permanent blindness to unenhanced vision. Such precautions shall include training of their armed forces and other practical measures.

Article 3

Blinding as an incidental or collateral effect of the legitimate military employment of laser systems, including laser systems used against optical equipment, is not covered by the prohibition of this Protocol.

Article 4

For the purpose of this protocol 'permanent blindness' means irreversible and uncorrectable loss of vision which is seriously disabling with no prospect of recovery. Serious disability is equivalent to visual acuity of less than 20/200 Snellen measured using both eyes.

6.14.5. Protocol on Prohibitions or Restrictions on the Use of Mines, Booby-Traps and Other Devices as amended on 3 May 1996 (Protocol II to the 1980 Convention as amended on 3 May 1996)

Article 1 – Scope of application

1. This Protocol relates to the use on land of the mines, booby-traps and other devices, defined herein, including mines laid to interdict beaches, waterway crossings or river crossings, but does not apply to the use of anti-ship mines at sea or in inland waterways.

2. This Protocol shall apply, in addition to situations referred to in Article I of this Convention, to situations referred to in Article 3 common to the Geneva Conventions of 12 August 1949. This Protocol shall not apply to situations of internal disturbances and tensions, such as riots, isolated and sporadic acts of violence and other acts of a similar nature, as not being armed conflicts.

3. In case of armed conflicts not of an international character occurring in the territory of one of the High Contracting Parties, each party to the conflict shall be bound to apply the prohibitions and restrictions of this Protocol.

4. Nothing in this Protocol shall be invoked for the purpose of affecting the sovereignty of a State or the responsibility of the Government, by all legitimate means, to maintain or re-establish law and order in the State or to defend the national unity and territorial integrity of the State.

5. Nothing in this Protocol shall be invoked as a justification for intervening, directly or indirectly, for any reason whatever, in the armed conflict or in the internal or external affairs of the High Contracting Party in the territory of which that conflict occurs.

6. The application of the provisions of this Protocol to parties to a conflict, which are not High Contracting Parties that have accepted this Protocol, shall not change their legal status or the legal status of a disputed territory, either explicitly or implicitly.

Article 2 – Definitions

For the purpose of this Protocol:

1. 'Mine' means a munition placed under, on or near the ground or other surface area and designed to be exploded by the presence, proximity or contact of a person or vehicle.

2. 'Remotely-delivered mine' means a mine not directly emplaced but delivered by artillery, missile, rocket, mortar, or similar means, or dropped from an aircraft. Mines delivered from a land-based system from less than 500 metres are not considered to be 'remotely delivered', provided that they are used in accordance with Article 5 and other relevant Articles of this Protocol.

3. 'Anti-Personnel mine' means a mine primarily designed to be exploded by the presence, proximity or contact of a person and that will incapacitate, injure or kill one or more persons.

4. 'Booby-trap' means any device or material which is designed, constructed or adapted to kill or injure, and which functions unexpectedly when a person disturbs or approaches an apparently harmless object or performs an apparently safe act.

5. 'Other devices' means manually-emplaced munitions and devices including improvised explosive devices designed to kill, injure or damage and which are actuated manually, by remote control or automatically after a lapse of time.

6. 'Military objective' means, so far as objects are concerned, any object which by its nature, location, purpose or use makes an effective contribution to military action and whose total or partial destruction, capture or neutralization, in the circumstances ruling at the time, offers a definite military advantage.

7. 'Civilian objects' are all objects which are not military objectives as defined in paragraph 6 of this Article.

8. 'Minefield' is a defined area in which mines have been emplaced and 'mined area' is an area which is dangerous due to the presence of mines. 'Phoney minefield' means an area free of mines that simulates a minefield. The term 'minefield' includes phoney minefields.

9. 'Recording' means a physical, administrative and technical operation designed to obtain, for the purpose of registration in official records, all available information facilitating the location of minefields, mined areas, mines, booby-traps and other devices.

10. 'Self-destruction mechanism' means an incorporated or externally attached automatically-functioning mechanism which secures the destruction of the munition into which it is incorporated or to which it is attached.

11. 'Self-neutralization mechanism' means an incorporated automatically-functioning mechanism which renders inoperable the munition into which it is incorporated.

12. 'Self-deactivating' means automatically rendering a munition inoperable by means of the irreversible exhaustion of a component, for example, a battery, that is essential to the operation of the munition.

13. 'Remote control' means control by commands from a distance.

14. 'Anti-handling device' means a device intended to protect a mine and which is part of, linked to, attached to or placed under the mine and which activates when an attempt is made to tamper with the mine.

15. 'Transfer' involves, in addition to the physical movement of mines into or from national territory, the transfer of title to and control over the mines, but does not involve the transfer of territory containing emplaced mines.

Article 3 – General restrictions on the use, of mines, booby-traps and other devices

1. This Article applies to: (a) mines; (b) booby-traps; and (c) other devices.

2. Each High Contracting Party or party to a conflict is, in accordance with the provisions of this Protocol, responsible for all mines, booby-traps, and other devices employed by it and undertakes to clear, remove, destroy or maintain them as specified in Article 10 of this Protocol.

3. It is prohibited in all circumstances to use any mine, booby-trap or other device which is designed or of a nature to cause superfluous injury or unnecessary suffering.

4. Weapons to which this Article applies shall strictly comply with the standards and limitations specified in the Technical Annex with respect to each particular category.

5. It is prohibited to use mines, booby-traps or other devices which employ a mechanism or device specifically designed to detonate the munition by the presence of commonly available mine detectors as a result of their magnetic or other non-contact influence during normal use in detection operations.

6. It is prohibited to use a self-deactivating mine equipped with an anti-handling device that is designed in such a manner that the anti-handling device is capable of functioning after the mine has ceased to be capable of functioning.

7. It is prohibited in all circumstances to direct weapons to which this Article applies, either in offence, defence or by way of reprisals, against the civilian population as such or against individual civilians or civilian objects.

8. The indiscriminate use of weapons to which this Article applies is prohibited. Indiscriminate use is any placement of such weapons:

(a) which is not on, or directed against, a military objective. In case of doubt as to whether an object which is normally dedicated to civilian purposes, such as a place of worship, a house or other dwelling or a school, is being used to make an effective contribution to military action, it shall be presumed not to be so used; or

(b) which employs a method or means of delivery which cannot be directed at a specific military objective; or
(c) which may be expected to cause incidental loss of civilian life, injury to civilians, damage to civilian objects, or a combination thereof, which would be excessive in relation to the concrete and direct military advantage anticipated.

9. Several clearly separated and distinct military objectives located in a city, town, village or other area containing a similar concentration of civilians or civilian objects are not to be treated as a single military objective.

10. All feasible precautions shall be taken to protect civilians from the effects of weapons to which this Article applies. Feasible precautions are those precautions which are practicable or practically possible taking into account all circumstances ruling at the time, including humanitarian and military considerations. These circumstances include, but are not limited to:

(a) the short- and long-term effect of mines upon the local civilian population for the duration of the minefield;
(b) possible measures to protect civilians (for example, fencing, signs, warning and monitoring);
(c) the availability and feasibility of using alternatives; and
(d) the short- and long-term military requirements for a minefield.

11. Effective advance warning shall be given of any emplacement of mines, booby-traps and other devices which may affect the civilian population, unless circumstances do not permit.

Article 4 – Restrictions on the use of anti-personnel mines

It is prohibited to use anti-personnel mines which are not detectable, as specified in paragraph 2 of the Technical Annex.

Article 5 – Restrictions on the use of anti-personnel mines other than remotely-delivered mines

1. This Article applies to anti-personnel mines other than remotely-delivered mines.

2. It is prohibited to use weapons to which this Article applies which are not in compliance with the provisions on self-destruction and self-deactivation in the Technical Annex, unless:

(a) such weapons are placed within a perimeter-marked area which is monitored by military personnel and protected by fencing or other means, to ensure the effective exclusion of civilians from the area. The marking must be of a distinct and durable character and must at least be visible to a person who is about to enter the perimeter-marked area; and
(b) such weapons are cleared before the area is abandoned, unless the area is turned over to the forces of another State which accept responsibility for the maintenance of the protections required by this Article and the subsequent clearance of those weapons.

3. A party to a conflict is relieved from further compliance with the provisions of sub-paragraphs 2 (a) and 2 (b) of this Article only if such compliance is not feasible due to forcible loss of control of the area as a result of enemy military action, including situations where direct enemy military action makes it impossible to comply. If that party regains control of the area, it shall resume compliance with the provisions of sub-paragraphs 2 (a) and 2 (b) of this Article.

4. If the forces of a party to a conflict gain control of an area in which weapons to which this Article applies have been laid, such forces shall, to the maximum extent feasible, maintain and, if necessary, establish the protections required by this Article until such weapons have been cleared.

5. All feasible measures shall be taken to prevent the unauthorized removal, defacement, destruction or concealment of any device, system or material used to establish the perimeter of a perimeter-marked area.

6. Weapons to which this Article applies which propel fragments in a horizontal arc of less than 90 degrees and which are placed on or above the ground may be used without the measures provided for in sub-paragraph 2 (a) of this Article for a maximum period of 72 hours, if:

(a) they are located in immediate proximity to the military unit that emplaced them; and
(b) the area is monitored by military personnel to ensure the effective exclusion of civilians.

Article 6 – Restrictions on the use of remotely-delivered mines

1. It is prohibited to use remotely-delivered mines unless they are recorded in accordance with sub-paragraph 1 (b) of the Technical Annex.

2. It is prohibited to use remotely-delivered anti-personnel mines which are not in compliance with the provisions on self-destruction and self-deactivation in the Technical Annex.

3. It is prohibited to use remotely-delivered mines other than anti-personnel mines, unless, to the extent feasible, they are equipped with an effective self-destruction or self-neutralization mechanism and have a back-up self-deactivation feature, which is designed so that the mine will no longer function as a mine when the mine no longer serves the military purpose for which it was placed in position.

4. Effective advance warning shall be given of any delivery or dropping of remotely-delivered mines which may affect the civilian population, unless circumstances do not permit.

Article 7 – Prohibitions on the use of booby-traps and other devices

1. Without prejudice to the rules of international law applicable in armed conflict relating to treachery and perfidy, it is prohibited in all circumstances to use booby-traps and other devices which are in any way attached to or associated with:
(a) internationally recognized protective emblems, signs or signals;
(b) sick, wounded or dead persons;
(c) burial or cremation sites or graves;
(d) medical facilities, medical equipment, medical supplies or medical transportation;
(e) children's toys or other portable objects or products specially designed for the feeding, health, hygiene, clothing or education of children;
(f) food or drink;
(g) kitchen utensils or appliances except in military establishments, military locations or military supply depots;
(h) objects clearly of a religious nature;
(i) historic monuments, works of art or places of worship which constitute the cultural or spiritual heritage of peoples; or
(j) animals or their carcasses.

2. It is prohibited to use booby-traps or other devices in the form of apparently harmless portable objects which are specifically designed and constructed to contain explosive material.

3. Without prejudice to the provisions of Article 3, it is prohibited to use weapons to which this Article applies in any city, town, village or other area containing a similar concentration of civilians in which combat between ground forces is not taking place or does not appear to be imminent, unless either:

(a) they are placed on or in the close vicinity of a military objective; or
(b) measures are taken to protect civilians from their effects, for example, the posting of warning sentries, the issuing of warnings or the provision of fences.

Article 8 – Transfers

1. In order to promote the purposes of this Protocol, each High Contracting Party:

(a) undertakes not to transfer any mine the use of which is prohibited by this Protocol;
(b) undertakes not to transfer any mine to any recipient other than a State or a State agency authorized to receive such transfers;
(c) undertakes to exercise restraint in the transfer of any mine the use of which is restricted by this Protocol. In particular, each High Contracting Party undertakes not to transfer any anti-personnel mines to States which are not bound by this Protocol, unless the recipient State agrees to apply this Protocol; and
(d) undertakes to ensure that any transfer in accordance with this Article takes place in full compliance, by both the transferring and the recipient State, with the relevant provisions of this Protocol and the applicable norms of international humanitarian law.

2. In the event that a High Contracting Party declares that it will defer compliance with specific provisions on the use of certain mines, as provided for in the Technical Annex, sub-paragraph I (a) of this Article shall however apply to such mines.

3. All High Contracting Parties, pending the entry into force of this Protocol, will refrain from any actions which would be inconsistent with sub-paragraph I (a) of this Article.

Article 9 – Recording and use of information on minefields, mined areas, mines, booby-traps and other devices

1. All information concerning minefields, mined areas, mines, booby-traps and other devices shall be recorded in accordance with the provisions of the Technical Annex.

2. All such records shall be retained by the parties to a conflict, who shall, without delay after the cessation of active hostilities, take all necessary and appropriate measures, including the use of such information, to protect civilians from the effects of minefields, mined areas, mines, booby-traps and other devices in areas under their control. At the same time, they shall also make available to the other party or parties to the conflict and to the Secretary-General of the United Nations all such information in their possession concerning minefields, mined areas, mines, booby-traps and other devices laid by them in areas no longer under their control; provided, however, subject to reciprocity, where the forces of a party to a conflict are in the territory of an adverse party, either party may withhold such information from the Secretary-General and the other party, to the extent that security interests require such withholding, until neither party is in the territory of the other. In the latter case, the information withheld shall be disclosed as soon as those security interests permit. Wherever possible, the parties to the conflict shall seek, by mutual agreement, to provide for the release of such information at the earliest possible time in a manner consistent with the security interests of each party.

3. This Article is without prejudice to the provisions of Articles 10 and 12 of this Protocol.

Article 10 – Removal of minefields, mined areas, mines, booby-traps and other devices and international co-operation

1. Without delay after the cessation of active hostilities, all minefields, mined areas, mines, booby-traps and other devices shall be cleared, removed, destroyed or maintained in accordance with Article 3 and paragraph 2 of Article 5 of this Protocol.

2. High Contracting Parties and parties to a conflict bear such responsibility with respect to minefields, mined areas, mines, booby-traps and other devices in areas under their control.

3. With respect to minefields, mined areas, mines, booby-traps and other devices laid by a party in areas over which it no longer exercises control, such party shall provide to the party in control of the

area pursuant to paragraph 2 of this Article, to the extent permitted by such party, technical and material assistance necessary to fulfil such responsibility.

4. At all times necessary, the parties shall endeavour to reach agreement, both among themselves and, where appropriate, with other States and with international organizations, on the provision of technical and material assistance, including, in appropriate circumstances, the undertaking of joint operations necessary to fulfil such responsibilities.

Article 11 – Technological cooperation and assistance

1. Each High Contracting Party undertakes to facilitate and shall have the right to participate in the fullest possible exchange of equipment, material and scientific and technological information concerning the implementation of this Protocol and means of mine clearance. In particular, High Contracting Parties shall not impose undue restrictions on the provision of mine clearance equipment and related technological information for humanitarian purposes.

2. Each High Contracting Party undertakes to provide information to the database on mine clearance established within the United Nations System, especially information concerning various means and technologies of mine clearance, and lists of experts, expert agencies or national points of contact on mine clearance.

3. Each High Contracting Party in a position to do so shall provide assistance for mine clearance through the United Nations System, other international bodies or on a bilateral basis, or contribute to the United Nations Voluntary Trust Fund for Assistance in Mine Clearance.

4. Requests by High Contracting Parties for assistance, substantiated by relevant information, may be submitted to the United Nations, to other appropriate bodies or to other States. These requests may be submitted to the Secretary-General of the United Nations, who shall transmit them to all High Contracting Parties and to relevant international organizations.

5. In the case of requests to the United Nations, the Secretary-General of the United Nations, within the resources available to the Secretary-General of the United Nations, may take appropriate steps to assess the situation and, in cooperation with the requesting High Contracting Party, determine the appropriate provision of assistance in mine clearance or implementation of the Protocol. The Secretary-General may also report to High Contracting Parties on any such assessment as well as on the type and scope of assistance required.

6. Without prejudice to their constitutional and other legal provisions, the High Contracting Parties undertake to cooperate and transfer technology to facilitate the implementation of the relevant prohibitions and restrictions set out in this Protocol.

7. Each High Contracting Party has the right to seek and receive technical assistance, where appropriate, from another High Contracting Party on specific relevant technology, other than weapons technology, as necessary and feasible, with a view to reducing any period of deferral for which provision is made in the Technical Annex.

Article 12 – Protection from the effects of minefields, mined areas, mines, booby-traps and other devices

1. Application

(a) With the exception of the forces and missions referred to in sub-paragraph 2(a) (i) of this Article, this Article applies only to missions which are performing functions in an area with the consent of the High Contracting Party on whose territory the functions are performed.
(b) The application of the provisions of this Article to parties to a conflict which are not High Contracting Parties shall not change their legal status or the legal status of a disputed territory, either explicitly or implicitly.

(c) The provisions of this Article are without prejudice to existing international humanitarian law, or other international instruments as applicable, or decisions by the Security Council of the United Nations, which provide for a higher level of protection to personnel functioning in accordance with this Article.

2. Peace-keeping and certain other forces and missions

(a) This paragraph applies to:

   (i) any United Nations force or mission performing peace-keeping, observation or similar functions in any area in accordance with the Charter of the United Nations;
   (ii) any mission established pursuant to Chapter VIII of the Charter of the United Nations and performing its functions in the area of a conflict.

(b) Each High Contracting Party or party to a conflict, if so requested by the head of a force or mission to which this paragraph applies, shall:
   (i) so far as it is able, take such measures as are necessary to protect the force or mission from the effects of mines, booby-traps and other devices in any area under its control;
   (ii) if necessary in order effectively to protect such personnel, remove or render harmless, so far as it is able, all mines, booby-traps and other devices in that area; and
   (iii) inform the head of the force or mission of the location of all known minefields, mined areas, mines, booby-traps and other devices in the area in which the force or mission is performing its functions and, so far as is feasible, make available to the head of the force or mission all information in its possession concerning such minefields, mined areas, mines, booby-traps and other devices.

3. Humanitarian and fact-finding missions of the United Nations System

(a) This paragraph applies to any humanitarian or fact-finding mission of the United Nations System.
(b) Each High Contracting Party or party to a conflict, if so requested by the head of a mission to which this paragraph applies, shall:
   (i) provide the personnel of the mission with the protections set out in sub-paragraph 2(b) (i) of this Article; and
   (ii) if access to or through any place under its control is necessary for the performance of the mission's functions and in order to provide the personnel of the mission with safe passage to or through that place:
   (aa) unless on-going hostilities prevent, inform the head of the mission of a safe route to that place if such information is available; or
   (bb) if information identifying a safe route is not provided in accordance with sub-paragraph (aa), so far as is necessary and feasible, clear a lane through minefields.

4. Missions of the International Committee of the Red Cross

(a) This paragraph applies to any mission of the International Committee of the Red Cross performing functions with the consent of the host State or States as provided for by the Geneva Conventions of 12 August 1949 and, where applicable, their Additional Protocols.
(b) Each High Contracting Party or party to a conflict, if so requested by the head of a mission to which this paragraph applies, shall:
   (i) provide the personnel of the mission with the protections set out in sub-paragraph 2(b) (i) of this Article; and
   (ii) take the measures set out in sub-paragraph 3(b) (ii) of this Article.

5. Other humanitarian missions and missions of enquiry

(a) Insofar as paragraphs 2, 3 and 4 above do not apply to them, this paragraph applies to the following missions when they are performing functions in the area of a conflict or to assist the victims of a conflict:

(i) any humanitarian mission of a national Red Cross or Red Crescent Society or of their International Federation;
(ii) any mission of an impartial humanitarian organization, including any impartial humanitarian demining mission; and
(iii) any mission of enquiry established pursuant to the provisions of the Geneva Conventions of 12 August 1949 and, where applicable, their Additional Protocols.

(b) Each High Contracting Party or party to a conflict, if so requested by the head of a mission to which this paragraph applies, shall, so far as is feasible:
(i) provide the personnel of the mission with the protections set out in sub-paragraph 2(b) (i) of this Article, and
(ii) take the measures set out in sub-paragraph 3(b) (ii) of this Article.

6. Confidentiality

All information provided in confidence pursuant to this Article shall be treated by the recipient in strict confidence and shall not be released outside the force or mission concerned without the express authorization of the provider of the information.

7. Respect for laws and regulations

Without prejudice to such privileges and immunities as they may enjoy or to the requirements of their duties, personnel participating in the forces and missions referred to in this Article shall:

(a) respect the laws and regulations of the host State; and
(b) refrain from any action or activity incompatible with the impartial and international nature of their duties.

Article 13 – Consultations of High Contracting Parties

1. The High Contracting Parties undertake to consult and cooperate with each other on all issues related to the operation of this Protocol. For this purpose, a conference of High Contracting Parties shall be held annually.

2. Participation in the annual conferences shall be determined by their agreed Rules of Procedure.

3. The work of the conference shall include:

(a) review of the operation and status of this Protocol;
(b) consideration of matters arising from reports by High Contracting Parties according to paragraph 4 of this Article;
(c) preparation for review conferences; and
(d) consideration of the development of technologies to protect civilians against indiscriminate effects of mines.

4. The High Contracting Parties shall provide annual reports to the Depositary, who shall circulate them to all High Contracting Parties in advance of the Conference, on any of the following matters:

(a) dissemination of information on this Protocol to their armed forces and to the civilian population;
(b) mine clearance and rehabilitation programmes;
(c) steps taken to meet technical requirements of this Protocol and any other relevant information pertaining thereto;
(d) legislation related to this Protocol;
(e) measures taken on international technical information exchange, on international cooperation on mine clearance, and on technical cooperation and assistance; and
(f) other relevant matters.

5. The cost of the Conference of High Contracting Parties shall be borne by the High Contracting Parties and States not parties participating in the work of the Conference, in accordance with the United Nations scale of assessment adjusted appropriately.

Article 14 – Compliance

1. Each High Contracting Party shall take all appropriate steps, including legislative and other measures, to prevent and suppress violations of this Protocol by persons or on territory under its jurisdiction or control.

2. The measures envisaged in paragraph 1 of this Article include appropriate measures to ensure the imposition of penal sanctions against persons who, in relation to an armed conflict and contrary to the provisions of this Protocol, wilfully kill or cause serious injury to civilians and to bring such persons to justice.

3. Each High Contracting Party shall also require that its armed forces issue relevant military instructions and operating procedures and that armed forces personnel receive training commensurate with their duties and responsibilities to comply with the provisions of this Protocol.

4. The High Contracting Parties undertake to consult each other and to cooperate with each other bilaterally, through the Secretary-General of the United Nations or through other appropriate international procedures, to resolve any problems that may arise with regard to the interpretation and application of the provisions of this Protocol.

6.14.6. Technical Annex

1. Recording

(a) Recording of the location of mines other than remotely-delivered mines, minefields, mined areas, booby-traps and other devices shall be carried out in accordance with the following provisions:
   (i) the location of the minefields, mined areas and areas of booby-traps and other devices shall be specified accurately by relation to the coordinates of at least two reference points and the estimated dimensions of the area containing these weapons in relation to those reference points;
   (ii) maps, diagrams or other records shall be made in such a way as to indicate the location of minefields, mined areas, booby-traps and other devices in relation to reference points, and these records shall also indicate their perimeters and extent;
   (iii) for purposes of detection and clearance of mines, booby-traps and other devices, maps, diagrams or other records shall contain complete information on the type, number, emplacing method, type of fuse and life time, date and time of laying, anti-handling devices (if any) and other relevant information on all these weapons laid. Whenever feasible the minefield record shall show the exact location of every mine, except in row minefields where the row location is sufficient. The precise location and operating mechanism of each booby-trap laid shall be individually recorded.

(b) The estimated location and area of remotely-delivered mines shall be specified by coordinates of reference points (normally corner points) and shall be ascertained and when feasible marked on the ground at the earliest opportunity. The total number and types of mines laid, the date and time of laying and the self-destruction time periods shall also be recorded.

(c) Copies of records shall be held at a level of command sufficient to guarantee their safety as far as possible.

(d) The use of mines produced after the entry into force of this Protocol is prohibited unless they are marked in English or in the respective national language or languages with the following information:
   (i) name of the country of origin;
   (ii) month and year of production; and

(iii) serial number or lot number. The marking should be visible, legible, durable and resistant to environmental effects, as far as possible.

2. Specifications on detectability

(a) With respect to anti-personnel mines produced after 1 January 1997, such mines shall incorporate in their construction a material or device that enables the mine to be detected by commonly-available technical mine detection equipment and provides a response signal equivalent to a signal from 8 grammes or more of iron in a single coherent mass.
(b) With respect to anti-personnel mines produced before 1 January 1997, such mines shall either incorporate in their construction, or have attached prior to their emplacement, in a manner not easily removable, a material or device that enables the mine to be detected by commonly-available technical mine detection equipment and provides a response signal equivalent to a signal from 8 grammes or more of iron in a single coherent mass.
(c) In the event that a High Contracting Party determines that it cannot immediately comply with sub-paragraph (b), it may declare at the time of its notification of consent to be bound by this Protocol that it will defer compliance with sub-paragraph (b) for a period not to exceed 9 years from the entry into force of this Protocol. In the meantime it shall, to the extent feasible, minimize the use of anti-personnel mines that do not so comply.

3. Specifications on self-destruction and self-deactivation

(a) All remotely-delivered anti-personnel mines shall be designed and constructed so that no more than 10% of activated mines will fail to self-destruct within 30 days after emplacement, and each mine shall have a back-up self-deactivation feature designed and constructed so that, in combination with the self-destruction mechanism, no more than one in one thousand activated mines will function as a mine 120 days after emplacement.
(b) All non-remotely delivered anti-personnel mines, used outside marked areas, as defined in Article 5 of this Protocol, shall comply with the requirements for self-destruction and self-deactivation stated in sub-paragraph (a).
(c) In the event that a High Contracting Party determines that it cannot immediately comply with sub-paragraphs (a) and/or (b), it may declare at the time of its notification of consent to be bound by this Protocol, that it will, with respect to mines produced prior to the entry into force of this Protocol defer compliance with sub-paragraphs (a) and/or (b) for a period not to exceed 9 years from the entry into force of this Protocol.

During this period of deferral, the High Contracting Party shall:
(i) undertake to minimize, to the extent feasible, the use of anti-personnel mines that do not so comply, and
(ii) with respect to remotely-delivered anti-personnel mines, comply with either the requirements for self-destruction or the requirements for self-deactivation and, with respect to other anti-personnel mines comply with at least the requirements for self-deactivation.

4. International signs for minefields and mined areas

Signs similar to the example attached and as specified below shall be utilized in the marking of minefields and mined areas to ensure their visibility and recognition by the civilian population:

(a) size and shape: a triangle or square no smaller than 28 centimetres (11 inches) by 20 centimetres (7.9 inches) for a triangle, and 15 centimetres (6 inches) per side for a square;
(b) colour: red or orange with a yellow reflecting border.

6.15. CONVENTION ON THE PROHIBITION OF THE USE, STOCKPILING, PRODUCTION AND TRANSFER OF ANTI-PERSONNEL MINES AND ON THEIR DESTRUCTION

Preamble

The States Parties,

Determined to put an end to the suffering and casualties caused by anti-personnel mines, that kill or maim hundreds of people every week, mostly innocent and defenceless civilians and especially children, obstruct economic development and reconstruction, inhibit the repatriation of refugees and internally displaced persons, and have other severe consequences for years after emplacement,

Believing it necessary to do their utmost to contribute in an efficient and coordinated manner to face the challenge of removing anti-personnel mines placed throughout the world, and to assure their destruction,

Wishing to do their utmost in providing assistance for the care and rehabilitation, including the social and economic reintegration of mine victims,

Recognizing that a total ban of anti-personnel mines would also be an important confidence-building measure,

Welcoming the adoption of the Protocol on Prohibitions or Restrictions on the Use of Mines, Booby-Traps and Other Devices, as amended on 3 May 1996, annexed to the Convention on Prohibitions or Restrictions on the Use of Certain Conventional Weapons Which May Be Deemed to Be Excessively Injurious or to Have Indiscriminate Effects, and calling for the early ratification of this Protocol by all States which have not yet done so,

Welcoming also United Nations General Assembly Resolution 51/45 S of 10 December 1996 urging all States to pursue vigorously an effective, legally-binding international agreement to ban the use, stockpiling, production and transfer of anti-personnel landmines,

Welcoming furthermore the measures taken over the past years, both unilaterally and multilaterally, aiming at prohibiting, restricting or suspending the use, stockpiling, production and transfer of anti-personnel mines,

Stressing the role of public conscience in furthering the principles of humanity as evidenced by the call for a total ban of anti-personnel mines and recognizing the efforts to that end undertaken by the International Red Cross and Red Crescent Movement, the International Campaign to Ban Landmines and numerous other non-governmental organizations around the world,

Recalling the Ottawa Declaration of 5 October 1996 and the Brussels Declaration of 27 June 1997 urging the international community to negotiate an international and legally binding agreement prohibiting the use, stockpiling, production and transfer of anti-personnel mines,

Emphasizing the desirability of attracting the adherence of all States to this Convention, and determined to work strenuously towards the promotion of its universalization in all relevant fora including, inter alia, the United Nations, the Conference on Disarmament, regional organizations, and groupings, and review conferences of the Convention on Prohibitions or Restrictions on the Use of Certain Conventional Weapons Which May Be Deemed to Be Excessively Injurious or to Have Indiscriminate Effects,

Basing themselves on the principle of international humanitarian law that the right of the parties to an armed conflict to choose methods or means of warfare is not unlimited, on the principle that prohibits the employment in armed conflicts of weapons, projectiles and materials and methods of warfare of a nature to cause superfluous injury or unnecessary suffering and on the principle that a distinction must be made between civilians and combatants,

Have agreed as follows:

Article 1
General obligations

1. Each State Party undertakes never under any circumstances:

   a) To use anti-personnel mines;
   b) To develop, produce, otherwise acquire, stockpile, retain or transfer to anyone, directly or indirectly, anti-personnel mines;
   c) To assist, encourage or induce, in any way, anyone to engage in any activity prohibited to a State Party under this Convention.

2. Each State Party undertakes to destroy or ensure the destruction of all anti-personnel mines in accordance with the provisions of this Convention.

Article 2
Definitions

1. 'Anti-Personnel mine' means a mine designed to be exploded by the presence, proximity or contact of a person and that will incapacitate, injure or kill one or more persons. Mines designed to be detonated by the presence, proximity or contact of a vehicle as opposed to a person, that are equipped with anti-handling devices, are not considered anti-personnel mines as a result of being so equipped.

2. 'mine' means a munition designed to be placed under, on or near the ground or other surface area and to be exploded by the presence, proximity or contact of a person or a vehicle.

3. 'Anti-handling device' means a device intended to protect a mine and which is part of, linked to, attached to or placed under the mine and which activates when an attempt is made to tamper with or otherwise intentionally disturb the mine.

4. 'Transfer' involves, in addition to the physical movement of anti-personnel mines into or from national territory, the transfer of title to and control over the mines, but does not involve the transfer of territory containing emplaced anti-personnel mines.

5. 'Mined area' means an area which is dangerous due to the presence or suspected presence of mines.

Article 3
Exceptions

1. Notwithstanding the general obligations under Article 1, the retention or transfer of a number of anti-personnel mines for the development of and training in mine detection, mine clearance, or mine destruction techniques is permitted. The amount of such mines shall not exceed the minimum number absolutely necessary for the above-mentioned purposes.

2. The transfer of anti-personnel mines for the purpose of destruction is permitted.

Article 4
Destruction of stockpiled anti-personnel mines

Except as provided for in Article 3, each State Party undertakes to destroy or ensure the destruction of all stockpiled anti-personnel mines it owns or possesses, or that are under its jurisdiction or control, as soon as possible but not later than four years after the entry into force of this Convention for that State Party.

Article 5
Destruction of anti-personnel mines in mined areas

1. Each State Party undertakes to destroy or ensure the destruction of all anti-personnel mines in mined areas under its jurisdiction or control, as soon as possible but not later than ten years after the entry into force of this Convention for that State Party.

2. Each State Party shall make every effort to identify all areas under its jurisdiction or control in which anti-personnel mines are known or suspected to be emplaced and shall ensure as soon as possible that all anti-personnel mines in mined areas under its jurisdiction or control are perimeter-marked, monitored and protected by fencing or other means, to ensure the effective exclusion of civilians, until all anti-personnel mines contained therein have been destroyed. The marking shall at least be to the standards set out in the Protocol on Prohibitions or Restrictions on the Use of Mines, Booby-Traps and Other Devices, as amended on 3 May 1996, annexed to the Convention on Prohibitions or Restrictions on the Use of Certain Conventional Weapons Which May Be Deemed to Be Excessively Injurious or to Have Indiscriminate Effects.

3. If a State Party believes that it will be unable to destroy or ensure the destruction of all anti-personnel mines referred to in paragraph 1 within that time period, it may submit a request to a Meeting of the States Parties or a Review Conference for an extension of the deadline for completing the destruction of such anti-personnel mines, for a period of up to ten years.

4. Each request shall contain:

a) The duration of the proposed extension;
b) A detailed explanation of the reasons for the proposed extension, including:
    (i) The preparation and status of work conducted under national demining programs;
    (ii) The financial and technical means available to the State Party for the destruction of all the anti-personnel mines; and
    (iii) Circumstances which impede the ability of the State Party to destroy all the anti-personnel mines in mined areas;
c) The humanitarian, social, economic, and environmental implications of the extension; and
d) Any other information relevant to the request for the proposed extension.

5. The Meeting of the States Parties or the Review Conference shall, taking into consideration the factors contained in paragraph 4, assess the request and decide by a majority of votes of States Parties present and voting whether to grant the request for an extension period.

6. Such an extension may be renewed upon the submission of a new request in accordance with paragraphs 3, 4 and 5 of this Article. In requesting a further extension period a State Party shall submit relevant additional information on what has been undertaken in the previous extension period pursuant to this Article.

Article 6
International cooperation and assistance

1. In fulfilling its obligations under this Convention each State Party has the right to seek and receive assistance, where feasible, from other States Parties to the extent possible.

2. Each State Party undertakes to facilitate and shall have the right to participate in the fullest possible exchange of equipment, material and scientific and technological information concerning the implementation of this Convention. The States Parties shall not impose undue restrictions on the provision of mine clearance equipment and related technological information for humanitarian purposes.

3. Each State Party in a position to do so shall provide assistance for the care and rehabilitation, and social and economic reintegration, of mine victims and for mine awareness programs. Such assistance may be provided, inter alia, through the United Nations system, international, regional or national organizations or institutions, the International Committee of the Red Cross, national Red Cross and Red Crescent societies and their International Federation, non-governmental organizations, or on a bilateral basis.

4. Each State Party in a position to do so shall provide assistance for mine clearance and related activities. Such assistance may be provided, inter alia, through the United Nations system, international or regional organizations or institutions, non-governmental organizations or institutions, or on a bilateral basis, or by contributing to the United Nations Voluntary Trust Fund for Assistance in Mine Clearance, or other regional funds that deal with demining.

5. Each State Party in a position to do so shall provide assistance for the destruction of stockpiled anti-personnel mines.

6. Each State Party undertakes to provide information to the database on mine clearance established within the United Nations system, especially information concerning various means and technologies of mine clearance, and lists of experts, expert agencies or national points of contact on mine clearance.

7. States Parties may request the United Nations, regional organizations, other States Parties or other competent intergovernmental or non-governmental fora to assist its authorities in the elaboration of a national demining program to determine, inter alia:

a) The extent and scope of the anti-personnel mine problem;
b) The financial, technological and human resources that are required for the implementation of the program;
c) The estimated number of years necessary to destroy all anti-personnel mines in mined areas under the jurisdiction or control of the concerned State Party;
d) Mine awareness activities to reduce the incidence of mine-related injuries or deaths;
e) Assistance to mine victims;
f) The relationship between the Government of the concerned State Party and the relevant governmental, inter-governmental or non-governmental entities that will work in the implementation of the program.

8. Each State Party giving and receiving assistance under the provisions of this Article shall cooperate with a view to ensuring the full and prompt implementation of agreed assistance programs.

Article 7
Transparency measures

1. Each State Party shall report to the Secretary-General of the United Nations as soon as practicable, and in any event not later than 180 days after the entry into force of this Convention for that State Party on:

a) The national implementation measures referred to in Article 9;
b) The total of all stockpiled anti-personnel mines owned or possessed by it, or under its jurisdiction or control, to include a breakdown of the type, quantity and, if possible, lot numbers of each type of anti-personnel mine stockpiled;
c) To the extent possible, the location of all mined areas that contain, or are suspected to contain, anti-personnel mines under its jurisdiction or control, to include as much detail as possible regarding the type and quantity of each type of anti-personnel mine in each mined area and when they were emplaced;
d) The types, quantities and, if possible, lot numbers of all anti-personnel mines retained or transferred for the development of and training in mine detection, mine clearance or mine destruction techniques, or transferred for the purpose of destruction, as well as the institutions

authorized by a State Party to retain or transfer anti-personnel mines, in accordance with Article 3;

e) The status of programs for the conversion or de-commissioning of anti-personnel mine production facilities;

f) The status of programs for the destruction of anti-personnel mines in accordance with Articles 4 and 5, including details of the methods which will be used in destruction, the location of all destruction sites and the applicable safety and environmental standards to be observed;

g) The types and quantities of all anti-personnel mines destroyed after the entry into force of this Convention for that State Party, to include a breakdown of the quantity of each type of anti-personnel mine destroyed, in accordance with Articles 4 and 5, respectively, along with, if possible, the lot numbers of each type of anti-personnel mine in the case of destruction in accordance with Article 4;

h) The technical characteristics of each type of anti-personnel mine produced, to the extent known, and those currently owned or possessed by a State Party, giving,where reasonably possible, such categories of information as may facilitate identification and clearance of anti-personnel mines; at a minimum, this information shall include the dimensions, fusing, explosive content, metallic content, colour photographs and other information which may facilitate mine clearance; and

i) The measures taken to provide an immediate and effective warning to the population in relation to all areas identified under paragraph 2 of Article 5.

2. The information provided in accordance with this Article shall be updated by the States Parties annually, covering the last calendar year, and reported to the Secretary-General of the United Nations not later than 30 April of each year.

3. The Secretary-General of the United Nations shall transmit all such reports received to the States Parties.

Article 8
Facilitation and clarification of compliance

1. The States Parties agree to consult and cooperate with each other regarding the implementation of the provisions of this Convention, and to work together in a spirit of cooperation to facilitate compliance by States Parties with their obligations under this Convention.

2. If one or more States Parties wish to clarify and seek to resolve questions relating to compliance with the provisions of this Convention by another State Party, it may submit, through the Secretary-General of the United Nations, a Request for Clarification of that matter to that State Party. Such a request shall be accompanied by all appropriate information. Each State Party shall refrain from unfounded Requests for Clarification, care being taken to avoid abuse. A State Party that receives a Request for Clarification shall provide, through the Secretary-General of the United Nations, within 28 days to the requesting State Party all information which would assist in clarifying this matter.

3. If the requesting State Party does not receive a response through the Secretary-General of the United Nations within that time period, or deems the response to the Request for Clarification to be unsatisfactory, it may submit the matter through the Secretary-General of the United Nations to the next Meeting of the States Parties. The Secretary-General of the United Nations shall transmit the submission, accompanied by all appropriate information pertaining to the Request for Clarification, to all States Parties. All such information shall be presented to the requested State Party which shall have the right to respond.

4. Pending the convening of any meeting of the States Parties, any of the States Parties concerned may request the Secretary-General of the United Nations to exercise his or her good offices to facilitate the clarification requested.

5. The requesting State Party may propose through the Secretary-General of the United Nations the convening of a Special Meeting of the States Parties to consider the matter. The Secretary-General of the United Nations shall thereupon communicate this proposal and all information

submitted by the States Parties concerned, to all States Parties with a request that they indicate whether they favour a Special Meeting of the States Parties, for the purpose of considering the matter. In the event that within 14 days from the date of such communication, at least one-third of the States Parties favours such a Special Meeting, the Secretary-General of the United Nations shall convene this Special Meeting of the States Parties within a further 14 days. A quorum for this Meeting shall consist of a majority of States Parties.

6. The Meeting of the States Parties or the Special Meeting of the States Parties, as the case may be, shall first determine whether to consider the matter further, taking into account all information submitted by the States Parties concerned. The Meeting of the States Parties or the Special Meeting of the States Parties shall make every effort to reach a decision by consensus. If despite all efforts to that end no agreement has been reached, it shall take this decision by a majority of States Parties present and voting.

7. All States Parties shall cooperate fully with the Meeting of the States Parties or the Special Meeting of the States Parties in the fulfilment of its review of the matter, including any fact-finding missions that are authorized in accordance with paragraph 8.

8. If further clarification is required, the Meeting of the States Parties or the Special Meeting of the States Parties shall authorize a fact-finding mission and decide on its mandate by a majority of States Parties present and voting. At any time the requested State Party may invite a fact-finding mission to its territory. Such a mission shall take place without a decision by a Meeting of the States Parties or a Special Meeting of the States Parties to authorize such a mission. The mission, consisting of up to 9 experts, designated and approved in accordance with paragraphs 9 and 10, may collect additional information on the spot or in other places directly related to the alleged compliance issue under the jurisdiction or control of the requested State Party.

9. The Secretary-General of the United Nations shall prepare and update a list of the names, nationalities and other relevant data of qualified experts provided by States Parties and communicate it to all States Parties. Any expert included on this list shall be regarded as designated for all fact-finding missions unless a State Party declares its non-acceptance in writing. In the event of non-acceptance, the expert shall not participate in fact-finding missions on the territory or any other place under the jurisdiction or control of the objecting State Party, if the non-acceptance was declared prior to the appointment of the expert to such missions.

10. Upon receiving a request from the Meeting of the States Parties or a Special Meeting of the States Parties, the Secretary-General of the United Nations shall, after consultations with the requested State Party, appoint the members of the mission, including its leader. Nationals of States Parties requesting the fact-finding mission or directly affected by it shall not be appointed to the mission. The members of the fact-finding mission shall enjoy privileges and immunities under Article VI of the Convention on the Privileges and Immunities of the United Nations, adopted on 13 February 1946.

11. Upon at least 72 hours notice, the members of the fact-finding mission shall arrive in the territory of the requested State Party at the earliest opportunity. The requested State Party shall take the necessary administrative measures to receive, transport and accommodate the mission, and shall be responsible for ensuring the security of the mission to the maximum extent possible while they are on territory under its control.

12. Without prejudice to the sovereignty of the requested State Party, the fact-finding mission may bring into the territory of the requested State Party the necessary equipment which shall be used exclusively for gathering information on the alleged compliance issue. Prior to its arrival, the mission will advise the requested State Party of the equipment that it intends to utilize in the course of its fact-finding mission.

13. The requested State Party shall make all efforts to ensure that the fact-finding mission is given the opportunity to speak with all relevant persons who may be able to provide information related to the alleged compliance issue.

14. The requested State Party shall grant access for the fact-finding mission to all areas and installations under its control where facts relevant to the compliance issue could be expected to be collected. This shall be subject to any arrangements that the requested State Party considers necessary for:

a) The protection of sensitive equipment, information and areas;
b) The protection of any constitutional obligations the requested State Party may have with regard to proprietary rights, searches and seizures, or other constitutional rights; or
c) The physical protection and safety of the members of the fact-finding mission.

In the event that the requested State Party makes such arrangements, it shall make every reasonable effort to demonstrate through alternative means its compliance with this Convention.

15. The fact-finding mission may remain in the territory of the State Party concerned for no more than 14 days, and at any particular site no more than 7 days, unless otherwise agreed.

16. All information provided in confidence and not related to the subject matter of the fact-finding mission shall be treated on a confidential basis.

17. The fact-finding mission shall report, through the Secretary-General of the United Nations, to the Meeting of the States Parties or the Special Meeting of the States Parties the results of its findings.

18. The Meeting of the States Parties or the Special Meeting of the States Parties shall consider all relevant information, including the report submitted by the fact-finding mission, and may request the requested State Party to take measures to address the compliance issue within a specified period of time. The requested State Party shall report on all measures taken in response to this request.

19. The Meeting of the States Parties or the Special Meeting of the States Parties may suggest to the States Parties concerned ways and means to further clarify or resolve the matter under consideration, including the initiation of appropriate procedures in conformity with international law. In circumstances where the issue at hand is determined to be due to circumstances beyond the control of the requested State Party, the Meeting of the States Parties or the Special Meeting of the States Parties may recommend appropriate measures, including the use of cooperative measures referred to in Article 6.

20. The Meeting of the States Parties or the Special Meeting of the States Parties shall make every effort to reach its decisions referred to in paragraphs 18 and 19 by consensus, otherwise by a two-thirds majority of States Parties present and voting.

Article 9
National implementation measures

Each State Party shall take all appropriate legal, administrative and other measures, including the imposition of penal sanctions, to prevent and suppress any activity prohibited to a State Party under this Convention undertaken by persons or on territory under its jurisdiction or control.

Article 10
Settlement of disputes

1. The States Parties shall consult and cooperate with each other to settle any dispute that may arise with regard to the application or the interpretation of this Convention. Each State Party may bring any such dispute before the Meeting of the States Parties.

2. The Meeting of the States Parties may contribute to the settlement of the dispute by whatever means it deems appropriate, including offering its good offices, calling upon the States parties to a dispute to start the settlement procedure of their choice and recommending a time-limit for any agreed procedure.

3. This Article is without prejudice to the provisions of this Convention on facilitation and clarification of compliance.

Article 11
Meetings of the States Parties

1. The States Parties shall meet regularly in order to consider any matter with regard to the application or implementation of this Convention, including:

a) The operation and status of this Convention;
b) Matters arising from the reports submitted under the provisions of this Convention;
c) International cooperation and assistance in accordance with Article 6;
d) The development of technologies to clear anti-personnel mines;
e) Submissions of States Parties under Article 8; and
f) Decisions relating to submissions of States Parties as provided for in Article 5.

2. The First Meeting of the States Parties shall be convened by the Secretary-General of the United Nations within one year after the entry into force of this Convention. The subsequent meetings shall be convened by the Secretary-General of the United Nations annually until the first Review Conference.

3. Under the conditions set out in Article 8, the Secretary-General of the United Nations shall convene a Special Meeting of the States Parties.

4. States not parties to this Convention, as well as the United Nations, other relevant international organizations or institutions, regional organizations, the International Committee of the Red Cross and relevant non-governmental organizations may be invited to attend these meetings as observers in accordance with the agreed Rules of Procedure.

Article 12
Review Conferences

1. A Review Conference shall be convened by the Secretary-General of the United Nations five years after the entry into force of this Convention. Further Review Conferences shall be convened by the Secretary-General of the United Nations if so requested by one or more States Parties, provided that the interval between Review Conferences shall in no case be less than five years. All States Parties to this Convention shall be invited to each Review Conference.

2. The purpose of the Review Conference shall be:

a) To review the operation and status of this Convention;
b) To consider the need for and the interval between further Meetings of the States Parties referred to in paragraph 2 of Article 11;
c) To take decisions on submissions of States Parties as provided for in Article 5; and
d) To adopt, if necessary, in its final report conclusions related to the implementation of this Convention.

3. States not parties to this Convention, as well as the United Nations, other relevant international organizations or institutions, regional organizations, the International Committee of the Red Cross and relevant non-governmental organizations may be invited to attend each Review Conference as observers in accordance with the agreed Rules of Procedure.

Article 13
Amendments

1. At any time after the entry into force of this Convention any State Party may propose amendments to this Convention. Any proposal for an amendment shall be communicated to the Depositary, who shall circulate it to all States Parties and shall seek their views on whether an

Amendment Conference should be convened to consider the proposal. If a majority of the States Parties notify the Depositary no later than 30 days after its circulation that they support further consideration of the proposal, the Depositary shall convene an Amendment Conference to which all States Parties shall be invited.

2. States not parties to this Convention, as well as the United Nations, other relevant international organizations or institutions, regional organizations, the International Committee of the Red Cross and relevant non-governmental organizations may be invited to attend each Amendment Conference as observers in accordance with the agreed Rules of Procedure.

3. The Amendment Conference shall be held immediately following a Meeting of the States Parties or a Review Conference unless a majority of the States Parties request that it be held earlier.

4. Any amendment to this Convention shall be adopted by a majority of two-thirds of the States Parties present and voting at the Amendment Conference. The Depositary shall communicate any amendment so adopted to the States Parties.

5. An amendment to this Convention shall enter into force for all States Parties to this Convention which have accepted it, upon the deposit with the Depositary of instruments of acceptance by a majority of States Parties. Thereafter it shall enter into force for any remaining State Party on the date of deposit of its instrument of acceptance.

Article 14
Costs

1. The costs of the Meetings of the States Parties, the Special Meetings of the States Parties, the Review Conferences and the Amendment Conferences shall be borne by the States Parties and States not parties to this Convention participating therein, in accordance with the United Nations scale of assessment adjusted appropriately.

2. The costs incurred by the Secretary-General of the United Nations under Articles 7 and 8 and the costs of any fact-finding mission shall be borne by the States Parties in accordance with the United Nations scale of assessment adjusted appropriately.

Article 15
Signature

This Convention, done at Oslo, Norway, on 18 September 1997, shall be open for signature at Ottawa, Canada, by all States from 3 December 1997 until 4 December 1997, and at the United Nations Headquarters in New York from 5 December 1997 until its entry into force.

Article 16
Ratification, acceptance, approval or accession

1. This Convention is subject to ratification, acceptance or approval of the Signatories.

2. It shall be open for accession by any State which has not signed the Convention.

3. The instruments of ratification, acceptance, approval or accession shall be deposited with the Depositary.

Article 17
Entry into force

1. This Convention shall enter into force on the first day of the sixth month after the month in which the 40th instrument of ratification, acceptance, approval or accession has been deposited.

2. For any State which deposits its instrument of ratification, acceptance, approval or accession after the date of the deposit of the 40th instrument of ratification, acceptance, approval or accession, this Convention shall enter into force on the first day of the sixth month after the date on which that State has deposited its instrument of ratification, acceptance, approval or accession.

Article 18
Provisional application

Any State may at the time of its ratification, acceptance, approval or accession, declare that it will apply provisionally paragraph 1 of Article 1 of this Convention pending its entry into force.

Article 19
Reservations

The Articles of this Convention shall not be subject to reservations.

Article 20
Duration and withdrawal

1. This Convention shall be of unlimited duration.

2. Each State Party shall, in exercising its national sovereignty, have the right to withdraw from this Convention. It shall give notice of such withdrawal to all other States Parties, to the Depositary and to the United Nations Security Council. Such instrument of withdrawal shall include a full explanation of the reasons motivating this withdrawal.

3. Such withdrawal shall only take effect six months after the receipt of the instrument of withdrawal by the Depositary. If, however, on the expiry of that six- month period, the withdrawing State Party is engaged in an armed conflict, the withdrawal shall not take effect before the end of the armed conflict.

4. The withdrawal of a State Party from this Convention shall not in any way affect the duty of States to continue fulfilling the obligations assumed under any relevant rules of international law.

Article 21
Depositary

The Secretary-General of the United Nations is hereby designated as the Depositary of this Convention.

Article 22
Authentic texts

The original of this Convention, of which the Arabic, Chinese, English, French, Russian and Spanish texts are equally authentic, shall be deposited with the Secretary-General of the United Nations.

6.16. UN General Assembly Resolution 52/38A

UNITED NATIONS

General Assembly

Resolution 52/38
General and complete disarmament

Date: 9 December 1997

Meeting: 67

Report: A/52/600

Vote: A – 142-0-18

A. Convention on the Prohibition of the Use, Stockpiling, Production and Transfer of Anti-Personnel Mines and on Their Destruction

The General Assembly,

Determined to put an end to the suffering and casualties caused by anti-personnel mines that kill or maim hundreds of people every week, mostly innocent and defenceless civilians and especially children, obstruct economic development and reconstruction, inhibit the repatriation of refugees and internally displaced persons, and have other severe consequences for years after emplacement,

Believing it necessary to do the utmost to contribute in an efficient and coordinated manner to facing the challenge of removing anti-personnel mines placed throughout the world, and to assure their destruction,

Wishing to do the utmost in assuring assistance for the care and rehabilitation, including the social and economic reintegration, of mine victims,

Recalling its resolution 51/45 S of 10 December 1996 urging all States to pursue vigorously an effective, legally-binding international agreement to ban the use, stockpiling, production and transfer of anti-personnel landmines with a view to completing the negotiation as soon as possible,

Stressing the role of public conscience in furthering the principles of humanity as evidenced by the call for a total ban on anti-personnel mines and recognizing the efforts to that end undertaken by the International Red Cross and Red Crescent Movement, the International Campaign to Ban Landmines and numerous other non-governmental organizations around the world,

Recalling the Ottawa Declaration of 5 October 1996 and the Brussels Declaration of 27 June 1997 urging the international community to negotiate an international and legally binding agreement prohibiting the use, stockpiling, production and transfer of anti-personnel mines,

Emphasizing the desirability of attracting the adherence of all States to the Convention on the Prohibition of the Use, Stockpiling, Production and Transfer of Anti-Personnel Mines and on Their Destruction, and determined to work strenuously towards the promotion of its universalisation in all relevant forums including, inter alia, the United Nations, the Conference on Disarmament, regional organizations and groupings, and review conferences of the Convention on Prohibitions or Restrictions on the Use of Certain Conventional Weapons Which May Be Deemed to Be Excessively Injurious or to Have Indiscriminate Effects,

Basing itself on the principle of international humanitarian law that the right of the parties to an armed conflict to choose methods or means of warfare is not unlimited, on the principle that prohibits the employment in armed conflicts of weapons, projectiles and materials and methods of warfare of a nature to cause superfluous injury or unnecessary suffering and on the principle that a distinction must be made between civilians and combatants,

Welcoming the conclusion of negotiations on 18 September 1997 at Oslo, Norway, on the Convention on the Prohibition of the Use, Stockpiling, Production and Transfer of Anti-Personnel Mines and on Their Destruction,

1. Invites all States to sign the Convention, which will be opened for signature at Ottawa, Canada, on 3 and 4 December 1997, and thereafter at United Nations Headquarters in New York from 5 December 1997 until its entry into force;

2. Urges all States to ratify the Convention without delay subsequent to their signatures;

3. Calls upon all States to contribute towards the full realization and effective implementation of the Convention to advance the care and rehabilitation, and the social and economic reintegration of mine victims, and mine-awareness programmes, and the removal of anti-personnel mines placed throughout the world and the assurance of their destruction;

4. Requests the Secretary-General of the United Nations to render the necessary assistance and to provide such services as may be necessary to fulfil the tasks entrusted to him by the Convention;

5. Decides to include in the provisional agenda of its fifty-third session an item entitled "Convention on the Prohibition of the Use, Stockpiling, Production and Transfer of Anti-Personnel Mines and on Their Destruction".

6.17. UN General Assembly Resolution 53/77N

UNITED NATIONS

General Assembly

Distr. GENERAL
A/RES/53/77

12 January 1999

Fifty-third session
Agenda item 71

RESOLUTIONS ADOPTED BY THE GENERAL ASSEMBLY
[on the report of the First Committee (A/53/584)]

53/77. General and complete disarmament
79th plenary meeting
4 December 1998

N. Convention on the Prohibition of the Use, Stockpiling, Production and Transfer of Anti-Personnel Mines and on Their Destruction

The General Assembly,

Recalling its resolution 52/38 A of 9 December 1997,

Reaffirming its determination to put an end to the suffering and casualties caused by anti-personnel mines, which kill or maim hundreds of people every week, mostly innocent and defenceless civilians and especially children, obstruct economic development and reconstruction, inhibit the repatriation of refugees and internally displaced persons, and have other severe consequences for years after emplacement,

Believing it necessary to do the utmost to contribute in an efficient and coordinated manner to facing the challenge of removing anti-personnel mines placed throughout the world, and to assure their destruction,

Wishing to do the utmost in assuring assistance for the care and rehabilitation, including the social and economic reintegration, of mine victims,

Recalling the conclusion of negotiations on 18 September 1997 at Oslo on the Convention on the Prohibition of the Use, Stockpiling, Production and Transfer of Anti-Personnel Mines and on Their Destruction 40/ and the opening for signature of the Convention at Ottawa, on 3 and 4 December 1997, and thereafter at Headquarters in New York until its entry into force,

Welcoming the addition of new States signatories to the Convention since its opening for signature, the rapid ratification by many signatories and the early achievement of the fortieth ratification of the Convention on 16 September 1998, which, according to the provisions of article 17 of the Convention, will result in the entry into force of the Convention on 1 March 1999,

Emphasizing the desirability of attracting the adherence of all States to the Convention, and determined to work strenuously towards the promotion of its universalisation,

1. Invites all States that have not yet done so to sign or, after entry into force, to accede to the Convention on the Prohibition of the Use, Stockpiling, Production and Transfer of Anti-Personnel Mines and on Their Destruction; 40/

2. Urges all States that have not yet done so to ratify the Convention without delay subsequent to their signature;

3. Renews its call upon all States to contribute towards the full realization and effective implementation of the Convention to advance the care and rehabilitation, and the social and economic reintegration of mine victims, and mine awareness programmes, and the removal of anti-personnel mines placed throughout the world and the assurance of their destruction;

4. Welcomes the generous offer by the Government of Mozambique to act as host for the First Meeting of the States Parties;

5. Requests the Secretary-General, in accordance with article 11, paragraph 2, of the Convention, to undertake the preparations necessary to convene the First Meeting of the States Parties, to take place in Maputo during the week of 3 May 1999;

6. Invites all States parties to the First Meeting of the States Parties and, in accordance with article 11, paragraph 4, of the Convention, States not parties to the Convention, as well as the United Nations, other relevant international organizations or institutions, regional organizations, the International Committee of the Red Cross and relevant non-governmental organizations to attend the Meeting as observers in accordance with the agreed rules of procedure.

40/ See CD 1478.

6.18. Meeting of the States Parties to the Convention on the Prohibition of Anti-Personnel Mines

APLC/MSP.1/1999/1

20 May 1999

Original: ENGLISH

First meeting
Maputo, 3-7 May 1999
Agenda item 17

FINAL REPORT

The Final Report of the First Meeting of the States Parties to the Convention on the Prohibition of the Use, Stockpiling, Production and Transfer of Anti-Personnel Mines and on Their Destruction consists of two parts and five annexes as follows:

I. Organization and Work of the First Meeting
II. Maputo Declaration
Annexes:
Annex I: List of Documents
Annex II: Reporting Formats for Article 7
Annex III: President's Paper on Circulation of Article 7 Reports
Annex IV: President's Paper on Intersessional Work
Annex V: Statement by His Excellency Mr. Joaquim Alberto Chissano, President of the Republic of Mozambique, at the opening ceremony of the First Meeting

6.18.1. Part I
Organization and work of the first meeting

A. Introduction

1. The Convention on the Prohibition of the Use, Stockpiling, Production and Transfer of Anti-Personnel Mines and on Their Destruction provides in Article 11, paragraphs 1 and 2:

"1. The States Parties shall meet regularly in order to consider any matter with regard to the application or implementation of this Convention, including:

"(a) The operation and status of this Convention;
"(b) Matters arising from the reports submitted under the provisions of this Convention;
"(c) International cooperation and assistance in accordance with Article 6;
"(d) The development of technologies to clear anti-personnel mines;
"(e) Submissions of States Parties under Article 8; and
"(f) Decisions relating to submissions of States Parties as provided for in Article 5.

"2. The First Meeting of the States Parties shall be convened by the Secretary-General of the United Nations within one year after the entry into force of this Convention. The subsequent meetings shall be convened by the Secretary-General of the United Nations annually until the First Review Conference."

2. At its fifty-third session, the General Assembly of the United Nations in resolution 53/77 N welcomed the generous offer by the Government of the Republic of Mozambique to act as host for

the First Meeting of the States Parties, and requested the Secretary-General, in accordance with Article 11, paragraph 2, of the Convention, to undertake the preparations necessary to convene the First Meeting of the States Parties, to take place in Maputo during the week of 3 May 1999.

3. To prepare for the First Meeting, States Parties convened two rounds of open-ended informal consultations at the Palais des Nations, Geneva, to which they also invited States not parties to the Convention, as well as the United Nations, other relevant international organizations or institutions, regional organizations, the International Committee of the Red Cross and relevant non-governmental organizations.

4. The first round of informal consultations was held on 1 March 1999, the day the Convention entered into force. During the consultations, participants considered a number of issues relating to the organization of the First Meeting including papers containing a draft provisional agenda, a draft programme of work, draft rules of procedure, and provisional estimated costs for convening the First Meeting. No objections were raised in connection with any of the papers considered and it was agreed that they would be finalized in all six languages of the Convention to be put before the First Meeting.

5. The second set of informal consultations took place on 13 April 1999. At that meeting, participants reviewed elements for a proposed draft political declaration to be issued on the occasion of the First Meeting; possible modalities for intersessional work under the Convention; practical ways of circulating the reports to be submitted under Article 7 of the Convention; and the issue of the venue and format of future meetings of the States Parties.

B. Organization of the First Meeting

6. The First Meeting was opened on 3 May 1999 by His Excellency Mr. Joaquim Alberto Chissano, President of the Republic of Mozambique. The opening statement of the President of the Republic of Mozambique is contained in annex V to this report. The First Meeting elected by acclamation the Minister of Foreign Affairs and Cooperation of the Republic of Mozambique, Dr. Leonardo Santos Simão, as its President in accordance with rule 7 of the Draft Rules of Procedure.

7. At the opening session, statements were made by Mrs. Louise Fréchette, Deputy Secretary-General of the United Nations; Dr. Salim Ahmed Salim, Secretary-General of the Organization of African Unity; His Royal Highness Prince Zeid Ra'ad Zeid Al Hussein delivering a message to the First Meeting from Her Majesty Queen Noor of the Hashemite Kingdom of Jordan; Ms. Jody Williams, Ambassador for the International Campaign to Ban Landmines; and Ms. Fárida Gulamo of the Mozambican Campaign Against Landmines. In addition, the President of the Meeting read a message addressed to the First Meeting by the President of the United States of America, Mr. William Jefferson Clinton.

8. At its first plenary meeting, on 3 May 1999, the First Meeting adopted its agenda as contained in document APLC/MSP.1/1999/L.1. On the same occasion, the First Meeting adopted its Rules of Procedure as contained in document APLC/MSP.1/1999/L.3, the estimated costs for convening the First Meeting as contained in document APLC/MSP.1/1999/L.5, and its programme of work as contained in document APLC/MSP.1/1999/L.2.

9. Also at its first plenary meeting, the Meeting elected by acclamation the representatives of Honduras, Jordan, Norway and Turkmenistan as Vice-Presidents of the First Meeting in accordance with rule 7 of the Rules of Procedure.

10. The Meeting unanimously confirmed the nomination of Mr. Carlos dos Santos, Ambassador and Permanent Representative of the Republic of Mozambique to the United Nations in New York, as the Secretary-General of the Meeting. The nomination had been the result of informal consultations among States Parties.

C. Participation and Credentials in the First Meeting

11. Forty-three States Parties participated in the Meeting: Austria, Belgium, Benin, Bolivia, Bosnia and Herzegovina, Bulgaria, Burkina Faso, Canada, Croatia, Denmark, France, Germany, Guinea, Holy See, Honduras, Hungary, Ireland, Jamaica, Japan, Jordan, Malawi, Mali, Mauritius, Mexico, Mozambique, Namibia, Nicaragua, Norway, Panama, Paraguay, Peru, San Marino, Senegal, Slovenia, South Africa, Sweden, Switzerland, Thailand, The former Yugoslav Republic of Macedonia, Turkmenistan, United Kingdom of Great Britain and Northern Ireland, Yemen and Zimbabwe.

12. Eighteen States which had ratified the Convention, but for which the Convention had not yet entered into force, participated in the Meeting as observers, in accordance with Article 11, paragraph 4, of the Convention and rule 1, paragraph 1, second sentence, of the Rules of Procedure of the Meeting: Antigua and Barbuda, Australia, Brazil, Chad, Ecuador, El Salvador, Guatemala, Italy, Lesotho, Malaysia, the Netherlands, New Zealand, Niger, Portugal, Slovakia, Spain, Swaziland and Uganda.

13. A further forty-seven States not parties to the Convention participated in the Meeting as observers, in accordance with Article 11, paragraph 4, of the Convention and rule 1, paragraph 1, second sentence, of the Rules of Procedure of the Meeting: Albania, Algeria, Angola, Argentina, Bangladesh, Burundi, Cambodia, Cameroon, Cape Verde, Chile, China, Colombia, Côte d'Ivoire, Cuba, Cyprus, Czech Republic, Dominican Republic, Ethiopia, Finland, Gabon, Georgia, Ghana, Greece, Iceland, Indonesia, Israel, Kazakhstan, Kenya, Libyan Arab Jamahiriya, Lithuania, Luxembourg, Mauritania, Morocco, Nepal, Philippines, Poland, Romania, Rwanda, Saint Vincent and the Grenadines, Singapore, Sri Lanka, Sudan, Togo, Turkey, Ukraine, United Republic of Tanzania and Zambia.

14. Credentials issued by the Head of State or Government or by the Minister for Foreign Affairs or by a person authorized by one of the above, as required by rule 4 of the Rules of Procedure of the Meeting, or credentials in the form of photocopies or facsimiles of such a document, or credentials in the form of information concerning the appointment of representatives to the Meeting received in the form of letters or notes verbales or facsimiles thereof from embassies, permanent missions to the United Nations or other intergovernmental organizations or other government offices or authorities, were received from all 108 States mentioned in paragraphs 11 through 13 above.

15. The Meeting accepted the credentials of the representatives of all of the States mentioned in paragraphs 11 through 13 above.

16. In accordance with Article 11, paragraph 4, of the Convention and rule 1, paragraphs 2 and 3, of the Rules of Procedure, the following international organizations and institutions, regional organizations, entities and non-governmental organizations attended the Meeting as observers: Palestine, United Nations, United Nations Children's Fund, United Nations Development Programme, United Nations Office for Project Services, World Food Programme, United Nations High Commissioner for Refugees, United Nations Institute for Disarmament Research, World Health Organization, European Commission, Organization of African Unity, Organization of American States, International Organization of The Francophonie, International Committee of the Red Cross, International Federation of Red Cross and Red Crescent Societies, Sovereign Military Order of Malta and International Campaign to Ban Landmines.

17. A list of all delegations to the First Meeting is contained in document APLC/MSP.1/1999/INF.1.

D. Work of the First Meeting

18. The First Meeting held seven plenary meetings from 3 to 7 May, when it concluded its work.

19. The first four plenary meetings were devoted to the general exchange of views under agenda item 10. Eighty-three delegations to the First Meeting made statements in the general exchange of views.

20. At the fifth plenary meeting, on 5 May 1999, the Meeting considered the submission of requests under Article 5 of the Convention. The President informed the Meeting that he had not been notified that any State wished to make such a request at the First Meeting. The Meeting took note of this.

21. At the same meeting, the Meeting considered the submission of requests under Article 8 of the Convention. The President informed the Meeting that he had not been notified that any State wished to make such a request at the First Meeting. The Meeting took note of this.

22. In addition to the plenary meetings, the Meeting held informal consultations on issues related to the operation of the Convention. These included the consideration of international cooperation and assistance in accordance with Article 6 on the topics of mine clearance, victim assistance, socio-economic reintegration and mine awareness, destruction of stockpiled anti-personnel mines, and development of technologies for mine action.

E. Decisions and recommendations

23. At its fifth plenary meeting, on 5 May 1999, the Meeting considered matters arising from and in the context of reports to be submitted under Article 7, including consideration and adoption of the reporting formats. The reporting formats were adopted as amended and are contained in annex II to this report.

24. At its sixth plenary meeting, on 6 May 1999, the Meeting agreed that the content of the President's Paper on Circulation of Article 7 Reports as amended (APLC/MSP.1/1999/Informal 3/Rev.1) should guide the technical ways and means of circulation of the reports. That Paper is contained in annex III to this report.

25. Following consultations on the President's Paper on Intersessional Work (APLC/MSP.1/1999/Informal 2), the Meeting recognized the importance of having intersessional Standing Committees of Experts on issues related to the operation of the Convention. Subsequently, at its seventh plenary meeting, on 7 May 1999, the Meeting decided that the intersessional work would be guided by the President's Paper which is contained in annex IV to this report. Further consultations identified the following States Parties as Co-chairs and Rapporteurs for the intersessional work programme:

Mine clearance
Mozambique and the United Kingdom of Great Britain and Northern Ireland, Co-Chairs; Peru and the Netherlands, Rapporteurs.

Victim assistance, socio-economic reintegration and mine awareness
Mexico and Switzerland, Co-Chairs;
Nicaragua and Japan, Rapporteurs.

Stockpile destruction
Hungary and Mali, Co-Chairs;
Malaysia and the Slovak Republic, Rapporteurs.

Technologies for mine action
Cambodia and France, Co-Chairs;
Yemen and Germany, Rapporteurs.

General status and operation of the Convention
South Africa and Canada, Co-Chairs;
Zimbabwe and Belgium, Rapporteurs.

26. The Meeting further noted that the first sessions of the Standing Committees of Experts would take place in Geneva on the following dates:

Mine clearance 13-15 September 1999

Victim assistance socio-economic reintegration and mine awareness 15-17 September 1999

Stockpile destruction 9-10 December 1999

Technologies for mine action 13-14 December 1999

General status and operation of the Convention 10-11 January 2000

27. At its seventh plenary meeting, the Meeting agreed that the Second Meeting of the States Parties would be held on 11-15 September 2000 in Geneva.

28. At the same plenary meeting, the Meeting adopted the Maputo Declaration, which is contained in part II of this report.

F. Documentation

29. A list of documents of the First Meeting is contained in annex I to this report.

G. Adoption of the Final Report and conclusion of the First Meeting

30. At its seventh and final plenary meeting on 7 May 1999, the Meeting adopted its Final Report as contained in document APLC/MSP.1/1999/L.7 and as orally amended by the President.

6.18.2. Part II Maputo Declaration

Maputo, Mozambique
7 May, 1999

1. We, the States Parties to the Convention on the Prohibition of the Use, Stockpiling, Production and Transfer of Anti-Personnel Mines and on Their Destruction, together with signatory States, are gathered in Maputo, Mozambique, joined by international organizations and institutions and non-governmental organizations, to reaffirm our unwavering commitment to the total eradication of an insidious instrument of war and terror: anti-personnel mines.

2. Even now, at the end of the century, anti-personnel mines continue to maim and kill countless innocent people each day; force families to flee their lands and children to abandon their schools and playgrounds; and prevent long-suffering refugees and displaced persons from returning to rebuild their homes and their lives. The real or suspected presence of anti-personnel mines continues to deny access to much-needed resources and services and cripples normal social and economic development.

3. We raise our serious concern at the continued use of anti-personnel mines in areas of instability around the world. Such acts are contrary to the aims of the Convention; they exacerbate tensions, undermine confidence and impede diplomatic efforts to find peaceful solutions to conflicts.

4. Therefore, even as we celebrate this First Meeting of the States Parties two months after the rapid entry-into-force of the Convention, we recognize that the enduring value of this unique international instrument rests in fully realizing the obligations and the promise contained within the Convention

- to ensure no new use;
- to eradicate stocks;
- to cease development, production and transfers;
- to clear mined areas and thus free the land from its deadly bondage;
- to assist the victims to reclaim their lives and to prevent new victims.

5. We believe these to be common tasks for humanity and therefore call on governments and people everywhere to join us in this effort.

6. To those who continue to use, develop, produce, otherwise acquire, stockpile, retain and transfer these weapons: cease now, and join us in this task.

7. To those who can offer technical and financial assistance to meet the enormous challenges of humanitarian mine action: intensify your efforts and help build the capacity of mine-affected countries themselves to increasingly take on these tasks.

8. To those who can offer assistance: help with the physical and psycho-social treatment and social and economic reintegration of mine victims, support mine awareness education programmes, and help those States in need to meet treaty obligations to demine and to destroy stockpiles, thus facilitating the widest possible adherence to the Convention.

9. To those that have not yet joined this community of States Parties: accede quickly to the Convention. To those who have signed: ratify. If ratification will take more time: provisionally apply the terms of the Convention while you put in place the necessary domestic legislation.

10. To the international community: promulgate, implement and universalise the Convention, the new international standard and norm of behaviour it is establishing.

11. In this spirit, we voice our outrage at the unabated use of anti-personnel mines in conflicts around the world. To those few signatories who continue to use these weapons, this is a violation of the object and purpose of the Convention that you solemnly signed. We call upon you to respect and implement your commitments.

12. Know that, as a community dedicated to seeing an end to the use of anti-personnel mines, our assistance and cooperation will flow primarily to those who have foresworn the use of these weapons forever through adherence to and implementation of the Convention.

13. Driven by the sad reality that the people of the world will continue to suffer the consequences of the use of anti-personnel mines for many years to come, we believe it crucial that we use this First Meeting of the States Parties to ensure that we make continued, measurable progress in our future efforts to eradicate anti-personnel mines and to alleviate the humanitarian crisis caused by them.

14. We recognize that anti-personnel mines represent a major public health threat. The plight of mine victims has revealed the inadequacy of assistance for victims in the countries most affected. Such assistance must be integrated into broader public health and socio-economic strategies to ensure not simply short-term care for victims, but special attention to the serious long-term needs for social and economic reintegration. Mine victims must be permitted to realize, with dignity, their place within their families and their societies. These issues must be accorded the highest political importance and practical commitment by States Parties and all those in the international community who care about this issue.

15. To this end, we commit ourselves to mobilise resources and energies to universalise the Convention, alleviate and eventually eradicate the human suffering caused by anti-personnel mines, including by striving to meet the goal of "zero victims".

16. For these purposes, we, the States Parties, will implement an intersessional work programme to take us steadily forward to the next Meeting of the States Parties, which will take place in Geneva from 11 to 15 September 2000. This will enable us to focus and advance our mine action efforts and to measure progress made in achieving our objectives. This work will be based on our tradition of inclusivity, partnership, dialogue, openness and practical cooperation. In this regard, we invite all interested governments, international organizations and institutions and non-governmental organizations to join us in this task.

17. Our work programme will draw together experts, building on the discussions held here in Maputo, to address the key thematic issues of:

- the general status and operation of the Convention;
- mine clearance;
- victim assistance and mine awareness;
- stockpile destruction; and,
- technologies for mine action.

This intersessional work will, inter alia, assist us in developing, with the United Nations, a global picture of priorities consistent with the obligations and time-frames contained within the Convention, including with regard to international cooperation and assistance. It will also take into account important work done at the international, regional and sub-regional levels.

18. The work of our experts will begin just four months from now, in Geneva. We appreciate and accept the offer of the Geneva International Centre for Humanitarian Demining to support our efforts. Our work will complement and reinforce the important mine action activities being undertaken by mine-affected States working in partnership with other States, international and regional organizations, non-governmental organizations and the private sector--also recognizing the United Nations system as an important actor in global mine action efforts.

19. Meeting here in one of the most mine-affected continents on earth and in a country which has experienced the ravages wreaked by these weapons on the Mozambican people and the social fabric of the nation, we focus our minds and strengthen our conviction on the need to make the killing fields of anti-personnel mines that have terrorized, maimed and killed people, destroyed lives and hope for too long, a relic of the past.

We are determined to succeed in our common task.

We are determined to work in partnership to this end.

We are determined to apply the principle of international humanitarian law, enunciated in the final preambular paragraph of the Convention itself that '...the right of the parties to an armed conflict to choose methods or means of warfare is not unlimited...'

This is our firm pledge to future generations.

[Annexes omitted]

7. ACKNOWLEDGEMENTS

It seems almost superfluous to recognise that the preparation of a work of this nature owes much to the sustenance wrested from others. Originally submitted in October 2000 as a doctoral thesis to the University of Tilburg in the Netherlands, my thanks go first to Professor Guy Goodwin-Gill of Oxford University for suggesting and supporting the idea, and to my two supervisors Professor Willem van Genugten and Roel Fernhout (now the Dutch National Ombudsman) for their patience, insight and, above all, their kindness.

Professor Françoise Hampson of Essex University had previously gifted me a passion for international humanitarian law that was subsequently kindled by Louise Doswald-Beck and Peter Herby.

And many colleagues and friends, past and present, have suffered my pious musings about the topic with relentless forbearance and good humour: Jody Williams of the International Campaign to Ban Landmines; Samir Basta, Jack Glattbach, Stephen Lewis and Bilge Ogun-Bassani at UNICEF; Lou Maresca and Johanne Dorais-Slakmon at the ICRC; Eric Filippino and Paddy Blagden at the Geneva International Centre for Humanitarian Demining; and David Atwood of the Friends World Committee for Consultation.

My family has been ever supportive, as good families always are. But my greatest thanks must go to my long-suffering wife, Françoise, who with Sisyphean determination persists in trying to convince me that the law simply isn't everything.

www.ingramcontent.com/pod-product-compliance
Lightning Source LLC
LaVergne TN
LVHW090308210926
848480LV00001B/175
* 9 7 8 1 5 7 1 0 5 2 4 4 5 *